BIR

D0504526

RCLWOOD LIBRA 91

COLOSSUS
The Secrets of Bletchley Park's Codebreaking Computers

Thomas H. Flowers

COLOSSUS

The Secrets of Bletchley Park's Codebreaking Computers

B. Jack Copeland and others

(Edited by B. Jack Copeland)

OXFORD
UNIVERSITY PRESS

OXFORD
UNIVERSITY PRESS

Great Clarendon Street, Oxford OX2 6DP

Oxford University Press is a department of the University of Oxford.
It furthers the University's objective of excellence in research, scholarship,
and education by publishing worldwide in

Oxford New York

Auckland Cape Town Dar es Salaam Hong Kong Karachi
Kuala Lumpur Madrid Melbourne Mexico City Nairobi
New Delhi Shanghai Taipei Toronto

With offices in

Argentina Austria Brazil Chile Czech Republic France Greece
Guatemala Hungary Italy Japan Poland Portugal Singapore
South Korea Switzerland Thailand Turkey Ukraine Vietnam

Oxford is a registered trade mark of Oxford University Press
in the UK and in certain other countries

Published in the United States
by Oxford University Press Inc., New York

© Oxford University Press 2006

British Library Cataloguing in Publication Data

Data available

Library of Congress Cataloging in Publication Data

Colossus : the secrets of Bletchley Park's codebreaking computers / B. Jack Copeland.
    p. cm.
  ISBN-13: 978–0–19–284055–4 (alk. paper)
  ISBN-10: 0–19–284055–X (alk. paper)
1. Lorenz cipher system. 2. World War, 1939–1945—Cryptography. 3. World War, 1939–1945—
Electronic intelligence—Great Britain. 4. Cryptography—Germany—History.
5. Cryptography—Great Britain—History. I. Copeland, B. Jack, 1950–
  D810.C88C66 2006
  940.54'8641—dc22   2005030993

Typeset in Adobe Minion
by RefineCatch Limited, Bungay, Suffolk
Printed in Great Britain by
Clays Ltd., St. Ives plc

ISBN 0–19–284055–X   978–0–19–284055–4

1 3 5 7 9 10 8 6 4 2

For Reg, an engineer

Preface

Flowers was speaking in his quiet, modest way. He was telling me about the giant electronic computer he had built for codebreaking during the war. The story was riveting. 'There should be a book about Colossus,' I suggested. 'A book about Colossus . . .' he said softly, almost disbelievingly. His computer's role in the Allied victory had been secret for so long. I began the search for the codebreakers who could provide the rest of the complex picture. People said 'We can't talk about a lot of it—Official Secrets Act.' But then British Intelligence declassified a crucial wartime report: 500 pages of previously ultra-secret material. Suddenly doors opened and tongues loosened . . .

Contents

List of Photographs x
Notes on the Contributors xii

Introduction 1
Jack Copeland

SECTION 1. BLETCHLEY PARK AND THE ATTACK ON TUNNY

1. A Brief History of Cryptography from Caesar to Bletchley Park 9
Simon Singh
2. How It Began: Bletchley Park Goes to War 18
Michael Smith
3. The German Tunny Machine 36
Jack Copeland
4. Colossus, Codebreaking, and the Digital Age 52
Stephen Budiansky
5. Machine against Machine 64
Jack Copeland
6. D-Day at Bletchley Park 78
Thomas H. Flowers
7. Intercept! 84
Jack Copeland

SECTION 2. COLOSSUS

8. Colossus 91
Thomas H. Flowers
9. Colossus and the Rise of the Modern Computer 101
Jack Copeland
10. The PC-User's Guide to Colossus 116
Benjamin Wells

11. Of Men and Machines   141
    Brian Randell
12. The Colossus Rebuild   150
    Tony Sale

                SECTION 3. THE NEWMANRY

13. Mr Newman's Section   157
    Jack Copeland, with Catherine Caughey, Dorothy Du Boisson,
    Eleanor Ireland, Ken Myers, and Norman Thurlow
14. Max Newman—Mathematician, Codebreaker, and Computer
    Pioneer   176
    William Newman
15. Living with Fish: Breaking Tunny in the Newmanry and the Testery 189
    Peter Hilton
16. From Hut 8 to the Newmanry   204
    Irving John (Jack) Good
17. Codebreaking and Colossus   223
    Donald Michie

                SECTION 4. THE TESTERY

18. Major Tester's Section   249
    Jerry Roberts
19. Setter and Breaker   260
    Roy Jenkins
20. An ATS Girl in the Testery   264
    Helen Currie
21. The Testery and the Breaking of Fish   269
    Peter Edgerley

       SECTION 5. T. H. FLOWERS' LABORATORY AT DOLLIS HILL

22. Dollis Hill at War   281
    Jack Copeland, with David Bolam, Harry Fensom, Gil Hayward,
    and Norman Thurlow
23. The British Tunny Machine   291
    Gil Hayward
24. How Colossus was Built and Operated—One of its Engineers
    Reveals its Secrets   297
    Harry Fensom

SECTION 6. STURGEON, THE FISH THAT GOT AWAY

25. Bletchley Park's Sturgeon—The Fish That Laid No Eggs   307
    Frode Weierud
26. German Teleprinter Traffic and Swedish Wartime Intelligence   328
    Craig McKay

TECHNICAL APPENDICES—TO DIG DEEPER

A1.   Timeline: The Breaking of Tunny   337
A2.   The Teleprinter Alphabet   348
     Jack Copeland
A3.   The Tunny Addition Square   350
     Jack Copeland
A4.   My Work at Bletchley Park   352
     William T. Tutte
A5.   The Tiltman Break   370
     Friedrich L. Bauer
A6.   Turingery   378
     Jack Copeland
A7. $\Delta\chi$-Method   386
     Max Newman
A8.   Newman's Theorem   391
     Friedrich L. Bauer
A9.   Rectangling   396
     Frank Carter
A10. The Motor-Wheels and Limitations   406
     Jack Good, Donald Michie, and Geoffrey Timms
A11. Motorless Tunny   409
     Jack Good and Donald Michie
A12. Origins of the Fish Cypher Machines   411
     Friedrich L. Bauer

     Notes and References   419
     Sources of Photographs   452
     Index   453

List of Photographs

Frontispiece: Thomas H. Flowers
1. Alastair Denniston
2. Edward Travis
3. Alan Turing
4. Bill Tutte
5. Max Newman
6. Catherine Caughey
7. Dorothy Du Boisson
8. Jack Good
9. Eleanor Ireland
10. Donald Michie
11. Ralph Tester
12. Helen Currie
13. Peter Hilton
14. Jerry Roberts
15. Harry Fensom
16. Gil Hayward
17. The Mansion, Bletchley Park
18. Enigma
19. Enigma with lamps and encoding wheels exposed
20. Dismantled Enigma wheel
21. Top brass from Bletchley Park
22. Marian Rejewski
23. Alan Turing
24. Enigma in use during the Battle of France
25. The Bombe

26. German submarine *U-110* under attack
27. Survivors from *U-110* in mid-Atlantic
28. Tunny
29. Tunny with encoding wheels exposed
30. British replica of Tunny, used in deciphering
31. Robinson, precursor to Colossus
32. Electronic valves used in Colossus
33. Colossus and two operators
34. Colossus X
35. Colossus VII
36. Colossus V
37. Control panel from Colossus VI
38. Aquarius, forerunner of rewritable internal memory
39. Tape processing in the Newmanry
40. Flowerdown intercept station
41. The Post Office Research Station at Dollis Hill
42. Human computers in the 1890s
43. Charles Babbage
44. The Manchester 'Baby', first electronic stored-program computer
45. Pilot Model of Turing's Automatic Computing Engine
46. Bendix G15, early personal computer
47. MOSAIC, used for secret work during the Cold War
48. Turing at the console of the Ferranti Mark I computer
49. The ENIAC
50. John von Neumann
51. Sturgeon
52. Sturgeon's encoding wheels and inner connections

Notes on the Contributors

Friedrich Bauer was Professor of Mathematics at the University of Gutenberg before becoming Professor of Computer Science at Munich University of Technology. He is the author of the classic *Decrypted Secrets: Methods and Maxims of Cryptology* (2nd edition 2000).

David Bolam is one of the engineers who built the Colossi. After the war he was involved in the automation of the national telephone system and eventually its computerisation.

Stephen Budiansky is a writer and historian. His books include the bestseller *Battle of Wits: The Complete Story of Codebreaking in World War II* (2000), *Air Power* (2004), and *Her Majesty's Spymaster* (2005), a biography of the Elizabethan spymaster Sir Francis Walsingham. He is a correspondent for *The Atlantic Monthly*.

Frank Carter is a specialist in the history of codebreaking. He is the author of a series of booklets on codebreaking published by the Bletchley Park Trust and lectures regularly at Bletchley Park, now a museum.

Catherine Caughey volunteered for the Women's Royal Naval Service (WRNS) in 1943 and was allocated to 'Special Duties X' at Bletchley Park, where she joined the Newmanry and worked as one of Colossus's operators from the beginning of 1944. Later she took responsibility for the Newmanry's teleprinter room, where Tunny messages were received from the main intercept station in Kent. After the war Caughey trained as an occupational therapist.

Jack Copeland is Director of The Turing Archive for the History of Computing and is Professor of Philosophy at the University of Canterbury, New Zealand, where he specialises in mathematical logic. His books include *Artificial Intelligence* (1993), *Logic and Reality* (1996), *The Essential Turing* (2004), and *Alan Turing's Automatic Computing Engine: The Master Codebreaker's Struggle to Build the Modern Computer* (2005).

Helen Currie joined the Auxiliary Territorial Service (ATS) in 1938, training as an intercept operator in 1942. This led to her transfer to Bletchley Park, where she joined the Tunny-breaking section called the 'Testery'. Initially her job was to translate punched paper tape into German by sight; later she operated a British copy of the German Tunny machine which produced the German plaintext automatically. After the war she entered local government and served as a magistrate.

Dorothy Du Boisson joined the WRNS in 1943 and was posted to Bletchley Park. In the Newmanry during the pre-Colossus period she operated Heath Robinson; she then moved on to the prototype Colossus and the 'Mark 2' Colossi. Finally she became a registrar in the Newmanry's 'Ops Room', where she was responsible for distributing and tracking the tapes containing the encrypted messages. The war over, she went into the Air Ministry as Controller of Typists and later became a senior administrator in the Ministry of Defence in Whitehall.

Peter Edgerley was recruited to Bletchley Park in 1942. He joined the attack on Tunny in the Testery, where he specialised in breaking Tunny messages 'by eye'. After the war he became a research scientist with ICI Plastics.

Harry Fensom joined Flowers' inner circle of engineers at the Research Branch of the British Post Office in 1942. He participated in the construction of various codebreaking machines, including Heath Robinson, Colossus I, and Colossus II, and was responsible for keeping the machines in continuous operation at Bletchley Park. Following the war Fensom designed ERNIE, the electronic randomiser used to produce winning numbers in the government-run premium bond lottery. He patented the first fully-electronic telephone and designed various electronic systems for use in telephone exchanges.

Thomas Flowers joined the Post Office Research Branch in 1930, where he became Head of Switching Research. During the 1930s Flowers pioneered large-scale digital electronics. In 1943 he designed and constructed the prototype Colossus, followed in 1944 by the first of the Mark 2 Colossi. After the war he developed the concept of the all-electronic telephone exchange. Flowers left the Post Office in 1964 to join Standard Telephones and Cables, publishing his text *Introduction to Exchange Systems* in 1976. He completed his chapters 'Colossus' and 'D-Day at Bletchley Park' shortly before he died in 1998.

Jack Good joined Bletchley Park in 1941, where he worked first on Enigma and then on Tunny, becoming principal statistician in the Newmanry. After the war he was offered a lectureship in mathematics at the University of Manchester but in 1948 returned to codebreaking at Bletchley Park's peacetime successor, GCHQ. Since 1967 he has been Professor of Statistics at Virginia Polytechnic Institute. His books include *Probability and the Weighing of Evidence* (1950) and *Good Thinking: The Foundations of Probability and its Applications* (1983).

Gil Hayward joined Flowers' group at the beginning of 1944. He had special responsibility for the British Tunny machines, used to decrypt messages once the codebreakers had deduced the 'settings' of the message. After the war he worked on a secret voice-encipherment system at the Post Office Research Branch. Later he joined the Special Branch of the Royal Malaysian Police, designing 'special techniques devices' for use against insurgents.

Peter Hilton was recruited to Bletchley Park at the beginning of 1942 and worked first on Enigma, breaking 'Offizier' ('Officers' Eyes Only') naval traffic. He transferred to Tunny towards the end of 1942 and soon became chief cryptanalyst in the Testery. Hilton went on to become a distinguished mathematician: he was appointed Professor of Pure Mathematics at the University of Birmingham in 1958, then moved to the United States to become Professor of Mathematics at Cornell University and finally Distinguished Professor of Mathematics at the State University of New York. His books include *Homology Theory* (1955) and *Course in Homological Algebra* (2nd edition 1996).

Eleanor Ireland joined the WRNS early in 1944 and was posted to Bletchley Park. In the Newmanry she operated the Colossus computers until the end of the war, and helped to break up the machines after the Allied victory. She went on to become an artist and illustrator. Her paintings have been exhibited in the Royal Academy.

Roy Jenkins joined the newly formed Testery in 1942, and worked on Tunny until the fall of Berlin. He entered the House of Commons in 1948 and was Home Secretary (1965–67 and 1974–76), Chancellor of the Exchequer (1967–70), and President of the European Commission (1976–81). Jenkins co-founded the Social Democratic Party in 1981. He became Lord Jenkins of Hillhead and Chancellor of the University of Oxford in 1987. He died in 2003.

Craig McKay is an expert on the history of signals intelligence. His books include *From Information to Intrigue* (1991) and *Swedish Signal Intelligence 1900–1945* (2003).

Donald Michie joined Bletchley Park in 1942 and worked on Tunny, first in the Testery and then as Max Newman's assistant in the Newmanry. He made an all-important contribution to the design of the Mark 2 Colossi. After the war he became a geneticist and then in the 1960s switched careers, founding the first European centre for Artificial Intelligence research and becoming

Professor of Machine Intelligence at the University of Edinburgh. His books include *On Machine Intelligence* (1974) and *The Creative Computer* (1984).

Ken Myers joined the team of engineers building Colossus I in Flowers' laboratory in 1943, and at the beginning of 1944 moved to Bletchley Park to install and maintain codebreaking machinery. After the war he worked on the problem of coordinating London's traffic lights.

Max Newman joined Bletchley Park in 1942 to work on Tunny in the Research Section. His vision of mechanised codebreaking led to the formation of the Newmanry and the use of high-speed electronic machinery. At the end of the war he became Professor of Mathematics at the University of Manchester, where he founded the Computing Machine Laboratory and oversaw the development of the first 'stored-program' electronic computer. His classic book *Elements of the Topology of Plane Sets of Points* (1939) remained in print for sixty years. Newman died in 1984. His essay in Appendix 7, written in 1943, would probably have been destroyed with the Colossi at the end of the war, had it not been smuggled out of Bletchley Park by an engineer. It was rediscovered only recently.

William Newman designs interactive computer systems. He wrote the first textbook on computer graphics, *Principles of Interactive Computer Graphics* (1973); his other books include *Interactive System Design* (1995). He is Max Newman's son and biographer.

Brian Randell is Emeritus Professor of Computing Science at the University of Newcastle upon Tyne and a distinguished historian of computing. His books include *The Origins of Digital Computers* (3rd edition 1992).

Jerry Roberts joined the Testery on its formation in July 1942 and went on to become a senior member of the organisation, working on Tunny until the end of the war. From 1945–47 he was a member of the War Crimes Investigation Unit. Thereafter he pursued a career in marketing, forming his own market research company in 1970.

Tony Sale worked in MI5 before directing a computer software company. He founded Bletchley Park Museum in 1994 and has there rebuilt Colossus.

Simon Singh is a writer and broadcaster. His BBC television documentary about Fermat's Last Theorem won a BAFTA award and his subsequent book *Fermat's Last Theorem* (1997) was a UK No. 1 bestseller (the first mathematical book to achieve this distinction). His history of cryptography *The Code Book* (1999) was turned into a Channel 4 television series *The Science of Secrecy*. Singh's most recent book is *Big Bang: The Origin of the Universe* (2005).

Michael Smith specialised in signals intelligence as a member of the British Army's Intelligence Corps and now writes on defence and security issues for the *Sunday Times*. His books include the UK No. 1 bestseller *Station X: The Codebreakers of Bletchley Park* (1998), *Foley: The Spy Who Saved 10,000 Jews* (1999), and *The Spying Game* (2003).

Geoffrey Timms joined Bletchley Park in 1944 and worked on Tunny in the Newmanry. At the end of hostilities he wrote *General Report on Tunny* with Good and Michie. Timms remained with GCHQ after the war, applying computer techniques to codebreaking. He died in 1982.

Norman Thurlow joined the Post Office Research Branch in 1937 and was recruited to the engineering side of the codebreaking operation in 1942. At first he dealt with machines for use against Enigma, but soon moved to the Newmanry and was closely involved with Heath Robinson and the Colossi. Thurlow remained with GCHQ after the war.

Bill Tutte was recruited to Bletchley Park in 1941, becoming a leading member of the Research Section. For a few months he worked on Italian ciphers, then turned his attention to the problem of Tunny. Tutte made three major breakthroughs which formed the backbone of the operation against Tunny: he deduced the structure of the Tunny machine, he devised the 'statistical method' which made Heath Robinson and the Colossi possible, and he invented the method of 'rectangling' necessary to keep pace with the Germans' daily changes to the Tunny code-wheel patterns. At the end of the war Tutte was elected a Fellow of Trinity College, Cambridge, and subsequently became Professor of Mathematics at the University of Waterloo, Ontario. His books include *Introduction to the Theory of Matroids* (1971) and *Graph Theory* (1984). He died in 2002.

Frode Weierud is the leading expert on the German cipher machine that was codenamed 'Sturgeon' by Bletchley Park. He is a computer specialist at the European Organisation for Nuclear Research (CERN) in Geneva.

Benjamin Wells is Professor of Mathematics and Computer Science at the University of San Francisco. He has lectured widely on Colossus. His books include *The Metamathematics of Algebraic Systems* (1971).

Introduction

Jack Copeland

The story of the Enigma cipher machine and its defeat by the Bletchley Park codebreakers astounded the world. This book describes Bletchley's success against a later and more advanced German cipher machine that the British codenamed *Tunny* (see photograph 28). How Bletchley Park broke Tunny has been a closely guarded secret since the end of the war.

Unlike Enigma, which dated from 1923 and was marketed openly throughout Europe, the ultra-secret Tunny was created by scientists of Hitler's Third Reich for use by the German Wehrmacht. Tunny was technologically more sophisticated than Enigma and—theoretically—more secure. From 1942 Hitler and the German High Command in Berlin relied increasingly on Tunny to protect their communications with Army Group commanders across Europe. The Tunny network carried the highest grade of intelligence.

Tunny messages sent by radio were first intercepted by the British in June 1941. After a year-long struggle with the new cipher, Bletchley Park had its first successes against Tunny in 1942. Broken Tunny messages contained intelligence which changed the course of the war, saving an incalculable number of lives.

Central to the Bletchley attack on Tunny was Colossus, the world's first large-scale electronic digital computer. The first Colossus was built during 1943 by Thomas H. Flowers and his team of engineers and wiremen, a tight-knit group who worked in utmost secrecy and at terrific speed. The construction of the machine took them ten months, working day and night, pushing themselves until (as Flowers said) their 'eyes dropped out'.

The racks of complex electronic equipment were transferred from Flowers' laboratory at Dollis Hill in London to Bletchley Park, where Colossus was reassembled. Despite the fact that no such machine had previously been

Notes and references begin on page 419.

attempted, the computer was in working order almost straight away and ready to begin its fast-paced attack on the German messages.

The name 'Colossus', devised by the members of the Women's Royal Naval Service who operated the computer, was certainly apt. Colossus was the size of a room and weighed approximately a ton. By the end of the war in Europe there were ten Colossi. The computers were housed in two vast steel-framed buildings—a factory dedicated to breaking Tunny. There are photographs of some of the Colossi in the centre of the book.

Shortly after Germany fell, Winston Churchill ordered that most of the Colossi be broken up. Two were retained by the peace-time descendant of Bletchley Park, the Government Communications Headquarters (GCHQ). Details of their postwar use have not been disclosed. The last Colossus is believed to have stopped running in 1960.

The war over, key Bletchley personnel moved to Manchester University. Various of the electronic panels from dismantled Colossi were taken to the newly created Computing Machine Laboratory there, although not before every trace of their original purpose had been removed. Colossus itself was a special-purpose computer, custom-built for codebreaking. In June 1948, in the Computing Machine Laboratory, the world's first truly general-purpose electronic digital computer ran its first program. Soon a Manchester engineering company developed the university's rough-and-ready prototype into the Ferranti Mark I, the first electronic digital computer to go on the market. It was the start of a new era.

All involved with Colossus and the breaking of Tunny were gagged by the Official Secrets Act. The very existence of Colossus was classified. A long time passed before the secret came out that Flowers had built the first large-scale electronic computer. During his lifetime (he died in 1998) he never received the full recognition he deserved. Many history books, even recently published ones, claim that the first electronic digital computer was a well-publicised American machine called the ENIAC (Electronic Numerical Integrator and Computer). The ENIAC, however, was not operational until the end of 1945, two years after Colossus first ran. British science and British industry suffered as a result of the total secrecy surrounding Colossus during the postwar years. Flowers writes bitterly in Chapter 6 of the long-lasting effects of the secrecy.

Until the 1970s, few had any idea that electronic computation had been used successfully during the Second World War. In 1975, the British government released a set of captioned photographs of the Colossi. By 1983, Flowers had received clearance to publish an account of the hardware of the first Colossus. Details of the later Colossi remained secret, and so, even more importantly, did all information about how Flowers' computing machinery was actually used by the codebreakers. Flowers was told by the British authorities that 'the technical description of machines such as COLOSSUS may be disclosed', but that he must not disclose any information about 'the functions which they performed'. It was rather like being told that he could give a detailed technical description of the insides of a radar receiver, but must not say anything about what the equipment did (in the case of radar, reveal the location of planes, submarines, etc., by picking up radio waves bouncing off them). He was also allowed to describe some aspects of Tunny—but there was a blanket prohibition on saying anything at all relating to 'the weaknesses which led to our successes'. In fact, a clandestine censor objected to parts of the account that Flowers wrote, and he was instructed to remove these prior to publication.

There matters more or less stood until 1996, when the US Government declassified some wartime documents describing the function of Colossus. These had been sent to Washington during the war by US liaison officers stationed at Bletchley Park. Even so, a vital report remained classified. Five hundred pages in length and called *General Report on Tunny*, this was written in 1945 by three Bletchley Park codebreakers, Jack Good, Donald Michie, and Geoffrey Timms. Thanks largely to Michie's tireless campaigning, the report was declassified by the British Government in June 2000, finally ending the secrecy. The full report is available electronically on this book's companion website <www.AlanTuring.net/tunny_report>.

The release of *General Report on Tunny* made this book possible. At last the wartime records were open to inspection, and the whole incredible story of Colossus and the assault on Tunny was ripe for the telling. Declassification meant that the codebreakers, engineers, and machine operators responsible for the defeat of Tunny could at last speak freely. Much of this book is in their words.

THE DECRYPTS

The immediate products of the codebreakers' attack on Tunny were German *decrypts*—decoded messages in plain German. Unfortunately, most Tunny decrypts appear to have been destroyed at the end of the war, along with their enciphered counterparts, in an effort by the British to cover up the whole attack.

What does survive is a huge number of English texts, prepared on the basis of German decrypts by intelligence officers at Bletchley Park. These texts seldom consisted of a word-for-word translation of a German decrypt, however. The material was altered by the intelligence officers as they saw fit. Part of the job of these officers was to disguise the origin of the intelligence, and the texts they prepared naturally gave no indication that the information came from German cipher traffic, let alone any indication of whether it came from Tunny or Enigma.

Many of the messages sent by Tunny would seem dull to us. Often messages consisted of lengthy lists—the cargo list of a ship, for example, or a list of the munitions and equipment in the possession of a particular army unit. Sometimes, though, the content of a message was dramatic and its significance palpable. Of special interest, of course, were messages signed by Hitler himself.

This short text affords a glimpse of what might turn up in the secret traffic. Dated December 1944, it details an order from Hitler to General Guderian:

```
On thirtieth November by order of the Fuehrer, Guderian ordered
centre of Budapest East of Danube to be put into state of defence at
once. Evacuation without fighting in case of unfavourable
development of situation was out of question. Every house to be
contested. Measures to prevent troops being endangered by the armed
mob of the city to be taken ruthlessly.
```

Below is a rare survivor—a word-for-word translation of an intercepted Tunny message. Dated 25 April 1943 and signed by von Weichs, Commander-in-Chief of German Army Group South, this message was sent from the Russian front to the German Army High Command ('OKH'— *Oberkommando des Heeres*). It gives an idea of the nature and quality of the intelligence that Tunny yielded. The enciphered message passed along the 'Squid' radio link shown on the map of the Tunny system on page 41.

The message concerns plans for a major German offensive in the Kursk area codenamed '*Zitadelle*'. Operation *Zitadelle* was Hitler's attempt to regain the initiative on the Eastern Front following the Russian victory at Stalingrad in February 1943. *Zitadelle* would turn out to be one of the crucial battles of the war.

Von Weichs' message gives a detailed appreciation of Russian strengths and weaknesses in the Kursk area. His appreciation reveals a considerable amount about the intentions of the German army. British analysts deduced from the decrypt that *Zitadelle* would consist of a pincer attack on the north and south flanks of a bulge in the Russian defensive line at Kursk (a line which stretched from the Gulf of Finland in the north to the Black Sea in the south). Highly important messages such as this were conveyed directly to Churchill, usually with a covering note by 'C', Chief of the Secret Intelligence Service. On 30 April an intelligence report based on the content of the message, but revealing nothing about its origin, was sent to Churchill's ally, Stalin.

(Ironically, however, Stalin had a spy inside Bletchley Park: John Cairncross was sending raw Tunny decrypts directly to Moscow by clandestine means.)

To OKH/OP. ABT. and to OKH/Foreign Armies East, from Army Group South IA/Ol, No. 411/43, signed von Weichs, General Feldmarschall, dated 25/4:—

Comprehensive appreciation of the enemy for "Zitadelle"

In the main the appreciation of the enemy remains the same as reported in Army Group South (Roman) IIA, No. 0477/43 of 29/3 and in the supplementary appreciation of 15/4. *[In Tunny transmissions the word 'Roman' was used to indicate a Roman numeral; '29/3' and '15/4' are dates.]*

The main concentration, which was already then apparent on the north flank of the Army Group in the general area Kursk—Ssudsha—Volchansk—Ostrogoshsk, can now be clearly recognised: a further intensification of this concentration is to be expected as a result of the continuous heavy transport movements on the lines Yelets—Kastornoye—Kursk, and Povorino—Svoboda and Gryazi—Svoboda, with a probable (B% increase) *['B%' indicated an uncertain word]* in the area Valuiki—Novy Oskol—Kupyansk. At present however it is not apparent whether the object of this concentration is offensive or defensive. At present, (B% still) in anticipation of a German offensive on both the Kursk and Mius Donetz fronts, the armoured and mobile formations are still evenly distributed in various groups behind the front as strategic reserves.

There are no signs as yet of a merging of these formations or a transfer to the forward area (except for (Roman) II GDS *[Guards]* Armoured Corps) but this could take place rapidly at any time.

According to information from a sure source the existence of the following groups of the strategic reserve can be presumed:— A) 2 cavalry corps (III GDS and V GDS in the area north of Novocherkassk). It can also be presumed that 1 mech *[mechanised]* corps (V GDS) is being brought up to strength here. B) 1 mech corps (III GDS) in the area (B% north) of Rowenki. C) 1 armoured corps, 1 cavalry corps and probably 2 mech corps ((Roman) I GD Armoured, IV Cavalry, probably (B% (Roman) I) GDS Mech and V Mech Corps) in the area north of Voroshilovgrad. D) 2 cavalry corps ((B% IV) GDS and VII GDS) in the area west of Starobyelsk. E) 1 mech corps, 1 cavalry corps and 2 armoured corps ((Roman) I GDS (B% Mech), (Roman) I GDS Cavalry, (Roman) II and XXIII Armoured) in the area of Kupyansk—Svatovo. F) 3 armoured corps, 1 mech corps ((Roman) II Armoured, V GDS Armoured, (B% XXIX) Armoured and V GDS Mech under the command of an army (perhaps 5 Armoured Army)) in the area of Ostrogoshsk. G) 2 armoured and 1 cavalry corps ((Roman) II GDS Armoured, III GDS Armoured and VI GDS Cavalry) under the command of an unidentified H.Q., in the area north of Novy Oskol.

In the event of "Zitadelle", there are at present approximately 90 enemy formations west of the line Belgorod—Kursk—Maloarkhangelsk. The attack of the Army Group will encounter stubborn enemy resistance in a deeply echeloned and well developed main defence zone, (with numerous dug in tanks, strong artillery and local reserves) the main effort of the defence being in the key sector Belgorod—Tamarovka.

In addition strong counter-attacks by strategic reserves from east and southeast are to be expected. It is impossible to forecast whether the enemy will attempt to withdraw from a threatened encirclement by retiring eastwards, as soon as the key sectors *[literally, 'corner-pillars']* of the bulge in the front line at Kursk, Belgorod and Maloarkhangelsk, have been broken through. If the enemy throws in all strategic reserves on the Army Group front into the Kursk battle, the following may appear on the battle field:— On day 1 and day 2, 2 armoured divisions and 1 cavalry corps. On day 3, 2 mech and 4 armoured corps. On day 4, 1 armoured and 1 cavalry corps. On day 5, 3 mech corps. On day 6, 3 cavalry corps. On day 6 and/or day 7, 2 cavalry corps.

Summarizing, it can be stated that the balance of evidence still points to a defensive attitude on the part of the enemy: and this is in fact unmistakable in the frontal sectors of the 6 Army and 1 Panzer Army. If the bringing up of further forces in the area before the north wing of the Army Group persists and if a transfer forward and merging of the mobile and armoured formations then takes place, offensive intentions become more probable. In that case it is improbable that the enemy can even then forestall our execution of Zitadelle in the required conditions. Probably on the other hand we must assume complete enemy preparations for defence, including the counter attacks of his strong mot*[motorised]* and armoured forces, which must be expected.

The Germans finally launched operation *Zitadelle* on 4 July 1943. Naturally the German offensive came as no surprise to the Russians—who, with over two months warning of the pincer attack, had amassed formidable defences. The Germans threw practically every panzer division on the Russian front into *Zitadelle*, but to no avail. On 13 July Hitler called off the attack. A few days later Stalin announced in public that Hitler's plan for a summer offensive against the Soviet Union had been 'completely frustrated'. *Zitadelle*—the Battle of Kursk—was a decisive turning point on the Eastern front. The counter attack launched by the Russians during *Zitadelle* developed into an advance which moved steadily westwards, ultimately reaching Berlin in April 1945.

Section 1

Bletchley Park and the Attack on Tunny

Chapter 1

A Brief History of Cryptography from Caesar to Bletchley Park

Simon Singh

THE SUBSTITUTION CIPHER

In Julius Caesar's *Gallic Wars*, he describes how he sent a message to the besieged Cicero. The messsage was encrypted by substituting Greek letters for Roman letters, then delivered in the most dramatic way imaginable. The messenger, unable to reach the camp, hurled a spear with the letter fastened to it with a thong. Although the spear lodged itself in a tower, nobody spotted it for two days. Eventually, it was taken down and delivered to Cicero, who read out the vital news to the entire camp, bringing enormous joy to his troops.

This was the first documented use of a substitution cipher for military purposes. Substitution ciphers, as the name suggests, encrypt messages by replacing the original characters with different characters. This is in contrast to a transposition cipher, in which the characters remain the same, but they are transposed or rearranged to create an anagram.

One of the most famous substitution ciphers is the so-called *Caesar cipher*, which simply replaces each letter in the message with the letter that is, say, three places further down the alphabet. Cryptographers often think in terms of the *plain alphabet*, the alphabet used to write the original message, and the *cipher alphabet*, the letters that are substituted in place of the plain letters, both of which are shown below.

Plain Alphabet	a b c d e f g h i j k l m n o p q r s t u v w x y z
Cipher Alphabet	D E F G H I J K L M N O P Q R S T U V W X Y Z A B C
Plaintext	ve ni, vi di, vi ci
Ciphertext	Y H Q L, Y L G L, Y L F L

The *plaintext* is the technical name for the original message, while the *ciphertext* is the encrypted message. In this chapter, the plaintext is written in lower case and the ciphertext in upper case. Although this example involves a shift of 3, lesser or greater shifts are of course possible. The Caesar cipher can be generally stated as substituting each plain letter with the letter that is x places later in the alphabet, where x is between 1 and 25. This illustrates one of the basic principles of cryptography, namely the relationship between the *algorithm* and the *key*.

In the Caesar cipher, the algorithm is the general idea of replacing the original letters with those that lie a fixed number of places further along the alphabet. The key, x, specifies the distance of the shift. In other words, the key is a flexible component within the algorithm, which needs to be specified in order to determine the exact method of encryption. The key is usually selected by the sender and has to be communicated to the receiver so that the message can be deciphered.

A codebreaker can crack the cipher by identifying the correct key. In this case, the codebreaker can check every key, known as a brute force attack, because there are only 25 keys.

A stronger version of the substitution cipher is the general substitution cipher, which allows the cipher alphabet to be any rearrangement of the alphabet. In this case, there are roughly 400,000,000,000,000,000,000,000,000 possible keys, because this is the number of ways to rearrange the alphabet. Although a large number of keys is not the sole requirement for a secure cipher, it certainly makes the codebreaker's job harder, because checking every single possible key would be impractical.

Typically, a communications network will use a single algorithm for several months or years, but will employ a variety of keys. For example, a different key can be used each day. This means that if a key is captured by the enemy, then only one day's communications are immediately jeopardised. It is assumed that the enemy already knows the algorithm, because it is inevitable that details of the system will have been leaked or stolen. The significance of the key, as opposed to the algorithm, is an enduring principle of cryptography, and it was definitively stated in 1883 by the Dutch linguist Auguste Kerckhoffs von Nieuwenhof in his famous article 'La Cryptographie Militaire': the security of a cryptosystem must not depend on keeping secret the crypto algorithm; the security depends only on keeping secret the key. This is *Kerckhoffs' Principle*.

CRACKING THE SUBSTITUTION CIPHER

One method for cracking a ciphertext is to guess the true meaning of part of the encrypted message, which is known as a *crib*. For example, the code-breaker might know that a ciphertext that begins 'XBKJ . . .' is a letter, so XBKJ might stand for 'dear . . .', which means that the true values for four letters have been established, which in turn might be helpful in deciphering the rest of the message.

Without a crib, and with so many keys, the general substitution cipher seemed impregnable for centuries, but eventually a flaw was revealed. One of the first scholars to exploit the weakness of the substitution cipher was the ninth-century Arab philosopher al-Kindi, who recorded his code-breaking technique, now known as frequency analysis, in 'A Manuscript on Deciphering Cryptographic Messages'.

Frequency analysis focuses on the fact that the letters in the Arabic, Roman, or any other alphabet have a distinct variation in frequency. In English, for example, e is the most common letter, accounting on average for roughly 13 per cent of all letters in a piece of text. The next most common letters are t, a, and n, whereas letters such as x, q, and z are very rare, as any scrabble player will testify.

Al-Kindi realised that if a letter was substituted for another letter (or symbol), then the new letter would take on the frequency of the original letter. Therefore, by studying the frequency of the letters in the ciphertext, it should be possible to establish their true value. For example, if L is the most common letter in the ciphertext, then L probably represents e.

Each letter has a personality and its overall frequency is just one part of that personality. Other traits include its relationship to other letters (q is always followed by u) or how often it appears at the start of a word. No matter how a letter is disguised during substitution, it will continue to carry its personality and should still be recognisable.

Once news of frequency analysis spread, it was clear that a better form of encryption was required. An ideal cipher would generate a ciphertext that bore no relation to the plaintext, unlike simple substitution which carries the frequencies across to the ciphertext as a hint to help identify the true value of each letter. The perfect ciphertext should appear to be random, because the codebreaker is impotent unless there is the slightest pattern that can be recognised.

THE VIGENÈRE CIPHER

There were numerous attempts to improve the simple substitution cipher. The *homophonic* cipher usually has a cipher alphabet that consists of numbers, with several possible number substitutions for the most common letters and one number for each of the rare letters. This results in a much flatter frequency distribution for the elements of the cipher alphabet, which makes the cipher much more secure. However, the ciphertext still retains recognisable qualities that allow it to be cracked. For example, if a number is always followed by a small set of other numbers, then the former is probably q and the latter is probably u.

An alternative to a cipher is a *code*. Although the word is used loosely to cover a whole range of encryption techniques, a code is technically a system with only one key. A code book might be a dictionary that lists thousands of words and alongside each one a five-digit number. A message would be encrypted by looking up each word of the plaintext and replacing it with the corresponding number.

This system is relatively strong, because the number of elements in the ciphertext will be smaller and there will be fewer repeated elements, but the lack of keys is a drawback. The same code book will be used for months or years, because creating and distributing a new code book is a major undertaking. During this lengthy period, it is highly likely that the code book will be deduced or stolen.

While some continued to use the old-fashioned, weak ciphers, others used inflexible codes or a combination of the two known as a *nomenclator*. But a better solution was the *Vigenère cipher*, named after Blaise de Vigenère, a French diplomat born in 1523, one of the cryptographers who contributed to its development.

The strength of the Vigenère cipher relies on using not one, but 26 distinct cipher alphabets to encrypt a message. The first step in encipherment involves drawing up a so-called Vigenère square, shown below, a plaintext alphabet followed by 26 cipher alphabets, each one shifted by one more letter with respect to the previous one. Hence, row 1 represents a cipher alphabet with a Caesar shift of 1, row 2 represents a cipher alphabet with a Caesar shift of 2, and so on. The top row of the square, in lower case, represents the plaintext letters, and you could encipher each plaintext letter according to any one of the 26 cipher alphabets. For example, if cipher alphabet number 2 is used, then the letter a is enciphered as C, but if cipher alphabet number 12 is used, then a is enciphered as M.

Plain	a	b	c	d	e	f	g	h	i	j	k	l	m	n	o	p	q	r	s	t	u	v	w	x	y	z
1	B	C	D	E	F	G	H	I	J	K	L	M	N	O	P	Q	R	S	T	U	V	W	X	Y	Z	A
2	C	D	E	F	G	H	I	J	K	L	M	N	O	P	Q	R	S	T	U	V	W	X	Y	Z	A	B
3	D	E	F	G	H	I	J	K	L	M	N	O	P	Q	R	S	T	U	V	W	X	Y	Z	A	B	C
4	E	F	G	H	I	J	K	L	M	N	O	P	Q	R	S	T	U	V	W	X	Y	Z	A	B	C	D
5	F	G	H	I	J	K	L	M	N	O	P	Q	R	S	T	U	V	W	X	Y	Z	A	B	C	D	E
6	G	H	I	J	K	L	M	N	O	P	Q	R	S	T	U	V	W	X	Y	Z	A	B	C	D	E	F
7	H	I	J	K	L	M	N	O	P	Q	R	S	T	U	V	W	X	Y	Z	A	B	C	D	E	F	G
8	I	J	K	L	M	N	O	P	Q	R	S	T	U	V	W	X	Y	Z	A	B	C	D	E	F	G	H
9	J	K	L	M	N	O	P	Q	R	S	T	U	V	W	X	Y	Z	A	B	C	D	E	F	G	H	I
10	K	L	M	N	O	P	Q	R	S	T	U	V	W	X	Y	Z	A	B	C	D	E	F	G	H	I	J
11	L	M	N	O	P	Q	R	S	T	U	V	W	X	Y	Z	A	B	C	D	E	F	G	H	I	J	K
12	M	N	O	P	Q	R	S	T	U	V	W	X	Y	Z	A	B	C	D	E	F	G	H	I	J	K	L
13	N	O	P	Q	R	S	T	U	V	W	X	Y	Z	A	B	C	D	E	F	G	H	I	J	K	L	M
14	O	P	Q	R	S	T	U	V	W	X	Y	Z	A	B	C	D	E	F	G	H	I	J	K	L	M	N
15	P	Q	R	S	T	U	V	W	X	Y	Z	A	B	C	D	E	F	G	H	I	J	K	L	M	N	O
16	Q	R	S	T	U	V	W	X	Y	Z	A	B	C	D	E	F	G	H	I	J	K	L	M	N	O	P
17	R	S	T	U	V	W	X	Y	Z	A	B	C	D	E	F	G	H	I	J	K	L	M	N	O	P	Q
18	S	T	U	V	W	X	Y	Z	A	B	C	D	E	F	G	H	I	J	K	L	M	N	O	P	Q	R
19	T	U	V	W	X	Y	Z	A	B	C	D	E	F	G	H	I	J	K	L	M	N	O	P	Q	R	S
20	U	V	W	X	Y	Z	A	B	C	D	E	F	G	H	I	J	K	L	M	N	O	P	Q	R	S	T
21	V	W	X	Y	Z	A	B	C	D	E	F	G	H	I	J	K	L	M	N	O	P	Q	R	S	T	U
22	W	X	Y	Z	A	B	C	D	E	F	G	H	I	J	K	L	M	N	O	P	Q	R	S	T	U	V
23	X	Y	Z	A	B	C	D	E	F	G	H	I	J	K	L	M	N	O	P	Q	R	S	T	U	V	W
24	Y	Z	A	B	C	D	E	F	G	H	I	J	K	L	M	N	O	P	Q	R	S	T	U	V	W	X
25	Z	A	B	C	D	E	F	G	H	I	J	K	L	M	N	O	P	Q	R	S	T	U	V	W	X	Y
26	A	B	C	D	E	F	G	H	I	J	K	L	M	N	O	P	Q	R	S	T	U	V	W	X	Y	Z

If the sender were to use just one of the cipher alphabets to encipher a message, then this would be a simple Caesar cipher, which would be easy for an enemy interceptor to crack. However, the Vigenère cipher involves using several rows of the Vigenère square (i.e. different cipher alphabets) to encrypt the letters of the message. In other words, the sender might encrypt the first letter according to row 7, the second according to row 24, the third letter according to row 21, and so on. In order to communicate, the sender and receiver must agree on a system for switching between rows. This agreement is achieved via a keyword. To demonstrate the Vigenère cipher, let us use the keyword 'WHITE' to encrypt the message 'Divert troops to east'.

Before encrypting, the keyword is spelt out above the message, and repeated over and over again so that each letter in the message is associated with a letter from the keyword. Then, to encrypt the first letter, *d*, begin by identifying the key letter above it, *W*, which in turn defines a particular row in the Vigenère square. The row beginning with *W*, row 22, is the cipher alphabet that will be used to find the substitute letter for the plaintext d. Hence, we identify the column headed by d and see where it intersects the row beginning with W, which turns out to be at the letter Z. Consequently, the letter d in the plaintext is represented by Z in the ciphertext.

Keyword	W	H	I	T	E	W	H	I	T	E	W	H	I	T	E	W	H	I
Plaintext	d	i	v	e	r	t	t	r	o	o	p	s	t	o	e	a	s	t
Ciphertext	Z	P	D	X	V	P	A	Z	H	S	L	Z	B	H	I	W	Z	B

To encipher the second letter of the message, i, the process is repeated. The key letter above i is H, so encryption involves a different row in the Vigenère square, namely the H row, the seventh row. To encrypt i, identify the column headed by i and see where it intersects the row beginning with H, which turns out to be at the letter P. Consequently, the letter i in the plaintext is represented by P in the ciphertext. Each letter of the keyword indicates a particular cipher alphabet within the Vigenère square, and because the keyword contains five letters, the sender encrypts the message by cycling through five rows of the Vigenère square.

The Vigenère cipher is strong because it is impregnable to simple frequency analysis. For example, a cryptanalyst applying frequency analysis to a piece of ciphertext would usually begin by identifying the most common letter in the ciphertext, which in this case is Z, and then assume that this represents the most common letter in English, e. In fact, the letter Z represents three different letters d, r, and s, but not e. This is clearly a problem for the cryptanalyst. Equally confusing is the fact that a letter that appears several times in the plaintext can be represented by different letters in the ciphertext. For example, the oo in 'troops' is substituted by two different letters, namely H and S.

The Vigenère cipher is called *polyalphabetic*, because a single message is encrypted using a variety of cipher alphabets. This is in contrast to the substitution ciphers that have been previously discussed, which are known as *monoalphabetic*.

The Vigenère cipher seemed so strong that it was dubbed *le chiffre indéchiffrable*. It remained unbroken for centuries, until Charles Babbage, the Victorian pioneer of computing, and Friedrich Wilhelm Kasiski, a retired Prussian army officer, discovered a flaw.

Imagine that a long text has been encrypted according to the Vigenère cipher with a keyword of five letters. If the word *the* appears a dozen times in the text, then there will be occasions when it will be encrypted in the same way, as there are only five different ways it can be encrypted. A codebreaker would identify repetitions in the ciphertext and appreciate that these indicate that a repeated word has been encrypted using the same piece of the repeated keyword. Furthermore, the number of letters between repetitions can be used to deduce the length of the keyword, which in turn allows the ciphertext to be cracked.

The history of cryptography is a battle between codemakers and codebreakers. Each time a code is broken, a new one has to be developed. Codes and ciphers evolve under the pressure exerted by codebreakers. Technology can accelerate this evolution, as both codemakers and codebreakers can develop devices to make and break codes. Technology is doubly important, because new communication systems, such as telegraph and radio, demand greater security and increase pressure on the codemakers.

ENIGMA, THE MECHANICAL VIGENÈRE CIPHER

As soon as the First World War ended, the German inventor Arthur Scherbius patented one of the most notorious cipher machines in history, the Enigma (see photographs 18–19 and 24). He was anxious to bring security up to date and his device was electromechanical, replacing the previous pencil and paper systems.

The basic form of Scherbius's invention consists of three elements connected by wires: a keyboard for inputting each plaintext letter, a scrambling unit that encrypts each plaintext letter into a corresponding ciphertext letter, and a display board consisting of various lamps for indicating the ciphertext letter. The diagram on page 17 shows the German military version of the Enigma machine. The most important feature is the set of wheels (sometimes also called *rotors*) that acts between the keyboard and the lampboard. To get to grips with the machine, we shall focus on these wheels or rotors.

Each wheel has 26 inputs and 26 outputs, and fixed wiring inside the wheels scrambles these connections, thereby encrypting each letter (see photograph 20). With the wheels in certain orientations, typing A would send the signal into the first wheel and it might emerge from the third wheel as P. The set of wheels effectively determines a cipher alphabet. At the moment, this is a simple monoalphabetic substitution cipher, but as each letter is typed, the first wheel rotates by one place, completely altering the cipher alphabet.

When the first wheel completes one revolution it nudges the second wheel forward one place, and after 26 nudges the second wheel nudges the third one. The wheels behave like a car odometer. The cipher alphabet is changing after each letter and the pattern will not repeat until all three wheels return to their original positions, which means that the cipher alphabet will be changing in a pseudo-random manner for any message of any reasonable length. The

Enigma machine essentially generates a polyalphabetic cipher. It behaves like a Vigenère cipher with thousands of possible cipher alphabets.

The sequence of cipher alphabets used for a particular message depend on the key chosen by the user. The key is the initial setting of the machine, which includes the starting positions of the three wheels, and which three are selected from the total number of wheels available to the operator (eight for most of the war), and also includes the way the plugboard is connected, bringing the total number of keys up to 159 million million million or more, depending on the type of machine.

At the outbreak of the Second World War, the German military believed that the Enigma cipher was unbreakable. Indeed, this was *le chiffre indéchiffrable* with an effectively unrepeating key, thereby removing the greatest weakness of the Vigenère cipher. The Enigma, however, was a machine with tiny flaws which could be exploited. The battle between codemakers and codebreakers continued during the war, with British codebreakers at Bletchley Park building on the work of their Polish allies and cracking the Enigma cipher.

Meanwhile, Germany was developing new and better cipher machines from 1940 onwards, such as the Lorenz SZ40 machine, codenamed 'Tunny' by the British (see photographs 28–29). This was one of a new generation of teleprinter machines. Each letter was translated into a 5-bit binary code according to the international Baudot–Murray system. Baudot–Murray code is not dissimilar to Morse code, each letter being translated into a binary code of dots and crosses.

Tunny encryption occurred by taking the plain letter and 'adding' it to a pseudo-randomly generated letter to create the encrypted letter, with addition occurring at the bit level. The letters that transformed plaintext into ciphertext were generated by a set of rotating wheels, so the system had something in common with the Enigma machine, although the SZ40 and other teleprinter machines were more complex than the Enigma.

The teleprinter cipher machines were the next stage in the evolution of cryptography. The challenge for the Allied codebreakers was to find a weakness in this formidable encryption system. It was a challenge that could only be completed with a tremendous combination of mathematics, science, engineering, and ingenuity.

Bletchley Park's attack on the Tunny machine culminated in the building of Colossus, the large-scale special-purpose electronic computer dedicated to breaking the new *chiffre indéchiffrable*.

<http://www.simonsingh.com> has a section on the history of cryptography and a directory of links to sites concentrating on codes and codebreaking. See also Singh, S. *The Code Book* (London: Fourth Estate, 1999).

The Enigma Machine

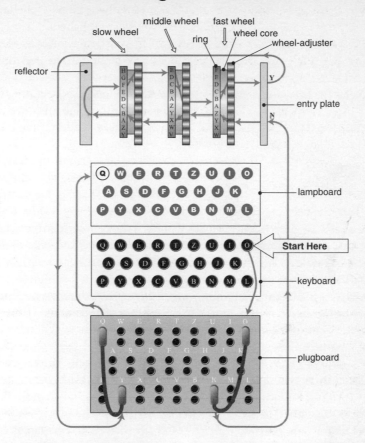

Diagram by Dustin Barrett and Jack Copeland.

Pressing a key at the keyboard causes a letter to light up at the lampboard. The diagram shows the path of the electric current through the Enigma.

The core of each wheel contains a maze of 26 insulated wires, with each wire joining one of 26 contacts on the right-hand side of the wheel to one of 26 contacts on the left-hand side. The wiring is different in each wheel.

Each time the operator presses a letter, one or more of the wheels turns, altering the wiring between the keyboard and the lampboard. Thus each letter of the message is enciphered using a different cipher alphabet.

The function of the plugboard is to provide an extra layer of scrambling. At the start of his shift the operator connects letters together with plug leads. A printed table of instructions, valid for the day, tells him which letters to connect to which.

Jack Copeland

Chapter 2

How It Began: Bletchley Park Goes to War

Michael Smith

THE GOVERNMENT CODE AND CYPHER SCHOOL

The breaking of the German teleprinter cipher that led to the construction of the Colossus computer was the culmination of a series of triumphs for British codebreakers. British interception of other countries' radio communications had begun in earnest during the First World War. The War Office 'censored' diplomatic communications passing through the hands of the international telegraph companies, setting up a codebreaking operation to decipher the secret messages. The British Army intercepted German military wireless communications with a great deal of success. E. W. B. Gill, one of the army officers involved in decoding the messages, recalled that 'the orderly Teutonic mind was especially suited for devising schemes which any child could unravel'. One of the most notable successes for the British cryptanalysts came in December 1916 when the commander of the German Middle-East signals operation sent a drunken message to all his operators wishing them a Merry Christmas. With little other activity taking place over the Christmas period, the same isolated and clearly identical message was sent out in six different codes, only one of which, until this point, the British had managed to break.

The army codebreaking operation became known as MI1b and was commanded by Major Malcolm Hay, a noted historian and eminent academic. It enjoyed a somewhat fractious relationship with its junior counterpart in the Admiralty, formally the Naval Intelligence Department 25 (NID25) but much better known as Room 40, after the office in the Old Admiralty Buildings in Whitehall that it occupied. The navy codebreaking organisation had an even more successful war than MI1b, recruiting a number of the future employees of Britain's Second World War codebreaking centre at Bletchley Park, including Dillwyn 'Dilly' Knox, Frank Birch, Nigel de Grey, and Alastair Denniston, who by the end of the war was head of Room 40. Among the many successes of the Royal Navy codebreakers was the breaking of the Zimmermann telegram, which showed that Germany had asked Mexico to join an alliance against the United States, offering Mexico's 'lost territory' in Texas, New Mexico, and Arizona in return, and brought the United States into the war.

That success appears to have contributed to the turf war between the army and navy codebreakers and what Denniston described as 'the loss of efficiency to both departments caused originally by mere official jealousy'. The two departments did eventually begin to exchange results in 1917, but there remained little love lost. At the end of the First World War, there were a number of people within Whitehall who were keen to axe the codebreakers as part of a peace dividend. But they were far outnumbered by those who were anxious not to lose the intelligence that the codebreakers had been producing. The army and navy codebreaking operations were amalgamated into a single organisation. Denniston was given charge of the Government Code and Cypher School (GC & CS), as it was to be known, with a staff of just over 50 employees, around half of whom were actual codebreakers. 'The public function was "to advise as to the security of codes and ciphers used by all Government departments and to assist in their provision",' Denniston later recalled. 'The secret directive was "to study the methods of cipher communications used by foreign powers".'

The main source of those communications was the international cable companies. A section in the 1920 Official Secrets Act allowed the Home Secretary to order the companies to hand over the cables to the codebreakers. Two Royal Navy intercept sites at Pembroke, in South Wales, and Scarborough, Yorkshire, also provided GC & CS with coded wireless messages.

GC & CS came under the control of the Director of Naval Intelligence Admiral Hugh 'Quex' Sinclair, a noted bon-viveur who installed it in London's fashionable Strand, close to the Savoy Grill, his favourite restaurant. But the only real intelligence the codebreakers were able to provide came from Soviet diplomatic communications and in 1921, when Sinclair was transferred to another post, the Admiralty handed GC & CS over to the Foreign Office. The codebreakers moved briefly to Queen's Gate. A year later, Sinclair was made Chief of the Secret Intelligence Service, now commonly known as MI6, and brought them back under his control. As a result, when MI6 moved to new offices in Broadway, Victoria, the codebreakers went with them, becoming in Denniston's words 'a poor relation of SIS, whose peacetime activities left little cash to spare'.

The codebreakers were recruited, as with their MI6 colleagues, from a limited circle of people within the establishment. J. E. S. 'Josh' Cooper, who would become a leading member of Bletchley Park and subsequently its Cold

War successor GCHQ, recalled being recruited as a 'Junior Assistant' in October 1925.

Like many other recruits (most probably) I had heard of the job through a personal introduction – advertisement of posts was at that time unthinkable. There was very little or no formal training for anybody in those days. The structure of the office was pretty hopeless. It had begun as six Senior Assistants and eighteen Junior Assistants but by the time I joined it was, I think, one Senior Assistant with a responsibility allowance (Denniston), twelve Senior Assistants and twelve Junior Assistants. Supporting staff consisted of a few misemployed typists, some women on SIS books and, I believe, a few women employed as 'JAA' (Junior Assistant's Assistant). For it was the Treasury's understanding that Senior Assistants broke new ciphers and Junior Assistants deciphered and translated the texts. Recruitment by personal introduction had produced some very well-connected officers, especially among the seniors. At best they were fine scholar linguists, at worst some of them were, frankly, 'passengers'.

THE TARGET COUNTRIES

GC & CS worked on the codes and ciphers of most European countries plus a number of other countries around the world. The main target countries were America, France, Japan, and Russia, the latter providing what Denniston said was 'the only real operational intelligence'. The value of that traffic, disclosing a concerted attempt to provoke a Bolshevik revolution in Britain in 1920 and repeated attempts to subvert British society throughout the 1920s and 30s, was a double-edged sword. First in 1920 and then again in 1923 and 1927, it persuaded the British government to disclose that GC & CS had broken the Russian codes and ciphers, leading to changes in Soviet cipher systems that by the late 1920s had all but ended the efforts to break Soviet diplomatic ciphers. After the Government's 1927 admission that GC & CS was reading Moscow's secret messages, the Russians began using the one-time-pad system which, when used properly, was unbreakable.

Similar problems had hampered the British attempts to read Germany's communications. The publication of the Zimmermann telegram had brought the Americans into the war, but it had also revealed Room 40's ability to read the German codes and ciphers. Germany had learned its lesson, and during the 1919 Paris Peace Conference, its delegation used the one-time pad system, blocking British attempts to read its communications with Berlin.

Very little interest was shown in naval or military messages in the immediate wake of the First World War and responsibility for assessing the value of these was left largely to naval and military intelligence. But in 1924,

GC & CS set up a small naval section under W. F. 'Nobby' Clarke, a veteran of Room 40. It obtained its intercepts from the Scarborough station; from a new Royal Navy site at Flowerdown, near Winchester, which had replaced Pembroke; and from operators on board Royal Navy ships who intercepted foreign naval messages in their spare time. By now the army had an intercept site at Fort Bridgewoods, Chatham, and in 1930, a military section was formed, under the command of Captain John Tiltman. The RAF set up its own intercept station at Waddington, Lincolnshire, in 1927, but it was not until 1936 that an air codebreaking section was created in GC & CS with Cooper in charge. Two years later, the RAF intercept site moved from Waddington to Cheadle, in Staffordshire. There were also a number of intercept stations at various sites overseas at the end of the First World War, including Malta, Sarafand in Palestine, Baghdad, and Abbottabad on the North-West Frontier. A Royal Navy intercept station was set up in Hong Kong in 1934 as the threat from Japan became more evident. The messages provided by this network and the international cable companies were augmented by diplomatic and clandestine messages intercepted by a small Metropolitan Police wireless unit based initially in the attic at Scotland Yard and from the mid-1930s in the grounds of the Metropolitan Police Nursing Home at Denmark Hill, south London. The unit, which was controlled by Harold Kenworthy, a Marconi wireless expert, was co-opted by Sinclair to provide GC & CS both with intercepts and technical advice.

ATTACKING ENIGMA

The publicity given to the success of the British codebreakers during the First World War led a number of nations to adopt machine ciphers, which were seen as more difficult to break. The most famous of these was the Enigma machine. The first British contact with the machine came in 1921, when it was still in development. It was shown to the British military attaché in Berlin, in the hope of persuading the British armed forces to use it.

The German Navy introduced the Enigma machine cipher in 1926 and for a brief while it remained a possibility that both the British and the German armed forces might use it. In 1927, Commander Edward Travis, a member of GC & CS who oversaw the construction and security of British codes and ciphers, asked Hugh Foss, a specialist in machine ciphers, to test a commercially available Enigma 'C', which had been bought by Dilly Knox during a visit to Vienna.

The Enigma machine (see photographs 18–19 and 24) resembled a small typewriter encased in a wooden box. It had a typewriter-style keyboard, set out in the continental QWERTZU manner, which differed slightly from the standard British/American QWERTY keyboard. Above the keyboard, on top of the box, was a lampboard with a series of lights, one for each letter of the alphabet. The operator typed each letter of the plaintext message into the machine. The action of depressing each key sent an electrical current through the machine, which lit up the enciphered letter on the lampboard (see the diagram on page 17). There were two crucial features to the machine. A letter could not be enciphered as itself, so the only letter that would not light up on the lampboard if the operator pressed 'T', for example, would be 'T' itself, and the machine was reciprocal, so, if 'P' was enciphered as 'T', then 'T' would encipher as 'P'.

As explained in Chapter 1, the encipherment mechanism consisted of three or, on some later models, four wheels or rotors, each having 26 different electrical contacts, one for every letter of the alphabet, on each side. Each contact, or letter, was connected to another on the other side of the wheel (see photograph 20). These connections were different for each of the three wheels. The wheels could be set at different positions to allow any one of the 26 contacts to form part of a complete circuit and could also be placed in different orders within the machine to add further difficulties for anyone attempting to break the cipher.

The action of depressing each key turned the first wheel one position. When that wheel had moved a set number of times, the second wheel moved round one position, and when the second wheel had turned 26 times, the third wheel moved round one position. The number of different settings for the machine was put at several million. But Foss determined that while it had a 'high degree of security', it could be broken if accurate 'cribs' were available. 'Cribs' are predictions of possible original plaintext, usually standard parts of routine messages, such as situation reports sent out every day. One of the most common was *Keine besondere Ereignisse*, 'nothing to report', which because of its brevity and common usage in situation reports was easy to spot.

Foss later recalled: 'I wrote a paper entitled "The Reciprocal Enigma" in which I showed how, if the wiring was known, a crib of fifteen letters would give away the identity and setting of the right-hand wheel and how, if the wiring was unknown, a crib of 180 letters would give away the wiring of the right-hand and middle wheels.'

The British decided not to buy the machine, although the RAF used it as the inspiration for a much more secure wheel-based cipher machine known as Typex, which British armed forces used with great success during the Second World War. A year after Foss's investigation, the German Army began using the Enigma machine and within two years had introduced an enhancement that greatly improved its security.

The *Steckerbrett* (*Stecker* = 'plug', *brett* = 'board') was an old-fashioned telephone-style plugboard, which allowed the operator to introduce an additional encipherment, using cables and jacks to connect pairs of letters: 'B' to 'Z', 'V' to 'L', etc. (see the diagram on page 17). This made the machine very much more secure, increasing the variations of encipherment to 159 million million million possible settings and blocking British attempts to read the Wehrmacht systems for around eight years. But the Spanish Civil War brought a flood of operational Enigma messages and on 24 April 1937, Dilly Knox managed to break the basic non-steckered machine—i.e. lacking the plugboard—which Germany supplied to its Italian and Spanish allies. Shortly afterwards he began working on the steckered systems used by the Wehrmacht for high-grade communications between Spain and Germany. The British codebreakers made some progress but no enciphered traffic was read and they remained ignorant of the precise nature of the stecker system until the French lent a hand.

THE ROLE OF THE POLISH CRYPTOGRAPHERS

The British had exchanged information on Russian ciphers with the Deuxième Bureau's codebreaking operation since 1933. But it was not until 1938 that the two sides began to discuss the Enigma machine in any detail. Given that the exchange on Russian material had been somewhat one-sided, with the British providing far more than they received in return, the French had a surprisingly large amount of material on the Enigma machine. Since they arrived via the MI6 station in Paris in the same red jackets the British secret service used for all its reports, the French contributions were nicknamed 'Scarlet Pimpernels'. They came not from the French codebreakers but from a Deuxième Bureau agent codenamed Asché. Hans Thilo Schmidt worked in the German Defence Ministry's cipher centre and, in exchange for money and sex, had provided the French with comprehensive details of the Wehrmacht Enigma systems.

The Scarlet Pimpernels included documents on how to use the machine as well as photographs showing the stecker system and how it worked, Cooper recalled. They also suggested that the French were not working alone. 'They had not disclosed that they had other Sigint partners,' he said. 'But a Scarlet Pimpernel on the German Air Force Safety Service traffic had obviously been produced from material intercepted not in France but on the far side of the

Reich. It gave data on stations in eastern Germany that were inaudible from Cheadle, but was weak on stations in the north-west that we knew well. Eventually, the French disclosed that they had a liaison with the Poles, and three-sided Anglo-Franco-Polish discussions began on the Enigma problem.'

The first meeting took place in Paris in January 1939 and was attended by Denniston, Knox, and Foss. By now the British had brought in a number of mathematicians to assist in breaking the machine, among them Alan Turing, and had made more progress. But Peter Twinn, another of the mathematicians brought in by Denniston, recalled that they had been held up by their inability to work out the order in which the keys of the machine were wired to the encipherment mechanism:

Dilly, who had a taste for inventing fanciful jargon, called this the QWERTZU. We had no idea what the order was. We had tried QWERTZU, that didn't work. There are 26 letters in the alphabet. Our ordinary alphabet has them in a certain order. But the Germans weren't idiots. When they had the perfect opportunity to introduce a safeguard to their machine by jumbling it up that would be the sensible thing to do. After all, there were millions of different ways of doing it.

The British codebreakers had high hopes that the meeting with the Polish and French codebreakers would produce the answer. But it was to be a major disappointment. The French codebreakers described their own method of breaking Enigma, which was even less refined than the basic system used by Foss in 1927. Knox described his improved version of Foss's system, which used a process known as rodding. The Poles were under orders to disclose nothing substantive and explained only how lazy operators set the machines in ways that produced pronounceable settings, such as swear words or the names of their girlfriends. This was something the British had already worked out and it was a great disappointment, Foss recalled: 'Knox kept muttering to Denniston, "But this is what Tiltman did," while Denniston hushed him and told him to listen politely. Knox went and looked out of the window.'

The Poles however were far more impressed with Knox and specifically asked that he be present at a second meeting between the Polish, British and French codebreakers, to be held at the Bureau Szyfrów, the Polish cipher bureau, in the Pyry Forest just outside Warsaw, in July 1939. It was only then that the Poles revealed the full extent of the progress they had made in reconstructing the Wehrmacht's steckered Enigma machine.

The Bureau Szyfrów had broken a number of German codes during the early 1920s but the introduction of Enigma had left them unable to read the Wehrmacht's messages. Their response was to recruit mathematics students and put them through a codebreaking course. Only three passed. Their names were Jerzy Różycki, Henryk Zygalski, and Marian Rejewski. All three were recruited but worked initially on a part-time basis, and it was only in September 1932 that Rejewski, the best of the three, was given the steckered Enigma machine and asked to solve it. By the end of that year, assisted by Enigma key lists obtained by the French from Schmidt, he had reconstructed the wiring mathematically, using permutation theory. By the beginning of 1938, assisted by the fact that the Germans were not changing the settings frequently, Rejewski and his colleagues were able to solve 75 per cent of the Poles' intercepts of German Enigma messages. In the autumn of that year, they began using electromechanical machinery known as *Bomby* to identify 'females', repetitive letters in the Enigma keys, to break the messages. But the introduction, in December, of two additional wheels, allowing further different permutations of wheel order, brought the Polish successes to a halt. Rejewski succeeded in reconstructing the wiring of the two new wheels but the Poles no longer had enough Bomby to run through the much greater number of possibilities the new wheels had created. They needed help and believed the British could provide it, said Colonel Stefan Mayer, the officer in charge of the Bureau Szyfrów: 'As the danger of war became tangibly near we decided to share our achievements regarding Enigma, even not yet complete, with the French and British sides, in the hope that working in three groups would facilitate and accelerate the final conquest of Enigma.'

The Poles explained how they used the Bomby and the *Netzverfahren* or 'grid system' invented by Zygalski. The latter used lettered sheets of paper with holes punched in them to help to break the keys by identifying the 'females'. But the introduction of the fourth and fifth wheels had meant they had to use far more Bomby and sheets than they could possibly produce. Knox was furious to discover that the Poles had got there first, sitting in 'stony silence' as they described their progress and produced a clone of the Enigma machine, reconstructed using the knowledge they had built up over the previous six years. But his good humour soon returned after they told him that the keys were wired up to the encipherment mechanism in alphabetical order, A to A, B to B, etc. Although one female codebreaker had suggested this as a possibility, it had never been seriously considered, Twinn recalled: 'It was such an obvious thing to do, really a silly thing to do, that nobody, not Dilly Knox or Tony Kendrick or Alan Turing, ever thought it worthwhile trying it. I know in retrospect it looks daft. I can only say that's how it struck all of us and none of the others were idiots.'

THE COMING OF WAR

A few weeks later the Poles gave both the French and British codebreakers clones of the steckered Enigma. Gustave Bertrand, the head of French codebreaking, who had been given both machines and asked to pass one on to the British, later described taking the British copy to London on the Golden Arrow express train and handing it over to Sinclair's deputy Colonel Stewart Menzies, who was wearing a dinner jacket with the rosette of the Legion d'Honneur.

The signing of the Molotov–Ribbentrop Pact between the Soviet Union and Germany, on 23 August 1939, left little doubt that war was now inevitable. Two days later, the codebreakers moved from Broadway to Bletchley Park, a mansion in the small town of Bletchley, about 40 miles north of London (see photograph 17). It had been bought by Sinclair, out of his own funds, as the War Station for MI6. It was given the cover-name Station X, not as a symbol of mystery but simply because it was the tenth of a number of MI6 sites all designated using Roman numerals.

Denniston, who realised that the elderly classicists who made up the bulk of his codebreakers desperately needed an injection of new talent, had spent the months before the war touring the universities looking for the mathematicians and linguists needed to break the German Enigma cipher. 'He dined at several High Tables in Oxford and Cambridge and came home with promises from a number of dons to attend a "territorial training course",' Cooper said. 'It would be hard to exaggerate the importance of this course for the future development of GC & CS. Not only had Denniston brought in scholars of the humanities, of the type of many of his own permanent staff, but he had also invited mathematicians of a somewhat different type who were specially attracted by the Enigma problem. I have heard some cynics on the permanent staff scoffing at this. They did not realise that Denniston, for all his diminutive stature, was a bigger man than they.'

The academics who attended the course were made to sign the Official Secrets Act and told that on receipt of a telegram they should report to Bletchley Park. Initially, all the codebreakers were crowded into the Mansion, with the exception of Knox and his small team of mathematicians, Turing, Twinn, and John Jeffreys, who were working on the Enigma traffic in an adjoining cottage. But a number of wooden prefabricated huts were erected in the grounds of Bletchley Park itself and a neighbouring school was taken over to house the commercial and diplomatic sections. Soon the various sections began to move out of the mansion into the newly constructed buildings, adopting the name of the hut they were in as their section title, in part for security reasons.

Bletchley Park's first break into Enigma traffic occurred in December 1939 when Turing managed to break five days of Naval 'Home Waters' Enigma, codenamed 'Dolphin' by the British, which had been intercepted in November 1938. But despite the Polish assistance, the codebreakers were unable to break any wartime Enigma. They managed the immense task of preparing the necessary number of punched Zygalski Sheets but could not get the system to work, because details of the internal wiring of the fourth and fifth wheels given to them by the Poles had been copied down incorrectly. Fortunately, Rejewski and his fellow codebreakers had moved to France shortly before the German invasion of Poland (see photograph 22). So, in the second week of January 1940, Turing was sent to see them at the French Army codebreaking base at the Château de Vignolles, in Gretz-Armainvillers, near Paris, to find out what was wrong. He took a large number of the newly made Zygalski Sheets with him. This allowed the Poles to make the first break into wartime Enigma traffic on 17 January 1940, when they read the cipher used for communications between the army's military districts inside Germany, the Wehrkreise, using traffic from 28 October 1939.

The operation at Bletchley Park to break Enigma was now undergoing a major reorganisation. Gordon Welchman, one of the new mathematicians brought in by Denniston, had recognised even before the break into Enigma that it would produce a wealth of intelligence on German military operations, which would have to be processed far more efficiently than GC & CS was then capable of doing. He suggested that the codebreaking operation needed to be much larger than Knox's research section, and would have to incorporate a separate intelligence reporting system if the decrypts were to be passed on both securely and efficiently. It would also need to have far more contact with the intercept sites that provided the Enigma traffic.

This represented a major revolution in the British Sigint operation. 'GC & CS had always tended to take too little interest in the radio by which they lived,' Cooper recalled. Similarly the three services had been dismissive of the work of the codebreakers. They believed their intercept operations, known as *Y Services*, produced sufficient intelligence simply by analysing the activities of the radio networks they were monitoring: indeed the new RAF site at Cheadle was completely ignoring the Enigma traffic. When Cooper suggested that it should begin taking Enigma, the head of the RAF intercept operation replied: 'My Y Service exists to produce intelligence, not to provide stuff for people at Bletchley to fool about with.'

Welchman was given the go-ahead to set up the new system and began his own recruitment drive. He brought in a number of leading mathematicians to work in his new codebreaking section, which was to be housed in one of the new prefabricated buildings, Hut 6. Stuart Milner-Barry, the chess correspondent of *The Times* and a fellow student of Welchman's at Cambridge, was one of the first to join Hut 6, as it was to be known. When the war broke out, he had been in Argentina, playing chess for Britain, along with his friends Hugh Alexander and Harry Golombek. They too soon joined, as did Dennis Babbage from Magdalene College, Cambridge, John Herivel, a former student of Welchman's, and Howard Smith, like Welchman from Sydney Sussex College, Cambridge, and later the head of MI5. Continuity with Knox's efforts was provided by John Jeffreys.

The organisation of Hut 6 reflected Welchman's vision of a totally integrated interception organisation. At one end of what would eventually become something of a production line was Bletchley Park Control, which was initially staffed by begging and borrowing the brightest young men from the top London banks. Control was to be manned 24 hours a day and in constant touch with the intercept sites to ensure that their coverage of radio frequencies and networks was coordinated and that as little as possible was missed. Where an important station was difficult to hear, it was to be 'double-banked', taken by two different operators, normally at different stations, so that the chances of picking up a false letter that might throw a spanner into the works were cut down.

'We were told what we would cover and that came from Station X,' recalled Joan Nicholls, one of the army intercept operators. 'The intercept control there would tell us what to cover that day with what priority. They would tell us if they wanted them double-banked, two people to take them, or if one good quality operator would be sufficient. We didn't know that Station X was Bletchley Park. We never knew where it was. You were only told what you needed to know and we just needed to know that Station X was controlling what we actually monitored.'

FROM INTERCEPTION TO CODEBREAKING

The main pre-war intercept sites in the UK were the two Royal Navy sites at Scarborough and Winchester, the army site at Fort Bridgewoods, Chatham, the new RAF site at Cheadle, and the Metropolitan Police site at Denmark Hill, south London. In the months leading up to the war, the Post Office built a number of other intercept sites for diplomatic traffic to allow the armed forces to concentrate on military and naval traffic. One of these, at Sandridge, near St Albans, was already in place working directly under the control of

Bletchley Park. Two more would shortly be opened in Scotland at Cupar and Brora.

The messages arrived from these outstations by motorcycle courier. But 'Traffic Registers' giving the preambles and first six groups of the messages intercepted by the outstations were sent by teleprinter to the Hut 6 Registration Room. Here a number of female graduates recruited by Milner-Barry from Newnham College, Cambridge, where his sister had been vice-principal, tried to establish the specific Enigma cipher in use from the preambles, carefully examining them to see if there was any intelligence that could be garnered before the codebreakers got to work. A description of each message, containing the frequency and callsigns, the message number, whether or not it was urgent, and the first two groups, was carefully logged on so-called 'B-Lists', a contraction of Banister Lists, named after Michael Banister, the codebreaker who designed them. These became known colloquially as Blists and the female graduates were dubbed 'Blisters'.

Early Hut 6 attempts to break into the keys for the Army and Air Force Enigma ciphers centred on the sheet-stacking room, where codebreakers used Zygalski Sheets to try to break the key in the same way as the Poles. Once a key was broken, the messages were passed to the Machine Room, which contained a number of the British Typex cipher machines, modified to act like Enigma machines. Here they were deciphered. 'When the codebreakers had broken the code they wouldn't sit down themselves and painstakingly decode 500 messages,' said Twinn. 'I've never myself personally decoded a message from start to finish. By the time you've done the first 20 letters and it was obviously speaking perfectly sensible German, for people like me that was the end of our interest.'

Diana Russell Clarke was one of a group of young women in the Hut 6 Machine Room, deciphering the messages. 'The cryptographers would work out the actual settings for the machines for the day,' she said. 'We had these Typex machines, like typewriters but much bigger. They had three wheels, I think on the left-hand side, all of which had different positions on them. When they got the setting, we were to set them up on our machines. We would have a piece of paper in front of us with what had come over the wireless. We would type it into the machine and hopefully what we typed would come out in German.'

Once the message had been deciphered it had to be passed on to someone who could make use of it. Since there had been no deciphered Enigma messages to pass on, no system was in place to do this. So a team of what was initially four intelligence officers was set up in Hut 3, an L-shaped building which nestled behind Hut 6. Their task was to use their knowledge of German to work out what should have been in the numerous gaps in the messages, translate them, and decide to whom they should be sent. The original section was headed by Lieutenant-Commander Malcolm Saunders of the Royal Navy. He was assisted by an Army captain, an RAF squadron-leader, who remarkably spoke not a word of German despite allegedly having acquired his knowledge of the Luftwaffe while carrying out 'field work' on behalf of MI6, and F. L. Lucas, a Fellow of King's College, Cambridge, and author of *The Decline and Fall of the Romantic Ideal*.

On his return to Britain, Turing used the correct data about the wiring of the wheels to lead a successful attack on a recent day's worth of the Wehrkreise Enigma, known at Bletchley Park as 'Green', a result of the coloured crayons used to indicate different keys on the Hut 6 wall charts. The codebreakers were understandably jubilant, but the Wehrkreise messages they had broken contained no intelligence for Hut 3 to report. Lucas said:

On a snowy January morning in 1940, in a small bleak wooden room with nothing but a table and three chairs, the first bundle of Enigma decodes appeared. The four of us who then constituted Hut 3 had no idea what they were about to disclose. Something fairly straightforward like German Police, or something more like diplomatic — neat and explicit documents straight from the office-tables of the Fuhrer and the Wehrmacht that would simply need translating and forwarding to ministries? They were neither. In after-years, even the Fuhrer's orders were duly to appear. But meanwhile here lay a pile of dull, disjointed, and enigmatic scraps, all about the weather, or the petty affairs of a Luftwaffe headquarters no one had heard of, or trifles of Wehrkreis business; the whole sprinkled with terms no dictionary knew, and abbreviations of which our only guide, a small War Office list, proved often completely innocent. Very small beer, in fact, and full of foreign bodies.

Shortly afterwards, Hut 6 broke a second Enigma cipher, the Red, the main Luftwaffe cipher which was widely used for both administrative and operational purposes, including crucially liaison with the army. This would prove to be an important break for two reasons. First, it was on traffic for 6 January 1940, demonstrating that the Germans had not, as feared, changed the indicating system on 1 January. Second, the Red was to become the most productive of the Enigma ciphers and Hut 6's staple diet throughout the war. But in the first few months of 1940, with little activity taking place, it could be broken only sporadically.

Then in the early hours of 9 April 1940, the Germans invaded first Denmark and then Norway. The Phoney War was at an end. Almost immediately, a new Enigma cipher made an appearance. Five days later, the 'Yellow', as it was dubbed by Hut 6, was broken, producing a mass of material on the German operations in Norway which totally overwhelmed Hut 3. Until now, all the reports had been bagged up at the end of the day and sent by van to MI6 headquarters in Broadway, from where they were passed on to the War

Office, the Air Ministry, and the Admiralty. This was clearly no longer sufficient and teleprinters allowing direct contact with MI6 were put into Hut 3.

The staff of Hut 3 was expanded rapidly by borrowing people who spoke German from other huts and by recruiting others from the universities. Each watch consisted of four intelligence officers, a Watch No. 1 and three others, together with a number of typists and clerical assistants. 'Hut 3 and Hut 6 were side by side,' said Ralph Bennett, one of the watch intelligence reporters. 'They were linked by a small square wooden tunnel through which a pile of currently available decodes were pushed, as I remember by a broom handle, in a cardboard box, so primitive were things in those days.'

In order to keep the number of people aware that the German ciphers had been broken to a minimum, Hut 3 totally rewrote the messages to remove any evidence of a deciphered radio signal. They were presented so as to give the impression that they had come from Source Boniface, a supposed British spy with a network of agents inside Germany.

Then, on 1 May 1940, the Germans changed the Enigma indicating system, rendering the Zygalski Sheets useless on all keys except Yellow (in use in Norway). The need for Hut 6 to get back into the Red intensified on 10 May when Germany invaded France. It was Herivel who came up with the answer. Herivel surmised that in many instances the operator would be too lazy or too pushed for time to change the wheel settings properly at the beginning of a new message. So, for messages at the start of the day, the wheel settings would be close to the day's settings:

If the intercept sites could send us the indicators of all the Red messages they judged to be the first messages of the day for the individual German operators there was a sporting chance that they would cluster around the ring settings for the day and we might be able to narrow down the 17,576 possible ring settings to a manageable number, say twenty or thirty, and simply test these one after the other in the hope of hitting on the right answer.

The 'Herivel tip', as it was known, worked in late May 1940 and Hut 6 never lost the Red again. It was used by countless Luftwaffe units and, because they needed to liaise closely with both the army and the navy in order to provide them with air support, gave a good overall insight into all the major German plans and operations. 'From this point on it was broken daily, usually on the day in question and early in the day,' recalled Peter Calvocoressi, one of the members of Hut 3. 'Later in the war, I remember that we in Hut 3 used to get a bit tetchy if Hut 6 had not broken Red by breakfast time.'

THE INTRODUCTION OF THE BOMBES

For several months in 1940, the Herivel tip and similar lapses by operators, such as using settings which spelt out words, were the only ways into the Army and Air Force Enigma systems. But the codebreakers' ability to break Enigma was enhanced immeasurably by the introduction of the *Bombe*. This was a fast-running electrical machine invented in the second half of 1939 by Alan Turing (see photograph 25). The Bombe used 'cribs' to break Enigma messages. Despite the similarity in names, the British machine bore little resemblance to the Polish Bomba and was much more capable of breaking the Enigma settings. It was built to Turing's specification by Harold 'Doc' Keen, the chief engineer of the British Tabulating Machine Company in Letchworth.

The Bombe was a bronze cabinet $6\frac{1}{2}$-feet high, 7-feet 4-inches wide and $2\frac{1}{2}$-feet deep. It initially contained a series of 30 rotating drums, equating to the wheels of 10 Enigma machines, although later versions simulated the action of 12 machines. It was designed to run through all the various possibilities of wheel settings at high speed in order to see if the suspected piece of plaintext appeared in the message. The codebreakers provided the operators with a 'menu' suggesting possible equations of clear letters to enciphered letters, which was fed into the Bombe. Each time the machine found a possible match, it was quickly tested on a replica Enigma machine to see if it produced German text. If it did, it was passed on for decryption.

The first Bombe, christened 'Victory', was installed in March 1940 in part of Hut 1, the other end of the hut being the station sick bay. For five months, it was effectively on trial, attempting to break Naval Enigma. Then Turing and Keen incorporated an idea of Welchman's into the design. Called the 'diagonal board' after the chessboard-like device Welchman produced to prove his theory, it exploited the fact that the Enigma encryptions were reciprocal. If P produced C, then C would produce P. By wiring up the Bombes to test both possibilities simultaneously, the process could be cut dramatically. On 8 August, a second Bombe, known as 'Agnus Dei', later corrupted to 'Agnes', and incorporating the diagonal board became operational, providing assistance to both Hut 6 and a small Enigma research section set up in the Naval Section Hut 4. Initially comprising just Turing and Twinn, this research section would become Hut 8, the naval equivalent of Hut 6.

Despite his early intervention into Army Enigma, Turing had concentrated on the much more difficult Naval Enigma from the start 'because I could have it to myself'. The difficulties lay in a more secure method of allocating key settings and a lack of cribs that could be used on the Bombes, caused by the failure to break enough messages to reveal common streams of plaintext. The lack of vital continuity made breaking the daily settings even more difficult and after his initial success in December 1939, Turing struggled. In May and June of 1940, Turing managed to solve six days of Dolphin, the German Navy Home Waters Enigma from April. He achieved this with the aid of two of the three new wheels that had been captured, or 'pinched', from the *U-33* in February 1940, and signals instructions taken from a German patrol boat. In November, after another pinch had given the codebreakers a full set of naval wheels, Foss managed to break the keys for 8 May, and those for 7 May succumbed shortly afterwards. The newly created Hut 8 enjoyed sporadic breakthroughs, helped by pinches, over the next six months. It was assisted substantially by the capture of key tables for February 1941 on board an armed German trawler off Norway and the discovery that messages being sent on Dolphin were also being sent using an easily read hand cipher. But still there was no continuous break.

The solution came when Harry Hinsley, a young intelligence analyst in Hut 4, spotted messages to and from German weather-ships among the Enigma traffic. These ships, stationed in two places, north of Iceland and in the mid-Atlantic, would need to have exactly the same equipment and keys as any other ship using Enigma but would be far more vulnerable to raids designed to furnish a 'pinch'. Just as importantly, the same messages were being passed in both the Dolphin Enigma key and the German Naval Meteorological Cipher which was much easier to break and would provide vital cribs throughout the war.

The German weather-ship *München* was captured in early May, providing the settings for June. A few days later, more material was captured when the *U-110* was forced to surface off Iceland (see photographs 26–27). A second weather-ship captured at the end of June gave Hut 8 the settings for July. Turing and his team read through June and July using the captured ciphers. From the beginning of August they were on their own. But as a result of the continuity established over the previous two months, the increased availability of cribs, the much larger number of Bombes that were now coming on stream, and a process called *Banburismus*, invented by Turing, which drastically cut the amount of time needed on the Bombes, they remained on top of Dolphin until the end of the war.

Hut 8 passed the deciphered messages on to Hut 4's Z Watch, the naval equivalent of Hut 3, which sent them to the Admiralty's Operational Intelligence Centre (OIC) by teleprinter. The breaking of Dolphin allowed the OIC to re-route the convoys bringing supplies across the Atlantic away from the German U-boats. The results were dramatic, although they cannot all be ascribed to the work of the codebreakers. Between March and June 1941, the U-boats had sunk 282,000 tons of shipping a month. From July, the figure dropped to 120,000 tons a month and by November, when the wolf packs were temporarily withdrawn from the Atlantic, to 62,000 tons. 'It has been calculated that, allowing for the increased number of U-boats at sea, about one-and-a-half million tons of shipping (350) ships were saved,' Hinsley later said. 'This intermission was invaluable for the level of British supplies, the building of new shipping and the development of anti-submarine defences.'

THE SHARK BLACKOUT

But in February 1942, the Atlantic U-boats began using a new four-wheel machine, producing a cipher which the British codenamed 'Shark'. It began a ten-month period known at Bletchley as the 'Shark Blackout'. America's entry into the war had given the U-boats a new target and for the first half of 1942 they were concentrating on sinking undefended merchant ships off the US eastern seaboard. But they returned to the Atlantic in August 1942 and over the next four months ran riot, sinking 43 ships in August and September alone. October and November brought no relief and the Admiralty began to step up the pressure on Hut 8. In a tersely written memorandum, it urged Hut 8 to pay 'a little more attention' to the U-boat cipher and complained that the Battle of the Atlantic was the only area of the war in which Bletchley was having no influence.

But the solution to Shark was almost in place thanks to the bravery of three young men. Two days after the Admiralty memorandum, a pinch of two German 'short signal' codebooks arrived at Bletchley, providing new cribs for the U-boat messages. The books had been recovered from the *U-559*, which was scuttled by its crew after being attacked by the British destroyer HMS *Petard* off the Egyptian coast. Lieutenant Anthony Fasson and Able-Seaman Colin Grazier swam to the submarine before it sank and managed to recover its signal documents. They were joined by the 16-year-old Tommy Brown, who worked for the Naafi, the organisation responsible for armed forces canteens. He succeeded in getting out with the codebooks. But Fasson and Grazier went down with the submarine. They were both awarded the George Cross posthumously. Brown received the George Medal. The honours were well deserved. The short weather messages were to provide the way into Shark. In order to allow the U-boats to receive messages from the weather-ships, which only had the three-wheel Enigma, the four-wheel machine also had the capacity to operate like a three-wheel machine. This gave Hut 8 a way in, using the short weather signals as cribs, and, on 12 December 1942, they broke Shark. Within hours, the Atlantic convoys were being re-routed around the Wolf Packs and, with the assistance of superior US Bombes, which entered effective service in September 1943, Hut 8 had no more major problems breaking the Naval Enigma ciphers.

TUNNY

By now Hut 6 was already preparing for D-day. It had broken a large number of Army and Air Force Enigma systems, which had provided vital intelligence during the campaigns in North Africa, in the Balkans, and on the Italian and Eastern Fronts. But its staple diet remained the Red Luftwaffe air liaison system. This was so rich in detail on air force operations that it shaped the direction of Bletchley Park's attacks on the German teleprinter ciphers, known collectively by the codename *Fish*. The easy availability of intelligence about Luftwaffe operations culled from Enigma led to the decision to concentrate on Tunny, the German Army's Lorenz SZ40 teleprinter cipher machine, at the expense of Sturgeon, the Siemens and Halske T52, used mostly by the Luftwaffe.

Chapter 3

The German Tunny Machine

Jack Copeland

ENIGMA'S HI-TECH SUCCESSOR

The Enigma cipher machine was slow and cumbersome to use. Sending a message was a complicated procedure requiring the participation of several operators (see photograph 24).

The process started with the German plain-language, known as the 'clear' or the 'plaintext'. Encrypting this produced the 'ciphertext'. Typically, the plaintext or clear consisted of ordinary German words mixed with military abbreviations and jargon (such as WEWA for *Wetter Warte*, meaning 'weather station', and BINE, literally 'bee', meaning 'very very urgent').

A cipher clerk typed the plaintext at the keyboard of an Enigma machine (see the diagram on page 17). Each time the clerk pressed a key, a letter on the lampboard would light. For example, typing HITLER might produce the letters FLKPIM. As the letters of the ciphertext appeared one by one at the lampboard, they were painstakingly noted down by an assistant.

Various items of information were then added to the ciphertext, including the intended recipient's radio call-sign, and a radio operator transmitted the complete message in Morse code.

At the receiving end, the process had to be carried out in reverse. The radio operator turned the dit-dit-dahs of the Morse transmission back into letters of ciphertext and handed the result to the cipher clerk. The clerk typed the ciphertext at the keyboard of an Enigma, which had been set up identically to the sender's machine. The letters of the plaintext lit up at the lampboard one by one and were recorded by the assistant.

The Tunny system was much more sophisticated. The process of sending and receiving a message was largely automated. Encryption and decryption were entirely automatic. The transmitted ciphertext was never even seen by the German operators. At the sending end, a single operator typed plaintext at the keyboard of a teleprinter. At the receiving end, the plaintext was printed out automatically by another teleprinter. (A teleprinter is called a teletypewriter in the US.)

The sender could switch his teleprinter equipment from 'hand mode' to 'auto mode'. In auto mode, a pre-punched paper tape was fed into the equipment. The plaintext punched on the tape was encrypted and transmitted at high speed. Many long messages could be sent one after another in this way. The operators would usually converse in hand mode before switching to auto mode. In case of difficulties, the sender could interrupt an auto transmission, dropping back into hand mode and typing something like KOMME ICH KLAR, 'Am I coming clear?'

Morse code was not used at all. The output of the Tunny machine—encrypted teleprinter code—went directly to air.

TELEPRINTER CODE

There was nothing at all secret about teleprinter code. It was in widespread use, both before and after the war, for transmitting information via teleprinter. This included telegrams and telexes sent via the worldwide telegraph system.

In teleprinter code—also called Baudot–Murray code after its creators—letters and other keyboard characters are represented by patterns of electrical pulses. The letter Q, for example, is pulse – pulse – pulse – no-pulse – pulse.

The basic units of teleprinter code are simply the pulse and the absence of a pulse. Each character is assigned a pattern of five basic units, pulse and no-pulse. (Morse code is a quite different: the basic units are the short pulse, dit, and the long pulse, dah, and the number of basic units assigned to a letter varies from 1 to 4. For example, E is dit, T is dah, and K is dah-dit-dah. Up to 6 basic units are used for numbers and punctuation.)

In peacetime use, the groups of pulses were transmitted unenciphered by telephone line from the sender's teleprinter to the recipient's.

The Bletchley Park codebreakers adopted the convention of representing a pulse by a cross and no-pulse by a dot. So Q is ×××•×. More examples: M is ••×××, N is ••××•, C is •×××•, L is •×••×, and S is ×•×••. The dot-and-cross equivalents of the other letters and keyboard characters are shown in Appendix 2 *The Teleprint Alphabet*.

When a message in teleprinter code is placed on paper tape, each letter (or other keyboard character) takes the form of a pattern of holes punched across the width of the tape. A hole corresponds to a pulse.

Using 'x' to mark the position of a hole and '•' to mark the absence of a hole, the short stretch of tape shown in Figure 1 contains M followed by N.

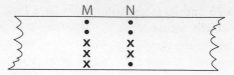

Figure 1. Teleprinter code.

Murray modified Baudot's original form of the code so that the letters most frequently used in English are represented by the fewest holes in the tape. For instance E, the commonest letter of English, is x••••, and T, the next most frequent, is ••••x.

The tape shown in Figure 2 contains the letters COLOSSUS. The small holes along the centre of the tape are sprocket holes. These engaged with a toothed wheel, called the sprocket wheel, which drove the tape through the teleprinter.

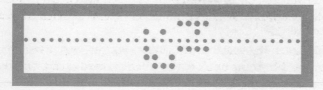

Figure 2. Punched paper tape containing the letters COLOSSUS.

Each of the five horizontal rows along the tape was known in BP (Bletchley Park) jargon as an *impulse*. In Figure 1 the fifth impulse, for example, is x• and in Figure 2 the fifth impulse is •xxx••••. Impulses are sometimes referred to as *channels*.

TELEPRINTER ENCRYPTION

British radio operators first intercepted transmissions in enciphered teleprinter code during the second half of 1940 (see Chapter 7). It was realised that the Germans had developed several different types of cipher machine for use in association with teleprinter equipment. The British gave these machines the general cover name 'Fish'.

Three different types of Fish were known to Bletchley Park: Tunny, Sturgeon, and the unbreakable Thrasher. Sturgeon was used mainly by the German air force and Tunny mainly by the German army. Sturgeon is the subject of Chapters 25 and 26 (see photographs 51–52). It was upon Tunny that Bletchley Park chiefly focused.

THE TUNNY MACHINE

The Tunny machine had a rectangular footprint of 19 inches by $15\frac{1}{2}$ inches and was 17 inches high. It was a cipher *attachment* (see photograph 28). The Tunny was attached to a teleprinter, in order to encrypt the stream of pulses produced by the teleprinter, and to decrypt incoming messages before the teleprinter printed them. Sturgeon, on the other hand, was not an attachment but a combined teleprinter and cipher machine.

Tunny was manufactured by the Lorenz company. The first model bore the designation SZ40. 'SZ' stands for *Schlüsselzusatz*, meaning 'cipher attachment'. A later version, the SZ42A, was introduced in February 1943, followed by the SZ42B in June 1944. ('40' and '42' seem to refer to years, as in 'Windows 97'.)

Like the Enigma, the heart of the Tunny machine was a system of wheels (see photograph 29). Some or all of the wheels moved each time the operator typed a character at the teleprinter keyboard (or in the case of an auto-transmission from pre-punched tape, each time a new letter was read in from the tape). There were 12 wheels in all. They stood side by side in a single row, like plates in a dish rack. The Germans numbered the wheels 1 to 12, from the left.

The Tunny system worked like this. The sending operator typed a message at the keyboard of his teleprinter, or fed in a tape for auto-transmission. The stream of pulse/no-pulse generated by his teleprinter equipment then passed through the Tunny machine on the way to the radio transmitter. The Tunny masked the plaintext with a stream of obscuring letters. These obscuring characters, known as *key*, were produced by the Tunny machine's wheels.

The receiver's Tunny, a duplicate of the sender's, took the stream of pulses delivered by the radio receiver and stripped away the key, producing unenciphered teleprinter code. The teleprinter to which the Tunny was attached then converted the teleprinter code to letters and other characters. The resulting plaintext was usually printed out on sticky tape, which the operator stuck in strips across a sheet of paper, like an old-fashioned telegram. In addition to (or instead of) printing the text, the receiving teleprinter could be made to punch a tape.

As in the case of Enigma, the rim of each of the Tunny's 12 wheels was marked with numbers, visible to the operator through a small window. Like the numbers on the rotating parts of a combination lock, these showed the positions to which the wheels could turn. Wheel 1, on the far left, had a total of 43 positions. The numbers of positions of the other 11 wheels were (travelling towards the right): 47, 51, 53, 59, 37, 61, 41, 31, 29, 26, 23.

In comparison, the Enigma had three rotating wheels, each wheel having only 26 positions. The version of Enigma used by the German military also contained the plugboard, which in effect functioned as an extra wheel, also with 26 positions, but with variable connections (see the diagram on page 17). For additional security, some later Enigmas were fitted with a fourth wheel.

Each Enigma wheel replaced one letter with another. For example, if the letter 'N' goes into the first wheel, 'Z' may come out. 'Z' is then passed to the next wheel, where a second substitution is performed, 'Z' being replaced by 'X', say, and so on. When a letter of plaintext entered the three-wheeled Enigma, a series of nine such substitutions led to the letter which lit up at the keyboard (see the diagram on page 17).

The Tunny wheels operated quite differently. All 12 wheels acted together to produce a single letter of key, which was then merged with one letter of the plaintext. The letters of the plaintext were obscured one by one in this way.

The process of merging two letters is described later in this chapter.

TUNNY LINKS

The first Tunny radio link, between Berlin and Athens/Salonika, went into operation on an experimental basis in June 1941. In October 1942 this experimental link closed down, and for a short time it was thought that the Germans had abandoned the Tunny machine. Later that same month Tunny reappeared in an altered form, on a link between Berlin and Salonika and on a new link between Königsberg and South Russia. At the time of the allied invasion in 1944, when the Tunny system had reached its most stable and widespread state, there were 26 different links known to the British. The map in Figure 3 shows 19 links (which is based on a wartime map drawn by the British).

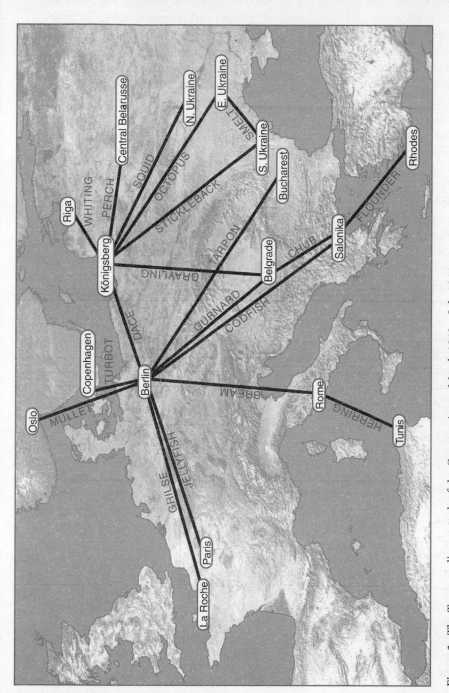

Figure 3. The Tunny radio network of the German Army, March 1943 – July 1944.

By Dustin Barrett and Jack Copeland.

BP gave each link a piscine name: Berlin–Paris was Jellyfish, Berlin–Rome Bream, Berlin–Copenhagen Turbot. The links carried messages from Hitler and members of the High Command to the various Army Group commanders in the field—intelligence of the highest grade.

The two central exchanges for Tunny traffic were Strausberg near Berlin for the Western links, and Königsberg for the Eastern links into Russia. In July 1944, the Königsberg exchange closed and a new hub was established for the Eastern links at Golssen, about 20 miles from the Wehrmacht's underground command headquarters south of Berlin (see Appendix 1 *Timeline: The Breaking of Tunny*). There were also fixed exchanges at some other large centres, such as Paris; otherwise, the distant ends of the links were mobile.

Each mobile Tunny unit consisted of two trucks. One carried the radio equipment, which had to be kept well away from teleprinters for fear of interference. The other carried the teleprinter equipment and two Tunny machines, one for sending and one for receiving. This truck also carried a device for punching tapes for auto-transmission.

Sometimes a land line was used in preference to radio. In this case, the truck carrying the Tunnies was connected up directly to the telephone system. Only Tunny traffic sent by radio was intercepted by the British.

During the final stages of the war, the Tunny network became increasingly disorganised. By the time of the German surrender, the central exchange had been transported from Berlin to Salzburg in Austria.

The last Tunny message was sent on 8 May 1945.

HOW TUNNY ENCRYPTS

The Tunny machine encrypted each letter of the plaintext by *adding* another letter to it. This process of adding—or merging—letters together is not quite the same as adding numbers, but there are similarities.

Like number-addition, Tunny letter-addition obeys fixed rules, which are set out in an 'addition table', rather like the multiplication tables that we learned at school. For example, one entry in the addition table is M + N = T. The complete table is shown in Appendix 3 *The Tunny Addition Square*.

The internal mechanism of the Tunny machine produces its own stream of letters, the 'key-stream'. Each letter of the ciphertext is produced by adding a letter from the key-stream to the corresponding letter of the plaintext. So, if the first letter of the plaintext happens to be M and the first letter of the key-stream happens to be N, the first letter of the ciphertext is T.

LETTER ADDITION

The Tunny machine adds letters by adding the individual dots and crosses that compose them. The rules that the makers of the machine selected for dot-and-cross addition are simple. Dot plus dot is dot. Cross plus cross is dot. Dot plus cross is cross. Cross plus dot is cross. Two sames add up to dot; two differents add up to cross.

$$
\begin{aligned}
DOT &+ DOT &= DOT \\
CROSS &+ CROSS &= DOT \\
DOT &+ CROSS &= CROSS \\
CROSS &+ DOT &= CROSS
\end{aligned}
$$

The following table shows the addition of M and N. Their sum, ••••×, is the teleprinter code for T.

M		N		T
•	+	•	=	•
•	+	•	=	•
×	+	×	=	•
×	+	×	=	•
×	+	•	=	×

HOW TUNNY DECRYPTS

The German engineers selected the rules of dot-and-cross addition so that the following is always true, no matter which letters, or other keyboard characters, are involved: adding one letter (or other character) to another and then *adding it again a second time* leaves you where you started. For example, adding N to M produces T, as we have just seen, and then adding N to T leads back to M:

T		N		M
•	+	•	=	•
•	+	•	=	•
•	+	×	=	×
•	+	×	=	×
×	+	•	=	×

This explains how the receiver's Tunny decrypted the ciphertext. The ciphertext was produced by adding a stream of key to the plaintext, so by means of adding exactly the same letters of key to the *ciphertext*, the receiver's machine wiped away the encryption, exposing the plaintext again.

Suppose the plaintext is the single word 'COLOSSUS'. The stream of key added to the plaintext by the sender's Tunny might be: WZHI/NR9. These characters are added serially to the letters of COLOSSUS:

$$C + W \quad O + Z \quad L + H \quad O + I \quad S + / \quad S + N \quad U + R \quad S + 9.$$

This produces XDIVSDFE (as you can check by using the addition table in Appendix 3). Then XDIVSDFE is transmitted over the link. The Tunny at the receiving end adds the same letters of key to the encrypted message:

$$X + W \quad D + Z \quad I + H \quad V + I \quad S + / \quad D + N \quad F + R \quad E + 9.$$

This uncovers the letters COLOSSUS.

THE OPERATING PROCEDURE

In order for the receiving machine to generate the same key as the sending machine, the receiving operator had to synchronise his Tunny with the sender's.

So long as both machines had their wheels in the same positions at the start of the message, the machines would automatically stay in synchronisation throughout the transmission. The receiving operator, then, needed to know the positions of the 12 wheels of the sending machine at the start of the message.

At Bletchley, these 12 positions were called the *wheel settings* for that particular message. Two different procedures were used to convey the wheel settings to the receiver. The first was used on the experimental Tunny link and the other was adopted once the experimental phase was over.

During the days of the experimental link, the wheel settings for a message were selected by the sending operator. Before sending the message, the operator would use his thumb or fingers to turn the wheels to the combination of his choosing. Each wheel was fitted with a toothed grip-ring to enable him to turn it easily (these are visible in photograph 29). As mentioned previously, the rim of each wheel was inscribed with numbers, 01, 02, 03, etc., each number marking a position of the wheel.

The sending operator was supposed to ensure that the wheels were never placed in the same positions at the start of two different messages. However, owing to operator error, this did sometimes occur—providing a way in for the codebreakers.

The sender transmitted his selected settings to the receiver in the form of a sequence of 12 letters. The 12 letters were sent in clear (i.e. unenciphered) before the enciphering of the message began. At Bletchley, these 12 letters in clear were called the message's *indicator*. Each letter of the indicator denoted the position of one wheel. So, for example, if the sender transmitted the indicator HQIBPEXEZMUG, the receiver knew that he must turn the left-hand wheel of his machine to position 'H', the next wheel to position 'Q', and so on.

All operators on the experimental link used the same letters to name the same wheel positions. Probably the operators were issued with tables setting out the correlations between letters and positions. The correlations were different for each individual wheel. 'E' might mean position 22 in the case of wheel 6, but position 10 in the case of wheel 8. Each month, a different set of correlations came into force.

To safeguard against operator error, the indicator was expanded into a sequence of common names before transmission: 'Anton' for 'A', 'Berta' for 'B', 'Caesar' for 'C', and so on (see Figure 1 of Appendix 5).

This system of conveying the wheel settings to the receiver had the effect of limiting the number of wheel settings that were available for use during any one month. Wheel 5, for example, had 59 possible positions, but because this exceeded the number of letters in the alphabet, less than half of the 59 positions could be used as starting positions. It was like having a combination lock some of whose combinations could not be used.

When the experimental Tunny link closed down in October 1942 and two links opened in its place (Octopus from Königsberg to the Ukraine and Codfish from Berlin to Salonika), a new procedure was introduced for conveying the wheel settings from sender to receiver. The use of the 12-letter indicator was discontinued. The new method, which remained in force for the rest of the war, involved what was called a *QEP book*.

A QEP book contained a list of one hundred or more different wheel settings. The operators at each end of a Tunny link had the same QEP book. Different links were issued with different books. After a QEP book had been used once, it was discarded and the operators moved on to the next book.

Each line of a typical QEP book looked like this:

> 001   20 47 26 50 17 35 13 02 12 10 24 09

Here 001 was called the 'QEP number'. The other 12 numbers specified the positions of the wheels. Each line of the book began with a different QEP number, 002, 003, and so on. Usually the QEP number was between 1 and 100 (although occasionally four-figure QEP numbers were used).

The sending operator selected a QEP number from the current book and transmitted it in clear, preceded by the letters 'QEP'. Once both operators had set the wheels of their machines to the positions shown beside that number in the book, the message could be transmitted.

The *General Report on Tunny* describes the complete process of transmission:

Tunny operators can transmit to each other either in cipher or in clear according to whether the Tunny machine is switched IN or OUT, and either in HAND or in AUTO. If sending and receiving machines were working simultaneously, transmission is described as DUPLEX, otherwise as SIMPLEX.

After Oct. 1942 the normal routine was somewhat as follows: The operator sits at the keyboard of the sending teleprinter with the printer of the receiving teleprinter directly in front of him. He makes contact with the operator at the other end by hand transmission in clear, and may carry on a brief conversation in Q-code to ensure that conditions are satisfactory for cipher transmission.

Q-code is an international code used by radio operators. To give an illustration, the strength of the received signal is represented on a scale of 1 to 5, with 5 meaning 'excellent'; transmitting 'QSA 5' means 'Your signal strength is excellent.' The procedure continues:

Before the Tunny machine is switched in, the operator sets the wheels to the settings opposite the next number in the QEP book and transmits QEP followed by the last 2 figures of the number. Just before switching in he transmits UMUM in clear.

After the machine is switched in, all outgoing transmission is in cipher. Further chat by the operator may be answered in clear, or, if the receiving Tunny is also switched in, in cipher. The text of the operator's chat (clear or cipher) is received on the printer but not preserved.

As soon as the operator is ready to transmit his message (which should have been previously perforated) he switches in the auto transmitter and ceases to operate the keyboard. The message starts with an address and serial number and as it is received it is stuck on a message form by the receiving operator.

The transmission of a complete tape is usually followed by operators' chat in hand and then mixed hand and auto transmission while the sender tries to discover if the message has arrived in comprehensible form, makes any necessary corrections, or retransmits any part of the tape. When the receiver is satisfied, he sends a receipt in clear or cipher according to whether his outgoing Tunny is switched in or not.

After the receipt, the sender may switch off or send another message before resetting. One transmission therefore may contain several serial messages. On the other hand, very long message tapes may be transmitted partly in one QEP and partly in the next, and resetting may also take place during a message if something goes wrong.

GENERATING THE KEY

The Tunny machine produces its key-stream by adding together two other letter streams which it generates, called at BP the *psi*-stream and the *chi*-stream (from the Greek letters psi ψ and chi χ). The psi-stream and the chi-stream are produced by the wheels of the Tunny machine. It is time to consider the wheels in detail.

The 12 wheels form three groups: five *psi-wheels*, five *chi-wheels*, and two *motor-wheels*. Wheels 1–5 are the psi-wheels, wheels 6 and 7 are the motor-wheels, and wheels 8–12 are the chi-wheels.

Each wheel has cams—sometimes referred to as 'pins'—arranged evenly around its circumference. The function of the cam is to push a switch as it passes, so that as the wheel rotates a stream of electrical pulses is generated.

It is the number of cams around a wheel that determines how many positions the wheel can adopt. Wheel 1 has 43 cams and therefore 43 positions, wheel 2 has 47 cams, and so on.

The Wheel Patterns

The cams can be adjusted by the operator. He can slide any of the cams sideways, so that they become inoperative and no longer push the switch when they pass it (see Figure 4). The wheel now causes not a uniform stream of pulses as it turns, but a pattern of pulses and no-pulses—crosses and dots.

The arrangement of the cams around the wheel, either operative or inoperative, is called the *wheel pattern*. For example, if the first and second

Operative   Inoperative

Figure 4. A wheel cam in the operative and inoperative position.

cams are operative, and the third and fourth inoperative, the wheel pattern begins ××••. . .

Lists of wheel patterns were issued to Tunny units so that the machines at each end of a link could be set up identically. Different links used different wheel patterns. Prior to the summer of 1944, the Germans changed the cam patterns of the chi-wheels once every month and the cam patterns of the psi-wheels at first quarterly, then monthly from October 1942. The motor-wheel patterns were changed daily, even on the experimental link. After 1 August 1944, all wheel patterns were changed daily.

It is the patterns of the cams around the chi-wheels that produce the chi-stream, and the patterns of the cams around the psi-wheels that produce the psi-stream.

With the arrival of each new letter of the message at the Tunny attachment (unenciphered if outgoing, enciphered if incoming), the five chi-wheels turned in unison, just far enough for one cam on each wheel to pass its switch. Cams in the operative position produced a pulse. For example, suppose that in the case of the first chi-wheel the cam that has reached the switch—the 'active' cam—produces a pulse; and suppose that the active cams on the second and third chi-wheels also produce pulses, but that the active cams on the fourth and fifth chi-wheels produce no pulse:

1st chi-wheel produces: ×
2nd chi-wheel produces: ×
3rd chi-wheel produces: ×
4th chi-wheel produces: •
5th chi-wheel produces: •

The letter that the chi-wheels produce at this point in their rotation is ×××••. That is to say, the chi-stream at this point contains the letter U. The five psi-wheels also contribute a letter (or other keyboard character). Perhaps the psis produce ×××•×, i.e. Q.

The letter produced by the psi-wheels is added to the letter produced by the chi-wheels in order to create a letter of key:

$$U + Q = T.$$

The wheel patterns were arranged so that the key-stream contained each character of the teleprinter alphabet approximately an equal number of times. This meant that, on average, the same was true of the stream of ciphertext.

The Staggering Psis

The chi-wheels all moved forward together by one cam with the arrival of each new letter (from the keyboard, tape, or receiver), but the psi-wheels moved irregularly. The psis might all move forward with the chis, or they might all stand still, missing an opportunity to move. This motion was described as 'staggering' at BP.

Whether the psi-wheels moved or not was determined by the motor-wheels. If the first motor-wheel showed ×, the psis advanced; and if the first motor-wheel showed •, the psis stood still. The first motor-wheel itself staggered, under the control of the second motor-wheel. Depending on whether the second wheel showed × or •, the first wheel would either advance or stand still (• meant 'stop', × meant 'go'). The second motor-wheel stepped on regularly like the chis.

While the psis remained stationary, they continued to contribute the same letter to the key. So the chis might contribute

... KDUGRYMC ...

and the psis might contribute

... GGZZZWDD ...

Here the chis have moved eight times and the psis only four.

The psi-stream is the stream of letters that the psi-wheels produce *as they turn*, here ... GZWD. .. The stream of letters that the psis actually contribute to the key, here ... GGZZZWDD ..., is called the *extended* psi-stream.

Limitation

In the SZ40, it was solely the movements of the motor-wheels which determined whether or not the psi-wheels moved. In the SZ42A and SZ42B, further factors also played a role in determining whether the psis moved. At BP these other factors were called 'limitations'.

One example is 'P_5 limitation', where the movement of the psis is determined partly by the letters of the plaintext itself. 'P_5' refers to the fifth impulse of the plaintext. In P_5 limitation, the presence or absence of a cross at a certain position in the fifth impulse of the plaintext (e.g. two letters back from the letter most recently encrypted) was one of the determinants of whether or not the psis moved.

P_5 limitation is an example of what BP called an 'autoclave', from the Greek for 'self' and the Latin for 'key'. The plaintext played a role in the creation of the key used to encipher it.

Appendix 10 *The Motor Wheels and Limitations* describes the detailed action of the motor-wheels and the various limitations used by the Germans.

BREAKING THE TUNNY MACHINE

As mentioned above, German operators from time to time used the same wheel settings for two different messages, a circumstance called a *depth*. It was through depths that the group known as the Research Section found its way into Tunny.

A depth could be used to retrieve a portion of key-stream. A long depth transmitted in August 1941 yielded approximately 4000 consecutive characters of key. This important event is described in the next chapter, and further detail is given in Appendix 5 *The Tiltman Break*.

In January 1942, one member of the Research Section, Bill Tutte, managed single-handedly to deduce the fundamental structure of the Tunny machine—previously a mystery—from these 4000 characters of key. Tutte, a quiet and modest man, had arrived at Bletchley Park from Cambridge University in mid-1941. Originally studying for a doctorate in chemistry, Tutte had become fascinated with mathematics instead. 'Tutte appeared, like Turing himself, taciturn and abstracted, staring for long periods into the middle distance,' recollected one of the Tunny group.

Tutte focused on just one of the five 'slices', or impulses, of the key-stream: the top-most row were the key-stream to be punched on tape. This impulse of the key-stream, Tutte managed to deduce, was the result of adding two streams of dots and crosses. Further, the two streams were produced by a pair of wheels, which he called 'chi' and 'psi'. The chi-wheel, he determined, always moved forward one place from one letter of text to the next, and the psi-wheel sometimes moved forwards and sometimes stayed still.

It was, to say the least, a remarkable feat. At this stage the rest of the Research Section joined in and soon the whole machine was laid bare, without any of them ever having set eyes on one.

Tutte describes in detail how he broke the Tunny machine in Appendix 4 *My Work at Bletchley Park*.

THE WHEEL-SETTING PROBLEM

Now that BP knew the workings of the machine, the problem was how to read the message traffic.

Depths could often be read, but depths were relatively infrequent. An important method for finding wheel patterns from depths, known as 'Turingery', was invented by Alan Turing in July 1942. Turingery is described in Appendix 6 *Turingery*. Turing was at that time on loan to the Research Section from Hut 8 and the struggle against Naval Enigma. Turingery was the third of the three strokes of genius that Turing contributed to the attack on the German codes, along with his design for the Bombe and his unravelling of the form of Enigma used by the Atlantic U-boats. As fellow codebreaker Jack Good observed, 'I won't say that what Turing did made us win the war, but I daresay we might have lost it without him.'

Thanks to Tutte's feat of reverse-engineering, the wheel patterns were known for August 1941, and while the number of links remained small and the chi- and psi-wheel patterns did not change frequently, the Research Section (and later the Testery) could break new patterns by hand.

Knowing the wheel patterns was not enough, however. Each message had its own wheel settings—its own 'combination'—and could not be read until its combination was known. During the era of the 12-letter indicator, the German operator obligingly told the codebreakers what the wheel settings were. But in October 1942, with the introduction of QEP books, the luxury of the indicator was no more. The codebreakers were thrown back on depths. How to discover the wheel settings for the rest of the message traffic was the fundamental problem facing the Tunny breakers in the autumn of 1942. The next chapter describes how Tutte solved the problem, by means of the fundamental '1 + 2 break in'.

Chapter 4

Colossus, Codebreaking, and the Digital Age

Stephen Budiansky

THE ACCIDENTAL CRYPTANALYSTS

The paths that took men and women from their ordinary lives and deposited them on the doorstep of the odd profession of cryptanalysis were always tortuous, accidental, and unpredictable. The full story of the Colossus, the pioneering electronic device developed by the Government Code and Cypher School (GC & CS) to break German teleprinter ciphers in the Second World War, is fundamentally a story of several of these accidental paths converging at a remarkable moment in the history of electronics—and of the wartime urgency that set these men and women on these odd paths. Were it not for the wartime necessity of codebreaking, and were it not for particular statistical and logical properties of the teleprinter ciphers that were so eminently suited to electronic analysis, the history of computing might have taken a very different course.

The fact that Britain's codebreakers cracked the high-level teleprinter ciphers of the German Army and Luftwaffe high command during the Second World War has been public knowledge since the 1970s. But the recent declassification of new documents about Colossus and the teleprinter ciphers, and the willingness of key participants to discuss their roles more fully, has laid bare as never before the technical challenges they faced—not to mention the intense pressures, the false steps, and the extraordinary risks and leaps of faith along the way.

It has also clarified the true role that the Colossus machines played in the advent of the digital age. Though they were neither general-purpose nor stored-program computers themselves, the Colossi sparked the imaginations of many scientists, among them Alan Turing and Max Newman, who would go on to help launch the post-war revolution that ushered in the age of the digital, general-purpose, stored-program electronic computer.

Yet the story of Colossus really begins not with electronics at all, but with codebreaking; and to understand how and why the Colossi were developed and to properly place their capabilities in historical context, it is necessary to understand the problem they were built to solve, and the people who were given the job of solving it. It is a story that really begins with a man who knew nothing about electronics, and almost nothing about statistics or Boolean logic.

John Tiltman was the accidental cryptanalyst par excellence. His clipped mustache and regimental bearing made him look like a British Army colonel from central casting—'Every inch a soldier,' friends said (see photograph 21). He had been severely wounded on the Somme in the First World War, winning the Military Cross for his troubles. Given a desk job to recuperate, he landed totally by fluke in the small postwar bureau of codebreakers that would soon be known as GC & CS.

Tiltman years later said he had had no knowledge of higher mathematics, not even statistics or probability. But he did have that indefinable knack of sensing patterns, combined with that indispensable tenacity that is the hallmark of all great codebreakers. Within a year he was on his way to Simla, in the Himalayan foothills of British India, with the assignment of breaking coded Soviet diplomatic traffic passing between Moscow and Kabul and Tashkent. His success fully justified the effort, for it revealed that the 'Great Game' had hardly ended with the overthrow of the Czar and the coming of Bolshevism: messages Tiltman broke throughout the 1920s revealed a concerted effort by Moscow to foment anti-British feeling and subversion along the frontier of the Raj.

Tiltman was definitely of the old school of codebreakers, the kind who could have walked off the pages of Edgar Alan Poe's or Arthur Conan Doyle's stories. He always worked by himself, standing at a specially made desk, following leads and hunches for days and weeks on end—more like a detective than a modern cryptanalyst, said one of his more modern, and mathematically inclined, colleagues, Hugh Alexander. He had a knack for seat-of-the-pants cryptography, and an even greater knack for languages, acquiring Russian, German, and Japanese. Beneath the Colonel Blimp exterior lay an extraordinarily supple mind and a certain humorous impatience with conventional authority as well. A private assigned to the military codebreaking section at Bletchley Park never forgot his introduction to Tiltman as he reported for duty. Approaching the colonel's desk, he stamped the floor in proper drill fashion and saluted, ending with another thunderous crash of his army boots on the wooden floor. Tiltman looked up wordlessly, looked down at the private's feet, and then back up at the young soldier's face. 'I say, old boy,' he finally said after a long pause, '*must* you wear those damned boots?'

It wasn't usual for privates to wear battle dress and white running shoes, but it wasn't usual for colonels to address privates as 'old boy' either, and both, to the delight of the private and the disgust of the regular army adjutant assigned to Bletchley Park, became the norm in Tiltman's section.

Tiltman's follow-the-hunches approach to sniffing out the weak point of an enemy code was actually, in many cases, the best way to tackle the coded signals of the Japanese and German forces that British and American listening posts began intercepting in the 1930s. Many of the enemy codes were hand systems that used code books or key squares in which words or letters or pairs of letters were substituted according to a prescribed pattern, and a trained human mind's ability to spot such patterns—in coded messages just as in chess games or crossword puzzles—was still the best tool for tackling them. In July 1941, as German panzers thundered into Russia, Tiltman's group broke the hand cipher used by the German Police in the East and began to read the first hints of unimaginable horrors to come: tallies were recorded of numbers of Jews shot in 'cleansing' operations by the advancing German troops, who had been told by Hitler that this was to be no contest 'in the knightly fashion'.

THE MACHINE CIPHERS APPEAR

But the Germans themselves were fully aware of the weakness of hand ciphers and, on a scale unlike any other nation, had built and deployed in the field thousands of coding machines. These electrical machines, using wired rotors that would turn to generate a new scrambling pattern as each letter of a message was typed in—A standing for E in one spot, A standing for X in another—were capable of millions upon millions of permutations that defied hand methods of decipherment. The most famous of these machines was the Enigma, which the German armed forces had been using since the mid-1930s. But following the invasion of Russia in June 1941, another sort of signal started appearing in the operational radio traffic of the German army. Clearly, this was the product of a machine cipher of even greater complexity. The signals were being sent not in Morse code, but in a 5-bit binary code; that immediately suggested to Bletchley's experts that the signals were being generated by a teleprinter machine. It was also at once apparent, however, that the standard teleprinter code was being scrambled—probably, the codebreakers surmised, by coding wheels attached to the teleprinter that automatically masked the standard teleprinter code as the text was transmitted.

These signals would subsequently be known by the British codename Tunny, and it would eventually be learned they were the product of an enciphering machine made by the Lorenz firm, the Schlüsselzusatz 40, or SZ40. Another teleprinter machine codenamed Sturgeon (the Siemens T52) would come into use by the Luftwaffe over the next year. By the end of the war, Bletchley Park was routinely cracking hundreds of Tunny signals a month in an operation that involved hundreds of men and women, including some of the finest mathematical minds in the country, aided by a battery of ten specially built digital electronic computers—machines of unprecedented size and complexity. The historian of cryptography Ralph Erskine has called the breaking of Tunny 'the greatest cryptanalytical feat of World War II'. Because Tunny links connected Berlin directly to the headquarters of theatre and army group commanders, the messages that Bletchley's codebreakers broke revealed German intentions and strategy at the highest levels. In the weeks leading up to D-day, decoded Tunny traffic provided a series of strategic appreciations by the German Commander-in-Chief West, Field Marshal Gerd von Runstedt, of the Allied invasion threat. These provided important reassurance to Allied commanders that their audacious deception plan was succeeding.

Breaking Tunny was also the feat that irrevocably hurled codebreaking headlong into the modern age of computing and mathematical analysis. It is no exaggeration to say that it helped to launch the entire modern digital revolution by providing an urgent impetus to the development of some of the key foundations of the modern computer that might otherwise have taken years more to mature.

The mathematical intensity of the work was unlike anything that had come before. By the end of the war, the theorems, reasoning, statistics, and Boolean logic that underlay the attack against Tunny had filled thousands of pages of notebooks. Many, indeed perhaps all, of the notebooks may have been lost by GC & CS's successor agency, but a detailed technical history of the work—the *General Report on Tunny*—does survive (and is available on the Internet at <www.AlanTuring.net/tunny_report>).

FIRST BREAK

Yet it was Lieutenant Colonel John Tiltman, a relic of the old pre-mathematical, pre-computing days of codes and codebreaking, who—ever so fitting to the quirky ways of cryptography—lit the spark of revolution. On 30 August 1941, British radio operators picked up two Tunny signals both bearing the same 12-letter starting code: HQIBPEXEZMUG. The Bletchley codebreakers already had established that these starting groups were 'indicators'; that is, they told the recipient of the message how to set the starting position of the wheels on the coding attachment. They had also figured out that these wheels generated a series of quasi-random 5-bit numbers that would be added bit by bit to each letter; the recipient at the other end of the link would turn his wheels to the same setting to automatically strip off this added 'key' and reveal the original text of the incoming signal.

In the case of the August 30 messages, however, the German teletype operator had committed a fabulous breach of security procedures. He had resent the same 3976-character-long message at the same setting of the coding machine, but the second time he had begun by abbreviating the word *spruchnummer* ('message number'), which he had spelled out in full the first time round. He had also in the course of retyping the message made other slip-ups, such as misspellings and changes in spacing. By the 3976th letter the two messages were off by about 100 characters.

This was a gift from heaven. The machine's code wheels had of course generated exactly the same sequence of key in both messages. So simply adding the first message to the second zeroed the key out of the equation altogether; what was left was a stream of 5-bit binary numbers that represented *only* the plaintext of the two messages added to one another. Tiltman was given the job of trying to figure out the actual text of both messages. This was a crossword-solver's delight. By guessing at likely words in one of the messages and seeing what letter that implied for the second, Tiltman in short order had teased out the full text. (His procedure is described in Appendix 5 *The Tiltman Break.*) Even more important, by adding the plaintext to the original coded signal, the Bletchley codebreakers now had an actual 3976-character long stretch of key that just might reveal how the Tunny machine was constructed: how many wheels it had, how they turned, how they were wired.

The Bletchley codebreakers would never see an actual Tunny machine until the end of the war. Their job was thus, sight unseen, to imagine how it was constructed, with nothing but this external evidence to go on. This was clearly a job for a mathematician.

GC & CS had begun the war with an extreme reluctance to hire anyone with a scientific or technical background at all. Recruiting was done through an old-boy network with a vengeance. The principal contacts that GC & CS had with the academic world were through men who had worked in the Admiralty's famous 'Room 40' codebreaking operation during the First World War; and these were mainly linguists who were now Oxford and Cambridge dons in such fields as classics, history, and modern languages. Alastair Denniston, GC & CS's operational head, explained that these men 'knew the type required', professors and bright undergraduates alike, and discreet enquiries were accordingly made. Of the first 21 'men of the professor type' (as Denniston called them) who were hired by GC & CS immediately after the outbreak of war in September 1939, 18 were humanists—historians of art, professors of medieval German, lecturers in ancient Greek. This was partly just an inevitable reflection of the contacts Denniston had, but it was also partly a manifestation of the enduring British public-school prejudice against anything even remotely associated with 'trade'; properly educated boys studied Latin and Greek, not science or engineering. Peter Twinn, one of the very few early recruits who did have a technical background, later recalled that there had been grave doubts about hiring him because mathematicians 'were regarded as strange fellows'; if hiring someone with scientific training 'were regretfully to be accepted as an unavoidable necessity,' as Twinn facetiously put it, the prevailing view was that it might be better 'to look for a physicist on the grounds that they might be expected to have at least some appreciation of the real world'.

Alan Turing, the brilliant theoretical mathematician whose prophetic 1936 paper on computability had laid the foundation of the stored-program digital computer, was at once the most notable confirmation of, and exception to, the rule. Brought in to work on the Enigma problem in 1939, he was almost completely unworldly in some ways, eccentric, given to scribbling out his analyses in such atrociously sloppy handwriting that, one of GC & CS's senior officials fumed, he often made mistakes because he couldn't even read his own writing. Yet his astonishing group-theoretical attack on Enigma in the autumn of 1939—and in particular his heavily statistical method for defeating the extremely difficult indicator system used by the German navy for its version of the Enigma—made it clear to a number of people in authority at GC & CS that mathematically adept recruits would be needed to deal with this new world of cryptanalysis.

Thus, by late autumn of 1941, when three months of frustrating work with Tiltman's recovered key sequence had gone nowhere, the GC & CS authorities were accustomed enough to the idea that mathematicians might actually be of some use that they were willing to risk turning the job over to one of these 'strange fellows'. What was more, they actually had some of them around to turn to. The job of trying to reconstruct the key wheels of Tunny thus fell to William Tutte, a young Cambridge graduate. Tutte tried writing out the key sequence for each of the 5 bits in grids with varying numbers of columns, looking for any recurring patterns. When he tried a grid with 41 columns for the first bit, a pattern suddenly popped out. Eventually Tutte was able to determine that each of the 5 bits generated for each letter was encoded by two separate wheels, a total of ten wheels in all, five chis and five psis, with a final pair of motor wheels which sent out 1s or 0s (×s or •s) that would determine whether the psi-wheels turned or not.

At first all of the work was done by hand. The trick was to find two messages that had been sent with very similar indicators. It was clear that the 12 letters of the indicator represented the start positions of the 12 coding wheels, and so two messages that differed by only one indicator letter would likely share a long sequence of overlapping key. Messages sent with the same key were said to be 'in depth' in the cryptanalysts' jargon, and these 'near-depths' proved vital especially for figuring out new wheel pattern sequences, which were changed every month ('wheel-breaking'). The indicators carried on each message then told the codebreakers how to set up those recovered wheel patterns to decode each subsequent message received for that month. By July 1942, the first actual German messages were read currently; from July to October 1942, virtually every message was read.

THE 1 + 2 TRICK

That sudden success, however, hit a just as sudden catastrophe in October, when the Germans, recognising the inherent insecurity of the 12-letter indicators, abruptly changed the indicator system. In place of the 12 letters that specified directly how to set the 12 wheels, they began using a simple number. The codebreakers concluded that the number was probably keyed to a daily list of settings provided to all users (the 'QEP' book described in the previous chapter); in any case, it was no longer possible, simply by looking at the message indicators, to tell whether two messages were near-depths. The only hope now for wheel-breaking was to find two messages sent on the same day with identical indicators, a much longer shot. Even worse, wheel setting of subsequent messages was likewise only possible when two messages were sent the same day with an identical indicator. Depths were now required for every message that was to be read, an almost impossible limitation for practical intelligence production.

It was then that Tutte made one of the most crucial mathematical discoveries in the project. Building on an initial insight by Turing, he realised that adding a string of enciphered letters to itself, but shifted one letter over, could yield information not apparent in the original string. Since the psi-wheels often did not advance from one letter to the next, that meant that, when a psi-wheel generated a × (1), it would more often than not generate a × again for the next letter. Likewise, a • (0) would more often than not be followed by another •. That meant that when a whole string of psi-wheel key was added to itself with a shift of 1, the resulting string would have a predominance of •s, since in non-carrying binary addition $0 + 0 = 0$ but also $1 + 1 = 0$.

Tutte subsequently calculated that such a shift-and-add treatment would in fact produce a string containing about 70 per cent •. Likewise, he discovered that because of the appearance of repeated letters, diphthongs such as *ei*, and other patterns in the German language—and just by the chance way that letters were rendered in the standard teleprinter code—the first two bits of the plaintext when shifted over one and added to itself also had a preponderance of •, about 60 per cent on average. And *that* meant that if the first two bits of a string of coded traffic were subjected to this same shift-and-add treatment, the effect of both plaintext and the psi-wheels would more often than not zero out. What would be left was a pattern of × and • that tended to track the contribution of the chi-wheels only.

This '1 + 2 break in' procedure depended heavily on statistical calculations, and the trick was clearly going to be devising a way to 'slide' the chi-wheels in all possible positions against a string of intercepted ciphertext, hunting for the one that gave the best statistical fit. Tutte's idea was tried by hand with stencils and paper to test its logical feasibility, and it worked. But the experiment also confirmed, if confirmation were even necessary, that operationally it was simply impossible to think of doing such a task manually. No one could possibly try thousands upon thousands of possibilities, calculate the statistics for each, and find the best fit for *every single message* by hand. The Germans were by now transmitting hundreds of Tunny messages a day. It was intelligence of the greatest importance, clearly—and appropriately of the greatest corresponding technical difficulty to break. What would be required was mechanisation on a scale that no one had ever dared dream of before.

The job of putting Tutte's idea into practical effect fell to three of the oddest of Bletchley Park's odd assortment of men and women. Not odd in the sense of eccentric, but certainly odd in the paths that brought them to this task, for none seemed on the face to be well suited to organising what would become a huge engineering and management task. Max Newman, who headed the effort, was a theoretical mathematician of the purest kind. His research at Cambridge before the war had focused on the foundations of mathematics and issues related to Gödel's famous proof of the impossibility of a mathematical system being both complete and consistent. 'I never saw him do anything except write on paper. He was not really of a mechanical bent,' recalls his son William. Max Newman at first assumed he would be ineligible for war work because of his German ancestry. But a close friend introduced him to someone at Bletchley, and by 1942 he was brought in and assigned to work on Tunny under Tiltman.

Newman found the heavily linguistic sort of pencil-and-paper work frustrating and almost considered returning to Cambridge. But the October 1942 set-back changed everything. In December, Newman was given the green light to explore the idea of mechanising a purely statistical attack on Tunny.

Newman's first assistant was an even unlikelier candidate to work on a pioneering project in automated computing. In the spring of 1943, Donald Michie was all of 19 years old. He had won a scholarship to study classics at Balliol College, Oxford, and had no experience with either machines or mathematics. But hoping to do something for the war effort—and assured that he was automatically guaranteed a place at university once the war ended if he postponed his enrolment to take up war service—he decided to enrol in a crash Japanese language course that he had learned about through a family friend who was an official of the War Office.

It was in fact none other than the ever resourceful John Tiltman who had launched this six-month training course for intelligence officers, brashly ignoring the sober advice of the experts at London's School of Oriental and African Studies, who insisted that no one could possibly master even the rudiments of such a difficult language as Japanese in less than two years. The course took place in a nondescript room above the Gas Company's offices in the city of Bedford, 15 miles from Bletchley. Michie went at once and presented himself for an interview, and was crestfallen to be told that he had been misinformed: the course was already full and the next enrolment was not until autumn. What happened next changed his life. 'Cheer up,' the officer said, seeing how disappointed he was, and went on to explain that there was a cryptography course starting the next Monday that might interest him as a way of filling in the time.

Michie—and his teachers—immediately discovered that he had an amazing natural talent for the subject. He shot ahead of the rest of the class and just six weeks later, when an officer from Bletchley arrived to recruit someone to work on Tunny, 'my selection was pretty much a foregone conclusion,' Michie recalls. He was assigned to a section at Bletchley Park that had been established in July 1942 under Major Ralph Tester—the 'Testery'—that was tackling Tunny using hand methods. In no time he was in charge of the mathematically intensive, and extremely tedious and laborious, task of determining the start settings of individual Tunny messages. When it came time for Newman to 'poach' an assistant, he wanted someone who was intimately familiar with the ins and outs of the hand methods, and Michie fitted the bill.

Michie's discovery that he had an aptitude for probability, statistics, and Boolean logic—and was even able to hold his own with his far more mathematically trained colleagues in the coffee-break and lunchtime competitive exchanges of brain-teasers and recreational mathematics—had an extraordinary impact on a subsequently extraordinary career. After the war he did take up his classics scholarship, but soon found it boring and abruptly switched to human anatomy and physiology, did important work in mammalian genetics, and then in the early 1960s shifted again, to computer science, and became a leading researcher in artificial intelligence.

The third member of Newman's core group was, like Newman, another extremely theoretical mathematician. But I. J. 'Jack' Good was recruited to Bletchley in a more conventional way in one sense, for he was an extremely good chess player, and Bletchley was teeming with extremely good chess players. The two men who would eventually head the Naval Enigma and Army–Air Enigma sections for most of the war—Hugh Alexander and Stuart Milner-Barry—were both members of the British national chess team and were convinced that good chess players made good cryptanalysts.

Good had won the Cambridge chess championship one year ('but what I was *very* good at,' he says, 'was five-minute chess') and knew both Alexander and Milner-Barry from the chess world. He also knew that they were working on some secret project. A Cambridge colleague, Good recalls, 'was fairly sure it was codebreaking'. (In general it was extraordinary how tight the security surrounding Bletchley's work was; the records of Bletchley at the National Archives note only two instances in which anyone shot off his or her mouth even to friends, family, and trusted colleagues about what was going on there.) Good, now 90 years old and a professor emeritus of statistics at Virginia Tech in the mountains of south-western Virginia, spent a decade after the war working for GC & CS's successor agency on cryptanalytic studies, where, among other things, he carried out some crucial statistical analyses for Project VENONA—the ultra-secret British–US effort that successfully broke Soviet espionage codes, despite the fact they were enciphered using theoretically unbreakable one-time pads. Good's car bears the self-dramatising licence plate '007IJG'.

Newman's section at Bletchley Park was known simply as the 'Newmanry'. Michie says that Newman was a 'terrific' manager, with 'a will of steel—but flexible steel. Obstinate as a mule, but bearing no grudge if obliged to yield.' William Newman believes his father was ahead of his time in practising an 'open' style of management; partly it was simply that he was awkward with people who were not his intellectual equals, so he was sure to recruit people who *were* on his level and whom he could therefore trust. The Newmanry kept a series of log books in which anyone could write an organisational suggestion or technical idea, and every few weeks a 4 p.m. 'tea party' was held at which ideas were put on the board and debated openly. ('It was a democratic assembly with legislative powers,' noted an official glossary of terms produced by the Newmanry.)

MECHANISING THE SOLUTION

It was odd that it was Newman, the theoretician's theoretician, who proposed mechanising the Tunny problem. Yet the idea of using a machine to do what humans could not was in the air, and in Newman's consciousness, for several reasons. Newman had taught Turing at Cambridge and was familiar with Turing's famous paper on computability, in which he had advanced what became known as the 'Turing machine', a conceptual device for representing the solution of a formal problem in mathematics in terms of a sequence of mechanical steps. Turing's brilliant success in developing a method to break Enigma in 1939 had relied fundamentally on a mechanised approach—the Bombes, which were large electromechanical analogues of a series of Enigma machines. Turned by a high-speed motor through all possible wheel starting positions, the machines would electrically test for certain consistent patterns that revealed the daily settings the Germans were using on their various Enigma networks. Now came Newman's suggestion that a machine be built to attack the Tunny traffic. His idea was pivotal, propelling codebreaking into the computer age.

By the time of the German surrender, ten Colossi were in operation. Most of them were promptly dismantled after the war, but their influence on the history of computing was inextinguishable. The Colossi were programmable only by plugging cords and flipping switches; a great deal of the 'programming' work that Good and Michie did was in fact in plotting out decision trees that the operators would follow in deciding what tests to run next, depending on the counts they obtained from the previous test. Nor were the Colossi by any stretch of the imagination general-purpose machines. Geoffrey Timms, one of the Newmanry mathematicians, after the war worked out an elaborate system of plugging up the machine so that it could in theory perform base-10 multiplication—but it was such a stretch and so complicated a process for the Colossus's circuits that the machine could not in fact complete the operation before the next clock pulse turned over. The Colossi were designed to solve a problem of extraordinary complexity and extraordinary wartime urgency, and at this they succeeded remarkably well. While Michie says he finds it improbable that any of the 'proto-programming tricks' they developed for Colossus had any impact on the development of post-war general-purpose computers, Good emphasises that the Boolean programming facilities of Colossus led him to suggest the concept now known as 'microprogramming' (see Chapter 16).

Flowers pointed out that Colossus did have one unmistakable impact for the future of computing: 'Showing Turing, Newman, and others what electronics could do'. Newman and Turing and Good all worked at the University of Manchester's computing project after the war, developing a stored-program digital electronic computer. Without the urgency of wartime necessity, the experience and confidence that they gained from seeing 'what electronics could do' might simply never have happened.

Chapter 5

Machine against Machine

Jack Copeland

THE WHEEL-SETTING PROBLEM

As explained in the preceding chapter, Tutte invented a way of finding the settings of the Tunny's chi-wheels, but the rub was that his method seemed impractical. It involved calculations which, if done by hand, would consume a vast amount of time—probably as much as several hundred years for a single, long message, Newman once estimated.

The necessary calculations were straightforward enough, consisting basically of comparing two streams made up of dots and crosses, and counting the number of times that each had a dot, or cross, in the same position. Today, of course, we turn such work over to electronic computers. When Tutte shyly explained his method to Newman, Newman suggested using high-speed electronic counters to mechanise the process. It was a brilliant idea. Within a surprisingly short time, Newman's factory of monstrous electronic computers, dedicated to breaking Tunny, was affording a glimpse of the future.

Electronic counters had been developed in Cambridge before the war. Used for counting emissions of subatomic particles, these had been designed by C. E. Wynn-Williams, then like Newman a Cambridge don. Newman knew of Wynn-Williams' work, and in a moment of inspiration he saw that the same idea could be applied to the Tunny problem.

Tutte invented his method in November 1942 and the following month Newman was given the job of developing the necessary machinery. Newman worked out the cryptanalytical requirements for the planned machine and called in Wynn-Williams to design the electronic counters. Wynn-Williams was by then involved in wartime research at the Telecommunications Research Establishment (TRE) in Malvern. Newman and TRE approached an expert on teleprinter equipment, F. O. Morrell, head of the telegraph and teleprinter group of the Post Office Research Station at Dollis Hill in North London, to engineer the other parts of the machine.

HEATH ROBINSON, THE PROTOTYPE TUNNY-BREAKING MACHINE

Construction of Newman's machine started in January 1943 and a prototype began operating in June of that year, in the newly formed Newmanry. The Newmanry consisted initially of Newman himself, Michie, two engineers, and 16 'Wrens'—members of the Women's Royal Naval Service. The section was housed in a two-roomed hut, Hut 11, originally the first Bombe room.

Smoke rose from the prototype machine the first time it was switched on (a large resistor overloaded). The Wrens, who operated it in shifts, soon named the machine 'Heath Robinson', after a famous cartoonist who drew overly ingenious mechanical contrivances. Part of Heath Robinson consisted of a huge angle-iron metal frame resembling an old-fashioned bed standing on end; this quickly became known as the 'bedstead' (see photograph 31). Around the bedstead wound two long loops of teleprinter tape, each made by gluing together the two ends of a length of tape. The two tapes were supported by a system of pulleys and wooden wheels of diameter about 10 inches.

The tapes were driven by toothed sprocket-wheels which engaged a continuous row of sprocket-holes along the centre of each tape (see Figure 2 in Chapter 3). Both tapes were driven by the same drive-shaft and moved in synchronisation with each other. The maximum speed of the tapes was 2000 characters per second. To the amusement and annoyance of Heath Robinson's operators, tapes would sometimes tear or come unglued, flying off the bedstead at high speed and breaking into fragments which festooned the Newmanry.

The hole/no-hole patterns punched on the tapes were read photoelectrically. Once these patterns had been converted by the photoelectric reader into electrical pulses, they were modified and combined by a 'combining unit' (a logic unit, in modern terminology). The number of pulses in the result was counted by Wynn-Williams' counting unit. The way the combining was done could be varied by means of replugging cables (a primitive form of programming). Dollis Hill made the combining unit and the bedstead, and TRE made the counting unit.

TUTTE'S METHOD

Initially both Robinson and Colossus used essentially the method that Tutte had described to Newman (although the method was elaborated by members of the Newmanry). The machine running the method produced the settings of the chi-wheels. Knowing the chi-wheel settings gave the codebreakers enough of a head-start that they were able to discover the settings of the psi-wheels and motor-wheels by eye, given (as a wartime document described it) a 'knowledge of "Tunny-German" and the power of instantaneous mental addition of letters of the Teleprint alphabet'.

As explained in Chapter 3, the Tunny machine produces ciphertext by adding the letters from a stream of key to the letters of the plaintext, and the key-stream is produced by adding together the stream of letters contributed by the chi-wheels and the stream contributed by the psis. If, say, the plaintext is 10,000 letters long, then 10,000 consecutive letters from the chi-stream are used in the course of encrypting the message. Let us call this strip of 10,000 letters from the chi-stream 'the chi' of the message. Tutte's method exploits a fatal weakness in the design of the Tunny machine. The central idea of the method (which came to be known as the 'statistical method') is this: *the chi is recognisable on the basis of the ciphertext, provided the wheel patterns are known.*

Once the message's chi has been determined, then it is an easy step to find the positions of the chi-wheels at the start of the message. This is done by surveying the entire chi-stream until the message chi is located. For example, the place in the chi-stream where the message chi begins may be where the first chi-wheel, χ_1, is at position 27, χ_2 at position 30, χ_3 at 11, χ_4 at 21, and χ_5 at 18. These, then, are the positions to which the operator turned the chi-wheels before beginning to encipher the message.

THE NEWMANRY AND THE TESTERY

Tunny-breaking involved close cooperation between the Newmanry and Ralph Tester's section, the Testery.

The Newmanry determined the settings of the chi-wheels using Robinson, or later Colossus, and then prepared what was called the 'de-chi' of the message. This was the result of stripping away the chi-wheels' contribution to the ciphertext. (Chapter 21 contains a sample of de-chi from the spring of 1945.) The de-chi was produced by a replica of the German Tunny machine, designed by the Post Office engineers at Dollis Hill (see photograph 30). These replicas were called 'Newmanry Tunnies' (or simply 'Tunny machines'). Once the chi-wheel settings had been determined, the cipher tape was run through a Newmanry Tunny which subtracted the chi.

The de-chi was then passed to the Testery. Here a cryptanalyst would break into the de-chi by pencil-and-paper methods. This part of the process, which somewhat resembled solving a crossword puzzle, is described in later chapters.

The reason it was easier to break the de-chi than the intercepted ciphertext is this. The de-chi is the plaintext with letters of the (extended) psi-stream added to it (the idea of the extended psi-stream is explained on page 49). This is because the de-chi is the result of subtracting the chi from the ciphertext, and the ciphertext is itself the result of adding the chi plus the extended psi to the plaintext: stripping away the chi from chi + extended psi + plaintext leaves extended psi + plaintext. As explained in Chapter 3, the extended psi contains distinctive patterns of repeated letters, e.g. ...GGZZZWDD... By latching onto these repetitions, the cryptanalyst could uncover a few words of the plaintext.

Once some words of the message had been broken, the psi-wheel and motor-wheel settings could be determined (see Chapter 21). When all the wheel settings were known, the ciphertext was keyed into one of the Testery's replica Tunny machines, and the German plaintext would emerge.

THE DELTA

At the heart of Tutte's method lies what is called the 'delta' of a character stream. The delta is the character stream that results from adding together each pair of adjacent letters in the original stream. For example, the delta of the short stream MNT (sometimes written ΔMNT) is produced by adding M to N and N to T (using the rules of dot-and-cross addition given previously). The delta of MNT is the pair TM, as the following table shows:

M	N	T	M + N	N + T
•	•	•	•	•
•	•	•	•	•
×	×	•	•	×
×	×	•	•	×
×	•	×	×	×

The idea of the delta is that it tracks *changes* in the original stream. If a dot follows a dot or a cross follows a cross at a particular point in the original stream, then the corresponding point in the delta has a dot. A dot in the delta means 'no change'. If, on the other hand, there is a cross followed by a dot or a dot followed by a cross in the original stream, then the corresponding point in the delta has a cross. A cross in the delta means 'change'.

The concept of delta was first introduced by Turing in July 1942. It formed the basis of 'Turingery' (see Appendix 6 *Turingery*). Tutte discovered, a few months later, that delta provided the vital clue to finding wheel settings.

Tutte showed by a clever mathematical deduction that the delta of a message's ciphertext and the delta of the chi would usually correspond slightly. That *slightly* is the key to the whole business—any degree of regularity, no matter how weak, is the cryptanalyst's friend. The slight regularity that Tutte discovered could be used as a touchstone for finding the chi.

SEARCHING FOR THE CHI

In order to illustrate the basic ideas of Tutte's method, we will assume that we have an intercepted ciphertext 10,000 characters long. This ciphertext is punched on a tape (we call this the 'message-tape'). An assistant, who knows the chi-wheel patterns, provides us with a second tape (the 'chi-tape'). This assistant has worked out the machine's entire chi-stream, beginning at an arbitrarily selected point in the revolution of the chi-wheels, and stepping through all their possible joint combinations. (Once the wheels have moved through all the possible combinations, their capacity for novelty is exhausted, and should the wheels continue to turn they merely duplicate what has gone before.) The complete chi-stream is, of course, rather long, but eventually the assistant does produce a roll of tape with the stream punched on it. The sequence of 10,000 consecutive characters of chi-stream that forms the chi of our message is on this tape somewhere—our problem is to find it.

We select the first 10,000 characters of the chi-tape; we will compare this stretch of the chi-tape with the message-tape. Tutte showed (as he explains in Appendix 4 *My Work at Bletchley Park*) that in fact we need examine only the *first* and the *second* of the five horizontal rows punched along the chi-tape— the first and second impulses, in the Tunny-breakers' jargon (see page 38). These two rows are the contributions of the first and second chi-wheels, χ_1 and χ_2, respectively. Accordingly we need consider only the first and second impulses of the message-tape. This simplifies the task of comparing the two tapes considerably. It was because Tutte's method focused on the first and second chi-wheels that it was dubbed the '1 + 2 break in'.

This is how we compare the message-tape with the stretch of chi-tape we have picked. First, we add the first and second impulses of the message-tape and form the delta of the resulting sequence of dots and crosses (so, for example, if the sequence produced by adding the two impulses begins ×•× . . ., the delta begins ×× . . .). Why are we adding the impulses? Because Tutte's method tells us to! Readers interested in the mathematical rationale of the method will find it on pages 363–4. Second, we add the first and second impulses of the 10,000-character strip of chi-tape, and again form the delta of the result. Next we lay these two deltas side by side and count how many times they have dots in the same places and how many times crosses. We add the two tallies to produce a total score for this particular strip of the chi-tape. We are looking for a match between the two deltas of around 55 per cent. Tutte showed that this is the order of correspondence that can be expected when the strip of chi-tape under examination contains the first and second impulses of the actual chi.

The first score we obtain probably won't be anything special—for we would be extremely lucky if the first 10,000 characters of chi-stream we examined were the chi of the message. So next we shift along one character in the chi-stream and focus on a new candidate for the message's chi, the 2nd through to the 10,001st character on the chi-tape. We add, delta, and count once again. Then we shift along another character, repeating the process until we have examined all candidates (see Figure 1). A buoyant score reveals the first and second impulses of the actual chi (we hope).

The location of a winning segment of tape within the complete chi-stream tells us the positions of the χ_1 and χ_2 wheels at the start of the message. Once these settings are known, a similar procedure is used to chase the settings of the other chi-wheels (see Chapter 17).

The two tapes running on Heath Robinson's bedstead were the message-tape and the chi-tape. In practice the chi-tape might contain, for example, only the first and second impulses of the complete chi-stream, resulting in a shorter tape. The two tapes ran on the bedstead in such a way that the message-tape progressively stepped through the chi-tape one character at a time. The combining unit did the adding and the delta-ing, and Wynn-Williams' electronic counters produced the scores.

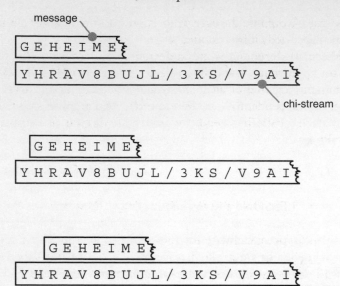

Figure 1. Stepping the ciphertext through the chi-stream, looking for the starting position of the chi-wheels.

THE MISTAKE IN THE TUNNY MACHINE

The cause of the slight regularity which Tutte latched onto is at bottom the intermittent or 'staggering' movement of the psi-wheels—the great weakness of the Tunny machine. (As explained previously, the psis would either all step forward together, like the chis, or all remain still, missing one or more opportunities to move.) While the psis remained stationary, they continued to contribute the same letter to the key. So, since delta-ing tracks change, the delta of the stream of characters contributed by the psis contained more dots than crosses. Tutte calculated that there would usually be about 70 per cent dot in the delta of the sum of the contributions of the first two psi-wheels.

The delta of the plaintext also contained more dots than crosses, thanks both to statistical properties of the German language and to the practices of Tunny operators, who habitually repeated certain characters (e.g. punctuation). Tutte investigated a number of broken messages and discovered to his delight that the delta of the sum of the first two impulses was as a rule about 60 per cent dot. Since these statistical regularities in the delta of the psi and the delta of the plain both involved a predominance of dot over cross, they tended to reinforce one another. Tutte deduced that their net effect, in favourable cases, would be the agreement, noted above, of about 55 per cent between the processed ciphertext and the processed chi.

Tunny's security depended on the appearance of randomness, but here was a crack in the appearance. The British seized on it. If, instead of the psi-wheels either all moving together or all standing still, the designer had arranged for them to move independently—or even to move regularly like the chis—then the chink that let Tutte in would not have existed. (See also Appendix 11 *Motorless Tunny*.)

LESSONS FROM HEATH ROBINSON

Newman's prototype machine, Heath Robinson, was a qualified success. It worked, proving in a single stroke that Newman's idea of attacking Tunny by machine was worth its salt and that Tutte's method succeeded in practice. However, Heath Robinson suffered from 'intolerable handicaps'.

Despite the high speed of the electronic counters, Heath Robinson was not really fast enough for the codebreakers' requirements, taking several hours to elucidate a single message. Moreover, the counters were not fully reliable—Heath Robinson was prone to deliver different results if set the same problem twice! Mistakes made in hand-punching the two tapes were another fertile source of error, the long chi-tape being especially difficult to prepare. At first undetected tape errors prevented Heath Robinson from obtaining results at all. And paramount among the difficulties was that the two tapes would get out of synchronisation with each other as they span, throwing the calculations out completely. The loss of synchronisation was caused by the tapes stretching, and also by uneven wear around the sprocket holes.

The question was how to build a better machine—a question for an engineer. In a stroke of genius, the electronics expert Thomas H. Flowers solved all these problems.

ENTER FLOWERS

Tommy Flowers (he preferred 'Tom' in later life) had joined the Telephone Branch of the Post Office in 1926, after an apprenticeship at the Royal Arsenal in Woolwich, well known for its precision engineering. He entered the Research Branch at Dollis Hill in 1930, achieving rapid promotion and establishing his reputation as a gifted and innovative electrical engineer. At the outbreak of war he headed the switching group at Dollis Hill (which was located in the same building as Morrell's telegraph and teleprinter group).

During the 1930s Flowers pioneered the large-scale use of electronic valves to control the making and breaking of telephone connections. (Photograph 32 is a close-up of some valves.) When (on his own initiative) he started to investigate this area, he was swimming against the current: the idea of large-scale electronic equipment was regarded with scepticism by many at the time. The common wisdom was that valves—which, like light bulbs, contained a hot glowing filament—could never be used satisfactorily in large numbers, for they were unreliable, and in a large installation too many would fail in too short a time. However, this opinion was based on experience with equipment that was switched on and off frequently, such as radio receivers, radar, and the like. What Flowers discovered was that, so long as valves were switched on and left on, they could operate reliably for very long periods, especially if their 'heaters' were run on a reduced current. 'Once switched on, the Colossi were never switched off until after the end of the war,' explains Harry Fensom, one of Flowers' engineers.

At that time, telephone switchboard equipment was based on the *relay*. A relay is a small automatic switch. It contains a mechanical contact-breaker—a moving metal rod that opens and closes an electrical circuit (see Figure 1 in Chapter 8). The rod is moved from the 'off' position to the 'on' position by a magnetic field. A current in a coil is used to produce the magnetic field; as soon as the current flows, the field moves the rod. When the current ceases, a spring pushes the rod back to the 'off' position. Flowers recognised that electronic valves, whose only moving part is a beam of electrons, were not only potentially very much faster than relays but also, since not prone to mechanical wear, would actually be more reliable.

In 1934 Flowers wired together an experimental installation containing three to four thousand valves (by contrast, Wynn-Williams' electronic counters of 1931 contained only three or four valves). This equipment was for controlling connections between telephone exchanges by means of tones, like today's touch-tones. A thousand telephone lines were controlled, each line having three or four valves attached to its end. Flowers' design was accepted by the Post Office and the equipment went into limited operation in 1939. Flowers had proved that an installation containing thousands of valves would operate very reliably, but this equipment was a far cry from Colossus. The handful of valves attached to each telephone line formed a simple unit, operating independently of the other valves in the installation, whereas in Colossus large numbers of valves worked in concert.

During the same period before the war, Flowers explored the idea of using valves as high-speed switches. Valves were used originally for purposes such as amplifying radio signals. The output would vary continuously in proportion to a continuously varying input, for example a signal representing speech. Digital computation imposes different requirements. What is needed for the purpose of representing the two binary digits, 1 and 0, is not a continuously varying signal but plain 'on' and 'off' (or 'high' and 'low'). It was the novel idea of using the valve as a very fast switch, producing pulses of current (pulse for 1, no pulse for 0) that was the route to high-speed digital computation. During 1938–9 Flowers worked on an experimental high-speed electronic data store embodying this idea. The store was intended to replace relay-based data stores in telephone exchanges. Flowers' long-term game plan was that electronic equipment should replace all the relay-based systems in telephone exchanges. After the war, he once again pursued his dream of an all-electronic telephone exchange, and was closely involved with the groundbreaking Highgate Wood exchange in London (the first all-electronic exchange in Europe).

By the time of the outbreak of war with Germany, only a small number of electrical engineers were familiar with the use of valves as high-speed digital switches. Thanks to his pre-war research, Flowers was (as he himself remarked) possibly the only person in Britain who realised that valves could be used reliably on a large scale for high-speed digital computing. When Flowers was summoned to Bletchley Park—ironically, because of his knowledge of relays—he turned out to be the right man in the right place at the right time.

Turing, working on Enigma, had approached Dollis Hill to build a relay-based decoding machine to operate in conjunction with the Bombe (the Bombe itself was also relay-based). Once the Bombe had uncovered the Enigma settings used to encrypt a particular message, these settings were to be transferred to the machine requisitioned by Turing, which would automatically decipher the message and print out the German plaintext. Dollis Hill sent Flowers to Bletchley Park. He would soon become one of the great figures of Second World War codebreaking. In the end, the machine Flowers built for Turing was not used, but Turing was impressed with Flowers, who began thinking about an electronic Bombe, although he did not get far. When Morrell's group was having difficulty with the design of the Heath Robinson's combining unit, Turing suggested that Flowers be called in. Flowers and his switching group improved the design of the combining unit and manufactured it.

Flowers did not think much of the Robinson, however. The basic design had been settled before he was called in and he was sceptical as soon as Morrell, from whom he first learned of the Robinson, told him about it. The difficulty of keeping two paper tapes in synchronisation at high speed was a conspicuous weakness. Moreover, the use of relays in the counters slowed everything down: Heath Robinson was built mainly from relays and contained no more than a couple of dozen valves. Flowers doubted that the Robinson would work properly, and in February 1943 he presented Newman with the alternative of a fully electronic machine that would be able to generate the chi-stream (and psi- and motor-streams) internally. Colossus was entirely his idea.

COLOSSUS

Flowers' suggestion was received with 'incredulity' at TRE and Bletchley Park. It was thought that a machine containing the number of valves that Flowers was proposing (between one and two thousand) would be 'too unreliable to do useful work'. In any case, there was the question of how long the development process would take—it was felt that the war might be over before Flowers' machine was finished. Newman pressed ahead with the two-tape machine. He offered Flowers some encouragement but effectively left him to do as he wished with his proposal for an all-electronic machine. Once Heath Robinson was a going concern, Newman placed an order with the Post Office for a dozen more relay-based two-tape machines (it being clear, given the quantity and very high importance of Tunny traffic, that one or two machines would not be anywhere near enough). Meanwhile Flowers, on his own initiative and working independently at Dollis Hill, began building the fully electronic machine that he could see was necessary. He embarked on Colossus, he said, 'in the face of scepticism' from Bletchley Park (BP) and 'without the concurrence of BP'. 'BP weren't interested until they saw it [Colossus] working,' he recollected. Fortunately, the Director of the Dollis Hill Research Station, Radley, had greater faith in Flowers and his ideas, and placed 'the whole resources of the laboratories' at Flowers' disposal.

The prototype Colossus was brought to Bletchley Park in lorries and reassembled by Flowers' engineers. It had approximately 1600 electronic valves and operated at 5000 characters per second. Later models, containing approximately 2400 valves, processed five streams of dot-and-cross simultaneously, in parallel. This boosted the speed to 25,000 characters per second. Colossus generated the chi-stream electronically. Only one tape was required, containing the ciphertext—the synchronisation problem vanished. (Flowers' original plan was to dispense with the message-tape as well and set up the ciphertext, as well as the wheels, on valves; but he abandoned this idea when it became clear that messages of 5000 or more characters would have to be processed.)

The arrival of the prototype Colossus caused quite a stir. Flowers said:

I don't think they [Newman et al.] really understood what I was saying in detail—I am sure they didn't—because when the first machine was constructed and working, they obviously were taken aback. They just couldn't believe it! . . . I don't think they understood very clearly what I was proposing until they actually had the machine.

On what date did Colossus first come alive? In his written and verbal recollections Flowers was always definite that Colossus was working at Bletchley Park in the early part of December 1943. In three separate interviews he recalled a key date quite specifically, saying that Colossus carried out its first trial run at Bletchley Park on 8 December 1943. However, Flowers' personal diary for 1944—not discovered until after his death—in fact records that Colossus did not make the journey from Dollis Hill to Bletchley Park until January 1944. On Sunday 16 January Colossus was still in Flowers' lab at Dollis Hill. His diary entry shows that Colossus was certainly working on that day. Flowers was busy with the machine from the morning until late in the evening and he slept at the lab.

Flowers' entry for 18 January reads simply: 'Colossus delivered to B.P.' This is confirmed by a memo dated 18 January from Newman to Travis (declassified only in 2004). Newman wrote 'Colossus arrives to-day'. Colossus cannot therefore have carried out its first trial run at Bletchley Park in early December. What did happen on 8 December 1943, the date that stuck so firmly in Flowers' mind? Perhaps this was indeed the day that Colossus processed its first test tape at Dollis Hill. 'I seem to recall it was in December,' says Harry Fensom. If Flowers kept a diary for 1943 this might settle the matter, but none has been discovered.

By February 1944 the engineers had got Colossus ready to begin serious work for the Newmanry. The computer attacked its first message on Saturday 5 February. Flowers was present. He noted laconically in his diary, 'Colossus did its first job. Car broke down on way home.'

Colossus immediately doubled the codebreakers' output. The advantages of Colossus over Robinson were not only its greatly superior speed and the absence of synchronised tapes, but also its greater reliability, resulting from Flowers' redesigned counters and the use of valves in place of relays throughout. It was clear to the Bletchley Park authorities—whose scepticism was now completely cured—that more Colossi were required urgently.

Indeed, a crisis had developed, making the work of Newman's section even more important than before. Since October 1942, when the Germans introduced the QEP system (see Chapter 3), the codebreakers using hand methods to crack Tunny messages had been reliant upon depths. With the tightening up of German security, however, depths became increasingly scarce, and by late 1943 only a trickle of messages was being broken by hand methods. Then things went from bad to worse. In December 1943 the Germans started to make widespread use of what Bletchley called 'P_5 limitation' (see Chapter 3 and Appendix 10). P_5 limitation made depth-reading impossible. The hand-breakers had been prone to scoff at the weird contraptions in the Newmanry, but suddenly Newman's machines were essential to all Tunny work.

In March 1944 the authorities demanded four more Colossi. By April they were demanding twelve. (The order for Robinsons was curtailed.) Great pressure was put on Flowers to deliver the new machines quickly. The instructions he received came 'from the highest level'—the War Cabinet—and he caused consternation when he said flatly that it was impossible to produce more than one new machine by 1 June 1944.

Flowers had managed to produce the prototype Colossus at Dollis Hill only because many of his laboratory staff 'did nothing but work, eat, and sleep for weeks and months on end'. He needed greater production capacity, and proposed to take over a Post Office factory in Birmingham. Final assembly and testing would be done at his Dollis Hill laboratory. Flowers estimated that once the factory was in operation he would be able to produce additional Colossi at the rate of about one per month. He recalled how one day some Bletchley people came to inspect the work, thinking that Flowers might be 'dilly-dallying': they returned 'staggered at the scale of the effort'. Churchill for his part gave Flowers top priority for everything he needed.

By means of repluggable cables and panels of switches, Flowers deliberately built more flexibility than was strictly necessary into the logic units of the prototype Colossus. As a result, new methods could be implemented on Colossus as they were discovered. In February 1944 Michie and Good quickly found a way of using Colossus to discover the Tunny wheel patterns (see Chapters 16 and 17). Flowers was told to incorporate a special panel for breaking wheel patterns in Colossus II.

Colossus II—the first of what Flowers referred to as the 'Mark 2' Colossi—was shipped from Dollis Hill to Bletchley Park on 4 May 1944. The plan was to assemble and test Colossus II at Bletchley Park rather than Dollis Hill, so saving some precious time. Promised by the first of June, Colossus II was still not working properly as the final hours of May ticked past. The computer was plagued by intermittent and mysterious faults. Flowers struggled to find the problem, but midnight came and went. Exhausted, Flowers and his team dispersed at 1 a.m. to snatch a few hours sleep. They left Chandler to work on, since the problem appeared to be in a part of the computer that he had designed. It was a tough night: around 3 a.m. Chandler noticed that his feet were getting wet. A radiator pipe along the wall had sprung a leak, sending a dangerous pool of water towards Colossus.

Flowers returned a few hours later to find the computer running perfectly. 'Colossus 2 in operation,' he noted in his diary. The puddle remained, however, and the Wren operators had to don gumboots to insulate themselves. During the small hours Chandler had finally tracked down the fault in Colossus (parasitic oscillations in some of the valves) and had fixed it by wiring in a few extra resistors. Flowers and his 'band of brothers' had met BP's deadline—a deadline whose significance Flowers could only have guessed at.

Less than a week later the Allied invasion of France began. The D-day landings of 6 June placed huge quantities of men and equipment on the beaches of Normandy. From the beachheads the Allies pushed their way into France through the heavy German defences. By mid-July the front had advanced only 20 or so miles inland, but by September Allied troops had swept across France and Belgium and were gathering close to the borders of Germany, on a front extending from Holland in the north to Switzerland in the south. Since the early months of 1944, Colossus I had been providing an unparalleled window on German preparations for the allied invasion (including German appreciations of allied intentions), and in the next chapter Flowers describes how Colossus II contributed to the success of the D-day landings.

The Germans tightened Tunny security in the weeks following the start of the invasion. Operators were instructed to change the patterns of the chi- and psi-wheels daily instead of monthly. By August there were daily wheel changes on almost all Tunny links. The methods the codebreakers had been using to discover new patterns were overwhelmed. With impeccable timing, Colossus II's device for breaking wheel patterns came to the rescue.

Once Flowers' factory in Birmingham was properly up and running, new Colossi began arriving in the Newmanry at roughly six-week intervals. Eventually three were dedicated to wheel breaking. Flowers was a regular visitor at BP throughout the rest of 1944, overseeing the installation programme for the Mark 2 Colossi. By the end of the year, the seventh was in operation. The Colossi provided the codebreakers with the capacity to find all 12 wheel settings by machine, and this was done in the case of a large proportion of decrypted messages. Colossus X was installed in April 1945 and by the time of the German surrender in May an 11th was almost ready. (There are photographs of some of the Colossi in the centre of the book.)

If Flowers could have patented the inventions that he contributed to the assault on Tunny, he would probably have become a very rich man. As it was, the personal costs that he incurred in the course of building the Colossi left his bank account overdrawn at the end of the war. Newman was offered an OBE for his contribution to the defeat of Germany, but he turned it down, remarking to ex-colleagues from Bletchley Park that he considered the offer derisory. Tutte received no public recognition for his vital work.

Chapter 6

D-Day at Bletchley Park

Thomas H. Flowers

Before the war in Europe started in 1939, I worked as an engineer in the Dollis Hill communications research laboratories of what was then the British Post Office and is now British Telecom. During the war I continued to work in the laboratories; luckily I was not conscripted into the armed forces.

Early in 1942 I was directed to go to GCHQ, the Government Communications Headquarters, then at Bletchley Park. I was told that there I would be briefed concerning some top-secret work which they wanted our laboratories to do for them. At Bletchley Park I met Alan Turing. Turing was working on Enigma at that time, and it was he who wanted the top-secret work done—a machine to assist with decoding Enigma messages once the Bombe had produced the message settings. From then until the end of the war, I was a frequent visitor to GCHQ.

In the early years of the war, Alan Turing had saved Britain from defeat by the U-boats, by breaking the Enigma code used by the German Navy to communicate by radio with their ships at sea. Radio broadcasting is the only possible way of maintaining contact with mobile units like ships, tanks, and troops, but it is not secret—the transmissions can be intercepted by anyone with a suitable radio receiver. Therefore the messages must be encrypted before transmission. Even then the transmissions are secure only so long as the code remains unbroken by the enemy. The Germans were very sure that their high-grade ciphers could not be broken!

British intelligence services had many radio receiving stations at home and abroad, listening continuously to German military radio broadcasts. These stations sent the coded messages they intercepted to Bletchley Park.

In 1940 Bletchley Park started to receive teleprinter messages in a code that they could not recognise. The Germans had invented a new coding machine specifically for teleprinter messages. Messages typed into this machine in plain language were automatically encoded before being transmitted. At the receiving end an identical machine automatically decoded the message and printed the plaintext on paper tape. Operationally, this was a great advance on the Enigma machine, for which the encoding and decoding of the messages was a slow process, requiring two operators at each end of the link. The Germans used the new system operationally from 1941 until the end of the war. They entrusted their most secret messages to this system, such as Hitler's orders to his generals on the battlefront.

Without ever seeing one of the new machines, the mathematicians at Bletchley Park deduced its characteristics and devised mathematical processes that, when applied to the messages by specially made machine processors, would break the code. However, because of the complexity of the code, these processors would have to be able to work at least one hundred times as fast as any processor that had been made up to that time. How could such a processor be made? This was the problem that faced Bletchley Park. But they were not the first to face it. The need for superfast processing had arisen in the telephone industry in the years immediately before the war. A solution to the problem had been devised. Thermionic valves were used as switches to turn electric circuits on and off. This they can do thousands of times faster than the metal-contact mechanical switches (relays) which had been used to make processors up to that time. (The valves used were like the ones found in radio sets, but in radios valves do not function as switches.)

This new way of using valves was to create a new technology and eventually a new industry, which we now call digital electronics, but in 1942 nobody knew that that was about to happen. The subject was still in the research domain and known to very few people in very few places in the whole world. By chance Dollis Hill was one of those places. My own work just before the war had included research into this new technology. But Bletchley Park did not know that. They gave the problem to someone else, who designed a processor—later named 'Heath Robinson'—which used the new technology, but only for part of the processing. This design was then given to Dollis Hill to make, which we did. But the processing speed was much too slow and there were difficulties in operating the machine. I could see that processors using the new technology for all the processing, instead of just part, would solve the difficulties of speed and operation. The fully electronic machine would be much bigger and more complicated, and would take longer to produce. Since the technology was new, I estimated that it would take a year or more to get the first of the processors into service. For this and other reasons, Bletchley was unable to accept my offer to make processors of this type for them. But, on my own initiative, I proceeded to make processors to my own design, thinking that these would be available for the Bletchley Park cryptanalysts if no speedier solution could be found.

From the laboratory staff at Dollis Hill I assembled a team of about fifty scientists, professional engineers and technicians who were capable of designing the machine and making many of the parts. We commandeered a Post Office factory in Birmingham which we knew was able to manufacture the parts we could not make ourselves. I had to tell a few trusted members of my staff the purpose of the machine, and some of the details of its operation, in order to enable them to do the work I expected of them. Apart from this, nobody could be told anything about what they were making, other than that it was top secret, very urgent, and the most important war project in the country. With that assurance, everyone willingly worked very hard, up to twelve hours a day, often six and sometimes six and a half days of the week. We produced the first processor in ten months.

The first processor contained 1600 valves and occupied a room. It was the largest machine that Bletchley Park had ever had to operate and they called it 'Colossus'. It worked as designed well enough, but we had not been able to make the processing fast enough, and with use we could see that it needed to be improved in several ways. With that experience and some new ideas, we revised the design and made a second machine. This we put into service at Bletchley Park on 1 June 1944. It contained 2400 valves and worked at a processing speed of 25,000 alphabetical characters per second. This was 125 times the speed of mechanical processors, and sufficiently fast for the task in hand.

June 1 was to have been D-day. The fact that our first fully satisfactory Colossus was put into service on that day was no coincidence. I had been told in February that if it was not ready by that date it would be too late to be of much use. We worked flat out for four months and met the deadline, but only just. I was at Bletchley Park myself on that historic day and had been there since the morning of the previous day, with a number of other men, dealing with the last few difficulties that remained. In fact, the machine was fully ready for service for the first time during the small hours of the morning of 1 June.

June 1 should have been D-day, but General Eisenhower needed three subsequent days of fine weather to get enough men and materials across the channel in order to resist the inevitable counter-attack. In the event the weather was not good and the invasion had to be postponed until it improved. On 5 June, Eisenhower was in conference with his staff when a courier arrived from Bletchley Park and handed him a piece of paper to read. Hitler had sent Field Marshall Rommel battle orders by radio transmission, which Bletchley Park had decoded with the aid of the new Colossus. Hitler had told Rommel that the invasion of Normandy was imminent, but that this would not be the real invasion. It was a feint to draw troops away from the channel ports, against which the real invasion would be launched later. Rommel was not to move any troops. He was to await the real invasion, *which could be expected five days after the Normandy landing.* This was what Eisenhower read from the paper. He then knew that he could start the invasion of Normandy assured of five days without determined opposition—enough time to build up his forces even with indifferent weather. But he could not tell his assembled officers what he had read. He just handed the paper back to the courier and said, 'We go tomorrow.' And on the morrow, 6 June, they went.

When Hitler realised that Normandy was the real thing, he took command of the situation himself. He committed his forces in north-west Europe to one mighty offensive, a hammer blow intended to drive the invaders back into the sea. And his hammer blow could well have been successful had he not communicated details by radio, which Bletchley Park decoded. The result was a defeat of the German army so overwhelming that the Allies were able to sweep rapidly eastwards across France.

The war continued for another year, during which time a total of ten Colossus machines were installed in Bletchley Park. These supplied the armed services with information right up to the end of the war in Europe. Much later, when some of the activities of Bletchley Park had been made public, Eisenhower was asked to give his assessment of the effect that the operation there had had on the war. He said that, without the information Bletchley had supplied, the war would have gone on for at least two years longer than it did, during which time the occupied countries would have been devastated and hundreds of thousands of lives lost as the German army was driven back.

Bletchley Park changed the course of history and the praise that the cryptanalysts have received is well merited, but nothing has ever been said about the many people who worked like slaves for over a year to create Colossus and get it into service by D-day. The British Government kept the existence of Colossus secret for thirty years, and when it was at last made public it attracted little notice. However, academics interested in the history of computers have recognised that Colossus was the world's first electronic computer. It was not designed as a computer: computers had not yet been invented. It resembled a modern computer about as much as George Stephenson's Rocket locomotive of 1829 resembled the Royal Scot and other steam locomotives of the twentieth century. The basic technology used in a modern computer—data storage and retrieval, ultrafast processing, variable programming, the printing out of the results of the processing, and so forth— was all anticipated by Colossus, some of it by as much as ten years.

Luck played a large part in the creation of Colossus and in its being ready for service in time for D-day. The luck started right at the beginning of the war. I was in Berlin on laboratory business only days before hostilities began.

A telephone call from the British Embassy made me go home at once, and I crossed the border into Holland only hours before the German frontier was closed. If I had been caught and had spent the war interned in Germany, Colossus would not have been built because there would have been no-one at Dollis Hill with sufficient knowledge of the new technology to make it. If Dollis Hill had not made Colossus, some other organisation may have made something similar, but we now know that none could have done so by D-day. Those chance events changed the course of the Second World War. If they had not, history would now record the devastation of a large part of Europe and a death toll much greater than actually occurred.

It is astonishing that the Germans never realised that their secret code could be broken. Every time decoded information was used to initiate some action against the Germans, there was a risk of raising suspicion that the code had been broken. Often no use was made of decoded information because the risk was too great. If luck had been on the German side, as on ours, they could have found out for themselves that their code was not unbreakable. When Colossus had been made public, a German scientist and engineer came to see me in order to tell me that he himself had possessed the ideas and the technical knowledge that made Colossus possible. This man had asked Hitler for resources to develop his knowledge, but his estimate of the time that would be required before any practical use could be made of his work had been two years, and this had caused Hitler to refuse the request. Hitler believed that the war would be over, won by himself, in less time than that. If he had not refused, the Germans would have become aware of ultra-high-speed processing, and would perhaps have realised that even the complexity of their code was not proof against its being broken by this means. Possibly they would then have found some way of making it very unlikely that anyone could have broken—or continued to break—the code.

When, after the war ended, I was told that the secret of Colossus was to be kept indefinitely, I was naturally disappointed. I was in no doubt, once it was a proven success, that Colossus was a historic breakthrough, and that publication would have made my name in scientific and engineering circles—a conviction confirmed by the reception accorded to ENIAC, the US equivalent made public just after the war ended. I had to endure all the acclaim given to that enterprise without being able to disclose that I had anticipated it.

What I lost in personal prestige, and the benefits that commonly accrue in such circumstances, can now only be imagined. But at the time I accepted the situation philosophically and, in the euphoria of a war that was won, lost any concern about what might happen in the future.

If I thought about it at all, it did not occur to me that the secrecy would be maintained for so long. Colossus was part of a team effort, the success of the effort was sufficient, and none so far as I knew or know looked for any other. With the war over, and everyone eager to make up for lost time, it must have seemed to me that there were plenty of opportunities ahead of me to exploit the new knowledge and techniques in civil applications. I might even have thought that the withholding of the existence of Colossus from possible competitors gave me some advantage over them.

Now, however, I am moved to question the effects that the secrecy, imposed for so long, had on the industries of this country. Subsequent events did not turn out to my advantage, quite the reverse, and matters would have been different, I am sure, both for myself and for British industry, if Colossus had been revealed even ten years after the war ended.

The lead that I had given to this country in the new technology was not lost in the computer field, despite the imposed secrecy. This was due to Bletchley mathematicians, in particular Alan Turing and Professor Max Newman, being in positions where they could use their knowledge effectively without disclosing the source. I was in a similar position in the telephone industry—except for having no power or opportunity to use the knowledge effectively. With no administrative or executive powers, I had to convince others, and they would not be convinced. I was one-eyed in the kingdom of the blind.

The one thing that I lacked was prestige, which knowledge of Colossus would have amply provided. Personal rivalries also played their part. These were exacerbated, and some were even provoked, by what was considered pretentiousness on my part. Little or none of that would have been possible had Colossus been known.

The result was that this country found itself years behind some others in the development of electronic exchanges of the type I pioneered. Events would have been different had the existence of Colossus been known. It is unlikely then that I would have been overlooked in the Post Office research reorganisation of 1947, unlikely then that incredulous exchange manufacturers would have failed to take notice when I tried to tell them that telephone exchanges of the future would be electronic, and unlikely, once market pressure did finally compel them to consider production of an electronic system in 1956, that they would have gone their own way, irrespective of what I had to say.

Chapter 7

Intercept!

Jack Copeland

'Y'

A top-secret cryptographic dictionary compiled by Bletchley Park in 1944 defined 'Y Service' as 'The organisation responsible for the interception of all enemy and neutral radio transmissions'. The job description was succinct, the task huge. The Y Service staff who intercepted and recorded the German and Japanese transmissions are unsung heroes of the attack on the enemy codes. Many of them were women. Their difficult and painstaking work was less glamorous than codebreaking, but without Y the Bletchley cryptanalysts would have had nothing to decrypt.

Chapter 2 sketches the growth of the Y Service between the wars, including the establishment of the Royal Navy intercept site at Flowerdown, the Royal Air Force site at Cheadle, and the Army site at Chatham (see photograph 40). These and other military sites in the UK tended to focus on Morse transmissions. Curiously, the interception of the non-Morse transmissions associated with Fish fell at first to the London Police.

THE POLICE LEND A HAND

Collaboration between the Foreign Office signals interception programme and Scotland Yard's Metropolitan Police wireless service began in 1926. ('Wireless' means 'radio'.) The Police wireless service, which started life in an attic at Scotland Yard, was originally set up to develop wireless for police vehicles. From 1926 the police operators began actively to intercept material of interest to the Foreign Office. In 1930 the Foreign Office started to finance the police Y section, which in turn became increasingly involved in the development of experimental equipment for Y work. Following successes against European traffic, the police operators received carte blanche to investigate 'any curious type of transmission'. In the mid-1930s the section expanded and relocated to buildings in the grounds of the Metropolitan Police Nursing Home at Denmark Hill in south London.

Police operators first intercepted German non-Morse transmissions in 1932, on a link between Berlin and Moscow. These transmissions, which went on for ten months, were clearly experimental, and the police monitored them in conjunction with the Post Office's Central Telegraph Office. It seems that the pre-war transmissions were unenciphered. Y's first wartime encounter with non-Morse transmissions came in the latter half of 1940, when two stations broadcasting enciphered teleprinter code were intercepted. Sadly the intercepted material was put aside, owing to a shortage of crypt-analysts. The transmissions were monitored and after a time they ceased. Probably the two stations had been carrying out tests. The British operators intercepted further non-Morse transmissions during the early part of 1941. These consisted both of teleprinter code and *Hellschreiber*, an early form of fax. Some transmissions were supersonic—what appeared to the intercept operator to be a steady tone was revealed by the monitoring equipment to consist of a stream of characters.

The first experimental Tunny traffic was intercepted in June 1941. The messages were distinctive, beginning with a plaintext list of 12 German names, such as 'Anton', 'Berta', 'Caesar', and 'Dora'. These lists turned out to be the message indicators, revealing the wheel start positions (see Chapter 3). Early Tunny transmissions were sent via *Hellschreiber*, but from March 1942 each of the Tunny machines on the experimental link was wired to a tone transmitter. As the name implies, this transmitted tones—somewhat like those produced by the keys of a modern touch-tone phone.

Denmark Hill was instructed to pay special attention to the newly dis-covered Tunny traffic. Assistance was provided by a small outstation with special aerials that was set up on the south coast near Dover. The Admiralty, Air Force, and Army all loaned first-class operators. But by February 1942, it was clear that a large intercept station dedicated to Tunny was required. A search was made for a suitable location and eventually, in May 1942, a farm-house about 15 miles south-east of London was requisitioned, at Knockholt in Kent. Situated on top of a rise, the farmhouse had an altitude of about 600 feet—ideal for snooping on radio transmissions from across the Channel. There were 160 acres of land to accommodate aerials and new buildings.

FOREIGN OFFICE STATION KNOCKHOLT

Knockholt, under the command of Harold Kenworthy, previously head of the Denmark Hill Y section, was the ears of the operation against Tunny. In June 1942 there was a staff of six at Knockholt. By the end of the war, over 800 people worked there.

The 'Set Room', the heart of the Y station, contained 30 receiving sets at its peak, each with ancillary equipment for printing intercepted material and perforating tapes. At the start of a shift 30 highly-trained operators (about a quarter of them women) donned their headphones; each worked side by side with an assistant, who managed the recording equipment. Two receiving sets were needed to monitor a single Tunny link, one for each end of the link. A dozen or so priority links were covered during a shift, and the remainder of the sets were used to search the airwaves for Tunny transmissions. The day's priorities were decided in a morning meeting at Bletchley Park. Despite the shift system, there were times when the priorities set by Bletchley exceeded Knockholt's capacity.

Knockholt intercepted about 12,000 Tunny transmissions during November and December 1942. In 1943 the number of intercepted transmissions increased sharply, peaking at over 34,000 during the three months from October to December. Thereafter the number of intercepts declined, falling to less than 7000 during the same period in 1944. Conversely, the number of message tapes despatched by Knockholt to Bletchley Park rose steadily throughout the war, climbing from 73 messages in the period April–June 1943 to 10,555 messages during the last four months of fighting. Knockholt intercepted more messages than Bletchley could possibly decrypt, and the selection of messages for despatch was governed by cryptanalytical and intelligence priorities (any suspected depths were teleprinted immediately to Bletchley Park). In all, 27,631 Tunny messages were sent from Knockholt to the Bletchley codebreakers, of which 13,508 were deciphered successfully—a total of 63,431,000 letters of decode.

Kenworthy summed up the challenge that faced his operators once Bletchley's attack on Tunny got under way: 'New methods were being developed at Station "X" which called for a hitherto unknown degree of accuracy in interception.' A single wrong or omitted character in the middle of a message of several thousand characters would almost certainly prevent the Newmanry from finding the wheel settings.

Difficulties facing the intercept operators included (besides such routine hazards as interference and poor weather conditions) the high speed of transmission when the Tunny machine was in auto mode, and the German's use of directional antennae to beam the signal towards the receiving end of the Tunny link, meaning that the signal picked up at Knockholt was usually weak. In addition, the German operator would suddenly and unpredictably change the frequency of the transmission—the intercepted signal would vanish abruptly, leaving the interceptor to guess which of the 25 or so available frequencies the German operator might have selected for the remainder of the transmission. Meanwhile Knockholt lost some number of letters of the message. Missing letters—known as a 'slide' in the message—could make the whole intercept worthless.

READING THE SLIP

In the early years of the war, the only teleprinters available at Denmark Hill were too slow for recording the non-Morse transmissions. Kenworthy was forced to fall back on *undulator* tape, known colloquially as 'slip' (see Figure 1). As the undulator tape unwound from a spool it was marked with a continuous ink trace by an automatic pen connected to the receiving equipment. Undulators were hardly at the cutting edge of technology, yet slip proved so accurate a recording medium that it remained the gold standard for Tunny interception work, even when fast teleprinters and in-line tape-perforating equipment became available.

A skilled reader could discern letters on the undulator tape at the rate of some 30 words per minute (the speed of Tunny transmissions was 66 words per minute). By scanning the undulator tape as the transmission was received, the intercept operator could glean information about shifts in frequency,

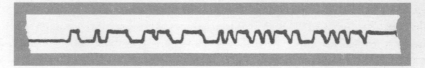

Figure 1. Undulator tape.

The tape bears the letters COLOSSUS. The teleprinter code for each letter is represented on the tape by a sequence of peaks and troughs. Dots are peaks, crosses are troughs. A peak representing •• is twice as broad as a peak representing •, a trough representing ××× is three times as broad as a trough representing ×, and so on. C, •××ו, consists of a peak of 1 unit length, followed by a trough of 3 units length, followed by a peak of 1 unit length. The code for a letter is always preceded by a 'start signal' and followed by a 'stop signal' (these control the teleprinter). The start signal is represented by a peak of 1 unit and the stop signal by a trough of 1.5 units. So C with its start and stop signals consists of a peak of 2, followed by a trough of 3, followed by a peak of 1, followed by a trough of 1.5. O, •••××, and its start and stop signals form a peak of 4 followed by a trough of 3.5.

Tape supplied by Don Hobbs.

since—surprisingly—the German operator would often use plaintext when informing the other end of the link what the new frequency would be.

Specialised personnel known as 'slip readers' worked on the undulator tape post-reception. They were able to tell how many letters had been missed in a slide, by measuring the length of the corrupted portion of tape. Armed with this information the codebreakers were usually able to compensate. Slip reading was done by 'civilian girls'. 'Girls are used exclusively for slip reading,' a contemporary report said. 'Extended observations have proved the advisability of using the superior patience of women in this monotonous work.'

Eventually, once special high-speed equipment was available, each receiving set was connected not only to an undulator but also to a teleprinter and a tape perforator. The tape perforator punched out the intercepted message on paper tape. The teleprinter printed the letters of the ciphertext on paper strip, which was then cut into sections and pasted onto a sheet known as a 'Red Form' (see Figure 1 of Appendix 5 *The Tiltman Break*). The teleprinter and perforator tended to be inaccurate unless reception was excellent, and the Red Form had to be checked against the undulator tape post reception. When the signal was poor, the operator switched off the teleprinter and the perforator, leaving the undulator to take down the message.

By the end of 1944, there were about 200 people at Knockholt whose job was to read, check, and transcribe slip. This was done in the Slip Reading Room, where the slip readers compared the Red Form against the undulator tape (or created a Red Form from the slip if none was provided). Slides were measured and bad characters were reconstructed from the undulator record. Corrections, and counts of missing letters, were marked on the Red Form. There were never enough slip readers—two months' training was necessary before a recruit could be let loose in the Slip Room. Consequently a proportion of the slip produced by the Set Room was never read.

Once the slip readers had corrected the Red Form it was passed to the Perforation Room (along with the punched tape from the Set Room if one was made), and the undulator tape was filed away. In the Perforation Room, operators made a punched tape from the Red Form, checking it against the Set Room tape where possible. Once an accurate punched tape was obtained it was transmitted twice to Bletchley Park, where the two copies were compared against each other. If the tapes agreed then it was assumed that the transmissions were error-free; often they did not agree, necessitating retransmission. Finally Knockholt sent the Red Form and a copy of the punched tape to Bletchley Park by motorcycle despatch rider, allowing further checking there if necessary.

Section 2

Colossus

• •

Chapter 8

Colossus

Thomas H. Flowers

SWITCHES

Machines such as counters, computers, and Colossus process information. Items of information are given a physical identity which can be recognised and transmitted over distance. The identity is transmitted by what is called a signal and the relationship between the signals and the information they represent is called a code (as distinct from a cipher). Certain types of numbers are commonly used to identify items of information, because they are universally known and endless in quantity: the information, processors, and processing are then said to be digital. Processing consists of logical operations carried out serially on the numbers until a conclusion has been reached, expressed in numbers which can be converted to information by the code.

Automatic number processors may be wholly or in part mechanical, electromechanical, or electronic. For the present purpose, electromechanical operation is the easiest to describe and to understand and so will be used as the starting point of this exposition.

Electromechanical processors comprise electrical circuits consisting of switches interconnected by wire conductors. A switch is a device which can be set into one of two states, the unoperated or OFF state and the operated or ON state. The earliest switches used movable metal elements called contacts which could be pressed together to connect, or separated to disconnect, two wires that were attached to the contacts. Some metal contact switches used electric motors to operate them.

All switches are stable in their OFF states. In their ON states, they may be stable only so long as the operating force is maintained. When this force is removed, they may remain in the ON state or revert to the OFF state. An electric light switch is an example of a manually operated switch which is

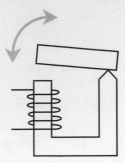

Figure 1. Electromagnetic switch.

stable in both the OFF and the ON states. A bell 'push-button to ring' switch reverts to the OFF state when the operating force is removed.

Electromechanical (i.e. electromagnetically operated) switches usually take the form of relays, each of which consists of a U-shaped iron structure, as shown in Figure 1, around part of which a coil of wire has been wound. A hinged iron armature bridges the open end of the U. The armature rotates on its hinge between two positions. In one, the OFF position, a spring impels the armature to open a gap in the iron circuit. In the other, the ON position, electric current through the coil of wire causes the iron structure to become a magnet and to attract the armature, leaving only a very small air gap in the iron circuit; not shown in the diagram is an arm on the armature which closes metal contacts on the relay so producing the ON state. With no current in the coil the relay is stable in its OFF state; with current in the coil it is stable in the ON state but returns to the OFF state when the current is switched off. It can be made stable in the ON state by a 'make' contact (as in 'make and break') on the relay itself to maintain current through the coil. A break contact on another relay has to be operated to restore the first relay to its OFF state.

Electronic switching systems use switches with no visibly moving parts, mostly thermionic valves until these were superseded by transistors and solid-state devices. Colossus, which was built before the transistor had been invented, used valves.

A thermionic valve has three electrodes: an electrically heated 'cathode' (C in Figure 2), a metal 'anode' (A), and a third electrode called a 'grid' (G). All three electrodes exist in a vacuum enclosed by a glass envelope. A battery maintains the anode at a positive potential relative to the cathode. The heated cathode emits electrons. These electrons reach the anode if the grid potential is positive with respect to that of the cathode, but not if it is negative. (The flow of electrons from the cathode to the anode is always described as a

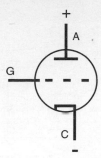

Figure 2. Thermionic valve.

current flowing from anode to cathode, according to the usual convention whereby the flow is said to be from positive to negative.)

The thermionic valve is a two-state device which can be used as a switch, but unlike the metal contact switch, the current that is switched can flow in only one direction. It is therefore not a direct substitute for a relay and the design techniques for the two types of switching are necessarily different. Nevertheless, most if not all digital machines using mechanical or electro-mechanical switches can be redesigned using electronic switches. A fundamental difference between the two types of machine is the speed of operation. The fastest that metal-contact switches can be made to operate is about a thousand operations per second. Electronic valve switches can attain speeds of millions of operations per second.

MEMORY

Memory for digital information in large quantity is now easy—and cheap—to provide electronically, but when Colossus was designed it was neither simple nor cheap. To store one bit (0 or 1) of information requires a device with two stable states, together with some means of setting the device to either of these two states. Numerous devices with those properties were in existence: the problem was to choose the most suitable device for each usage. Two types of memory were needed: one in which stored information could be read but not changed during the whole of the processing, and another in which information could be both stored and read during the processing. Colossus used five principal types of memory device.

The largest quantity of information that had to be stored during the whole of the processing was the message to be decoded. Bletchley Park received the messages stored as holes punched in five-hole paper tape. These were

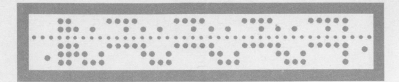

Figure 3. Punched paper tape. The two single punches are the start hole and the stop hole.

processed by Colossus in that form. The tape, half an inch wide, had a line of small holes down the centre (see Figure 3) by which it could be mechanically advanced by a sprocket wheel, one hole at a time. Across the paper, in line with a sprocket hole, up to five larger holes were machine-punched to store the binary digits 0 and 1 (known as dots and crosses at Bletchley Park). The message on the tape is preceded and followed by lengths of tape which are blank except for the sprocket holes.

The two ends of the tape were stuck together to form a loop, which wound round pulleys on a frame, enabling it to be rotated continuously. A pulse of electricity was produced by each hole as it passed through a photoelectric reader. The continuous stream of *sprocket-hole* pulses thus produced was communicated to the processor's master control and provided a time-base for the operation of the whole machine. Small holes hand-punched just before and just after the message on the tape indicated to the master control the start and the end of the message (see Figure 3). Hand operation of a key started the rotation of the tape, and when it had reached processing speed another hand-operated key caused processing to commence the next time a start-hole pulse was received from the tape. Thereafter the machine operated automatically until the end of the scan. During each revolution of the tape, the message was read into the processor, followed by a pause before being read again. The pause was due to (and its duration was controlled by) the length of blank tape in the loop. Its purpose was to give time, if required, for some necessary processing before the next scan of the message began.

Much data that was not subject to change during the processing was stored by means of plugs and sockets. Figure 4 shows three rows of sockets mounted on a strip of insulating material. The sockets on each of the two outer rows are connected together and to sources of electric potential, + and −, representing dot or cross. U-shaped links enable each centre-row socket to be connected to one of the sockets on either side of it, and thus to represent a stored digit, dot or cross. The processor accesses the centre sockets by means of switches in order to read the stored digits.

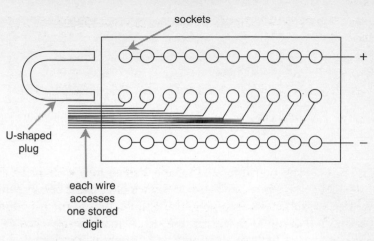

Figure 4. Plug-board data-store.

A mechanical rotating-arm multistate switch is illustrated in Figure 5. This is called a *uniselector*. A uniselector is often used to store a group of items of information. Usually a number of such switches are mounted and rotated on the same spindle to enable several items of information to be stored at each position of the switch. Items are retrieved by rotating the switch to a given position. Colossus used switches of this kind for some slow-speed operations.

The Eccles–Jordan *trigger circuit*, invented in 1921, is a device used in electronic switching machines, including Colossus, in order to store and use single-digit information generated during processing. It comprises two valves used as switches, either of which, but not both, can be switched on at any time and remain stable.

Instead of a two-valve trigger, a single *thyratron* valve can sometimes be used, with resulting economy in components. A thyratron is the same as a

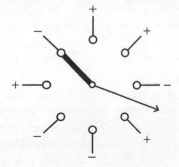

Figure 5. Uniselector or rotary switch.

thermionic valve but with a small quantity of neon or other gas in the envelope, instead of a vacuum. It is switched to the ON state when the grid becomes positive with respect to the cathode but can then be switched OFF only by reducing the anode potential to stop the flow of current.

THE COLOSSUS MACHINE

Colossus was a special-purpose machine designed primarily to perform processes devised by Bletchley Park for discovering the settings of the code wheels made by the machine operators before the messages were sent. Much of Colossus was an electronic analogue of the Lorenz Tunny machine. Bletchley Park also eventually found ways of using the machine to discover the Tunny wheel patterns when they were routinely changed. (Colossus did not itself decode intercepted messages. This was done by other machines, specially modified teleprinters, also known as Tunny machines.)

Figure 6 is a diagrammatic representation of Colossus. The message to be broken (it is assumed that the Tunny wheel patterns are already known to the cryptanalysts) was formed into a loop and mounted on Colossus so that it could be scanned repeatedly by a photoelectric reader. The output from the reader consisted of electrical pulses from the holes in the tape. The sprocket holes produced a continuous stream of pulses—called timing pulses—which were sent to the master control and used to control the timing of the whole of

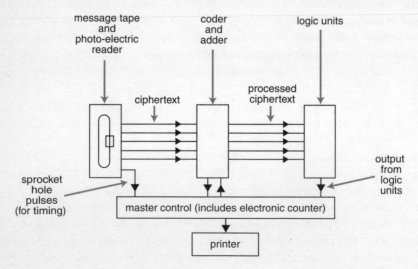

Figure 6. Colossus system.

the processing. The message holes produced five-digit numbers which were communicated to a coder.

The master control supplied pulses to the coder synchronised with sprocket hole pulses, but only while the message was actually being read. The coder consisted of a number-generator, driven by the master pulses, and an adder which added the generated numbers to the message numbers as they were read from the tape. The number-generator produced the same streams of pulses that the wheels of the Lorenz Tunny machine produced. The output from the coder was five single-digit streams of pulses, which could be selected by plugs and jacks for individual processing.

Once started, the tape did not cease to revolve until every possible combination of digits on the Tunny wheels producing the selected streams (e.g. the chis) had been used at the start of a scan of the message. Thus the combination of digits which had been used to code the message must have been used for one of the scans. The problem for the cryptanalysts was to identify that unique scan.

Once started, Colossus continued to function under the control of the master unit, the equivalent of a modern computer's central processing unit (CPU). The master control sequenced the various functions that it was called upon to do, as decided by the operators of the machine.

The wheel patterns themselves were generated by rings of thyratron valves stepped by pulses synchronous with sprocket-hole pulses and supplied by the master control. Electromagnetic uniselectors stepped during the blank part of the tape to advance the starting positions of those wheels in use.

The electronic storage of all the information—the ciphertext as well as the key—would have avoided all problems relating to speed of operation. Although this was possible at the time, it was impractical.

IDENTIFYING THE CORRECT SCAN

Each of the single-digit streams (or 'impulses', in BP jargon) from the coder consisted of a dot or a cross for every character of the message. For every scan except the unique one, the occurrence of dots and crosses was more or less random. Knowing the total number of characters in the message, the probability of any particular total of dot or cross could be calculated. For the unique scan, the output of dots and crosses was not random, but that of a Baudot-coded message, and therefore influenced by the peculiarities of language. However, the differences in simple counts of the dots and crosses of each stream were not enough to identify with certainty the unique scan from all the others.

Bletchley Park discovered processes involving two streams or 'impulses' which produced dot outputs greater in number for the unique scan than for all the others (see Chapter 5). The processes were performed by logic units to which two selected digit streams could be connected by plugs and cords. The output of a logic unit so connected could be applied, also by plugs and cords, to a counter in the master control (as shown in Figure 6). The logic units consisted of Boolean addition modules, OR gates, AND gates, unit delay, and trigger circuits.

Since none of the starting positions of the code wheels were known at the beginning of processing a message, the first run of scans was necessarily a long one. Once the starting positions for one or more code wheels had been discovered, the digit streams produced by these wheels could be paired with others in turn, making it possible to determine the starting positions of other wheels with very much shorter scans.

THE COUNTER

The master control contained a four-decimal number counter which counted the dots and showed the total score at the end of each scan of the message. The unique scan would show up as the one that produced the largest score. To identify that scan, scans using every possible combination of starting positions of the chi- and psi-wheels involved would have to be made, with a typewriter recording the starting positions and their scores. The unique scan could then be picked out from the record.

However, it was not necessary to record the count for every scan. The small proportion of scans which produced the highest scores would be sufficient. To select that proportion, the counter had four decade switches which could be set to any number up to 9999. The cryptanalyst had to decide, for each message, the number to which the counter should be set (the 'set total'). If the count for a scan did not reach the set number, no record was made for that scan. If the score did reach or exceed the set number, the score and the starting positions of the code wheels used for that scan were stored on relays. These relays were capable of operating during the blank part of the tape, thus allowing the processing of the next scan to proceed without interruption.

PRINT-OUT

A permanent record of the stored information was made by an electro-magnetically operated typewriter which occupied the time of several scans, during which the set number could be reached again. If that happened, the processing was stopped, but not the tape rotation, until the relays and the typewriter were free. Scanning was then restarted by the next occurrence of a start pulse from the tape. Most of the loss of time due to the mechanical slowness of the typewriter was thus avoided.

When the typewriter recordings started to repeat, all the combinations of code-wheel settings had been used, and scanning could be stopped. The scan that had produced the highest count had a high probability of being the unique scan that was being sought.

THE SPAN COUNTER

When, as sometimes happened, scanning as just described did not yield a satisfactory result, the reason was usually corruption of the message on the tape. Errors in reception could occur due to noise or fading of the German transmission, resulting in a character not being received or a false character being generated. After the corruption, the coder operation would be out of synchronism with the message.

To deal with this situation, a decimal number counter was provided in the control unit to count the sprocket-hole pulses supplied to the coder between the receipt of start and stop pulses from the tape. Decade switches on the counter enabled the selection of two numbers. Pulses were produced when these numbers were reached by the counter. These two pulses were used to start and stop the processing, instead of the start and stop pulses from the tape. Hence processing could be limited to any span of the message on the tape. The counter was in consequence called the span counter.

Scanning the message in two halves, for instance, could show in which half the corruption existed. Having found a span of the message without corruption, the span could be increased in both directions until the corruption was encountered.

THE SHIFT REGISTER AND PARALLEL PROCESSING

The Lorenz machine generated and processed numbers at the rate of about five numbers per second: Colossus generated and processed them at the rate of 5000 per second. That speed was limited not by the processing but by the speed at which the paper tape could be safely driven, as determined by experiment. A long tape was mounted and driven at ever increasing speed until it broke at something over 9000 characters per second. Tape flew all over the place; it was festooned over everything and everybody. We decided from this test that 5000 characters per second was the highest speed that could be used with safety. (At that speed the tape was travelling at nearly 30 miles per hour.)

Every message to be decoded had to be processed individually, and processing speed was very important in order to gain the maximum advantage from the decrypts. Limitation of the processing speed to 5000 characters per second would have seriously reduced the quantity and value of decrypts. This limitation was surmounted by the invention of the shift register, probably the most important of the several new inventions which made Colossus possible. The shift register enabled a plurality of identical processors each to process one scan of the message but from consecutive starting points on the number-generator cycle. Using five processors working in parallel from five consecutive starting points increased the processing speed to 25,000 characters per second.

A shift register comprised trigger circuits in series, providing storage of consecutive digits of a single stream of digits. Just before the next digit in a stream became available, all the digits already stored in the chain were advanced to the next positions, exiting the digit in the last store and leaving the first in the chain free to receive the next digit. A six-position shift register was allocated to each of the five single-digit streams of the message. Each register stored characters of a message as they were received. Thus six consecutive characters of a message were available. Consecutive pairs of digits of a stream were applied to two of five individual logic units. Master controls provided from a single scan of the tape the results of five consecutive scans. One piece of equipment for recording the results of the scans was sufficient for all five scans.

The five-fold increase in the speed of processing that became possible meant a five-fold reduction in the time taken to break each message and a five-fold increase in the number of messages which were broken, with incalculable advantage to the war effort.

Chapter 9

Colossus and the Rise of the Modern Computer

Jack Copeland

GETTING THE STORY WRONG AT THE START

Secrecy about Colossus has bedevilled the history of computing. In the years following the Second World War, the Hungarian-born American logician and mathematician John von Neumann, through writings and charismatic public addresses, made the concept of the electronic digital computer widely known. Von Neumann knew nothing of Colossus, and he told the world that the American ENIAC—first operational at the end of 1945, two years after Colossus—was 'the first electronic computing machine'. Others familiar with the ENIAC and unaware of Colossus peddled the same message.

The myth soon became set in stone, and for the rest of the twentieth century book after book—not to mention magazines and newspaper articles—told readers that the ENIAC was the first electronic computer. In 1971, a leading computer science textbook gave this historical summary: 'The early story has often been told, starting with Babbage and . . . up to the birth of electronic machines with ENIAC.' The present chapter revisits the early story, setting Colossus in its proper place.

FIRST—WHAT *IS* A COMPUTER?

In the original sense of the word, a computer was not a machine at all, but a human being—a mathematical assistant whose task was to calculate by rote, in accordance with a systematic method supplied by an overseer prior to the calculation. The computer, like a filing clerk, might have little detailed knowledge of the end to which his or her work was directed. Many thousands of human computers were employed in business, government, and research establishments, doing some of the sorts of calculating work that nowadays is performed by electronic computers (see photograph 42).

The term 'computing machine' was used increasingly from the 1920s to refer to small calculating machines which mechanised elements of the human computer's work. For a complex calculation, several dozen human computers might be required, each equipped with a desktop computing machine. By the 1940s, however, the scale of some calculations required by physicists and engineers had become so great that the work could not easily be done in a reasonable time by even a roomful of human computers with desktop computing machines. The need to develop high-speed large-scale computing machinery was pressing.

During the late 1940s and early 1950s, with the advent of electronic computing machines, the phrase 'computing machine' gave way gradually to 'computer'. As Turing stated, the new machines were 'intended to carry out any definite rule of thumb process which could have been done by a human operator working in a disciplined but unintelligent manner'. During the brief period in which the old and new meanings of 'computer' coexisted, the prefix 'electronic' or 'digital' would usually be used to distinguish machine from human.

A computer, in the later sense of the word, is any machine able to do work that could, in principle, be done by a human computer. Mainframes, laptops, pocket calculators, palm-pilots—all are computing machines, carrying out work that a human rote-worker could do, if he or she worked long enough, and had a plentiful enough supply of paper and pencils.

GRANDFATHER BABBAGE

The Victorian Charles Babbage, many decades ahead of his time, was one of the first to grasp the huge potential of the idea of using machinery to compute. (See photograph 43.) Babbage was Lucasian Professor of Mathematics at the University of Cambridge from 1828 to 1839, a position once held by Isaac Newton and held today by cosmologist Stephen Hawking. Babbage's long-time collaborator was Ada, Countess of Lovelace (daughter of the poet Byron). Her vision of the potential of computing machines was in some respects more far-reaching even than Babbage's own. Lovelace envisaged computing machines going beyond pure number-crunching, suggesting that one of Babbage's planned 'Engines' might be capable of composing elaborate pieces of music.

In about 1820 Babbage proposed an 'Engine' for the automatic production of mathematical tables (such as logarithm tables, tide tables, and astronomical tables). He called it the 'Difference Engine'. This was, of course, the age of the steam engine, and Babbage's Engine was to consist of more accurately machined versions of the types of components then found in railway locomotives and the like—brass gear wheels, rods, ratchets, pinions, and so forth. Decimal numbers were represented by the positions of 10-toothed metal wheels mounted in columns. Babbage exhibited a small working model of the Engine in 1822. He never built the full-scale machine he had designed, but did complete several parts of it. The largest of these—roughly 10 per cent of the planned machine—is on display in the London Science Museum. Babbage used it successfully to calculate various mathematical tables. Babbage's 'Difference Engine No. 2', designed during 1846–9, has recently been constructed by Doron Swade and his team at the Science Museum—a glorious machine of gleaming brass.

Babbage also proposed the 'Analytical Engine', considerably more ambitious than the Difference Engine. Had it been completed, the Analytical Engine would have been an all-purpose mechanical digital computer (whereas the Difference Engine could perform only a few of the tasks that human computers carried out). A large model of the Analytical Engine was under construction at the time of Babbage's death in 1871, but a full-scale version was never built. The Analytical Engine was to have a memory, or 'store' as Babbage called it, and a central processing unit, or 'mill'. The behaviour of the Analytical Engine would have been controlled by a program of instructions contained on punched cards connected together by ribbons (an idea Babbage adopted from the Jacquard weaving loom). The Analytical Engine would have been able, like Colossus, to select from alternative actions on the basis of the outcomes of its previous actions—a facility nowadays known as 'branching' (see Chapter 10).

Babbage's idea of an all-purpose calculating engine was well known to some modern pioneers of automatic calculation. In the United States during the 1930s, Vannevar Bush and Howard Aiken, both of whom built successful computing machines in the pre-electronic era, spoke of using modern technology to accomplish what Babbage had set out to do. Babbage's ideas were remembered in Britain also, and his proposed computing machinery was on occasion a topic of lively mealtime discussion at Bletchley Park.

TURING AND THE STORED-PROGRAM CONCEPT

As everyone who can operate a personal computer knows, the way to make the machine perform the task you want—word processing, say—is to open the appropriate program stored in the computer's memory. Life was not always so simple. Colossus did not store programs in its memory. To set up Colossus for a different job, it was necessary to modify some of the machine's wiring by hand, using switches and plugs. The larger ENIAC was also programmed by re-routing cables and setting switches. (See photograph 49.) The process was a nightmare: it could take the ENIAC's operators up to three weeks to set up and debug a program. Colossus, ENIAC, and their like are called 'program-controlled' computers, in order to distinguish them from the modern 'stored-program' computer. Babbage's Analytical Engine, too, was to be a program-controlled, not a stored-program, computer.

This basic principle of the modern computer, that is, controlling the machine's operations by means of a program of coded instructions stored in the computer's memory, was thought of by Alan Turing in 1936. At the time, Turing was a shy, eccentric student at Cambridge University. He went up to King's College in October 1931 to read mathematics and was elected a Fellow of King's in the spring of 1935, at the age of only 22. In 1936 he left England to study for a PhD in the United States, at Princeton University, returning in 1938. Turing's 'universal computing machine', as he called it—it would soon be known simply as the universal Turing machine—emerged from research that no-one would have guessed could have any practical application. In 1936 Turing was working on an obscure problem in mathematical logic, the so-called 'decision problem', which he learned of from lectures on the foundations of mathematics and logic given by Newman. While thinking about this problem, Turing dreamed up an abstract digital computing machine which, as he said, could compute 'all numbers which could naturally be regarded as computable'.

The universal Turing machine consists of a limitless memory in which both data and instructions are stored, in symbolically encoded form, and a scanner that moves back and forth through the memory, symbol by symbol, reading what it finds and writing further symbols. By inserting different programs into the memory, the machine can be made to carry out any calculation that can be done by a human computer. That is why Turing called the machine *universal*.

Turing's fabulous idea was just this: a single machine of fixed structure that, by making use of coded instructions stored in memory, could change itself, chameleon-like, from a machine dedicated to one task into a machine dedicated to a completely different task—from calculator to word processor, for example. Nowadays, when many have a physical realisation of a universal Turing machine in their living room, this idea of a one-stop-shop computing machine is apt to seem as obvious as the wheel. But in 1936, when engineers thought in terms of building different machines for different purposes, the concept of the stored-program universal computer was revolutionary.

It is not known whether Turing had heard of Babbage's work when he invented the universal Turing machine. In their specifics, the Analytical Engine and the universal Turing machine are chalk and cheese. Turing later emphasised that the Analytical Engine was universal (a judgement that was possible only from the vantage point of the mathematical theory of universal machines that Turing himself developed). Nevertheless, there is an important logical difference between the two types of machine. In Turing's machine, but not Babbage's, program and data both consist of symbols in memory, and the machine works on both using exactly the same operations. Reading the program is no different from reading the data. This is the stored-program concept. Implicit in the concept is the possibility of the computer operating on and modifying its own program as it runs, just as it operates on the data in its memory. Turing was later to suggest that this ability of the stored-program computer to modify its own instructions might form the mechanism for *computer learning*—a topic now at the forefront of research in Artificial Intelligence.

In 1936 the universal Turing machine existed only as an idea. Right from the start Turing was interested in the possibility of building such a machine, as to some extent was Newman. But it was not until their Bletchley Park days that the dream of building a miraculously fast all-purpose computing machine took hold of them. Before the war they knew of no practical way to construct a stored-program computer: it was at Bletchley that they learned how it might be done. Large-scale electronics was the secret.

FROM COGWHEELS TO ELECTRONICS

The transition from cogwheel computers to electronic computers took just over a century. Various largish, purely mechanical computing machines were built, including the Scheutz Difference Engines, modelled on Babbage's, and Bush's (analogue) Differential Analyser, completed at Massachusetts Institute of Technology in 1931. It took a skilled mechanic equipped with a lead hammer to set up the mechanical Differential Analyser for each new job.

The next generation of computing machines used electromechanical technology. Their basic components were the small electrically driven switches called 'relays' (see Chapter 5). Electromechanical program-controlled digital computers were built during 1939–45 by (among others) George Stibitz at Bell Telephone Laboratories, Aiken at Harvard University and IBM, and Konrad Zuse in Berlin. Turing himself built a very small electromechanical multiplier while at Princeton (it multiplied binary numbers).

Electromechanical is not electronic. Electronic valves operate very many times faster than relays, since the valve's only moving part is the beam of electrons. It was the development of high-speed digital techniques using valves that made the modern computer possible.

Flowers' pioneering work before the war on large-scale electronics in connection with telephone exchanges has already been described in Chapter 5. In the United States, a somewhat comparable use of valves, although on a much smaller scale and with an entirely different purpose, was by John Atanasoff, during the period 1937–42. At this time Atanasoff, an applied mathematician, was working at Iowa State College. His aim was to use valves to carry out numerical calculations. In 1939, with the assistance of his student Clifford Berry, Atanasoff began building what is nowadays sometimes called the Atanasoff–Berry Computer, or ABC, a small-scale electronic digital computing machine for a specialised purpose, the solution of systems of linear algebraic equations. (This is just one of the huge variety of different tasks that can be performed by a human computer or an all-purpose computing machine.) Atanasoff's digital computer contained approximately 300 valves. Although the electronic part of this small-scale machine was a success, the computer as a whole never worked properly, because errors were introduced by an unsatisfactory binary card-reader. Work on the computer was discontinued in 1942, when Atanasoff left Iowa State for the US Naval Ordnance Department. In 1941 John Mauchly, a professor at a small American college, visited Atanasoff's laboratory. He showed great interest in Atanasoff's computer. Mauchly later went on, with engineer Presper Eckert, to design and build the ENIAC.

COLOSSUS—THE MISSING LINK

Soon after the end of the war Turing and Newman embarked on separate projects to create a universal Turing machine in hardware (Turing in London, Newman in Manchester). Historians who did not know of Colossus tended to assume that Turing and Newman inherited their vision of large-scale electronic computing machinery from the ENIAC group in the United States. In reality, Colossus was the link between Turing's pre-war work and his and Newman's post-war projects to build an electronic stored-program computer. (Flowers' view of the ENIAC, which he saw just after the war: it was just a number-cruncher—Colossus, with its elaborate facilities for logical operations, was 'much more of a computer than ENIAC'.)

Although Colossus possessed a certain amount of flexibility, it was far from being an all-purpose computer, and nor did it conform to Turing's stored-program concept. (Colossus's 'program store consisted of a bank of binary mechanical switches by which variable connections could be made between selected streams of data from the data stores and function units corresponding to the arithmetic unit of a modern computer,' Flowers explained.) Nevertheless, Flowers had established decisively and for the first time that large-scale electronic computing machinery was practicable.

Even in the midst of the attack on Tunny, Newman was thinking about the universal Turing machine. He showed Flowers Turing's 1936 paper about the universal machine, 'On Computable Numbers', with its key idea of storing symbolically encoded instructions in memory, but Flowers, not being a mathematical logician, 'didn't really understand much of it'. There is little doubt that by 1944 Newman had firmly in mind the possibility of building a universal Turing machine using electronic technology. It was just a question of waiting until he 'got out'. In February 1946, a few months after his appointment to the Fielden Chair of Mathematics at the University of Manchester, Newman wrote to von Neumann (like Newman considerably influenced by Turing's 1936 paper, and himself playing a leading role in the post-ENIAC developments taking place in the United States):

I am ... hoping to embark on a computing machine section here, having got very interested in electronic devices of this kind during the last two or three years. By about eighteen months ago I had decided to try my hand at starting up a machine unit when I got out. ... I am of course in close touch with Turing.

The implication of Flowers' racks of electronic equipment was obvious to Turing too. Flowers said that once Colossus was in operation, it was just a matter of Turing's waiting to see what opportunity might arise to put the idea of his universal computing machine into practice. By the end of the war, Turing had educated himself thoroughly in electronic engineering (during the later part of the war he gave a series of evening lectures 'on valve theory').

TURING'S ACE

Turing's opportunity came along in 1945, when John Womersley, head of the Mathematics Division of the National Physical Laboratory (NPL) in London, invited him to design and develop an electronic stored-program digital computer. Womersley named the proposed computer the Automatic Computing Engine (ACE)—a homage to Babbage.

Turing's technical report 'Proposed Electronic Calculator', dating from the end of 1945 and containing his design for the ACE, was the first relatively complete specification of an electronic stored-program digital computer. The slightly earlier 'First Draft of a Report on the EDVAC', produced in about May 1945 by von Neumann, was much more abstract, saying little about programming, hardware details, or electronics. The EDVAC, the Eckert–Mauchly group's proposed successor to the ENIAC, was to be a stored-program machine. Harry Huskey, the electronic engineer who subsequently drew up the first detailed hardware designs for the EDVAC, stated that the 'information in the "First Draft" was of no help'. Turing, in contrast, supplied detailed circuit designs, full specifications of hardware units, specimen programs in machine code, and even an estimate of the cost of building the machine.

Turing's ACE and the EDVAC differed fundamentally in design. For example, the EDVAC (which was not fully working until 1952) had what is now called a central processing unit, or CPU, whereas in the ACE the various logical and arithmetical functions were distributed across different memory units. Another deep difference between the ACE and both the EDVAC and its British derivative the EDSAC (built by Maurice Wilkes at the University of Cambridge Mathematical Laboratory) was that, in Turing's design, complex behaviour was to be achieved by complex programming rather than by complex equipment. Turing's philosophy was to dispense with additional hardware, such as special units for division and long multiplication, and to carry out these functions by means of programming (or coding, as it was then called). Concerning his and Wilkes' differing outlooks, Turing said:

I have read Wilkes' proposals for a pilot machine . . . The 'code' which he suggests is however very contrary to the line of development here [at the NPL], and much more in the American tradition of solving one's difficulties by means of much equipment rather than thought.

Turing saw that speed and memory were the keys to computing (in the words of his assistant, Wilkinson, Turing was 'obsessed with the idea of speed on the machine'). His design for the ACE had much in common with today's RISC (Reduced Instruction Set Computer) architectures and called for a high-speed memory of roughly the same capacity as an early Macintosh computer (enormous by the standards of his day). However, delays beyond Turing's control meant that by 1947 little progress had been made on the physical construction of the ACE (although much effort had gone into writing programs or 'instruction tables'). The world's first stored-program electronic digital computer was the 'Manchester Baby', which ran its first program on 21 June 1948 in Newman's Computing Machine Laboratory at the University of Manchester (see photograph 44). As its name implies, the Baby was a very small computer, and the news that it had run what was only a tiny program—just 17 instructions long—for a mathematically trivial task was 'greeted with hilarity' by Turing's team.

Had Turing's ACE been built as planned it would have been in a different league from the other early electronic computers, but his colleagues at the NPL thought the engineering work too ambitious, and a considerably smaller machine was built. Known as the Pilot Model ACE, this machine ran its first program on 10 May 1950. (See photograph 45.) With an operating speed of 1 megahertz it was for some time the fastest computer in the world; more than 30 of the production version, DEUCE, were sold—confounding the suggestion, made in 1946 by Sir Charles Darwin, Director of the NPL and grandson of the great Darwin, that 'it is very possible that ... one machine would suffice to solve all the problems that are demanded of it from the whole country'.

The delays that cost NPL the race with Manchester were to an extent the fault of Dollis Hill. Turing knew that Flowers was uniquely qualified to build the ACE, and it had been agreed between the NPL and Dollis Hill in February 1946 that a team under Flowers' direction would carry out the engineering work for the ACE. In March 1946 Flowers said that a 'minimal ACE' would be ready by August or September of that year. Unfortunately, however, Dollis Hill was overwhelmed by a backlog of urgent work on the national telephone system and it proved impossible to keep to Flowers' timetable. As Flowers has said, his section was 'too busy to do other people's work'. In February 1947, Turing suggested that the NPL set up its own electronics section in order to build the ACE. This was done but, sadly, inter-departmental rivalry hindered the work and in April 1948 Womersley reported that hardware development was 'probably as far advanced 18 months ago'. Meanwhile, in the autumn of 1947, Turing retreated in disgust to Cambridge for a year's sabbatical leave, during which he did pioneering work on Artificial Intelligence. Before his leave was over, he lost patience with the NPL altogether and Newman's offer of a job lured a 'very fed up' Turing to Manchester University. In May 1948

Turing was appointed Deputy Director of the Computing Machine Laboratory (there being no Director).

The basic principles of Turing's ACE design were used in the G15 computer, built and marketed by the Detroit-based Bendix Corporation (see photograph 46). The G15 was designed by Huskey, who had spent 1947 at the NPL in the ACE Section. The first G15 ran in 1954. It was the first commercially available personal computer. By following Turing's philosophy of minimising hardware in favour of software, Huskey was able to make the G15 small enough (it was the size of a large domestic refrigerator) and cheap enough to be marketed as a single-user computer. Yet thanks to the ACE-like design, the G15 was as fast as computers many times its size. Over 400 were sold worldwide and the G15 remained in use until about 1970. (Other derivatives of the ACE included the EMI Business Machine, a relatively slow electronic computer with a large memory, designed for the shallow processing of large quantities of data that is typically demanded by business applications, and the low-cost transistorised Packard-Bell PB250.)

One computer deriving from Turing's ACE design, the MOSAIC (Ministry of Supply Automatic Integrator and Computer), played a role in Britain's air defences during the Cold War period. (See photograph 47.) In 1946 Flowers had established a two-man team at Dollis Hill to build a computer to Turing's logical design; the team consisted of Allen 'Doc' Coombs and William Chandler, Flowers' right-hand men from the Colossus days. Coombs and Chandler carried out the engineering design of the MOSAIC, a large computer based on Version VII of Turing's logical design for the ACE (Version VII dated from 1946). The MOSAIC first ran a program in 1952 or early 1953. The computer was installed at the Royal Radar Establishment, Malvern, where it was used to calculate aircraft trajectories from radar data, in connection with anti-aircraft measures (the details remain classified).

Of the various ACE-type computers that were built, the MOSAIC was closest to Turing's original conception, although slower (570 hertz) and with much less high-speed memory. Given that two engineers working alone succeeded in completing the MOSAIC (Coombs emphasised: 'it was just Chandler and I—we designed every scrap of that machine'), there is no doubt that, given sufficient manpower, a computer conforming more closely to Turing's grand-scale requirements could have been up and running in the early 1950s. Thanks to their wartime involvement with Colossus, Chandler and Coombs possessed unrivalled expertise in large-scale digital electronics and had a substantial lead on everyone else in the field. Turing, of course, was well aware of this, but the Official Secrets Act prevented him from sharing his knowledge of Colossus with Sir Charles Darwin. Had he been able to do so, the NPL might have acted to boost the resources available to Chandler and Coombs, and so made Turing's dream a reality.

THE TRIUMPH AT MANCHESTER

Newman had laid plans for his Computing Machine Laboratory following his appointment at Manchester in September 1945, applying to the Royal Society for a sizeable grant (approved in July 1946) in order to develop an electronic stored-program computer. Newman introduced Frederic Williams and Tom Kilburn—recruited to Manchester University from the Telecommunications Research Establishment (TRE)—to the idea of the stored-program computer. Williams and Kilburn knew nothing of Colossus. At TRE during the war they had worked on radar and were experts in electronic circuit design. At the time he left TRE, Williams was developing a method for storing patterns of zeros and ones on the face of a cathode ray tube—an idea that, with Kilburn's help, was rapidly to lead to the type of high-speed random access memory (RAM) known as the Williams tube.

Williams' description of Newman's Computing Machine Laboratory is vivid:

It was one room in a Victorian building whose architectural features are best described as 'late lavatorial'. The walls were of brown glazed brick and the door was labelled 'Magnetism Room'.

Here, Kilburn and Williams built the Manchester Baby. The first program, stored on the face of a Williams tube as a pattern of dots, was inserted manually, digit by digit, using a panel of switches.

Once Turing had arrived in Manchester, he designed the input mechanism and programming system of, and wrote a programming manual for, the Baby's successor, the Manchester Mark I. At last Turing had his hands on a stored-program computer (see photograph 48). He was soon using it to model biological growth, a field nowadays known as 'Artificial Life'. While the rest of the world was just waking up to the idea that electronics was the new way to do binary arithmetic, Turing was talking very seriously about programming digital computers to think.

At the time of the Baby machine and the Mark I, Kilburn and Williams, the men who had translated the logico-mathematical idea of the stored-program computer into hardware, were given too little credit by the mathematicians at Manchester, where they were regarded as excellent engineers, but not as 'ideas men'. Now the tables have turned too far and the triumph at Manchester is credited to them alone. During the official celebrations of the 50th anniversary of the Baby, held at Manchester in June 1998, Newman's name was not so much as mentioned. Fortunately the words of the late Williams survive to set the record straight:

Now let's be clear before we go any further that neither Tom Kilburn nor I knew the first thing about computers when we arrived in Manchester University . . . Newman explained the whole business of how a computer works to us.

Tom Kilburn and I knew nothing about computers . . . Professor Newman and Mr A. M. Turing . . . knew a lot about computers . . . They took us by the hand and explained how numbers could live in houses with addresses . . .

During the period December 1946 to February 1947 Turing and Wilkinson gave a series of nine lectures covering Versions V, VI, and VII of Turing's design for the ACE. The lectures were attended by representatives of various organisations which planned to use or build an electronic computer. Among the audience was Kilburn, who usually said, when asked where he got his basic knowledge of the computer from, that he could not remember; for example, in a 1992 interview he said: 'Between early 1945 and early 1947, in that period, somehow or other I knew what a digital computer was . . . Where I got this knowledge from I've no idea.' In his first report on the Manchester computer work, dated 1947, Kilburn referred to 'unpublished work' by Turing, and he helped himself to various of Turing's technical terms.

Whatever role Turing's lectures may have played in informing Kilburn, there is little doubt that credit for the Manchester computer belongs not only to Williams and Kilburn but also to Newman, and that the influence on Newman of Turing's 1936 paper was crucial—as, of course, was the influence of Flowers' Colossus.

THE PHILADELPHIA CONNECTION

Meanwhile, momentum was gathering on the other side of the Atlantic. After visiting the United States in January 1947, Turing reported that the 'number of different computing projects is now so great that it is no longer possible to have a complete list'. The most visible players were Eckert, Mauchly, and von Neumann. Eckert and Mauchly had entered into a contract with the US Army Ordnance Department in June 1943 to build an electronic machine, the ENIAC. Construction got under way in Philadelphia at the Moore School of Electrical Engineering (part of the University of Pennsylvania). Von Neumann was involved in the Manhattan Project at Los Alamos, where human computers armed with desk calculating machines were struggling to carry out the massive calculations required by the physicists. Hearing about the ENIAC by chance, he saw to it that he was appointed as a consultant to the ENIAC project. By the time he arrived at the Moore School, the design of the program-controlled ENIAC had been frozen in order to complete construction as soon as possible. The ENIAC was not an all-purpose computer, having been designed with only one very specific task in mind, the calculation of trajectories of artillery shells, and nor of course was it a stored-program machine. Von Neumann brought his knowledge of Turing's 'On Computable Numbers' to the Moore School. Thanks to Turing's abstract logical work, von Neumann knew that, by making use of coded instructions stored in memory, a single machine of fixed structure could in principle carry out any task that can be done by a human computer. It was von Neumann who placed Turing's abstract universal computing machine into the hands of American engineers. When Eckert explained his idea of using mercury 'delay lines' to form a high-speed recirculating memory, von Neumann saw that this was the means to make concrete the universal machine of 'On Computable Numbers'.

After extensive discussions with Eckert and Mauchly, von Neumann wrote the 'First Draft of a Report on the EDVAC'. Von Neumann's colleague Herman Goldstine circulated the 'First Draft' with only von Neumann's name on it. Eckert and Mauchly were outraged, knowing that von Neumann would be given credit for everything in the report—their ideas as well as his own. There was a storm of controversy. As a result, von Neumann abandoned the proposed EDVAC and in 1946 established his own project to build a stored-program computer, in the Institute for Advanced Study at Princeton University. The completed machine, with a high-speed memory consisting of 40 Williams tubes, was working by the summer of 1951. (See photograph 50.) It had approximately the same number of valves as Colossus II. Known as the IAS computer, this was not the first of the various stored-program computers under construction in the United States to work, but it was the most influential, and served as the model for a series of what were called 'Princeton class' computers.

THE TWO COLOSSI

Von Neumann became familiar with ideas in 'On Computable Numbers' during Turing's time at Princeton (1936–8) and was intrigued by Turing's concept of a universal computing machine. Von Neumann is often said to have invented the stored-program computer, and many books on the history of computing in the United States place him centre stage and make no mention of Turing. Von Neumann himself, however, repeatedly emphasised the fundamental importance of 'On Computable Numbers'. For instance, in a letter to the mathematician Norbert Wiener, von Neumann spoke of 'the great positive contribution of Turing': Turing's mathematical demonstration that 'one, definite mechanism can be "universal"'.

Stanley Frankel (the Los Alamos physicist responsible, with von Neumann and others, for mechanising the large-scale calculations involved in the design of the atomic and hydrogen bombs) recorded von Neumann's view of the importance of 'On Computable Numbers':

I know that in or about 1943 or '44 von Neumann was well aware of the fundamental importance of Turing's paper of 1936 'On computable numbers . . .', which describes in principle the 'Universal Computer' of which every modern computer (perhaps not ENIAC as first completed but certainly all later ones) is a realization. Von Neumann introduced me to that paper and at his urging I studied it with care. Many people have acclaimed von Neumann as the 'father of the computer' (in a modern sense of the term) but I am sure that he would never have made that mistake himself. He might well be called the midwife, perhaps, but he firmly emphasized to me, and to others I am sure, that the fundamental conception is owing to Turing— insofar as not anticipated by Babbage, Lovelace, and others. In my view von Neumann's essential role was in making the world aware of these fundamental concepts introduced by Turing and of the development work carried out in the Moore school and elsewhere.

When von Neumann established his computer project at Princeton, he gave his engineers 'On Computable Numbers' to read. Julian Bigelow, von Neumann's chief engineer and the person largely responsible for the engineering design of the IAS computer, remarked:

The person who really . . . pushed the whole field ahead was von Neumann, because he understood logically what [the stored-program concept] meant in a deeper way than anybody else. . . . The reason he understood it is because, among other things, he understood a good deal of the mathematical logic which was implied by the idea, due to the work of A. M. Turing . . . in 1936–1937 . . . . Turing's [universal] machine does not sound much like a modern computer today, but nevertheless it was. It was the germinal idea. . . . So . . . [von Neumann] saw . . . that [ENIAC] was just the first step, and that great improvement would come.

BACK TO THE FUTURE

Given our knowledge of the achievements at Dollis Hill and Bletchley Park, the history of computing must be rewritten. Histories written in ignorance of Colossus are not only incomplete, but give a distorted picture of the emergence and development of the idea of the modern computer. Turing's logical work in 1935–6 and Flowers' work at Bletchley led, via Newman's desire to put the concept of the stored-program universal computing machine into practice, to the Manchester Laboratory and the Manchester Mark I computer. From this in turn came another momentous development, the first mass-produced computer to go on sale, a copy of the Mark I built by the Manchester engineering firm Ferranti Ltd. In the United States, Turing's work steered von Neumann to the underlying logical principles of the EDVAC and the IAS computer. Technology transferred from Manchester, the Williams tube random-access memory, was crucial to both von Neumann's IAS machine and its commercial spin-off, IBM's first mass-produced stored-program computer, the IBM 701. The 701 was a foretaste of the global transformation soon to flow from this criss-crossing pattern of invention and influence set in motion by Alan Turing in 1936.

Chapter 10

The PC-User's Guide to Colossus

Benjamin Wells

MAY I TOUCH THE COMPUTER?

Personal computers (PCs) dominate today's digital landscape. The two-letter name started with the 1981 IBM PC. Desktop machines based on single-chip microprocessors—and thus called microcomputers—were widely used before the IBM PC, but that is the name that has stuck. Many would consider a Packard-Bell tabletop computer of the early 1960s to be the first personal computer. But as far as single-user/operator commercial machines go, there is also the Bendix G15 from the mid-1950s, described in Chapter 9.

PC users are likely to have forgotten or never known the atmosphere of early-generation computers. The 'operating system' was a schedule for the human staff who mounted large reels of tape, toggled inputs at the long control panel, pushed the load-and-run switch, and stacked punch cards and fanfold sheets of printed output. The numerous operators wore white lab jackets, worked in large air-conditioned spaces, and appeared to be high priests and acolytes in a vocational order. The users were supplicants. Apart from experimental machines at universities—such as MIT's famed TX-0 (1955–6), which was controlled by the first computer hackers once it moved to the MIT campus in 1958—the users entreated the operators through written requests heading a card deck. Back then, the users as well as the general public stood behind a velvet rope, even a window wall. The operators continued to rule the machine long after users had electronic connection through time-sharing remote terminals. But those who had hacked the small machines like the TX-0 knew that the goal was the direct, immediate access of personal computers. Colossus already had that personal touch.

Designed to be used by a single cryptanalyst assisted by one Wren, and later

Grateful recognition is given to M. C. W. Conner, Greg Benson, Jack Copeland, and Karl Fant.

often run by the Wren solo, Colossus was in that sense a personal computer. But just how close was Colossus to being a PC? This chapter compares and contrasts the architecture of Colossus with that of today's personal computers.

WHAT IS COMPUTER ARCHITECTURE?

Boxes, Circuits, Logic, and Programs

An architect designs a building by balancing needs and functions with resources and aesthetics. The availability and cost of components constrain her work. Physical limitations and dynamics of use further impact on it. The building reflects the architect's imagination and skill. The computer architect shares the goal of realising function aesthetically within a framework of constraints. But a physical computer reveals far more about the design and designer of the casing than the architecture, much less the architect. This is to be expected, for computer architecture bridges abstract logic and electronic circuits. Neither of these is particularly visible, especially today when microscopic wiring on silicon chips determines the behaviour of our computers. Photos reveal that far more was on view with Colossus than with PCs, but one reads most of the architecture from diagrams and descriptions, not from open racks of electronic gear. Before following any of these clues, let us consider what a computer is.

Our modern view of computers is that they are general-purpose machines for calculation and logical decision. The term 'general-purpose' stems from their flexible programmability, which arises from two properties. First, they accept programs specifying streams of commands from a small but powerfully complete set of basic instructions. Second, they can store and access these programs internally, much as they manipulate the data used and produced by a program. From the very beginning of computers, there was a choice of keeping the program and data separate or letting the program modify itself just like any other data. In time, large programs and modern operating systems led to an uncrossable barrier between program and data stores. Self-modifying programs were distrusted. More recently, there has been a rebirth of interest in letting the program change itself. In genetic programming, for example, programs mutate on their own in the style of biological genes. The important point is that the general-purpose computer can read a program's instructions from its memory.

It is the computer's architecture that specifies the set of instructions and how they are executed when the program runs. It also specifies how program and data memory are used. Usually, some of this is controlled by wiring, and some by software. Today's computer provides far more programming than the user may notice. When you launch a favourite word processor, your operating system, such as Windows, Linux, or MacOS, performs many tasks handed off by that application program. Chores like scheduling, using the cache and virtual memory, and handling input–output are invisible—not only to the user, but also usually to the programmer. Both can be grateful for this support, which was not there during the first two decades of computing. Modern architecture complements these facilities. Nevertheless, many of the features of our most common general-purpose machine, the personal computer, can already be detected in the architecture of the much earlier Colossus.

An Example you can Grasp with One Hand

A suggestive parable here is the four-function handheld calculator. From the earliest consumer versions, these were general-purpose computers. Although their programmability was not apparent or accessible, they ran specific programs on general hardware. The user saw only the keys on the face and the digits in the display. But the machine ran a program that repeatedly checked to see if a key had been pressed. The program used this information to control a set of subroutines that calculated the four functions $(+, -, \times, \div)$ and drove the display. These actions depended on data and program memory stores— pressing a key was not so simple as playing a piano note or even ringing a doorbell. The calculator's behaviour resulted from inflexible programming (or firmware), but other firmware could be installed with no change to the hardware. A PDA (personal digital assistant) does more today than such a calculator because miniaturisation allows more resources to be housed in the same-sized box. The features have also increased, largely through consumer 'education' and demand. Your Palm appears to be more general than a calculator. It has an operating system, many applications, and varied interactions with the user and other devices. It is new hardware indeed, but the greater difference lies in the architecture of the PDA's software, not its hardware. The moral of this parable is that, at the heart, the two handhelds are the same.

WHAT DID COLOSSUS LOOK LIKE?

Colossus from the Outside

We have discussed how computer architecture specifies connected and coordinated structures to support logic, decision making, and communication with the user. Architecture maps function onto hardware. Like climate control and earthquake bracing for buildings, the imposition of the real world can be felt in building computers, too. Temperature and heat flow, electronic signal speeds, and a technology's limited capabilities and compatibilities can dictate design. Such forces will shape and circumscribe the computer's architecture. They will affect its overall size, compactness, features, and utility.

But few of these things are linked directly to a PC's external form. In fact, the case hides a computer's architecture more now than in the first decade of computing. A series of SGI, NeXT, and Apple computers have taken the look of the so-called central processing unit (CPU) to new heights of elegance. No longer squarish metal boxes, they suggest nothing about the chips and boards that constitute the actual CPU. Even mass-market cloners package their machines in sculpted housings. Ubiquitous computing, wearable computers, and eventually nanotechnology will further cloak the electronic anima.

It will be helpful, therefore, in comparing early computers with today's, to keep in mind that little was hidden and no thought, much less money, was wasted on packaging. The few forces promoting any casing at all aimed at achieving neatness, safety, professionalism, and—to a far lesser extent—usability. Front panels could provide indicator lamps and switches, but leaving the back open facilitated reconfiguration, expansion, experimentation, maintenance, and frequent repair. All versions of Colossus had open racks with few panels. So, if anything of the architecture could be found from physical observation, it was not hard to see.

The Physical Evidence

Only a few fragments remain of the eleven completed Colossus machines and their support hardware. There were some contemporary photographs. The photography does suggest that productivity was paramount, not good looks. Just a glance at the physical embodiment of Colossus might convince you that it was quite another species than your PC (see photographs 33–37). But push on: there are numerous common architectural features that span these quite distinct implementations.

Moving closer to Colossus, you can observe a rhythm of structure in the stacks of electronic chassis. You note similar components and assemblies, reminding you of the racks of cards or banks of memory chips in a PC, if you have ever added these. Interconnecting cables cross boundaries of functional units. Telephone-type plugs and cables (called plug cords at Bletchley, and also jack patches beyond) highlight modules subject to customisation and frequent alteration. Input–output devices need electrical wiring to control them and transfer data. Switch and pilot-lamp panels show where the operators work. So you can tell something from the general layout after all, just about as much as removing the shell of a PC shows. But the logical structure always remains indecipherable.

Ignoring Limitations

In our exercise of comparing today's machines to Colossus, we prefer that its size not be a distinguishing feature. This does not mean the physical dimensions, such as volume, footprint, or weight, although these were large, if not colossal. It means putting no limits on resources such as memory, tape, time, and the speed and number of CPUs. We generously assume that a computer design can be supplied with unbounded resources: the memory goes beyond what the addressing structure allows, the speed is faster than the latest chip from the foundry, etc. It's not like comparing two models of the latest laptop for a Consumer's Choice Award. So we can be happy if Colossus adds $1 + 1$, and forgive it for not having CPU capacity to add 20-digit integers.

Besides ignoring scale limitations, we need to discount the intended use of Colossus by decrypters. Instead, with hindsight we propose capacities undreamt by the builders. Although Colossus was only targeted to attack Tunny traffic, Good makes it clear in Chapter 16 that execution of tasks beyond its design demonstrated its flexibility. Other users have mentioned running demonstration programs after the war ended. At the same time, we must beware of exaggerations, including an outrageous claim by one author that Colossus printed English plaintext from German ciphertext!

In short, we are talking general architectural features—not full-blown, detailed design appropriate to the salesroom. We'll also count any feature from any of the eleven built Colossi as fair game. We will discern branching, program and data store, program control, and more.

To help organise our architectural exploration, let us partition time and its flow. We shall consider, in this order: what happens at particular times in Colossus; sequences of these events; how past events are remembered; and how several things can be done at the same time. We conclude by studying how these happenings are orchestrated by programming. In this journey, present and past tense merge: architecture is timeless, even when machines fade away.

AN INSTANTANEOUS VIEW—LOGIC, ARITHMETIC, COUNTERS, INSTRUCTIONS, REGISTERS

This is a snapshot view of the computing capabilities of Colossus in modern terms. It covers what happens in a single machine cycle—the basic unit of time—or in several if the particular feature considered takes more than one cycle. The apparently rudimentary arithmetic and logic unit in Colossus differs from that of a PC in important ways, but these may be more superficial than essential. The comparison requires some technical discussion.

Logic

First comes the logic. Colossus had the internal power to implement Boolean logic (also known as propositional logic). This is a set of logical operations based on True and False, and called XOR, NOT, AND, OR, and so forth. OR corresponds to connecting two assertions in English with 'or', and XOR, short for 'exclusive or', is the more restrictive 'either . . . or'—as in 'Either the butler or the bailiff murdered the heiress (but not both)'.

The rules for XOR are just the same as the rules for dot-and-cross addition given in Chapter 3, but with True replacing × and False replacing •: 'False XOR False' is False (if it's False that the butler murdered the heiress and False that the bailiff murdered the heiress, then 'Either the butler murdered the heiress or the bailiff murdered the heiress' is False). 'True XOR False' is True, and 'False XOR True' is True, but 'True XOR True' is False (because XOR is exclusive). These rules are set out in Table 1, where True and False are

Table 1. XOR

XOR	0	1
0	0	1
1	1	0

abbreviated by the bits (*binary digits*) 1 and 0, respectively. The other Boolean operations are described by similar tables. Table 2 gives the rules for NOT.

Table 2. NOT

NOT	
0	1
1	0

Colossus had circuits that computed XOR and OR. These two logic operations are insufficient to generate all the other possible ones; in particular, you cannot combine them to make NOT. There were various hardware options for expressing NOT. Flowers mentions that there were hardware units 'performing the logical functions of negation, add modulo-2, A not equivalent to B, and several others'. (In Boolean logic, 'not equivalent to' and XOR are the same thing.) Colossus could in fact compute any Boolean operation, because XOR and NOT together *do* generate them all.

In Colossus, bits were represented by voltage difference on a pair of wires (Table 3), not by the presence or absence of a voltage pulse on a single wire, a common scheme today.

Table 3. The representation of bits by voltage difference

Voltage	0	1
wire 1	high	low
wire 2	low	high

If the first wire has high voltage and the second low voltage, a 0 by the table, then reversing the voltage to low and high makes it a 1. NOT could be obtained by simply crossing the two wires over. Flowers mentioned a one-valve inversion unit, which probably implemented NOT. In addition, somewhat restricted 'not' switches were provided in later models of Colossus. There are also more technical ways of achieving NOT.

Arithmetic

Binary arithmetic is governed by the rules of bit addition and multiplication shown in Table 4. (Note the carry in adding $1 + 1$.)

Table 4. Addition and multiplication

+	0	1		×	0	1
0	0	1		0	0	0
1	1	10		1	0	1

With regard to arithmetic in Colossus, XOR is the heart of binary addition, for A XOR B is the column value of the sum of two bits A and B. The carry bit from this sum can be computed as *A* AND *B*. In fact, AND has the same rules as those for single-bit multiplication shown in Table 4. Counting, delta-ing, and so forth was what Colossus was designed to do, rather than ordinary addition. Nevertheless, with some adroit use of the plug panel, the addition of at least a few bits could be managed. The other arithmetic operations can be based on addition. So one can argue that Colossus had the latent capability, if not the available capacity, to compute all four standard arithmetic functions.

Counters and Rings

The logical and arithmetic operations described above are found, appropriately, in the part of the machine designated the ALU (arithmetic-logic unit) by Flowers. Colossus had three other types of arithmetic elements: the output counters (up to five), the span counter, and the thyratron rings.

The first type of counter counted the number of 1-bits (up to 10,000) seen at a selectable position in the ALU circuitry. Each output counter could be set up to count the matches found for some chosen codebreaking attack. So these counters delivered the information for which Colossus was built. The span counter tracked the input in order to start—and later stop—processing at two intermediate places on the input tape. By this means an interesting interval on the tape could be isolated and analysed.

All these counters employed *biquinary* representation. Biquinary representation uses a 2-state component (0+, 5+) combined with a 5-state component (0, 1, 2, 3, 4) to represent any decimal digit 0 (= 0 + 0), 1, 2, . . ., 9 (= 5 + 4). ('Biqui' was a common solution on later machines that used decimals in addition to, or instead of, binary internal data, including the IBM 650, one of the last widespread valve, or vacuum tube, machines.) According to Flowers, the advantage of this almost decimal representation lay in the electronics. The valve circuit used could count to five reliably, but not to six (and certainly not to ten). For this reason, the resulting module was called a 'penta-stable'.

Why not use binary counters as computers do now? The engineering of the day could support a biqui approach, which made it easy to print the counter values in the familiar decimal notation. Circuit analysis shows that it is more economical than binary. With five counters of four decimal places each in Colossus, there is a saving of nearly a hundred valves over the binary solution. This represents, however, a small percentage of the total number of valves. Nonetheless, biqui was simpler and more reliable with the valve circuits of the time.

The Thyratron Rings

The major innovation with Colossus was to simulate the 12 wheels of the Tunny machine electronically and automatically, using thyratron ring circuits. Thyratrons—high-powered gas-filled valves used in numerous electronic devices even today—acted as easily-triggered latches in Colossus: a small voltage turned them on, and they stayed on until reset.

Arranging n thyratrons in a circle leads to a ring that can count from 1 to n. Thyratron rings computed chi and psi data and the motor control on psi. The lengths of the rings were the deduced sizes of the Tunny wheels: 41 for the ring representing χ_1, 31 for χ_2, and so on (see Chapter 3). The movement of the wheels—the uniform advance of the chis, and the 'staggering' of the psis under the control of the motor-wheels—was mirrored automatically.

How should we view these 12 thyratron rings? Flowers suggested they are data in semi-permanent memory—like the CMOS tables that provide start-up information for PCs. Another, modern, view is that they serve as subroutines that calculate the sequences directly on the fly.

Controlling the Rings

A wheel's cam settings (called a 'trigger' in Colossus jargon) were made via a special panel, using U-shaped pins or 'U-links' (see Figure 4 in Chapter 8). Setting a cam was called 'putting in a pin'; later, some triggers could be set more conveniently with regular plug wires. A wheel had as many as seven preset triggers that could be selected by the operator through a switch. Two could even be in effect at once.

After the input tape had run through the reader, a wheel's start setting could be stepped automatically. (This stepping of an individual wheel's start position should not be confused with the advance of the wheels after each letter was processed.) This was accomplished by electromechanical rotary switches, like those used in dial telephone exchanges of the day. The user could also select rotary stepping by five instead of one to accommodate the parallel processing described below. An advanced feature called 'slow stepping' delayed the stepping of a wheel according to positions of other wheels.

So there were different control mechanisms for each of these four parameters: cam positions, starting position, step interval, and stepping mode. The ring configuration was very flexible; with hindsight, the rings were programmable.

Instructions and their Storage

Flowers stated that the output of a thyratron ring went to the ALU controller rather than directly XORing with the corresponding input stream, as happened in the more rigid Robinsons. That raises the issue of exactly what the controller of the ALU could do: what instructions did Colossus implement? The schematic diagrams we have do not give these in detail. At the same time, the functional descriptions in *General Report on Tunny* may be cryptologically complete, but do not discuss architecture or implementation. Even a rebuild of Colossus from complete diagrams, however, might not reveal the full scope of the instructions, for these depend on what could be wired to what. Some of this is known from design and architecture, but experimentation is required to determine the limits even of a plugboard. Flowers and Coombs affirmed increasing flexibility with successive versions.

At first plug-wiring was required; later models provided more convenient switching at a control board. Configuring a plugboard allows maximal customisation but requires bit-level programming by hand. The number of connections a plug-wire could make was very large. On the other hand, switching made commonly used patterns of wiring invocable by the operator through a single switch setting. Neither of these sounds much like a member of a PC instruction set, but let's look closer. Plugging resembles an instruction in ROM (or firmware), or even a frequently invoked PC instruction waiting in the cache for the next execution. Switching resembles software macros and scripts, or even library functions (like extensions or .dll).

A crucial difference between Colossus and PCs is that in Colossus the program is not stored internally. Think about the visible change that programming creates in a PC and in Colossus. The insides of a PC look no different at any scale after you launch a program from the hard-drive. After Colossus was programmed, it gained a jumble of plug-cables and pins and a hotchpotch of switch positions. While the mess emphasises the difference on the visible level, the real distinction is that every memory location in the PC's program store can hold any instruction. The program store in Colossus may have been as plastic in spirit as a PC's, but it did not have that homogeneity, that isogenericity, that . . . well, let's just say that blank-slate quality. We shall study instructions and programs and their storage further in the next four sections.

Registers

The last feature to discuss in this section is the presence or absence of registers. These are fast memory elements often performing arithmetic, logic, memory addressing, or instruction handling. They have been considered crucial for CPU architecture since the 1950s. Colossus had no registers in the modern sense. But there are four structures that show some qualifications for the register job. These are the ring output stores, the input shift registers (important additions to later versions of Colossus, these are described in the section below on parallelism), part of the master (program) controller, and the combining unit. Although the first two look like intermediate storage, or buffers, they more closely resemble internal temporary storage registers because their output is to the ALU. Possibly just a schematic convention, the combining unit is nonetheless the closest thing to a CPU register architecturally. It's a stretch to claim that an instruction register or address counter exists anywhere in the machine, but the master control does orchestrate the next instruction. This brings us to sequencing.

THE SEQUENCE OF ACTIVITY—CLOCK, INSTRUCTION/DATA FETCH, BRANCHING, INTERRUPTS, INPUT

Timing

'What next?' is a question most appropriate to a sequential or serial computer, in which only one thing happens at a time; the beads must be strung together for coherent effects. The *primum mobile* in PCs is the clock. Based on an electronic oscillator built into the CPU chip, a PC's metronome may now beat faster than 4 gigahertz (GHz), or 4,000,000,000 cycles per second. One cycle is the smallest interval for the machine, its atomic time-period. (In PCs it is common, however, to provide for several actions to overlap in a way that seems to slice the time even finer.) By contrast, the basic timing in Colossus was around 5 kilohertz (kHz), or 5000 cycles per second. Even more different was the source of the timing signal: the sprocket holes in the input tape, which had run on toothed wheels during the tape's creation. In playback the tape ran through the smooth rollers of the Colossus bedstead apparatus, but the holes were recruited as the source of synchronisation between the electronics and the tape drive.

Colossus could have been 'overclocked' by running the tape faster. Even at 15–18 kHz, the valves would have operated within heat limits according to

Chandler. This could not be done with a paper tape, for 10 kHz speed would reliably break the tape (contrary to rumour, it would not set it ablaze). But a stationary, pulsing light source could generate the timing signal, with no rewiring, if internal speed were the only consideration. The speed of Colossus actually compares well with the first home computer kits running the Intel 4004 CPU chip at 108 kHz. That chip performed 60,000 instructions a second, only about six times faster than a cranked-up Colossus. By contrast, the first IBM PC had a clock rate of 4.77 megahertz (MHz), or 4,770,000 cycles per second, and executed 800,000 instructions per second. (A legend about the speed of Colossus holds that a simulation on the first Pentium microprocessor ran at half the speed of the BP machine. That Pentium ticked at 60 MHz, so the relatively slow simulation may have been an artefact of the programming language used rather than a quality of Colossus.)

Good Old Times at Colossus

Something has to read the clock or be driven by its ticking. One clock consumer inside Colossus was the internal mechanism that stepped the master controller; it thus resembled the PC's instruction counter. In the stored-program paradigm of PCs, instructions are fetched from the program store and put into an instruction register under the control of an instruction address counter working in tandem with memory access mechanisms. The decoded instruction specifies its data requirements. The data may already be in registers if the instruction is an operation on the registers. If data needs to be fetched, then cache, RAM, disk, or other memory must be accessed.

In Colossus, the instructions were not fetched: they were already there in the CPU and on the plugboards and switch panels, waiting to be activated by data. The master control, selected wiring, branching, and interrupts channelled the flow of data to the processing elements. This is reminiscent of analogue computers, now largely superseded by digital simulations of them. They consisted of electrical circuit boxes that continuously changed the qualities of signals coming to them via plug-wires. There are also three modern analogies: (1) dataflow machines, where data streams to the functional elements; (2) object-oriented programming, whose data objects process messages streaming through them; and (3) quantum computer gate circuits. In Colossus, as in these other models, the flow and the processing—in other words, the instructions and their execution—are direct and immediate.

Additionally, two clock signals, differing in phase only, were distributed to four components. These were the input shift registers, the thyratron rings, the ring store registers, and the combining unit logic of the ALU. All danced in step with the timing signals from the sprocket holes.

Although the clock did provide lock-step sequencing for most elements in the computation path in Colossus, in a sense the ALU itself was free of the clock. It had to complete its work without timing, because it had to finish in one cycle, in just one tick of the clock! Whatever processing could fit into that interval, it was untimed, unsequenced, unsupervised. Micro-processors have been built that have no clock at all; their operation is determined completely by logic and not by any timing sequence. Colossus shares an additional element of some of these so-called asynchronous designs: the two-wire bit representation shown in Table 3, today called 'dual rail'.

Overall, though, Colossus was as clocked as it gets. The sequencing of counters and rings, the distribution of input data streams, and the overall logical operations on those streams were all under the influence of the clock, rhythmically locked to the flying tape. Boring computer, about to be surprised.

When Plans Change: Branches and Interrupts

The surprise in running any program comes from two events that can defeat periodicity and defy predictability: branches and interrupts. A branch occurs in a program (or device) when there are two choices for the next action, and the decision is determined by the current internal state of affairs. An interrupt means news has arrived from the outside that changes what happens next. Both surprises are typically mediated by registers in PCs, but not in Colossus.

Branches come in several flavours. For example, some decisions depend only on the timing or position in the computation, while others depend on input and computed values. The latter are unpredictable in advance. The most important kind of unpredictable branch decision leads to a choice between different next actions, not just a different counter value or lit pilot lamp. We can call this 'action branching'.

Branches are implemented at several places in the Colossus architecture. Here are five examples that coordinate several parts of the architecture. The first four concern branching that is fairly inflexible and predictable.

(1) The multiple passes of the input tape may be terminated by a rotary stepper (functioning as a simple counter) cycling back to its start, and more generally affected by displays and status signals given to the operator, who might then press STOP. (2) In later models, a span counter controls the active interval of the tape in accord with the span limits determined by the crypt-analyst (e.g. 'start reading at character 100, stop after character 500'). These

first two branch situations—pass control and the span interval—are fixed, predictable loop decisions, or else involve the cryptologist in completing the branch.

The next two branchings involve the thyratron rings. (3) The output of the thyratron psi rings is controlled by the output of the motor rings. Surely this complexity added to the Tunny machine must make the psi rings quite unpredictable! Not so, since you could replace a particular psi wheel with a much larger wheel that would have the motor effects built in from the start. Such a wheel would be impractically large, for Tunny or for Colossus, but it shows that the motor effect is predictable. Motor modifications added later to Tunny and known at Bletchley as 'limitations' made the key stream from the wheels depend on the plaintext stream itself (see Appendix 10 *The Motor Wheels and Limitations*). Now do we have real unpredictability? No, for we can just make another single wheel, enormously bigger but still predictable. (4) The slow-stepping of a ring during multiple scans through the message is determined by another ring's return to its initial start position. Stepping— fast and slow—is also predictably periodic. But Colossus could not take advantage of the theoretical predictability of combined motor wheels and slow-stepping. Indeed, it was much simpler to simulate and connect the smaller individual wheels, providing a measure of unpredictability but far greater speed in the end.

The final example in this section is a truly unpredictable action branch. (5) The decision to print is controlled by a result counter. This counter's effect is unpredictable, as well as automated. It has a parameter—the 'set total' described by Flowers in Chapter 8—externally keyed by the operator on switches, but the printing decision is controlled by the computed data. (In Colossus X, an operator could even choose to have all counter contents printed when any one of them reached the set total.) In other words, print- ing could not be predicted, only observed. This is real branching, for the next action depends on the branch decision.

We now turn to the issue of branching wholly within the processor.

Program Branching

There are a lot of unpredictable calculations in the area of Colossus that we can call the CPU. These are often of the form 'if A matches B, then pass along the value 1' (perhaps sending it to counter #2, for example). This is often called a 'conditional branch' by programmers.

Programmers know that *if . . . then . . .* is a fully adequate foundation for 'instruction branching,' a very important property for programming lan- guages. So that must mean Colossus had instruction branching? Not quite.

Although conditional branching was implemented by the Colossus CPU in multiple places and styles, it is an unfair stretch to claim instruction branching as a general architectural feature based on this evidence. Why is *if–then* weaker in Colossus? The distinction is that in Colossus a value may (or may not) be sent to a *specific* counter or logic unit. There is no hint that as a result of the branch it might be sent instead to a *different* counter, or, say, to AND rather than XOR. A change in values occurs as a result of the branch, but not a change in control or logic. Using the language of the last section, *if–then* in Colossus is an unpredictable branch, but not an action branch. (It is still possible that Colossus could have provided true instruction branching depending on computed results. If it did, however, this significant element seems to have found no official historian or publicist.)

Two Interrupts in Colossus

Interrupts and their automated handling occur at two places in Colossus. The first are the start–stop signals on the input tape. The start signal initiates combining the input with the thyratron ring output simulating the wheels. The stop brings electronic and electromechanical resets of counters and sequencing of the wheel starts. These conditions and activities do not block anything. This meant that operators had to provide sufficient blank paper tape between stop and start on the input loop in order to allow time to finish the resetting before the next tape-reading cycle began.

The second interrupt is the printer-busy condition that suspends processing till the printer, an electric typewriter, is free. It is required by performance limitations in the printer and motivated by a wish to preserve computed data. It occurred when both a stop signal on the input and a set-total-exceeded signal from the output counter meant there was something to print, but the printer had not finished a previous print order and returned to the printer-ready state. Because the advent and duration of the busy condition could not be predicted, it brought a full block to all processing and other activity except the printing and the rolling of the input tape. Both a ready signal from the printer and a new stop signal from the input tape are required to initiate the readout and resets. The handling of this interrupt is one of the most sophisticated and yet most mechanical features of Colossus.

The Input Stream

The last issue of sequencing brings us back to the input tape. The tape provides the data, of course, as well as the timing and start–stop interrupt signals. Two things are worth noting. First, the input has no associated internal memory beyond the combination of the tape reader and shift registers, holding at most six characters at a time (plus the fifth-row bit delayed for two cycles during 'limitation' calculations). Thus the data from the next pass of the tape loop cannot be influenced by the previous one. Second, the vertical alignment of data punches with sprocket holes guarantees automatic synchrony of clock and reader, handy but not essential.

The tape can be viewed as simply a very big wheel, apart from the timing. It could be implemented, in principle, in a monster thyratron ring. If there were such an automatic input stream, it and the clocking signals derived from it could be wired directly to Colossus, bypassing the optical reader (now no longer necessary). Even though it needed to be read repeatedly, the prepunched paper tape was the simple, flexible, reliable input mechanism of choice for that era. Had Colossus developed further, the tape might have played a quite different role. *General Report on Tunny* lists fantasy improvements wished for future Colossi, including setting the triggers electronically from punched cards. Eventually, a hybrid Robinson–Colossus might have had a fully electrical configuration loaded from paper tape, already the case with the support machine Aquarius (see Chapter 24). Such a configuration could have included limited memorised input data read directly from a tape of encrypted text. Then Colossus could indeed run tapeless.

STORING THE SEQUENCE OF ACTIVITY—MEMORY, BUFFERS, OUTPUT

If a tree falls in the forest when nobody is there, does it make a sound? If a computer runs, and nobody knows about it, did computation occur? We demand not only that the computing machine change state, but also that we can read a record of changes. In addition, there is the need for data and instruction storage. With these, the computer has continuity plus its own sense of change. No wonder that, next to speed, memory is the most valued commodity in computing. Memory is also an index of the history of PCs. The first computers named 'PC' had 64 kB of RAM fast memory and a maximum file size of half that; indeed, the very first IBM-PCs off the assembly line had only 16 kB of RAM. These are now minimum sizes of files produced by some applications. Today, PC desktop RAM is up to 16 GB (someday soon on one memory chip?), and a 1 terabyte (1000 GB) off-the-shelf hard-drive will hold very big files.

Program Memory

We have already discussed several memory components of Colossus. The input tape, the shift registers, the counters (with their keyable limits), and the rings (with their cam settings, start positions, and 1-bit stores) fall in the categories of sequencers, registers, and arithmetic elements. Let's delay for a moment the discussion of input–output buffers. Then there remains a single type of memory in Colossus to consider. This is the program store, the all-important memory represented by the fixed, pluggable or switchable wiring of the main control and ALU routing. In other words, the program memory was exactly the programmer's interface. Without a program, there were unset switches and rows of empty jacks. Without a program, there was still a storage structure and a capability of storing instructions in it. This is similar to what we see with a PC's RAM, hard-disk, or CD/DVD-R drive. These provide separate electronic, magnetic, or optical structures that exist independently of their contents, and independently of whether they even have contents. Colossus too had actual storage for potential programs. There are, however, four significant differences in the program stores of Colossus and your own PC: (1) instructions in Colossus were limited to valid plug-cord wiring, switch patterns, etc.; (2) the use of one instruction could rule out the use of another through prior occupancy of a required jack; (3) Colossus did not fetch program instructions in a sequence; and (4) the program memory was not an electronic circuit. Given these differences, the analogy between the program stores of Colossus and of a modern computer becomes stretched.

Buffers, Data Memory, and Lasting Records

Buffers store data temporarily, aggregating it for further processing or input/output. According to Flowers, there was a temporary data store at the tape reader. (It probably aided electronic circuits transforming the approximately rectangular pulses from the photocells in the tape reader to the polarity representation of high/low used on the data lines.) This would constitute an input buffer that then fed to the shift register, which also buffered the input. The ring output store, characterised above as a register, acted as an input buffer as well, because the output of a ring—a flow of current or not—needed to be collected and converted to +/− representation. Other ring buffers delayed wheel bits one cycle for key-stream feedback calculations. There was also an output buffer that connected the printer counter with the printer, and yet another buffer that printed the rings' start positions. Several mentions are made in *General Report on Tunny* of status lamps and even visual output. So perhaps some buffering was involved with these functions as well.

There were flexible data memory elements in Colossus: buffers, registers, counters, and ring and counter settings. Of course, we have classified the input tape as a type of read-only memory. But the machine lacked even a miniature version of the large working RAM memories of PCs, which typically are erased when the power is turned off. Moreover, there was no electrically based non-volatile memory of any kind to hold data without power. The printout served as the only lasting record of the computation on early Colossus models, for there was also no secondary, archival memory, and output via pilot lamps and other signals to the operators was evanescent. *General Report on Tunny* refers to a five-row punch on Colossus VI, so on that machine it seems that paper tape could have served as intermediate storage as well as output.

Memories in Colossus

One might conclude from several dismal assessments in the last few paragraphs that Colossus had poor memory. In fact, Colossus had many different kinds of memory, worthy of a modern system, but they were all terrifically limited in capacity. Memory venues included registers, counters, rings, buffers, parameter settings, logic and arithmetic components, plugboards, switches, and tape. Each of these could preserve part of the state of the computation at least from one cycle to the next, which deserves to be called memorising.

SIMULTANEOUS ACTIVITY—PARALLELISM

Having greater respect for the flexibility of Colossus, we are ready to consider another of its capabilities. Much is made today of parallel computing, now that even mail-order machines have dual processors. Did Colossus act in parallel?

Parallel Aspects of Colossus

Multiple and parallel output counters have already been discussed. Another parallelism was implicit from the start. Each of 32 possible 5-bit characters could be represented by punches at some of the five positions across the input tape. The five input bit streams (called 'impulses' at BP) were processed in parallel even in Heath Robinson. That is, they were being combined simultaneously with the parallel data of the wheel sequences. (In the case of Robinson, these sequences were read in synchronously from a second input tape. Colossus, of course, generated them internally on the parallel thyratron rings.) We tend to forget that moving a byte rather than a bit may connote parallelism (depending on the electrical bus connections that do the moving). In fact, a bus made parallel can be a more effective speed-up than multiple CPUs.

Another element of parallelism was not peculiar to Colossus, for it had already appeared in Robinson's capacity to read two characters in parallel from the ciphertext input tape. This design responded to requirements of cryptographic algorithms that needed to delta pairs of adjacent characters. Therefore, the Robinson photocell array was constructed to read two characters at once, for Robinson had no input buffering. Colossus I continued reading a pair at a time. This type of photocell would not have been required in Colossus II, which achieved pair processing directly with the shift register.

More importantly, general parallel speed-up was seen as a way to overcome the physical limit on tape speed, so the shift register in later models provided access to not one but five pairs of successive tape characters. That is, if the input is AVTRMH, processing can take place independently and simultaneously on A and V, V and T, T and R, R and M, and finally M and H. The economic and logistic advantage of processing multiple input characters at once was a reduction (initially) in the number of machines to be built and also in the number of people required to operate and maintain them.

Implementation of Parallel Processing

The simultaneous reading of 6 hole positions running lengthwise along the tape had no engineering solution at the time. It was decided to serialise the process slightly by storing 6 successive characters from the tape reader in five 6-bit shifting and delaying buffers, one for each tape row, or impulse. These shift registers then delivered six 5-bit characters to the ALU: five pairs of characters to the five independent logical processors—in other words, to five parallel copies of the current program. These copies were wired separately; today, they might be instances or downloads of a master program, but back then nothing prevented their being set up as different programs. Because this could happen unintentionally, the parallel programming required special care.

It may help to continue the example above with a guess on how the processing proceeded. Suppose AVTRMHBKJI is on the input tape and AVTRMH has already been read. Then the shift register currently holds HMRTVA, in the order of reading, that is, the pair VA, eldest from the reader, goes to the fifth processor, and HM, the youngest, goes to the first processor. The five pairs are now processed simultaneously with the current 5-bit letter that is the net result from the dozen thyratron rings. Next, B is read from the tape. The shift register now holds BHMRTV; HM has moved up the delay chain to the position of the second pair, while BH becomes the new first pair. VA has now been completely processed, and A is no longer available, for it has been shifted out of the register. By the time the pair BH is completely processed and H shifts out, five wheel characters have been used with it, and five new characters have been read from the tape. On the next tape pass, the rotary switches might crank the starting place of the thyratron rings five notches forward, because each pair, starting with VA, has seen five outputs from the rings.

Parallels with Today's Parallel

The data tapped off from the shift registers were sent to the same, identically parallel cryptanalytic program in analogy with present-day SIMD, or single-instruction multiple-data parallel computers. Flowers indicated that switch panels were configured to facilitate this parallel programming. But if it was the same program, then why process each pair five times as it moved along the delay chain in the shift register? Because at each stage, new data arrived from the simulated Tunny machine embodied in the thyratron ring assembly. The operation of the machine was not only parallel but also interlaced in the same way that modern structures called 'pipelines' interlace instructions.

Another style of parallel computing was feasible. The parallel streams of data from the shift registers could be directed to separate and different logical manipulations performed by distinct programs running simultaneously (and synchronously). Apart from the lockstep clocking, this resembles the programming of MIMD, or multiple-instruction multiple-data parallel computers, exemplified by modern multiprocessor PCs, clusters of workstations, and networked distributed processors.

SIMD or MIMD, it is like five copies of Colossus I running at once. In the first case, they compute the same thing on different data; this is the only parallel use described by Flowers. But the second style of parallel computing was at least feasible, and the five 'submachines' were capable even of running five different cryptographic methods on the same or different input characters. To put this in modern perspective, high-end consumer PCs typically use dual processors, but parallel supercomputers employ as many as 131,000 such CPUs.

A Parallel Conundrum

Parallelism is also demonstrated by a 'multiple test' feature discussed in *General Report on Tunny*—the simultaneous examination of more than one wheel setting (two in Colossus I, five in Colossus II). Unlike the process of 'multiple reading' into a shift buffer described by Flowers and just discussed, multiple testing took a single letter from the input tape, and used the current and four previous outputs from a chosen wheel to make five simultaneous calculations, feeding to the five result counters. To do this, in the Colossi so equipped, thyratron ring output would be remembered in a buffer for up to six cycles.

Curiously, Flowers did not mention multiple testing directly (see Chapter 8), while *General Report on Tunny* has only two vague references to multiple reading. The two parallel modes seem incompatible, although both could take advantage of 5-stepping. Perhaps multiple testing and reading both occurred in some fashion (*General Report on Tunny* speaks of throwing 'the multiple test switch')—although neither the builders nor the users give a clue how that might work.

CONTROL AND COMMAND—PROGRAMMING, OS, APPLICATIONS, EXTENSIONS, INSTRUCTION SET

Flexible Programming

Programming the Colossus was tedious, and there was no high-level programming language. Although the architecture offered support and scope for ingenious programs, it did not make the programmer's life easy. Tightly refined codebreaking algorithms were implemented in plug-wiring and switches. But the crucial story is that the same machine supported many different algorithms via flexible programming. Flowers said that the programs tended to become hardwired for convenience. This appears to counteract the programming flexibility that we are trying to detect. But the evolution of a plug-wire program fragment to soldered hardware circuits is similar to burning firmware permanently on silicon. What we lose in versatility by freezing the program, we gain in variety by having a new type of programming analogue.

Diversity of Program Capabilities

There were so many different things to program on Colossus: counter settings, the cams and starts on wheels, and, most of all, the plugging and switching to set up the main arithmetic-logic processing. Perhaps it does not sound much like a modern computer, where the programs don't have such messiness. Or do they? Consider the PC with its control panels, extensions, and libraries. Consider the installation of industrial software, a notoriously tedious and touchy enterprise. Consider setting your own preferences in your web browser.

As a PC user, you know that there is an operating system, or OS. This program runs independently of and prior to any application program you might use to write a letter, perform scientific calculations, or communicate with friends. With the advent of Linux and OSX, you may have become aware that your computer's architecture supports different operating systems on the same hardware. Apart from the Wren and her training, Colossus had no operating system, but there were architectural elements that relate to operating systems. The master control, the interrupts and their handling, the printer port driver, the counter interfacing, all of this sounds like OS. We might call it by today's name: hardware support.

Think of the software that defines PC productivity (those fondly called 'killer applications') for PCs: VisiCalc, WordStar, PageMaker, Netscape, Photoshop. What are the killer applications for Colossus? At least here we can easily identify the analogue. As a dedicated machine, Colossus ran critically important Tunny-cracking code—and only that. The significant thing for us was that this code could change within broad limits, especially on Colossus II and its successors.

General Report on Tunny indicates the use of special-purpose 'gadgets', including one that subtracts a selected number. These might be viewed both as hardware add-ons and as software plug-ins, with the effect of extending the processing repertoire, much as PCI cards or Photoshop plug-ins extend the power of a PC system.

Instructions by Cable

Let us return to the heart of computer architecture, the structure of the instructions. The Colossus instruction set was externalised as a manual of plug-wiring and switch-setting followed by the Wrens. Each different cable patch could specify some difference in behaviour. Thus the instruction repertoire in Colossus was large for the first machine and grew larger for its successors. Although the modern tension between reduced and complex instruction sets (Mac vs. PC, or RISC vs. CISC) plays no role here, a count of different Colossus instruction types might well be in the thousands. For example, 40 source jacks and 40 destination jacks could give $40 \times 40 = 1600$ possible distinct instructions for a single cable.

Counting the instructions can be tricky. *General Report on Tunny* says that a particular switch panel (the improved Q panel) could enforce the majority of 2^{32} (around 4000 million) logical conditions representable by sets of the 32 Baudot characters. Another calculation shows that the 206 switches on this panel actually allow the vastly larger number of 3×10^{58} different settings. Both are poor ways, however, to count instructions, because we should focus on the different instruction types, not all the different instances or combinations of them. Indeed, the panel may implement only 206 instructions, or just eight, for the eight different types of switches on it.

Flowers said that the direct, wired coding by switch or plug was necessary in Colossus, even if they had thought of stored-program logic, in order to get the required performance using the components of the time. The wired-program paradigm persisted for decades in various computers and peripheral machines. It even influenced internal programming. The Pilot ACE materialised Turing's earlier design of the first realistic stored-program computer (see Chapter 9). Their program instructions were an automation of a plug-wired instruction architecture. Functionality depended on the location to which data was sent, in perfect analogy to the destination jack of a jumper cable; for example, routing a number to destination #17 in the Pilot ACE caused it to be added to the number stored in register #16, while routing it to destination #18 caused it to be subtracted from the number in register #16.

So ACE and Colossus share an architectural dependence on plug-wiring. Let's go one step further. The PC machine instruction is similar to the ACE's, although their instruction architectures differ. In both, there are parts of each machine instruction word that indicate memory address, function and destination, and other parameters. PCs have special registers for doing arithmetic. Together with the associated register instructions that use them, these behave like the destinations in ACE. In other words, some PC registers resemble plug-wiring. Of course, they don't look the same, but there is an architectural homage to the days of drooping wires.

GRANTING COLOSSUS IS A COMPUTER (AND PERSONAL), IS IT A PC?

According to the analysis above, Colossus includes many individual architectural elements found in a generic modern PC. Indeed, there emerges a strong parallel. When resources, bandwidth, and program store are treated generously, the Colossus machines and modern PCs are not *too* different. A striking metaphor for Colossus is the modern microprocessor chip heading for an embedded application, like a four-function calculator, a pacemaker, or a rice cooker. Just as the embedded chip has all of its flexible talents bent to one dedicated purpose, so Colossus's candle burned brightly, but under the bushel of desperate cryptanalytical need. If the machine and the makers had had the freedom of an academic or commercial setting, they might have engendered a continuous line of machines with greater and greater capabilities.

Recent memoirs and releases of previously restricted documents have shown the general-purpose nature of Colossus. In order to determine cam settings, a wheel-breaking panel was introduced in later models: Michie considers this 'a degree of general-purpose programmability'. He also points to Timms' post-war programming of a Colossus to perform multiplication, limited to what could be accomplished in a single machine cycle, as demonstrating 'the in-principle applicability of the later Colossi to problem domains far beyond the original'.

It is similar to a future archaeologist's digging the chip out of an unearthed automatic frying-pan and, under electronic probes, finding an unexpected complexity and power. Neither Colossus nor the chip is diminished by its limited context, and neither should be minimised for its dedication. Colossus stood on the brink of the fully programmable computer era. Although it was removed from participation (by the post-war secrecy), it was not remote from it. The architecture may not have evolved directly, but the builders participated in post-war computer and network construction. So their ideas and experience did live on and grow. Was Colossus an indicator of a promised land, with its own entry barred? Or was it a harbour opening to the sea? Our odyssey may have shown you that it was both.

THE PHOENIX OF BLETCHLEY PARK

Between burying the pieces and burning the plans, they just about extinguished Colossus. But from those ashes, Colossus has arisen, most notably as Tony Sale's physical rebuild at Bletchley Park (see Chapter 12). There is also a virtual phoenix on the Internet. My students and I have used Java, Lisp, and VRML to construct a virtual Colossus and a virtual German Tunny machine. These are available for download at <http://www.AlanTuring.net/virtual_colossus>. Using these programs, we have successfully (and quickly) broken and set wheels for Tunny-encrypted ordinary English plaintext—disproving a myth that only military German, or more specifically its Tunny dialect, was amenable to attack by Colossus. Our next step is to demonstrate concretely the universality of computation on Colossus, by using our simulator to implement a so-called universal Turing machine (see Chapter 9). To show that Colossus is universal is to show that (speed and memory capacity aside) Colossus has the same computing power as your PC!

Chapter 11

Of Men and Machines

Brian Randell

EARLY REVELATIONS OF COLOSSUS

The first inkling I had of the work done at Bletchley Park during the Second World War on electronic codebreaking machines resulted from my efforts to find out what Alan Turing had done during the war. I had been assembling a set of original documents and papers for reproduction in a book on the origins of digital computers, when a colleague questioned the fact that Turing did not figure in the book. At this stage I knew only of Turing's pre-war work on what we now term 'Turing machines', which was purely theoretical, and of his post-war work at the National Physical Laboratory, which did not lead to a working computer in the pre-1950 period on which I was concentrating (see Chapter 9).

I responded to the implied challenge and gradually tracked down various brief published allusions to wartime work by Turing and others at Bletchley Park (in particular an article by Jack Good), which were then assembled into a draft article. This draft persuaded various people, especially Donald Michie and Jack Good—both of whom worked with Turing at Bletchley Park—to provide additional, although very guarded, information. I decided to try to get the British wartime work on electronic computers declassified. I wrote directly to the Prime Minister at the time, Mr Edward Heath. The reply I received, signed by the Prime Minister himself, although it politely refused my request, nevertheless constituted for several years what I think was the only unclassified official document admitting that there had been a wartime electronic computer project in Britain.

The result of this investigation was my 'On Alan Turing and the Origins of Digital Computers', which I presented at Michie's annual machine intelligence workshop at Edinburgh in October 1972. The proceedings of the workshop were due to be published by the University of Edinburgh Press, and after

I had given my presentation I overheard two people connected with the University Press voicing concern over whether they dare include it in the book. The conversation ended with them agreeing that it would be all right to go ahead since, if there were any repercussions, it would be the head of the University Press, namely Prince Philip, the Duke of Edinburgh, who would be held responsible.

There matters largely rested until the story of the breaking of the Enigma cipher started to come out, in particular via several books which made the term 'Ultra Secret' famous. I decided it was time to reopen the matter of declassifying the wartime computer project and I made some cautious enquiries. Before long, I received a somewhat encouraging response, accompanied by an intimation that it would be appreciated if I did not write directly to the Prime Minister again on the matter. Shortly afterwards I was invited to a meeting with some very senior government officials, where to my delight I was shown a set of wartime photographs of Colossus, plus a draft of the page of text that had been written to accompany these photographs when they were made public (which I was invited to help clarify). It was agreed that, once the photographs had been released, I could interview the people who had been involved at Bletchley Park and at Dollis Hill. In return I agreed to provide a draft of my article for vetting.

There followed one of the most exciting, and humbling, periods of my life, as I got to meet, or correspond with, a considerable number of the people who had been involved with Colossus. My main meetings, with Tommy Flowers and his colleagues Bill Chandler, Sid Broadhurst, and Allen (Doc) Coombs, were particularly memorable—since their evident immense expertise was exceeded only by their modesty and their friendliness to me. It was a fascinating task trying to piece together the story, since the wartime work had been highly compartmentalised on a 'need-to-know' basis, and the people involved had been under an oath of complete secrecy ever since. Now, for the first time, they were being asked to try to remember what had happened, and when, without the benefit of any notebooks or diaries. I revealed the vetted results of my investigation at the International Research Conference on the History of Computing at Los Alamos in June 1976. Given the dramatic story I had to tell, it was no credit to me that my presentation was the sensation of the conference. Doc Coombs had accompanied me to Los Alamos and another session was hurriedly arranged, at which Doc and I—particularly Doc—answered a torrent of questions. (He was being his usual ebullient self and I had to try to prevent him from committing any indiscretions, as I was still very mindful of the rules under which I had agreed to conduct and report on my investigation.)

The next development in which I was involved concerned the television series *The Secret War*. Unfortunately, the programme mentioning Colossus, and the accompanying book, wrongly identified the cipher machine attacked by Colossus. This was said incorrectly to be the encrypting teleprinter built by Siemens—Sturgeon, the subject of Chapters 25 and 26.

After this I played one further part in trying to ensure that Flowers got the recognition he deserved. The latter part of his career had been (unfairly) blighted by the failure of a post-war project to build an electronic telephone exchange. Very few people had any idea how brilliant an engineer he was, or of the vital contribution he had made to the Allied war effort. I persuaded my university to confer the honorary degree of Doctor of Science on Flowers—an event which featured large on the front page of *The Times*.

BIOGRAPHICAL BACKGROUND: FLOWERS, BROADHURST, CHANDLER, AND COOMBS

Flowers was in charge of the switching group at the Post Office Research Station; in 1941 the group—the biggest in the Research Station—contained fifty people in all, including perhaps ten graduate engineers. Flowers' major research interest over the years had been long-distance signalling, in particular the problem of transmitting control signals, in order to enable automatic switching equipment to replace human operators. His work on electronics had resulted in an experimental toll-dialling circuit which was operational in 1935 (he recalled using it to telephone his fiancée, whom he married later that year). He and his switching group worked on a great variety of different research projects in the pre-war years—as he put it 'work was fired at us from all directions'. He used thyratrons for counting purposes; and had some contact with C. A. Beevers, an X-ray crystallographer who was working on a special-purpose digital calculator made from electromechanical telephone switching components. This was perhaps Flowers' most direct early contact with digital computation. (On the analogue side, he had some knowledge of the differential analyser at Manchester University, having seen it there at an exhibition in about 1937, and later having had one of the graduates who worked on it, Alan Fairweather, as a member of his staff.) As war approached, Flowers became involved with various special projects. One (originated by the Royal Aircraft Establishment, Farnborough) involved an electromechanical digital device for anti-aircraft ranging by means of sound detection. This project was a cause of some embarrassment to Flowers, who since 1937 had been cleared to receive information about what later came to be known as radar. He therefore knew that the device was likely to be obsolete before completion, but was not able to tell the others.

In February 1941 Flowers was approached, via the director of the Research Station, W. G. Radley (later Sir W. Gordon), to work on a problem for Bletchley Park. Flowers had until this time reported to Radley through a division head. However, for security reasons even the division head was not told of the request from Bletchley Park, and from then on Flowers reported directly to Radley. It seems that Flowers and Radley were the first Post Office people to be initiated into the work at Bletchley Park. Flowers' next six months or so were spent building a special-purpose electromechanical device for Bletchley Park. The work was done mainly at Dollis Hill but Flowers spent a lot of time at Bletchley Park, where he interacted with Turing and Gordon Welchman. Turing paid a number of visits to Dollis Hill at this time for discussions with Flowers, but for security reasons the majority of their meetings were held at Bletchley Park.

Flowers' colleague Broadhurst was brought in to help with this project. Broadhurst had, in his own words, 'come up the hard way, but it was quite enjoyable', having joined the Post Office as a labourer. He had taken a job with the Post Office to tide him over while he continued to look for proper engineering work, after finishing his apprenticeship with the South-East and Chatham Railway in about 1923. He was soon upgraded by the Post Office, and later served for a period commissioning and maintaining one of the early automatic exchanges, before being transferred to the newly formed circuit laboratory at Post Office headquarters. From there he moved to the PO Engineering Training School, finally being transferred to Dollis Hill. Broadhurst's forte was electromechanical equipment. At Dollis Hill he taught courses on automatic telephony, which was then a fairly new subject within the Post Office. Eventually he was promoted into the Research Branch, joining Flowers' group, where he spent the first 18 months of the war working on various projects associated with radar.

The device that Flowers and Broadhurst built for Turing involved the use of high-speed rotary switches. It could perhaps be described as a sort of computer, with a lot of the data and logic being stored on banks of switches. However, there was nothing in the way of arithmetic or programming facilities. In the end the whole project turned out to have been a mistake, as the speed requirement that had been specified turned out to have been grossly underestimated. Flowers had the impression that one of the reasons he and Broadhurst were then introduced to other problems at Bletchley Park was that the people there felt somewhat guilty at having wasted his time!

At about this stage Chandler, another of Flowers' staff, was brought into the work for Bletchley Park. Chandler was the youngest of the three, having joined the Research Branch at Dollis Hill in 1936 as a trainee. He had begun his career in 1930 as an apprentice telephone engineer with Siemens Brothers. At Dollis Hill before the war he worked on long-distance signalling and dialling systems. He believed that during this work he made the first ever use of valves for switching purposes in Post Office communications. Flowers described Chandler as the most 'mathematical and computer-minded and electronic-minded' of the three of them.

The three engineers became involved in a different project, on which Wynn-Williams of TRE and H. M. Keen of the British Tabulating Machine Company were working, although once again Flowers and his colleagues found themselves getting much of their direction from Turing. Some years previously Keen had been responsible for the engineering design of Turing's electromechanical Bombe. The problem now was to produce a very much faster version of the equipment. With their prior experience, Flowers and his assistants were brought in to provide electronic forms of relays. Flowers and Chandler spent some time at Letchworth with Keen. They suggested the use of hot cathode gas discharge valves instead of relays and provided a demonstration, emphasising that valves would bring increased speed and increased reliability. For various reasons their solution was not adopted. However, through these various activities they established themselves as the leading exponents of electronics at Bletchley—in time, fortunately, to be entrusted with the details of Tunny.

Coombs, a relative latecomer to the group, joined them at about the time the first Colossus was commissioned. After leaving Glasgow University with a doctorate and joining the Post Office in 1936, Coombs had been involved in various items of war work and had become experienced with a great variety of electromechanical equipment and with electronics, although not with electronic switching. He was brought into the Foreign Office cipher work in about October 1943 and was initially involved in the production at Dollis Hill of additional Robinsons—but the advent of Colossus changed all that.

HEATH ROBINSON

Flowers and his team were not involved during the early stages of the Heath Robinson project (see Chapter 5). At TRE Wynn-Williams had assembled a small group of carefully selected people (all of whom had first to be approved by Bletchley). This group, together with the superintendent (A. P. Rowe) and assistant superintendent (W. B. Lewis) were the only people in TRE party to the secret. Wynn-Williams undertook to produce the electronic counters and necessary circuitry for the machine proposed by Newman, but recommended that a Post Office telegraph engineer be given the tape driving and reading problem. It was thus that Morrell, head of the telegraph group at Dollis Hill, became involved, in about the summer of 1942. Morrell commissioned E. A. Speight and A. C. Lynch of the physics group at Dollis Hill to produce a photoelectric reader. (Speight had designed much of the Post Office's 'Speaking Clock', which was accessible by public telephone.) Gil Hayward reports that Speight and Lynch had previously designed and produced a teleprinter tape reader for RAF fighter command headquarters at Bentley Priory; named the 'Auto Teller', this was for use in recording the flood of messages arriving from stations around the country (see also Chapter 24). Speight and Lynch used the Auto Teller as the basis for the new photoelectric reader. They were not told of the intended purpose of the new reader, which they knew as the Mark I Telegraph Transmitter—or more exactly the 'Transmitter, Telegraph, Mark I'. Because some of the components had originally been intended for fighter command headquarters, many people assumed that the apparatus destined for 'BP' was for Bentley Priory.

The photoelectric reader used double-crescent masks in order to produce a nearly rectangular pulse of light as a circular hole crossed the mask. It incorporated a number of lenses (much of the optical work was done by Speight's assistant, D. A. Campbell). Two successive rows of five-hole tape were read simultaneously, and the sprocket holes were detected in order to produce timing pulses. Although the electronics of Robinson were capable of operating at 2000 characters per second, in practice the operating speed was limited by several factors, including the length of the tape—long tapes placed more strain on the paper at the sprocket drive and were usually run more slowly. The TRE and Dollis Hill halves of the Heath Robinson were put together, it is believed, at Bletchley Park in about April 1943.

COLOSSUS

Flowers, of course, proposed building a very different and much more sophisticated machine (see Chapter 5). His approach contrasted greatly with that of Wynn-Williams, who preferred to use as few valves as possible, favouring electromagnetic relays. Unlike Wynn-Williams, Flowers was confident that switching circuit networks involving large numbers of valves could be made to work reliably. As one of his colleagues put it, 'the basic thing about Flowers was that he didn't care about how many valves he used'.

The electronic design for Colossus was done mainly by Flowers and

Chandler, with Broadhurst concentrating on the auxiliary electromechanical equipment. The photoelectric reader was a redesigned version of the one used in Heath Robinson, working at 5000 characters per second. The electronic counters were based on ones developed before the war by W. B. Lewis, who had been at the Cavendish Laboratory with Wynn-Williams. (Lewis played an important, although perhaps unwitting, role in the Colossus story, through his book on counting circuits—Flowers credits this book as a landmark in his own understanding of electronics.) When Flowers tried out Lewis' original circuit he found it would not work properly for him, so he produced a redesigned circuit that did not require such accurate components. This was later patented. Flowers' counting circuits were altogether more sophisticated than Lewis'.

Colossus was assembled and tested at Dollis Hill. Tests were made using short loops of tape on which repetitive patterns had been punched. The machine was then partially unwired prior to transportation to Bletchley Park, where it was reassembled. A small team of junior technicians, who had helped with the electronic design of Colossus, were mainly responsible for commissioning the machine. As luck would have it, the first job to be run on Colossus at Bletchley Park happened to take only ten minutes (jobs could equally well take several hours). The codebreakers had trouble believing their eyes. Flowers said, 'They just couldn't believe it when we brought this string and sealing wax sort of thing in and it actually did a job. They were on their beam ends at the time, Robinson just hadn't got enough output, they wouldn't go fast enough.'

Historically significant features of the prototype Colossus included:

- Binary electronic circuitry on a large scale. This contributed to the reliability of Colossus, since (except in the tape reader photocell amplifiers) all valves were either cut-off or conducting (representing 0 or 1, respectively).

- A clock pulse that synchronised and timed operations throughout the machine. It was this feature which made the size of the machine possible, eliminating cumulative timing errors.

- A (five-step) shift register.

- Two-state circuits and clock control meant that the machine could operate at any speed down to zero (except for the photocell amplifiers). In consequence Colossus could be 'hand-stepped' for test purposes.

- The operation of the switching circuits was isolated from the output (by the use of 'cathode followers').

Colossus II involved extensive redesigning, although the basic logic and Flowers' original circuit technology remained virtually unchanged. An additional counter was provided, more use was made of shift registers, and a number of detailed modifications were made to the original circuitry. The design work was divided up between Flowers, Broadhurst, Chandler, and Coombs—Coombs remembers Flowers literally tearing his basic logic diagram into pieces and handing out one piece to each of them. Their designs were then handed over to various less senior engineers, who laid out the circuits on standard panels and supervised the actual construction.

Production of the Colossi took up about half the total workshop and production capability at the Dollis Hill Research Station. Construction of the electronic panels for the first two or three machines was undertaken by a staff of wiremen there, but subsequently the panels were built at the Post Office factory in Birmingham. Frames on which the tape pulleys were mounted (the 'bedsteads') were built by the Dollis Hill workshops. The racks on which the electronic panels were installed were standard ones from Post Office stores. Racks were wired together for the first time at Bletchley Park, an operation which would take two or three weeks, there being a large amount of inter-rack wiring.

Design work continued right up to the end of the war and no two Colossi were exactly the same. In 1944 Coombs was placed in charge of the work at Dollis Hill when Flowers was promoted and ceased his full-time involvement (although Coombs continued to report to him). Flowers became involved in the planning of work to be carried out on the telephone system once the war had ended.

Colossus was a special-purpose program-controlled electronic digital computer. Program control by means of plugboards was available on contemporary punched-card machines and was well known to Flowers and his team. In fact Flowers described the prototype Colossus as probably less programmable than some IBM machines of the time. Colossus II, however, was much more flexible than the prototype, because of an additional logic switching panel.

Although a special purpose device, Colossus turned out to have considerable flexibility within its field. Once this flexibility was appreciated by the codebreakers, it was exploited fully, and Colossus ended up being used for a number of quite diverse tasks not anticipated when the machine was designed. Early in 1945 Shaun Wylie showed that, without any modifications or additions, Colossus could break the motor wheels, a task which had hitherto been the responsibility of the Testery, and had been thought of as one that could not be mechanised.

THE SUPER ROBINSON

Flowers designed at least one other machine after Colossus—the Super Robinson. This involved four data tapes, and to some extent went back to the use of sprocket wheels to keep the tapes synchronised. The problem which the machine addressed could have been solved electronically, but Flowers and his people did not have the time to do so. In any case, Robinson's earlier problems of tape wear caused by the sprocket wheels had largely been solved by Morrell, who had designed a system for driving the tapes by friction (by means of a pulley), using the sprockets only to keep the tapes in alignment. The Super Robinson was a hybrid, which to a very large extent used Colossus circuit technology, its multiple tape inputs being roughly synchronised by the sprocket drive and then electronically synchronised to the clock pulse derived from one tape.

Although Colossus had soon replaced the two-tape Robinson for wheel setting, the Robinson remained indispensable for 'crib runs'. A crib run involved comparing two tapes in all positions. One tape was derived from the ciphertext and one from probable plaintext (the crib). Colossus, which had no means of generating arbitrary patterns, could not mimic the crib tape. Cribbing was a method of wheel-breaking (the Newmanry began to use it in June 1944). A successful crib run usually produced a long enough stretch of key to make wheel-breaking easy. The demands of cribbing made it necessary to overcome some of the persistent handicaps of the Robinson and so four Super Robinsons were ordered.

The Super Robinson had four bedsteads and a plugboard that was rather more flexible than that of Colossus, although the Super Robinson lacked the immense elaboration of facilities provided by Colossus. The 'span' and 'set total' facilities of Colossus were incorporated (see Chapter 8). Two Super Robinsons had been completed by 8 May 1945.

Chapter 12

The Colossus Rebuild

Tony Sale

COMPUTER ARCHAEOLOGY

In 1991, some colleagues and I started the campaign to save Bletchley Park from demolition by property developers. At this time I was working at the Science Museum in London restoring some early British computers. I believed it would be possible to rebuild Colossus, but nobody else believed me.

In 1993, I gathered together all the information available. This amounted to no more than eight 1945 wartime photographs of Colossus (some of which are printed in this book), plus brief descriptions by Flowers, Coombs, and Chandler, and—crucially—circuit diagrams which some engineers had kept, quite illegally, as engineers always do!

I spent nine months poring over the wartime photographs, using a sophisticated modern CAD system on my PC to recreate machine drawings of the racks. I found that, fortunately, sufficient wartime valves were still available, as were various pieces of Post Office equipment used in the original construction.

In July 1994, His Royal Highness the Duke of Kent opened the Bletchley Park Museum and inaugurated the Colossus rebuild project. At that time I had not managed to obtain any sponsorship for the project, so my wife Margaret and I decided to put our own money into it, to get it started. We both felt that if the effort was not made immediately there would be nobody still alive to help us with memories of Colossus. Over the next few years various private sponsors came to our aid and some current and retired Post Office and radio engineers formed the team that helped me in the rebuild.

MORE INFORMATION COMES TO LIGHT

In 1995, the American National Security Agency was forced by application of the Freedom of Information Act to release about 5000 Second World War documents into the US National Archive. A list of these documents was put onto the Internet. When I read it I was amazed to see titles like 'The Cryptographic Attack on FISH'. I obtained copies of these documents and found that they were invaluable reports written by American servicemen seconded to Bletchley Park when America entered the war. I was also fortunate enough to be given access to the then still classified *General Report on Tunny* (parts of which are published for the first time in this book). Having this information enabled us to work out the function of many more of the circuits and program switches on Colossus.

I was helped by the memories of Dr Arnold Lynch, who had designed the optical paper-tape reader in 1942, and by 1995 the tape reader was working and some of the basic circuitry of Colossus had been recreated. At this stage the rebuilt Colossus operated only on two channels (out of the five channels from the paper tape).

THE SWITCH-ON

The Duke of Kent returned to the Park on 6 June 1996 to switch on the first stage of the rebuild. This was a marvellous occasion with Flowers present, together with people who had worked at Knockholt, in the Testery, and in the Newmanry.

One reason for wanting to get Colossus up and running in 1996 was to promote awareness of Flowers' contribution to the history of computing at the time of the 50th anniversary of the American ENIAC. For far too long the Americans had got away with the myth that the ENIAC was the first large-scale electronic computer in the world. It was not, but they got away with it because Colossus was kept completely secret until the 1970s.

GOING FOR A MARK 2 COLOSSUS

After the 1996 switch-on, we decided that we should try to rebuild a Mark 2 Colossus. The Mark 2 Colossi were far more powerful than the Mark 1 prototype (Colossus I), and it was a Mark 2 Colossus that was actually in the room in H Block where we were doing the rebuild. This was an extremely difficult task which took over 6000 man-days of effort—but by 2003 we had most of the computer working.

In January 2004, we decided to go all out to get the Mark 2 machine fully working by 1 June 2004—the 60th anniversary of the day that Colossus II first ran (see Chapter 5). The result was that, on 20 May 2004, I filmed the Colossus rebuild setting all five chi-wheels on an actual message from the Bream link. We have now, we think, incorporated nearly all the circuits, and although there may still be some parts which cannot be worked out, we think we have about 90 per cent of Colossus built, but not yet fully working.

The rebuild is on public display at Bletchley Park.

THE PERFORMANCE OF COLOSSUS

Colossus is hard-wired and switch-programmed, just like ENIAC. Because of its parallel nature it is very fast, even by today's standards. At 5000 characters per second—the speed at which Colossus reads the paper tape—the interval between sprocket holes is 200 microseconds. In this time Colossus will do up to 100 Boolean calculations simultaneously on each of the five tape channels and across a five-character matrix. The gate delay time is 1.2 microseconds, which is quite remarkable for very ordinary valves. Colossus is so fast and parallel that a modern PC programmed to do the same codebreaking task takes as long as Colossus to achieve a result.

RECTANGLING

Now that most of the information about the basic Colossus has been acquired, thoughts have turned to implementing 'rectangling'. This was the most advanced task that Colossus performed. It involved a procedure devised by Bill Tutte for iteratively deducing the wheel patterns used on Tunny for a particular message (see Appendix 9 *Rectangling*). When the required hardware is incorporated into the rebuilt Colossus, it will really demonstrate the enormous codebreaking power of the machine.

THE REBUILD OF HEATH ROBINSON

The acquisition of a fragment of circuit diagram of Heath Robinson opened the possibility of recreating the unique logic design of this machine. I have built a replica of Heath Robinson in my garage, including its two paper-tape readers.

Section 3

The Newmanry

Chapter 13

Mr Newman's Section

Jack Copeland
with Catherine Caughey, Dorothy Du Boisson, Eleanor
Ireland, Ken Myers, and Norman Thurlow

ORGANISATION OF THE ATTACK

When Turing arrived at Bletchley Park, the day after Chamberlain's announcement of war with Germany, he joined Dilly Knox's Research Section. The job of the Research Section was to study enemy ciphers and operating procedures, and to devise methods of attack. The techniques invented by this high-powered think-tank were then handed over to other sections where they were used operationally against the enemy traffic. In 1939, Enigma was the focus of research. By the time Tutte joined the Research Section, in mid-1941, Captain Gerry Morgan headed it. Tunny soon became the leading problem. Thanks to Tutte, the Research Section broke the Tunny machine in January 1942, and in July read up-to-date traffic for the first time.

Tunny could now be tackled operationally, and a Tunny-breaking section was immediately set up under Major Ralph Tester. Several members of the Research Section moved over to the 'Testery'. Armed with Turingery and other hand methods, the Testery read nearly every message from July to October 1942—thanks to the insecure 12-letter indicator system (see Chapter 3). In October, however, the 12-letter indicators were replaced by QEP numbers and the Testery, now completely reliant on depths, fell on leaner times (see Chapter 5). The Research Section renewed its efforts against Tunny, looking for a means of wheel setting that did not depend on depths. With the invention of Tutte's method, Newman was given the job of developing the necessary machinery, and when the Heath Robinson was delivered in June 1943 the 'Newmanry' became a separate section.

From December 1943 the Newmanry would be responsible for breaking and setting the chi-wheels, and the Testery for breaking and setting the remaining wheels manually. The two sections worked hand-in-glove.

Initially Newman's staff consisted of one cryptographer (Michie), two engineers, and 16 Wrens. Soon a second cryptographer arrived (Good), and after three months of experimentation, two or three messages were being set each week. 'Cryptographers', 'engineers', and 'Wrens' remained the principal staffing categories of the Newmanry throughout the war. By May 1945, there were 26 cryptographers, 28 engineers, and 273 Wrens.

During the period June 1943 to July 1944, two Americans joined the cryptographic staff of the Newmanry. It is not always appreciated that the United States was a relative latecomer to the attack on Tunny, and never played a major role. Coombs—one of Flowers' right-hand men at Dollis Hill and closely involved in the Newmanry—described how 'the Americans when they came into the war were told about the particular code system that was being used [Tunny], and they declared that it was impossible to break that code, couldn't possibly be done. ... We showed them the machines breaking it and producing clear text at the end, and they were absolutely amazed. It was way ahead of anything they had imagined.'

In November 1943, the Newmanry moved from its two rooms in the wooden Hut 11 to new quarters in Block F, and in a further expansion in September 1944 occupied Block H as well. Blocks F and H each contained Colossus Rooms, Tunny Rooms (holding replica Tunny machines manufactured at Dollis Hill), and a Registry, which received, circulated, and tracked tapes. Wheel breaking took place in Block H, under the charge of the shift's 'Wheel Man', and wheel setting was carried out in Block F, under the Duty Officer, the cryptographer who managed the work of the Newmanry during his shift.

The Newmanry Tunny machines were used for preparing and copying the tapes for the Colossi, and for de-chi-ing (see photograph 30). Once the chi-wheel settings had been found by Colossus (or, previously, by the Robinson), a Tunny was set up to strip away the chis' contribution to the ciphertext, and to print out the resulting de-chi. At that stage the de-chi was put in a bag and sent to the Testery for human attack.

The Colossi in Block H deduced Tunny wheel patterns by means of a method also devised by Tutte and known as 'rectangling' (see Chapter 17 and Appendices 4 and 9). By the end of 1944 the Colossi were also being used for motor-setting and psi-setting, and in March 1945 the responsibilty for psi-setting passed formally from the Testery to the Newmanry.

In a rare light moment, the official history of the Newmanry (*General Report on Tunny*) waxes lyrical about the Colossi:

```
It is regretted that it is not possible to give an adequate idea of
the fascination of a Colossus at work: its sheer bulk and apparent
complexity; the fantastic speed of thin paper tape round the
glittering pulleys; the childish pleasure of not—not, span, print
main heading and other gadgets; the wizardry of purely mechanical
decoding letter by letter (one novice thought she was being hoaxed);
the uncanny action of the typewriter in printing the correct scores
without and beyond human aid; the stepping of display; periods of
eager expectation culminating in the sudden appearance of the
longed-for score; and the strange rhythms characterising every
type of run: the stately break-in, the erratic short run, the
regularity of wheel-breaking, the stolid rectangle interrupted by
the wild leaps of the carriage-return, the frantic chatter of a
motor run, even the ludicrous frenzy of hosts of bogus scores.
```

In the following chapters some Newmanry cryptographers write about their work on Tunny and about their lives at Bletchley Park. This chapter tells the stories of some of those other breakers of the code, the Newmanry's Wrens and engineers.

THE NEWMANRY WRENS

The Newmanry Wrens were from HMS *Pembroke V*—since the Wrens were a naval organisation, their units were named as though they were ships. *General Report on Tunny* notes that 'a pass in mathematics in School Certificate or "good social recommendations" was normally considered essential'. Most recruits were between 17 and 20 years of age. Prospective recruits were interviewed and those selected for 'Special Duties X' were transported to Bletchley Park (Station X), where they received up to a fortnight's training in the teleprinter alphabet and the workings of the German Tunny machine. At the end of their training they were given a written test.

In those deeply sexist times no woman rose to a senior management position in the Newmanry, and none achieved the status of cryptographer, despite the fact that nine per cent of Newmanry Wrens had received a university education. 'The cheerful common sense of the Wrens was a great asset,' says *General Report on Tunny*. More significant assets went unmentioned or unnoticed. It is explained that 'Wrens (unlike men) were organised in fixed watches and given fixed jobs in which they could become technically proficient.' The Report notes approvingly that 'several' of the Newmanry's 273 Wrens 'showed ability in cryptographic work' and that 'several others were trained by the engineers to undertake routine testing of machines'.

Dorothy Du Boisson, the Wren with her back to the camera in the cover photograph (taken in 1945), was interviewed for the Newmanry in the spring of 1943. She recalls Newman's introductory lecture at Bletchley Park:

On arrival at BP, we were taken into a room and told that a certain Mr Newman would be informing us what we would be doing. Mr Newman was a very quiet man, reserved and not at ease with girls. He walked up and down in front of us with his eyes on the ground, talking about a machine with twelve wheels. When he had gone we were none the wiser. Later we discovered that he thought we had been told what the section did. Mr Newman decreed that everyone, except himself, be called by their first name. This was a marvellous idea — at once we were a team.

Catherine Caughey, who joined the Newmanry Wrens at the beginning of 1944, also remembers Newman's introduction to the work of the section:

We drove into Bletchley at about 0900 hours and stopped at high barbed wire fencing reminiscent of a high-security prison. RAF police boarded our bus and issued each of us with a security pass. We were then deposited in front of a hideous Victorian Manor. There was no one to meet us. The place was WEIRD. There were weedy looking boffin types walking in pairs or on their own. Some were very young, some middle-aged. Service personnel came in and out of huts. They did not address each other and never lifted their heads to notice us. After an hour of waiting — luckily we were able to stand in the sun, out of the wind — a bald-headed man wearing round, metal-framed utility spectacles approached us and introduced himself as Mr Newman. We followed him into Block F — the Newmanry. He sat us down at a long trestle table and began teaching us a new kind of mathematics and logic. He was a good teacher, but also impatient. He had not realised that we had no idea what this was all about. Our tuition continued for twelve days. Somebody else took over from Mr Newman as the days passed. Gradually we got the idea of what we were doing. On the evening of the last day of tuition, we sat an exam.

Eleanor Ireland arrived at Bletchley later in 1944, from a WRNS reception camp situated in a requisitioned castle near Glasgow:

We travelled down on the night train from Glasgow. This was packed with service personnel and we arrived at Bletchley completely exhausted. From the station we were taken by transport to Bletchley Park, only a few minutes away. The transport stopped at an entrance manned by guards. We were taken a few at a time into a concrete building where we were issued with our security passes. We were told to protect them with our lives.

Before us was a large Victorian mansion with a sward of grass in front of it. A Wren officer escorted us into a low building adjacent to the Mansion, where she gave us an intimidating lecture about the extreme secrecy of every aspect of the work that was being done at

Bletchley Park. We were never to divulge any information about our work nor about the place where we worked, on penalty of imprisonment. We were never to discuss our work when 'outside', not even with those with whom we worked. We were not to ask anyone outside our own unit what they did. We were not to keep diaries. Our category, we were told, was PV Special Duties X — 'PV' stood for *'Pembroke V'*, our notional ship. We would wear no category badges and if anyone asked us what we did we were to say that we were secretaries. We were told that we would never be posted anywhere else, because the work was too secret for us to be released. Everyone had to sign the Official Secrets Act. So effective was this lecture that each time I left the building where I worked, I just dropped a shutter and blanked it all out. There were Foreign Office, army, navy, and air force personnel at the Park, but we never knew what was done in other sections.

We returned to the transport subdued and puzzled by the lecture, still with no idea where we were going. The transport left the sleepy town of Bletchley and drove nine miles into the country, through woodland, until we came to the village of Woburn. We turned by a church and drove through a very imposing set of gates into beautiful parkland. In front of us stood the stately home of Woburn Abbey. This was HMS *Pembroke V*. After climbing up the grand staircase to the second floor we were allocated temporary accommodation. The rooms were very grand — formerly they were bedrooms used by the Duke of Bedford and his family. Walls were lined with red silk. The bathrooms were impressively large, with the bath on a 'throne' two steps above the floor, encased in mahogany and very gloomy.

After we finished our fortnight's initiation at Bletchley we were allocated to watches, A, B, C or D. At that stage we were moved out of our temporary accommodation and up into a room under the eaves at the front of the house, the servants' quarters, where eight of us shared a 'cabin'. The cabin was spartan: four bunk beds, four chests of drawers, and a built-in cupboard where we kept our cases, food, and so on — until we discovered the resident mice. The Duke lived in a house in the grounds and he would come and have a look round every now and then to make sure everything was all right. All the family pictures and furniture were stored away in another wing of the Abbey. Some of my friends had a lovely cabin on the ground floor, which I recognised when I went back many years later. It is now a dining room, hung with yellow silk and a magnificent collection of Canaletto paintings. The park was also magnificent, with seven lakes and several herds of rare deer.

The day after we had arrived at the Abbey, we were driven back to Bletchley Park in an old army transport bus. From the Mansion we were escorted past a tennis court and some hideous low concrete buildings — we later learned that the buildings were bomb-proof. At the entrance to Block F, another grim concrete building, we were met by

Mr Newman, who introduced himself and welcomed us. We were taken into a long, low room with a large blackboard and long tables. Mr Newman took his position in front of the blackboard. He had a very pleasant manner and put us at our ease. He told us that this section had only quite recently been set up and that we would be working with mathematicians and engineers. He said he had specifically asked for Wrens to staff the section, run the machines, and organise the Registry Office.

For a fortnight we went in every day and he lectured us on a new type of binary maths which he would write up on the blackboard. We were shown the tapes that were used on the machines. We learned the teleprinter alphabet and we had to become adept at reading tapes. We were taken round the section and shown what everyone was doing. We saw the room where the messages came in on teleprinter tape on two separate machines. Most of the messages came from Knockholt. The section had two Colossi at that time: I was overawed by them, a mass of switches, valves, and whirring tape. I thought they were incredible — quite fantastic. We were shown into a long room where tapes were cut and joined, and tapes that had split on the machines were repaired. Then we went to the Registry itself, or 'Ops' as it was called, where all tapes were registered and tabulated and put into a series of cubby holes.

At the end of the fortnight we were tested on our knowledge, and depending on how well we performed were selected for various tasks — administration, dealing with the tapes as they came in, and so forth. I was delighted to be chosen to operate Colossus, which I considered the plum job!

Ireland and her Wren companions were the first members of a new profession—computer operator. Du Boisson arrived at the Newmanry in the pre-Colossus days. She was set to work on the first Newmanry Tunny and then on Heath Robinson, before eventually moving to Colossus. Du Boisson writes:

My first job was Tunny operator. Tunny was an upright machine with panels of plug holes, which we plugged up in accordance with the settings received from 'Heath Robinson' (as we dubbed it). Tunny had a tape reader, into which the message tape was threaded. Tunny was plugged up just like an old fashioned telephone exchange — it used to give me electric shocks as I put in the plugs.

At that time there were only four of us on watch, so we had to be versatile. I learned how to operate Heath Robinson — a large machine with numerous wooden wheels. After we got a result with Heath Robinson, the message tape went into the Tunny machine. Despite the best efforts of the engineers, Heath Robinson was always breaking down and had to be patched up. It was difficult getting the tapes out of the machine without doing too much damage to them. Sometimes spinning tapes would break and fly all over the place.

Eventually Colossus appeared. We were told the valves gave off the heat of over 100 electric fires. If we got too hot or sleepy we went out for a splash from the static water tank (for use in the event of enemy action or fire). Someone suggested that we went topless, but we did not take up the offer.

We operated Colossus under the direction of a cryptographer. He told the operator what settings were required and monitored the results. After a while, a formula was developed so that the operator could do it herself, releasing a cryptographer for more important work. Despite this, we never really knew what we were doing — we just did as we were told. If we could not get the required result, we went to the Duty Officer for further instructions.

There were some messages that we could not break however hard we tried. There was great jubilation when we broke one particularly important link. To celebrate, someone decorated the room with daffodils.

The first of each month was hectic, since this was when the wheel patterns changed. The new patterns were often broken before the day watch came on. If they were still unbroken by lunch time, we got a bit worried.

When more WRNS were posted to the Newmanry, I came off the machines and went into the Ops Room as a registrar, where I was responsible for logging the tapes in and out and distributing them to the machines. Two of us worked in the Ops Room. We kept a register in which we recorded the date and the identity of each tape, and we logged the time that the tape went onto and came off Colossus, and likewise for Tunny. We knew exactly where every tape was, and how much machine time had been spent on it.

We had soon learned to unwind tapes into a bucket — otherwise they went all over the floor and it was easy to tread on them. Each tape that was to go onto Robinson or Colossus had to be joined into a loop. It was difficult to get the join right, and if we didn't the tape might not stand up to the speed of the machine. After many experiments, we found that special glue, a warm clamp, and French chalk produced a good joint — the art was using just the right amount of glue. Then the tape went onto a shelf to await a machine.

Ireland was also a Colossus operator:

I was taught how to operate the machine by another Wren. She explained what all the switches were for, and showed me how to peg a wheel pattern on the grid at the back of the machine with pins that looked like very large, very strong hairpins, copper-nickel plated.

The tape was shut into position in front of the photoelectric reader, which had a small gate for the tape to slide through. The operator used as many pulley-wheels as were necessary to make the tape completely taut. This was a tricky operation, getting the tape to the right tension. It took a little time and had to be done with great care. We were terrified of the tape breaking should the tension be wrong. Breaks meant that valuable time was lost. (I can remember that when I was given a new Wren to instruct, I was worried about leaving her alone for very long, and would hurry back from meal-break to make sure nothing awful had happened.) All the jobs we put on the machine were timed. They generally took about one hour to run. Every single tape was logged on and off in a book — the time we received the tape and the time it was taken off the machine. It was instilled into us that time was of the very essence. We knew we were working against the clock and that people's lives depended on what we were doing.

We worked in four watches. Watches A and C interchanged and so did B and D. I was on C watch. We worked 8 a.m. to 4 p.m., 4 p.m. to 12 p.m., and 12 p.m. to 8 a.m. A week of days, a week of evenings, a week of nights, and a week of 'changeovers' during which we filled in any gaps in A watch. The changeover week could be very tiring — off at 8 a.m. and on again at 4 p.m., for instance. We had one weekend off every month and an occasional additional weekend.

Another big block was put up to house two more Colossi. I was sent to work on Colossus III which stood in an enormous room with Colossus IV. I operated Colossus III alone under the direction of a cryptographer. He would sit at a long table facing Colossus. Others such as Jack Good and Donald Michie would come in to discuss what was going on and to make suggestions. On the table in front of the cryptographer were sheets of symbols and he used a slide rule to make his calculations. He would tell me what he wanted from the machine. On the grid at the back of the machine I would pin up whatever pattern he was working on, and would put on the tape that he wished to run. At the front of the Colossus were switches and plugs. We could set switches to make letter counts. Sometimes I was given a norm and as each figure came up on the typewriter I did a calculation and wrote down against the figure how much above or below the norm it was. I became very good at mental arithmetic.

If anything went wrong with Colossus we would contact the maintenance team. The officer in charge of the team was an extraordinarily clever man, Harry Fensom. Another brilliant engineer working with us was Ken Myers, who after the war worked on the coordination of the London traffic lights. The magnificent work done by these engineers has had little or no recognition.

Engineer Gil Hayward remembers the Wrens curing a problem with the printer arrangements: 'The output from Colossus was recorded by an electric typewriter, which was mounted on a tubular metal stand some four feet high. The carriage return action of the machine was very vigorous and caused the whole assembly to move rapidly away from its correct position. The Wrens obtained a length of stout rope and, in true nautical fashion, moored the stand to Colossus.'

Caughey too began her work in the Newmanry as a Colossus operator, and later was transferred to the room where the intercepts came in by teleprinter from Knockholt:

When I arrived at the Newmanry I was taken into what they called the 'Rob' room. Apparently there had been Robinson machines there before, but I was introduced to Colossus. Colossus – what a sacred word – had to function 24 hours round the clock. I was given a tape with letters marking the start position. I found it a terrible strain to remember all the things that we were told to do. The tape had to be threaded round spools top and bottom. Next there were plugs to set in. (I now find it all hard to remember in any detail, after keeping the secret for so long – I tried to blot out of my mind everything that happened at BP, for fear that I might talk in my sleep or under an anaesthetic.) Often the machine broke down. The engineers worked next door across the passage and a phone call brought one immediately. They seemed like magicians.

Somehow it got around that I was good at Morse. I had learned it as a girl guide at the age of 11, and had amused myself trying to read the blinking lights from ships sending messages. I was promoted to a leading Wren and my pay went up to three pounds ten shillings a fortnight – I had received only 30 shillings a fortnight as an operator of Colossus. I was put in charge of Room 12, with one assistant. This small room contained two teleprinters and a telephone. 'Fish' was picked up by the high masts at Knockholt and transmitted directly to Room 12 by teleprinter. Each message was sent twice, once to each of my two teleprinters. The first five or six inches of each tape were in Morse code. The tapes had to be checked against each other to make sure there were no errors. Concentration was necessary, since if we made a single mistake then decoding would not work. We used to write the Morse in letters, roll the tapes, and take them up to the 'Rob' room (as the room where Colossus lived was still named). This work was a strain on the eyes, because at all times of day we worked under neon lighting. The windows were covered in an opaque mesh (I imagined for two reasons – nobody could look in and see what we were doing, and there would be no glass to break if we were bombed). I had to get spectacles while working in Room 12.

Mr Newman was greatly looked up to and we all recognised his brilliance. Yet he was remote. I doubt whether he knew any of our names. He always passed us with a preoccupied expression on his face. One day, waiting for the train to take me home on leave, I saw him on the platform. He was dressed in a shabby old Burberry raincoat and was carrying a dead hare by the hind legs. He appeared to be searching the platform for something so I went up to ask if I could help. He gave me a distressed look and said that he had lost his ticket. We searched together but were unsuccessful, and as my train came in I tried to cheer him by saying I was sure the guard would believe him. His reply was: 'Oh no, that is not my problem — until I find my ticket I cannot remember whether I am going to Oxford or Cambridge.'

As D-day approached our work increased in volume. In March 1944 a ban on travel outside a 20 mile radius was imposed on us, for reasons of security (with 80 days confinement to barracks for anyone who disregarded the ban). This meant that one could not get home for a weekend's rest. From about that time we were also no longer permitted to eat in the cafeteria, and were banished to a concrete block room with no windows where we ate horrid hashed-up meals out of containers. It had always been exciting for us to eat in the cafeteria, because we never knew whom we might see there — Anthony Eden, General Montgomery, Air Commodore Cunningham, Admiral Cunningham, Admiral Tovey. Psychologically this was a great help and made us realise that our work was vital. General Eisenhower was a frequent visitor just before D-day.

Living and working conditions were hard at first for the Newmanry Wrens. It was the same for the engineers, who were given temporary accommodation in the attic of a building used by the codebreakers. The attic was cold and very damp—Harry Fensom remembers 'having to put newspapers on the bed to keep warm'. Ken Myers recalls that one night the terrible damp drove them to chop up some wooden shelves with an axe and start a fire. Caughey describes the plight of the Wrens:

We suffered from exhaustion and malnutrition. The Wrens at Quarters gave us very poor food. I shared one of the servants' poky little rooms under the roof with three others. It was freezing cold, with dreary brown wallpaper and an unstained floor. The unaccustomedly large number of residents was too much for the plumbing and all water was contaminated.

One reason things were so bad was because those in charge at Woburn Abbey had no idea of what we were doing. They made us do an hour's squad-drill on the gravel in front of the Abbey every morning. Worse still, different watches were mixed up in the cabins. Comings and goings disturbed those trying to sleep. This was torment. Night duty was particularly hard for most of us. It took three or four nights for our eating and sleeping patterns to adjust — then, just as we became settled, our duty would change again. We were all being killed by the constant changes of shift. Church Parade on a Sunday was compulsory. On my first Sunday, when I was on nights, I had to assemble with the others. We had to march two miles each way to the village church, along an icy road.

Some of us were fainting after squad-drill and our health was clearly deteriorating. Once this was noticed, there were some improvements in our living conditions. They sorted out our cabins. At last, after three months, we were given meals to match our watches – cornflakes and toast for our breakfast before going onto night duty, instead of the 6 p.m. dinner kept warm to be dished up at 10 p.m.! The soggy cabbage smelt like drains.

The Wrens knew little of Bletchley's successes. 'Occasionally they would pass on information,' says Caughey. 'I remember being told when the German battleship *Tirpitz* was sunk. We danced a jig in the corridor.'

'The biggest upset was Arnhem,' recalls Du Boisson. 'BP knew that the Germans were moving their troops, but did not get the details through in sufficient time for anything to be done about it, so we were told.' Du Boisson remembers that later in the war the authorities decided regular feedback would improve morale:

Towards the end of the war it was decided that once a month we would be given some information about what we had been doing. It was then we were told that every little detail in the messages was important. Every German officer had a card and each time his name appeared in a message, all the details were noted. Once, we were told, a senior German officer had sent a coded message asking for the luggage of his mistress to be forwarded. Our people were delighted to read it, since his regiment had not been heard of for several months.

THE NEWMANRY ENGINEERS

Newman, describing his section in a tape-recorded interview, drew the distinction between maintenance engineers and designing engineers: 'Then there were the engineers—and I am not speaking only of the engineers who looked after the machine, but the designing engineers who contributed very much to the design of all these machines.' Coombs, himself a designing engineer, described the nature of this contribution in another tape-recording: '[W]e used to go out regularly [to Bletchley Park, from Dollis Hill]. . . . We'd get an idea, or a complaint would come, "Look, we can't make this work, it's not right." We would suggest new modifications and new machines, and we built those . . . [A]ll sorts of off-shoots of Colossus were built, a lot of them due to our ideas as to extra things we could add—once we were well and truly in the work and not just plumbers doing the work for somebody else. . . . We were busy inventing new machines to do other bits of the job that the mathematicians hadn't thought of asking for, because they hadn't thought they would be possible. Once we had cottoned on to the mathematical side, and knowing the technical side as well, we were able to say, "Well, look, we can do so-and-so, how about that?" We weren't supposed to know anything about the mathematical side of it to begin with, but Professor Newman used to laugh and say, "Well, you can't keep them out of it, can you?" '

The maintenance engineers were also supplied by Dollis Hill. They were recruited from the best available Post Office telephone engineers in the country—'[W]e went round pinching good people from all over the place, the best we could get,' said Coombs. The recruits worked first at Dollis Hill, or at Flowers' factory in Birmingham, building the equipment in order to become thoroughly familiar with it, and then they were sent to the Newmanry to take up their maintenance duties. Most were aged between 20 and 22. Month after month they worked gruelling shifts of 70 hours a week or more.

Engineer Norman Thurlow was recruited by Dollis Hill in June 1942 and was transferred to Bletchley Park as soon as his security clearance came through. His job was installing equipment for use against Enigma. Later he joined the newly formed Newmanry and was charged with keeping the Heath Robinson running. Thurlow went on to design 'Mrs Miles', a Newmanry machine for combining several tapes (see photograph 39). This had four tape-reading heads: at the time the newspapers were running stories about a Mrs Miles and her new-born quads.

Thurlow recollects:

The original Bombe room, Hut 11, which previously held five Bombes, was divided longitudinally to house the new experimental machine, Heath Robinson. The room was further divided, with the machine to the west and a large 'lead acid' battery, having 25 large glass cells, to the east. This battery powered the experimental machine and was probably intended to serve several other machines. Later machines, in Block F annex, all worked directly from the main electricity supply. (A separate room accommodated a stand-by petrol-driven generator for Colossus and the teleprinter machines in case the mains supply failed.)

The experimental machine consisted of two racks, each 6 feet high and 19 inches wide. Rack 1 contained mainly electrical components and rack 2 was equipped with wheels to carry two punched paper tapes. Optical tape readers used photo-cells to detect both the five digit teleprint code on each tape and also the sprocket holes in the centre of the tape (which synchronised operations). The same room also contained ancillary machines to punch tapes from a teleprinter keyboard and to copy tapes.

For several weeks the experimental machine was in continuous use, operated by Wrens working three eight-hour shifts. The number of tape rolls rapidly increased, presenting a storage problem. This was solved by means of a clothes line and plastic clips, produced by the Wrens. When new accommodation in Block F became available, the group moved to the Annex. The trial Robinson machine was returned to Dollis Hill and a new Robinson, eliminating some of the deficiencies, was installed in Block F.

The Colossus machines were well designed and well built – they gave little trouble. Although I remember Colossus II had a novel fault, producing random data distortion. Col. II was installed near a south facing window and it was noticed that data errors occurred as clouds interrupted the sunlight. The optical housing was redesigned to cure the trouble.

As the number of machines increased and the cryptanalysts extended their activities, it became apparent that more 'operator errors' were occurring. A team of Wrens was set up to act as 'First Aid' on reported faults, with the aim of assisting the machine operators before reporting faults to the watch engineers.

Tapes were the lifeblood of the section. Many Wrens were occupied with machines to punch, copy, and check tapes. Checking tapes, after copying, involved holding the two tapes together and observing each character in turn. Two holes coinciding would be completely transparent. If neither tape carried a hole then the position would appear opaque. In the event of a copying error, a hole would appear on one tape only. Fortuitously, the tapes were translucent, so the error was immediately apparent. A single added or missing character would make a tape useless. Expert operators could check at high speeds. One became electrically charged. Receiving a shock when next touching the keyboard, the operator complained that the machine was live. The engineer's log showed: 'machine OK, earthed operator'.

Ken Myers was involved in the construction of Colossus I at Dollis Hill and then moved to Bletchley Park early in 1944. His job was to install, commission, and maintain Colossi and other machines. Myers writes:

I would work an eight-hour maintenance shift, and then move on to a further shift of six hours or longer, installing and commissioning machines, and updating earlier machines. My 21st birthday was spent chasing a miscounting fault on one of the Colossi!

Early failures on the racks were mainly due to faulty valves and low insulation between heaters and cathodes. Sometimes this could be seen as a blue spark in the valve envelope, but often we had to resort to removing the valves one by one until the fault disappeared. Once the 'rogues' had been dealt with, valve failures were rare indeed. This was mainly because the machines, and therefore the valves, were never switched off, so failures due to thermal stresses were never a problem. Mechanical failures did occasionally occur, mainly on the uniselectors used to mark the wheel start positions, and on the 'chasers' used in producing visual

display. The 'printout' uniselector, which also got quite a
hammering, sometimes failed too.

Otherwise, Colossi gave us little trouble after commissioning.
Occasionally tapes were faulty (the sprocket holes indistinct),
and so were selenium light cells (used to convert the tape holes into
electrical pulses). I remember we used to rest the selenium cells in
darkness for a period, after which they recovered. (I believe these
cells were originally intended for use as proximity fuses in anti-
aircraft shells.)

The electric typewriters that were used to print out the results
on Colossus came from the USA — in the bomb bays of Flying Fortresses,
we were told. In order to provide an electrical printout, all the
typewriter keys had solenoids fitted under them. An electrical
pulse to the appropriate solenoid pulled the key down to print the
figure or letter. These typewriters gave us more trouble than our
electronics. So much so that we used to swap them over with spare ones
every few weeks in order to overhaul them.

Documentation for all our machines was minimal and mostly drawn
freehand. I remember early on in the Signalling Group at DH, when we
were wiring up panels for Colossus, one bright lad spent a tea break
converting his wiring schedule into a theoretical circuit, and
pronounced that it looked like part of a counter. Little did he know
how right he was.

We had two Tunny machines in the Newmanry. At two o'clock in the
morning, a Wren operator was prettying herself with a mirror before
going to the canteen for a meal. The Wrens made their handbag mirrors
out of highly polished metal plates purloined from the drawer fitted
to the front of GPO 300-type telephones. She propped the mirror on
top of a large transformer panel used to power the Tunny machine. It
slid down across two large brass terminals. There was a bright flash,
the mirror evaporated, and the lipstick shot across her throat. I
was working nearby on a Miles machine. The scream made me look up. I
thought she had cut her throat.

The official history of the Newmanry mentions a fire on 15 November
1944. Two Newmanry Tunny machines and several smaller machines were
damaged. Myers explains that the fire was caused by spilt benzene:

A black concoction made fluid by benzene was invented to join the two
ends of a tape to form a loop. The mixture was pasted on both tape ends
which were then put into something like a tape splicer. This
resulted in a tough, flexible joint capable of standing the stresses
produced as the tape passed over the pulleys at 30 miles per hour. The
benzene was stored in glass Winchester jars on racks in F Block
workshop, adjacent to the room containing the two Newmanry Tunny
machines. A benzene jar broke when it was knocked off the shelf and
the contents seeped under the door by the Tunny machines. There was a
flash. The pitchmastic floor caught fire and black smoke filled the

machine room. I and two other engineers were delighted to have a genuine reason to use the fire extinguishers. The local fire brigade had been summoned but were having difficulty getting past the security people at the gate. Afterwards a proper brick store for the benzene was quickly built.

THE END OF THE NEWMANRY

Caughey, on night shift in the Newmanry during the final hours of the war, witnessed the end of the wartime Tunny traffic:

On Tuesday 8 May 1945 the wireless said that the fighting would stop at one minute past midnight. At that exact time my teleprinters ceased. The European war was over. We were the first to know. Oh what rejoicing. We all took two days off. I went home. We got cheered and whistled at in the streets. Near my home the RAF sent off rockets. Aeroplanes did victory rolls. Churchill broadcast a marvellous speech, and the King too. Our leave was more or less unofficial and after two days I reported back for duty. Only twelve of us returned out of about twenty.

No more transmissions came over the teleprinters from Knockholt. All night duty ceased, but we had to turn up for the days and evenings. Then suddenly the section became very busy again, with material coming through from Knookholt. We were mystified, and naturally felt the work was pointless.

Things went to pieces at the Abbey. The food was even worse. We got no clean linen for several weeks. Then, on the 22nd of June, we were told we would be drafted to Gayhurst Manor, a beautiful Elizabethan house belonging to the Carlisle family (who were still living in part of it). Wrens working on Enigma had been quartered there. I was put into a room where Guy Fawkes had slept. Two hundred Wrens from Stanmore, another Wren Enigma depot, were moved to Woburn Abbey.

We were still driven to BP to do our watches. Then on the 13th of July we were told that we were redundant. It was an emotional moment when we handed in our security passes and once more signed the Official Secrets Act. That night a farewell dance was held for us in Bletchley town. The following morning we had a terrific send off at the railway station. Our duty officers were there, engineers, and other Wrens from BP. Our train carried us away from the 'Human Whipsnade' — the name given by the locals to Bletchley Park, after the well-known zoo. We arrived at Stanmore, where we were to be rehabilitated and re-drafted. My emotions were confused. I knew how privileged I had been. I was in fear of the secret that I must keep. But keep it I did. My great sadness is that my beloved husband died in 1975 without knowing what I did in the war.

Du Boisson recalls that 'we were told we might go out East to work on Japanese codes—but a few days later we were told it was all off.' About this time, she remembers, she 'was taken by Shaun Wylie to see a captured German Tunny machine in its lorry'. Then, unthinkably, orders came to smash the Colossi into fragments. 'Suddenly the Colossi were gone,' Du Boisson says, 'broken up on the orders of Churchill, we were told at the time. All that was left were the deep holes in the floor where the machines had stood.' Ireland helped break up the Colossi—'A sad job,' she recollects. 'Then we were made to sign the Official Secrets Act again.'

The Newmanry's Colossi might have passed into the public domain at the end of the fighting, to become, like the ENIAC, the electronic muscle of a scientific research facility. The Newmanry's brilliant engineers would quickly have adapted the equipment for peacetime applications (see Chapter 24). The history of the computer might have unfolded quite differently with such a momentous push right at the beginning. Perhaps we in the twenty-first century would be reaping benefits impossible now to specify. Churchill's order to break up the Colossi was an almighty blow in the face for science.

Most of the work of destroying the Colossi fell to the engineers who had devoted themselves to keeping them running. Myers remembers that (presumably under Newman's instructions) they 'sent some of the panels of the Colossi (counters, shift registers, etc.) to Manchester University for use in their early computer experiments—but not before all traces of the original use were removed, for example signwriting on keys, and jack labels such as CHI, PSI, MU1, MU2, DELTA.' It may have been a consolation, in those final days of the Newmanry, to think that parts of the Colossi might live on in another incarnation. Although, as things turned out, it is very unlikely that any hardware from the Newmanry found its way into the Manchester computer; Williams and Kilburn were supplied gratis with all the components they needed by Kilburn's employer, the Telecommunications Research Establishment (see Chapter 9).

Thurlow describes the last days of the Newmanry, recalling a prediction, made by the authorities in 1945, that is fulfilled by the publication of this book:

A large bonfire occurred in the courtyard of Block H to signal the end of the war. During the next few days, as operations rolled to a halt, dismantling of the Colossus machines began. Our instructions ruled that no element remaining should be sufficient to give any indication of its possible use (and also required that all the work should be carried out on site).

A thanksgiving meeting held at the front of the house covered the lawns with people from the various areas of the site, and gave an

```
indication of the large number employed. Staff evaporated back to
civilian duties. HMS Pembroke V with her smart WRNS crew sailed away
into the sunset. A final memo to staff reminded us of the continued
need for secrecy, but noted that many years in the future it might be
possible to tell our grandchildren of '... the tapes that span on
silver wheels ...'.
```

GCHQ AND THE SURVIVING COLOSSI

In April 1946, the British codebreaking headquarters was transferred from Bletchley Park to buildings in Eastcote in suburban London. At the time of the move, the old name of the organisation, 'Government Code and Cypher School', was formally changed to 'Government Communications Head-quarters' (GCHQ). Six years later another move commenced, and during 1952–4 GCHQ transferred its personnel and equipment, including its code-breaking machinery, away from the London area to a large site in Cheltenham.

Some machines did survive the dissolution of the Newmanry. Two Colossi made the move from Bletchley Park to Eastcote, and then eventually on to Cheltenham. They were accompanied by two of the replica Tunny machines manufactured at Dollis Hill. One of the Colossi, known as 'Colossus Blue' at GCHQ, was dismantled in 1959 after 14 years of post-war service. The remaining Colossus is believed to have stopped running in 1960.

During their later years the two Colossi were used extensively for training. Details of what they were used for prior to this remain classified. There is a hint of the importance of one new role for these Newmanry survivors in a letter written by Jack Good:

I heard that Churchill requested that all Colossi be destroyed after the war, but GCHQ decided to keep at least one of them. I know of that one because I used it myself. That was the first time it was used after the war. I used it for a purpose for which NSA [National Security Agency, the US counterpart of GCHQ] were planning to build a new special-purpose machine. When I showed that the job could be carried out on Colossus, NSA decided not to go ahead with their plan. That presumably is one reason I am still held in high regard in NSA. Golde told me that one of his friends who visits NSA told Golde that I am 'regarded as God' there.

After Bletchley's own spectacular successes against the German machines, GCHQ was—not unnaturally—reluctant to use key-generating cipher machines to protect British high-grade diplomatic traffic. More attractive was the idea of using *one-time pad*. This involves issuing both sender and receiver with identical key (e.g. in the form of a roll of teleprinter tape). The sender uses the key to encipher a message (e.g. by adding the key to the message Tunny-style) and then disposes of the one-time-only tape. The recipient deciphers the message by means of an identical copy of the key (which is then destroyed).

The advantage of one-time pad is that the code is unbreakable, provided the key is well made. Even if the enemy is able to acquire the key used for a number of messages, this should not assist the enemy codebreakers with the rest of the traffic, since each serving of key is unrelated to all the other servings (assuming that the key is well made). The *disadvantage* of one-time pad is that a complex and highly efficient distribution network is required to supply users with key. GCHQ decided to bite the bullet: the security offered by one-time made it worth tackling the problem of distribution. (Although it is probably true to say that those who proposed the use of one-time underestimated the difficulties involved in distribution.)

The next issue was how to make the key. The weakness of Tunny key, of course, was that it was far from devoid of pattern—a reflection of the mechanical regularities that underlay its production. Absolutely patternless key was the cryptographers' ideal. That way no matter how many characters of key might fall into enemy hands, there could be no method of using these to predict further characters of key.

Employing some of Flowers' circuitry from Colossus, ex-Newmanry engineers developed a random noise generator that could produce random teleprinter characters on a punched tape. This device, codenamed 'Donald Duck', exploited the random way in which electrons are emitted from a hot cathode. The tapes churned out by Donald Duck were the desired one-time pad. Copies were made (by Newmanry-type machines) and the tapes were distributed to GCHQ's clients.

There was an additional step. Not all the tapes produced by means of a random generator will be completely patternless. To take an extreme example, there is no reason why the generator, even though entirely random in operation, should not produce a tape consisting entirely of A's—just as a long run of tosses of a fair coin might all come up heads. The tapes produced by Donald Duck had to be vetted, and any that exhibited pattern were discarded. A Colossus was used in this vetting procedure, making counts of the characters on the tape in order to detect any pattern.

Probably the Colossi had additional post-war applications. They could have been used to make character counts of enemy cipher traffic, searching for features that might give GCHQ's cryptanalysts a purchase (see Table 1 of Chapter 17, which shows character counts for Tunny traffic). Perhaps the GCHQ Colossi were even used against reconditioned German Tunny machines. Many Tunnies were captured by the invading armies during the last stages of the war. If the national interest so dictated, Tunny machines may have been sold to commercial organisations or foreign powers, and the resulting traffic read by GCHQ.

To complete this fascinating final chapter of the story of Colossus, historians must wait for the declassification of the relevant post-war documents. Who can say whether this will happen while the grandchildren of the men and women who built and first operated the Colossi are alive.

Chapter 14

Max Newman—Mathematician, Codebreaker, and Computer Pioneer

William Newman

PROLOGUE

Like many British children in my age group I can pinpoint my first memory of my father to the particular day when he and I were reunited after being separated since my infancy. It happened in October 1943, at Poole Docks on the south coast of England. My mother Lyn, my older brother Edward, and I had spent three years as evacuees to the United States, and after a lengthy and hazardous journey by ship and flying boat had arrived back, exhausted. I remember a crowd of people on the dockside, from which a thin, bald, agitated man emerged and strode up to us saying, 'Oh, there you are!' This was my father, Max Newman.

While I retain a clear image of that meeting, I was to discover almost nothing of what my father was doing at the time until many years later. I was placed in the same position as others in codebreakers' families. During the war I knew of Bletchley only as the place where my father went to work. After the war ended I came to know it more as a railway station where we changed trains in order to travel between Cambridge and the North. Then a silver tankard appeared in our house, resplendent with the inscription: 'To MHAN from the Newmanry, 1943–45'. After much pestering from me to know what this was about, my mother took me aside and whispered conspiratorially in my ear, 'Codes . . . but you must never tell anyone!' My father, although one of the most discreet of men, must have trusted my mother enough to tell her this much, and she must have trusted me.

By the time the first account of Colossus and the Newmanry was published my father was nearing his eighties, and the habit of keeping quiet about these events was as ingrained in him as eating, sleeping, and solving crossword puzzles. Furthermore the authorities would allow him to mention only certain aspects of the Colossus work. He was obviously pleased to be free at last to talk about his war work, but he did so hesitantly, choosing his words carefully and sometimes describing things only by oblique reference. Few of us close to him chose to push him to tell us the wartime stories that he had kept from us for so long. Perhaps we felt there was plenty of time, and perhaps he hoped that the authorities would ease their restrictions. But at the age of 85 he began to suffer from Alzheimer's Syndrome, and he died two years later having told little about his exploits and experiences at Bletchley Park.

PRE-WAR

My paternal grandfather, Herman Neumann, was born in 1864 in the German town of Bromberg, now Bydgoszcz, Poland. The third son of Jacob Neumann and his wife Betty, Herman emigrated to London at the age of 15 with his parents and six brothers and sisters. There he trained as a bookkeeper, and in 1896 he married Sarah Pike, a gifted 26-year-old schoolteacher whose family hailed from Somerset. Maxwell, their only child, was born on 7 February 1897 in Chelsea. A few years later little Max and his parents moved to the south London suburb of Dulwich. Sarah found a teaching position at the nearby Goodrich Road school, where she taught until her retirement in 1935. After war broke out in 1914 Herman was interned by the British, and on his release he left Sarah and returned to Germany, where he died in 1926. In 1916 both Sarah and Max changed their names to Newman by deed poll.

Max attended school at Goodrich Road and then at the City of London School. He excelled in classics and mathematics, played chess well, and also became an accomplished piano player. Opting for mathematics, he won a scholarship to St John's College, Cambridge, and began his studies there in 1915. The First World War soon intervened, and he took up a teaching post at Archbishop Holgate's School in York, followed by service in the Army Pay Corps and a further spell of teaching at Chigwell School. He returned to Cambridge in October 1919 and graduated two years later. Max then worked towards a Fellowship of St John's, which he achieved in 1923. In his dissertation he was already writing about the use of 'symbolic machines' in making physics predictions, and thus turning his mind towards the roles of machines in mathematics.

For the next twenty years, Max was to channel much of his energy and intellectual power into establishing himself as a mathematician, and in particular as a world expert in modern topology. This was a field that few in Britain had tackled before him, but for Max it typified the kind of challenge he constantly sought. His plan of attack was to build on the work of pioneers in the field, taking short, simple steps that led him gradually towards solving the major topological problems. Between 1926 and 1942 he published over twenty papers and generated theories that have remained important to topologists ever since. He taught his first course of topology lectures in 1925, and was appointed a lecturer in 1927. In 1939 his classic book *Elements of the Topology of Plane Sets of Points* was published; it was to remain continuously in print for the next sixty years.

By the 1930s Max was helping postgraduate students rise to maturity; one of them was Alan Turing. As Andrew Hodges has told, Alan attended Max's foundations course in the spring of 1935, in which Max lectured on Gödel's theorem and on related questions of provability. At one point he posed his class a question: could the provability of mathematical statements be discovered by a mechanical process? This question lodged in Alan's mind, and gradually he developed the paper that was to make his reputation in the mathematical world, and later in computer science: 'On Computable Numbers, with an Application to the *Entscheidungsproblem*'. Painfully shy, Alan delayed speaking about his endeavours until the spring of 1936, when he gave Max the draft typescript.

Max's first sight of Alan's masterpiece must have been a breathtaking experience, and from this day forth Alan became one of Max's principal protegés. There was an immediate threat to the publication of Alan's work, because in Princeton a competing proof had just been produced by Alonzo Church. Max canvassed vigorously to gain support for Alan's paper, writing to F. P. White (a fellow Johnian) to argue for its publication in the *Proceedings of the London Mathematical Society*, which White edited. On the same day Max wrote to Church himself, asking if he could help arrange for Alan to visit Princeton. Both of these initiatives bore fruit, with Alan departing in September 1936 for Princeton, and his paper (incorporating changes suggested by Max) appearing in that year's *Proceedings*.

As he established himself in Cambridge, Max built up a circle of long-lasting Cambridge friends. Foremost among these were Patrick Blackett and his wife Pat. A towering intellect like Max, Patrick would achieve renown as a leading physicist and a consummate power-broker in academic and government circles. Other close friends included topologist and collaborator Henry Whitehead and his pianist wife Barbara, and the distinguished geneticist Lionel Penrose and his wife Margaret.

Max also made friends with Lyn Irvine, a young writer and daughter of a presbyterian minister in Aberdeen. She was working in London as a book reviewer for Leonard Woolf, husband of Virginia and co-founder of the Hogarth Press. Like Max, Lyn had studied at Cambridge, and it was their mutual friend Ceceley Creasy who introduced them at a Cambridge party in 1932, with the veiled warning, 'Max is our local solipsist!' Max and Lyn were married in 1934, with Patrick Blackett as best man. In 1935 they moved into Cross Farm, a converted farmhouse with an adjoining dovehouse, situated at the village crossroads of Comberton, five miles from Cambridge. Their first son Edward was born later that year.

In September 1937 the family sailed to Princeton, where Max had been invited to work for six months. In a letter to her parents Lyn described his idyllic life:

Max has no job here. He simply sits at home doing anything he likes. That is what the Institute of Advanced Studies [sic] exists for. They know Mathematicians can be trusted to like doing Mathematics better than anything else. He has taken a little rest from his book and is doing some pet problem at the moment. He goes to a couple of seminars in the week and has tea most days with his brother Mathematicians at the Institute.

The 'pet problem' to which Lyn referred was to lead to a pivotal event in Max's career, for it was the Poincaré conjecture, a celebrated theorem in topology that had resisted all attempts on it for the past thirty years. Max worked on it steadily while in Princeton, and believed he had found a proof. In his final weeks in America he presented the proof in a five-hour talk, spread over four days, to the assembled Princeton professors—including almost certainly such renowned mathematicians as Weyl, Gödel, Lefschetz, and von Neumann. None could see a flaw in it. When Max returned to Cambridge in April 1938, he faced the happy prospect of joining the Cambridge immortals and securing both his prosperity and his place in mathematical history.

It was not to be, however, for in July Max found a fatal flaw in his proof. It was four days before he could bring himself to tell Lyn. She too was devastated. Early the next morning she awoke, remembering that something dreadful had happened the previous day, but unable in her drowsiness to recall what it was. At first she thought the infant Edward must have died. When she realised that Max's proof had failed, it seemed even worse.

At 41 Max had many years of mathematics ahead of him, but he had passed the stage in his life when mathematicians usually make their greatest research contributions. His long-term strategy of stalking the big problems by taking small steps had brought him great success, including the award in 1939 of a Fellowship of the Royal Society. But his one attempt at taking a very big step—the Poincaré conjecture—had failed. With war looming, the future must have appeared to him, and to Lyn, to be clouding over.

WARTIME

Max and his family were to face many upheavals during the Second World War. The first was under way even before the declaration of war on 3 September 1939. Lyn now found herself with two young children of part-Jewish descent (for I had been born in May of that year) in a country going to war with a virulently anti-semitic German regime. The solution, adopted by many parents in this situation, was to seek refuge in America. Lyn, Edward, and I sailed for New York on the *Western Prince*, leaving Liverpool on 31 July 1940. Our tickets were paid for out of a wartime refugee fund established by Lionel Penrose.

Alone now in Cambridge, Max continued his teaching and research, but gradually became disillusioned with Cambridge life as his colleagues left to join the war effort. His first thought was to seek work in America so that he could join his family and support them more easily; at this time he probably thought his German background would rule out war work. Strenuous efforts were made by his Princeton friends Lefschetz and Weyl to secure him a fellowship. However, the scheme was strongly opposed by topologist Oswald Veblen, professor at the Princeton Institute for Advanced Study. Veblen believed, according to Lyn, 'that every able-bodied man ought to be carrying a gun or a hand-grenade and fight for his country'. So Max stayed in England, and was eventually to vindicate Veblen.

In the spring of 1942 Max began to consider war work seriously. It was Patrick Blackett who started the ball rolling for Max, writing in May to recommend him to the Director of Naval Intelligence:

The man I mentioned to you is M. H. A. Newman, FRS, of St John's College, Cambridge. He is about 45, and was born in England, his father being German and his mother English. He is one of the most intelligent people I know, being a first-class pure mathematician, an able philosopher, a good chess player and musician. He has also had a considerable amount of University and College administrative experience. Do you think you could use him in any way?

A few days later F. E. Adcock, who had been involved in codebreaking since the First World War, wrote to Max: 'Dear Newman, There is some work going at a government institution which would I think interest you and which is certainly important for the War . . .' Max must have written back expressing interest coupled with concern about his German parentage, for he shortly received a letter from another celebrated cryptographer, Nigel de Grey (who had decrypted the Zimmermann telegram in 1917). De Grey could not reassure Max about his eligibility, but was keen for him to meet 'one of our Principals' during the week of 8 June.

Max's continuing worries about his family background must have led him to contact Blackett again and inquire whether there might be other opportunities for war work, should his background prove a problem. 'I rang up a friend in the Ministry of Reconstruction, but gather the organisation is rather at a low ebb,' Blackett responded. 'I was advised that the Ministry of Works might be more suitable for you, as it has more relation to Architecture, etc. . . . Let me know what you would like me to do.' In the same letter Blackett reminded Max of the possible job at 'B.' doing work that would be 'very important'. In July Max received the long-awaited confirmation from Bletchley Park that his German ancestry would not be a bar to employment, together with an offer of an appointment as a Temporary Senior Assistant.

Max nevertheless continued to vacillate and to seek Blackett's advice. Would there be a job big enough to keep him interested? How would it compare with his current existence? What about the living conditions? Blackett wrote back after attending a meeting at Bletchley in which Max had been discussed 'at considerable length'. He strongly advised Max to accept the Bletchley Park offer, described the work as preferable to university life in every way, and, while admitting that the locality was 'a bit dim', commended the Bletchley Park atmosphere.

Meanwhile a small tussle appears to have broken out between two Bletchley Park groups competing for Max's services: Colonel John Tiltman's group, working on Tunny, and F. L. ('Peter') Lucas' Enigma intelligence section. Choosing his words carefully, Lucas wrote to Max:

I gather from Blackett that you are thinking of coming here; and he asks me to write you a word on the subject. I need not say how glad I should be to have anyone of your standing. The work is hard but, to me, fascinating. It is, in my section, a matter not of specialised gifts, but of general intelligence and quick thinking. I don't at all want to minimise the drawbacks. It is essential you should choose with open eyes. So I repeat that the work leaves one at times pretty exhausted and that, in the overcrowding of the area, you may not find a comfortable billet. On the other hand I myself can think of few things I would sooner be doing.

A week later Max wrote to Dr Benians, the Master of St John's, to say he wished to accept the position at Bletchley Park and to ask for leave of absence. This granted, he was able to decide in favour of Tiltman's offer and to agree a starting date of 31 August 1942. Max arrived at Bletchley Park to find Tiltman's group engrossed in the problem of Tunny.

Max was initially assigned to the Research Section, joining Tutte and others working on Tunny. Part of his work involved decrypting messages by the existing slow hand methods, which were somewhat akin to solving crossword puzzles. Max found the company congenial, but the work frustrated him at times and left him feeling ineffectual. He even thought of returning to Cambridge. It was around this time, however, that Max made his first breakthrough—the idea of mechanising Tutte's method using high-speed electronic counters. He took his proposal to the Bletchley Park management. The whole scheme must have seemed hopelessly overambitious at the time, but Max won his superiors round, and in December 1942 was put in charge of developing an experimental machine (later to be dubbed 'Heath Robinson'). Shortly afterwards the head of Bletchley Park, E. W. Travis, confirmed Max's appointment to lead research on special codebreaking machinery.

Max must have faced stern challenges from the very outset. He appears to have overcome them by drawing to the full on his Cambridge experiences, supplementing them with a combination of ingenuity, perseverance, and intellectual firepower. The organisation he set up, the Newmanry, certainly bore all the hallmarks of the collegiate community he had just left. It was egalitarian to a degree unusual even for Bletchley Park. Most people were on first-name terms, despite Max's insistence that he and his cryptanalysts be addressed as 'Mr' by the other staff while on duty. When the Newmanry moved onto three-shift working its team spirit could have suffered, so Max instituted a system of log-books in which staff could suggest topics for discussion at 'tea parties', meetings open to all staff. Indeed the esprit de corps was such that people would work extra hard to avoid handing on a backlog, and sometimes stayed on at work after their shift was over.

For Max the intellectual challenge was as great as for the more junior cryptanalysts, for they were all groping their way into the domain of research that became known years later as computer science. They were learning, as future computer scientists did, how to solve problems through a combination of analysis and practical experiments. Max was at his best when drawing on his analytical intuitions, although if he was asked for an instant reaction he could become defensive, brushing aside the proposal until he had had time to consider it thoroughly. Once he had fully taken in the situation, however, he would become fully engaged, bringing to bear his unique combination of critical analysis, intellectual leaps, wit, turn of phrase, and—where dangers lurked—reticence. Max's intellectual stance, frustrating though it must at times have been for others, undoubtedly helped him to maintain his relentless drive towards the Newmanry's spectacular breakthroughs.

The workload was unremittingly heavy, as Peter Lucas had warned. In 1943 Max was at the Newmanry from 9 a.m. to midnight for weeks on end. He and his small team, under great pressure to deliver results, grappled constantly with Heath Robinson's complexity, unreliability, and lack of speed. Max might typically be found listening to the machine's relays and estimating a job's running time by counting each eighth pulse; or when a new routine showed promise he might try it out at once, marching off with a colleague to stop the 'run' in progress and test the new method. He was in regular discussions with Flowers about improvements to Heath Robinson, and was starting to report to Travis on Flowers' 'more ambitious machine' which promised to set fifty messages a day—Colossus. He made visits to Knockholt to investigate sources of inaccuracies and methods for reducing them. All of this took its toll on him—a letter to Lyn in July told of a bad throat, pink eye, and toothache, but no time to go to the dentist. In August Lyn wrote to a friend that Max 'after a week's holiday only said he felt ready for another week.' The lack of jokes in his letters worried her particularly, for Max usually managed to find something humorous in describing the most dire situations.

It was with great relief, mixed with some trepidation, that Lyn was able to return with us to England from the United States in the autumn of 1943. From the summer of 1942 her letters to Max had constantly raised the matter of returning, and her letters to her parents chronicled Max's series of reasons for putting it off. By the spring of 1943, however, there were clear signs that the Allies were winning the Battle of the Atlantic, and Max agreed to booking us berths homeward on the SS *Nyassa*, sailing to Lisbon. We endured a long wait in Portugal for a flight to England, during which time Edward came down with dysentery. It was several weeks before we could complete our journey and meet Max at Poole docks.

We moved into a small house in Gawcott Fields, on the outskirts of Buckingham and about twenty miles from Bletchley. I began to adapt to the novelty of having a father around. With him my reading lessons were a novel experience: he would help me through the printed words, 'This Man is Ill, He Must Take a Pill,' and then add his own sequel, 'The Pill Will Kill Him,' laughing wickedly. I got used to his quick and often unexpected actions: a shake of his newspaper, like a terrier with its prey, or a sudden deafening sneeze. A car came by in the morning to take him to work, and in the evening to bring him home. My mother would spend the day searching for ingredients for his evening meal, washing and ironing him a clean shirt, and snatching a few moments with Edward and me. Occasionally we experienced the dramas of war, such as a fighter plane crashing and burning in a nearby field. In May 1944 we were able to leave the isolation of Gawcott Fields and return to Cross Farm.

Max spent the last twelve months of the war billeted at the Duncombe Arms, a small hotel in the village of Great Brickhill near Bletchley. Every week or so he came home for two nights, travelling by train to our local station and bicycling the last two miles. I was rarely up late enough to see him arrive, but I remember the rush and bustle in the mornings when Max left for the station. Once in the confusion he left without any money. He was saved by the station-master, who (and I can still hear my delighted mother telling the story) '*gave* him his ticket and *lent* him a pound!' I began—I was only five— to gain an impression of the people my father worked with, including the frequently mentioned Wrens, whose name inevitably suggested small bird-like people, and whose welfare was of obvious concern to my father. Often in the final flurry of activity before his departure for Bletchley he would say, 'Oh, the Wrens!' and my mother would quickly find him a cake or other treat for them.

The nature of Max's worked changed in January 1944 with the arrival of Colossus, for his direct involvement in the technical work became less essential. He spent more of his time in his office with the door shut, alone or with his assistant John Herivel (of Enigma's 'Herivel Tip' fame). The Wrens assumed Max was still engaged in codebreaking work, unravelling the last vestiges of a decrypt after they had done their best with it. In fact he was in constant negotiation to obtain the necessary staff—over 300 by the war's end—to operate the growing complement of Colossus machines. In November 1943, the Testery had come up with proposals of their own for a 'cribbing machine' to reduce their reliance on hand methods; Max had had to argue diplomatically against its construction. By March 1944 he was drawing up a detailed argument for more staff, showing how the Newmanry's output would otherwise be restricted. For all this he gained the respect of his colleague Ralph Tester, who was later to sum up Max as 'a genial colleague, but he knew what he wanted, in material or human resources, and he usually got it.'

Max left lasting impressions on many at Bletchley Park. To some he could come across as a detached, slightly remote person, absent-minded at times, but with an intellectual quickness and impatience that could be intimidating. His patience was sometimes tried beyond its limits. For example, he had an intolerance for 'horseplay' between Wrens and young engineers, and lost his temper over this more than once. But many experienced and appreciated a warmth in him, and a quiet wit that could break the ice. There was joy to be had in people's achievements and in their misfortunes, as far as Max was concerned. He revelled in battles of wits, their cut and thrust, and, whenever possible, their comic elements. By dwelling on the humour in his stories he was able to downplay and often hide entirely his own part in them. One family anecdote came from a pre-war Cambridge philosophical meeting at which Ludwig Wittgenstein was roused to declare, 'Max, you should have been drowned at birth,' but of course Max never told us what he had said to provoke this, though it possibly demolished an argument of Wittgenstein's. He would tell these anecdotes with infectious enjoyment. There was an absent-minded Cambridge don who worked surrounded by piles of books, among which Max had once found an ancient lamb cutlet on a plate, and a Yorkshire-born engineer at Bletchley Park called Higginbottom who told Max about another engineer with 'sich a funny nyme—*Ramsbottom*'.

POST-WAR

In the final months of the war, with an Allied victory inevitable, Max and his Bletchley Park colleagues began to make plans for the future. Some wanted nothing better than to return to the academic departments they had left, while others decided to make new careers in cryptography, offered to them by the British government. Max was content with neither, however. His sights had been set on 'something big' even before joining Bletchley Park, and he was now seeking a further challenge to follow his success in setting up and managing the Newmanry. He had begun to perceive exciting applications in mathematics for electronic computing machines. He wanted an opportunity to pursue two goals in parallel, building up a first-class team of mathematicians and mounting a mathematics-led effort to explore computing. But there was little prospect of achieving either of these at Cambridge, where the mathematics faculty remained resistant to the kinds of innovations Max had in mind, and where computing was already in the hands of a separate department, the Mathematical Laboratory, headed by Wilkes. Where would he find the opportunity he was seeking?

Early in 1945 Patrick Blackett, who had been appointed head of Manchester University's physics department in 1937, began to make strong overtures to Max to join him there as head of mathematics. There were good prospects of funding for research into computers at Manchester. Around him in the Newmanry were just the sort of people—mathematicians with computing experience—that Max would need to build a first-class research team. Things began to fall rapidly and smoothly into place. Max took up his new post in Manchester in the autumn of 1945, and we moved to a house in Bowdon, Cheshire, in January 1946.

It was in December 1946 that Max learned he had been put forward to receive the Order of the British Empire in the 1947 New Year's Honours. At this time he was in Princeton, where Johnny von Neumann was now working on computing machines. Alan Turing had been awarded the OBE six months earlier, and now it was Max's turn. But Max had been incensed by such inadequate recognition of Alan's huge contribution to winning the war, and he turned the offer down. As he wrote later, 'I was, in fact, also offered an OBE but declined it. I am not sure now whether this was the best thing to do, but I had heard a little earlier of the ludicrous treatment of Turing and felt impelled to do something.'

For Max the first few years at Manchester were a period of exciting developments. They saw the mathematics department, under his leadership, make its initial steps towards achieving world-class status. Max continued to rely on strategies that had worked well for him in the past. He took great care in recruiting staff of the highest calibre. He applied equal care to planning his campaigns for resources, and he created the same kind of Cambridge-style collegiate atmosphere that he had brought with him to Bletchley Park. Some key appointments were made in stages: when he found the right person to fill a professorship, he appointed them as a senior lecturer or reader for a couple of years and then, if all was well, promoted them. At the committee meetings where promotions were approved, Max could get his way through his careful preparation and through the trust he established with committee members. It became known that if Max said that his candidate was of high standing, there was no need to question him.

Among the initial post-war intake of staff at Manchester were David Rees and Jack Good, both ex-Newmanry; Alan Turing was to join later. Meanwhile Max had secured in July 1946 a grant of £35,000 from the Royal Society to fund computer research, and had most likely had a hand in the appointment of F. C. Williams to the chair of Electrical Engineering. Although an enthusiastic champion of the computer work, Max took relatively little part in the actual design of the machine that was to become the Manchester 'Baby' computer (see photograph 44). His main contributions were an algorithm for computing prime numbers, and participation in the design of the 'B-tube', essentially an index register and one of the machine's most significant features. But Williams gave Max and Alan credit for the 'running start' they were able to make (see Chapter 9).

It was a considerable coup when in 1948 Max persuaded Alan Turing to leave the National Physical Laboratory and take up a readership in the department; and Alan now became a close family friend of ours. Despite his shyness he seemed to me more approachable than the other mathematicians who visited us. His choice of presents on my birthdays was especially thoughtful and generous: a splendid steam engine one year, a little hobbyist's toolkit another. He played games with me and Edward, and lost ignominiously to us at Monopoly. He came with us on a brief spring holiday in Criccieth, North Wales, where we rented a house. There were lively discussions in our sea-front living room between him, my father, Bertrand Russell, Rupert Crawshay-Williams, and others. I also remember Alan running on the beach, disappearing into the far distance and coming racing back. When he later bought a house in Wilmslow he would sometimes run the dozen or so miles from there to our house in Bowdon. Once I heard a noise in the early hours of the morning and went to the front door to find Alan dressed in running gear. He wanted to invite us to dinner and, thinking us all asleep but having nothing on which to write, was posting through our letter box an invitation scratched on a rhododendron leaf with a stick.

In the summer of 1949 the Manchester computing work became headline news, sparked off by a lecture by Professor Geoffrey Jefferson but then fuelled by some typically unguarded remarks of Alan's reported in *The Times*:

I do not see why [the computer] should not enter any one of the fields normally covered by the human intellect, and eventually compete on equal terms. I do not think you can even draw the line about sonnets, though the comparison is perhaps a little bit unfair because a sonnet written by a machine will be better appreciated by another machine.

Max, who fielded numerous telephone calls from reporters, wrote a clarifying letter to *The Times* describing the more mundane computing work on checking Mersenne prime numbers.

Max had hoped that mathematicians would play a major role in computing. At Manchester, however, it was the design and construction of the computer's general-purpose stored-program hardware that took priority. Meanwhile Max gradually withdrew from the computing activity. He would explain this later by saying that 'the engineers took over', but it seems likely that his decision was influenced by his opposition to using the Manchester computer in the development of nuclear weapons.

Max instead returned to his old love, topology, and devoted himself to building up the mathematics department into one of high renown. He hired others who had worked with him at Bletchley Park, including Peter Hilton and Sandy and Margaret Green. A stream of mathematician visitors passed through Manchester, many of them staying at our house. One that I remember particularly well was the cyberneticist Norbert Wiener. He sat in our garden, falling asleep in the June sun and waking up at intervals to say 'Excuse my snoring' in his sonorous voice, before falling asleep again. He walked around the house with our tiny kitten on his shoulder licking his large bald head.

Max remained at the helm of the Manchester department until 1964. Even then he was still active in research, taking it with him wherever he went. During a 1960 family holiday in Scotland he sat almost every day working on a paper that was to surprise many for its quality and topicality. Indeed Max seemed rarely if ever to let his mind rest. When he was not doing mathematics he was quite likely to be solving *The Times* crossword puzzle in his head or playing a Bach four-part fugue. He continued to enjoy running his department, even though the exciting formative period was over—'suspended animation' was how he now described his job to Lyn. His eventual retirement was accompanied by many tributes and much celebration of his achievement. As usual Max enjoyed the humour of the event as much as the accolades. He had insisted for many years that the corridor floors in his department should not be polished, because he feared slipping and falling; when he went back the day after his official retirement to retrieve some papers, he was greatly amused to find a cleaner already laying down a thick layer of polish.

Lyn died in May 1973. With the death in 1972 of Lionel Penrose, Max had lost one of his oldest friends. Margaret Penrose and Max, both thus bereft of their partners, married in November 1973. Until his cruel final illness struck in 1982 Max was, I believe, as happy as he had been for many years. His mathematical days were over, but other less taxing pursuits had come to take their place. His wartime exploits were at last being made public (thanks largely to the determination of Brian Randell) and could be placed alongside the many other achievements of his long, distinguished career.

Chapter 15

Living with Fish: Breaking Tunny in the Newmanry and the Testery

Peter Hilton

ACTION THIS DAY

I should begin by explaining how I happened to find myself, on 12 January 1942, at the age of 18, awaiting permission to enter the gates of Bletchley Park, to undertake work, on behalf of the British Foreign Office, of whose nature I had essentially no knowledge. In October 1941, four very distinguished members of the Bletchley Park team (Alan Turing, Hugh Alexander, Stuart Milner-Barry, and Gordon Welchman) had written a letter to Churchill, drawing his attention to the importance of the work being done at BP on deciphering Enigma, and, therefore, the urgency of recruiting appropriately trained people (principally mathematicians), and of making funds available for building more of the high-speed Bombes needed to expedite the decoding process. Churchill, to his great credit, did not react like a bureaucrat appalled that the writers of the letter had not gone through the proper channels; he immediately saw the importance and good sense of the letter and minuted it 'Action this day' to his chief of staff, General Ismay. The result was the empanelling of an interviewing team which toured the universities looking for mathematicians with a knowledge of modern European languages. Such people, however, were not easy to find, since the British higher education system of the time, based as it was on the principle of premature specialisation, virtually guaranteed that no such people would exist. (Ironically there were many German Jewish refugee mathematicians in Britain at that time, but they were 'enemy aliens' and so not to be trusted!) The team came to Oxford and I was, I believe, the only person presenting himself for interview. I was not a mathematician, merely a second-year undergraduate specialising in mathematics, and my knowledge of German was very rudimentary, acquired by self-study. But the interviewing team snapped me up, and offered me a position in the Foreign Office, to carry out certain entirely unspecified duties, provided I was willing to start in January 1942. I suspect the interviewing team did not themselves know the nature of the work I would be doing. I, of course, knew nothing of the background to the setting up of the interviewing team. How then was I to decide whether to accept the offer?

I was at the time undergoing training in the Royal Artillery. Under wartime conditions in Britain, undergraduates had to enrol in officer cadet training units to prepare themselves for subsequent military service. I had enrolled in the artillery training unit, naively supposing this would familiarise me with modern technological warfare. But I had discovered ruefully that the Royal Artillery had certainly not been modernised recently, nor had its favoured methods of instruction. To give one example, we were being instructed by Sergeant Major Cope in the use of the 'director', a device to determine the angle of elevation of the target, which had undoubtedly been state-of-the-art at the time of the Crimean War. The War Office manual was quite explicit: one took six readings of the angle of elevation, computed the average by a fixed algorithm, and communicated the average to the guns. The enemy, presumably, had been indulging meanwhile in some warm-up exercises like community singing, waiting for the real action to begin. I took six readings of the angle of elevation of the nearby church steeple, getting $22°11'$, $22°9'$, $22°11'$, . . ., and to get the average proceeded as any intelligent person would do, guessing $22°10'$ and adding up the corrections. I recall getting a sum of zero, so I could announce that the average was $22°10'$. Sergeant Major Cope came round and asked me where I had calculated the average. 'Actually sir,' I replied, 'it is not always necessary to add the six readings in order to compute the average.' ' 'Ilton,' Cope shouted, 'I've 'ad trouble with you before. When I come round next I want to see those six readings added up and divided by 6.' So, with nerves of steel, I added 22 to itself six times and divided the resulting sum by 6. Miraculously, 22 re-emerged from the process. When Cope came round again, he said, 'Well, 'Ilton, did you get the same answer?' 'Yes sir.' 'There you are, you see, the book's right.'

Experiences like this convinced me I would not be happy in the Royal Artillery, and so, despite the fact that I would lose six lovely months at Oxford (my age group was scheduled for conscription in the summer of 1942), and despite my ignorance of the nature of the work, I did not long hesitate to accept the Foreign Office offer—one of the best decisions I have ever taken— and so presented myself on that cold January morning in 1942. As it transpired, I was to work on deciphering German Naval Enigma messages in Hut 8. Then I started working on Fish in late 1942, in the Research Section. Many of those who worked on Fish worked earlier on the Air or Naval

Enigma, moving across as Fish took over many channels from the Enigma machines.

I will be writing of the 'steady-state' period which lasted (with very minor and temporary changes) from mid-1943 until the end of the European war. The two sections devoted to the deciphering of Fish, the Newmanry and the Testery, had been formed, and were working together with steady success on the decryption of the high-grade German ciphers. In Chapter 18 Jerry Roberts describes the work on Fish prior to the steady state.

THE PROBLEM

By early 1943, the German *Geheimschreiber* (secret writer) machine—which we irreverently called 'Fish' and which I will call Fish throughout this chapter—was not only in regular, but in heavy use for the encryption of military and diplomatic signals. I understand that today the official name for the *Geheimschreiber* is the Lorenz machine, but that is a name I heard for the first time more than 50 years after the war, and I shall not use it in this chapter.

During the build-up to the steady-state period, many changes were made in the enemy procedure, all designed to make the traffic more secure. In the steady state, the Germans were changing wheel patterns daily (but fortunately they started by changing them monthly). Our tasks were twofold: on a daily basis we had to determine the patterns on the 12 wheels (wheel-breaking), and then we had to determine the starting position of each of the 12 wheels for each message transmitted on that particular day (wheel-setting).

Our attack on the problem was partly statistical, partly linguistic. By taking advantage of certain statistical biases in the German military language, we were able to determine, with some degree of certainty, the starting positions of the chi-wheels for a given message, assuming that the wheel patterns were already known. Thus, for example, the Germans imposed a rule on the wheel patterns of the *extended* psi-wheels (i.e. the psi-wheels as they were extended by the 'staggering' due to the action of the motor-wheels—see Chapter 3). This rule said that, on each extended psi-wheel, a *change* (from 0 to 1 or 1 to 0) should be as frequent as a non-change (00 or 11). They saw this as a randomising device; but we could exploit it, since it had the consequence that certain statistical features of the clear text (or plaintext) were reflected, albeit imperfectly, in the cipher, enabling us to set the chi-wheels with very high probability of correctness.

As previously explained, this part of the job was done in the Newmanry, with the essential assistance of the Colossi. (Alan Turing contributed to the thinking in developing these machines, as did Max Newman and several others, but an enormous part of the credit for designing Colossus, and all the credit for building it, goes to Tommy Flowers. Jack Good pointed out that in a 1998 article I exaggerated Turing's role in the designing of Colossus. I am happy to have this opportunity to do full justice to the contribution of Flowers.) Once a given message was 'de-chied', as we called it, it would be sent over from the Newmanry to the Testery for the setting of the psi-wheels and the motor-wheels. Typically this would be achieved by running a conjectured segment of 'clear'—that is, a 'crib'—through the de-chi to detect a stretch of extended psi-wheels. Knowing the patterns of the (unextended) psi-wheels and having available a significant segment of the extended psi-wheels, the setting of the motor-wheels, whose patterns we also assume known, was a fairly routine and rapid process.

The process of determining the wheel patterns themselves was, usually, a matter of battening on procedural errors committed by the German operators and thereby obtaining long stretches of key. I will describe a typical exploitation of a procedural error in the next section. However they were obtained, it was from such long stretches of key that the wheel patterns were inferred. This part of the process, which was done by hand, was typically carried out in the Testery, but, both in principle and in fact, it could be performed in the Newmanry. Although we carried out the process by hand, a procedure was developed in theory, and put to practical test at the end of the war, whereby Colossus could be used for the entire decoding process. But this procedure was never adopted in real time.

USE OF DEPTHS

Following an initial period—very valuable to us—when the initial positions of the wheels were indicated by letter labels, the Germans adopted a more sophisticated approach. Each operator was provided with a QEP book—a form of 'one-time pad', sheets of paper on which were printed sequences of 12 numbers indicating the starting positions of the 12 wheels. The German operator, preparing to transmit a message, would set the wheels of his machine in the positions indicated by the next unused sequence of numbers. Of course, the receiving operator would have to set his machine to the same starting position, so that (as explained in Chapter 3) he could receive in clear the message being transmitted in encrypted form.

However, it happened, remarkably frequently, that the transmitting operator forgot to move on to a new set of 12 numbers after setting the wheels of his machine. The result was that he would start to transmit a second message using exactly the same key as for the earlier message. Very likely the process would not get very far, as the receiving operator—who had faithfully moved on to the next starting sequence—would find himself receiving absolute gibberish. However, it might be some time before the error was corrected; for the receiver, apparently, did not always pay full attention to the early part of the message being received; and, in any case, if the receiver simply intervened to tell the transmitter something was wrong—*Wiederholen Sie bitte* (please repeat)—*his* enciphered message would not be understood by the transmitter for the same reason. The resulting confusion would be monitored by our signals people who were intercepting the German transmissions, and they would tell us that it seemed highly likely that a certain pair of messages constituted a depth (i.e. two messages enciphered on the same key). Astonishingly, there were even examples of more than two messages enciphered on the same key; I am at a loss to provide a plausible scenario for so gross an error.

When we in the Testery received word that two messages probably were enciphered on the same key—and the signals people were rarely wrong—we went to work. Our method was as follows. There are two messages: in the first, the machine added the key K to the clear, Cl_1, to produce the cipher, Ci_1; and, in the second, the machine added the *same* key K to the clear, Cl_2, to produce the cipher, Ci_2. Symbolically, we have

$$Cl_1 + K = Ci_1$$
$$Cl_2 + K = Ci_2$$

Let us add these two equations. Since addition and subtraction are the same, the key drops out! We obtain

$$Cl_1 + Cl_2 = Ci_1 + Ci_2$$

Thus, if we add the two messages (i.e. the two ciphers) we obtain the sum of the two clears. The job is then to separate the sum of the two clears into the two individual clears. Let me illustrate with an example. Suppose

Ci_1 contains ... T E P Q I T R A 9 D D P C Z X ...
Ci_2 contains ... B K I + S A K S B C D A C H Q ...

(The six extra symbols of the teleprinter alphabet were designated 9, 8, +, 3, 4, /. The numeral 9 was the space between words, 8 denoted letter shift (the shift from numbers to letters), and + denoted figure shift (the shift from letters to numbers).)

So, we have

$$Cl_1 + Cl_2 = Ci_1 + Ci_2$$
$$= \ldots D\ C\ T\ N\ A\ W\ S\ I\ X\ U\ /\ Y\ /\ S\ R \ldots$$

We succeed in analysing this stretch of 15 letters into the two constituent clears:

$$Cl_{1(2)} = \ldots C\ H\ E\ F\ 9\ D\ E\ S\ 9\ H\ E\ E\ R\ E\ S \ldots$$
$$Cl_{2(1)} = \ldots U\ G\ Z\ E\ U\ G\ 9\ A\ B\ W\ E\ H\ R\ 9\ K \ldots$$

We recognise the final letter K in the second clear as the beginning of 'KANONE', since *Flugzeug Abwehr Kanone* means 'anti-aircraft gun'. This enables us to extend the first clear correspondingly. Similarly, we can go back in the second clear with '9FL', thus extending the first clear backwards, too. In this way we extended our 'break-in' in both directions. Perhaps we have other break-ins which can be linked up. I confess I enormously enjoyed this particular activity, which called for the exercise of all sorts of intellectual arts as well as familiarity with German military language.

One difficulty was that, since $Cl_1 + Cl_2 = Cl_2 + Cl_1$, we do not know which of the clears is Cl_1 and which Cl_2. (It is for this reason that we earlier labelled the two clears $Cl_{1(2)}$ and $Cl_{2(1)}$.) There may be external evidence to indicate which is which; for example, if one of the messages is a weather report, it can probably be identified by the time at which it was transmitted. However, this ambiguity only means there are two candidates for the key, namely, $Ci_1 + Cl_{1(2)}$ and $Ci_1 + Cl_{2(1)}$. So two of us would start the process of analysing the key, either to obtain wheel patterns or simply the starting positions of the wheels. In a short time one of us would be triumphant, the other frustrated!

It is impossible to exaggerate the importance of such procedural errors as depths in tipping the balance in our favour. Ultimately I believe that it was Nazi arrogance and Nazi propaganda to their own people about the master race which led them to believe their machine was unbreakable and, hence, to pay totally inadequate attention to the requirements of secure procedures.

THE DAY'S WORK

Some of us, in both the Newmanry and the Testery, enjoyed 'joint appointments', thus spending much time in each. Among those officially in the Testery, Donald Michie and I were especially privileged to have many opportunities to work with the Newmanry team; and we interacted especially closely with Shaun Wylie, Jack Good, and David Rees in the Newmanry. Life, for Donald and myself, was as interesting as it could possibly be.

The day was divided into three shifts—the night shift, the day shift, and the afternoon shift. The night shift was remarkably popular. This was partly because one could then better get on with the job free of bureaucratic interruption. But also the first task of the day, determining the day's wheel patterns, typically fell to the night shift in the Testery (where we would usually have a sufficient length of key to do the job, obtained from a depth or from some reliable crib). Then the Newmanry, armed with the wheel patterns, would go into action, using the Colossus machines to set the chi-wheels for the individual messages of the day. The de-chi of a given message would be rushed back to the Testery, where hand methods were used to set the psi-wheels and motor-wheels (methods described by Peter Edgerley in Chapter 21). Once this was done, the message disappeared from our view; presumably, somewhere, a full decryption was produced and made available to the appropriate intelligence people.

Once the wheels were set, the cryptanalyst's job was done for that message. The process of obtaining the clear was from then on purely mechanical. Thus we never knew more than a few short stretches of the actual text of a message—the decoders never saw a complete decode! (This was in keeping with the paramount principle of the authorities that nobody should ever know more than was absolutely necessary for doing the job. The fallacy in the operation of this principle was, of course, that it was the authorities, and not those doing the job, who determined what was necessary!) Most people might suppose that, since we were the codebreakers, we must have seen the clear text of every message we deciphered, and must thus have been privy to a huge amount of fascinating secret information about enemy movements and dispositions. In fact, we commonly saw no more than some 30 consecutive characters of any given message that we 'decoded', and this stretch of decrypt might be, in fact was likely to be, a very routine part of the message whose presence in the text we had been able to anticipate.

The German operator would typically start his transmission by sending a sentence or phrase by hand. He would presumably await an indication from the receiver that he was receiving the message clearly and would then switch over to automatic transmission. This opening material fabricated by the operator we called 'Quatsch'—and the Quatsch was often very stereotyped and predictable. Sometimes, though, it had a strong human element. I recall *'Ich bin so einsam'* (I am so lonely) from an operator on the Leningrad front, and *'Mörderische Hitze'* (Murderous heat) from an operator on the Italian front. It was one of the serious mistakes committed by German Intelligence that they seemed to believe we would be uninterested in material transmitted that we expected to have no intelligence content—yet another example of the procedural errors to which an overconfident authority, fed on ridiculous propaganda of racial superiority, was prone. In fact, of course, such material contained a high proportion of predictable text, and predictable text was just what we needed for our work in the Testery. One particularly egregious error committed frequently by the German operator was to mark the end of the Quatsch and the beginning of the message proper by a sequence of, say, ten '+' symbols (go into figure shift), followed by ten 'Z' symbols (spacers), followed by ten '8' symbols (go into letter shift). Those 30 letters of text had absolutely no content, but their presence in the message, at a recognisable place, was invaluable to us. Thus it could even happen that the text used to set the psi-wheels and motor-wheels—the only stretch of decrypt usually seen by the codebreaker—was almost literal nonsense.

We were not always current in our work. Decoding the day's transmissions was, of course, the top priority, but there were always tasks left over from previous days, to which we reverted if there were no more of the day's 'catch' to be treated. This was true, too, in the Newmanry, where there were always recalcitrant messages which had, for some reason or another, so far failed to yield to our attempts.

In respect of both the machine- and hand-methods that we used to carry out the decryption, one of our problems was the possibly imperfect nature of the original text presented to us by the signals people. These people were wonderful at their job; but sometimes conditions—say, weather conditions—were so bad that many characters of the messages were misread or even completely lost. The signals people were extraordinarily good at determining just how many characters had been lost; but, of course, they were not infallible, and a single error in the determination could be devastating to our prospects of decoding such a message.

We enjoyed each other's successes; and would often temporarily drop our own task to help a colleague who was in difficulty. There was, among us, a real camaraderie. My memories of those days are entirely unclouded by any recollection of dispute or bad spirit; there must, I suppose, have been some, but, if so, I was never involved. For this happy atmosphere, we had much to thank Max Newman and Ralph Tester, and the constant awareness, on our part, of the potential importance of the work we were doing.

I have good reason to believe that the general demeanour of our group—a numerically insignificant number of individuals among the thousands employed at BP—was quite different from that of most people working there. We were a group of '*je m'en foutiste* intellectuals' (intellectuals who couldn't give a damn), as the American cryptanalyst Alfred Friendly described us, meaning that we acknowledged only the discipline we imposed on ourselves. I have heard and read such epithets as 'dull', 'gloomy', and 'dreary' used to describe life at BP, by people I never even came across during my three and a half years there. These descriptions are the antithesis of those I would use to describe my life at BP and the lives of my friends and colleagues in the Newmanry and the Testery.

Max Newman introduced into the Newmanry a kind of variant of 'sabbatical leave'. Despite the urgency of our work, Max would systematically release two members of his team to do 'research' for a fortnight, to think about how to improve our methods and procedures. (Such leave was not compulsory, however.) This is just one among many examples of Max's superb understanding of how to be an effective administrator. He remains unique in my experience (I write after more than fifty years in academia) as the model of the supreme facilitator, introducing those arrangements and procedures, and only those arrangements and procedures, which enabled the members of his team to do their jobs to the very best of their ability. He never imposed on us a chore which could only be justified on bureaucratic grounds. It was no surprise to me that when he went, after the war, to Manchester University to be the Fielden Professor of Mathematics, he built up a superb department (my only surprise was that in 1948 I was invited to join this talented group).

TURING: A VISITOR TO FISH

Alan Turing played a unique and absolutely essential role in the breaking of high-grade German ciphers—and thus in winning the war. He was not formally a member of the Newmanry or the Testery, but his work and his ideas made our work possible, and even when not himself present, he remained an inspiration.

Alan Turing was a genius. For a person of such extraordinary brilliance, he was remarkably willing to share his ideas with those genuinely interested in understanding them. Moreover, he was an unusually versatile genius, whose ideas ranged very widely. I was fortunate to know him from the time of my arrival at BP in January 1942 until his tragic death on 7 June 1954. We were colleagues not only at BP, but during my first four years on the faculty of the mathematics department in the University of Manchester. He was a warm, friendly human being, with a very good sense of humour. Even in the straitened circumstances in which he found himself following his trial and conviction, in 1952, for a homosexual act carried out with a willing adult partner in private, he retained his enormous zest for life and for the free exchange of ideas. Turing was bound over, having given an undertaking not to repeat the offence. This verdict meant that there was no official penalty, but he was thereby branded a felon, losing his security clearance and becoming unable to obtain a visa to travel to the United States.

It is not my purpose to describe the details of Turing's contributions to the winning of the war, but to relate two incidents in his life at Bletchley Park which illustrate both his original approach to problems of any kind and his quirky and infectious sense of humour. When the danger of an invasion of the UK by German paratroops seemed a really serious one, Turing volunteered for the Local Defence Volunteers, popularly known as the Home Guard, in order to become an expert at firing a rifle and hitting his target. In order to be enrolled, it was, of course, necessary to complete a massive form full of irrelevant questions. As all those experienced in government bureaucracy know, when completing such forms the only essentials are to give one's name, to sign and date the form, and to answer every question. The answers themselves don't matter, because they are never likely to be read. One of the questions was: 'Do you understand that, by enrolling in His Majesty's Local Defence Volunteers, you render yourself liable for military discipline?' Turing, who always reasoned from first principles, argued as follows: 'I can imagine no set of circumstances under which it would be to my advantage to answer this question yes.' So he answered it no. He was duly enrolled and soon became a first-class shot—he usually did very well the things that he set himself to do. But then the danger of invasion receded. Turing found attending parades increasingly tedious, so he stopped going, and started receiving nasty notes of increasing irritability. These culminated in a summons to his court-martial, presided over by Colonel Fillingham, Officer Commanding the Buckinghamshire Division of His Majesty's Local Defence Volunteers.

'Is it true, Private Turing, that you have attended none of the last eight parades?'

'Yes, sir.'

'Do you realise this is a very serious offence?'

'No, sir.'

'Private Turing, are you trying to make a fool out of me?'

'No, sir, but if you look up my application for admission to the Home Guard, you will see that I do not understand I am subject to military discipline.'

The form was produced, Colonel Fillingham read it, and became apoplectic. All he could say was, 'You were improperly enrolled. Get out of my sight!'

Turing would rather suddenly develop a tremendous passion for some form of activity, or some study, and wish to devote a lot of his time and energy to it. On my first encounter with him at Bletchley Park he was obviously very much fascinated by chess problems. At BP he developed a real delight in playing tennis, and especially enjoyed playing doubles. He was very good up at the net, where his speed and good eye enabled him to make many effective interceptions. However, he was dissatisfied with his success rate: too often he intercepted a return from an opponent, but sent the ball into the net. Applying his remarkable thinking processes to a mundane problem, he reasoned as follows: 'The problem is that, when intercepting, one has very little time to plan one's stroke. The time available is a function of the tautness of the strings of my racquet. Therefore I must loosen the strings.' And, being Alan Turing, he then carried out the necessary alterations to his racquet himself. At this point my recollection may be coloured by the great distance in time, but I seem to recall Turing turning up for his next game with a racquet somewhat resembling a fishing net. He was absolutely devastating, catching the ball in his racquet and delivering it wherever he chose—but plainly in two distinct operations and, therefore, illegally. He was soon persuaded to revert to a more orthodox racquet!

OUR LEISURE ACTIVITIES

What about the daily lives of the members of our group—how did we spend our leisure time, what were our living arrangements? In the nature of things, there could not be a great deal of organised leisure activity. The three-shift system militated against our availability, and even when our evenings were officially free, it could well happen that we would, in fact, be working. I recall some impressive amateur theatrical productions, but these were rare events. There was tennis and (if my memory is not misleading me) squash. There were visits to the pub, but these depended on the very uncertain availability of beer during the war. There were discussions on matters of concern to all thinking people at that time—political, economic, educational, philosophical. A series of informal seminars was arranged by Testery member Peter Benenson, later founder of Amnesty International. These discussions were always lively and never rancorous, though attended by people of fundamentally different political viewpoints. One detected no trace of '*je m'en foutisme*' in our exchanges of opinion!

Much chess was played while we were off duty. We had some of the finest players in the United Kingdom in our group—Hugh Alexander, then the British chess champion, Harry Golombek, who was for many years chess correspondent of the London *Times*, J. M. Aitken, Scottish chess champion, Jack Good, Mac Chamberlain, Tony Perkins, and many others. Once a match was arranged with a team representing Oxford University. I recall vividly how puzzled our opponents were as to just what chess club they were playing against.

HOUSING ARRANGEMENTS: LIVING WITH MRS BUTLER

Among the many advantages which our group of cryptanalysts had over the female service personnel—mostly Wrens, but also ATS (Women's Army)—was the fact that, while the women had to live communally in assigned accommodation, we were free to find our own billets, and to move, according to our choice, from billet to billet.

Finding a billet was not so easy, however. Few of us had a car, and there was a substantial element of luck involved in the process. Searching for accommodation I presented myself at a small semi-detached house in the village of Fenny Stratford to interview the householder, Mrs Butler. It was clear that Mrs Butler was a sweet, kind lady who was, moreover, seriously in need of the money which renting a room would bring. She was a widow and her husband had been a train-driver. But he was very right-wing and had refused to join the union, so that when, tragically, he was killed in an accident, she did not receive a union pension. All this I learned in the first few minutes of our conversation. Mrs Butler showed me a framed photograph of her late husband, gripping the back of a chair, and said, ' 'E was only railway, but 'e was me 'usband.' I decided quickly that life with Mrs Butler had possibilities, and, indeed, I remained with her for my entire stay at BP. There were usually three of us in Mrs Butler's house. The other two were very close friends of mine; with one I had to share a bedroom.

It soon became evident that Mrs Butler was a modern Mrs Malaprop. I took to sharing the best Butleriana with my friends at work, and soon they came to expect their regular dose of malapropisms. (In fact, I had taken on more than I had bargained for: some of my friends were moved to intelligence outposts throughout the world—Cairo, Washington, Rome—and I was expected also to keep them supplied regularly with Mrs Butler's *bons mots*.) On one occasion, after she had been reading an article in her favourite newspaper, the *News of the World*, suggesting that the Pope had not done all that he might to save the lives of European Jews, I said that we should be careful about criticising when we did not know all the facts. Mrs Butler replied, 'I'm sorry, Peter, but I don't reckon much to the Pope—that there Vatican, 'im and 'is cardigans. I don't reckon much to that lot.'

Once the *News of the World* contained a long front-page article announcing that the Allies, advancing up Italy, had come across some diaries implicating Mussolini with Clara Petacci (in fact his mistress).

Mrs Butler started reading the article and said, 'Well, Peter, who'd 'ave thought there were two people called Mussolini?'

'What makes you think there are two, Mrs Butler?' I asked.

'Well, there must be,' she replied, 'because there's another one 'ere 'aving a love affair.'

'No, Mrs Butler,' I said, 'I think this is a front-page sensation just because it's the Mussolini you know.'

'Oh, it can't be 'im—'e's the head of a big Fascite State.'

'He's only human, Mrs Butler,' I replied.

'Well, I'll read some more and see,' she said.

There then began the frequently enacted pantomime of her search for her spectacles. On this occasion she located them, mysteriously, in the potato dish; and, in my mind's eye, I can clearly see her putting them on and clearing the lenses by rubbing them with her thumbs. She then came across references to Rome, Italy, and the 'Palaze Veneze' and said, 'Well, you're quite right what you say, Peter. Well, I never—and 'im a big Fascite, too.'

Then she read out: 'Clarita was a very passionate woman and used to pay nightly visits to eleven deuce.' The newspaper was, of course, referring to *Il Duce*, Mussolini.

'Are you sure it's eleven deuce, Mrs Butler?' I asked.

'Well, I don't know,' she answered. 'It might be two deuce.'

SECRECY

Have I painted too rosy a picture of our life and work at BP? Do I have no criticism of any kind of the arrangements made for us to do our work on the codes? I do have some criticisms of the rules under which we functioned at BP. They are all concerned with the application of the principle of total secrecy.

Nobody denies the necessity of maintaining secrecy about the work of the codebreakers during the actual course of the war, but it is difficult to understand, let alone justify, the blanket embargo on all mention of our activities for years after the end of the war. It is also difficult to justify the failure to reward the people who did so much to help to win the war. I have especially in mind Tommy Flowers, who had to endure so many years in which his pioneering work designing and building Colossus went unrecognised, and who had to listen in silence as others got the credit for creating the electronic computer. It cannot have helped his frame of mind or relieved his bitter taste to know that Churchill had given instructions at the end of the war to destroy most of the Colossi.

There is a different aspect of the secrecy issue that is, in some ways, even more oppressive, and which militates against the efficiency of those working under its weight. This is the tendency of the bureaucrats who control the freedoms of the people doing the real work to try to compartmentalise the activities of those in their charge. Thus we, the cryptanalysts, were not allowed to know anything of what went on outside our own sections, and presumably those concerned with the intelligence context of the messages we decoded were not allowed to know anything of the methods, or problems, involved in deciphering those messages. (I must write 'presumably' because, of course, I was not allowed to know if the intelligence people were told anything of our methods, but I am not paranoid, and do not assume that the cryptanalysts alone were especially distrusted!) One obvious respect in which this isolation of each individual unit in the intelligence chain is disadvantageous is that it stopped us from warning our own codemakers of the specific dangers of faulty procedures; another aspect is that we lost the opportunity to profit from the experience of those deciphering Japanese codes, and vice versa. It was especially galling to me that the issue of the impact of the impenetrable security blanket could never be discussed—we were simply given the rules by which we had to abide.

This aspect of our work—or, rather, of the ambience in which our work was done—has left a lasting impression on me. I have often, in the past fifty years, had to advise students as to whether to take up positions involving codemaking or codebreaking, either in government departments or in industry. I have always warned the student of the effects of the security aspects of the work. One accepts the restrictions that security considerations impose on one's freedom when one is helping to fight a war. But these restrictions are irksome and very unnatural under normal conditions. To do that sort of job well one must become involved in the work and be excited by it. But then one would naturally want to talk about one's work to family, friends, colleagues— and this one may not do. One's conversation must be carefully self-censored to ensure one does not inadvertently give something away. Moreover, to establish one's reputation and enhance one's mobility one must publish one's original ideas and results, and this one may not do.

DIASPORA

None of the cryptanalysts in the Newmanry and the Testery wanted to stay on after the end of the war. It was all too obvious that the freedom we had enjoyed to create optimal conditions for doing our difficult and demanding job would not survive into peacetime, even if we would have wanted to do that kind of work when our nation was at peace. As 1945 wore on, it became increasingly clear that the war was coming to an end, and, as they prepared for working under the less exigent peacetime conditions, so the bureaucrats became increasingly intolerant of the unorthodox behaviour of the '*je m'en foutiste*' cryptanalysts. So it was that, early in the spring of 1945, a memorandum was sent by the BP administrators to all heads of sections announcing that the habits of certain members of staff of arriving at, and departing from, their offices at arbitrary times would have to cease. (Of course, this is a grotesque description of our practice—we would stay for very long hours, perhaps more than 24 hours even, if there was a real crisis, but we might also leave early if the difficult work was done and only routine tasks remained.) Heads of sections were told to report, in specific detail, on the habits of each member of their staff, thus: 'Mr X arrived in his office at nine a.m. (0900) and departed at five thirty p.m. (1730).' Mr Foss, in peacetime a curator at the British Museum, who knew he would very soon be returning to his peacetime duties, replied as follows: 'Mr Foss thanks Mr . . . very much for his memorandum and is pleased to inform him that he will provide no (0) such information.'

Chapter 16

From Hut 8 to the Newmanry

Irving John (Jack) Good

I ARRIVE AT BP

During the Second World War the Germans used two kinds of high-grade cryptographic system: Enigma, and what we called 'Fish'. There were two forms of Fish. The official name for one was the *Schlüsselzusatz* (cipher attachment) SZ40 and 42, made by Lorenz, and which we called 'Tunny'. The other was the Siemens T52, which we called 'Sturgeon'. I worked on Enigma and on Tunny.

After the outbreak of war I had to wait more than a year before I obtained suitable war work. My personality is not that of an officer and a gentleman, rather that of a philosopher and a mathematician, so I was not expected to join the army, other than, later on, the Home Guard. (On my first day in the Home Guard I was taught how to throw a hand grenade, although in years of compulsory cricket I was never taught how to bowl!) Eventually I was interviewed by the twice British chess champion Hugh Alexander, and the Cambridge mathematician Gordon Welchman. I knew Alexander in the chess world. I had another job offer which, unknown to me, would probably have involved work on radar. I chose Bletchley Park which I thought would be somewhat romantic.

A few weeks before I joined Bletchley Park, when I was playing in a chess match where the chess master Stuart Milner-Barry, later knighted, was playing, probably on the top board, I was tactless enough to ask him whether he was working on German ciphers. He replied, 'No, my address is Room 47, Foreign Office.' Shortly thereafter, when I joined BP, he was there, sure enough working on German ciphers! At first the official address at Bletchley Park was indeed Room 47, Foreign Office, Whitehall, London, but soon it became permissible to give one's private Bletchley address.

I joined BP on 27 May 1941, the day the *Bismarck* was sunk, and was met at

Bletchley railway station by Hugh Alexander. As we walked across a field, on the way to the office, Hut 8, he told me the exciting news that we were just beginning to read the German naval cipher system (which used the Enigma). I shall never forget that sensational conversation. It was a breach of security to discuss such secrets outside the office, but being secretive was somewhat out of character for Alexander.

The main activity in Hut 8 was the analysis of the Naval Enigma. When I joined Hut 8, Alexander was the deputy head, while the head was the famous mathematician Alan Turing. I regarded myself as Turing's main statistical assistant. Hut 8 was divided into two sections, a linguistics section, headed by Shaun Wylie, and a somewhat mathematical section in another room. There was a large third room where young ladies, known as 'the girls', did routine clerical work. Turing used to refer jocularly to people who are forced to do mechanical operations as 'slaves'. There was a hatch connecting the two smaller rooms for rapid communication. Once, Alexander bounded towards the hatch, in some excitement, and banged his head badly at the top of the hatch, almost knocking himself out. He always worked with great energy and infectious enthusiasm.

My bosses during the war, Alexander, Turing, and later Newman, were also my friends. They were entirely non-bossy. Turing and Newman both had a dry mathematical wit. As an organiser and topologist, Newman once said, 'It's wonderful how many shapes the neck of a bottle can take.' Alexander's humour was more down to earth. For example, he once said, 'We'll have to wait, thumbing our twiddles.' Newman differed from Alexander in being an excellent father symbol rather than an excellent older-brother symbol, whereas Turing didn't like administration and left nearly all of it to Alexander.

In a discussion in 1941 Alexander said he could see no reason for fearing death—an example perhaps of what a member of Hut 8 called his 'frightening objectivity'. According to Alexander, ability in chess depends on the same qualities that lead to success in ordinary life and the 'will to win' is very important. Alexander was very observant. On one occasion, when he was making a remark about the document in front of him, he saw me start although I was standing behind his right shoulder. Perhaps his bulging eyes improved his peripheral vision! He once said that the worst fault an administrator can have is to be jealous of those who work for him. Alexander took a military IQ test (I think the matrix test) and scored at the level of a four-star general. Turing told me his own IQ was only at about the median of the undergraduate mathematics students at Cambridge. His logical thinking was profound but it wasn't fast—the IQ is a measure of speed of logical thinking more than of its depth. Turing was a poor chess player, presumably because he tried to work everything out in too much detail. (Turing and Alexander both had considerable athletic ability. Milner-Barry said of Alexander's table tennis, 'He was remarkably effective in an ugly and contorted style that enabled him to retrieve endlessly.' Turing might well have competed as a marathon runner in the Olympic Games, but he developed a neurological problem in a leg.)

Turing visited the US in 1942. Soon after his visit he put the following problem to me. Consider a barrel of gunpowder at all points in a plane having integer coordinates. We are given the probabilities that if one barrel blows up then adjacent barrels also blow up. What is the probability of the explosion diverging to infinity? In retrospect the problem reminds one of atomic energy. Turing had been a student at Princeton before the war and knew John von Neumann well. Von Neumann was one of the architects of the atomic bomb. What is the probability that Turing discussed atomic energy with von Neumann during his 1942 visit?

ENIGMA AND BANBURISMUS

The linguistics section of Hut 8 built up more and more knowledge about potential cribs (*mots probables*). It was a case of success leading to more success. In the mathematical section, during my time there, the emphasis was on a technique called 'Banburismus' because the stationery for it was printed in the town of Banbury. This was also the origin of Turing's names 'ban', 'deciban', and 'natural ban' as units for expressing weights of evidence which were called 'scores'. Turing invented Banburismus, which was an elaboration of a method called the 'clock method' by Rejewski, who attributes the method to Jerzy Różycki. The primary aim of Banburismus was to produce information about the right-hand wheel of the Enigma (and sometimes the middle wheel). Successful use of Banburismus would lead to a big reduction in the number of wheel combinations ('wheel orders') to be tried by the Bombes. Without Banburismus there would be 336 wheel combinations to be tried. (The number 336 arises as $8 \times 7 \times 6$ because there were, in 1941, three wheels in the machine, fixed for a day, selected from a 'library' of eight wheels.) Banburismus would lead also to a 'menu' for the Bombes (but a better menu would sometimes have been obtained from a crib). The Bombe operators followed the menu supplied by the cryptanalyst when setting up the Bombe for the search.

I will here mention only one important aspect of Banburismus, the method of scoring whether two cipher messages are in 'depth' at a given offset. (Two messages are said to be in depth over a stretch if the states of the cryptographic machine are the same for the two messages in that stretch or offset or overlap.) The scores were calculated for each possible overlap between pairs of cipher messages having the same settings for the slow (left-hand) wheel and also for the middle wheel. As with Tunny, such pairs of messages were known from the nature of the message indicating system (if the so-called bigram, or digraph, tables were known). At Alexander's suggestion I worked out a more accurate scoring system. This was known as ROMSing, where ROMS stood for the Resources of Modern Science—Alexander's joke. The theory resembles 'Fuzzy Bayes', employed post-war for estimating probabilities of various events in a hospital, from a necessarily small sample, while taking into account statistics from a larger sample from a group of hospitals.

The game of Banburismus was enjoyable, not easy enough to be trivial, but not difficult enough to cause a nervous breakdown. I was quite good at this game, but Alexander was the champion. If he was on a working shift (we worked on a three-shift system, each shift being eight hours), he usually had broken most of the right-wheel alphabet by the time the next shift came on duty. I obtained the most probable *wrong* alphabet—it was about 3000 to 1 on at its peak, and then gradually slipped back when I allowed for the middle-wheel information.

When I first arrived at BP, the scores were recorded as decibans to one place of decimals. My first reaction was to think why not drop the decimal point and call the unit a centiban? But I then noticed that most of the entries would be single digits if they were entered to the nearest half-deciban (hdb) and I calculated that not much information would thereby be lost by this 'rounding'. The use of centibans, being a very small unit, can be regarded as treating weight of evidence as a continuous variable. So I didn't only propose a new unit. The problem of how much evidence is lost by rounding to hdbs, and its solution, is very similar to Max Planck's resolution, in 1900, of the 'ultraviolet catastrophe' by assuming uniformly spaced discrete energy levels. My proposal led to a very great saving in time in Banburismus. It exemplifies how valuable a very simple idea can be. Alexander said, 'We found simplicity in scoring most important.' He mentions that originally the girls would record the number of 'vertically repeated' monographs (single letters), digraphs (letter pairs), etc., and the length of the comparison (the overlap), and that then two improvements were made. The first was to enter the score in decibans to one place of decimals, and later to the nearest half-deciban. He said, 'These changes did not merely save us trouble, they enabled us to succeed, where we would otherwise have failed, by making it possible to try so many more alternatives.' Thus the modest half-deciban was vastly more important than it might seem. The famous American financier John Pierpont Morgan had a point when he said, 'I don't want it perfect, I want it Thursday'—but perfectionism also has its place of course, especially in engineering.

I MOVE TO THE NEWMANRY

In April 1943 I was transferred to Hut F, the Newmanry, to work on Tunny—a very high-grade system, containing messages from the megamurderer to his generals. I have previously said my transfer to the Newmanry was in October 1943 because this date is written on a book that I was given as a present from former colleagues in Hut 8 (*Introduction to Mathematical Probability*, by J. V. Uspensky). But I have since remembered that the publishers took several months to deliver the book. It is autographed by Candida Aire, Hugh Alexander, Michael Ashcroft, Hilary Brett-Smith (later married to Sir Harry Hinsley), Arthur Chamberlain, Joan Clarke (later Murray), Al Clifford (US), Sylvia Cowgill, Pauline Elliott, A. P. Mahon, Rolf Noskwith, Richard Pendered, June Penny, Alan Turing, and Shaun Wylie (my friend Leslie Yoxall had left Hut 8 by then). Turing wrote, 'A wondrous arithmetician who never thought but only counted.' At a guess his satirical quotation comes from Voltaire's *Candide*. Turing's satire was, of course, friendly badinage. This book is one of my treasured possessions.

The function of the Newmanry was to work on machine attacks on Tunny, and it complemented the Testery where hand methods were used. Some of the members of the Testery, apart from Major Ralph Tester, were Roy Jenkins (later Chancellor of the Exchequer), Alan Turing occasionally (on loan from the Research Section), Peter Benenson (founder of Amnesty International), Peter Hilton (who also helped the liaison with the Newmanry), Peter Ericsson, and Donald Michie (well known to the artificial intelligentsia and previously Curator of the Balliol Book of Bawdy Verse). Peter Hilton had an interest in palindromes (sentences that read the same forwards and backwards). He once spent a sleepless night composing the masterly palindrome DOC NOTE, I DISSENT. A FAST NEVER PREVENTS A FATNESS. I DIET ON COD. (This palindrome has been incorrectly attributed to others.)

Max Newman felt inferior in the Testery, where he probably compared his efforts to those of people such as Hilton, who was able mentally to see two teleprinter characters merging modulo 2. Newman was thinking of exerting his right to return to Cambridge. But then he judged that much of the purely non-linguistic work (including the testing of cribs) done in the Testery could be mechanised and that electronic machinery would be essential. He

1. Alastair Denniston. Head of the Government Code and Cypher School from its formation in 1919.

2. Edward 'Jumbo' Travis. Deputy head of the Government Code and Cypher School under Denniston and head from 1942.

3. The legendary Alan Turing.

4. Bill Tutte. A brilliant codebreaker, Tutte deduced the design of the German Tunny machine from a single intercept.

5. Max Newman. Head of the Tunny-breaking section called the 'Newmanry', Newman was in charge of the Colossi.

6. Catherine Caughey (née Harvey). Caughey was a Colossus operator in the Newmanry.

7. Dorothy Du Boisson. Colossus operator Du Boisson is standing with her back to the camera in photo 33.

8. Jack Good. Codebreaker, chess player, and distinguished mathematician and philosopher.

9. Eleanor Ireland (née Outlaw). Another Colossus operator, Ireland helped the engineers to break up the Colossi at the end of the war.

10. Donald Michie. One of Bletchley's youngest recruits, Michie went on to become a leading expert in computer intelligence.

11. Ralph Tester. Head of the Tunny-breaking section called the 'Testery'.

12. Helen Currie (née Pollard). Currie operated a British 'Tunny machine' in the Testery.

13. Peter Hilton. Codebreaker in the Testery and the Newmanry, and subsequently an eminent mathematician.

14. Jerry Roberts. Codebreaker and shift leader in the Testery.

15. Harry Fensom. A gifted engineer, Fensom was one of Flowers' 'band of brothers'.

16. Gil Hayward. An engineer in the Intelligence Corps, Hayward is pictured here in Egypt; he returned to Britain in 1944 and joined Flowers' Colossus group.

17. The Mansion, Bletchley Park. Wartime headquarters of the Government Code and Cypher School.

18. A three-wheel Enigma machine. Behind the keyboard is the lampboard. The three wheels are visible behind the lampboard. Beside each wheel-slot is a small window, through which letters marked on the wheels are visible to the operator.

19. Enigma machine with its wheels and lamps exposed. Once the operator has inserted the correct wheels for the day, he closes the inner lid and encryption can begin.

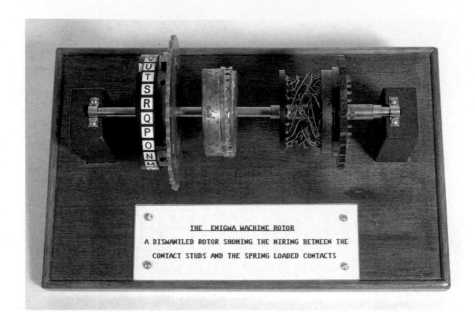

20. A dismantled Enigma wheel showing the internal wiring.

21. Top brass from Bletchley Park. Colonel John Tiltman (RIGHT), Alastair Denniston, and Italian expert 'Vinca' Vincent (CENTRE). Tiltman achieved the first break into Tunny.

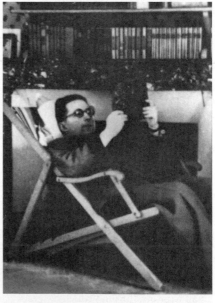

22. Polish codebreaker Marian Rejewski taking a rest from the attack on Enigma.

23. Alan Turing. Turing made numerous fundamental contributions to code-breaking, and he is the originator of the modern ('stored-program') computer.

24. An Enigma machine and operators in General Guderian's command vehicle during the Battle of France.

25. The Bombe. Turing's Bombes turned Bletchley Park into a codebreaking factory.

26. The stricken *U-110* shortly after depth charges blasted it to the surface. A Royal Navy boarding party captured the *U-110*'s Enigma machine.

27. German survivors from the *U-110* in mid-Atlantic.

28. The Tunny machine.

29. Tunny with its twelve encoding wheels exposed.

30. A British 'Tunny machine', used in the deciphering process. The racks of electrical equipment imitated the actions of the German Tunny.

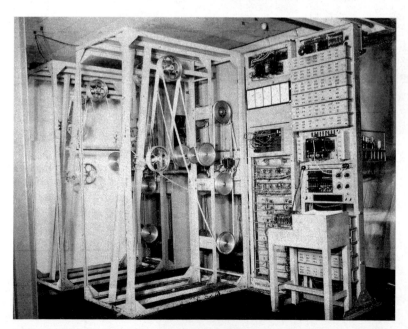

31. Robinson, precursor to Colossus. This machine, eventually called 'Old Robinson', replaced the original 'Heath Robinson' (the two were similar in appearance).

32. Some of the types of electronic valve used in Colossus. On the far right is a photocell from the tape reader.

33. Colossus with two operators, Dorothy Du Boisson and Elsie Booker (RIGHT).

34. Colossus X. In the foreground is the automatic typewriter for output. The large frame to the right (the 'bedstead') held two message tapes. As one job was being run, the tape for the next job would be loaded onto the bedstead, so saving time. Using a switch on the selection panel, the operator chose to run either the 'near' or the 'far' tape (SEE PHOTO 37).

35. Side view of Colossus VII. The four large boxes on the rear frame are the power supply units.

36. Colossus V, back view. The racks of valves on the right simulated the movements of the Tunny machine's wheels.

37. Some of the controls on Colossus VI. TOP: rotary switches for the span counters. LEFT: plug panel for programming. RIGHT: selection panel. Notice the switch at the top left of the selection panel for choosing the 'near' or 'far' tape. Other switches on this panel enable the operator to select chi or delta chi, psi or delta psi, and so on.

38. Aquarius. This codebreaking machine contained an early form of computer memory. Data read in from a punched paper tape were stored in the form of electrical charge.

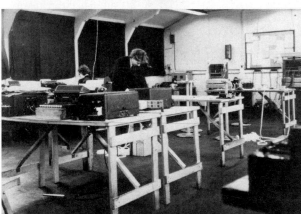

39. At work in the Newmanry. On the trestle tables are machines for copying and correcting paper tapes, sticking tape-ends together, and counting perforations. Against the wall are two 'Mrs Miles' machines for combining tapes. Notice the blacked-out windows.

40. The intercept station at Flowerdown.

41. The Post Office Research Station at Dollis Hill. Here Flowers pioneered digital electronics and built Colossus.

42. Human computers in the 1890s— the Accounting Department at J. Lyons and Co.

43. Charles Babbage, grandfather of the computer.

44. The Manchester 'Baby'. The first electronic stored-program general-purpose computer, the Baby ran its first program in June 1948, in Newman's Computing Machine Laboratory.

45. The Pilot Model of Turing's Automatic Computing Engine. Turing's ACE was the fastest of the early electronic computers.

46. Advertisement for the Bendix G15, a personal computer based on Turing's design.

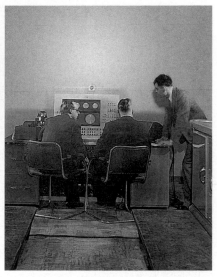

47. The MOSAIC. A large computer built to Turing's design, the MOSAIC was used for secret work during the Cold War.

48. Turing standing at the console of the Ferranti Mark I computer at Manchester University. Here Turing pioneered the field of research now called Artificial Life.

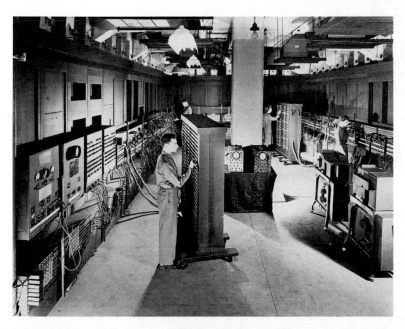

49. The ENIAC. Although standardly described as the 'first electronic computer', the ENIAC in fact went into operation two years later than Colossus.

50. John von Neumann beside the Princeton IAS computer. The row of cannisters is the memory—each cannister contains a single cathode ray tube ('Williams tube').

51. Sturgeon. Sideways view of the Siemens T52d cipher machine with its protective cover removed.

52. Sturgeon's code wheels and inner plug connections. Each of the ten code wheels of the T52d consists of four cams. The plug connections select the code wheels used in the addition and transposition circuits.

convinced Commander (later Sir) Edward Travis, by then the head of BP, that work on such machinery should be begun, and thus the Newmanry was born. Its purpose, at first, was to set the chi- and psi-wheels for individual messages after the patterns of the wheels had been recovered in the Testery.

Michie was Newman's first cryptanalytic assistant. He joined the Newmanry in April 1943, a few weeks before me. Michie had been a major scholar in Classics at Balliol College in Oxford but his wartime experiences converted him into a scientist. After about five months we were joined by Shaun Wylie and later by about another 12 mathematicians. One of them was the famous topologist, J. H. C. (Henry) Whitehead. He had a low opinion of the theological speculations of his uncle, the famous philosopher A. N. Whitehead (he once remarked, 'Bertrand Russell would have been a better philosopher if he had been a better mathematician' and that Russell had used up his mathematical energy on his and A. N. Whitehead's famous work on the foundations of mathematics, *Principia Mathematica*). In spite of these caustic remarks, Henry Whitehead was genial and enthusiastic. Some other cryptanalysts in the Newmanry, in alphabetical order, whose names I recall with clarity, were Michael Ashcroft, Oliver Atkin, Howie Campaigne (US), Michael Crum, Sandy Green (for a short time), John Herivel (mainly in administration), Walter Jacobs (US), Kenneth LeCouteur, Tim Molien (US), Gordon Preston, and David Rees. Crum, who broke Sturgeon, was a son of a Deacon of Canterbury. He had a first-class intellect, with very high ethical standards both for himself and others. I would rather have told a risqué story to a lady than to Michael Crum. When saying anything he would ask himself, 'Is it true, is it kind, is it wise?'

Wylie married Odette, the head of one of the shifts of the first 16 Wrens. They were both very thin but healthy. After the war, Wylie wrote a well-received joint book with Peter Hilton on homology. Wylie had, and probably still has, a very exact logical mind; when he understood anything, he seemed to understand it completely. He was a human embodiment of the philosopher Wittgenstein's saying that if anything can be said at all it can be said clearly (a saying that hardly applies to Wittgenstein himself). Wylie never mentioned any of his successes. Once I noticed an acknowledgement to him in Hardy and Wright's *Theory of Numbers* and when the next morning I called him 'Dr Wylie', he said, 'You must have been reading Hardy and Wright.' He was a perfect gentleman who never lost his temper except on purpose, and was an extremely good listener. I was tempted to believe he wouldn't interrupt a conversation even to mention that the war was over! About the time Wylie joined us, we moved into part of a large brick building called Block H. We needed plenty of space to house the ten Colossi that would ultimately be built.

In the Newmanry I was especially friendly with Donald Michie and Peter Hilton. We used to go to a pub where the manageress was named Mrs Conquest. Her dog seemed to try to bite customers' legs and she would complain if they retaliated. I understand there is now a pub in Bletchley called *The Enigma*; perhaps it is the same pub. We often went to dances at Woburn Abbey where many of the Wrens were billeted. On the way back to Bletchley by coach Peter Hilton would entertain us by singing bawdy songs such as My Brother Silvest. He was an excellent raconteur of the dirty joke: before saying one in company, when the conversation had lagged, he would ask 'Is it all right?' In two recent articles, Hilton gave too much credit to Turing in regard to Colossus. It was Newman who specified the cryptanalytical requirements for Colossus, not Turing, although Turing probably had some influence. Hilton confessed to me that he was misled by his respect and sympathy for Turing.

The organisation of the Newmanry cryptanalysts was somewhat democratic. There were so-called 'tea parties' which could be called by any cryptanalyst by writing an idea in the current research log-book, and a note on the blackboard in the research room. These 'tea parties' were free-for-all informal meetings where many decisions were made (but there was no tea). By the end of the war five or six research log-books had been filled with notes.

THE ART OR SCIENCE OF CRYPTOLOGY

Before going into details about the breaking of Tunny, let us consider generalities concerning the art or science of cryptology, the two main branches of which are *cryptography* and *cryptanalysis*. (I am using the modern definitions—we did not speak of 'cryptanalysis' at Bletchley Park.) The aim of the cryptographer is to produce a system that is convenient to use legitimately but is too expensive or complex, or impossible in principle, for the cryptanalyst to break (or to break too often or too soon). Systems of the latter type—impossible to break in principle—using large quantities of 'one-time tape' are liable to be inconvenient for the legitimate users, especially if these users form an intercommunicating network.

The Enigma and Tunny were both 'finite-state' machines with a large number of possible states. But the number S of possible states is not necessarily a good measure of the security of a cryptographic machine, though a large S helps to sell the machine! It measures only the cost of an *exhaustive* or 'British Museum' attack (i.e. an attack that examines all possibilities). The cryptographer should consider also cryptanalytic shortcuts and whether cipher clerks are likely to make dangerous mistakes. For example, a simple substitution system has a $26 \times 25 \times 24 \times \ldots \times 3 \times 2 \times 1$ (called 26!) $= 4.03 \times 10^{26}$ different possible substitution alphabets, yet such a system can usually be easily broken by a 12-year-old, given a message of, say, 200 words. To get an even larger British Museum Work Factor (BMWF), consider having one simple substitution in even positions in a message and another one in the odd positions. Then the BMWF would be 1.6×10^{53}. But this system would have little security. Thus a large BMWF is necessary but by no means sufficient for the security of a cryptographic machine. Incidentally, the cryptanalyst's task, even for a simple substitution system, is of course helped a lot if he has a correct crib.

We can regard a cryptographic machine of given structure as a device that converts the input P ('plain language' or encoded language not usually encrypted, for example international teleprinter code) into cipher Z. (The play 'Breaking the Code', about Turing, could now more precisely be called 'Breaking the Cipher'.) The conversion from P to Z is carried out by means of an operation (in fact a function, in the mathematical sense) f, that is, $Z = f(P, K)$, where K denotes the key. A sensible cryptographer will assume that the operation f is known to his 'enemy' the cryptanalyst. Suppose K has N possible values. Then we can think of N as the BMWF for the analyst.

As a 'thought experiment', let us imagine a cryptanalyst who is able to carry out a British Museum attack on one cipher message. That is, he knows f and decides to try all possible values of K for that message. For each of the N possibilities he has to see whether plain language is produced by the deciphering operation f^{-1}, the inverse of the enciphering operation f. (In modern public key systems, anybody can encipher a message, but only a few can decipher it because the inverse f^{-1} can be very difficult to determine. For example, the enciphering might use the known product of two large prime numbers, while the deciphering requires the knowledge of those two primes themselves in order to use them in a certain manner other than by multiplying them together.) Thus the cost to the analyst is N times the cost c of testing whether the output is plain language, for any given assumption about K. The cost c might be low if the beginnings of the plain-language messages are stereotyped.

Enigma and Tunny both attain a high value for N, although the wheels are entirely different for the two machines. The wheels in the Enigma were wired from one face to the other one (see photograph 20); the Tunny wheels had cams on their circumferences, each capable of two states. The two states are often called 'mark and space' or 'effective and ineffective' but we called them 'cross and dot' or 'one and zero'. The Germans called them *Nocke* and *Keine*. For Tunny the period of the entire 12 wheels is the product of the lengths (where the 'length' of a wheel is the number of cams around the circumference) of all 12 wheels, which is about 1.6×10^{19}. This would be the work factor for a cryptanalyst wheel-setter from the British Museum. (Wheel setting is finding the settings at the beginning of a message of wheels of known patterns. *Discovering* the wheel patterns is wheel breaking.) The number of cams to be positioned by a cipher clerk, on a given day or month (or 'cryptoperiod'), is the sum of the lengths of the 12 wheels, namely 501, which gives the cipher clerk a lot of work. But the German cryptographers must have thought this inconvenience was acceptable and would keep the cipher clerk off the streets.

The BMWF for a Tunny wheel-breaker is 'only' about $2^{501} \div (1.6 \times 10^{19})$, or about 4×10^{131}, because a rotation of a pattern is the same pattern as far as the wheel-breaker is concerned. Such a work factor could never be achieved, even if the moon were completely converted into an electronic computer. (The number of particles in our universe is 'only' about 10^{80}.) The British Museum attack is out of the question, both for the Enigma and for Tunny. The cryptanalyst has to break the problem down.

TUNNY

The cryptographic machines Enigma and Tunny had very different designs; and a single Tunny transmission often contained thousands of letters or characters (even up to 60,000), whereas an Enigma message was seldom longer than a few hundred letters. It isn't surprising that the main *cryptanalytic* machines for attacking Enigma and Tunny were also entirely distinct. They were known respectively as Bombes and Colossi. This point deserves mention because, for example, even Rejewski, the great Polish cryptanalyst, implies incorrectly (in the penultimate paragraph of his article of 1981) that Colossus was used against the Enigma. The original Bombe, and its much smaller and less sophisticated Polish version the Bomba, were electromagnetic whereas Colossus was of course electronic. Eventually the US navy built 120 electronic Bombes, the first one in the middle of 1943. The main engineer of the American Bombes was Joseph Desch, a near genius. Computer historian J. A. N. Lee remarked (when chairing a meeting in 1998, at which I was the speaker) that the meaning of 'the first electronic computer' depends on what adjectives are used. Note that an electronic Bombe is much further from being general-purpose than is a Colossus.

In Tunny, $Z = P + K$ where Z, P, and K are all 'pentabits' and the addition is modulo 2 in each of the five levels or impulses (i.e. $0 + 0 = 0$, $0 + 1 = 1 + 0 = 1$, but $1 + 1 = 0$). This is just as in Vernam's patent of 1918 (see Appendix 12

Origins of the Fish Cypher Machines). As explained earlier in the book, the wheels of Tunny fall into three categories, the five chi-wheels, the five psi-wheels, and the two motor-wheels $\mu 37$ and $\mu 61$. The chi-wheels move regularly and produce a sequence of teleprinter letters called $\chi = (\chi_1, \chi_2, \chi_3, \chi_4, \chi_5)$. The psi-wheels all move together, but not regularly, and produce a letter called $\psi = (\psi_1, \psi_2, \psi_3, \psi_4, \psi_5)$ before 'extension'. The psi-wheels are driven by $\mu 37$ in the sense that, in the original design, they all rotate one place when $\mu 37$ shows a cross (or one), and don't move when $\mu 37$ shows a dot (or zero). Likewise $\mu 37$ is driven by $\mu 61$ in the same sense, whereas $\mu 61$ itself moves regularly. The output of the psi-wheels is called the extended psi and is denoted by ψ'. (This distinction is unnecessary for the chi-wheels because they move regularly.) The key K is equal to $\chi + \psi'$. Thus we can write $Z = P + \chi + \psi'$. Note that $P = Z + K$, so decipherment is the same process as encipherment, just as for the Enigma, but for an entirely different reason. This feature has the same convenience for the cipher clerk as it has in the case of Enigma.

The 'lengths' of the chi-wheels are 41, 31, 29, 26, 23; since these numbers are relatively prime (i.e. have no common divisors except 1), the period of the set of chi-wheels is about 20 million, so of course no message would be long enough to 'bite its own tail' with respect to the chi-wheels. When the period of use of the wheel patterns was a month, there might well have been some pairs of messages which *by chance*, at a suitable displacement or shift, used the same stream of chi-wheels where the two messages overlap.

For example, if there were a thousand messages, there would be half a million *pairs* of messages. If each pair were compared at 10,000 relative shifts, to the right, and also to the left, then there would be about 10 billion opportunities of a depth. So the expected number of 'chi depths', so to speak, would be about 10 billion divided by 20 million, that is, 500. But to find such chance chi depths, if they existed, would have been very expensive. It would have required a sort of all the traffic, hoping for hexagraph (i.e. six-letter) repeats, between the two messages, in both P and ψ' at the same place. (There are 32^6, or about a billion possible hexagraphs.) We never tried to look for such pairs of chance depths and I don't know whether anyone thought of trying. (One might believe there is oil but can't afford the expense of looking for it.) The depths actually discovered were 'causal' in the sense that some German cipher clerks omitted to cross a setting off a list or else they used a button whose function was to return the wheels to their original settings in a message. The cipher clerks were tempted to make use of this reset button so as to save themselves the work of resetting the wheels. The existence of the button, although of some convenience to a cipher clerk, was a serious cryptographic weakness. Perhaps the *cryptographers* thought the cipher clerks wouldn't make such blunders for fear of having their throats cut by Nazis.

The lengths of the psi-wheels are 43, 47, 51, 53, 59, while the lengths of $\mu37$ and $\mu61$ are, not surprisingly, 37 and 61. (When taken in pairs, the lengths of the 12 wheels are always relatively prime, even the non-prime lengths 26 and 51.) If the patterns of all 12 wheels are known, but nothing is known about their initial settings for a given message, then the number of possible settings of the 12 wheels is about 1.6×10^{19}. So the cryptanalyst, lacking a massively parallel computer, has to find shortcuts such as attacking one or two wheels at a time.

We didn't capture a German Tunny until the last days of the war in Europe. A handful of us were privileged to visit an interrogation station, soon after the surrender of Germany on 8 May 1945. We saw a real Tunny machine in the truck that contained it, together with two German prisoners who had operated the machine. They appeared to be content. I recall that in the truck there was some bark of a tree used instead of tobacco. This confirmed the bad economic conditions in Germany at the end of the war. When I saw the prisoners they weren't smoking, not even tobacco.

HEATH ROBINSON: TEETHING PROBLEMS

When I joined the Newmanry, Heath Robinson had recently been installed. Heath Robinson had several teething problems. As you may guess from its name, this machine had been put together with emphasis on speed of completion more than on reliability. For its time, Heath Robinson was a good machine but it suffered at first from numerous mistakes in its use, as well as from its own imperfections. Some of the problems were: sprockets tearing and stretching the tape; tapes breaking and coming unstuck (thereby making a mess on the floor!); incorrect setting up of wheel settings and wheel patterns; putting tapes on Robinson back to front; inaccurate punching of start and stop signals on the tapes; prevalence of transient faults; badly written figures and figures incorrectly written down; inadequate handing over from one shift to the next; guessing the average of readings in the run, instead of calculating it in advance; using even lengths of tape in runs involving χ_4, whose length is even (!); inaccurate counting by Heath Robinson; damaging tapes by maltreatment; numerous gaps (or 'slides') in tapes incurred at that time by an intercept station; running out of office supplies, and of benzene (used in ungluing tapes which were glued with Bostik); sickness due to intolerable working conditions; intercept station perforating a wrong tape;

mechanical relays developing 'pips' (irregular bumps that form on the surface of the metal contacts); and overemphasis on operational results at the expense of research.

The main imperfection in the design of Heath Robinson was the driving of the tapes partly by their sprocket holes at hundreds of times the speed of the tapes in normal teleprinter usage, causing stretching and tearing. The stretching was a nuisance largely because the distance from the sprocket driving to the photoelectric reading was not as short as it might have been. The amount of stretching between two letters of the tape would be proportional to the number of sprocket holes or letters in that part of the tape. If the two tapes on the machine didn't stretch by almost exactly the same amount, then the synchronisation between the two tapes could be destroyed. Also, from time to time the machine would begin to smoke, a fault that could be detected by the sense of smell. It was not perfect but it was completed by 'Thursday'. One was often able to recognise that Heath Robinson had gone wrong and to diagnose the fault from the kind of noises it made. Colossus was much more carefully engineered, so its much less frequent faults could rarely be diagnosed by sound.

As a consequence of these troubles, the success rate was for several weeks extremely low and the future of the Newmanry was in jeopardy. We introduced elaborate checking to counteract these troubles, and ironed out most of them. I developed the maxim: *If it's not checked it's wrong.* In later life this habit of thought tended to irritate my secretaries! There were other reasons why progress was slow when I joined the Newmanry. One very important problem was that some of the best runs (with appropriate 'set totals' for deciding what to print) were not being made. Michie and I did research in the evenings on the statistics of plain language and wheel patterns, with some algebra and experimental runs, and that improved matters. We studied communication links such as Bream (Berlin–Rome) and Jellyfish (Berlin–Paris) and were interested in what were the numbers of dots and crosses in χ, ψ, and ψ', and in their deltas (first differences), and in $\mu 37$, and in the probabilities of such things as $\Delta P_1 + \Delta P_2 = $ dot, or $\Delta P_4 + \Delta P_5 = $ dot *given* that $\Delta P_1 + \Delta P_2 = $ dot. This research was important for the selection of computer runs at various stages in the setting of the chi- and psi-wheels. (The delta or forward difference operator Δ, in which a binary digit or a 'letter' is added modulo 2 to the next binary digit or letter, is the same as the forward difference used in the calculus of finite differences, except that our differences are modulo 2.)

WHEEL SETTING

Wheel setting is the problem of determining the initial settings of the wheels when their patterns are known. Its solution depends on the main weakness of Tunny, the fact that the psi-wheels have to move in unison. In other words $\Delta\psi'$ is often equal to $(0, 0, 0, 0, 0)$ which is known as a slash $(/)$. To take advantage of this weakness, the cryptanalyst often used the delta operator.

Suppose then that we try to set just one chi-wheel, say χ_1, by adding $\Delta\chi_1$ to ΔZ_1. This gives us $\Delta(P + \psi')_1$, the sum of the first levels (impulses) of ΔP and $\Delta\psi'$. A one-wheel run could in principle have enabled us to set χ_1, but the German cryptographers thought of this and arranged the extended ψ_1 in such a way that there would be no statistical 'bulge' we could search for. Their precaution applied to all five levels. So a one-wheel run wouldn't work. But a two-wheel run, say for the first two chi-wheels, using their deltas, does often work because any two levels of the extended delta psi are correlated. This is because the psi-wheels often pause in unison. Statistics of plain language showed that three-wheel runs although just practicable wouldn't have been much better than two-wheels runs. Perhaps the cryptographers thought or hoped we couldn't do even a two-wheel run in a reasonable time. The thought was mistaken, the hope forlorn.

The most common initial run, for the beginning settings of the wheels for a message, was a two-wheel run for χ_1 and χ_2, although these two wheels have the greatest lengths of the chis. Any other pair would take less time to run but was less likely to succeed because the delta properties of the plain language were not as favourable for them. Recall that by 'plain language' we don't mean simply German, but German together with special characters for carriage return, line feed, shift, etc., and everything is encoded (not encrypted) by Baudot, the international teleprinter alphabet. The run was done by adding $\Delta Z_1 + \Delta Z_2$ to $\Delta\chi_1 + \Delta\chi_2$ (by means of the plugging or switching of Heath Robinson) where the cipher terms were obtained from the cipher or Z tape and the chi terms from a chi tape. Start and stop holes were punched on the Z tape so that the part used would be of length 1 less than a multiple of 1271 (41 $\times$ 31), whereas the chi tape was of length 1271, also with start and stop holes. There was trouble if a mistake was made in punching the start or stop holes on either tape! A 'set total' was included in the program so that not too many solutions were proffered. The name of the run was abbreviated to $1 + 2/$. If the run was regarded as successful, then the next run would usually be $4 + 5/1,2$ meaning a run for χ_4 and χ_5 with the initial settings of χ_1 and χ_2 having known values. If that seemed to be successful, then a run for χ_3 would be done with the (beginning) settings of all four of the other chis given their presumed values.

When we succeeded in setting the chis for (the beginning of) a message, then we added them to Z (or subtracted them, which is the same thing in mod 2 arithmetic). We sometimes called this operation 'stripping off the chis' and the effect is to produce the 'de-chi', which is denoted by D. Thus $D = Z + \chi = P + \psi'$.

A run for one or more wheels can be expected to succeed only if 'what's left' (after those wheels have been stripped off) is expected to be 'rough' enough, that is, sufficiently non-flat-random. (A flat-random sequence is one in which the 'letters' of the 'alphabet' are statistically independent and have probabilities $1/t$, where t is the size of the alphabet. For the Enigma, $t = 26$, whereas it is $2^5 = 32$ for Tunny.) This principle could be called the 'what's left principle'. As applied to χ_1 and χ_2 its meaning is that $\Delta(P_1 + P_2 + \psi'_1 + \psi'_2)$ must be rough enough. This requires that both $\Delta(P_1 + P_2)$ and $\Delta(\psi'_1 + \psi'_2)$ must be rough enough. (P and ψ are very nearly independent.) The first term is rough because of the nature of the 'plain language' and the second one is rough because of the main weakness of the Tunny enciphering machine, the fact that all five psis move in unison.

With all five chis set one could run programs for the psis, but this time the Z tape would be replaced by a D or de-chi tape. Heath Robinson couldn't cope electronically with extending the psi-wheels, so the de-chi tape was contracted instead! This required more tricky tape preparation.

USING COLOSSUS

The Colossus Mark I was built by 'Thursday' and was nearly perfect too, apart from some teething troubles. Later, I estimated that, at its best, a Colossus could do about 10^{11} (100 billion) Boolean operations without making an error that would affect the outcomes of the runs. A switching operation took 10 microseconds, so the effective speed of Colossus was limited primarily by the speed of the tape. That ordinary teleprinter tape could be run on pulleys at nearly 30 miles per hour without tearing was one of the great secrets of the war. Another was the knowledge that valves that didn't die in their infancy were reliable if the machine was left switched on all the time. (Chandler once said, 'There is little doubt that expansion and contraction of valve heaters being switched on and off caused many valve failures in computing equipment built soon after the war.') The advantages of having the key information incorporated in the electronics were—apart from avoidance of the need to synchronise two tapes and to drive tapes by their sprocket holes—the ease of changing the key information; the avoidance of much tape preparation, with the consequence that errors in key tape preparation would be very greatly reduced and much time would be saved; and the fact that the 'clock pulses' could reliably be provided by the sprocket holes of a single tape. The cost, of course, was that far more valves were needed than had been used in Heath Robinson.

The programming of Colossus was done by Boolean plugging and toggle switches. The flexible Boolean nature of the programming was proposed by Newman and perhaps also supported by Turing, both of whom were familiar with Boolean logic, and this flexibility paid off handsomely. The engineers, as well as the cryptanalysts, appreciated the flexibility of the Boolean design of Colossus. As Chandler remarked, 'It says much for the flexibility of the original design that . . . modifications could be incorporated' in later Colossi.

For a time, the mode of operation was for a cryptanalyst to sit at the typewriter output and call out instructions for changes in the program to be made by a Wren. (These changes were, of course, made in the light of results that had been printed.) At this stage there was a close synergy between man, woman, and machine, a synergy that was not typical during the next decade of large-scale computers. But, after some experience, I worked out some decision trees (in addition to one proposed by Newman), with Michie's cooperation, so that Wrens could operate Colossus in a more routine manner. (Otherwise we would not have been able to keep all the Colossi running without hiring more cryptanalysts.) The Colossi produced quite a bit of heat, so much that it was once facetiously proposed, but not by the operators, that they should be topless!

When a decision tree failed in its aim, or was inconclusive, a record from the printer was presented to the cryptanalyst on duty, called a 'duty officer', to make suggestions for further runs or for abandonment. The record contained all the high scores in the runs together with a frequency count of the best partial de-chi, with the alphabet written out in what we called 'reflection order'. Reflection order was convenient for the cryptanalyst because it readily revealed whether one of the five levels in the setting was faulty. In this reflection order, the third level was treated as the 'least significant' of the five because it usually contained less information than the other levels.

The reflection order has the property that each letter is obtained from the previous one by changing only one binary digit. I thought of the reflection order by a weak analogy with the interesting infinite sequence: •xx•x••xx••x•xx• etc., which the mathematician and world chess champion M. Euwe had used in a 1929 article on infinitely long games of chess (with a modified rule for a drawn game). After two signs, four signs, eight signs, etc., in Euwe's sequence, all is repeated with dots and crosses interchanged. The reflection order is now called the Gray code and is useful for analogue-to-digital conversion. Gray thought of the reflection order independently, but I don't know at what date.

Another of my discoveries whose significance was not limited to codebreaking was a remarkable phenomenon that I named *coalescence*. I hit on it during a night shift on Colossus in 1944. To my great surprise I found that after a few thousand letters it made little difference where one of the wheels, ψ_5, was assumed to be set at the start of the message—different wheel starting positions 'coalesced' after a sufficient length of text. This effect was in fact the result of a limitation in use at the time, where the motion of the psi-wheels depended on the fifth level of the plain language two positions back in the message (see Appendix 10 *The Motor Wheels and Limitations*). It turned out that coalescence occurred also for ψ_1 when that wheel was involved (one back) in the limitation. I explained coalescence in terms of the 'gambler's ruin' problem. There was a later exposition by LeCouteur which I believe depended on the theory of random motion on a circle. It is most interesting that since 1998 the concept of coalescence has turned out to be very useful in connection with what is called the Markov Chain Monte Carlo (MCMC) method.

The original function of Heath Robinson and of Colossus was to find the settings of the chi- and psi-wheels. For the first few months of the operation of Colossus this was its sole function, the rest of the work being completed in the Testery, and we got into the habit of thinking that wheel-breaking should be done by carbon units. But one morning Donald Michie came into the office with a simple idea for using Colossus to help to produce the $\Delta Z_1 + \Delta Z_2$ 'rectangles' used by the Testery for wheel breaking (see Appendix 9 *Rectangling*). With a little help from me we verified that his idea was correct. This was the source of various attachments made to successive Colossi and, from that time onwards, Colossi were used both for setting and for speeding up the breaking of the chi-wheels. Timms wrote in *General Report on Tunny*: 'Colossus rectangling has been slightly disappointing; although the rectangle is produced in the required form, it has been found necessary to copy it onto squared paper for convergence.' Note that he did say 'slightly'! Michie's idea was certainly valuable. Once again then, a simple idea that we had been overlooking led to a very useful saving of time—and time was often of the essence. Since the mid-1960s, if there is a laborious calculation to be done, everybody thinks of programming it for a computer; but the mid-1940s were not the mid-1960s. Novel ideas in science, mathematics, and chess are often basically simple at first and later increase in complexity. When T. H. Huxley first heard of the theory of natural selection, he said, 'How extremely stupid of me not to have thought of that myself.'

THE FIRST LARGE-SCALE ELECTRONIC COMPUTER

Colossus could be regarded as the first large-scale electronic computer, albeit for a specialised purpose, but leaning towards being general-purpose. By and large the machine was comparable with the ENIAC, although Colossus was completed, and was reliable, two years earlier. Soon after the victory in Europe, Shaun Wylie showed that Colossus could have been used for breaking the motor-wheels. (He was unaware of my very early hand-breaking of the motor-wheels, from a de-chi, for Bream or Jellyfish message #5521. This took a few days to do, probably in May 1943.) Thus Newman's dream of total mechanisation could have been completed.

After the end of the war in Europe, it was shown by Timms that multiplication to base 10 was almost possible on Colossus, by complicated plugging. I say 'almost' because the calculation could not be completed in the time between 'clock' pulses, but the exercise was interesting in verifying how flexible was the Boolean plugging of Colossus in principle. (It wouldn't have helped to slow down the clock pulses, by slowing the tape, because the unit or quantum of time in the computer was determined by the sprocket holes in the tape itself!) Although there was not much point in doing base-10 multiplication at the time, the capability shows that the machine was in principle more general-purpose than its designer intended. Basically this is because ordinary calculations can be expressed in Boolean terms. Another feature of the Colossus was conditional branching, but only in the weak sense that at times the motion of the wheels depended on the putative plain language, specifically on P_5 two positions back.

Part of the program could be changed quickly by means of toggle switches which were connected to produce circuits in series or in parallel as required. Another less important but amusing aspect of the flexibility of the design was a way of using the span counter. Spanning, introduced in Colossus II, was an extremely important part of wheel setting and wheel breaking. As soon as the first wheels were set, the message was invariably spanned for possible slides (omitted or inserted letters). If slides were detected, later runs were done on a slide-free portion. Although the original purpose of my suggestion of the span counter was to span long stretches of the tape, such as several thousand characters, for which purpose it was extremely useful, I noticed it could also be used to span just one character. It could thus be used to decipher a message one letter at a time—rather slowly, of course. (Perhaps an attachment to Colossus could have been made to carry out this process rapidly and this would have been very valuable and not merely amusing. But such an attachment was never proposed to my knowledge.) This enabled us to check, after setting the wheels for a message, that the wheels had been correctly set, before removing the message tape from the Colossus. This check was done by deciphering the first few letters of the message at the putative settings. On one occasion, by an extraordinary coincidence, when the wheels were *not* correctly set, the decipherment of the first five letters read IJGOO. I remember saying that if the sixth letter had been a D, I would assume either that a miracle had occurred or that someone had played a practical joke on me.

The Boolean programming on Colossus caused me to suggest, in February 1947, a concept that I called 'machine building'. In December 1947 Newman mentioned the idea in a discussion with Harry Huskey and Jim Wilkinson, both influential pioneers of computing. At the opening ceremony of the Manchester computer in 1951, Maurice Wilkes, the designer of the Cambridge University EDSAC, independently proposed the idea, with much more detail. It is now called 'microprogramming'. The distinction between his suggestion and mine is that Wilkes had engineering in mind, whereas, by a very strong analogy with the Colossus programming, I proposed it for the *users* of computers. A thought that seems somewhat creative is often suggested by previous experience and is less creative than it appears.

Flowers gave a lecture on 15 October 1981 at the Digital Computer Museum in Marlboro, Massachusetts (he was introduced by Wilkes). After Flowers spoke, J. D. Andrews, who worked for him (although not during the war) said that the Flowers group apparently had the following 'firsts' in Colossus (I have changed Andrews' wording a little):

1. The first application of logic controlled by an *alterable program*.

2. The first use of clock-synchronising pulses sent to a *large* block of logic.

3. The first use of *parallel processing*.

4. The first use of *interrupt*—to prevent overloading of the printer.

5. The first use of a *higher-level description* of a machine program. Andrews must here be referring to the use of abbreviated notations such as $4 + 5/1,2$ meaning a run for $\Delta Z_4 + \Delta Z_5 =$ dot, given the initial settings of wheels 1 and 2. Such notations were already in use with Heath Robinson.

6. The first use of *optical reading* of paper tape. Andrews is, of course, counting Colossus and Heath Robinson in one and the same breath—and we must remember also the Dollis Hill Auto-Teller (see Chapter 24).

7. The first use of *shift registers*. ('There are many,' said Andrews, 'like myself who think that the world was created with shift registers as part of the package—to imagine a world without them is difficult.')

Andrews also noted that, incredibly, all of these developments were put into service without any prior experimental 'breadboarding': there was no time.

The degree to which Colossus led the field was illustrated at a computer conference which I attended in Cambridge (England) in 1949. In the discussion Coombs gave a twenty minute discourse on the behaviour of electromagnetic relays under heavy use, and on how to discourage them from forming 'pips'. The delegates were surprised that anyone could know so much about this topic. They would have been more surprised if Coombs had told them where he obtained his information!

EXEUNT

Most of the cryptanalysts in the Newmanry dispersed into various universities and most of us achieved some measure of success in our unclassified work. But the success of our efforts during the war, and the feeling that we were helping substantially, and perhaps critically, to save much of the world (including Germany) from heinous tyranny, was a hard act to follow. Flowers and the other engineers cannot be praised enough. (A few years after the war Coombs told me that he had been deprived of credit by the Dollis Hill administration for his contributions to trans-Atlantic communication and he felt like committing suicide.) I think Flowers deserved to be knighted, and Newman too.

Chapter 17

• •

Codebreaking and Colossus

Donald Michie

SORRY, WRONG INFO

In late 1941, following my 18th birthday, a normal next phase would have been two further terms at boarding school, with an option for scholarship holders to proceed to a shortened University degree course before joining up. But over that Christmas my teenage imagination was fired by a tale from my father concerning a mysterious establishment at Bedford. He had it on the authority of the then War Minister, Sir James Grigg, that as preparation for doing something unspecified but romantic behind enemy lines there were opportunities to sign up for a Japanese course starting in a couple of months' time. I duly journeyed to Bedford and presented myself at the address given.

My request to enrol elicited from the Intelligence Corps officer at Bedford a somewhat puzzled reply: 'Who told you that we have a Japanese course now? That particular exercise is planned for the autumn.' Noting my confusion he added: 'But we have courses on codebreaking. There's a new intake just starting. Would that interest you instead? I'll have someone find you a billet nearby. Be back here at 9 a.m. Monday.'

In the Second World War one did not mess about. Returning to the London suburbs just long enough to pack a suitcase, I was back and signed in to the School of Codes and Ciphers, Official Secrets Act and all, on the Monday morning. With the rest of the new class I was soon held in thrall by our instructor, a certain Captain Cheadle, and by the black arts of codes and ciphers.

With nothing to occupy my evenings, I arranged to have my own key to the building and classroom. My habit became to return after hours to the texts and exercises. The resulting accelerated learning curve made my selection inevitable when a Colonel Pritchard arrived from Bletchley. He was on a mission to recruit for the new section that was being formed by Ralph Tester to follow up John Tiltman's and William Tutte's successive coups—the hope was that breaking and reading Tunny traffic could be placed on a regular basis. The Pritchard interview lasted no more than a few minutes. I was to present myself within 48 hours at the entrance to Bletchley Park with a sealed letter.

After admission and a visit to the billeting office, I was parked in the Mansion House. My first task was to memorise teleprinter code until I could fluently sight-read punched paper tape. Pending completion of the Hut assigned to Major Tester's new section I sat as an ugly duckling in a large room filled to capacity by members of the Women's Auxiliary Air Force. What were they doing? Who knows? New arrivals were imprinted with a draconian DON'T ASK DON'T TELL principle in regard to anyone's immediate business but their own. I did, however, discover that those whose boyfriends were on active service felt only contempt for an apparently fit young male in civilian attire. Some of them had lost boyfriends in the RAF, and many had boyfriends still alive but in daily peril.

The experience did nothing to ease my sense of disorientation in the new surroundings. Relief appeared in the person of a uniformed and exquisitely charming Intelligence Corps officer, Second Lieutenant Roy Jenkins. My task was to bring him up to my own recently acquired sight-reading skills. Roy's post-war career was to include Cabinet Minister and Chancellor of Oxford University. In my isolation, his company was rescue and balm. We departed to swell the ranks of Tester's new section, in my case via a most curious diversion.

FORTY MEN AND A TEENAGER

On reporting to Ralph Tester I was immediately dispatched to take charge of a room like a small aircraft hangar. It was located at some distance from his new Hut. Within it there sat at tables several dozen uniformed men who remain in my memory as being all of the rank of lance corporal. What I can attest beyond error is that I quickly became convinced of the infeasibility of the operation which it was now my job to supervise.

When two intercepts were known to constitute the same message retransmitted with the same key, but with the plain-language message at a different offset with respect to that key—a type of depth—they could be added so as to cancel out their common key. The resulting 'depth-sum' text must logically then consist of the addition to itself at that offset, or 'stagger', of a German plain language message. Given such a text, if one guessed that some character sequence, say GESELLSCHAFT (company), was likely to appear somewhere in the plaintext, then the experiment could be tried of adding that 12-character sequence (a 'crib') to the depth's first 12 characters, inspecting the result, then to characters 2–13, 3–14, etc, in tedious progression through the text. This procedure was known as 'dragging'.

'Adding', of course, refers to modulo-2 addition, which makes addition and subtraction indistinguishable (see Chapter 3). In consequence, if, say, HONES + OBDZE = NEST9, then NEST9 + OBDZE = HONES.

THE TELEPRINTER ALPHABET

Discussion of depths involves a look at certain properties of the teleprinter code on which the logic of the German Lorenz ciphers was based. To bridge the gap between symbols and physical paper tape, recall that '1' ('×') designates a hole punched in the tape and '0' ('•') designates a no-hole. So the character symbolised as '9' (00100) is encoded by a single hole punched in channel (or impulse) 3 and causes the teleprinter that reads that tape to advance one character without printing, which is why it is the typographical equivalent of 'space'. The character symbolised as '/' (00000) is encoded by the absence of holes from all channels and is known as 'blank'. Its action when read by the teleprinter is nil. Unlike 'space', 'blank' cannot form a legal character in a plain language teleprint message. The characters symbolised as '3' (00010) and '4' (01000), and called 'line feed' and 'carriage return', were not used in German military communications. The complete repertoire is given in Appendix 2 *The Teleprinter Alphabet*. (The non-alphabet character meaning 'shift to upper case' (11011) is in my memory symbolised as '+', although in *General Report on Tunny* it is symbolised as '5'. This stirs an echo. But I shall here use '+' throughout, pending resolution of the divergence of usage.)

To cause a FULL STOP to be printed at the receiving end, the operator has first to hit '+' for 'shift to upper case', then 'M' for 'full stop', then '8' (11111) for 'shift to lower case', then '9' for 'space-bar', making the character sequence +M89. Teleprinter keyboards, unlike those of typewriters, lack means for effecting such shifts as single key-presses.

'Differencing', or 'delta-ing', a string of teleprint code produces what we called its delta form. Recall from earlier chapters that the first character of the delta text is got by adding characters 1 and 2 of the undifferenced text, the second character is the sum of characters 2 and 3, and so on. Each successive repetition of any character in the undifferenced text is automatically flagged in the delta text as a '/', as can be inferred from the table in Appendix 3 *The Tunny Addition Square.*

DIFFERENCING—EXAMPLES

Differencing +M89 for FULL STOP produces UA+. To make sure that the case-shifts have 'taken', the operator often represented the FULL STOP by doing ++M889 for safety. Differencing this yields:

```
+  +  M  8    8  9  ?
?  +  +    M  8  8  9
?  /  U  A  /  +  ?
```

In a five-channel tape representation, ++M889 and /UA/+ look like this:

```
+ + M8 8 9      / U A / +
1 1 0 1 1 0     0 1 1 0 1
1 1 0 1 1 0     0 1 1 0 1
0 0 1 1 1 1     0 1 0 0 0
1 1 1 1 1 0     0 0 0 0 1
1 1 1 1 1 0     0 0 0 0 1
```

To give some idea of how non-randomness can be unmasked by the simple operation of differencing, try adding either the top two or the bottom two channels of this delta text. In both cases the answer is:

$$0\ 0\ 0\ 0\ 0$$

In this particular case it so happens that the additions chance to have the same effect using the undifferenced text. So to show how just any abundance of repetitions gets picked up, I will invent an imaginary Australian tribal word 'Boonnaawoolloo':

```
B O O N N A A W O O L L O O 9
1 0 0 0 0 1 1 1 0 0 0 0 0 0 0
0 0 0 0 0 1 1 1 0 0 1 1 0 0 0
0 0 0 1 1 0 0 0 0 0 0 0 0 0 1
1 1 1 1 1 0 0 0 1 1 0 0 1 1 0
1 1 1 0 0 0 0 1 1 1 1 1 1 1 0
```

Differencing this string of characters we get:

E /	H /	K /	T J	/	R /	R /	/	M
1 0 0 0	1 0 0	1 0 0	0 0	0 0	0
0 0 0 0	1 0 0	1 0 1	0 1	0 0	0
0 0 1 0	1 0 0	0 0 0	0 0	0 0	1
0 0 0 0	1 0 0	1 0 1	0 1	0 0	1
0 0 1 0	0 0 1	0 0 0	0 0	0 0	1

Addition of channels 2 and 4 is observed to give the sequence:

$$0\ 0\ 0\ 0\ 0\ 0\ 0\ 0\ 0\ 0\ 0\ 0\ 0\ 1$$

with 13 out of 14 zeros where random expectation is 6.5. This near-perfection arises from the fact, unintended when I concocted the example, that addition of these same channels in the *undifferenced* text yields:

$$1\ 1\ 1\ 1\ 1\ 1\ 1\ 1\ 1\ 1\ 1\ 1\ 1\ 0$$

Whether or not this 'delta $(2 + 4)$' tendency holds up in large samples of plain language, even as a modest but exploitable statistical bulge over the random expectation of 50 : 50 for 0s and 1s, would remain for investigation by the cryptanalysts—supposing that they wished to read Fish-encoded messages in the imagined tribal language. My purpose here is to illustrate that large-scale machine analysis of the statistical properties of plain language, by cryptanalysts trained in statistics rather than in linguistics or in the language itself, is an essential first step in any attempt to break a new code for a new traffic. Empiricism is all.

To give the reader a feel for the *kind* of mass statistics needed at the most basic level, I include a table of letter counts from *General Report on Tunny* (see Table 1). This well illustrates the extraordinary departures of German military plain language from the characteristics of random sequences drawn from the same alphabet. Notice how the frequency of characters other than / depends on the number of crosses in them. Notice also the bulges in the counts of P, ΔP, $\Delta \psi'$, ΔD. On the other hand, ψ', χ, Z, show for all practical purposes typical random counts in which every letter occurs an approximately equal number of times. (All counts are taken from a single message sent on the Grilse link on 10 January 1945.)

The small example of plaintext regularity given above, resulting from the keystroke sequence used to implement the full stop, was not actually a 'small' example operationally. Military German was crammed with abbreviations, marked by full stops, or by other punctuation signs whose keystroke profiles showed similar statistical regularities. These were found to be most marked in

Table 1. Some typical letter counts

	P	ΔP	ψ'	$\Delta\psi'$	ΔD	χ	Z	
/	4^a	91	118	1159	128	98	110	/
9	544	78	107	4	127	99	81	9
H	67	82	97	17	128	99	94	H
T	123	56	108	4	98	101	124	T
O	89	121	107	18	128	101	108	O
M	180	69	100	47	105	106	89	M
N	212	66	98	7	78	95	95	N
3	1^a	157	99	2	118	101	114	3
R	159	77	87	11	87	105	110	R
C	44	73	84	53	84	98	105	C
V	21	64	100	153	80	99	89	V
G	94	127	109	32	125	114	93	G
L	87	76	85	17	98	118	104	L
P	51	90	116	47	99	110	123	P
I	137	50	121	10	94	89	87	I
4	3^a	52	79	5	71	105	93	4
A	161	136	96	13	96	90	82	A
U	81	224	109	52	148	103	99	U
Q	23^b	79	103	186	92	97	88	Q
W	38	67	108	52	70	114	104	W
5	200	326	106	160	170	108	106	5
8	197	144	75	572	101	107	112	8
K	60	45	106	154	66	99	95	K
J	6	194	96	46	115	96	77	J
D	71	83	91	14	71	91	85	D
F	42	156	103	56	107	83	104	F
X	1	83	79	168	87	93	106	X
B	57	32	111	47	55	104	101	B
Z	26	65	81	13	81	103	108	Z
Y	7	84	94	62	88	95	106	Y
S	110	90	121	14	109	75	110	S
E	304	63	106	5	96	104	98	E
Total	3200	3200	3200	3200	3200	3200	3200	

a /, 3, 4 should not occur in P. Their occurrence is due to corruption.
b Q rarely occurs in letter-shift, but is quite frequent in figure-shift, where it corresponds to 1 (see Chapter 18).
Source: *General Report on Tunny*, p. 21.

plaintext when the first and second delta channels were combined by addition. By cancelling out to zeros, this provided frequent 'windows' for viewing snatches of underlying key. As for the delta key itself, a component of it (delta-psi) was also sprinkled with blanks resulting from character-repetitions in the non-delta psi-stream. This provided a low but exploitable frequency of peep-holes through which to catch glimpses of delta-chi (see Chapter 5).

In exploitation of this psi behaviour, delta-ing keytext in order to recover delta chi-wheels was how Tutte got into the structure of pure key in the first place. As we have seen, interception of rare depths made it possible to recover and work on pure key. The Testery used delta key for the method known as 'Turingery', both to break wheel patterns, and then, less laboriously, for the wheel settings of each individual message subsequently intercepted in the period (initially a month) during which that particular set of wheel patterns was operative for the given link. But as the practice of German operators became more disciplined, so the already sparse samples of pure key became sparser for lack of new depths, and effectively dried up.

BACK TO THE DRAG

Let us return to the lance corporal dragging the crib GESELLSCHAFT step by step through the text of a depth-sum, pausing at each step to see what resulted from each successive trial addition. He stopped only if the result of his addition at any stage yielded, say, SELLSCHAFT9U, at once concluding from such a local break that the offset was 2 and that the plaintext contained the sequence GESELLSCHAFT9U. In the hands of a cryptanalyst the immediate next step would be to extend by two characters the 'crib' that had been dragged, yielding, perhaps, SELLSCHAFT9UNT, which would strongly suggest some further extension, say GESELLSCHAFT9UNTER (company under), which might possibly be rewarded by 'SELLSCHAFT9UNTER9A', and so forth.

A harder problem was posed by depths of a different kind, which also succumbed to a similar crib-dragging method. In this second category, the operator of the German enciphering machine had unaccountably reset all wheels to their original settings at the end of a transmission, and had then proceeded to transmit, not the same message at a stagger, but a brand new message. To the person dragging a crib through a suspected depth-sum, the only clue that he might have struck lucky would be if, after adding his crib (say GESELLSCHAFT) at a given point in the ciphertext, the resulting character string looked like some unrelated fragment of military German. Instead of a nonsense string of characters, the crib GESELLSCHAFT might trigger, say, EDER9MANN9WI. If the crib dragger thought this looked like German he would mark the spot, and any similar candidate spots he might find, and put the job in his out-basket. On receiving the possible break, a Testery cryptanalyst engaged on depth-breaking would doubtless next try adding 9JEDER9MANN9WI (every man) to the depth-sum text, getting D9GESELLSCHAFT (plausible). The depth-breaking continues, extending both plaintexts in both directions until, in the ideal case, the extension process extends to the limits of the shorter of the two superimposed messages (see Chapter 15).

Using the law 'when and only when HONES + OBDZE = NEST9, then NEST9 + OBDZE = HONES', it follows that HONES + NEST9 = OBDZE. Note that as the staggered messages are extended by the cryptanalyst, for example as

Decrypt 1:   H O N E S T 9 I S 9 A S 9 H O N E S T 9 D O E S 9
Decrypt 2:   / / H O N E S T 9 I S 9 A S 9 H O N E S T 9 D O E

so also is the length of depth-sum text that is 'explained':

Depth-sum: H O O B D Z E P E 4 I E U Z M O B D Z E B M 3 X S

I here underline the recurrence of the OBDZE sequence as pointing to one of a myriad small indicators (in this case a suspiciously long repeated sequence) which the cryptanalyst's ever-scanning eye unconsciously notes and exploits. The denouement, however, comes when extension is complete, yielding a complete plaintext message.

From the relation plaintext + ciphertext = keytext we know that

either we have only to add decrypt 1 to ciphertext 1 to recover keytext,
or we have only to add decrypt 2 to ciphertext 1 to recover keytext.

If the first succeeds, then decrypt 2 + ciphertext will also recover the same keytext. If the second succeeds, then decrypt 1 + ciphertext will also recover the keytext.

Clues as to which is the right way round for pairing intercepts with plaintexts were sometimes present. If not, then it was necessary for the Testery to process each candidate in parallel on the assumption that it was the true key, until one of the two was confirmed. Given true key, an elaborate manual procedure—Turingery—could reverse-engineer from it the patterns set up on the 12 wheels of the Tunny machine.

MISPLACED TASK-DECOMPOSITION

So what was wrong with the reasonable-seeming thought that the task could be decomposed into a brute force (crib-dragging only) component and a skilled (extending the breaks) component? Why not first throw brute force at it and then pass the text on to the cryptanalysts with candidate breaks already found and flagged? Take a few dozen Intelligence Corps clerks each equipped with a list of cribs to be dragged, together with rule-sheets for the addition of teleprint characters and for the recognition of common fragments of military German. Let them do the dragging, marking all local breaks found or suspected. Marked-up texts could then be sent on to the Testery proper, to receive the attention of cryptanalysts whose time would thus be conserved by prior delegation of the drag work.

It sounded good. Experience soon convinced me otherwise. But my conviction had to be validated in the eyes of others. My only course was to drive the project along until its futility became evident, not to the band of massed lance corporals, but to the authors of the original proposal, whoever they were (this I never knew).

The flaw lay in the non-decomposability of a task once talent and much practice has melded it into a fluent unity. The cognitive psychologists speak of 'automatisation'. To the eye of an observer from Mars, delivery of the serve at tennis might appear to be a sufficiently separate and stereotyped task to suggest a change of rules. The expert player might be allowed to employ a brute-force server (crib-dragging posse of lance corporals) who would on delivery of his service instantly quit the court, leaving the tactically highly skilled tennis professional (cryptanalyst) to continue the rally.

Trade-offs can be debated for each separate athletic or intellectual skill, but can only be quantified empirically, case by case. In tennis, as in depth-breaking, each opening move (the serve) flows smoothly and subliminally into the move sequence (the rally) that follows. The gains from continuity of the single-agent scheme probably outweigh in tennis the sacrifice of sheer serving speed. The same principles were eventually shown to dominate the depth-breaking case.

TO THE TESTERY

The dogged endeavours of my well-drilled force of crib-draggers in due course generated sufficient documentation for me to report that the 'human wave' assault was unlikely to contribute effectively and was best disbanded. After this interlude, depressing for all concerned, I gained the long-sought shore of the Testery proper. I was turned over to a young graduate, now the internationally distinguished mathematician P. J. Hilton, for instruction in Turingery.

Peter knew all the Testery hand procedures backward and forward, and played a massive part in perfecting them. My first and vivid memory was that, although only a year or two older than me, he smoked a pipe. My second was of his didactic strictures on my fetish of tidiness and aesthetics in paper-and-pencil work, such as using a carefully aligned ruler rather than drawing my lines freehand. I should say 'my *then* fetish'. With efficiency and speed at an unimaginable premium, not to mention justified awe of my new mentor, I was cured of this particular perfectionism on the spot!

Among other vivid images of my first encounter with the Testery is first and foremost that of Major (later Colonel) Ralph Tester himself. I recall his mesmeric impact on female spectators in the lunch break as he leapt, demonic and glowing, about the tennis court—with an animality that I had only ever envisaged as radiating from the great god Pan. Yet a year later when I was already in the Newmanry, engaged in a machine-based attack on the same Fish ciphers, the same man was ashen under his tan. He had had to summon me (presumably at Newman's request) to reprove my conduct. Why had I been canvassing the cryptographic staff of both Newmanry and Testery for signatures to a petition for the administrative merging of the two sections? With the naivety of a 19-year-old I was oblivious of such facts as that, even if a Foreign Office section and a War Office section could have been merged, one or other of Tester and Newman would have had to be dumped, and that it would not have been Newman. An ingenious administrative compromise resulted. A fictional 'Mr X' appeared on Newman's books whose fake identity four selected Testery staff assumed for periods in rotation, acting as a species of internal consultant. This gave good technical liaison, previously absent.

Tester had the sense of purpose and personal humility of an outstanding leader. At the time of Rommel's retreat to Tunisia, we suddenly found that some mysterious change in the system had locked us out of the Berlin–Tunis channel. In early 1943, shortly before my departure to the just-formed 'Newmanry', the lexicographer Jim Wylie from the Research Section was assigned to join me in a two-man assault on the conundrum. It took us three very anxious weeks to penetrate what became known as 'the χ_2 limitation' (see Appendix 10 *The Motor Wheels and Limitations*). All hands were now turned to the exploitation of our break. A group of us offered to go flat out round the clock. Ralph's cryptographic skills were really too unpractised to be of material help, as he and we knew. But he sat among us, bolt upright as was normal for him, pencil in hand and unflagging as the hours raced by. In the end the hours were not racing, and we young Turks were drooping. Ralph, focused and refulgent as ever, saw this. 'You know,' he said tactfully, 'it's easy for me. Most things go downhill with age. Stamina for some reason goes the other way. So you're no good for this sort of marathon stuff until you're at least forty. Another coffee, anyone?' During the glory days of the American space programme, when the mean age of space vehicle commanders seemed to be getting more and more venerable, I recalled Tester's words.

STRANGE INCIDENT, BEST FORGOTTEN

The Testery's machine operators were ATS girls ('Auxiliary Territorial Service', I think). One of them, Helen Pollard—now Currie—in her reminiscence of the Testery (Chapter 20) speaks not only of the thrill of it all but briefly hints at a romantic attachment. That attachment outlasted the war. If there is to be a dedication of this memoir, then let it be to her.

For all the attractions of the new life, or perhaps because of them, I could not drop from my mind the initial 'white feather' impact of that roomful of WAAF girls. While on leave visiting my home in Weybridge, I learned from my father of questions from his peers at the St Georges Hill golf club about what his son was doing for the war effort. Apart from knowing that I was not after all learning Japanese, his mind was unavoidably blank. It was out of the question to give information of any kind to any person outside the wire, beyond saying 'sort of clerical work' or the like. He asked me whether I had ever considered active service.

Back at BP I asked for an interview with Colonel Pritchard and requested a transfer to the North African desert. Pritchard let me finish. Then he said: 'Who's been getting at you?' Taken off guard, I waffled. 'No-one?' he enquired politely, and let his question hang in the air. Eventually I blurted out that my father had mentioned such a possibility, but had applied no pressure. Anyway, I maintained, it had nothing to do with my decision. There was another uncomfortable pause. Then: 'I have to instruct you to return to duty. You see, Mr Michie, we have a war on our hands. Inconvenient, but unfortunately true. Unless you have further questions, you are free to return at once to your section.' Pause. 'And by the way, I do not expect you to raise such matters again.' Pause. 'Either with me or with anyone else.' Longer pause. 'As for your father, I do not anticipate that he will raise them either.'

I returned to the Testery and I confess I felt relieved. I don't believe I gave it a further thought. But many years later my mother told me that my father had received a visit at his place of work in the City of London from an army colonel, who presented himself as my superior officer. Did I know anything about it? I shook my head. For a decade or two after the war, to reveal anything whatsoever about Bletchley Park and its activities continued to be embargoed under the Official Secrets Act. Inevitably its subjective restraints weakened over time. None the less, 25 years passed before the first mention appeared in the open literature of the British use in 1943–5 of electronic computers for a cryptanalytic purpose.

LODGINGS—A NOTE OF PERSONAL REMINISCENCE

It was Peter Ericsson who generously threw me a welcome rescue line when I confided my dissatisfaction with my current landlady digs. He made the astonishing suggestion that I shack up with him at Mr and Mrs Brown's in Fenny Stratford—astonishing because the Brown household consisted downstairs of one small hall-cum-kitchen and one small sitting room in the back, where meals were also dished up and eaten, one outside toilet in the yard shared with neighbours, and two small upstairs bedrooms, of which one was the Browns' and the other was Peter's. The latter was just about big enough to contain a large double bed and a small wardrobe.

This wardrobe became the sole available store for the totality of his and my material possessions, and the experience of sharing a bed was entirely new to me! But in the prevailing spirit of giving anything and everything a try, we did. Somehow we must have mastered the social skills of sharing the intimacies of daily life, not only with each other but also with the Browns. All in the household had to take turns to journey downstairs to the kitchen sink in the small front room for washing, cleaning one's teeth, etc. As for having a bath, this ritual occurred once a week—Saturdays if memory serves—when a tin bathtub was brought in (I think from the yard) and water was heated in relays in pot, pan, and kettle.

The logistics were intricate beyond measure. Peter and I were often working different shifts, which eased the personal *lebensraum* problem, but complicated the round-the-clock timings of exits and entrances. I recall once arriving from work and walking blithely in from the yard. I was rewarded by an amazing vision. Mrs Brown's vast naked bulk arose in startlement from the foam, a pink dream of abundance to put a Rubens masterwork in the shade.

Peter and I shared our digs for two years. He opened the world of visual arts to me, including everything, such as it is, that I know about filmmaking. He was also spellbinding on both the comical and the crazy aspects of urban cultures of many lands. After the war he and Lindsay Anderson, destined to become one of Britain's innovative film directors (remember *If. . .?*), launched an avant-garde film magazine *Sequence*. They worked on the floor of a virtually unfurnished London apartment. Occasionally I visited from Oxford and helped where I could.

TURING, CHESS, AND 'THINKING MACHINES'

It was through needing to consult the originator of Turingery that I first met Alan Turing. We soon discovered a common interest in chess, and also the fact that we were both sufficiently poor players to be able to give each other a level game. At BP a person was either a chess master, having been recruited for that reason (similarly with winners of national crossword competitions) or he did not count chess among his interests. We formed the habit of meeting once a week for a game of chess in a pub in Wolverton. On the pervasive need-to-know principle we never discussed his work in the naval section. When I was demobilised I still knew nothing about Enigma, except possibly its name. Our shared topics of interest were the possible mechanisation of chess-playing, and learning machines. These interests were inspired by him, and were shared with Jack Good, now internationally renowned in mathematical statistics. In the post-war years, 'thinking machines' continued to occupy the three of us in occasional correspondence and meetings until Turing's death, and thereafter the two survivors, Good and myself, to the present day.

The naval section had originally been founded to support Turing's great Enigma breakthrough. Hence it was natural that he be asked to head it. Unfortunately his uncanny intellectual gifts were tightly interwoven with an equally uncanny lack of what are ordinarily called 'social skills'. The predictable result was administrative chaos. Rapid *ad hoc* extemporisations came to the rescue from one of his brightest lieutenants, the one-time British chess champion Hugh Alexander. He had made his pre-war living (there was in those days no money in chess) as an experienced and fast-thinking manager of the John Lewis London department store. So a little job like quietly and tactfully reorganising Turing's bewildered section was to him an interesting challenge. In short order Alexander flowed into the *de facto* headship. Turing continued happily as *de jure* head, no longer distracted by these matters.

One day Turing arrived at the gate of the Park late for work. On such occasions one signed oneself into a book with ruled columns and headings that included 'Name of Head of Section'. Turing unexpectedly wrote 'Mr Alexander', and proceeded in to work. Nothing was said. But somewhere wheels turned silently. Records were updated. Alexander continued his miracles of inspired and often unorthodox deployment of human and material resources, but now as the official head of naval section. (I had this from a third party, and never asked Turing about it. I think he would have found my question uninteresting.)

DEPTH-BREAKING AND THE TESTERY DRAGON

At a much later stage of the war, the role of my crib-dragging posse of lance corporals was mechanised in the Testery by an electromechanical machine. Called the 'Dragon', it was the brainchild of Angus Macintosh. Some decades later I knew him again as a fellow member of the Edinburgh professoriate. The Dragon repaid its keep in a modest way. Recall that the idea was to drag a short string of commonly occurring plaintext through a depth-sum. Just as with the lance corporals, the search was for a local sequence of the depth-sum text that fitted; when added to the crib a recognisable plaintext fragment resulted—a 'local break' to be passed to a cryptanalyst for extension.

Occasionally one of the Dragon's local breaks flagged for the cryptanalyst's attention provided him with a useful start. However, particularly in the common case of a stagger of 1, the cryptanalyst's eye spotted local breaks through entirely different and scarcely mechanisable means. Endless practice had equipped us with relatively huge mental dictionaries of cribs, the latter in the form of subliminally coded character-string clichés. Take the above case of GESELLSCHAFT, and generalise it to form the class of all words ending SCHAFT. While scanning the text of a stagger-1 depth, the cryptanalyst's eye would be instantly caught if JGQCX occurred, and continued, say, so as to form JGQCXJQW+. Addition to itself at a stagger of 1 goes:

$$
\begin{array}{l}
\text{S C H A F T} \cdot \\
\cdot \text{ S C H A F T} \cdot \\
\cdot \text{ J G Q C X} \cdot
\end{array}
$$

By instinct, as it were, one would immediately feel like appending a space to the upper of the two plaintext lines,

$$
\begin{array}{l}
\text{S C H A F T 9} \\
\cdot \text{ S C H A F T}
\end{array}
$$

But the experienced Testery cryptanalyst wouldn't even try the new character sum 9 + T, get the answer H, and note that it doesn't fit into JGQCXJQW+. He would have already recognised another familiar sequence, namely QW+, which would trigger in his brain the sequence 'shift up, N, shift down, space', or +N89, which is teleprintese for 'comma'. So:

$$
\begin{array}{l}
\text{S C H A F T + N 8 9} \cdot \\
\cdot \text{ S C H A F T + N 8 9} \\
\cdot \text{ J G Q C X J Q W +} \cdot
\end{array}
$$

Good! Now for some backwards extension, the cryptanalyst would say. How about 9WISSENSCHAFT? 9GESELLSCHAFT? If none of one's stock clichés leapt to mind, either at plaintext or delta level, then one might ask the sole German-speaking worker in the Hut, Peter Ericsson. His linguistic gifts, matched with an even more fluent associative imagination, would kick in. If his first verbal suggestion didn't hit the mark, he'd be over to your desk with pencil and eraser. In minutes he would have extended your small break in both directions in a lightning succession of trials, retractions, and consolidations.

The mental style of another notable young colleague, Peter Benenson, was an almost unnerving contrast. Sheer concentrated doggedness was applied systematically, obsessively, hour after hour. That too, I noted, could garner miracles, less swiftly but perhaps more surely, sometimes reducing jobs that others had tossed onto the heap as intractable. After the war he went on to found Amnesty International, culminating in a colourful exit with psychiatric overtones. I did not follow the details.

It was essentially by such generate-and-test cycles of conjecture that Tiltman had got out the very first depth, intercepted on 30 August 1941. In his case, the displacement, or 'stagger', was three characters rather than one. This is more adverse than a stagger of one in terms of guessing candidate extensions, but is partly compensated by a gain in the length of each individual successful extension.

SECURE CONDUCT

German operators were, not surprisingly, forbidden to retransmit a message without changing the wheel settings. An analogous peacetime interdict is supposed to deter drivers from taking vehicles onto the road without fastening their seat belts. Reflection suggests a safer expedient. Road vehicles could by law incorporate interlocks in their manufacture, enabling the ignition to fire only when the driver's seat-belt is fastened. As we know, that is not the way that the minds of civil transport authorities work. Nor was it the way of wartime Germany's military authorities with the Lorenz machine. Rather than commission a redesign, they banned undesired operator behaviours, while not even disabling the reset button.

The curative effect of administrative enforcement proved patchy at best. By degrees the stable door was in the end closed. By then the horse had bolted. If German *cryptanalysts* had been given an opportunity to vet the Lorenz for design flaws, then the British project to crack it could never have got off the ground. In Britain the *codemakers* were the Royal Corps of Signals. The *code-breakers* were the mixed-services signals intelligence organisation built up at BP during the Second World War. We did not communicate. Similar compartmentalisation prevailed, so some of my colleagues ascertained, both in America and in Russia. Interlock, filtering, and other precautions would, of course, occur at once to a codebreaker. In like manner, the only dependable way of protecting corporate and governmental computer networks today from the criminal trespasses of hackers is to hire from their top echelon on the principle of fighting fire with fire.

Generating depths was but the first and most extreme of many human foibles that introduced unwanted regularities into messages. The habit, for example, of hitting the shift-up and shift-down keys twice in quick succession, just to make sure, could have been rendered harmless electromechanically. A simple logical filter, placed between the stream of characters from the keyboard and the wireless transmitter, could have done the trick. Examples could be multiplied.

At all events, one thing is sure. The day that the world's nations break the hermetic seal between codemakers and codebreakers will see the end of the military cryptology game as we know it.

NEWMAN'S PROPOSAL

The limitation on Turingery and on almost everything else done in the Testery was the requirement to have keytext to work on, obtained from depths. Newman's idea was to recover the wheel settings from *ciphertext* messages instead of just those where the underlying key had been handed over on a plate, as depths, by insufficiently disciplined German operators. These rare free gifts, which were all that we could so far decipher, were rapidly becoming rarer. Clearly large-scale statistical processing, impossible by hand methods, offered the only chance for breaking and reading the overwhelming majority of intercepts. Newman based his proposal for mechanising the attack on a frontal assault on the ciphertext itself, hoping for sufficient occurrence of non-random features of the enciphered plaintext, or specifically the differenced text.

His proposal extended to intercepted ciphertext some of the principles that were applicable by hand only to pure key. The idea was aimed at the statistical tendency for delta plaintext (and particularly Boolean combinations of selected channels of plaintext) to have more 0s than 1s and hence to represent a pale and fuzzy reflection of underlying delta key. Perhaps delta cipher would be just sufficiently like delta key that, although hand exploitation of this correlation was out of the question, fast machine processing might bring it within striking distance.

The plan was thus to operate on such a scale of sample-size and speed that the statistical properties of military German plaintext contained a sufficient frequency of character repetitions to combine with the strongly above-random frequency of repetitions in the stream of psi-wheel characters. Then, after delta-ing both character streams, a weakly above-random frequency of the all-zeros character:

$$0$$
$$0$$
$$0$$
$$0$$
$$0$$

would serve as an intermittent 'window' through which the delta-chi at this point could be glimpsed. A logical consequence would be that if the cryptanalysts were in possession of the chi-wheel patterns, but not of their settings (starting points), then hypothetically an exhaustive search through all the $41 \times 31 \times 29 \times 26 \times 23$ possible settings, on each trial setting adding the delta chi stream to the delta plain message stream, would leave just delta-psi + delta-plain. This might reveal itself by the afore-mentioned faint statistical excess or 'bulge' in the number of all-zero char-acters. Because of the astronomical combinatorics of such a search, Newman followed an earlier suggestion of Tutte's that logical combinations of, say, only two selected channels be processed at any one time, with an indication that combining the first two channels as delta $(1 + 2)$ might be the place to start.

ENTER HEATH ROBINSON, ENGINEERS, WRENS, AND GOOD

Funds for Newman's proposal had been granted. Two rooms, comprising Hut 11, were provided. A floorful of prefabricated parts was delivered and put under assembly-and-test by the engineers. Some Wrens arrived to operate the new machine, and the Newmanry sprang into energetic if disjointed activity.

I was one day sitting at my table in solitary wonderment when I saw in the further corner a smallish figure seemingly frozen in meditative yet enquiring reverie. He slowly approached with a deliberative step, right arm and hand in semi-extension. I rose and waited for the hand to come into range. At that point he stopped, and gazed composedly upon my bafflement. After what seemed a long while, he made an announcement in tones of quiet precision: 'I am Good!'

In April 1987 an international symposium on the *Foundations and Philosophy of Probability and Statistics* was held to honour Good's 70th birthday. In prefacing my own contribution to the symposium I remarked that my lifetime experience (continued today) had confirmed that he was indeed Good then, and has been getting better ever since. Newman remembered (in a letter) that Good was a valuable man to have around when anything went wrong: '[H]e was sort of the physician, and he would know what it was, that it was because a Wren had gone out to tea early, or that it was because something was dirty, or that we'd forgotten to add in some parameter in calculating it.'

Good's detective gifts were indeed remarkable. I recall his being brought urgently from his lodgings when a document or other item had been mislaid in the middle of a night shift. He had in fact been woken from his bed. Jack's seated figure in a heavy overcoat overlaying pyjamas and dressing gown, topped off with a grey scarf round the neck, woollen and fringed, formed the calm centre of a vortex. His method of search was instructive, being wholly abstract. That is, it was conducted solely within an evolving mental model. Others streamed to and fro, bringing him answers to carefully posed questions and setting out on missions to confirm or refute specific further predictions, as the logical map, invisible of course to the onlooker, was systematically shrunk to a point. This announced and the item duly found, Jack was conveyed back to his interrupted sleep. Sherlock Holmes' dictum has been much quoted to the effect that when all impossibilities have been eliminated, then whatever remains, however improbable, is the truth. That was the first occasion on which I ever saw the dictum put into action in its pure form, and the last.

A STATISTICIAN'S SLAVE

Exhaustive search of the combinations of all five chi-wheel settings at once was, of course, not remotely possible even for electronic machines. Therefore the strategy that Newman had proposed was, as mentioned above, to find combinations of channels in German plaintext messages that were so productive of statistical regularities that the rest could initially be disregarded without loss in the size of the statistical excesses over chance. In the event, the systematic studies that I helped Jack Good then to conduct, using the Heath Robinson as a statistician's slave, confirmed Newman's suspicion that adequate relative excesses ('proportional bulges' in our terminology) could be got even after disregarding channels 3, 4, and 5, leaving only $31 \times 41 = 1271$ combinations of possible settings of the χ_1 and χ_2 wheels to be tried.

Once these two chi-wheels were set, matters became more problematical. Tackling channels 4 and 5 in like manner sometimes found a marginally sufficient bulge, sometimes not. So more sophisticated statistical properties of plaintext had to be pressed into service. But first such properties had to be prospected for and discovered, perhaps properties that could be forced into the open by exploiting more complex relations between channels. The hope, therefore, was that by amassing such statistics, we might eventually operate on raw intercepts as input, without having to rely on depths.

The heaven-sent gift to the Testery of pure key from depths can be appreciated when one realises that key can be seen as key + plaintext in the special case that the plaintext consists of the message: 0 0 0 0 0 0 0 0 0 0 0 0 0 0 0 0 0 0 0 0 0 0 0 0 0 0 0 0 0 0 0 0, etc. Clearly, here the character repetition frequency is 100 per cent. In other words delta plaintext + delta key gives all zeros, just as it would if the plaintext message were 1 1 1 1 1 1 1 1 1 1 1 1 1 1 1 1 1, say, or G G G G G G G G G G G G G G G G G G G G G G G G G, etc. Sometimes, by the way, it was—at least for long stretches, even in the absence of a depth. A possible guess is that in manual mode the enciphering operator had either fallen asleep in mid-keystroke or had carelessly leaned on the keyboard, thus keeping some key depressed. In that case the corresponding character could simply repeat in every machine cycle and be transmitted. A more normal practice involved two stages. First the plaintext message was converted from keyboard to an output paper tape. Second the plaintext tape was input into the Lorenz for the encipher-and-transmit step in auto mode. The generation of a continuing string of repetitions of blank or other plaintext character could result from a jammed tape remaining immobile in the Lorenz's tape reader while enciphering and transmission continued as normal.

So much for free gifts. What of the harsh realities that supervened as the supply of depths and all other sources of keytext headed for extinction? When, as became the invariable rule, enciphered plaintext has the intended form of a one-off message in military German, then *only when this plaintext message has a repeated character* can this act as a little window of 'blank' in the delta ciphertext, through which a character of the underlying delta key can be seen.

SIZE AND FREQUENCY OF 'PEEP-HOLES'

How frequent, then, were the peep-holes? If delta plaintext gave 100 per cent zeros on all five channels then the delta plaintext would be fully transparent, as with the conjectural sleeping or leaning operator. What if delta plaintext were generally to give 50 per cent zeros on some given channel, but consistently more than 50 per cent when certain channels were combined in some way, such as by addition, the other channels being temporarily ignored? The idea then arises to enhance the peep-holes by imposing a logical restriction on some other, third, delta channel, or the sum of two others, gaining in return a more than compensating increase of the relative size of the effect— contingent on how well the logical constraints were designed to fit the actual statistical properties of plaintext.

Let us return to an earlier-mentioned example, namely the delta of ++M889 which encodes the punctuation mark 'full stop'. As earlier noted, it so happens that just as the sum of the first two channels of the delta gives all zeros, so also does the sum of channels 4 and 5. On channels 1 and 2 this regularity was usually enough, along with other channel 1 and 2 features of delta German plaintext, to find by machine the settings of χ_1 and χ_2. The features of plaintext on channels 4 and 5 were not always so favourable as to allow the same trick to be applied. Use of the plugboard to cause the machine only to look at channels 4 and 5 at those points which satisfied some condition on 1 and 2 (e.g. that delta of $1 + 2 = 0$) was found to increase the $4 + 5$ bulge to a degree that sometimes more than compensated for the loss in effective sample size. Other more sophisticated statistical interactions were required to cope with all channels in all cases. First, however, far-reaching knowledge of the intricate statistical characteristics of plaintext was required in order to discover what precisely these statistical interactions might be.

When the first Robinson machine became operational, Jack Good and I spent our day shift in frontal assault, with Max pacing around for positive results to announce. Although he agreed in theory with our argument that pure reconnaissance of the problem should be the first use of the newly operational machine, the need for credibility, with high-ranking military and others dropping in to see what results were being got, pressed sorely on him. Once he had laid it down, Max Newman was not someone that a person in his senses would oppose. From nine to six each day, Jack and I accordingly went through the motions.

GHOST SHIFTS

But many evenings were spent in clandestine ghost shifts, with one or two volunteer Wrens and an engineer. Our purpose was to use the new instrument to gather massive delta plaintext statistics, including in particular the frequencies of zeros (i.e. repetitions in the original plaintext) in the sum of selected pairs of channels, conditional on what was happening on other channels.

I say 'conditional on what was happening . . .'. This was all-important after the first two chi-wheels had been got, yielding knowledge of the first two channels of delta-psi + delta-plain. To get knowledge of further, and possibly more recalcitrant, chi-wheel settings, we needed somehow to sharpen the statistical 'bulges' characterising other channels of delta plaintext. On the Heath Robinson we could only screen out channels unwanted in a given run by concocting tapes in which the unwanted channels were left all blank. In the Colossus, this conditionalising was later done at the flick of a set of hand-switches, together with plugboard programming for forming arbitrary Boolean combinations of selected channels.

With the aid of Heath Robinson and our volunteer assistants we systematically extracted from Testery decrypts batteries of general rules governing the statistico-logical structure of military German, with and without delta-psi streams superadded. Owing to the action on the psis of the motor stream, this latter component was guaranteed to supply a stream of extra zeros.

Armed with these tabulations, statistical summaries, and empirical rules, we were now in a position to make frontal assaults in earnest. This yielded sufficient operational success for Newman to announce feasibility. I doubt if he ever knew of the clandestine operation. If he had, his forward-pressing propensity, and preference for focusing on the next big thing, would I believe have led him to smile and then dismiss it from mind.

The next big thing, of course, was Colossus.

COLOSSUS

Colossus possessed radically new properties, including facilities for plugboard programming which allowed the user to apply specified Boolean constraints to the machine's search of the data for statistical regularities. By manipulation of connections and hand-switches, up to 100 Boolean functions of selected channels of a running tape could be simultaneously evaluated on the fly.

Hard-wired branching was also possible, for example to effect conditional printing by the on-line typewriter—conditional, that is, on current values of intermediate computed results. Operation on a serious scale began in February 1944. As explained below, Good helped me to test a proposal for an unorthodox use of the machine which conferred a considerable extension of functionality. The resulting engineering crash programme leading to the Colossus II, III, . . ., XI machines nudged the design further in the direction of 'programmability' in the modern sense.

Long before that stage Good and I had been powerfully, indeed brilliantly, reinforced by four of Good's former colleagues from Naval Enigma—David Rees, Shaun Wylie, Arthur Chamberlain, and Michael Ashcroft, together with Newman's friend and pre-war mathematical co-worker J. H. C. Whitehead, whom he recruited directly from civilian life. From an early stage, five of us (Good, Rees, Wylie, Whitehead, and I) were the beneficiaries of a scheme which relieved each of us in turn for a week from all duties except to sit alone in the 'research room' and ruminate as we pleased. The resulting stimulus to the flow of new ideas and techniques was held to be sufficient justification— for things were indeed getting very tough, and innovation was at a correspondingly high premium.

PATTERN BREAKING

When Colossus became operational, wheel setting could only be done for the tiny proportion of traffic for which the wheel patterns for the given link and day had already been broken by laborious, slow, and chancy hand processes. The know-how and equipment for finding the settings perforce stood idle whenever we did not have in our hands, so to speak, wheels of known patterns. At a time when the Germans were beginning on link after link to change all 12 patterns not monthly but daily, the pace of manual wheel-breaking created a new cryptanalytic bottleneck, soon amounting almost to a roadblock.

At the heart of our means of pattern-breaking was 'rectangling', an inexpressibly tedious and time-consuming hand procedure due to Tutte, and initially for deriving the patterns of just the χ_1 and χ_2 wheels (see Appendix 9 *Rectangling*). Not only laborious at a mundane clerical and calculational level, rectangling was vulnerable to risks of small slips. A tiny copying error could lead to loss of precious codebreaker–hours in subsequent detection and rectification, or if undetected then to the job's eventual abandonment. Even without these hazards, the pace of manual breaking of wheels for the Newmanry machines to set would still have been glacial relative to the new demands now unleashed.

In April 1944, I made a technical proposal that was simple enough to allow Good and myself to validate its correctness in a couple of hours' experimentation. Using Colossus I in ways for which it had not been designed, we demonstrated the feasibility of machine-aided breaking of the wheel patterns themselves. So what did we do when, as Jack Good relates in the previous chapter, 'one morning Donald Michie came into the office with a simple idea for using Colossus to help to produce the . . . "rectangles" used by the Testery for wheel breaking'? Jack stood at the on-line teleprinter, calling out excerpts and summaries of what was being printed as the trial progressed. I stationed myself behind the machine. I think I had to stand on a chair to give me easier access to the top two strips of sockets representing the first two chi-wheels. The experiment succeeded! In principle Colossus could, if suitably modified, be used as a very high-speed interactive rectangling machine. We could see that the back-pins must be brought to the front and replaced by hand-switches. We could see also in broad outline the extensions needed to the machine's inner stepping and reporting logic. The rest was taken up, under Newman's urging, by the team already engaged in building Colossus II. It was decided to equip the new machine with what was referred to as a 'special attachment' or 'rectangling gadget'. The design, engineering, and patching-in of this attachment was led by Harry Fensom. The special attachment enabled Colossus II to begin a new kind of business, semi-automated pattern-breaking, a few days before D-day.

By the end of the war the closely interlaced operations of Colonel Tester's hand-cryptanalysis section and of Max Newman's machine section were breaking about 25 new sets of wheel *patterns* weekly and the complete *settings* of about 150 transmissions. On grounds of the relative cost-effectiveness of anticipated further effort, a rather larger number of intercepts were abandoned with some settings still not found. Under the coordinated control of 22 cryptographers and 273 Wrens on a three-shift regime, nine Colossus machines, each weighing over a ton, were working continuously round the clock. Peak monthly decryption reached in excess of 600 messages per month.

THE TESTERY REPORT

The release, in June 2000, of *General Report on Tunny* allows the level of detail as regards Newman's section and the machine procedures used there to be extended and refined. Still to reach the public domain is a technical report on the work of Colonel Tester's section. On cessation of hostilities, I was assigned to prepare the latter document, and completed it in a couple of months before joining Good on *General Report on Tunny*. Although the Testery report remains classified, I was recently enabled (by kind arrangement of the Director) to visit Bletchley Park's successor organisation, the Government Communications Headquarters (GCHQ) at Cheltenham, and to refresh my memory of it. I also received guidance from GCHQ's chief mathematician as to which details in it cannot yet be disclosed. A good deal of its content is directly inferable from other sources, including *General Report on Tunny*. The full Testery report amplifies this knowledge.

As was also necessary with *General Report on Tunny*, ultimate declassification of the Testery report will require that a decision be taken in concert by GCHQ and the US National Security Agency. Its eventual declassification can hardly be in doubt.

Section 4

The Testery

Chapter 18

Major Tester's Section

Jerry Roberts

THE SIGNIFICANCE OF BREAKING TUNNY

Tunny messages passed primarily between army headquarters in Germany and the various army groups. A great deal of traffic passed between headquarters and Army Group B, where the main fighting on the Western front was concentrated. On the Eastern front, messages between headquarters and Army Groups North, Central, and South dominated the traffic. Many messages were signed by top field marshals like von Rundstedt, Model, Rommel, and Keitel. Occasionally there were messages signed by Hitler himself.

Tunny provided information about the Germans' actions and planning from the spring of 1942 onwards—from the time of Hitler's decision to focus on the Russian front through to the final breakthrough of the Allied armies in 1945. The strategic value of the information was immense. One long message alone gave the whole disposition of the units within the army groups on the Eastern front, and, within each army, of the divisions, panzer-divisions, and all the other specialised units. Our problem was how to convey the gist of this information to the Russians without letting them know how we had derived it.

In June 1944 Hitler assembled the main body of his troops in the Pas de Calais, well north of the Allied landing beaches in Normandy, believing that the main Allied attack would come in the Calais region. If, instead, Hitler had committed these troops straight after the Normandy landings and thrown the Allied forces back into the sea, the consequences would have been incalculable. That he did not plan to do so was known through the decryption of Tunny. This is only one example of the many crucial contributions that Tunny made to the eventual Allied victory.

THE TESTERY

Bletchley Park was a medium-sized country house set in pleasant grounds; although it was a strange mixture of architectural styles, I found it came to be a likeable building. It housed some of the top army brass, including Brigadier Tiltman, the most senior army person there and himself a top cryptographer. I arrived at BP in late 1941 as a civilian and was interviewed by Tiltman. He wore his full uniform, complete with red tabs—it was an intimidating encounter.

At that time the Park still looked like a park, with trees and a lake on which there were even ducks. The huts which eventually came to occupy such a lot of the grounds were then fewer in number (we were soon lodged in one of these, close to the Mansion). The Intelligence units were already established in their various huts—prosaic as these looked, they had an aura about them, such as might attach to the vaults of the Bank of England: there, after all, was concentrated the most secret material in the country.

When I started in the Testery, in July 1942, its staff numbered only eight or nine. The Testery grew steadily as the war went on, numbering 118 in May 1945—small by comparison with the quantity of deciphered material produced. It was said that around 1000 people worked at the Park when I joined; towards the end of the war, it was estimated that over 10,000 people worked there.

During the first part of 1942 Major Tester headed a small unit breaking German military police traffic (which used a much simpler cipher than Tunny, called Double Playfair). This unit formed the main part of the fledgling Testery, founded in July 1942. Our small group, consisting of Tester, Colvill, Ericsson, Hilton, Oswald, and Roberts, was sufficient to break the relatively limited amount of traffic passing on Tunny at that time.

In the mature Testery there were four main groups:

Management   Major Tester himself ran the unit overall. Tom Colvill was the Testery's general manager. Peter Hilton played one of the most important roles on the cryptographic side, participating in system-breaking (i.e. dealing with any changes to the Tunny machine), and liaising with the Newmanry.

Senior executives   The four German linguists on whom the main burden of message-breaking fell were Major Denis Oswald, Captain Jerry Roberts (shift-leader), Captain Peter Ericsson (shift-leader), and Mr Victor Masters (shift-leader). Other message-breakers included Regimental Sergeant Major Peter Benenson, Mr Peter Edgerley, Captain Dobbins, Captain Roy Jenkins, Mr John Christie, and Mr Jack Thompson.

Tunny machine typists   Some 22 ATS girls (Auxiliary Territorial Service—

the equivalent of the army) dealt with typing clean copies of the decrypted messages. Their Tunny machines were set up so that when ciphertext was typed in, clear text came out.

Back-up staff This was a group made up mainly of non-commissioned army personnel who dealt with the registering of traffic and other administrative tasks.

In the Testery's early months (1942 into 1943) everyone worked on one shift, and most were engaged in the breaking process. As time went on, and the sheer volume of decrypting grew, it became necessary to have an evening shift, from 4 p.m. to midnight. A little later, as the wheels for more army groups were broken, a night shift was added, working from midnight to 9 a.m.

Each team would work for one week on days, one on evenings, and one on nights. During the daytime, the shift personnel could take any major problem to the management or the senior codebreakers, but this was not possible for the midnight shift, nor, after 6 p.m., for the evening group. So shift-leaders were appointed, the duties falling largely to three people, Ericsson, Roberts, and Masters. The shift-leaders would participate in message-breaking and had the responsibility of keeping the decrypting process going smoothly, including the setting of messages and the typing out of clear text.

A high proportion of the Testery's staff were very young. Two of the three shift-leaders were 21 when they joined and 23 when they were appointed, while the top mathematician, Hilton, was 19 when he joined. Edgerley and Michie were even younger—18. Most of the ATS staff were under 24 in 1944. Virtually all were away from their family, billeted in or around Bletchley Park.

TESTER AND COLVILL

Tester, a linguist and head of the unit, was recruited from Unilever (the manufacturers of 'Sunlight' soap), where he held a senior position in their accountancy division. The imperturbable, pipe-smoking Tester spoke fluent German, but did not pretend to be a codebreaker. The atmosphere in his unit was always positive and friendly, and the personnel were well selected—Tester seemed to find the right niche for everybody. Thanks to Tester's influence the work of the Testery was very well organised: it was rare to see members of the unit with nothing to do; absences were minimal; and the work spirit was good, even at 4 a.m. on the graveyard shift. Tester represented the unit authoritatively in its relations with other departments, including the

Newmanry, the top brass in Hut 3 (to which our deciphered material went when it left the Testery), and the administration at BP.

While the excellent organisation of the Testery was due in good part to the friendly but firm urbanity of Tester himself, he was greatly assisted in management by another senior man, Tom Colvill. Colvill was also recruited from business: he had been a manager in a major insurance company. As Tester spent more time liaising with other departments, Colvill handled progressively more of the management of the unit. A lot of the credit for the success of the Testery goes to Colvill. His actuarial background probably made it easier for him to understand the mindset of the mathematicians. Colvill eventually bore the burden of the administration of over 100 staff.

After the war, both men returned to their respective companies.

TRAFFIC THROUGH THE SECTION

Organisation of the Material

Each day, traffic came in from the various German army groups on both the Western and the Eastern fronts. The traffic had to be recorded and classified, and a check kept on its progress, right through to its machine-decoding and the despatch of the clear text to the intelligence officers in Hut 3. These functions, and other aspects of practical organisation, were in the charge of Regimental Sergeant Major 'Tubby' Roots, who was assisted by Staff-Sergeant Jim Walford and a small army team.

Breaking

Messages were distributed to cryptanalysts according to the day's priorities. When a cryptanalyst obtained a break-in, it could occur at any point in the message, not necessarily at the beginning. A unit known as 'Room 40' (see Table 1) had the task of working the clear text back to the beginning of the message so that the starting positions of the wheels could be established.

Machine Decoding

Once the patterns on the 12 wheels had been established and the wheel start positions found, the messages could be decrypted. The final clear texts were typed up by ATS girls. On each shift, a team of seven or eight ATS girls carried out the typing process, hammering away at their Tunny machines for the whole shift—eight or nine hours at a stretch. The night-watch, from midnight to 9 a.m., was particularly demanding. There was a break for forty minutes

Table 1. Shifts in the Testery during May 1945

	9.00a.m.–4.00p.m.	4.00p.m.–12.00m.	12.00m.–9a.m.
ROOM 41	Capt. Ericsson	Capt. Roberts	Mr. Masters
(Cryptographers)	C.S.M. Barratt	S/Sgt. Philps	Capt. Dobbins
	Lieut. Levenson	S/Sgt. Denman	Capt. Davies
	R.S.M. Wild	Mr. Christie	Capt. Jenkins
	S/Sgt. Holmes	Mr. Thompson	Sgt. Rollo
	Sgt. Uphill		Mr. Edgerley
	Mr. Michie		Sub. Worsley
	C.S.M. Pollard		
	Permanent days—**Major** Oswald, Capt. Marshall, R.S.M. Benenson,		
	Mr. Colvill, Mr. Hilton		
ROOM 40	Sgt. Mayo-Smith	Capt. Wesson	Mr. Jones
(Wheel setting)	Sgt. Gloster-Downing	Capt. Maddocks	Capt. Bancroft
	Cpl. Porter	R.S.M. Roots	Capt. Potts
	Cpl. Rees	S.S.M. Walford	Sgt. Cook
	Cpl. Williams	S.Q.M.S. Garner	Cpl. Rogers
	Cpl. Ramsey	Cpl. Mashiter	Cpl. Keyte
	Cpl. Nash	Cpl. Cook	L/Cpl. Langford
	L/Cpl. Bradley	L/Cpl. Taylor	Cpl. Maskell
	Permanent days—Sub. Bridgewater, Cpl. Saward, Cpl. Street		
ROOM 27	S/Sgt. Gutteridge	Sgt. Godsell	S/Sgt. Traynor
(Decoding by	S/Sgt. Owen	Sgt. Sproston	Sgt. Hampson
Tunny machine)	Sgt. Smith	Cpl. Cook	Cpl. Jaques
	Cpl. Mollier	Cpl. Eccleston	Cpl. Witty
	Cpl. Roberts	Cpl. Bell	Cpl. Davies
	Cpl. Wright	Cpl. Dorney	Cpl. Leverett
	Pte. Charlesworth		
	Under instruction—L/Cpl. Holloway		
ROOM 28	C.S.M. Collin	Sub. Palmer	Sub. Tickle
	Mr. Wood	Mr. Jeeves	Capt. Winter
	S/Sgt. Collings	Sgt. Beckingham	
ROOM 29	Lt. Van Der Wal	Capt. Peterson	C.S.M. Carney
	Cpl. Ashworth	Sgt. Alderton	
	Permanent days—**Capt.** Hayward		
ROOM 43	Permanent days—Cpl. **Hickman**, Cpl. Sayr		
ROOM 12	S.Q.M.S. Finch	Cpl. Danils	S.Q.M.S. Sinclair
(Registration)	Cpl. Enderby	Cpl. Gwyne	Sgt. Smith
	Cpl. Swadling	Cpl. Fitch	Cpl. Ansell
	L/Cpl. Thomas	Cpl. Smith	L/Cpl. Bailey
BLOCK F	Cpl. Marshall	Cpl. York	Cpl. Phillpot
	Pte. Harwood		
ROOM 31	Cpl. Ophen	Cpl. Hart	Cpl. Haddick
	L/Cpl. Price	Cpl. Marti	Cpl. Horton
		Cpl. Coons	
	Permanent days—S.S.M. Bloom, S/Sgt. Wheeler, Sgt. Maunsell,		
	Cpl. Gibbons, Cpl. Spreadborough, Cpl. Long		
	Statistics—Sgt. Nathan, Cpl. Cook, Cpl. Aspinall		

around 4 a.m. On a snowy or rainy night the hundred yard walk to the canteen rather took the shine off the break, and the wartime food reduced the appeal even more.

Routing of Broken Messages

A sub-unit, including some senior personnel, read the decrypts and sent them on to the relevant intelligence officers. Another sub-unit looked at decrypted messages to spot possible cribs.

RECRUITMENT OF THE BREAKING STAFF

A fair proportion of the senior personnel at BP came from the top universities, especially Oxford, Cambridge, and London (each was a 30- to 50-minute train ride from Bletchley station). The Testery, like BP itself, recruited primarily linguists and mathematicians to form its cryptographic staff. Graduates in both fields were contacted, as well as senior figures at the universities. Personal recommendations were important—it was almost impossible to sack someone once they were at BP, for fear they might subsequently prejudice security. Recommendations were often sought from academics and others who had worked in the Admiralty's Room 40 during the First World War.

In trying to foresee how useful a person might be at breaking ciphers, the recruiters saw as promising an affection for chess or crosswords. Both Peter Ericsson and myself were put through this hoop when interviewed at the War Office by a Major Masters. It went:

Masters   Do you play chess at all?
Roberts   Oh yes, I enjoy chess.
Masters   Do you tackle crosswords, such as the ones in *The Times* or the
          Observer?
Roberts   Oh yes, I have a go at them often.

Ericsson's responses were:

(Chess) Oh, no, I've never bothered with it.
(Crosswords) Oh no, no, no, waste of time.

This did not prevent us ending up in the same unit!

BREAKING, EARLY DAYS

In the earlier days (before the tightening up of German security) there were plenty of depths. Two longish messages were chosen and their ciphertexts were added together. Because the messages had had exactly the same encryption applied to them, this was the equivalent of adding the two clear texts together.

The addition might produce, say:

$$\ldots \text{F J M 5 X E K L R J J} \ldots$$

The cryptographer would test certain words against this and, if lucky, would find that at one position a choice of word produced possible clear text from the other message of the pair. For instance, if the cryptographer tried the common 9ROEM9 ('Roman'),

$$\text{F J M 5 X E}$$

could give

$$\text{9 R O E M 9}$$
$$\text{D E 9 G E S}$$

A lot of units in the German army were assigned Roman numerals, I, II, and so on. These could not be typed as they stood, and the Tunny operator handled them by typing the German equivalent of 'Roman 1'. The abbreviation for Roman—ROEM (from *Roemisch*)—therefore cropped up a lot. The character 9 was used to indicate a space between words.

DE9GES was possible clear, so the cryptographer would push on with a number after ROEM, in this case EINS (one), and find he had good clear:

$$\text{F J M 5 X E K L R J J}$$
$$\text{9 R O E M 9 E I N S 9}$$
$$\text{D E 9 G E S C H I C K}$$

The cryptographer would then assume that the text ran 9WURDE9GES-CHICKT9 ('was sent') and see what letters that gave in the first message. If WURDE did not work, he would try other likely words.

Cryptographers had to have all the letter 'additions' (such as $F + 9 = D$) at their fingertips. The whole vocabulary became second nature to us, so that we could quickly test out possible clear texts, discarding them if unsuccessful and trying new ones. More than 50 years later, I still find myself trying to 'break' car number plates with 9ROEM9 or 55M889 (the keyboard code for a full stop)!

It was here, of course, where the linguists were most needed. A break-in might show, for instance, HEITEN9 (a frequent ending in German) and the linguists would be able to try various likely words in order to extend the break, such as EINHEITEN (units). There were other frequent endings, UNGEN9 and KEIT9 for example. The linguist would have to test out various possibilities, such as 9SENDUNGEN9 (messages) and 9TAETIGKEIT9 (activity).

The breaker had to look for a whole variety of such pieces of text and rapidly test for them at different places in the ciphertext. We would recognise a cluster of cipher-letters which were the addition of two standard bits of clear. For example, the cipher-letters

$$8 \; Z \; 9 \; V \; A \; /$$

are the sum of

$$9 \; R \; O \; E \; M \; 9 \; \text{(roman)}$$
$$5 \; 5 \; M \; 8 \; 8 \; 9 \; \text{(full stop)}$$

A message breaker might eventually develop a kind of instinct for spotting a break-in.

It looks easy once you know how. And some messages did prove relatively easy, especially if they had a lot of punctuation in them. But there were many others which resisted for quite a long time—though rarely for more than 24 hours. These occasional 'toughies' could cause frustration and even desolation.

Once enough text had been broken, it was necessary to work out the wheel patterns in detail. Initially, Hilton played the major role in organising this important function, and also the setting of messages.

As the Germans opened more and more Tunny links, the volume of traffic increased and the quantity of broken messages rose sharply. By May 1943 a total of 1.4 million letters had been decrypted (by hand methods). The great majority of depths were broken. On the 'singles'—i.e. messages not in depth—it was mostly not possible to effect a break, except when we had a 'crib'. Cribs included cases where we might guess that the message was a resend on different wheel settings of a message that we had already broken.

Up to this point all the actual breaking was done by hand.

BREAKING, LATER DAYS

The need was recognised at the top level to try to mechanise that part of the work for which this was feasible. It was just as well that the Newmanry achieved their breakthrough in mechanisation. Depths started to dry up when the Germans introduced what we called 'P$_5$ limitation' on some links. The result of P$_5$ limitation was to make the key-stream dependent on the clear text—no more depths (see Appendix 10 *The Motor Wheels and Limitations*). In the summer of 1944, when the Germans brought in tightened procedures, message breaking in the Testery juddered to a halt. On top of an absence of depths, the wheel patterns were now changed every day. This meant that every day the wheel patterns must be broken anew—a massive amount of work for the Testery.

Using Colossus, it was possible to break 'single' messages, which now constituted all the traffic. As explained in previous chapters, Colossus stripped away from the ciphertext the contribution made by the chi-wheels. In order to break the 'de-chis' produced by Colossus, it was necessary to establish the patterns of the psi-wheels and the two motor-wheels. To do this, we in the Testery tried possible pieces of German text against the de-chi, attempting to generate what looked like a pattern of psi.

Two German practices in particular were a godsend to the Testery. The first was the treatment of Roman numerals discussed above. If one identified a likely sequence for 9ROEM9, one then had a run of six or more places already. (As previously mentioned, the German operator used 9 to divide words off, e.g. 9ROEM9EINS9.) If this clear was added to the ciphertext and gave, for instance, a pattern of repeating letters like the following, you knew you had probably struck gold—psi.

```
x  x  •  •  •  •  •  •
x  x  •  •  •  x  x  x
•  •  x  x  x  •  •  •
•  •  x  x  x  •  •  •
•  •  •  •  •  x  x  x
A  A  N  N  N  L  L  L
```

This pattern was typical of the contribution of the psi-wheels 'stretched out' with repeated letters due to the action of the motor-wheels.

A second highly useful practice was the way the Germans handled punctuation. The letter M was used for full stop, but it was necessary to indicate its use as punctuation so that it would not be taken as part of a word. This was done by using 55 going into punctuation mode and 88 coming out. We always wrote ++ instead of 55, so at the end of a sentence one might have

$$++M\ 8\ 8$$

or, with luck,

$$9++M\ 8\ 8\ 9$$

thereby giving, in the second example, seven places. Other punctuation was done in the same way. A comma used N instead of M, a colon C, and so on. Numbers were rendered similarly, the letters along the top row of the keyboard, Q, W, E, R, T, etc., being used for, respectively, 1, 2, 3, 4, 5, etc. For example, ++W889 was 2.

It was necessary to build up at least 50 or so letters of continuous text for a full break to be established. With a little more work the break would lay bare the patterns of all the wheels.

The techniques we used are described in more detail in Chapter 21.

HOW PEOPLE LIVED AT BP

Bletchley in 1939 was a modest town with, as the wit said, a lot to be modest about. It owed its development to the London, Midland & Scottish Railway, being the first main stop outside London on the route to Birmingham and the north-west. People changed trains there to get to Oxford and Cambridge, which were roughly equidistant from Bletchley. A fair number of rail workers lived at Bletchley.

Bletchley consisted principally of a long high-street, which ended near the station and had some pockets of better housing on one side. There were many two-storey terrace houses where, even in their main rooms, it would be difficult to swing the proverbial cat. Bletchley was quiet, perhaps dull, but worthy. The town offered relatively little in the way of entertainment, and the younger set at BP lived for the day they could flee to London and the social whirl, even if only for 24 hours.

Being a fairly early resident I was billeted in Bletchley itself. Many were lodged outside the town, often in stately homes in the case of ATS girls, WAAFs, and Wrens, or else in houses in the surrounding villages. If out-of-towners elected to spend an evening in Bletchley, or at BP, they were obliged to take the midnight coach back to their lodgings, getting to bed around 1 a.m. and needing to take an 8 a.m. coach to be at work by 9 a.m. (The shortage of petrol prevented the laying on of other coaches.) Social activity was a good deal blunted by this situation. In spite of this, clubs developed for various activities—amateur dramatics, chess, and so on. From time to time the Wrens in one of the stately mansions would organise a dance, for which special transport was permitted.

An interesting juxtaposition arose from the billeting of people with a professional or semi-professional background in working-class homes. It was not uncommon for one class to have contact with the other at the workplace, but at a time when the class divide was a great deal wider than it is today, it was highly unusual for the two classes to live side by side like this. War, and in particular the ration book, was a great leveller.

At the station end of the high-street and 300 yards up a hill was the small road leading to the security gates at the entrance to BP. There was a striking contrast between the town itself, the essence of everyday humdrumness, and BP with its dramatic work going on 24 hours a day, often affecting crucial decisions in the conduct of the war, and involving—not the least remarkable aspect of the work there—the first practical use anywhere in the world of the electronic digital computer.

While there was nobody in the town who knew just what went on at the Park (one rumour held that it was Littlewoods Pools), there were many in the Park itself who had no concrete—or even vague—idea of what really happened there. The basis was 'need to know': if you needed to know something to be able to do your work, you were told as much or as little as your seniors felt you needed. When Tiltman interviewed me in 1941, he emphasised that absolute silence must be preserved. I took this to heart—both my parents died in the 1970s without knowing anything of the work I had been engaged on during my four years at BP.

Chapter 19

Setter and Breaker

Roy Jenkins

There were two sections which worked on the German military cipher known as 'Fish'. One was called Mr Newman's section and consisted mainly of civilian mathematicians assisted by Wrens and by the embryonic computers. Their task was to strip the first layer of disguise off the intercepted messages. This they did purely by the techniques of probability mathematics, for their product had no more obvious meaning than their raw material.

Having got this far they sent the half-deciphered messages over to us in Major Tester's section. (The Major existed, but was always a shadowy figure, neither much encouraging nor admonishing, nor indeed performing great feats of cryptography himself.) We were a more mixed bag, army officers if we were already so, RSMs (Warrant Officer Class I) if not (this saved time; the rank, at least equally well paid, could be conferred without officer training), one American lieutenant, and a few civilians who were nominally on the strength of some section of the Foreign Office. We were assisted by ATS girls, but by no analytical machines, for our task was the more intuitive one of seeing the clear German (or at least German obscured only by Wehrmacht jargon) under the second layer of cipher, and this was thought to be beyond the help of machines. I would guess, however, that what we did could now be easily computerised. Another retrospective reflection from the perspective of half a century on is that it was very odd that in both sections, despite the fact that the processes called for no strength of physique or even exercise of authority, the question of giving women other than subordinate jobs simply never arose.

Tester's section was divided into two parts. There were the 'breakers' and the 'setters'. The breakers were obviously the elite. They were like matadors

This chapter is an extract from pp. 52–4 and 57 of Lord Jenkins' autobiography *A Life at the Centre* (London: Macmillan, 1991). It appears with the permission of the author and the publisher.

compared with picadors, except that they did their work first. Setting was relatively routine. You had to know all the properties of the cipher which had been discovered during the past three years or so, and work with logic and precision. But, if you did this, output for any individual was more or less predictable.

After about six weeks as a setter I was allowed to become a breaker, or at least a would-be breaker. Sometimes nothing would happen at all. It is the night shifts which remain engraved on my mind. We worked three shifts, for there was great urgency about the need to get the intelligence, and changed shifts within a compass of three weeks, one week of days, one of evenings, and one of nights. The night shift for some strange reason was the longest—nine hours—as it was certainly the bleakest. I remember quite a few absolutely blank nights, when nothing gave and I went to a dismal breakfast having played with a dozen or more messages and completely failed with all of them. It was the most frustrating mental experience I have ever had, particularly as the act of trying almost physically hurt one's brain, which became distinctly raw if it was not relieved by the catharsis of achievement.

On the other hand there could be nights when a cornucopia of success was upended on one's head. I remember one shift when I made 13 separate breaks. They just fell into my lap like ripe apples. I thought it was too good to be true, and grew rather superstitious towards morning, particularly when it became clear what the exact score was going to be. I was going to London immediately I came off duty, a journey which at the time was accomplished by walking down to Bletchley Junction and getting on the first night train from Scotland which heaved into the station. They were often two or three hours late and contained some fairly exhausted passengers. There were then a lot of flying bombs arriving in London by day as well as by night, and the thought crossed my mind that the unnatural success of the night might be a fine apotheosis before being caught by one.

Our ability to break depended crucially on the quality of the work sent over by the probability mathematicians. No one could break a transcript if the first process was wrongly done. The majority of their efforts they confidently and rightly marked 'certain'. Some they marked 'probable' or even 'possible'. These were hardly worth bothering with. But the mathematicians also invented a category to which they gave the interesting label of 'morally certain'. One lesson I took away is that there is a great difference between 'morally certain' and 'certain'. Once 'certain' is qualified it loses its meaning.

In September 1944 I went seriously off form for several weeks and was rightly returned to the setting room. It was a considerable blow, which ironic-ally coincided with my being promoted to captain, a good indication of how indifferent the whole operation was to rank. It took any gilt off my third pip. Fortunately, I was judged to have recovered form after a couple of months (I am not sure how anyone could tell without trying me out, but perhaps such insight was Major Tester's special contribution), and was allowed back.

Bletchley exhausted the mind, and to some extent, with the difficulty of adjustment to a frequent change of shift, the body. We tried extremely hard, feeling that it was the least that we could do as we sat there in safety while the assault on the European mainland was launched and V1s and V2s descended on London. And trying hard meant straining to get the last ounce of convoluted ingenuity out of one's brain, rather like a gymnast who tries to bend his bones into positions more unnatural than he has ever achieved before. It also meant doing everything as quickly as possible for, the break having been secured, messages had to be set, then decoded by machine and then sent in their entirety to what was known as Hut 3, where their intelligence value was appraised and decisions were made as to which commanders should be informed of what. And a lot of the information was of value only if it could be passed on within a day or so. Despite the intense secrecy we were encouraged if so minded, presumably on morale grounds, to read any of the decodes which we had helped to produce. But I never much did so. I think it was partly that an approach of professional detachment developed. The surgery completed or the case pleaded, one did not dwell too much on the fate of the patient or the prisoner. But partly it was just brain fatigue, at least for anything to do with ciphers.

When the Russians got to Berlin they took over the Fish machines in the War Ministry, somewhat changed the settings, and proceeded to use them for sending signals traffic to Belgrade and other capitals in their new empire. We continued to get the intercepts and played around with trying to break the messages. We never succeeded. I think it was a combination of the new settings being more secure (which raises the question of how much the Russians had found out about our previous success) and the edge of tension having gone off our effort. During this phase I was transferred for a few weeks to the Newman section, from which many of the star mathematicians had already gone. There I never really understood what I was trying to do. I would give random instructions to the Wrens who worked the machines. They would come back with reams of tape at which I would look uncomprehendingly while they waited to be told what to do next. Eventually I would give another equally random instruction. Fortunately it did not greatly matter. But there are few things more demoralising than pretending you understand something when you do not. I learned from this lesson 19 years later when I first became a minister in a fairly technical department.

The private utility came from the fact that when I retired hurt from this excursion beyond my intellectual capacity I acquired a room to myself in a remote part of Major Tester's section. There no-one disturbed me with work or anything else for days on end (night shifts had happily been abandoned). I settled down to read the 'tombstone' volumes which then formed the core of English modern political biography. I read all day, apart from getting up for a few minutes every one and a half hours or so and playing a ball game with arcane rules of my own devising against a wall of my solitary room. This immersion course transformed my knowledge of and interest in the lives and careers of British political figures of the previous hundred years.

Chapter 20

An ATS Girl in the Testery

Helen Currie

TYPISTS REQUIRED

I joined the Auxiliary Territorial Service (ATS) in 1938 during the Munich crisis. At that time I was working as a typist in Fleet Street, and 'Typist' duly appeared as the classification on my enrolment papers. Being a Territorial I was called up at the very beginning of the war. Then, in 1942, I volunteered for work as a signals operator, and was sent to the signals school in Trowbridge. I was trained to locate German stations by means of their call signs and to write down (in five-letter blocks) the Morse signals being sent by the German operator. It was difficult work. I was promoted to lance corporal—richly deserved, I thought!

Typists were going to be needed to operate the Tunny decoding machines, already in the process of being built. My record—typist, in the service since the outbreak of hostilities, trained in a branch of military intelligence, and with the rank of lance corporal (it was an army rule that only those with a rank could handle secret documents)—must have put me in the running.

In the summer of 1942, after I had completed my signals course, I was sent to London to be interviewed by an awe-inspiring gentleman. I remember only two of the questions that he asked me. Would I like to work in the country? Could I keep a secret? I answered 'yes' to the first and 'I think so' to the second (my young life had not so far tested me greatly in this respect). Puzzled, I went back to Trowbridge. About three weeks later I was on my way to Bletchley railway station with another ATS girl, Mary. We were met there by a genial Sergeant 'Tubby' (I never did find out his real name). He took us to Bletchley Park, a mere 150 yards away.

DECODING BY HAND

Major Ralph Tester was the head of the section that I now joined. He was a lovely, twinkly man and very kind. I signed the Official Secrets Act. Whatever the organisation was as a whole remained a mystery to me. It was emphasised again and again that not an iota of what I was doing should be talked about outside my section. At first I had no idea what I was doing anyway!

In those early days, Mary and I were the only two ATS girls in evidence. We were billeted in Fenny Stratford, which was a walk up the road from Bletchley Park. At first we worked in a room at the back of the Mansion, sitting at trestle tables. There were some army lads with us who knew more about the work. Every so often young men, some in uniform, some civilians, gave us sheets of squared paper covered with lines of dots and crosses. We were shown how to add these dots and crosses together with the aid of a chart. If we did it correctly, we produced a line of plain German language. I liked this work, it seemed like a game, and because I was able to do the adding in my head, without consulting the chart, I was very quick at getting results.

I noticed another clue to what I was doing. Very much in evidence at Bletchley were pads, printed in red, that were the same as those we used at the Signals School to take down the coded signals. These pads were covered with the familiar blocks of five letters. The young men worked from these pads, and it appeared that I was now engaged on the next step of the mammoth task of gathering intelligence of the enemy's movements.

Those first weeks were very pleasant. We worked from 9 a.m. to 4 p.m. There was always someone with whom to spend evenings. It was summer and we were young. It seemed as though our war was being spent in a quiet, sunlit backwater.

OPERATING THE TUNNIES

In the late autumn of 1942 we were moved into brick-built huts surrounded by protective walls. In these huts were huge machines—Tunny machines. Attached to them were teleprinters; the keyboard was similar to that of a typewriter, and so it was no problem to operate them, providing one had some typing skill. This was the work that I had been sent to Bletchley Park to do. The machines were watched over by engineers, who were on hand if anything went wrong. More and more ATS girls joined us during the summer months of 1943, to operate more and more machines. We were divided into three shifts to enable the machines to be operated round the clock—one week 9 a.m. to 4 p.m., the next midnight until 9 a.m., and the third (which we hated) 4 p.m. until midnight.

On the Tunny machine there were numbered circuits each operated by its own button, which was pressed to gain the correct setting. The operating procedure consisted of setting up the machine by pressing in the key numbers which were written on the message pad by the cryptographers. All the important codebreaking was done in the next room, separated from ours only by a partition. Provided that the machine was set correctly and the coded letters were accurately typed, what came out onto the roll of white paper fitted to the teleprinter was clear German. It seemed like magic at first.

Even without knowing the language it was easy to recognise German, and just as easy to see that gibberish was coming out when something went wrong. This happened when a letter was missed out, or one was typed that wasn't there. Mostly this occurred when a letter of the coded text had been missed during interception (or maybe many letters if reception was bad, as it often was). Then it would be necessary to step the impulses on until the text became clear again. This was often a matter of trial and error—pushing the buttons and then typing the text, and only when clear German again appeared could one breathe a sigh of relief and carry on typing. We typed to the end of the German message and placed it in an out-basket.

The gentle clack of the machines as they operated became a background to our working lives. The work never got tedious. There was something about the atmosphere at Bletchley Park that generated an all-pervading excitement. Everything was done to keep us happy and keen on the job. Dormitory huts were constructed on the site, with ablution blocks and a laundry, so that it was no longer necessary to spend time moving to and from billets. A splendid hall was built outside the main gate. There we danced, plays were put on, the Ballet Rambert gave a performance. We listened to gramophone concerts, watched films, had discussions. There were even boxing matches.

It seemed idyllic. However, on the radio the harsher side of the war reached us. I became personally involved in that when the young airman I married in August 1943 was killed ten weeks later. The whole section grieved for me. Peter Hilton, a very sweet man, brought me the best and clearest message he could find, which would give me no trouble to type. It was his way of bringing me comfort.

FULL THROTTLE

As time went on, and news from the various fronts was good and bad by turn, the volume of our work (and the number of people employed at Bletchley Park) increased enormously. Our fingers flew over the teleprinter keys. Clever young men hovered behind our chairs reading as we typed, waiting to take the message away to be analysed. Sometimes it was taken page by page: we knew those ones were very important.

I and many of my friends in the Testery made the most of life. There were some passionate romances! We lived totally in the present, greedy for life and with no thought for the future. We didn't know if there would be a future. Being so near the railway station, with direct trains to London, on days off we could travel up to town. We even did this during a long change-over from one shift to another. We might take in a morning film, then maybe a theatre matinee, perhaps followed by dinner and dancing. Catching the last train back to Bletchley, we arrived just in time to change into uniform and report for duty, to relieve the girls who had been bashing away at the machines all evening. It was a stimulating, exhausting life.

LAST DAYS

The last stages of the war were hectic. The traffic became almost more than we could cope with. Sometimes, having staggered off duty and dropped exhausted into bed, we were aroused from deep sleep a couple of hours later to return to the Testery and carry on.

I was with Donald Michie at the cinema in Fenny Stratford when the programme was stopped to announce the end of hostilities in Europe. Donald and I went to London the next day and danced round Trafalgar Square, kissing complete strangers.

The work at Bletchley Park continued until the war in the East came to an end, but since my assignment was German army traffic, my decoding work ceased. Donald Michie and Jack Good wrote a history, which I and the other ATS girls typed.

THE SILENT YEARS

We returned, somewhat sadly, to civilian life. It wasn't always easy to adjust. I remember Peter Hilton saying, many years afterwards, that it was a long time before he found work to compare with the heady excitement of his job at Bletchley Park. Then, of course, there was the state-imposed silence, lasting thirty years. My family had no idea what I had been doing. The memories faded, and if I did recall my experiences they took on a dream-like quality, almost as if I had imagined them. Then one day I saw some photographs of a Bletchley machine in the *Picture Post* and a description of the work that had gone on there during the war. I was excited, amazed, delighted. I could now talk about that unique part of my life, share it with other people. The years of silence were over.

Chapter 21

The Testery and the Breaking of Fish

Peter Edgerley

LEARNING THE GAME

In 1942 I was an 18-year-old schoolboy. My headmaster received a letter from a government department asking him to recommend candidates for work in military intelligence. There was, not unnaturally, little information given about the nature of the work, and certainly no mention of codes or ciphers—but I was sufficiently intrigued and decided to apply. I attended an interview in London, at an address just off Piccadilly. There were five or six interviewers on the panel, some of them civilians. It was a difficult interview, since there was no mention of what the job was. A few weeks later I received a travel warrant and was asked to report to 1 Albany Road in Bedford. I discovered on arrival that I was on a cryptology course.

My qualifications were in French and mathematics. Those of us with no German were put on a crash course, in a back room of a hotel a couple of minutes' walk away from the cryptology school. The German course was non-military in orientation, and the cryptology we were taught was in fact based entirely on English. The cryptology course covered a variety of methods of encryption—nothing hush-hush. We were each issued with a course book, and an instructor came round to give us help with the exercises at the end of each chapter. There were also encrypted messages which we were expected to decrypt.

The course lasted about two months. We all knew by then that, if chosen, our next move was to Bletchley Park. I was chosen, but unfortunately there was not enough local accommodation at Bletchley, and I had to stay in Bedford, along with several others who had taken the course. We caught the train to and fro each day, except when returning at midnight after a late shift, when a bus was laid on.

THE TESTERY

Tester's section—an army section, also employing some civilians on army reserve—was at that time located in Hut 15A, near Enigma Huts 3 and 6 and close to the far end of the tennis court provided for us by Winston Churchill. When Block F was completed we moved there, next door to the much expanded Newmanry with its Colossi. After the move to Block F many more people joined the section.

Room 41 of the Testery received and broke the de-chis supplied by the Newmanry. De-chi was ciphertext with the contribution of the chi-wheels stripped off. Superficially, de-chi looks just the same as ordinary ciphertext.

The Room 41 cryptanalysts included schoolmasters, students who had done a year or so at university, and school-leavers who had qualified but had not actually started their studies. Some studied or taught mathematics while others had some knowledge of languages, including German. Those who came with no German had to pick it up, or at least learn the vocabulary and ways of the Tunny traffic. As might be expected, the longer-serving personnel had an advantage over newer staff. It also helped to understand the techniques used by the Newmanry to produce the de-chis. The cryptanalysts working in Room 41 included Russell Barratt, John Christie, Mervyn Davies, H. 'Dobby' Dobbins, Roy Jenkins, Colin Rollo, and Arthur Levenson (from the US forces).

Once Room 41 had broken a de-chi it was sent to Room 40. Room 40's task was to get the break 'back to the start' of the message, in order to determine the positions of the wheels at the beginning of the message. I give an example later in the chapter, using a real Tunny message. If a break occurred well on in the ciphertext, then getting the break back to the start could be a tough task. This division of labour between Room 40 and Room 41 meant that the cryptanalysts in Room 41 could get on with cracking further de-chis while the wheel settings of broken de-chis were being worked out in Room 40.

Room 40 passed on the de-chi and the starting positions of the wheels to the ATS girls in Room 27. The ATS officer in charge would give the de-chi and the start positions to a Tunny machine operator, who would set up her machine appropriately and tap away. The full decryption of the message emerged from her Tunny. From there the decrypt went to the cribs section (known as 'Sixta' and located I think in Room 28 of the Testery) who kept a copy and sent the message on by pneumatic tube to the department which would deal with it. Most of the Testery's decrypts went to Hut 3 (Army) for translation and processing, but some went to Hut 4 (Navy), and some went directly to a certain Mr Page, who dealt with traffic relating to espionage.

DECIPHERING IN THE TESTERY, 1942–43

The Newmanry did not come into existence until the middle of 1943, and prior to this the Testery worked on Tunny unaided by de-chis. In those early days, the German operators often sent out messages on the same setting: depths. The two messages could be added together using the 'Tiltman triples' (such as A + B = G; see Appendix 3 *The Tunny Addition Square*). Figure 1 gives a fabricated example, involving hand and auto transmissions (see Chapter 3). The intercept operators at Knockholt (and, later, at Kedleston Hall in Derbyshire) could easily tell the difference between hand and auto transmissions, which were at different rates, and they would mark the intercepted text 'hand' or 'auto'. This information was a great help to us in breaking the message, as I shall explain.

When we added together the two ciphertexts, as in the examples in Figures 1 and 2, the key 'cancelled out'. This phenomenon has been explained by Peter Hilton in Chapter 15. What we obtained was a length of gibberish that was the sum of the two plaintexts. It was then a matter of worrying away at this gibberish, trying to tear it apart into two meaningful messages. For example, you might correctly guess one word of one of the messages, such as 'Abwehr' (the secret intelligence service of the German High Command), and also guess its correct position in the message. This gave you eight symbols of the two messages, including the space at each end of the word. By subtracting those letters from the characters in the combined text, you would be left with eight letters from the other message.

Those eight letters of the other message might have a space in the middle followed by 'flug'. So then you would think, 'Well that's going to be "flugzeug"—aircraft!' So you got 'zeug' followed by a space, which gave you five more letters of the other message. You kept extending forwards and going

```
AUTO          QEP 50     Z Y X 3 L F P A U + R O L E B 8 / / 3 G . . .
HAND          QEP 50     F J J T K R V B L W E P P C 9 J X 9 I E . . .

Added together           M V P O X U 3 G Y S J E 9 K X H X 9 C + . . .

Clear 1                  W I R 9 M A C H E N 9 M U S I K 9 + Z 8 . . .
Clear 2                  K O M M E 9 I C H 9 K L A R + + B 8 8 9 . . .

English (hand)           Am I coming out clear? (Operator suspects a hitch.)

English (auto)           We make music (Typical quatsch—padding which hid the start
                         of the real message, so making it difficult for any would-be
                         codebreaker to latch onto the address or other stereotyped
                         material at the beginning of the message.)
```

Figure 1. Breaking an auto/hand depth.

```
              QEP 51      Z Y X 3 L F P A U + R O L E B 8
              QEP 51      V T B O X 4 M J E L 3 J Z 8 C K
  Addition                K S 9 T X K R 3 I D 4 W A V Q T

  Clear 1                 W I R 9 M A C H E N 9 M U S I K
  Clear 2                 M A C H E N 9 M U S I K 9 + Z 8
```

Figure 2. A typical stagger. A stagger was a form of depth that occurred when the punched tape had to be re-fed by the German operator, following a break or other mishap. Sometimes the stagger was caused by the operator pulling the tape well back into the blank stretch that preceded the message, which he would do to make sure the first few characters of the message were not lost on retransmission. (The example shown here uses the same plaintext as Figure 1.)

backwards as well. You broke in in several places and you tried to join the pieces up. This was the real excitement, this business of getting the two texts out of a sequence of gibberish. It was marvellous. I never met anything quite as thrilling, especially since you knew that these were vital messages.

Once you got the two messages out, you took the enciphered message and the plaintext and add them together to get the key. Once you had the key, you had the wheel patterns.

At this time the wheel patterns were changed only once a month. To discover them, a complicated method called 'Turingery' was applied to depths sent at the beginning of the month. Turingery found the wheel patterns from the key stream and is described in Appendix 6 *Turingery*. Room 40 used the wheel patterns in order to work out the wheel start positions of each partly decrypted message.

BREAKING DE-CHIS

The success of Newman and his team in developing machines for tackling single messages (i.e. messages not in depth) led to major changes in the work of the Testery. The earliest prototype, Heath Robinson, produced some de-chis for the Testery to work on, but when Colossus came into action in early 1944 the main job of the Testery became setting the other wheels, the psis and the motors. Hundreds of de-chis were broken in Room 41 during the last year of the war. The success rate for the messages that we attempted hovered in the region of 90 per cent.

We were often able to break a de-chi by making use of any Hand, where the plaintext could be guessed more easily than in the case of Auto. Figure 3 gives an example: the codebreaker makes a guess at the clear, 'Your key is out', and

```
De-chi          R X G E P C E + X D + R O A 4 V U J N I 4 P Z L W
Guess           D E I N 9 S C H L U E S S E L 9 I S T 9 R A U S 9
Extended psi    A M M F L L K K K Y G G X 4 G G E C M 3 3 Y F Q Q

Psi             A M F L K Y G X 4 G E C M 3 Y F Q
       1        x • x • x x • x • • x • • • x x x
       2        x • • x x • x • x x • x • • • • x
       3        • x x • x x • x • • • x x • x x x
       4        • x x • x • x x • x • x x x • x •
       5        • x • x • x x x • x • • x • x • x
```

Figure 3. Breaking into a de-chi from Colossus.

adds the conjectured German clear to the de-chi, producing extended psi with its characteristic repeats.

A run of letters of unextended psi such as that shown in Figure 3 would normally be sufficient to set all five psi-wheels, assuming that the wheel patterns were known. The codebreaker would try to fit the first of the five impulses shown in Figure 3 on to ψ_1, the second on to ψ_2, and so on (see below for a worked example). If the run of letters was insufficient, more text would have to be decrypted. The two motor-wheels would then be set. That done, the positions of the wheels at the start of the message would be written on the top of the de-chi. For example:

$$21, 3, 46, 9, 53 \qquad 29, 2 \qquad 1, 30, 19, 6, 10$$
$$\text{psi-wheels} \qquad \text{motor-wheels} \qquad \text{chi-wheels}$$

The Tunny machine operator could now decode the message.

TRICKS OF THE TRADE

Hand was always a likely way into a message, since hand was almost always about breakdowns due to keying faults on the machine—hence 'Your key is out' and 'Am I coming clear?' Breaking auto was more difficult. 9TAGES-MELDUNG9 (daily report) was a good crib to 'drag' near the beginning of a message. If the crib appeared somewhere in the plaintext, then adding it to the de-chi at the correct place would give extended psi. There were naturally many other favourite cribs in our repertoire.

As previously mentioned, messages began with what we called 'quatsch'—an irrelevant sentence or phrase. The point of quatsch was to disguise the starting position of the message proper. The Germans did this because they knew that otherwise we would be able to use the stereotyped material occurring at the beginning of messages as cribs. Quatsch was generally not easy to break into, but if you got some promise at the real start of the message, with several repeated letters, you could extend backwards into the quatsch and get a full break that way.

The first part of the message proper began +Z89 and then came the priority, often SSD—*Sehr Sehr Dringend*, 'very very urgent'. (There were other priorities and SSD was probably overused.) The call-sign came next, followed by the message number and the time, using the 24 hour system. Helpfully, there were full stops between the numbers. Then came the address—we got to know these quite well after a time.

Searching the text of the message itself was perhaps more difficult, but there were a number of words that appeared frequently. Here are a few favourites:

ABSCHNITT	section	PANZERUNTERSTUETZTET	tank supported
ANGRIFF	attack	SICHERUNG	safety, protection
BRUECKE	bridge	STUETZPUNKT	strongpoint
FEIND	enemy	TAGESMELDUNG	daily report
KOMMANDO	command	WIDERSTAND	resistance
LAGEBERICHT	situation report	ZURUECK	back(wards)

There were of course many more. Naval affairs would have a different selection.

In Chapter 15 Hilton recalls some of the giveaways from hand and quatsch, such as MOEDERISCHE (murderous)—a possibility if the first few letters looked right. Realising that the message he was dealing with came from Southern Italy, Hilton added HITZE (heat) and was well on the way to a full break. Similarly ICH BIN SO EINSAM ('I'm so lonely') and HIER IST SO TRAURIG ('It's so sad here'). Another break or two were on the way! NIEDER MIT DEN ENGLANDER ('Down with the English') and HEIL HITLER also appeared quite frequently.

Sometimes the totally unexpected turned up. I was convinced that I had got onto a word beginning SCHED: the trigram SCH is common in German. Then the 'S' began to look a bit dodgy, and much later it transpired that the word was not German at all—it was CHEDDINGTON, a village about 10 miles from Bletchley! The Germans had discovered that a particular RAF bomber squadron was based there. Fortunately, it was near the end of the war and the Luftwaffe did not venture so far in those days.

In 1943 what we called χ_2 limitation was brought in on some links (see Appendix 10 *The Motor Wheels and Limitations*). This was a kind of mask for the extended motor key. The extended motor key was produced as before, but whenever there was a dot in the χ_2 wheel (one place back) there was an enforced cross in the motor stream. This change turned out to be an advantage for the Testery, because one knew where the motor dots could *not* be. So by writing out in lengths of 31 (the length of χ_2), you could tell where they *might* be. This technique was used mainly after the Newmanry started sending over de-chis from Colossus.

There was a tray of difficult de-chis which were re-examined when time was available. Somebody had written 9DAMPFSCHIFF9 on one of these. This fragment of clear was obviously right, giving several letters of extended psi, but getting more of a break was difficult. The message was solved a week later: it contained lots of figures giving the cargo on a ship going along the Yugoslav coast.

In February 1945 an American-made machine called the 'Dragon' was delivered (see Chapter 23). Up to this point all de-chis were broken by hand. The Dragon could 'drag' a de-chi with a possible crib and would stop when it found a position that worked. The Dragon had some success with old but undeciphered material. Hand methods were quicker on current messages, however. The machine was temperamental, and in any case came too late to be of any use.

Section 28 of *General Report on Tunny* is a deep study of Testery methods. Some of the methods discussed there are perhaps more suited to enthusiasts. In practice, the Testery's 'old hands' could frequently set the wheels by cruder methods, relying on minor short breaks pencilled in after a quick inspection of the de-chi.

A DE-CHI FROM 1945

The only de-chi to have found its way to the Bletchley Park Museum was obtained from a message sent a week before the end of the German war. All other Tunny messages may well have been destroyed. This message, intercepted on 30 April 1945, concerned a retreating German army group near the Czech–German border. It is horribly full of German operator errors. (Occasionally operator errors were so extensive that a message could not be translated.) A Colossus de-chied it and someone in the Testery did the rest. Figure 4 shows how the de-chi might have been broken. The message displays all the standard German procedure at the start, including the address and the date. (The line labelled 'χ_2' was written on the de-chi by someone in the Newmanry, to assist the Testery with χ_2 limitation.)

Some impression of how to set about the job can be gained from the examples given earlier. It is not known who broke the de-chi nor where the break was situated, but I assume that the possible break in the seventh line of

```
            De-chi                                  Plaintext

χ2      ••XX•XX••X••XX••XXXX•X••XXX••X
        SZIIY839WAF4+8/AOGZ4SZDDQUOLMAF        WOLLE.WI.R..AUCH.BLEIBEN.++Z--K
        UGUBTZPC3B+SSVAOAM+/SFC+8LRVFWY        R..GWFRL+X-.FUE..+.WPYP.CXT.QIP
        4N/GX4OF3CPDCZPDDCCXJHCYYU/IGVE        Q.V.AACQEM..+.AA-..QEE..+.AA-..
        E8LGS4MZDX+Y3CIQDOERZHW/XEGKFZE        .AN..OB+M-.SUEDWEST+V.AA-GEHEIM
        MUSLPOOQSEMFQFPJYYDNNPDZTZZBLET        E.KOMMANDOSACHE+AA-..+.AA-.NUR.
        SNMNVLIHPTXH+WLOI4ESBPXAL8OMT9X        ZUR.PERSOENLICHEN.UNTERRICHTUNG
LINE 7  MQTTJAZMZAFIMIVSIBN8TUP999+MC3B        +N--.WEITERGABE.VERBOTEN+MA.AA-
        HTVSA3MZPAOE94IYRJHCUWWLGPPSS4Z        LAGEBERICHT.VON..+.EPMM.-NN..VO
        DKTKTJEGA 4C8FQV+EXIXJ99RYXGGFJ        M..+.EPMRM.QORT.AA--.KATEN.NN.K
        UGW++VYBUR+ECCZWQ9XOJ3WYW8LLF9M        AT.NN.KARTEN..+.Q.C.Q.-PP.PPP.A
        PETDL++/PDTVBBI3QHTUYKGYAPPVEHG        .MA.---.ROEM.+.QM-.WESTEN..+.C-
        EXEGFXXCPJWSMFF/XZ/L9144+VGTHHH        ..AOK...L.V.C----.ROEM.+.OWM-.A
        8ULDNFRIK8SWSQ4WYSHSCJGVPN94VM4        +M-.K+MCMA.-.PANZERUNTERSTUEZ.N
        /HBNAEYGYH34LXZBCBVIQNV9Y4/SYVZ        N.PANZERUNTERSTUETZTE.FEINDANGR
        XOIXCFW39IMW3RPEMV9SKS8UPVRIPJ+        IFFE..GEGEN.EIGENE.STUETZP.UNKT


Break on line 7
                JAZMZAFIMIVSIBN8TUP999          Unextended psi from break:
                9WEITERGABE9VERBOTEN+M          X••X•X•XX•••X•X•
Extended psi:   KTTGE4UM888EOOII3QQ380          X•X•XX•X•••X•X•X•
                                                X•••X•X•••XX••X•X•
                                                X•X•••XX••X•X•XXX
Message date:   30.4.1945 (line 9)              •XX••••XX••••X•XX
```

Figure 4. Breaking a de-chi from April 1945.

the de-chi was found. The number of operator errors (indicated by '.NN.' in the plaintext—deletion was difficult with a teleprinter so operators used these symbols to indicate that there had been an error in the preceding word) would have made the message difficult to get back to the beginning if the break had been much further on. The length of this break (22 characters) is about half of ψ_1 (length 43) and about 37 per cent of ψ_5, so fitting the wheel patterns on to the break would not have been difficult.

This final phase of fitting the psi-wheel patterns on to the break is dead simple, given that the wheel patterns for the day are known. As Figure 5 shows, by simply counting from the left it is easy to see that ψ_1 is at position 29 at the start of the break, ψ_2 at position 42, and so on.

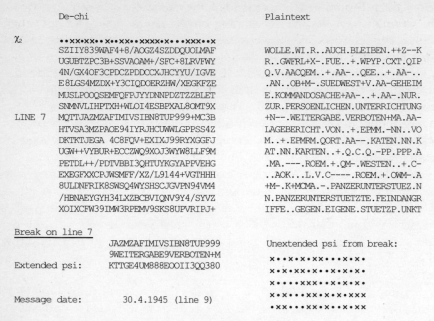

```
                                                                    POSITION
ψ1   X•XX•X••X•X•X•X•XX•••XXX•X•X•XXX••X•X•XX••X•                       29
ψ2   X•••X•X•X••XX•X•••••X•XXX•X•XX•••X•X•X•X••XXX•X•XX•                 42
ψ3   X•X•X••XX•X••X••X•X•XXX••••X•XX•X•••••XXX••X•X•X•                   35
ψ4   •X••X•X•X•X•X•XX•XX•X••X•X•••XX•X•XX•X•XXXX•••XX•                   31
ψ5   •X••X•XX•••X•X•XXXX•XX•X•X•X•X•X••••X•XX•X••X•XX•••XX                51
```

Figure 5. Fitting the psi-wheel patterns.

After the psi-wheel patterns were fitted, the two motor-wheels were fitted. This was pretty easy as well, depending on the rate at which more of the plaintext could be deduced. (Snags arose if there were errors, however minor, in the attempted decryption.) The first part of the process was obtaining the key from the plaintext by addition. Then the key was set out in rows of 61, the length of the longer motor-wheel. This procedure became known as the method of repeated columns, and was usually successful.

Once the motor-wheels had been fitted, the message would be 'brought back to the start' in readiness for typing. The de-chi would then pass down the production line to the ATS girls who churned out the German plain.

Section 5

T. H. Flowers' Laboratory at Dollis Hill

Chapter 22

Dollis Hill at War

Jack Copeland
with David Bolam, Harry Fensom, Gil Hayward, and Norman Thurlow

THE POST OFFICE RESEARCH STATION

The Dollis Hill building was erected in 1933 as the headquarters of the Post Office Engineering Department Research Station. Here T. H. Flowers pioneered digital electronics. The imposing brick building looks out from its hilltop site over the suburbs of North London (see photograph 41). It housed what was probably the most active telecommunications research centre in Europe. The building still stands today—now converted into condominiums, it flanks a road named Flowers Close.

Dollis Hill (DH) supplied much of the cryptanalytical machinery for Bletchley Park. Another of its roles was to provide an emergency alternative to the underground Cabinet War Rooms in Whitehall. Early in the war a secret underground citadel was excavated at DH. A massive reinforced concrete structure, the citadel extended three floors into the ground. It is said that Churchill took against the new bunker, and the War Cabinet met at DH only once.

Gil Hayward joined the Post Office Research Station in 1934. He describes the ethos of the new research laboratory:

I went to DH at the age of 16, straight from school. The Research Station had existed in permanent form for less than two years, having previously been accommodated in a series of wooden huts. 'Research is the Door to Tomorrow' was inscribed in stone above the main entrance to the new building. The atmosphere at DH was unique. Original thinking was encouraged and there was a substantial amount of freedom.

Engineer Norman Thurlow summarises the general position at DH at the start of the war:

The Post Office included the post and telephone businesses. The Engineering Department served both operations for all engineering work, including R&D. The Research Branch at Dollis Hill consisted of several different groups. Among them were the telegraph, switching, and physics groups, headed by Frank Morrell, Tom Flowers, and Eric Speight, respectively. These three groups all became involved in some way with the Bletchley Park operation. The state of the art was defined by the telephone and telegraph systems. Telephones were then controlled by lettered dials, signalling at ten pulses per second. All switches in the country-wide telephone network operated at ten pulses per second. The telegraph system ran at the somewhat higher speed of fifty pulses per second. The needs of the cryptanalysts at Bletchley Park meant that equipment designers at Dollis Hill and elsewhere had to push switching techniques towards higher speeds and greater reliability.

At 5000 characters per second the operating speed of Colossus I was orders of magnitude greater than the speed of the telegraph system. During tests, Flowers pushed up the processing rate to about 10,000 characters per second. The electronics coped, but the paper tape disintegrated. The parallelism adopted in Colossus II boosted the processing rate by a factor of five.

SPECIAL OPS

Codebreaking was not the only aspect of the secret war in which Dollis Hill was deeply involved. Hayward tells how, in 1940, he received his initiation into DH's clandestine activities:

I was happily at work in the lab one day when I was approached by a Senior Staff Officer, Mr James Doust. Doust took me off to one of the soundproof speech testing rooms on the first floor at DH, and there told me to say nothing to anyone of what he was about to say. He said there was a job overseas 'which might be dangerous'. I expressed interest and next day Doust came up to me and told me to get on my motorcycle and follow his car. I was surprised to find myself arriving at the gates of Wormwood Scrubbs prison. Inside I was conducted up a flight of stone steps leading to a long corridor with prison cells along one side. On entering a cell near the end of the row I was greeted by an army colonel in full uniform. Seating himself at a blanket-covered table beneath the small window, the colonel wasted no time. He had been told, he said, that I wished to join his 'mob'. I was to report to Room 246 at the War Office the next day. So began my career as an intelligence operative.

Next came some preparations at DH, reminiscent of agent 007's briefings with 'Q', the secret gadgets supremo of the Bond movies. I realised for the first time that many of the staff at DH were engaged in secret war work. I was given a suitcase with a false bottom. Inside was concealed a set of tools. I was also supplied with a sheaf of diagrams of the entire telephone network of Turkey, and told to await instructions. I later discovered that, in the event of Turkey entering the war on the German side, I was to be dropped by parachute and would join a band of resistance fighters, my mission to sabotage Turkey's communications system. 'Might be dangerous' seemed a bit of an understatement.

Turkey did not enter the war. Hayward found himself instead in Cairo, where he helped install bugging equipment in a prisoner-of-war camp. The listening devices enabled intelligence staff to eavesdrop on prisoners' conversations. 'The prisoners, usually of high rank, were kept two to a cell in a block of ten cells,' Hayward explains. 'I installed a secret microphone in each cell.' The special listening equipment was supplied by Dollis Hill, and on several occasions Hayward's superior, 'Mac', travelled to London for meetings with Doust, his liaison at DH. 'For security reasons Mac was not prepared to use any sort of communication except face-to-face contact,' says Hayward. He continues his story:

I set up a lot of POW listening facilities in the Middle East theatre. This meant extended trips to Khartoum, Mombasa, Jerusalem, Rehovoth (a small village in the centre of Palestine) and, via Damascus, to Baghdad. I also set up a facility in Malta. These outstations were small replicas of our main base unit in Cairo, fitted with equipment supplied by DH, and staffed by intelligence officers, with one of our signals personnel to keep the equipment running. In addition to our fixed stations we had a mobile unit, again supplied by DH, consisting of two single-decker London buses. One had been converted into sleeping quarters, and the other contained a fully equipped sound studio, complete with two recording/listening positions, a bank of microphone amplifiers, and a converter to produce 240 volts AC from the vehicle battery. This mobile unit was for eavesdropping on tents. It did sterling work in the desert and was finally destroyed behind enemy lines, when a German tank appeared over a low hill and opened fire with its machine gun.

In February 1944 Hayward returned from the Middle East to Dollis Hill, where he joined Flowers' group (see Chapter 23).

THE PRE-COLOSSUS ERA

The Bombes, designed by Turing and used against Enigma, were built not at Dollis Hill but by the British Tabulating Machine Company in Letchworth. Once the first Bombes were in operation, however, it was not long before DH—and Flowers—became involved in the attack on Enigma (see Chapters 5 and 11). Codebreaking machinery provided by DH included the Analyser, a decoder for extracting the German text from broken Enigma messages, and other relay-based machines used against the Hagelin and Sturgeon cipher machines. Thurlow describes some of the early equipment:

Early machines provided by Research Branch included the decoders used to translate coded messages into plain language, once the settings had been found. A hut to the south of the main building at BP held two such machines. These were under the control of army staff. The machines, operated by ATS typists, used standard Post Office relays and rotary stepping switches. Output was to a teleprinter. These machines, possibly for Enigma, and another known as 'Sturgeon' for decoding traffic encrypted by the Siemens T52 system, were designed by the Morrell and Flowers team.

Harry Fensom was recruited to DH in 1942, joining Flowers' group. He was involved with the Heath Robinson and the Colossi; and before that with the Analyser, the electronic 'Cobra', used in connection with the second-generation four-wheel Bombes, and 'Nightingale', a machine that imitated the Hagelin C38 cipher machine employed by the Italians (see Appendix 4). Fensom recollects:

Towards the beginning of the war I was working for the Post Office Engineering Department in the City of London at Clerkenwell telephone exchange as a trainee maintenance engineer (a reserved occupation). In August 1942 the inspector in charge of the exchange called me into his office and told me that he had received an order for my transfer. I was to report on the Monday to the Research Station at Dollis Hill. He could give me no further information about my duties. I found myself (at the age of 21) a recruit to a small, privileged group engaged on secret work. After a week spent wiring up equipment and getting to know the ropes, the new recruits were summoned to the office of the chief, Dr Gordon Radley, Controller of Research. Radley told us that we had been seconded to the Foreign Office. We signed the Official Secrets Act and were ordered not to communicate anything that we learnt henceforth concerning our work —not even to our fellow workers at Dollis Hill or Bletchley Park (where we would be going), unless they were also part of this select team. Radley then briefly explained that our work would be connected

with German cipher machines such as the Enigma. We formed the habit
of secrecy — we were all very aware that leaks could lead to the loss
of countless lives. No questions were asked and no information was
given. We kept our secrets, even from our wives and families, until
about 1975, when certain aspects of our work were declassified.

It turned out that I was to be one of the original few junior members
— all very young — of the team led by Thomas Flowers, head of the DH
switching group. From February 1942 onwards Flowers selected us
from among the maintenance engineers in automatic telephone
exchanges throughout the country. I believe I was chosen not only
because of my experience and technical qualifications, but because I
was a radio ham and also had City and Guilds certificates in radio
communication. However that may be, I found that my 'trouble-
shooting' know-how in nearly every type of automatic telephony
system, and my practical experience of valve circuits, was exactly
what was needed in order to get these entirely new — indeed out of
this world — devices working for BP.

I found myself helping the Flowers group to develop several
decrypting machines. Two were associated with Enigma. The Analyser
was entirely electromechanical and was commissioned by BP to
exploit the settings provided by the Bombes. The Analyser was,
however, scrapped after we had completed and tested it, because the
commissioning had been based on incorrect information. The other
machine was called 'Cobra', owing to the snake-like form of its
multi-wire connections, leading to the Bombe (approximately 2000
wires linked the two machines). Cobra provided the extra-fast read-
out required for the four-wheel Bombe, and used electronics for the
first time. We knew that electronics was the way to achieve the 26
times increase in speed necessitated by the fourth wheel of the
Enigma machine (since 26 new possibilities were provided by the
fourth wheel, there had to be a 26-fold increase in the number of
tests carried out by our machine). The Bombe, being
electromechanical, was running at its maximum speed, determined by
the relays it contained. The Cobra used gas-filled thyratrons as
electrical switches — no moving mechanical parts, only electrons in
a cloud of gas molecules — in order to perform the same function as
the relays but very much faster. (Cobra contained radio-type vacuum
valves as well as the gas-filled thyratrons.) I helped install the
first Cobra in the BP outstation at Stanmore.

I then very quickly became involved in another decrypting
machine, the 'Nightingale'. This was electromechanical, not
electronic, since no excessive speed was necessary. Made of
standard telephone parts, it was used to deal with Italian traffic
encrypted on the C38 Hagelin machine. Our Nightingale imitated the
Hagelin but was more flexible, and it offered the codebreakers a
number of useful facilities. Information yielded by Nightingale
helped sink convoys in the Mediterranean. I assisted Nightingale's

designer, Sidney Broadhurst, to install one in London at Berkeley Street (hence the name, after the popular song of the time 'A Nightingale Sang in Berkeley Square'). Here we manhandled the extremely heavy ten-foot steel rack of telephone exchange-type apparatus through a ladies' dress shop on the ground floor and then up to another floor — we had to break down the door frame in order to get Nightingale into its destined room. The other Nightingale went to BP.

BUILDING COLOSSUS

Fensom worked on the construction of Colossus I in Flowers' lab, and simultaneously on the production of redesigned Robinsons. He describes those busy times, and the eventual delivery of Colossus I to Bletchley Park:

We assembled and tested the entire Colossus in our special room at DH known as the AC lab, where our other codebreaking machines had been constructed in secret. It took us many months to build Colossus, working continuously, day and night. We even had a resident hairdresser to save valuable time!

We were privileged to have a visit from the King and Queen — who did not, however, get to see our prize exhibit. Their visit encouraged us, in this difficult part of the war, making us feel that we were playing a very important part.

In parallel with building Colossus, we were also making enhancements to the Robinson, using Colossus-type circuits (especially to replace the thyratron counters and XOR circuits that TRE had designed). Our modifications produced vastly improved machines. Also many improvements were made to the bedsteads as they came off the production line. A great advance was to install a friction drive for the tapes, with the sprocket wheels only idling to maintain the synchronism. Because some of the new Robinsons were completed before Colossus, we were able to prove some of the circuits and principles before Colossus was finally finished.

Once Colossus I had been tested in the AC lab we dismantled it into its separate racks. This involved disconnecting the innumerable leads at one end only, and of course labelling each one (very, very securely!). I was in charge of the installation of Colossus in the Newmanry.

Each panel was tested as it was assembled in the Newmanry, the valves being inserted step by step. The great day came when Colossus performed its first run, on a problem whose solution was already known to the codebreakers. Joy knew no bounds when Colossus gave the right answer in a fraction of the time of the Heath. There was further amazement among the cryptanalysts when several repeat runs on the same problem all gave exactly the same answer!

Fensom describes some of the innovative engineering practised by the Flowers group:

Because this was the first large-scale use of combined electromechanical and electronic systems, we had to develop construction techniques as we went. It was necessary to overcome the interference generated by the breaking of the relay and switch circuits. This interference had two effects: the sparking generated radio-frequency waves, which were picked up by the valve circuits, and blips and glitches occurred in the power lines. We used filter units to deal with this. We also had to learn how to avoid high-frequency cross-couplings in the panels. Mica capacitors were used for decoupling on the panels, signal leads were segregated, and power leads were decoupled with masses of paper capacitors (we avoided electrolytic capacitors).

Contrary to other peoples' practice, we mounted our 1500 valves horizontally on vertical steel panels (on standard steel telephone exchange racks). This allowed maximum cooling by convection. Horizontal trays would simply have trapped the heat. When Colossus was installed at BP, extractor ducts along the top of the racks helped the cooling process.

The counters were an essential part of Colossus and a large number were required for various operations. They had to be fast and accurate. We attempted to build a counter that W. B. Lewis had described in 1942 in his book on electrical counting techniques, but we used a different type of valve (our standard pentode instead of Lewis's 'magic-eye' valve). This altered various critical parameters and we found the resulting counter to be unstable and unreliable. So we redesigned the Lewis counter, producing a radically different model which was the subject of a patent. The final circuit was highly successful and never gave trouble in use – it could always be relied on to give results that were 100 per cent accurate.

The counter panel was at the very bottom of a rack and I remember reclining on the floor at DH for several days, helping Bill Chandler with the counter circuit, which at first refused to work. We tested each stage with an oscilloscope, deducing the likely causes of the trouble, rewiring here and there, and adding modifications. As a result of our experimentation, we finally came to understand the finer details of the circuit's operation and were able to optimise it. By the time we were finished, it performed way above its required maximum frequency, and the valves operated well below their quoted parameters – a large factor of safety.

ENEMY ACTION

Situated only about eight miles from the centre of London, the Dollis Hill laboratory was under constant threat of attack from the air. Hayward describes one narrow escape, and tells the story of a plastic grenade that came close to blinding Flowers—and to wiping Colossus from history before it was even conceived:

DH had its share of air-raid warnings. On one occasion DH was narrowly missed by a V2 rocket. I was walking to work from the bus stop and passed two housewives leaning out of upstairs windows of their adjacent houses, complaining to each other in loud voices about the meagreness of the food rations and other inconveniences. Suddenly a V2 fell nearby. The loud explosion caused a momentary pause in the ladies' conversation, and then one exclaimed, 'It didn't ought to be allowed!' At the lab I learned that Eric Speight had been caught in the explosion and was very lucky to have escaped unharmed. The course of the war would have been very seriously affected had DH received a direct hit.

Attack by German parachutists was an ever-present threat during the early part of the war and DH had its own Home Guard platoon, of which Tommy Flowers was a member. During a training exercise someone threw a flash grenade which unfortunately landed very close to Flowers. His face turned into a mass of blood, caught in the hail of minute fragments from the plastic grenade case. It was tremendously lucky that no real damage was done.

Incendiary bombs were another danger and Doc Coombs was a member of the roof-top fire-watch squad. When the air-raid sirens went off, Doc would grab his tin hat and rush up the stairs shouting, 'Bandits at 12 o'clock.' He was a great enthusiast in everything he did. Doc suffered from a violent nervous twitch, which could be quite unsettling until you were used to him. The twitch became more pronounced when he was talking animatedly, as he often did. While driving from DH to BP we often stopped off at a café for a meal. We scarcely noticed Doc's twitches, but customers at the café would become alarmed, especially if a sudden spasm sent a portion of food off Doc's fork and across the room.

THE DRUDGERY OF SECRECY

Secrecy may have held some glamour for those in on the secret, but for those not in the know, and this included many of the engineers and technicians working with Flowers, the extreme secrecy was simply an encumbrance. Not only was it a source of frustration—it was also de-motivating and prevented the men from feeling really a part of the project. David Bolam was one of those not in the know. He began work with the British Post Office Engineering Department as a technician in the middle of 1941. At first he maintained automatic telephone exchanges, and then assisted with the construction of the state-of-the-art telephone equipment that was being installed in London. In 1943 he received his summons to DH. Bolam writes:

In December 1943 I received a letter from the War Office instructing me to report to Dollis Hill Research Station, where, the letter said, I would undertake work of national importance.

I and about eight other new recruits all arrived at the Research Station on the same day. We were welcomed by Doc Coombs, who told us that we would be involved in top-secret work. We were given the Official Secrets Act to read, and were told of the severe penalties for divulging information. Coombs said it was unlikely that the project we were joining would be removed from the secrecy list during our lifetimes. He explained that the information each of us would be given would concern only the specific tasks we were allocated.

Much of the work consisted of wiring circuit boards and switching panels, and was similar to work I had often carried out at telephone exchanges. I did not understand why so many valves were required, though. Frequent modifications were made to whatever it was that we were building, and at times major changes were called for. Other tasks I was given included calibrating hundreds of resistors, and making up dozens of multi-pin leads for connecting the racks of equipment together. It was obvious to me that these leads would enable the racks to be interconnected very quickly when the equipment was installed elsewhere.

The wiring was done from hand drawings provided for the most part by Coombs or Flowers. Both men monitored our work. It had soon become apparent that these two were the project leaders. They often went missing — probably they were at Bletchley Park, but we didn't know that then. Sometimes they seemed unaccountably gloomy. No doubt there were technical or design problems which they could not discuss with us!

I was, of course, curious about what we were making. The only information I was ever given related to the wiring up of the circuit boards and other components. Once I asked why the work could not be undertaken by a manufacturing company, and was told there was a danger of information being passed to the Germans by fifth columnists. One day the door of the adjacent room was left open and I saw a framework holding paper tape which was being driven at high speed. There was some sort of control panel with flashing lights. I recognised the tape as that used for sending teleprinter messages, and supposed we must be building special communications equipment. Naturally I did not tell my fellow technicians what I had discovered. One day when I was helping to load some of the equipment we had made onto a vehicle, I asked the driver where it was going. He told me his job was simply to go to a rendezvous point, where someone would be waiting and they would exchange vehicles. Beyond that, he said, he knew nothing.

At times the secrecy was extremely frustrating. Having no information about the project, it was difficult to feel that I was actually contributing to anything. Our bosses did their best to encourage us and to keep our spirits up, but the secrecy got us down. Knowing nothing of the importance of what we were doing at Dollis Hill, I was constantly afraid that I would be seconded to work in the coal mines (as coal miners joined the armed forces, others were compelled to take their place in the mines).

From about February or March 1944, Flowers and Coombs required us to put in long hours of duty. I often worked 12-hour shifts. Of course, we were building Colossus II—but I didn't find that out until many decades later.

Chapter 23

The British Tunny Machine

Gil Hayward

THE DOLLIS HILL TUNNIES

Early in 1944 I returned to the UK from top-secret work in the Middle East. Two days after my arrival I received instructions to report to Tommy Flowers at Dollis Hill. I had joined DH in 1934 at the age of 16, straight from school, and had left in 1940 to carry out intelligence work overseas. Flowers introduced me to my new colleagues, Doc Coombs, Bill Chandler, and Sid Broadhurst, the last of whom I had met in 1938, during a course of training for the rank of probationary inspector—I had enjoyed his lectures on automatic telephony. The introductions over, an awkward silence fell. Here was an army captain in the intelligence corps who knew nothing about their project and who was still being vetted by the security services. This would preclude their discussing anything of a secret nature in my presence, probably for another two weeks, until my security clearance came through.

On the third day of this ridiculous state of affairs, Broadhurst could stand it no longer. After lunch he said, to no one in particular, 'Let's tell him.' The others agreed, and in less than an hour I had a fairly detailed outline of what our project was. By the end of the afternoon I was deeply immersed in the design of the wiring and layout of the rotary switches that would simulate the 12 wheels of the German Tunny machine. Broadhurst saved two precious weeks by taking the bull by the horns as he did. As it was, it was a near-run thing to get the equipment in operation by D-day.

Our Tunny would be deciphering the encrypted teleprinter traffic after the cryptanalysts had determined the wheel patterns and wheel settings. The tedious hand-work required to produce the decrypts, once the settings were known, had not been able to keep pace once Colossus went into operation. This situation called for a copy of the Lorenz machine to produce decrypts.

The Lorenz, one of which I was able to examine after the end of hostilities, was a beautifully made piece of mechanism, but it lacked the flexibility that our electromechanical copy possessed.

I settled back into the old DH routine as if I had never been away. All my old friends, with few exceptions, were still there, apparently doing the same jobs they had been doing when I last saw them. Only when we had a BP reunion about forty years later did I realise that most of them had been working either on Colossus or on the Bombes. We would meet for lunch as usual, but we never discussed what we were doing. The necessity for absolute secrecy was never questioned—as far as I know, no-one ever disclosed the nature of the job they were engaged on.

Soon after my arrival at DH, I accompanied Broadhurst, Chandler, and Coombs to BP in the DH staff car. (Flowers rarely came with us, being involved in yet another war project—we scarcely saw him apart from his daily visits to our small lab.) The free and easy and very informal atmosphere of BP struck me immediately. Everyone was called by their first name, irrespective of their position in the organisation. Army rank counted for nothing. I met Ralph Tester on that first visit. During my early visits, Coombs, Chandler, and Broadhurst were in conference with Max Newman and others on the final design of Colossus II, which at that point was not much more than a skeleton steel framework in an annexe to the Line Transmission Laboratory at DH (where we were also to assemble Tunny).

We completed our first Tunny in March 1944. Then arose the problem of how to test the thing. I devised a set of wheel patterns so that if one typed, at the keyboard of the Tunny's teleprinter, 'Now is the time for all good men to come to the aid of the party' (the standard test sentence used by telegraph people), the teleprinter responded with a line from Wordsworth's 'The Daffodils': 'I wandered lonely as a cloud that floats on high oer vales and hills' (teleprinters have no apostrophe). When Flowers popped in that morning to make his daily check on progress, I reset the wheels and asked him to type in 'Now is the time . . .'. I remember the look of surprise and boyish pleasure on his face as he read the printout. We used this set of wheel patterns to test all the Tunnies that were built.

Over the course of time we installed ten of our Tunny machines in Major Tester's section, and I was placed in charge of the maintenance team of 12 young Post Office engineers culled from various districts throughout the UK. Early on, Tester showed me an Enigma machine. This little machine, he explained, had been in use until recently, but had now been superseded by the teleprinter ciphers. This was a clever way to reduce my curiosity about other sections at BP. I realised much later that all the sections there were segregated, with no one curious enough or impolite enough to want to find out what went on elsewhere. (I never knew, until 1993, that in the building spur adjacent to the Testery, Japanese ciphers were being attacked.)

DECRYPTS

The Tunny machines in the Testery were operated by staff from the ATS, presided over by a small, jolly captain named Mavis Tickle. Most of the output that the machines produced was of a routine nature, uninteresting to operators and engineers alike. It usually consisted of lists of stores required, personnel details, ammunition stocks, and so forth. Occasionally, though, one of the ATS operators who understood German would let out a whoop of excitement—as when two German battleships, on their way back to Germany, tried to slip up the Channel under cover of darkness, but sent a message giving their expected time of arrival.

Frequently it was not easy to take any action on the information harvested at BP, for fear of alerting the enemy to the fact that we were reading their messages. An Enigma message decrypted by BP in 1942 posed such a dilemma. The information in the message prevented a small party of senior intelligence officers, including me in my technical capacity, from falling into the hands of the enemy. We were on our way to set up an outstation in Athens, and were in Alexandria waiting to take a small plane to Greece, via Crete. Unexpectedly we received a message saying that our plane had been diverted to another project and our departure would be delayed. Two days later we learned of the invasion of Crete by German paratroopers, and returned from Alexandria to Cairo with no inkling of the true facts behind our delayed departure. BP knew that Crete was about to be invaded. Although it was possible to save our party by means of this simple ploy, it was not possible to alert the small garrison on Crete, for fear of compromising Enigma. The entire garrison was captured, a sacrifice to the overriding need to maintain secrecy.

DRAGONS

In the summer of 1944, an American sergeant in the US signal corps arrived in the Testery, having escorted six pine crates from the USA, each about 8 feet high by 3 feet wide by 2 feet deep. My young lads were more interested in the crates than their contents—we had not seen such lovely timber for years. The escort, Sgt. Tom Collins, accepted my offer to dispose of this packing material for him, which he evidently regarded as trash. No sooner were the crates emptied than they were taken apart; the planks were divided among my small staff and quickly vanished from sight. We dubbed Tom Collins 'Sam Scram', after the American sergeant in the wartime radio show *ITMA* (*'It's That Man Again'*). Sam was a postmaster from a small rural town. At first he would not leave his precious charge, six racks crammed with relays, and carried a 45 Smith and Wesson at all times. It was several days before we convinced him that we were not planning to make off with his machinery, and he started leaving his side-arm in his billet.

Sam's 'baby', as he called it, was new to us. Its function was to 'drag' a short crib through a message de-chi, searching at each position for coincidences (see Chapter 17). Broadhurst came along for the switch-on, interested to see how the American cross-point relays, which were unfamiliar to us, would perform. Sam threw the main switch, causing the most deafening clatter and grinding noise we had ever heard coming from an assembly of relays. It sounded like a monster munching its way through sheets of tin plate. The load on the power supply was so great that the room lights dimmed as several hundred relays pulled in at once, and then brightened again on their release. Sam seemed to think this was normal.

Dragon, as we dubbed it, crashed and clanged on for about three weeks. Then I came in one morning to find a disconsolate Sam, who figured his baby was very sick. The thing spluttered on for a short time longer and then fell silent—Sam's Dragon was dead. Sid Broadhurst came to examine the wreckage. The relays that the designers had used were intended for telephone exchanges, where they would operate once per telephone call. In Dragon they operated about once per second, continuously. Their contacts had cut into each other, to the point where they no longer met. Sid took me on one side and said quietly, in that dry way of his, 'I think we could make one of those, don't you?' He went back to DH and in the remarkably short time of about three weeks had produced his own version of Dragon, which we installed in the same room as Sam's defunct baby.

Sam was late in arriving the morning when our Dragon was switched on. He came in and said in his usual breezy way, 'Hi, Cappy, when are you gonna run this thing?' I told him that it was already running. For once Sam was speechless. Except for a very faint pitter-patter from the relays, our Dragon was practically silent. Sam dismantled his machine, and it was taken away, although what they used for crates I do not know. The Dollis Hill Dragon worked happily until our operation closed down in 1946.

THE END OF STATION X

We moved the BP operation to Eastcote early in 1946, but before doing so we dismantled almost all our deciphering machinery on Churchill's command that no part larger than a man's fist should remain. My memory of the move to Eastcote is hazy, but Harry Fensom informs me that two each of Colossus and Tunny went there, and these finally ended up at GCHQ in Cheltenham.

Frank Crofts, one of my team of young lads, salvaged one unexpected treasure from our small workshop in the Testery. At the bottom of a heap of junk on a window-sill he found a brown foolscap envelope. This contained a 12-page description of the operation and function of our Tunny, written in Broadhurst's hand. Frank told no-one of his find, but took the envelope away and kept it safe for more than forty years. In about 1986 he gave me the envelope. Broadhurst's account gave us all the design information we needed to rebuild Tunny.

THE TESTERY TUNNIES: APPEARANCE AND CONSTRUCTION

Tunny consisted of a steel rack 7 feet 6 inches high and some 40 inches wide. The 12 wheels were represented by three rows of uniselectors or rotary switches (each having several banks of 25 contacts, arranged in a semicircle; *cf.* Figure 5 of chapter 8). The top 2 feet of the rack were occupied by these together with a duplicate set of uniselectors called 'chasers'. Below were arranged 12 rows of Post Office switchboard jacks, of the sort used in manual exchanges. Each row of jacks represented a wheel, with the number of jacks in the row corresponding to the number of cams around the wheel. The jacks were in strips of 20. The row representing $\mu 61$—the larger of the two motor wheels with 61 cams—had an extra single jack at the end of its three strips of 20. A brass plug was inserted into a jack to represent a cross. Dot jacks remained unplugged. Beneath each row of wheel-pattern jacks was a similar row into which one plug was inserted to indicate the start position of that wheel. A third row, below the wheel-start row, contained the lamp jacks. One lamp at a time would illuminate as the uniselectors rotated, showing the current position of the wheel as deciphering proceeded.

The lower section of the rack contained a series of key switches for resetting the wheels to any position, and to include or exclude a limitation. The bottom section of the rack held a large number of relays, involved with driving the wheels, diverting the incoming pulses into separate channels, and timing the operations (the timing unit used high-speed single-contact relays). There was also a section of 'remembering' relays (Broadhurst's term), which remembered the current sequence of dots and crosses from the wheels while the uniselectors stepped on to their next positions. The chasers were used to mark the position up to which a successful decrypt had been achieved. The chasers remained at this position while the working wheels stepped on. Should an error then occur, the wheels could be reset to the positions marked by the chasers. These refinements did not exist in the German Tunny machine.

Chapter 24

How Colossus was Built and Operated— One of its Engineers Reveals its Secrets

Harry Fensom

THE FIRST ACT: HEATH ROBINSON

Flowers' team, which included me, became involved with the design of the logic units of Newman's proposed machine after Morrell's Telegraph Group, which had been assigned the job, got into difficulties. For modulo-2 addition ('exclusive-or', or XOR) Morrell was proposing to use a type of frequency-modulator employed for voice-frequency telegraph signals. This might have been all right for adding only two signals, but it was useless for adding many signals, because the device was analogue in nature (i.e. not digital or discrete, but using continuously variable voltages). The small variations added up, with the result that the device often produced a wrong answer. After some clever work by Gil Hayward, it just about worked for the number of additions that were required.

The Heath Robinson's 'bedstead', containing the tape drive and the photo-electric tape-reader, was designed and built at Dollis Hill. Our people Eric Speight and Arnold Lynch had very recently used photoelectric cells to do what was required. Fighter Command had asked Dollis Hill for a fast means of recording the telegraphic signals from their aircraft observers. Speight and Lynch, working together with Morrell's group, had designed some photo-electric equipment that would record these signals directly from the tele-graphic punched tape. The device they built, called the 'Auto-Teller', was never in fact used, but this photoelectric technology formed the basis for the bedstead.

When we finished our part of Newman's machine at Dollis Hill I moved to Bletchley Park, and Alan Bruce from TRE accompanied their part of the machine, the counter and display rack. The Heath Robinson was installed in the wooden Hut 11—the Newmanry. I was privileged to be one of those present at the Heath's inauguration before the VIPs—and I can confirm that smoke did rise from it at switch-on. I was able to deal with this. A large resistor had overloaded, which I bypassed, and we carried on. (The machine never did catch fire, on this or any other occasion, but as mentioned in Chapter 13, we had a benzene fire in our workshop, at a much later date, and this may have contributed to the erroneous stories of Heath Robinson catching fire.)

The bedstead was found to be capable of running two continuous loops of teleprinter paper tape in synchronism at about 2000 characters per second, without tearing the tapes too often. After a few runs, however, the sprocket drive would eventually split the tape.

The message tape contained a blank section following the message. This allowed time for the machine to carry out the logical operations called for by the routine (our word for what would nowadays be called a 'program'). The other tape, containing the wheel patterns, was formed into a loop whose length was prime to that of the message tape. (Two numbers are prime to one another if they have no common factor.) The result was that after each revolution of the message, the wheel patterns started at a new position relative to the message. The run was stopped when the original position of the two tapes was reached again.

The number of characters—or sprocket holes—traversed during a complete run was equal to the product of the wheel lengths times the message length. At 2000 characters per second, a test of χ_1 and χ_2 (of lengths 41 and 31) against a message of about 2000 characters would take approximately half an hour.

Two sets of ten photoelectric cells were used to read the holes in the two tapes. Three other cells were used to read the sprocket holes and the start and stop holes. (The cells used in Heath Robinson were a gas-filled type with a limited high-frequency response. Subsequent bedsteads for Robinsons and Colossi used fast high-vacuum cells.) Much as in a cine projector, light from two low-voltage projector lamps was focused onto the cells, the light passing through lenses, shaping masks, and the tape gate. The use of two rows of five cells enabled two characters from each tape to be scanned simultaneously. The bedstead also contained amplifiers for the photocell outputs, which converted the signals produced by the cells into square-shaped pulses. The action of the light-shaping mask also helped to give square pulses. Unfortunately, the limited nature of the amplifiers restricted the number of consecutive crosses that could be read reliably.

The tapes were wound round a series of pulley-wheels about 10 inches in diameter. Tape length varied with the size of the message, and different lengths were accommodated by using different numbers and arrangements of pulleys. One movable pulley, on a sloping variable mounting, acted as a jockey to achieve fine adjustment of the tape tension.

An auxiliary rack constructed by Dollis Hill housed the logic units, which used the modulator-type XOR gates described earlier. The logic units were driven by the bedstead signals. The logic inputs and outputs were connected to switchboard-type jack sockets. These could be arranged in different combinations, by plugging appropriate ones together with cords. The cords, of the type used in telephone switchboards, were double-ended with plugs at each end. This logic rack was the heart of the exercise. It really did only one job initially, but in fact turned out to be quite versatile, since the logic units could be connected together in ways that were not originally planned.

The outputs from the logic rack went to TRE's counter rack. The counters used thyratron valves only for the first few stages, and relays for the rest—Wynn-Williams believed in using the minimum number of valves, because his experience was with equipment for mobile use. There were in fact two counters, which were used alternately in order to allow time for display and reset. There was also a counter for the number of message revolutions (i.e. the number of times that the start hole passed its photocell). The probability count, and the number of message revolutions at that point, were shown by lamps on the display panel. With the Heath there were problems when two or more successive high scores were similar to one another—it was difficult for the operator to read the display in the short time between each test.

Table 1 shows how the results of a run might look, for a message length of 4000 characters, and with the set-total switch at, say, 2070 (meaning that counts below this value were not displayed). Ideally the correct answer would stand out like a sore thumb, but sometimes it was accompanied by random high scores.

Since χ_1 and χ_2 were 41 and 31 cams long respectively, only 1271 positions

Table 1. Results of a run on Heath Robinson. The high score of 2236 indicates that the correct starting positions are 17 for χ_1 and 10 for χ_2.

χ_1	χ_2	Count
1	3	2077
2	8	2072
4	7	2083
9	8	2081
17	10	2236
31	6	2100
4	27	2111

had to be examined (a marked reduction on the 1.5×10^{19} positions that would have to be examined if all five chi-wheels were searched). However, this was still 1271 multiplied by, say, a message length of 10,000 letters— 12,710,000 tests per run. Ordinary state-of-the-art tape readers ran at ten characters per second. Using one of these, a χ_1, χ_2 run would require about two weeks of continuous operation. No wonder Hitler believed the Lorenz machine was impregnable! The path-breaking Heath would take only about two hours to do the run.

AUTOMATIC TELEPHONE EXCHANGES: PRECURSORS TO THE COMPUTER

Most of the logical concepts used in the design of Colossus were already present in the telephone exchanges of the time. Particularly important was the idea of the automatic *routiner*. This was a device that stepped through a routine, or program. A routiner put a large number of devices through a pre-selected series of electrical and logical tests. We usually let the routiner run overnight, when the exchange switches were lightly used, and thus mostly free for testing. The faulty ones were busied out and notified to the operator in the morning.

Counters were a necessity for all sorts of jobs in exchanges—not least for recording the number of telephone dial pulses. *Logic functions* abounded, for example in detecting that the called number had answered, so that the meter could be incremented and the call timed.

Another important device used in London was the *director*. This translated the three digits (or letters) of the exchange code into a (usually) longer series of different digits, which served to route the call through the necessary number of exchanges to its destination. The routing would be different for each calling exchange, just as the directions for finding one's way to a point across the city will be different for different possible starting points. The director was a very sophisticated machine.

All we needed to do was to take these ideas and make them electronic.

THE ELECTRONIC REVOLUTION

Flowers proposed an entirely new concept: an all-electronic machine to replace the Heath Robinson. In spite of BP's scepticism, Flowers pressed ahead with his idea. He had the complete backing of Dr Gordon Radley, then Controller of Research at DH. Radley put at Flowers' disposal as much of the DH workforce as Flowers wished, and then that of the Post Office factories as well.

Flowers had two superb engineers to do the intricate design work for this never-before-attempted job. Sid Broadhurst was a master of system design, and of the logic and timing of complicated relay circuits. Bill Chandler was the expert on digital valve design, and could produce a system that worked straight away when implemented from the drawing board. To complete his team Flowers had other engineers who drew the detailed layouts and thought through the fine print of the design, and some dedicated wiremen who soldered it all together—and a few like me, who assisted Broadhurst and Chandler, and then maintained the products at BP.

Flowers drew the logic diagram for Colossus in 1943 using rough sketches of the various gates and their implementation. Later in our time together his diagrams became more formalised, and employed a symbolism resembling that used by von Neumann in 1945 in the 'First Draft of a Report on the EDVAC' (see Chapter 9). Circles were used to represent gates (AND, OR, and NOT, other logic functions being composed of combinations of these); and 'sausages', as I called them, were used to represent time delays.

Flowers conceived the so-called one-back circuit (or more than one back), which subsequently became known as the shift register. It was first used to provide the delta function. Additionally the one-back circuit avoided the need to use two rows of photocells to read the message input, as in the Heath—Colossus II had only one row of cells.

In Colossus II we had a parallel machine doing five simultaneous tests on five consecutive message- and wheel-characters at a time. The effective speed increased five times. A run taking half an hour on Colossus I could now be done in six minutes! It meant more gates and counters, of course, but we didn't mind a thousand extra valves.

One machine, Aquarius, that we built for the Newmanry was very special, in my eyes anyway, in that it incorporated a relatively large semi-permanent memory. (See photograph 38.) A tape was run on a bedstead and all its characters were remembered in a dynamic store. The tape could then be removed, and all subsequent operations read the characters from the store, as many times as necessary and as and when required. The store used a large bank of capacitors, which were either charged or not, a charged capacitor representing cross (1) and an uncharged capacitor dot (0). Since the charge gradually leaked away, a periodic pulse was applied to top up those which were still charged (hence the term 'dynamic'). This form of memory is similar to random access storage on the screen of a cathode ray tube, as in the Williams tube memory (see Chapter 9).

A GENERAL-PURPOSE COLOSSUS

I realised at the time that Colossus's rings of thyratrons, simulating the wheels of the Tunny machine, were the only specialised part of what could otherwise have been a general-purpose computer—a truly universal machine. I did not then know of Turing's theoretical idea (although Flowers did). My thinking was more on the practical side of making machines that could cater for all sorts of input and output, such as text, pictures, movement, or anything which could be given a value. These values would be converted to electrical voltages or currents which Colossus, our logic machine, could manipulate. Present-day computers are very similar: these are probably used considerably more for text-processing and manipulating pictures than they are for simply doing numerical calculations. Flowers used to say that Colossus was much more of a computer than the number-crunchers which sprang up after the war—a data-processor rather than a mere calculator, and rich in logical facilities.

It was obvious to me that in Colossus we had all the elements to make a general-purpose device. For example, to obtain a calculator pure and simple all that was required was a keyboard for input, such as we had constructed earlier for our Analyser (a machine used against Enigma), a tape reader to handle masses of data, and a set of logic units, composed of a collection of our gates, to implement the algorithm (with the aid of some counters and fast electronic stores). A master control would organise the routine, the required algorithm being set up in advance at a control panel. Algorithms that were required frequently could of course be pre-set. Slow stores for read-out would feed a printer or tape-punch or electric motor, etc. The only snag I saw was that the machine would be colossal and vastly expensive. Colossus (like the gigantic ENIAC) was fine when the aim was to win a war, but it was hardly ideal for the laboratory or the classroom.

Shortly after the war our team did in fact make a general-purpose computer at Dollis Hill—the MOSAIC (see Chapter 9). Unlike Colossus this had stored-program control, and it saved considerably on valves by using 'delay lines' for high-speed storage.

THE OPERATION OF COLOSSUS I

One panel of Colossus contained the so-called 'master control'. This acted as a program sequencer, guiding the run through all its steps, from switch-on to print-out and then on to the end of the run. Flowers designed the routine, or program, carried out by the master control, using a timing diagram and logic diagrams that had almost a modern flavour, thanks to his anticipation of the future von Neumann style of diagram. The complexity of the routine in operation was analogous to that of present-day computer programs.

I will describe the master control from memory, since the records of it were destroyed. My description applies only to Colossus I. The subsequent Colossi had vastly more routines to deal with, and it would take a whole book to write out the programs.

Manual Actions
1. INITIATION
   1.1 Select normal or test cycle.
   1.2 Reset alarm (if necessary).
   1.3 Thread message tape around pulleys on bedstead.
   1.4 Switch on printer and load paper.
   1.5 Set wheel pins at back of machine to the required wheel patterns.
   1.6 Set wheel start positions by pegs in jacks on the control panel. *(Unknowns were usually set to position 1.)*
   1.7 Select which wheel starts were required to step (by moving control keys up to the 'step' position).
   1.8 Use RST (reset) key to clear storage of previous results.
   1.9 Choose the near or far tape on the bedstead by means of a switch on the select panel. *(Although only one tape was required on the bedstead, it was equipped to drive two, but separately. The second tape could be loaded up while the first was running, so saving time.)*
   1.10 Set up the desired algorithm at the plugboard.
   1.11 Adjust set-total dials to the value calculated for the type of run.
2. Start bedstead tape motor.
3. Operate master start (MAS on control panel) momentarily. *(This control was ineffective until the tape was running at the correct speed.)*

Automatic Operation of Master Control
4. Distributor reset to beginning. *(The distributor acted as a sequencer, or modern program counter, for the master control.)*
5. Clock pulses generating OK? If not, system alarm lamp lights; goto 3. *(If pulses still not OK, operator treats as a fault.)*
6. Wheel start uniselectors rotated to positions marked in 1.6.

7. Pause key operated? If yes, control waits until not.
8. Tape stop pulse received (end of message)? If not, waits until yes. *(The machine's processing cycle begins when the stop pulse is received and occurs while a blank section of tape is running through the reader.)*
9. All wheels cleared (i.e. wheel thyratrons extinguished). *(Clearing the wheels allows them to begin in 10.1 at the positions given by the uniselectors, either as started in 6 or as incremented in 16.)*
10. GENERAL RESET FOR THE NEW CYCLE
10.1 Wheel start thyratrons set (as indicated by uniselectors).
10.2 Result counters reset to zero.
10.3 Set-total counter set to indicated value.
10.4 All logic units reset to normal.
10.5 All stores cleared if not busy.
11. Tape start pulse received? If not, control waits until yes. *(New cycle starts.)*
12. System clock-pulse (CL1) sent to logic devices for one pulse period. *(CL1 is a continuous signal from the sprocket holes. It is produced simultaneously with the message character signals as the tape is read.)*
13. Clock-pulse signal (CL2) sent to wheels to step (selected) chis and μ_1 by one position, and psis and μ_2 if appropriate. *(CL2 is CL1 delayed by one-half of the clock period; this delay is necessitated by the design of the wheel-stepping circuits.)*
14. Clock-pulse signal sent to result counter—counter incremented if permitted by logic output.
15. Tape stop pulse received? If yes goto 17; if no goto 12.
16. Increment wheel starts (step uniselectors).
17. Is result count greater than set-total? If not goto 9. *(Repeat the process using the next wheel start settings.)*
18. Count and current wheel starts to print store if it is free. *(Free = empty.)*
19. Else if store not free, goto 8. *(Suspend test temporarily, by inhibiting tape start pulse.)*
20. Print from store if printer free until store empty.
21. Else if printer not free, wait and then goto 20.
22. Wheel start settings = original settings?
   If yes, end of run—goto 3. If not:
23. Goto 8. *(Next cycle with new wheel start settings.)*

Section 6

Sturgeon, The Fish That Got Away

• •

Bletchley Park's Sturgeon—The Fish That Laid No Eggs

Frode Weierud

INTRODUCTION

This chapter describes the Siemens & Halske T52 cipher machines and explains how Bletchley Park broke them. (See photograph 51.) Many authors have confused the T52 with the Tunny machine, and have erroneously linked the T52 to Colossus. The German armed forces employed three different types of teleprinter cipher machines during the Second World War: the Lorenz SZ40/42a/42b (Tunny), the Siemens & Halske *Schlüsselfernschreibmaschine* (*SFM*—Cipher Teleprinter Machine) T52, and the one-time-tape machine T43, also manufactured by Siemens. The Siemens T52 existed in four functionally distinct models: T52a/b, T52c, T52d, and T52e (there was also the T52ca, a modified version of the T52c). At Bletchley Park all T52 models went under the code name 'Sturgeon'. The Siemens T43 was probably the unbreakable machine that BP called 'Thrasher'. (This came into use relatively late in the war, and appears to have been used only on a few selected links.)

In 1964 Erik Boheman, the Swedish Under-Secretary of State, first revealed that Sweden had broken the T52 during the Second World War. The Swedish successes against the T52 are the topic of Chapter 26. It was only in 1984 that the British officially acknowledged that Bletchley Park had also enjoyed some success against the T52. Not only did BP intercept traffic enciphered on the T52; it also broke all the different models that it discovered.

The author would like to thank Bengt Beckman, Ralph Erskine, David Alvarez, Torbjörn Andersson, Jürg Drobick, Philip Marks, Jon Paul, Wolfgang Mache, Captain Jon Ulvensøen and the Armed Forces Museum (*Forvarsmuseet*) in Oslo, Donald Davies, Geoff Sullivan, Friedrich Bauer, and Jack Copeland.

It was clear from the beginning that the T52 was a very difficult machine to break. Probably it would have remained unbroken had it not been for German security blunders in using the machines. The blame should not be put entirely on the German teleprinter operators, however: the designers of the machines at Siemens, who failed to listen to the advice of the German cryptographic experts, were also responsible. The Siemens engineers seem to have focused more on the engineering problems than on the cryptographic security of the machine. The T52a/b and the original T52c were machines with quite limited security. The T52c is an extraordinary example of how not to go about designing a cryptographic machine. The wheel-combining logic, which was meant to strengthen the machine, had exactly the opposite effect—it eased the task of breaking the machine. The T52d, on the other hand, was a relatively well-designed machine. If this had been the first T52 to see service—and the teleprinter operators had been properly instructed in using the machine—there is little likelihood that it would have been broken.

A weakness of all the T52 machines was that, unlike Tunny, the wheel patterns were immutable. Presumably the designers thought that, given the complexity of the machine, it was not necessary to vary the code wheel patterns. However, variable wheel patterns would have strengthened the T52 machines considerably. Because of the permutation circuit of the T52 (discussed below), cribs could not lead to the recovery of the key-stream. Even complete plaintext of thousands of characters would not have enabled the recovery of the code wheel patterns.

Hinsley revealed that BP decided to concentrate on Tunny because of the need to husband resources and because of the scarcity of good intelligence on the German army from other sources. However, these were probably not the only reasons why BP abandoned its efforts against the Sturgeon machines. The cryptanalytical difficulties BP faced in attacking these machines, the small number of exploitable Sturgeon links, and the very limited intelligence that could be derived from the traffic, must also have been important factors in the decision to concentrate on Tunny. Given the poor intelligence content of the Sturgeon messages, we are left with the question: how much Sturgeon did BP capture and break? The question is still open, but there are indications that many of the more important links were perhaps never broken.

TUNNY, STURGEON, AND *SÄGEFISCH*

All the German teleprinter cipher machines were on-line machines. This means that when the operator types his plaintext message at the transmitting end of the link, the same plaintext appears immediately on the receiving machine. Neither of the operators ever sees the ciphertext. All these machines used the standard teleprinter speed of that time (50 baud). The Lorenz (Tunny) machines were designed to be suitable for use on high-frequency radio links (operating in the 3 to 30 MHz bands). Radio signals in this frequency range are affected by both slow and fast fading, Doppler shift, and multi-path propagation, which can easily play havoc with the digital teleprinter signals. The SZ40/42 machines had a better receiver design than the T52 and were therefore more successful in reconstituting severely distorted teleprinter pulses. Towards the end of the war, Lorenz worked on the development of an improved machine, the SZ42c, which applied the cryptographic process directly to the radio signal itself. The SZ42c was an advanced design—the German engineers were clearly leaders in the field of cryptographic machinery.

The Lorenz SZ40/42 machines were a German army development, while from an early stage the T52 was adopted by the navy and air force. The T52 machines were allowed to remain on board only while a vessel was in harbour, and would normally be connected by cable to the well-developed telegraph line network that covered most of German occupied territory. This was also the situation with the air force T52 machines. Lorenz machines, on the other hand, were used from the start on radio teleprinter links. Since a large part of the German army tended to be continually on the move, it was relatively seldom that their cipher machines could be connected to the fixed telegraph network. In due course, the T52 machines also appeared on radio links. Initially they were used on radio relay connections (a highly directional point-to-point radio link), using frequencies in the VHF and UHF range. Later they also appeared on ordinary links using frequencies in the HF range.

The Germans called their special radio equipment for use with teleprinters 'Sägefisch' (sawfish). The name was apparently derived from the sawfish-like shape of the signal observed at the output of the receiving detectors. At the end of the war a total of nine different *Sägefisch* models were in use, under construction, or planned. The two manufacturers involved were Telefunken and Siemens & Halske. *Sägefisch* I, II, IV, and V were made by Telefunken while WTK I and II (*Wechselstrom-Telegraphie über Kurzwellen*—voice-frequency telegraphy over short wave) were made by Siemens. There was some cooperation between the two firms, and EFFK I (*Einheits-Funkfernschreibgerät für Kurzwellen*—standard radio teleprinter equipment for short wave) was a joint development. *Sägefisch* III, a Siemens development, was never brought into service and *Sägefisch* V and WTK II reached only the prototype stage. The last *Sägefisch* equipment, EFFK II, was still under development when the war ended.

THE FIRST ENCOUNTER WITH STURGEON

BP first encountered T52 traffic in the summer and autumn of 1942. Most of the traffic passed on a radio link between Sicily and Libya, which BP called the 'Sturgeon' link. During the same period there was another T52 link in operation, from the Aegean to Sicily, which BP called 'Mackerel'.

The operators on these two links were in the habit of sending a large number of messages using the same machine settings, producing multiple depths. At BP the mathematician Michael Crum analysed the depths and discovered that the machine had ten code wheels whose patterns appeared to be fixed.

The Sturgeon and Mackerel links came to an end with the second battle of El Alamein, which began at the end of October 1942. One other signal transmitted on a T52c—the machine used on the Sturgeon and Mackerel links— was intercepted later in November. It was believed to have come from the Caucasus. Consisting of the usual messages in depth, it was successfully attacked. The messages dealt with the situation on the Russian front. That was the last appearance of traffic from a T52c machine.

In the first six months of 1943 other teleprinter links appeared which, like the Sturgeon and Mackerel links, also used 'UM UM' in clear to indicate that encipherment should commence (*Umschalten*—switch over). Some of the links were known to use the Tunny machine. It was often difficult for Bletchley Park to distinguish between links using Tunny and those using Sturgeon. Both types of link gave only a QEP number to indicate the machine settings. (The only exception to this rule was the Salmon link between Königsberg and Mariupol, where some groups of letters were sent, apparently to indicate settings.) The basic idea of QEP numbers is explained in Chapter 3.

GERMAN USE OF Q-CODES

QEP was a special code meaning 'cipher key specification' which the Germans added to the set of international abbreviations for radio operators, the so-called Q-codes (which are still in use). The code groups QRA to QUZ are meant for use by all radio services, while the groups QAA to QNZ are reserved for the aeronautical service, and QOA to QQZ for the maritime service. However, the German operators gave many of the more obscure codes new meanings, dealing with the use of teleprinters and cipher machines.

For example, QEH was used to mean *Handbetrib* (send by hand), QES *Komme mit Sender* (will use tape transmitter), QEX *Geben Sie Kaufenschleife* (send a test tape), QFL *Fliegerangriff* (air raid).

Some examples of German Q-codes having special reference to cipher machine use are: QDL QEP meaning 'set up', QDO GKDOS meaning '*Geheime Kommandosache*' (top secret traffic), QEO 'officers key', QGS '*G-Zusatz*' (Tunny machine), QSS 'cipher transmission', QTQ 'additional limitation in use', QZZ 'daily key setting'. QEK was used to indicate which cipher machine was in use—QEK alone indicated that the T52a/b was being used, QEKC indicated the T52c, and QEKZ indicated Tunny.

The form of the numbers and letters following QEP and specifying the settings would depend on which cipher machine was in use. The QEP details were given in the cipher instructions for each type of machine.

THE STURGEON MACHINE

Analysis of intercepts showed that the Sturgeon machine was using two operations, a modulo-2 addition—as explained in previous chapters, this is the same as the Boolean operation of 'exclusive-or' (XOR)—and a permutation, or rearrangement, of the resulting five teleprinter code elements.

Modulo-2 addition is really nothing more than a simple inversion. A plaintext element—i.e. a bit—will change from 0 to 1 or from 1 to 0 if the key element is 1, while if the key element is 0 it will remain unchanged. This can be seen from the XOR table in Figure 1, where Σ_i represents the key element, P_i the plaintext element, and C_i' the resulting ciphertext element. We use C' to indicate that this is an intermediate result—the real ciphertext character, C, will appear only after the permutation has taken place.

Σ_i	P_i	C_i'
0	0	0
0	1	1
1	0	1
1	1	0

Figure 1. XOR.

The permutation is a simple reordering of the teleprinter elements or bits. For example, the permutation 12345 is the 'identity' permutation, producing no change in the order of the elements, while the permutation 52413 takes bit 1 to position 4, bit 2 does not move, 3 goes to position 5, 4 goes to 3, and bit 5

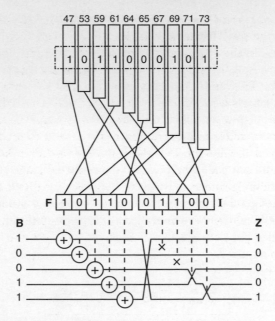

Figure 2. Functional diagram of the T52.

The ten rectangles of varying heights symbolise the ten code wheels. (The code wheels were labelled A to K from right to left, omitting I.) Protrusions around their circumferences were sensed by electrical contacts. The length of the code wheel sequences produced by the protrusions is written above each of the ten wheels. Below the wheels, the plug connections that make up the main inner key are shown connecting each of the ten wheels to the various elements of the XOR and transposition circuits.

In the T52a/b and T52d, each code wheel consisted of four identical cams, each fitted with a changeover contact that was used in either the XOR circuits or the transposition circuits of the transmitter and receiver part of the machine. In the T52c/ca and T52e this relatively complex circuit was modified by using relays with multiple contact sets for the functions in the XOR and transposition circuits. These so-called SR relays were controlled via a logic circuit driven by the cam contacts on four different code wheels. The code wheels in the T52c/ca and T52e had one single cam on each wheel; the other three cams became superfluous and were therefore removed. The relays SR1-SR5 were used in the permutation circuit, while SR6-SR10 made up the substitution circuit. The T52a/b and T52d included a flexible transposition circuit, which allowed full freedom in its configuration. This flexibility was absent from the T52c/ca and T52e—these machines used a standard configuration of the transposition units which was wired permanently in place.

ends up in position 1. This is the permutation shown in Figure 2, which depicts the basic functioning of all the T52 machines.

The cryptographic algorithm, transforming a plaintext character P into the corresponding ciphertext character C, consisted of adding an element of key to each of the five teleprinter elements of the plaintext character, and then permuting the order of the five resulting bits. The two cryptographic operations, modulo-2 addition and permutation, are controlled by two continuously changing key values. The modulo-2 key was called the *subtractor* at BP and was represented by the symbol Σ, while the permutation key was called the *permutor* and was represented by Π.

The two keys, Σ and Π, were each generated by five code wheels. The five Σ-wheels and the five Π-wheels could be chosen freely from the machine's ten code wheels. In the T52a/b and T52d this selection was done by plugging cables into the respective subtractor and permutor sockets (see photograph 52), while in the T52c and T52e the selection was done by a switch assembly. The T52 code wheels were similar in functionality to the wheels used in the Tunny machine. However, while the Tunny wheels had metal cams which could be set in an active or an inactive position—and so the wheel patterns could be changed at will—the T52 wheels were moulded in Bakelite (an early form of plastic). Each code wheel carried its own fixed pattern.

The decryption algorithm consisted of two steps: first an inverse permutation was applied to the ciphertext elements, and then a modulo-2 addition was performed. The inverse permutation is the permutation that restores the original bit order. For example, to restore 52413 to 12345, the inverse permutation 42531 is required.

Relays		Wheel Output Channels									
		1	3	5	7	9	I	II	III	IV	V
Permutor	SR1	X	X					X		X		
	SR2		X	X					X		X	
	SR3			X	X					X		X
	SR4				X	X	X				X	
	SR5	X				X		X				X
Subtractor	SR6			X	X			X		X		
	SR7		X	X					X			X
	SR8	X	X					X				X
	SR9	X				X		X	X			
	SR10				X	X	X				X	

Figure 3. The wheel combination logic of the T52c.

In the T52c/ca and T52e, plugging was not used for changing the wheel order. Instead, these machines contained ten switches, one for each wheel, which could be set to one of ten positions labelled 1, 3, 5, 7, 9 and I, II, III, IV, V. The plugs and sockets of the T52a/b and T52d machines were completely removed. The ten output channels from the wheel order selection circuit carried the same labels as the switch positions. These output channels would then enter the wheel combination logic and control the SR relays as shown in the figure.

A cross in the row for one of the SR relays means that the control of the relay depends on the output channels indicated, e.g. the function for the SR4 relay is given by the modulo-2 sum of the output channels 7, 9, and I, IV. Any of the ten wheels could be connected to any of the ten output channels going to the wheel combination logic, the only restriction being that a given output channel could be selected only once. (If this rule were disobeyed, a short circuit would result.)

In the T52c, T52ca, and T52e, each of the SR relays was controlled via a wheel combination logic that consisted of the modulo-2 sum of four different output channels.

Source: Davies, D. W. 'The Early Models of the Siemens and Halske T52 Cipher Machine', *Cryptologia*, vol. 7 (1983), pp. 235–53. (The author has verified Davies' findings by reference to documents in the archives of the FRA (*Försvarets Radioanstalt*), the Swedish signals intelligence organisation.)

The example depicted in Figure 2 illustrates how the machine works. A plaintext character, B say, is added bitwise to the subtractor character, F say. (B in teleprint code is ×••×× or 10011; Appendix 2 gives the complete teleprint alphabet.) The result of the modulo-2 addition is routed through the transposition circuit, which is controlled by the permutor character, I say. As the diagram indicates, an individual transposition unit is active when the controlling bit supplied by the permutor character is 0. The resulting ciphertext character is Z. The two key characters, F and I, are determined by the inner key configuration (plugs or switches) and the code wheel positions when the plaintext character B enters the machine.

The T52c and T52ca machines introduced yet another complexity, the message-key unit. This unit, consisting of 15 transposition units, was connected between the code wheel cam contacts and the wheel order selection circuit. Its function was to further permute the order of the wheels before their contacts were selected in the wheel order selection circuit. A new setting of the message-key unit was selected for each new message. This meant that even if the main inner key—the selection of the order and functionality of the wheels—remained the same, the wheels would still have a different function for each new message.

The T52d and T52e had irregular movement of the code wheels, a so-called stop-and-go movement. The movement of each wheel was controlled by contacts on two of the other wheels. These two machines also had a switchable autokey (autoclave) element. If the autokey element was switched in, the third bit of each plaintext character was involved in controlling the movement of the wheels.

THE PENTAGON

Analysis at BP of the T52 key generator showed that the ten code wheels were combined in fours. The circuit responsible for this combining was named the 'Pentagon' (after the shape of the graph mapping the different possible relationships provided by this circuit).

The Pentagon was cryptographically a weak device. Only four different subtractors could be associated with a given permutation. Furthermore, the subtractor character was always even, that is, the five code impulses always summed to zero. Therefore the plaintext character was even whenever the ciphertext character was even, and odd whenever the ciphertext character was odd. For the cryptanalyst this was similar to the Enigma's peculiarity that no letter can encipher to itself, and it was of great help in reading depths and placing cribs.

DEPTHS

The first Sturgeon message to be read was a depth of 40 (i.e. 40 messages enciphered with identical machine settings)—an almost incredible number. The German operators can have had no idea of the detailed functioning of the machine, and must have either disobeyed orders or been wrongly instructed. Eventually, with detailed knowledge of the limitations imposed by the Pentagon device, BP could read depths of four or five fairly easily.

The ten code wheels were selected and set to a new start position once a day; this base or initial setting remained in force during the whole day. This procedure would not have posed a problem if the machine had not been equipped with a reset device. A small crank allowed the operator to bring the machine back to its initial start position easily. This was the main reason for the large number of messages in depth. With this knowledge, it was possible to read messages at depths of two or three as soon as the daily wheel settings had been recovered. When the breakers could make a guess at a crib of about six letters, even single messages could be broken—thanks to the limitations of the Pentagon.

BP's analysis showed that the different messages were being sent using different wheel orders. The codebreakers guessed that there was some form of message-key device changing the connections between the code wheels and the Pentagon. But because the operators were bringing the machine back to its initial position, the binary streams from each of the wheels were always the same. This was the undoing of the message-key device.

For each message, five letters were given as a message key. These letters always came from the reduced alphabet: P S T U W X Y Z. (A letter could appear more than once in the group of five; even WWWWW was intercepted on one occasion.) BP noticed that, when two message keys agreed in n positions, it was usually, but not always, the case that $2n$ of the wheels had the same function in the Pentagon. However, the rule did not apply to message keys sent on different days. This message-key system was never broken—although the operators' habit of resetting the code wheels defeated the message-key device.

All this makes it evident that BP was initially confronted with the T52c. The T52a/b did not have the cryptanalytically helpful Pentagon. The T52c had a message-key unit with five levers that could be set in eight different positions, indicated by the letters P S T U W X Y Z. Like the T52a/b, the T52c also had a small crank that allowed the code wheels to be brought back to an index position. This was a conceptual error in the T52c, since the main reason for this wheel resetting mechanism was to allow the operator to set the message key easily on the wheels—the T52a/b was not equipped with a message-key unit like that of the T52c, and the message key was set directly on five of the ten code wheels. The ten wheels were brought back to their initial position by the resetting mechanism in preparation for sending a new message, and the five wheels selected as message-key wheels were then set to their new position. It is debatable whether even the limited wheel resetting available in the T52a/b was a good idea, but it was certainly a blunder of some magnitude to make complete wheel resetting available in the T52c.

BREAKING THE T52d

A new link appeared in July 1943, operating between Königsberg and Munich. Codenamed 'Halibut' by BP, this link went off the air in August, but reappeared in a changed form in 1944. In the period from July to August 1943 a few depths of four and one of five were intercepted. A depth of four from August was read and found to have been enciphered in the same way as depths that had appeared earlier on the Salmon T52a/b link between Königsberg and Mariupol. Like the Salmon messages, the depth of four consisted of operator chat. The July depth of five resisted all attempts to break it, however. It finally succumbed to a sustained attack a year later, in June 1944, and turned out to have been enciphered on a new machine, the T52d.

This was the first break into T52d traffic. The message did not use the autokey element (*Klartextfunktion*) of the T52d, but nevertheless the Halibut break was an outstanding achievement. The T52d machine was completely broken from the depth of five (actually it was only a depth of four in places). From BP's subsequent analysis of the machine, a depth of four appeared to be the absolute minimum required for a break.

How was it possible to break such a complicated machine from only one intercept in depth of four and five? Part of the answer is that BP was not confronted by a completely new machine: it was mainly the stop-and-go wheel movements that distinguished the T52d from the T52a/b. The code wheels themselves had the same patterns as those of the T52a/b and the T52c. It would turn out later that almost all the machines in the T52 series used the same code wheel patterns. As previously mentioned, the patterns were fixed and no changes were ever made to them—a very serious weakness.

The Halibut break was a manual operation (assisted by a large number of catalogues, showing the possible alphabets that resulted from an assumption that a certain plaintext character corresponded to a certain character in the ciphertext). Since all the operations were done by hand, setting was a slow and tedious process. BP did not develop a machine to assist with the deciphering.

Final proof that BP had broken a new Sturgeon model was provided by decrypts referring to experiments with a machine called 'T52d'. Later two captured T52d machines were found to contain the same motor wheel logic that had been derived cryptanalytically from the Halibut message.

The Halibut break showed the sheer cryptanalytic difficulty presented by the T52d. BP launched a substantial research effort to understand the T52d fully, and to explore possible attacks against it. The codebreakers realised that solutions through depths could not be relied upon in the future, because of the increasing use of the autokey function. Another problem that presented itself was how to differentiate between this traffic and Tunny. BP hoped to find statistical techniques that would enable identification of the traffic.

INSECURE BUT UNPROFITABLE

The link named 'Conger' appeared between Athens and Berlin in September 1943. Hundreds of messages were sent and all were in depth, so there was no great difficulty in reading them. However, their intelligence value was nil: the messages contained only operator chat.

Conger contained references to the T52b. A T52b had been captured in Tunisia, and by correlating the code wheel sequences recovered from Conger intercepts with those of the actual machine, it was found that at the initial starting position all wheels were set to one. The wheels were used in the order of their periods. In November, similar Conger messages in depth were sent; this time the wheels were all set to 2. This is amazing and shows a complete disregard for security.

It would seem that the machines were used by operators who had never read the instructions and who had not been issued with operational keys for these machines. One also gets the strong impression that the majority of Sturgeon links were not operational links, but reserve channels kept open mainly with operator chat and test messages. However, their use was cryptographically damaging to the machines.

Both Conger and Halibut reappeared early in 1944 in a slightly changed form. The new Halibut messages were all short, whereas previously they were often very long. Conger, on the other hand, often contained long messages.

Depths of up to four occurred. The messages had no repeats, however, indicating that the autokey function was being used—a hypothesis further supported by the intercept logs, which contained phrases like 'Mit KTF' (with KTF—*Klartextfunktion*) and 'Ohne KTF' (without KTF). BP did find one depth of two without the autokey function, but a depth of two was considered unbreakable.

Shortly after the reappearance of Conger and Halibut it was decided to cease interception of all links using Sturgeon machines, since the work was unprofitable. There is no evidence that much further effort was invested by BP in the Sturgeon machines and their traffic.

THE CAPTURES

As already mentioned, the first Sturgeon machine to be captured was a T52b found in Tunisia. It was discovered that the code wheels on this machine moved regularly and that they did not combine. It was therefore evident to BP that it was not the Pentagon machine (the first Sturgeon type of machine to be intercepted and broken).

Subsequently a full technical description of a machine that combined the functions of the T52a/b and T52c was captured on the island of Elba. It appeared from this description that the T52c machine was related to the Pentagon machine, since it combined the code wheels in fours. However, the number of alphabets was found to be 256 instead of the 60 possessed by the Pentagon machine. The machine described was in fact the T52ca. The Elba description also showed that the T52c machine was equipped with a wheel permuting mechanism corresponding to the message-key unit described earlier. It was found that the unit consisted of five levers, each of which controlled three switches out of a set of 15. When activated, each switch interchanged two wheels. A switch was active or inactive depending on the position of the controlling lever (although the correlation of active switch position and lever position was different for the three switches controlled by a given lever). In addition, it was found that all the machines were equipped with a set of switches or plugs constituting the main inner key setting. The switches or plugs selected which of the ten code wheels controlled a given function in the cryptographic process.

Following the capture of the Elba description, an actual machine of the type described was captured at Naples. This was clearly a T52c machine, but the message-key unit with the five levers had been removed. It was noted that the machine was very similar to the first captured T52b machine, which also had room for a message-key unit although none was actually fitted. A second machine was captured at Naples. The original type number of this machine, T52b, had been altered to T52d. The machine was equipped with wheel-stopping logic and had a switch to enable or disable the autokey function. Without the autokey function, the code wheels had the same movement as that derived cryptanalytically from the July Halibut message. When the autokey function was active, the wheel movement logic became more symmetrical, and the third impulse of the plaintext governed part of the logic. Two of the wheels were controlled by a plaintext cross, while two others were controlled by a dot. Later yet another T52d was captured. This machine had been altered from a T52a. When the machine was compared with the T52b, it became obvious that the T52a and T52b must have been very similar. It is known from German sources that the only real difference between the two was that the T52b was fitted with extra filters to reduce radio interference.

The Elba capture included not only the description of the T52c but also two key book pages, one for the T52d and one for the T52a/b and T52c. One side of each page gave the table for 3 June 1944, while on the other side was the table for 4 June. The table for the T52c is reproduced in Figure 5, and a similar table for the T52d/e is reproduced in Figure 4. The use of these tables, and the method of disguising the code wheel settings (transmitted as QEP numbers or letters), changed several times throughout the war, but the tables themselves largely retained their original structure and layout.

GERMAN SECURITY ALARMS

References to Sturgeon machines were frequent in both Tunny and Enigma traffic. During 1942, decodes referred only to the T52a/b and T52c machines. The *Wehrmacht Schlüsselfernschreibvorschrift* (*SFV*), the main instruction book for the use of teleprinter cipher machines, issued on 1 December 1942, refers only to the T52a/b, T52c, and SZ40 types of cipher machine. It is therefore very likely that these were the only machines available in 1942. (BP appears to have captured a copy of the *SFV* some time before November 1944.)

On 17 October 1942 an Enigma message from CSO *Luftflotte 2* (Chief Signal Officer Air Fleet 2) to *Fliegerführer Afrika* (Air Commander Africa) mentioned that the T52c had inadequate security. It gave orders that 'Secret' and 'Secret Commands Only' (probably a translation of *Geheime*

W. Fſchr. Spr. Schl.
SFM T 52 d/e   Prüfnr. ~~104~~

Geheim!

Norwegen Nr. 4
1. Tag ab 0900 Uhr DGZ

	1	2	3	4	5	6	7	8	9	10	
A	18	20	38	31	54	47	67	54	70	17	A
B	05	30	22	60	63	29	35	42	55	04	B
C	37	28	58	36	03	46	13	47	20	67	C
D	46	27	42	32	10	07	64	41	08	15	D
E	23	13	30	29	24	56	20	31	39	32	E
F	19	45	57	07	55	61	27	58	68	72	F
G	42	22	19	26	08	11	53	29	16	58	G
H	35	08	28	55	58	22	19	68	02	19	H
i	29	49	17	47	36	30	61	08	40	65	i
K	02	19	48	43	42	20	24	14	31	47	K
L	33	51	25	10	32	05	52	28	18	22	L
M	38	06	35	05	60	17	04	46	64	11	M
N	43	01	09	27	35	44	66	12	59	30	N
O	47	11	37	59	64	25	22	56	71	14	O
P	14	07	56	49	13	19	44	38	27	07	P
Q	44	25	11	21	48	28	51	17	35	29	Q
R	17	12	15	40	34	12	57	05	48	57	R
S	15	26	52	46	62	45	26	37	44	62	S
T	39	21	18	14	01	38	11	50	56	21	T
U	03	52	23	53	26	14	49	69	61	25	U
V	36	24	54	16	37	33	23	59	34	52	V
W	16	50	44	24	53	43	18	21	53	50	W
X	40	48	41	33	51	65	45	34	46	12	X
Y	34	37	20	39	18	23	33	63	36	73	Y
Z	10	53	34	45	59	02	48	16	54	37	Z
	1	2	3	4	5	6	7	8	9	10	

Figure 4. Daily key table for the T52d/e.
The message key QEP FF OO PP AA ZZ VV CC MM HH UU corresponds to setting the leftmost code wheel to 19, as shown in column 1, row F of the table. The next wheel to its right is set to 11, as shown in column 2, row O. And so on. The complete code wheel setting for this message key is: 19 11 56 31 59 33 13 46 02 25.

Geheim!

RB 51

Lw.-RB-Fs. Spr. Schl.
T 52c

Prüfnr.

1. Monatstag ab 0900 Uhr DGZ

	1	2	3	4	5	6	7	8	9	10	
A	11 z	19 x	49 u	27 s	59 p	61	19	42	10	17	A
B	26 y	29 w	50 t	08 p	07 z	08	24	63	14	62	B
C	05 x	10 t	39 s	56 z	22 y	04	26	12	52	65	C
D	36 u	09 s	13 z	12 x	17 w	32	30	11	17	06	D
E	09 s	17 z	25 x	13 u	15 t	47	45	41	34	11	E
F	47 p	14 y	38 w	14 t	03 s	12	19	03	15	66	F
G	12 w	16 t	56 p	09 y	42 u	30	27	02	58	57	G
H	08 t	32 p	17 y	23 w	46 x	65	09	44	02	64	H
İ	42 p	19 s	27 t	13 u	58 w	08	67	40	52	20	İ
K	34 x	28 y	26 z	21 p	10 s	11	45	61	57	50	K
L	29 t	20 u	43 w	32 x	52 y	23	09	60	49	11	L
M	27 z	27 p	33 s	41 t	15 u	52	11	09	12	59	M
N	28 w	09 x	34 y	59 z	47 p	40	53	66	39	24	N
O	45 s	23 t	14 u	44 w	19 x	48	57	67	32	48	O
P	35 y	43 z	09 p	53 s	10 t	52	49	30	43	31	P
Q	03 u	35 w	52 x	02 y	08 z	26	34	10	23	28	Q
R	46 p	14 s	06 t	32 u	18 w	62	15	66	24	17	R
S	16 z	38 y	32 x	30 s	12 p	12	35	50	20	15	S
T	14 w	04 t	27 p	29 x	45 z	20	32	04	47	40	T
U	19 s	27 u	28 z	21 w	39 t	31	38	57	66	48	U
V	45 x	05 w	09 u	03 z	46 y	45	14	19	05	03	V
W	44 t	34 p	20 s	56 y	05 u	38	62	62	34	16	W
X	33 p	03 x	10 t	59 u	24 w	15	24	37	39	10	X
Y	30 u	45 t	55 z	02 x	21 p	52	30	18	21	12	Y
Z	14 y	22 z	09 w	28 s	34 x	39	02	13	16	61	Z
	1	2	3	4	5	6	7	8	9	10	

Figure 5. Daily key table for the T52c.

The method of indicating the code wheel setting described in Figure 4 also applies to the table for the T52c, but in addition there are lever settings for the message-key unit as shown in the first five columns. The key QEP FF OO PP AA ZZ VV CC MM HH UU would in this situation give the code wheel settings 47 23 09 27 34 45 26 09 02 48, with the message-key levers at p t p s x.

Kommandosache—'Top Secret') were to be enciphered on Enigma before being sent over *Sägefisch* links. This message passed between stations served by the Sturgeon link using the T52c machine; but nevertheless seemingly important messages continued to pass over the link without first being enciphered on Enigma.

The message doubting the security of the T52c stands in contrast with the *SFV*, which authorises the T52c for use over radio and radio relay links and contains a clear instruction not to use the T52a/b over these links. The Luftwaffe for some reason did not obey these instructions, using the T52b for practice transmissions on the Salmon, Halibut, and Conger links. Luftwaffe cipher officers must have been unaware of the close similarity between the different T52 models and so did not see the threat that these transmissions posed to the other machines.

Decodes show that in February 1943 the Germans suddenly discovered that something was seriously wrong with their *Sägefisch* machines. A message from Madrid to Paris said that the T52 was very badly compromised and that enemy decipherment was possible. 'Secret' and 'Top Secret' messages were no longer to be sent using the T52.

On 18 February 1943 a new set of instructions for using the T52 machines was issued. The new instructions included the order that the device for setting all the wheels back to the 'zero position' be removed. This shows that the Germans had finally woken up to the peril of sending many messages on the same key by means of the wheel-resetting mechanism. Apparently the Germans also suspected some weakness in the method for indicating the settings of the machine to the recipient, and they introduced new, temporary measures. They would later abandon the use of QEP numbers and use a QEP structure with ten bigrams (letter pairs), as shown in Figure 4. It is not clear why this was considered a better procedure; possibly it offered more flexibility than QEP numbers in choosing message keys.

On 19 February another message gave further instructions. Traffic sent over teleprinter links had to be enciphered with Enigma first. The T52a/b was not to be used for 'Secret' and 'Top Secret' messages, except when no other means was available. Then on 6 March two messages said that traffic on the *Aptierte* (adapted) T52c no longer needed to be enciphered first on the Enigma. From then on there were references to the T52ca; 'a' probably stood for *Aptierte*. On 14 June 1943 there was a message saying 'On completion of the adaptation to SFM T52c, the designation T52ca will no longer be used. The designation T52c only is to be used from now on.' The changes made to the T52c concerned the wheel combining logic, which BP had found to be of great help when breaking the Pentagon machine. The Germans must have made a detailed analysis of the machine and found this part of the logic to be particularly weak.

In 1942 the T52c was studied by an army cryptanalyst, Doering. He showed that it could be broken on a text of 1000 letters. Investigations into the weaknesses of the T52c resulted in the production of the T52d. However, early in 1943, Doering showed that the T52d was insecure as well. This resulted in the production of the T52e. Yet it was known to the German experts that both the T52d and T52e were open to attack through depths, and that a depth of ten messages could be read without a crib. (Traffic from the T52e was never observed, or at least never identified, by any of the allied cryptanalytical services. They knew of the existence of the T52e from Enigma decrypts, but the machine itself remained unknown to them until the end of the war.)

The cries of alarm from the German cryptographers were not heard, or at least not acted on, by the German army and air force. In the summer of 1942 the totally insecure T52a/b was still in use and the equally insecure T52c was being distributed. The army's position was that the teleprinter traffic went over landlines and could not be intercepted; hence there was no need to worry about inadequate security. Evidence of tapping of teleprinter lines in Paris in 1942 and 1943 gave the army a serious jolt.

INDISCRETIONS AMONG FRIENDS

Colonel Ragnvald Alfred Roscher Lund was the Norwegian military attaché in Stockholm from March 1941. Roscher Lund was Norway's chief intelligence officer. In 1935 he initiated courses in cryptography and then created Norway's first signals intelligence and cipher office. Early on he made contact with Swedish cryptanalysts and quickly became a close friend of one of Sweden's most famous cryptanalysts, Yves Gyldén. Roscher Lund made frequent trips to Sweden before the war and became well known in Swedish military circles. He was held in high esteem.

The success of the Swedish cryptanalysts against the T52 is described in the next chapter. The Swedes tapped German teleprinter lines passing over Swedish territory and deciphered the T52 traffic. British Intelligence seems to have known by 1942 of the Swedish success against the T52. Roscher Lund, who had been informed by the Swedes about their deciphering of the landline traffic, was an important source of information to the British—so much so that there was immediate consternation in British circles when Roscher Lund was ordered to leave Stockholm in order to organise the Norwegian intelligence office in London. On 10 September 1941, Winston Churchill sent a letter to the Norwegian prime minister, Johan Nygaardsvold, asking him to reconsider his decision. Churchill wrote: 'This officer has been of great service to the British Intelligence organisation in Sweden, and his presence there is of special value to His Majesty's Government, and to the Allied Cause as a whole . . . I sincerely hope that your Excellency and your colleagues may feel able to reverse the decision which has been taken. It is a matter to which I attach great importance.' Nygaardsvold did not change his mind, however, and Roscher Lund arrived in London on 12 October 1941, taking office in the headquarters of the Norwegian government in exile at Kingston House, Knightsbridge.

Within a month Roscher Lund asked a Captain Howard if he could help him resolve questions that the Norwegians had about the security of their Hagelin cipher machines. The Norwegians had heard rumours, originating from British sources, that the Hagelin machine was unsafe and was being read (see Appendix 4). At the insistence of Captain Howard, a cryptanalyst from Tiltman's section at Bletchley Park went to London on 14 November and met Roscher Lund for lunch at the Royal Automobile Club. After lunch the unknown cryptanalyst accompanied Roscher Lund to Kingston House, where he was introduced to Erling Quande, chief of the Norwegian cipher office in London. The BP man was shown the Hagelin machines that the Norwegians were using and was asked about their security. Roscher Lund, perhaps wishing to show the British cryptanalyst that he was talking to a fellow expert, gave an impromptu overview of his experience. His disclosures included details of his contacts with the Swedish and Finnish cipher bureaux. Roscher Lund estimated the personnel in the Swedish Cryptographic Bureau to be about 150 and said, mistakenly, that Yves Gyldén was head of the Bureau (in fact Gyldén was leader of the French section). In his report of the conversation, the British cryptanalyst said: 'The Swedish Bureau had had considerable success in their attacks on French cyphers and which he [Roscher Lund] put at 95%, Italian military 85%, and fair progress on the German cyphers. Lund said the Germans were sending masses of messages to their troops in the north of Norway by teleprinter and that the telephone manufacturing firm L. M. Ericsson had built a machine which deciphered these messages which dealt mainly with personnel and administration.' This is an explicit reference to the Swedish breaking of the T52, even correctly naming the manufacturer of the deciphering machines. Roscher Lund also spoke in great detail about the Finnish cryptanalyst Reino Hallamaa and his success in breaking Russian codes and ciphers.

Roscher Lund was obviously trying to bargain some of his cryptographic secrets in exchange for British help in securing Norwegian communications.

Probably neither Swedish nor Finnish cryptanalytical security suffered any harm from this loose talk among friends.

The British cryptanalyst concluded his report: 'Major Lund gave me the impression of being most anxious to help the British Government, and having regard to the rumours referred to, his concern about the security of the Hagelin machine was quite genuine. I would therefore like to suggest that the appropriate steps be taken to put Major Lund's mind at rest on this matter.' Whether Roscher Lund got the information he wanted is not known. What he did get was an OBE for his services to British Intelligence.

STURGEON AFTER THE WAR

The Siemens T52 rose like a phoenix from the ashes of the Third Reich. It was not the only cipher machine to do so. Enigma in its many variations was used by several countries for a considerable number of years after the war. Most of these countries were Western powers. In Norway, for example, Enigma was used by the Security Police (*Overvåkingstjenesten*) until the 1960s. Enigma was also used by some Warsaw Pact countries (the new enemy). A prominent example is the use of Enigma by the East German State Police, the notorious *Stasi*. It is not known when the East Germans started to use the Enigma, nor for how long it was in use, but a US Armed Forces Security Agency document describing the deciphering process is dated 22 May 1952. This perhaps explains the report that some US Navy Bombes were taken out of storage and put back into service.

The Sturgeon machine created even more interest among prospective users than Enigma. The T52 was much more sophisticated and up to date, and in addition could be connected directly to modern telecommunication lines. Probably the first country to consider using the machine was Britain. By September 1945 the Royal Air Force had already started service trials with the machine:

In accordance with the Minutes of a Meeting to discuss the policy regarding radio teleprinting in the Royal Air Force, held at Air Ministry, Whitehall, on Friday 7th September, 1945, it is desired to determine the suitability of the G. *Schreiber* as a cypher machine or as a scrambler device associated with either landline or radio circuits. Arrangements are to be made to carry out service trials of this machine on a similar basis to those conducted for the GP 28.

The G. *Schreiber* is not clearly identified as the T52. It is possible, but unlikely, that the term was being used to refer to the Lorenz SZ42 (Tunny).

Since the SZ42 was less secure than the T52d, it is doubtful whether it would have been adopted for service trials.

The *G. Schreiber* trials started in early October and were completed in November. The GP 28, a cipher machine delivered to the Royal Air Force by the Telecommunications Research Establishment at Malvern, had already undergone service trials in June and July 1945. The final verdict was:

Tests on the *G. Schreiber* equipment were completed during the month and reports rendered to Air Ministry. It was decided at Air Ministry that the equipment should not be brought into use on RAF radio circuits.

Unfortunately the detailed test reports have not been found, and it is not known whether this negative outcome was a result of concerns about the machine's cryptographic security, or whether it was simply because the machine was found to be less well suited for the intended use than its competitor.

Other countries were a lot more receptive to Sturgeon's charms. In 1946 the Norwegian Cipher Office (under the leadership of Captain Nils Stordahl) started to test and modify T52d and T52e machines that had been left behind in Norway. A number of the modified machines were used to encipher teleprinter communications between the headquarters of the Security Police in Oslo and their regional stations. The total number of machines may have been as high as 70. Air Disarmament Wing No. 8801 had prepared this number of *G. Schreibers* for transfer to England, but in a meeting between Royal Air Force officers and Norwegian Post Office personnel in Oslo on 8 September 1945, it was agreed that most or all of the machines would be left with the Norwegians. Other T52 machines were used by the Norwegian Intelligence Service (*Etterretningstjenesten*) for their internal communications, and a few machines were given to Sweden to protect the intelligence link between Oslo and Stockholm.

Wolfgang Mache mentions that about 380 T52 machines survived at the end of the war, the greatest number being in Germany. The majority of these machines were collected at the Post Office central store in Elmshorn, formerly the communications equipment arsenal of the German navy. About 280 T52 machines and a few T43 machines were stored there. These machines were meant to have been destroyed or demilitarised, but apparently they were only dismantled. From 1948 onwards the electromechanical firm Willi Reichert in Trier started to rebuild T52d and T52e machines from a large stock of T52 parts. Quite possibly these were the dismantled parts from the Elmshorn store. Some electrical drawings for the T52d bearing the name of Willi Reichert are dated as late as 1959. During the period 1949–53 Willi Reichert delivered more than 235 T52 machines to the French Foreign Office and

French armed forces. The French were undoubtedly the largest users of T52 machines after the war. Perhaps there were post-war attacks on T52 traffic by the British and Americans—both are known to have had considerable interest in French post-war codes and ciphers.

The Dutch navy also found the T52 an attractive machine and used a number of them in the 1950s. It is not known where the machines were used—possibly on links between land stations in the Netherlands and on links to Dutch stations in Indonesia.

The East Germans took an interest in the T52. By 1951 the Stasi already had an extensive teleprinter network, consisting of six main centres servicing a total of 48 stations. Their equipment was mostly teleprinters, hand perforators, and tape transmitters and receivers, from Siemens, Lorenz, and Olivetti. Instead of using on-line ciphering equipment, the Stasi seem to have enciphered all their teleprinter messages by hand, using a manual cipher called TAPIR. Letters, numbers, signs, and all the special teleprinter characters, were first encoded using a five by ten encoding rectangle. The resulting numbers were set out in groups of five, which were super-enciphered by adding five-digit numbers from an additive book valid for a given teleprinter link. This must have been a long and tedious procedure, and it very much negated the advantages of using teleprinter communications.

In July 1951 a United States Intelligence report on 'Communications in the Soviet Zone of Germany' described the interest that the East Germans were showing in the T52. German communist officials approached a former Siemens employee, who had assembled T52 machines during the war and had remained with Siemens in East Berlin until 1947, eventually entering the communication service of the *Volkspolizei* (People's Police). When he subsequently defected to West Berlin, he disclosed that the officials had sought his advice on the feasibility of manufacturing T52e machines at the former Siemens plant in Chemnitz. Their plan was to buy a T52e in the Western Zone and have it copied by East German engineers. An engineer was sent to the Western Zone, but there our knowledge of the intriguing post-war history of the T52 peters out. Were T52e machines manufactured at Chemnitz for service behind the Iron Curtain? The veil of secrecy holds firm—for now.

Chapter 26

German Teleprinter Traffic and Swedish Wartime Intelligence

Craig McKay

BEURLING'S BREAK

As German forces marched into Norway in April 1940, the German ambassador to Sweden requested permission to lease a number of telephone lines running across Swedish territory. The lines would be used to carry communications between Germany and centres in Norway. The Swedish government agreed—and proceeded to tap the lines. Analysis showed that the Germans were using the lines for teleprinter traffic (among other things). Following suitable modifications to Swedish receiving equipment, the teleprinter signals were processed and printed out on paper tape. The initial traffic was in plaintext. From this traffic, and from telephone conversations, it was learned that the Germans were proposing to introduce something called the 'Geheimschreiber'—in fact the Siemens T52, known to the British as Sturgeon. The Swedes assumed that the Geheimschreiber was some kind of encryption device. The assumption was confirmed at the end of April, when intercepted text became unreadable.

It was at this point that Professor Arne Beurling, the magician of Swedish wartime cryptanalysis (and a future inheritor of Einstein's office at the Institute for Advanced Study at Princeton University) entered the game. Beurling had already played a major role in the solution of the five-digit code used by the Soviet Baltic fleet. The T52 traffic would also succumb to his charms. His

I am grateful to my friend Bengt Beckman for constructive comments on this chapter; his pioneering work *Svenska Kryptobedrifter* (Swedish Achievements in Cryptology) has been an important source of inspiration (Stockholm: Albert Bonniers Förlag, 1996). For a detailed account of the history of Swedish signal intelligence, the reader is referred to Beckman's and my book *Swedish Signal Intelligence 1900–1945* (London: Frank Cass, 2003).

solution, based on traffic of 25 and 27 May 1940, led to the emergence in Sweden of what was virtually an industry for the extraction of intelligence from German cable traffic.

Curiously enough, the exact details of Beurling's break remain unknown. He never explained his method in detail, far less wrote it down, and rather relished keeping it completely secret. It is clear that Beurling made his attack on what the British called a 'depth' (and the Swedes referred to as 'parallel texts')—that is to say, a set of telegrams enciphered using the same key. Depths could quickly be identified from an indicator known as the QEP. Two telegrams sent on the same day with the same QEP could be assumed to have been enciphered using the same key. Depths should never have occurred. In practice, they occurred all the time, due to an unholy alliance between a design fault in the T52a/b, operator error, and electrical disturbances on the line.

One theory about Beurling's break is that he used a technique he had developed previously against Soviet codes, teasing out plausible plaintext candidates for the corresponding letters in the ciphertext. Once he disentangled sufficient letters in the depth—100 or so—the structure of the encryption device emerged: a machine with ten wheels, of varying periods. As explained in the preceding chapter, five of the wheels were used to add a stream of five-bit numbers to the successive five-bit numbers representing plaintext characters, while the other five wheels were used to permute the results of this addition.

THE PRODUCTION PHASE

After Beurling's break into the Sturgeon traffic, the cryptanalytical work soon moved into the production phase. New staff were recruited, and found themselves working around the clock to keep pace with demand. In order to deal with the vast amount of incoming material, Beurling designed a special machine, known as an 'app' (from '*apparat*', plural '*apparna*'—apparatus), which automated the process of decryption. Engineer Vigo Lindstein was given the task of building the app; and in due course some 30 of them were produced, by the Ericsson company. Like the Testery Tunnies (and unlike Heath Robinson and Colossus) the apps played no analytical role—they produced plaintext from ciphertext once the cryptanalysts had determined the settings of the Sturgeon machine.

Operation 'Barbarossa'—the German invasion of Russia—brought an increase in the amount of Sturgeon traffic passing through Sweden. German landline communications with Finland assumed greater importance; and at the same time a T52a/b machine was brought into service at the German legation in Stockholm, in order to cope with the surge in diplomatic reporting to and from the Swedish capital. The offices of the German press attaché and the German air attaché received their own Sturgeons.

All this was grist to the mill of Swedish intelligence. Once routines had been established, an average of 5 kilometres of telegram text were broken each day. The year 1942 saw a grand total of some 2100 kilometres of text being solved, with a peak occurring in November, when more than 10,500 messages were circulated to the Defence Staff and the Ministry for Foreign Affairs. A special section was established to analyse the incoming material and to summarise it under appropriate subject headings.

THE SECRET LEAKS OUT

Neutral capitals were hotbeds of espionage during the Second World War and Stockholm was no exception. While Roscher Lund's revelations to the British, described in Chapter 25, were the result of leaks at the highest level, the Russians learned of the Swedish successes in solving both Soviet and German traffic from a much lowlier source. In the autumn of 1941 a venal messenger, employed by the Defence Staff to courier intercepts around Stockholm, approached the Soviet Legation and offered his services. He was duly kitted out with a camera and provided with a room where he could take snaps of the top secret contents of his bag.

There were other pointers to the vulnerability of Swedish security. A telegram of 8 January 1942 from the Czech intelligence service in Sweden to its London base reported that the Swedes had begun to target their activities. This tip off had come from 'an acquaintance in the Swedish General Staff cipher bureau', the telegram said. (Ironically, the telegram was deciphered by the Swedes.) On one occasion a Swedish Defence Staff liaison officer with access to intercepts of German traffic congratulated an Axis attaché on his forthcoming transfer to Berlin. The only trouble was that the transfer was news to the individual concerned! Somehow the Swedish officer managed to talk his way out of the situation, and so far as is known the incident caused no damage to security.

By far the most serious blow to the security of Swedish cryptanalytical work occurred in the summer of 1942, when the Germans themselves became aware that the Swedes were reading their traffic. The accepted version of events is that the Finnish military attaché in Stockholm, who had more or less free access to the Swedish Defence Staff and was treated as 'one of the family', had blurted out the facts to a German colleague. (The full story, however, may be more complex.)

With alarms bells ringing, the Germans naturally sought to introduce countermeasures. An order was immediately given forbidding the transmission over Swedish lines of material graded *Geheime Kommandosache* (Most Secret). However, the Germans failed to allow for human ingenuity in interpreting the order: in one case, the relevant officer merely struck out the classification on the telegram and forwarded it regardless. The ultimate goal was to avoid the use of Swedish cables for sensitive material altogether. This could be done by redirecting Finnish traffic via the Baltic countries, and using sea cables for traffic between Norway and Denmark. The problem, though, was that such a change could not be accomplished overnight. Nor could a supply of new, more secure machines be produced instantly. In the meantime, the pressure to maintain communication links between the various German offices and centres remained undiminished, and continuity of German practice worked in favour of the Swedish cryptanalysts.

COUNTERMEASURES AND COUNTER-COUNTERMEASURES

New teleprinters with an encryption/decryption facility were brought into play, among them the *Geheimschreiber* T52c. Considered more secure than the T52a/b, it was nevertheless configured so that it could be used as a T52a/b, enabling communication with any network station whose T52a/b was still awaiting replacement. Continuity features with the T52a/b were to prove the Achilles heel of the T52c. A team of Swedish cryptanalysts (Carl-Gösta Borelius, Lars Carlbom, Bertil Nyman, and Bo Kjellberg) was able to break T52c traffic and to reconstruct the essential operation of the machine. Lindstein and Bengt Florin were given the task of modifying the apps to deal with the new traffic. A variant of the T52c, the T52ca, was spotted on 23 February 1943. This machine was also broken after a depth of eleven telegrams was obtained on 8 March. Once again Lindstein provided apps to automate decipherment.

As part of their countermeasures, the Germans introduced the machine known to the British as Tunny. Tunny was used both for landline and radio traffic, and was first noticed by the Swedes in 1941. Initially traffic was comparatively sparse, and difficult to intercept in the case of radio transmissions. Owing to a lack of suitable material, the Swedes at first made little headway against Tunny. However, a fresh attack was made in March 1943, by Borelius, Kjellberg, and Tufve Ljunggren, ending in success. An electromechanical device was invented—built in part out of bicycle chains—for accelerating the decryption process. Yet a declining amount of raw traffic, which was in any case often of technically poor quality, meant that the intelligence dividend from this achievement remained modest.

As German countermeasures began to bite, the picture became similarly bleak elswhere. With improved discipline on the part of German operators, the solution of T52ca traffic encountered difficulties. Moreover, the proportion of diplomatic traffic using unbreakable 'one-time pad' increased significantly. A new *Geheimschreiber*, the Dora model (T52d), which took over in 1944, proved too hard a nut to crack. The Swedes mounted an operation to gain entry—softly, softly—to the German air attaché's office in Stockholm, with the aim of studying and experimenting with the cryptological equipment on the spot.

INTELLIGENCE VALUE OF FISH INTERCEPTS

Professor Harry Hinsley has singled out three significant landmarks in the gathering of Tunny intelligence by the British. First, the initial break into the link between Berlin and the HQ of Army Group E at Salonika allowed traffic to be read between November 1942 and the summer of 1943, a time when there was a drop in Enigma decrypts in this theatre. Second, the break at the end of April 1943 into the link from Berlin to Army Group South on the Russian front provided complete details of the proposed German offensive at Kursk (see the Introduction). Third, exploitation of the link between Berlin and Commander-in-Chief West from the beginning of 1944 gave an unrivalled insight into German appreciations of Allied invasion intentions. The Allied command was able to adjust the details of the invasion plan at the eleventh hour in the light of information received via Tunny.

How significant by comparison was the intelligence derived from Sturgeon intercepts? The traffic initially intercepted in Sweden was in transit between Germany and Norway, but the intelligence obtained from the intercepts was certainly not restricted to the Norwegian campaign. By far the most spectacular example of its worth as an indicator of strategic events was the build-up of evidence that the Germans would launch an attack on Russia in June 1941. Erik Boheman, Under-Secretary of State at the Swedish Ministry for Foreign Affairs, passed this vital evidence to Sir Stafford Cripps, British ambassador to the Soviet Union, as Cripps passed through Stockholm en route from Moscow to Britain.

In due course the Germany–Norway teleprinter traffic was supplemented by transit traffic between Germany and Finland and between Berlin and the German legation in Stockholm. Since the German service attachés were provided with situation reports and other updates on the progress of the war, a broad picture of military developments was obtained.

Access to German teleprinter traffic gave Swedish decision-makers a confidence-boosting advantage. This applied in particular to the diplomats at the Swedish Ministry for Foreign Affairs, who were able to study the effects of their diplomatic efforts in the reports passing between Stockholm and Berlin. For the Swedish security service, the decrypted traffic was a source of valuable information about the activities of the Abwehr (the German secret military intelligence and counter-intelligence organisation) in Sweden and elsewhere. Study of Abwehr traffic revealed the cover names of key officers and their agents, as well as their comings and goings. It is safe to say that very little of what the Abwehr got up to in Sweden remained hidden from the watchful eye of the Swedish authorities.

Sigint also yielded very tangible benefits in the field of trade negotiation. On one occasion, foreknowledge of the German's position enabled the Swedes to hold out for a more favourable agreement yielding a profit of 20 million crowns, a sum that greatly exceeded the entire budget for Swedish signals intelligence in 1942. In addition, intercepts of traffic between Berlin and the German legation in Stockholm provided indispensable information about German attempts to give covert financial subsidies to certain Swedish newspapers and to plant articles. But undoubtedly the greatest dividend from the flow of high-level intercepts was the knowledge that, should Germany decide to launch an attack on neutral Sweden, the Swedes could expect a margin of forewarning.

Technical Appendices

To Dig Deeper

Appendix 1

Timeline: The Breaking of Tunny

This chronology (reproduced from *General Report on Tunny*) begins with the appearance of the first Tunny link. Changes in the Tunny system are described, and the leading developments in the British attack are outlined.

1941	Changes in Tunny	Organisation Changes	Machines	Theoretical Discoveries and Achievements
June	SZ40 on first Tunny link	Work in Research Section starts		
July				
August	The depth HQIBPEXEZ- MUG sent—and read			
September				
October				
November				
December				

1942	Changes in Tunny	Organisation Changes	Machines	Theoretical Discoveries and Achievements
January				Machine broken for Aug. 1941
February				
March	Broken traffic shows $ab = \frac{1}{2}^a$ Tone transmission			
April			Decoding machine ordered	Machine broken for March 1943 First attempts at setting
May				Wheels broken before the end of the month by indicator method
June			First decoding machine arrives	
July		Testery founded to take over work on Tunny from Research Section		Current traffic read for first time Turingery
August	Introduction of Quatsch			
September				

^{a} This was a German precaution. a represents the proportion of crosses in the total motor stream (see Appendix 10) and b the proportion of crosses in each $\Delta\psi$ pattern. See further Appendix 8.

1942	Changes in Tunny	Organisation Changes	Machines	Theoretical Discoveries and Achievements
October	Experimental Tunny link closed Codfish and Octopus start with QEP system and monthly change of psi patterns	Testery confined to depths Research Section begin investigating Statistical Methods		
November			Newman suggests electronic counters	1 + 2 break in invented by Tutte Message set statistically using $\Delta Z_1 + \Delta Z_2$ rectangle [b]
December		Newman given task of developing machines for setting Tunny		

[b] Z is the ciphertext.

1943	Changes in Tunny	Organisation Changes	Machines	Theoretical Discoveries and Achievements
January			Early Robinson designed and ordered	
February	SZ42A (with χ_2 lim.) makes first appearance on Codfish[c]			Research Section breaks chis statistically from Z by rectangles
March	$\bar{\bar{\chi}}_2 \bar{P}_5$ lim. tried experimentally on Herring		Plans for mechanical setting of Tunny and Sturgeon well under way	$\bar{\chi}_2$ lim. broken
April		First 16 Wrens arrived		$\bar{\bar{\chi}}_2 \bar{P}_5$ broken by Testery and Research Section
May			Method of contracted de-χ successful	
June		Newmanry work starts	Arrival of Heath Robinson and first Newmanry Tunny	
July				
August		R0 started[d]		Recognition that 4σ in a break-in is not by any means certain[e]

[c] lim. = limitation. See Appendix 10.

[d] R0 was the first of six Research Logs kept by the Newmanry. R1 was begun in December 1943 and R5, the last, in February 1945.

[e] σ = standard deviation.

1943	Changes in Tunny	Organisation Changes	Machines	Theoretical Discoveries and Achievements
August				Discovery that Knockholt (at the time) were producing a lot of slides in tapes
September			Suggestion of 'and/or' machine and repeated use of character on Colossus or Robinson	Discovery that best ΔP letter is not necessarily / Expected score of motor run in terms of ΔD^f
October		Change over from two to three shifts		
November		Newmanry moved from Hut 11 to Block F	First (production) Robinson arrived	Recognition that de-χ's can be broken by hand / Discovery of $\hat{\chi}_2{}^g$
December	Reappearance of $\overline{\chi}_2 + \overline{\overline{P}}_5$ limitation in Bream and Codfish traffic	Testery take on psi and motor setting and Newmanry concentrate on chi setting and breaking	Second (production) Robinson arrived	Recognition that ΔD statistics (rather than ΔP) are the quickest way of finding new runs

^{f} D is the de-chi.

^{g} $\hat{\chi}_2$ is $\Delta\chi_2$ summed with the result of shifting χ_2 one place forwards.

1944	Changes in Tunny	Organisation Changes	Machines	Theoretical Discoveries and Achievements
January		General Registries of Newmanry and Testery amalgamated	Direct TP line from Knockholt to Block F installed[h] Robinson 3 (first double bedstead Rob.) installed	χ_3 now set in Newmanry, rather than sending de-χ's on only 4 impulses to Testery
February			Colossus I installed Spanning suggested	Colossus first used for wheel-breaking
March			Robinson IV installed	
April		First motor runs successfully done on Colossus	New Tunny machine, new Garbos and one Mrs. Miles installed[i]	Significance tests for rectangles
May				Cribs, predicted by Sixta, successfully used for wheel-breaking for first time
June	SZ42B first used on Codfish (with $\bar{\bar{\chi}}_2 \, \psi'_1 \, \bar{\bar{P}}_5$ lim.)	Daily meetings started	Colossus II installed	

[h] TP = teleprinter.
[i] A Garbo is a machine for printing a tape. It could carry out limited operations on the content of the tape before printing (e.g. deltaing).

1944	Changes in Tunny	Organisation Changes	Machines	Theoretical Discoveries and Achievements
July	Invasion of Europe. Daily wheel changes on Jelly. Koenigsberg Exchange closes and moves to Golssen	Slide-runs started, using test-tapes, to check machines[j]	Colossus III installed. More reliable Robinsons designed—suitable for work on cribs	New 'staircasing' method evolved for cribs. Significance tests for wheel-breaking runs introduced
August	Daily wheel changes on almost all Tunny links	No. of computers increased very considerably	First rectangles made on Colossus. Colossus IV finished	
September	Several links ceased using P_5 limitation	Work started in Block H	Colossus V installed	Thurlow rectangles first done. Combined χ_5 flag for key introduced, with significance test[k]
October	Further reorganisation of Tunny		Colossus VI and first Super-Robinson installed. Colossus VI takes tapes up [to] 25,000 long	Copy correction units (for correction of tapes) introduced

[j] A slide-run is a run with all five chis, searching for a location in the tape where cipher letters have been omitted (e.g. because of poor reception).

[k] A flag is a method of comparing rows of a rectangle.

1944	Changes in Tunny	Organisation Changes	Machines	Theoretical Discoveries and Achievements
November		15th November. The fire New type of test runs for checking Colossus – test runs Kedleston Hall started operating Reorganisation at Knockholt	Colossus VII installed	New adaptation of rectangling methods used to break short stretches of key Complete page of QEP nos. with corresponding wheel-settings recovered from Whiting decode Jacob's flag started
December	P_5 limitation largely abandoned by Germans	Extensive motor and psi setting by machine		Colossus decoding invented Theory of coalescence

1945	Changes in Tunny	Organisation Changes	Machines	Theoretical Discoveries and Achievements
January		Psi test-runs first made De-χ checks first done Education committee formed	Colossus VIII installed Second Super-Rob. finished	
February		$\hat{\chi}_2$ runs started	Device installed on Colossus VI enabling sum of squares of rectangle entries to be computed quickly Rectangles now produced on tape—to mechanise computing on keys	Tests carried out on Thrasher (on new Robs) gave negative results, with regard to Tunny-type machines
March	Exchange set up at Salzburg	Raw tapes sent from Knockholt 4 wheel runs instituted Setting of psis now considered as responsibility of Newmanry rather than Testery Wrens taught wheel-breaking	Colossus IX installed Mechanical flags instituted Machines tested regularly by Wrens	

1945	Changes in Tunny	Organisation Changes	Machines	Theoretical Discoveries and Achievements
April		Rectangle making started on Super-Robs	Colossus X installed '5202' arrived—to start work experimentally[1]	
May	Victory in Europe Last Tunny message sent	Change from 3 to 2 shifts Work on back traffic (1943–4) History and 5202 section formed		
June			Two sets of German Tunny equipment arrive	Experimental operations using 5202

[1] Produced just too late for the European war, the 5202 was a photographic machine for Tunny setting.

The Teleprinter Alphabet

Jack Copeland

The table on the next page gives the 5-bit teleprinter code for each character of the teleprint alphabet (see Chapter 3). The left-hand column shows the characters of the teleprint alphabet as they would have been written down by the Bletchley codebreakers. For example, the codebreakers wrote '9' to indicate a space (as in 'to9indicate') and '3' to indicate a carriage return.

The 'move to figure shift' character (which some at Bletchley wrote as '+' and some as '5') told the teleprinter to shift from printing letters to printing figures; and the 'move to letter shift' character (written '−' or '8') told the machine to shift from printing figures to printing letters. With the teleprinter in letter mode, the keys along the top row of the keyboard would print QWERTYUIOP, and in figure mode the same keys would print 1234567890.

Most of the keyboard characters had different meanings in letter mode and figure mode. In figure mode the M-key printed a full stop, the N-key a comma, the C-key a colon, and the A-key a dash, for example. (Unlike a modern keyboard, the teleprinter did not have separate keys for punctuation.) The meanings of the other keys in figure mode are given at the right of the table.

To cause the (sending or receiving) teleprinter to print 123 WHO ME? the operator must first press figure shift and key Q W E to produce the numbers. He or she then drops into letter mode and keys a space (or vice versa), followed by W H O. To produce the comma it is necessary to press figure shift then N. This is followed by letter shift, space, and M E. A final figure shift followed by B produces the question mark:

+QWE−9WHO+N−9ME+B

CONVENTIONAL NAME	IMPULSE 1 2 3 4 5	MEANING *IN LETTER SHIFT*	*IN FIGURE SHIFT*
/	• • • • •	(no meaning)	
9	• • × • •	space	space
H	• • × • ×	H	£
T	• • • • ×	T	5
O	• • • × ×	O	9
M	• • × × ×	M	full stop
N	• • × × •	N	comma
3	• • • × •	carriage return	carriage return
R	• × • × •	R	4
C	• × × × •	C	colon
V	• × × × ×	V	equals
G	• × • × ×	G	@
L	• × • • ×	L	close bracket
P	• × × • ×	P	0 (zero)
I	• × × • ×	I	8
4	• × • • •	line feed	line feed
A	× × • • •	A	dash
U	× × × • •	U	7
Q	× × × • ×	Q	1
W	× × • • ×	W	2
+ *or* 5	× × • × ×	move to figure shift	(none)
− *or* 8	× × × × ×	(none)	move to letter shift
K	× × × × •	K	open bracket
J	× × • × •	J	ring bell
D	× • • × •	D	who are you?
F	× • × × •	F	per cent
X	× • × × ×	X	/
B	× • • × ×	B	?
Z	× • • • ×	Z	+
Y	× • × • ×	Y	6
S	× • × • •	S	apostrophe
E	× • • • •	E	3

Source: General Report on Tunny, p. 3.

The Tunny Addition Square

Jack Copeland

The table opposite lists the sum of every pair of Tunny characters. (The rules of Tunny addition are explained in Chapter 3.)

To look up the sum of K and X, for example, find K in the boldface column on the left (or use the identical column on the right, if this happens to be easier) and then find X in the boldface row along the top (or in the identical row along the bottom). Moving horizontally from K and vertically from X, the sum lies at the intersection: $K + X = L$.

Notice that Tunny addition is symmetrical: selecting X in the column on the left and K in the row along the top again produces L. $K + X = X + K$, and so on for all other pairs of characters.

The character / has one of the properties that 0 has in ordinary addition: $A + / = A$, $B + / = B$, and so on, for all characters. It also has a property unlike anything found in ordinary addition. As the table shows, / results when any character is added to itself: $A + A = /$, and so on. Therefore / appears with a high frequency in the delta of any sequence—such as the extended psi—in which neighbouring letters are often the same.

Taken together, these two properties of / explain why adding the message key to the ciphertext restores the plaintext. Where P is a character of the plaintext and K is the corresponding character of the key, $(P + K) + K = P + / = P$.

The apparently haphazard order of the characters in the boldface row along the top of the table (repeated in the other boldface row and columns) is revealed as far from haphazard once the characters are written in teleprint code (see Appendix 2). Starting from the all-dot character /, each character differs by only one dot or cross from its immediate predecessor: / is •••••, 9 is ••×••, H is ••×•×, and so on.

This way of ordering the characters creates some striking regularities in the table. Notice, for example, that the four-by-four block at the top left (whose first row is / 9 H T) moves diagonally down the table from left to right. The diagonal from the top left of the table proper to the bottom right consists entirely of occurrences of /, while the opposite diagonal consists entirely of occurrences of E. Within each four-by-four block, each corner-to-corner diagonal consists of the same letter repeated.

Moreover the first row and first column of each four-by-four block are identical, as are the second row and the second column, and so on. Other regularities in the table are easily spotted.

Notice that in this table the figure shift and letter shift characters are written '5' and '8' respectively (see Appendix 2).

```
      / 9 HT   OMN3   RCVG   LPI4   AUQW   58KJ   DFXB   ZYSE

/    / 9 HT   OMN3   RCVG   LPI4   AUQW   58KJ   DFXB   ZYSE   /
9    9 / TH   MO3N   CRGV   PL4I   UAWQ   85JK   FDBX   YZES   9
H    HT / 9   N3OM   VGRC   I4LP   QWAU   KJ58   XBDF   SEZY   H
T    TH9 /    3NMO   GVCR   4IPL   WQUA   JK85   BXFD   ESYZ   T

O    OMN3    / 9 HT   LPI4   RCVG   58KJ   AUQW   ZYSE   DFXB   O
M    MO3N    9 / TH   PL4I   CRGV   85JK   UAWQ   YZES   FDBX   M
N    N3OM    HT / 9   I4LP   VGRC   KJ58   QWAU   SEZY   XBDF   N
3    3NMO    TH9 /    4IPL   GVCR   JK85   WQUA   ESYZ   BXFD   3

R    RCVG    LPI4    / 9 HT   OMN3   DFXB   ZYSE   AUQW   58KJ   R
C    CRGV    PL4I    9 / TH   MO3N   FDBX   YZES   UAWQ   85JK   C
V    VGRC    I4LP    HT / 9   N3OM   XBDF   SEZY   QWAU   KJ58   V
G    GVCR    4IPL    TH9 /    3NMO   BXFD   ESYZ   WQUA   JK85   G

L    LPI4    RCVG    OMN3    / 9 HT   ZYSE   DFXB   58KJ   AUQW   L
P    PL4I    CRGV    MO3N    9 / TH   YZES   FDBX   85JK   UAWQ   P
I    I4LP    VGRC    N3OM    HT / 9   SEZY   XBDF   KJ58   QWAU   I
4    4IPL    GVCR    3NMO    TH9 /    ESYZ   BXFD   JK85   WQUA   4

A    AUQW   58KJ    DFXB   ZYSE    / 9 HT   OMN3   RCVG   LPI4   A
U    UAWQ   85JK    FDBX   YZES    9 / TH   MO3N   CRGV   PL4I   U
Q    QWAU   KJ58    XBDF   SEZY    HT / 9   N3OM   VGRC   I4LP   Q
W    WQUA   JK85    BXFD   ESYZ    TH9 /    3NMO   GVCR   4IPL   W

5    58KJ    AUQW   ZYSE   DFXB   OMN3    / 9 HT   LPI4   RCVG   5
8    85JK    UAWQ   YZES   FDBX   MO3N    9 / TH   PL4I   CRGV   8
K    KJ58    QWAU   SEZY   XBDF   N3OM    HT / 9   I4LP   VGRC   K
J    JK85    WQUA   ESYZ   BXFD   3NMO    TH9 /    4IPL   GVCR   J

D    DFXB   ZYSE    AUQW   58KJ    RCVG   LPI4    / 9 HT   OMN3   D
F    FDBX   YZES    UAWQ   85JK    CRGV   PL4I    9 / TH   MO3N   F
X    XBDF   SEZY    QWAU   KJ58    VGRC   I4LP    HT / 9   N3OM   X
B    BXFD   ESYZ    WQUA   JK85    GVCR   4IPL    TH9 /    3NMO   B

Z    ZYSE   DFXB    58KJ   AUQW   LPI4   RCVG    OMN3    / 9 HT   Z
Y    YZES   FDBX    85JK   UAWQ   PL4I   CRGV    MO3N    9 / TH   Y
S    SEZY   XBDF    KJ58   QWAU   I4LP   VGRC    N3OM    HT / 9   S
E    ESYZ   BXFD    JK85   WQUA   4IPL   GVCR    3NMO    TH9 /    E

      / 9 HT   OMN3   RCVG   LPI4   AUQW   58KJ   DFXB   ZYSE
```

Source: General Report on Tunny, p. 5.

My Work at Bletchley Park

William T. Tutte

Introduction

It was January of 1941. Britain was at war with Germany and Italy. Germany had conquered Western Europe but Italy was suffering defeat in Greece, Egypt, and Libya. I was a research student at Trinity College, Cambridge. I remember an interview with my tutor, Patrick Duff, when he told me that I should go to a certain town about 50 miles away for an interview about a possible war job.

Gaps occur in one's memory after 50 years or so. I must have had the interview and something of interest must have been said in it. But I remember nothing of it. I fancy that town must have been Bletchley, but feel no surety even of that. However, I soon found myself in a cryptographical school in London, at a place near St James's Park and his Underground station. There I learned how to deal with cryptograms of the First World War.

Why did they pick me? I think it was because I had acquired a reputation as a solver of puzzles at Trinity. I had been one of the four undergraduates who had, for fun, worked out a solution of the problem of dissecting a square into unequal squares. (Curiously R. Sprague in Berlin had worked out a solution at about the same time. His square was the first to be published.)

Presumably my performance at the school was found satisfactory and I was recruited to Bletchley Park with the rank of temporary assistant clerk (of the Foreign Office). I was a member of a small group called the Research Section, which had a room in the Mansion. But after a year or so it moved into one of the temporary huts. I do remember the names and appearance of at least some of my fellow-members. There was Captain Gerry Morgan, the head of the section, and his brother Stanley, a lieutenant. There was Sergeant Rylands, smoking his pipe. There was Daphne Bradshaw, whose husband was also at the Park as an administrator. Others I remember but think they joined later. I noticed that differences of army rank seemed of no importance within the Research Section. Some of the people there were members of the armed forces and others, like myself, were civilians. We mixed together in the section on equal terms.

The Research Section was consulted by other sections about ciphers that were still unbroken or whose exploitation had not yet been reduced to a routine. When I arrived the section was chiefly concerned with an Italian naval cipher of the latter kind. The encipherment was done on a commercial machine of Swedish manufacture. We called it a Hagelin machine. I took it that a Mr Hagelin was either the inventor or the manufacturer. There being nothing secret about the machine, specimens were available at Bletchley.

The Hagelin Machine

The Hagelin machine produced what we called an 'additive cipher'. It used a 26-letter alphabet and the letters were taken as equivalent to the integers from 1 to 26 in their numerical order. With this convention letters could be added modulo 26, or mod 26.

The mechanical details have become vague in my memory. But somehow the operator fed plaintext into the machine. The machine generated a sequence of letters, of random appearance, that we called the key. Letter by letter the machine added the key to the plaintext and the result was the ciphertext. This would be sent by radio from originator to recipient. The latter would set his machine to subtract the key from the ciphertext, and so recover the plaintext. If the message was intercepted by a British station, say at Malta, the ciphertext would go to the Research Section at Bletchley Park with, of course, no information about the key.

There were many possible initial settings of the machine, and each one gave a different key. The originator could choose one of these settings and then he had to tell the recipient which one he was using. The sensible method would be to say in clear, 'I am using setting number n,' and then the recipient would look up setting number n in a secret book. I suppose this method was used but cannot remember. Perhaps it was something less secure.

The great weakness of an additive cipher is the danger that two messages may be sent on the same setting, i.e. same key. Cryptographers call this a depth of two. Three on the same setting would be a depth of three, and so on. Let us denote the common key of two messages in depth by K. Let the plaintexts be P_1 and P_2, yielding ciphertexts C_1 and C_2 respectively. Then we have two equations:

$$P_1 + K = C_1, \tag{1}$$

and

$$P_2 + K = C_2, \tag{2}$$

the addition being mod 26. Subtracting the second equation from the first we get

$$P_1 - P_2 = C_1 - C_2. \tag{3}$$

So the cryptanalyst only has to subtract one cipher text from the other to get the difference of the two plaintexts. The machine itself has vanished from his problem: all he has to do is disentangle the difference $P_1 - P_2$ into the two plaintexts P_1 and P_2. How did he know the two messages were on the same key? The originator had to say so in his preliminary clear messages to the recipient.

Disentangling P_1 and P_2 is simple in principle if not always easy in practice. Each clear message usually had an address very near the beginning. A likely one for a message going to Italy would be KSUPERMARINAKALTK. The Italian operators, having no other use for the letter K, made it a word spacer. One would put such an address into P_1 and calculate the corresponding part of P_2 from one's knowledge of $P_1 - P_2$. If that part made Italian naval sense, then that section of P_1 and P_2 could be assumed known. The next step was to guess a continuation of P_2 and verify it (or otherwise) by checking against P_1, and so on. With luck P_1 and P_2 could be read up to the point where one of them ended, and the information could be sent to those who would decide how to use it.

The cryptanalyst would be more interested in the fact that, having P_1 and C_1, he could now get the key K from equation (1). He could then contemplate the key and the machine and brood over the problem of what configuration of the machine would produce that key.

Users of additive cipher machines are, or ought to be, strictly forbidden to send two messages in depth. But evidence from the Second World War suggests that perfect obedience is difficult to get in practice. I confess I do not remember how good the Hagelin users were at avoiding depths. I do not remember having to break one myself but the danger was there and my explanation of it will, I hope, be helpful when I come to the discussion of another additive cipher machine—Tunny.

Let me now write about the structure of the key. First it was the sum of six periodic subkeys, which I will denote by $K_1, K_2, \ldots, K_6$. Each of these had a period of the order of 30. Each key K_i had an associated small positive integer n_i and was simply a sequence of numbers each of which was either 0 or n_i. We called these subkeys 'wheels'. For each of them was generated by an actual mechanical wheel with pins that could be punched in or out. The position in or out of such a pin would determine whether K_i had 0 or n_i in that position. It was also possible to adjust n_i for each K_i. Normally the sum of the n_i would not exceed 26. So the addition of the six subkeys, or wheels, could be regarded as ordinary addition, not addition mod 26. Also the n_i went in non-decreasing order from K_1 to K_6.

The number n_i and the arrangement of pins made the 'wheel pattern' of K_i, its periodic sequence. Wheel patterns would change from month to month, or from day to day, according as to how security conscious were the authorities, but not from message to message.

My task with the Hagelin machine came after the wheel patterns had been determined, I suppose by analysing a key derived from a depth. I was given messages to set on the known wheel patterns; that is, I had to find which pin on each wheel was active in the initial setting. I would guess an address in a likely part of the message and calculate, on that assumption, the corresponding part of the key. Some numbers in this key would be so high as to require a contribution of n_6 from K_6. Others would be so low as to demand 0 from K_6. So with luck K_6 could be set or the assumption could be disproved. Having succeeded with K_6, I would go on to treat K_5 similarly, and so on. I became fairly proficient at this. Sometimes, that is some nights, I would be invited to sleep in the Italian naval hut so that I could be awakened and consulted over some particularly awkward message.

It came to pass that the breaking of these messages was reduced to routine, or so nearly so that they needed no longer to be the concern of the Research Section.

I Meet Tunny

I think it was in October 1941 that I was introduced to a new German cipher called 'Tunny', the first of the Fish links. (The Germans referred to one of their radio links as 'Sägefisch'. Perhaps Bletchley's term 'Fish' derived from this.) Each cipher message of Tunny was preceded by a sequence of 12 letters belonging to the ordinary German alphabet. As a safeguard against error these might be expanded into common personal names (A for Anton, B for Berta, C for Caesar, D for Dora, E for Emil, F for Friedrich, and so on). This sequence of twelve letters we called the 'indicator'. Presumably it told the recipient how to set his machine.

Sometimes two messages would be found to have the same indicator. Some of these pairs were successfully read on the assumption that the cipher was additive and used mod 2 addition. It could now be asserted that Tunny was an additive cipher and that the 12 indicators determined the key. Very likely they specified the settings of 12 wheels, something like Hagelin wheels.

If θ is a letter of the teleprinter alphabet, then it satisfies the equation

$$\theta + \theta = 0 \quad \text{(i.e. \bullet\bullet\bullet\bullet\bullet, all-space).}$$

(For some reason cryptographers at Bletchley preferred to write 1 and 0 as cross and dot ($\times$ and $\bullet$) respectively. Electrical engineers used -1 and 1 and multiplied in the ordinary way where we added mod 2. It came to the same thing.)

Thus each letter is its own negative; subtraction is the same operation as addition. This fact introduces new difficulties into the process of reading depths. Equation (3) is now replaced by

$$P_1 + P_2 = C_1 + C_2. \tag{4}$$

The equation has acquired more symmetry. Now, even if we have found P_1 and P_2, the equation does not tell us which plaintext goes with which ciphertext. Plaintext P_2 may be the true P_1. However, if the messages are read up to the point where one ciphertext ends, then the plaintext that obviously ends there must go with the shorter ciphertext. So in that case the ambiguity may be resolved.

But in practice a depth is likely to be read in patches, with short or long gaps between consecutive patches. Perhaps a gap represents letters that, because of some natural interference, were not received at the British interception station, or were received only in a damaged form. Perhaps it appeared only because depth-reading is difficult. Then the ambiguity applies to each patch separately. There is nothing in the algebra to show which part-message of one patch goes with which part-message of another. Of course, the sense of the part-messages, if they are long enough, may indicate which goes with which.

On one occasion a German operator made a major error. A message about 4000 letters long was sent. There must have been some difficulty of reception, for the message was sent again. The sender made the mistake of using the same indicator as before. If the second version had been an exact copy of the first this would not have mattered. But evidently the sender did not insert a tape; he typed his message in letter by letter. His punctuation was different. He put in fewer word-spaces. So the old version was drawn out to a greater length than the new. The two messages were vulnerable to a cryptanalyst as a depth of two. Moreover, once they were recognised as differently punctuated versions of the same text, the reading of the depth was made much easier. Message 1 was about to say what message 2 had said a little way back. The depth was read by Colonel John Tiltman, next above Gerry Morgan in Bletchley's hierarchy. He even decided which plaintext went with each ciphertext; the one that had the complete message went with the shorter ciphertext. Adding P to C he got a piece of Tunny key 4000 letters long.

All this happened two or three months before I met Tunny. In those few months other Bletchleyites were trying to 'break the Tunny key', that is, to describe mathematically a machine that could produce that stretch of key. They worked hard, guided by an ingenious theory, but to no avail. Some time later I was told about this theory, but it is now gone from my memory. By then it was known to be wrong.

Was it a gesture of despair that Captain Morgan, that day in October, handed me the Tunny key, with associated documents, and said, 'See what you can do with this.' Apart from the 4000 letters of key there was just one other item of information that struck me as possibly significant. It was that 11 letters of the indicator could take all 25 values permitted by the German alphabet (omitting J). But the other letter took only 23 values. Did that mean that there was a wheel of period 23?

In the cryptographical school in London we often attacked our simulated cipher messages by writing them out on some period that seemed appropriate. Thus if the period was 29 we would write the first 29 letters in a row on squared paper, then the next 29 exactly below them, and so on. We would then look for repetitions from row to row. If there were significantly many, we knew we were well on the way to a solution. So I thought I would start on the Tunny key by writing it out on a period, or perhaps only one impulse of it. I do not think I had much faith in this procedure, but I thought it best to seem busy.

I chose to write the first impulse on some period. It would be less trouble to write a single impulse than to write the complete key. Besides, just possibly the part might be cryptographically simpler than the whole. But what period should I use? That information about the indicators suggested that 23 might be worth trying. So, but very doubtfully, might 25. Why not try both at once? The product 23×25 was only 575 and there were 4000 letters of key. So I wrote the first impulse of the key on a period of 575, filling about 7 rows.

The next step was to look for repetitions of sequences of five or more dot–cross symbols from row to row, the second group of the repetition exactly under the first. But there were not significantly many of these repetitions. Before taking the next logical step, that is, doing likewise with the second impulse, I checked the diagonals. It seemed that I would have got good results on a period of 574.

I wrote the first impulse on a period of 574 and marvelled at the many repetitions down the columns from row to row. But surely the Germans would not use a wheel of that length? Perhaps the true period was 41, this being a prime factor of 574? So I wrote the first impulse a third time, now on a period of 41. I got a rectangle of dots and crosses that was replete with repetitions. (See Figure 4 in Appendix 5.)

My interpretation of this effect was simple. The first impulse, K_1, was the sum of two sequences of dots and crosses. The first was periodic, of period 41. The second had the curious property that in it dot was more likely to be followed by dot than by cross, and similarly cross was more likely to be followed by cross than by dot. Careful study showed that the second sequence could be interpreted as the product of a wheel that sometimes moved on from one letter of text to the next and sometimes stayed still. The first sequence, of course, came from a wheel that always moved on one place from one letter to the next. I called the first wheel, of period 41, the χ-wheel and the second, which turned out to have a period of 43, the ψ-wheel. These names stuck. Owing to some German's carelessness, the part of the key produced by the ψ-wheel showed sequences of five or more dots more often than it should. Hence the complete first impulse of the key agreed with the χ-sequence to five or more places more often than it should. This made repetition from row to row more likely than it should have been.

At this stage the rest of the Research Section joined in the attack. Each other impulse of K was split into its χ and ψ components. It was found that the five ψ-wheels moved in step. From one letter to the next either they all moved on one place or they all stayed still. Besides the χ- and ψ-wheels there were the two 'motor-wheels'. One of period 61 moved regularly like the χ-wheels. The other moved on one place when the first showed cross and stayed still when the first showed dot. This second motor-wheel had period 37. The ψ-wheels moved on when it showed cross and stayed still when it showed dot. Thus were the entire workings of the Tunny machine exposed without any actual physical machine or manual thereof coming into our hands.

The reader will observe that the Germans could have arranged the patterns of the ψ-wheels so that in the resulting ψ-keys consecutive symbols were as likely to be different as similar. Then my method would have failed. We must class their failure to do so as their second major mistake, the first being the long message repeated with the same key. Either mistake alone I think they would have got away with, but the two together proved fatal.

About that indicator position that allowed only 23 letters. There was a corresponding wheel of period 23. It was the fifth χ-wheel. If I had not noticed those diagonal repeats and had accordingly applied my method to the other impulses, it would have succeeded on the fifth. Then I suppose my success would have been attributed entirely to close logical reasoning. As things were, I was supposed to have had a stroke of undeserved luck. (Think twice, O Gentle Reader, before thou takest an unexpected and opportune short cut.)

The Days of the Indicator

The indicator of that long depth was HQIBPEXEZMUG. Now that we knew the workings of the machine, albeit only in mathematical abstraction, we could analyse keys obtained from shorter depths. This involved writing each impulse of the key on the period of its χ-wheel, now known, and inferring for each consecutive pair of χ-symbols whether they were alike or different. If we assumed, and were right in our assumption, that the new key had the same wheel patterns as HQIBPEX-EZMUG, the problem became one of finding not wheel patterns but 'wheel settings'. We had to find for each wheel what symbol of its periodic pattern corresponded to the initial letter of the message. From a few successes of this kind we found that the wheel patterns changed only from month to month. The wheel settings, of course, changed from message to message, save when an operator carelessly sent a depth.

Our decodes were of messages too old to be of interest to our customers. There was a little current traffic but it provided no depths. Two or three months into 1942 there was more traffic and our German suppliers sent a few depths. There came one that seemed usable, being about 1000 letters long.

The depth was broken and the five impulses of the key could now be written on the appropriate periods. Alas, the resulting rectangles were just random-seeming arrays of dots and crosses. We supposed that the Germans had noticed the weakness of their early ψ-patterns and had corrected it. If so their ψ-patterns now had more changes than continuations, just sufficiently more to make my method of analysis ineffective. The alternative hypothesis that they had switched to an entirely different machine was too awful to contemplate.

I was now immersed in the theory of Tunny and, I suppose, worried as much as anyone in the section about this new impasse. Looking down the list of indicators one day, I noticed two that differed only in one of the 12 letters. This was something new, a 'near-depth'. I wondered if a near-depth could be read like a real depth, though no doubt with much greater difficulty.

If the old rules were still valid the two keys differed only in the setting of one χ-wheel. I do not now remember which one. For the purposes of explanation let me pretend it was the first, with period 41. Then the difference Δ between the two keys would be the mod 2 sum of the two versions of χ_1, corresponding to two different wheel settings. It would therefore have period 41. Once 41 places of Δ had been determined, the near-depth could be made effectively a true depth by adding Δ to one of the messages. A successful reading would give not only many letters of key but extra information about the first χ-wheel. I was optimistic that this extra information would make possible the breaking of the key.

So it turned out. We, being incapable of reading near-depths, asked for help from another section, one that abounded in linguists instead of mathematicians. At first the linguists were reluctant to tackle the problem. This was understandable: if you guessed a letter in one message there were now two alternatives for the corresponding letter in the other. But they set to and succeeded. After reading a stretch of 41 (or whatever it was) letters they converted the pair of messages to a true depth and carried on, with much reduced difficulty, to the end.

The problem now was what to do with Δ. I will go on pretending that Δ belonged to the first impulse. Then it gave rise to 20 possible patterns for χ_1, one for each of the possible relative settings of the first χ-wheel in the two messages (irrespective of which setting went with which message). At first sight it seemed that the 20 should be 40 since the χ-pattern could be reversed without altering Δ. (To reverse the pattern, change dot to cross and cross to dot.) However, it would not worry us if we were using not the German χ-pattern but its reverse. We would then use the reversed ψ-pattern of that impulse too, and the key would be correct. So there were really 20 different possibilities.

Most of the possibilities could be rejected as implausible. We were sure that a χ-pattern should have, roughly, as many crosses as dots and as many continuations as changes. Judging by the χ-patterns we had found for the old messages, the German operators agreed with us. We also imagined that the composers of wheel patterns received some such advice as this: 'Remember, Conrad, no excessively long blocks of dots, or of crosses.' So the 20 possibilities reduced to very few plausible ones. For each of these we had the χ-pattern and its settings in the two messages. But because of the peculiarities of mod 2 addition we did not know which setting went with which message. We would have to try both possibilities.

Suppose we are lucky enough to apply the correct χ_1-pattern in its correct setting to the first impulse of key. By addition we get the first ψ-impulse, ψ_1. When this has two different consecutive symbols we know that the ψ-wheels have moved from one symbol to the next. But when ψ_1 has two consecutive symbols the same we can say that, more likely than not, the ψ-wheels have stayed still from one symbol to the next. This is because we believe that the Germans have now put more changes than continuations into their basic ψ-patterns.

Since the five ψ-wheels move in step, we can apply the knowledge of ψ-movement thus obtained to any other impulse. Let us say the second, in which the χ-period is 31. For each consecutive pair of symbols there, we can say either 'Here the ψ-wheels have certainly moved' or 'Here, more likely than not, they have stayed still.' In the first case ψ_2 most likely shows a change, and in the second a repetition. This is because of the new German rules of ψ. Using this information we can deduce, pretty accurately, the succession of changes and repetitions in the χ_2-pattern. This, in turn, enables us to correct that succession in the ψ_2-sequence, making it more accurate if not perfectly so. Then we can go to the third impulse and get very accurate information about χ_3, and so on to the breaking of the key.

If there is more than one plausible pattern for χ_1 we simply have to try each possibility in turn, until the key collapses.

By such a procedure we broke the key of the near-depth, getting the wheel patterns of the corresponding month. I remember that a later near-depth gave us the patterns for a later month.

At this stage Alan Turing, tiring perhaps of Enigma, made a few weeks' visit to the Research Section. (By this time the Research Section had moved from a room in the

Mansion to one of the huts. I do not remember the number, but I was told recently at Bletchley that it must have been Hut 15.) Turing became interested in the problem of breaking a true Tunny depth and he found a method of doing so. Some people, though not myself, became expert in Turing's method. It seemed to me that it was more artistic than mathematical. To start with, you picked a pair of consecutive positions in some χ-wheel and assumed either a change or a repetition there. Whichever you chose you had a 50 per cent chance of being right. The pair would recur, with interval the χ-wheel period, throughout the key. Let us suppose χ_5 chosen so as to have the shortest period, 23, and the greatest number of recurrences. At each recurrence you could calculate the corresponding pair in ψ_5 and say whether it most likely represented a ψ-motion or a ψ-stoppage. Since the ψ-wheels moved in step, this information applied to all the impulses. You assumed the 'most likely' alternative for each recurrence. Then you could deduce information about some consecutive pair in the other χ-patterns and extend it through the key on their periods. Soon of course you got clashes. At each clash you rejected the alternative you felt in your bones was the less likely. With sufficiently reliable bones you might break all the wheel patterns. If you failed you tried again, perhaps with a different pair of symbols and perhaps with the other assumption about the first pair.

So by Turing's method and by the method of near-depths we got our monthly wheel patterns and whetted the appetites of our customers with the messages of the depths and near-depths. But those customers wanted more deciphered messages than that. So we had to work on another problem. Given a message not in depth, and given the wheel patterns, find its wheel settings.

I said in a previous essay that I could not remember how this problem was solved. Yet I do remember that I was sure it could be solved even before I found the near-depth. I remember saying to those linguists, 'If we can break this near-depth, we shall go on to break many more messages.' But now a memory of Sergeant Rylands has revived. Referring to a still-famous poster of the First World War, he said, 'If ever that little boy asks me "What did you do in the Great War, Daddy?" I shall have to say "I dragged Herring"' (or it may have been some other Fish-link).'Yes,' I say, 'We, and notably Sergeant Rylands, solved that problem by the device of dragging.'

We knew what indicator letters corresponded to the wheel settings of any depth or near-depth we had broken. For the next break we would choose a message not in depth but with at least one χ-indicator for which the corresponding wheel setting was known. I will now try to explain what could be done if the setting of one χ-wheel, say χ_1, was known. But I shall rely at least as much on reasoning as on memories of 1942. (I should mention that the indicator letters were not in alphabetical order on their wheels.)

Messages of that time commonly started with an address. There being few addresses in use on a given link, a cryptanalyst could use them as cribs. Of a given message he could say, 'This quite likely has 9OBERKOMMANDO9WEHRMACHT9 very near the beginning.' (It was customary with us to write the word-space symbol as 9.) Adding this address to the message in a possible position we would get a stretch of possible key. On the assumption that it really was key we would add the known χ_1

to the first impulse and so get ψ_1. Then in every impulse we could say of each consecutive pair of symbols whether it most likely represented a ψ-movement or a ψ-stoppage. Then for each consecutive pair of symbols of χ_2 we could say whether they were most likely to be a change or a continuation. We would then slide the actual χ_2-pattern along χ_2 until it clicked, until 'most likely' agreed sufficiently often with 'actual'. If there was clicking for the other three impulses as well, then the five χ-settings had been found. If there was no clicking, then the address had to be 'dragged' to the next position. If the settings of two χ-wheels happened to be known from the indicators then the process became much quicker.

When the χ-wheels had been set the χ-key could be added to the part of K under the address to get the corresponding part of the ψ-key. There the pattern of ψ-movement and ψ-stoppage would be known very accurately and so the ψ-wheels could be set too. After this the reading of the message could be completed. We would use the fact that there were just two possibilities for the next ψ-letter since the ψ-wheels either all moved on one place or all stayed still. The corresponding χ-letter would be known since χ-wheels moved regularly. So there would be two possibilities for the plain language letter and usually there would be no doubt which was right. When the entire ψ-key was known, it would be possible to tackle the motor-wheels.

With each new success the process of dragging became easier since the meanings of more indicator letters were known. If the crucial depth or near-depth came early in the month, we might soon find ourselves reading current traffic.

Waiting for that depth could be exasperating. I began to dream of breaking wheel patterns without any depth or near-depth, using only information from the indicators. All messages having the same letter in the same indicator place would have the same setting of the corresponding wheel. Perhaps, given enough messages of the same month, that information could break the wheel patterns.

Consider the first letter, say in the third impulse. The first clear letter was likely to be word-space (••×••). One would assume it to be enciphered by the first χ-symbol and the first ψ-symbol in relation to the indicator-letters concerned. Assuming the first χ_5 symbol at indicator A to be cross, we should be able to calculate the ψ_3-symbols at the appropriate indicator-letters by studying the set of messages with χ_3-letter A. From these we could expect to get all the first symbols at the χ_3-letters, and so on just to check. The process would, of course, be gone through for all the five impulses. Garbles and eccentric first-clear letters could be circumvented if few enough.

I remember that this process worked well for the first letter in the past month that I chose to study. It gave the unexpected information that the first letter of a message was enciphered by the χ-key only. This cleared up one of our minor problems. It explained why the first letters of our decodes so often seemed to be wrong. It also made it possible to resolve a familiar ambiguity: did we have the German wheel patterns in χ and ψ or their reverses? Not that anyone thought that resolution important.

The process could now be applied to the second symbols from each indicator-letter. It could now be assumed that the ψ-symbols could all be the same for a given impulse and indicator-letter. I remember that this attack succeeded too. Now the comparatively few plaintext letters that were not word-spaces could be deciphered. If they could be interpreted as the first letters of addresses then some third clear letters could be guessed. Unfortunately the ambiguity between German and reverse reappeared with this second letter. Eventually it would have to be resolved, for correlation with the first χ-symbols. Meanwhile one had to accept that there were two alternatives.

Difficulties increased with the third symbol from the indicator letter. Some messages would be enciphered from the second symbol of the active ψ-key and others from the first. The letter of the plaintext would be less likely to be word-space. But the other likely plaintext letters were few and could be guessed. There seemed to be good hope of deciphering the third letters. There was another comforting thought. No new independent ambiguity should appear. The third letter could be correlated with the second by way of the messages for which the ψ-wheels had stayed still.

My memory tells me that I coped reasonably well with the third letter but got confused with the fourth and made no further progress. Had that been the whole story it would hardly have been worth mentioning here. But my attempt aroused the interest of a new member of the Research Section, James Wyllie. Wyllie was an editor of the Oxford Latin Dictionary. He was willing to take over from me, for he said, 'This is just the task for a lexicographer!' He too chose a past month and he carried the procedure so far that he was able to put his wheel pieces together to make the complete wheel patterns. So I have called this method of Tunny-breaking 'Wyllie's method'.

In 1996 when I first began to be seriously questioned about my memories of BP I was unable to say just how much practical use had been made of Wyllie's method. But since then I have seen a report issued by the Newmanry soon after the German collapse. I gathered that the traffic of several months had been broken, at least partly, by that method. Its disadvantage was that it needed a large number of messages so it could only succeed late in a month. It might be cut short by the breaking of a depth or a near-depth. But even so its fragmentary wheel patterns would be of help in the process of dragging.

So the deciphering of Fish went on until November 1942. Then there came a black day. From then on, the cipher messages came to us without those helpful indicator letters. They were replaced by a simple number. No doubt a German cipher officer would look up that number in a little book and find 12 letters printed against it. But we did not have that little book. It seemed that just one way of attack was still open to us. We could still recognise depths; messages in depth had the same number. Near-depths might still occur but we had no way of recognising them. Production stopped, save for the occasional pair of messages in depth.

I suppose some German inspector had examined the process of encipherment and had exclaimed somewhat as follows: 'Hey, you're giving those bastards information that you don't need to give them! I don't suppose it has done them any good, but it's wrong in principle. Stop sending the 12 letters!' (Here I have assumed the inspector to have complete confidence in the security of Fish, believing that otherwise he would have demanded much more. On second thoughts it is easy to imagine that he did demand more but was overruled by his superiors. After the German collapse an anecdote came to BP, I know not how reliable its source. A German mathematician had queried the security of a cipher machine early in the war. An army officer had replied, 'So what? We're winning the war, aren't we?' 'Famous last words,' quipped Gerry Morgan.) Be that as it may, we had met with disaster. In spiritual metaphor we shouldered our pencils and squared paper and trudged glumly out of Eden. In some such manner did that unknown German gentleman, as judged at BP, set going the Computer Revolution.

The Winter of Our Discontent

We still got, at rare intervals, depths that could be broken by Turing's method. Then we would have the wheel patterns for the current month. We asked, 'How can we set these wheels on the messages that are not in depth?'

Dragging without a known wheel setting was not seriously considered. In theory I suppose 23 cryptographers could each have been given one of the 23 possible settings of the 5th χ-wheel and told to drag on the assumption that that was the correct one. That would have been an extravagant use of manpower, especially as the breaking of one message would no longer give wheel settings for others.

The Research Section had now been joined by Max Newman. Most of us worked together in one big room that occupied most of our Hut, but Gerry Morgan had his own enclosed office. There he and Max would foregather and discuss the problem. I gathered that they had an inkling of a possible method, which at times they would explain volubly to me and to others. I fear that I understood little of it and had little confidence in that little. For myself I dreamed of applying methods of linear algebra.

I have been asked, 'When did the study of $\Delta\chi$ and $\Delta\psi$ become usual at Bletchley?' Above I have been much concerned about whether two consecutive symbols in a stream T of dots and crosses were alike or different. Equivalently, but more simply, I could have asked whether ΔT had a dot or a cross. It seems that the Δ operation could have been used with advantage in Turing's method. I do not remember, but find it hard to doubt that it was. Using ΔK_1 instead of K_1 would certainly have helped in the breaking of the key of HQIBPEXEZMUG. Had I written ΔK_1 on a period of 41, each column would have been either predominantly dot or predominantly cross, and the dot–cross sequence would have been the pattern of the periodic sequence $\Delta\chi_1$. So I was probably doing no new thing when, in our emergency, I meditated on the possible use of Δ-sequences. But it is from that time that they are prominent in my memory.

A Δ-sequence of particular interest was $\Delta\psi$. It could be assumed that in encipherment the ψ-wheels would advance about half the time and stay still half the time. Then about half the letters in $\Delta\psi$ would be all-space (•••••). Considering only the ith impulse, $\Delta\psi_i$ would be dot when the ψ-wheels stayed still and it would sometimes be dot when they moved on.

I delta-ed the encipherment equation for the first impulse of a message:

$$\Delta C_1 = \Delta P_1 + \Delta\chi_1 + \Delta\psi_1. \tag{5}$$

After contemplating this for a while without enlightenment, I wondered if I could play one impulse against another since the ψ-wheels moved in step. So I wrote the corresponding equation for the second impulse:

$$\Delta C_2 = \Delta P_2 + \Delta \chi_2 + \Delta \psi_2. \qquad (6)$$

I noted that $\Delta \psi_1$ and $\Delta \psi_2$ were very much alike. When the ψ-wheels stayed still they were both dot. When the ψ-wheels moved on, wouldn't $\Delta \psi_1$ and $\Delta \psi_2$ be alike as often as not? I calculated that the sequence $\Delta \psi_1 + \Delta \psi_2 = \Delta(\psi_1 + \psi_2)$ would be about 70 per cent dot. It seemed that I could achieve an imperfect elimination of ψ by adding my two equations together. The operator Δ is distributive over addition, so I could write my result as

$$\Delta(C_1 + C_2) = \Delta(P_1 + P_2) + \Delta(\chi_1 + \chi_2) + \Delta(\psi_1 + \psi_2). \qquad (7)$$

All now, I thought, depended on $\Delta(P_1 + P_2)$. I investigated it for some known plaintext and was delighted, but surprised, to find that it was as a rule about 60 per cent dot. The upshot was that $\Delta(C_1 + C_2)$ and $\Delta(\chi_1 + \chi_2)$ would agree with one another more often than not. In favourable cases, such as one deciphered message that I checked, there might be 55 per cent agreement.

Here was a method of wheel setting! $\Delta(\chi_1 + \chi_2)$ was a periodic sequence, supposed known, with a period of $41 \times 31 = 1271$. Lay it against $\Delta(C_1 + C_2)$ in each of the 1271 possible relative positions and count the number of agreements for each one. One position should give significantly more agreements than any of the others, and that one would give the correct settings of χ_1 and χ_2. The procedure was not to be recommended as a hand method, but no doubt our electrical engineers could find a way of mechanising it. One hoped that the method would work for other pairs so that the settings of all five χ-wheels could be found.

I went into Gerry Morgan's office to tell of these results. Max Newman was there. They began to tell me, enthusiastically, about the current state of their own investigations. When I had an opportunity to speak I said, rather brashly, 'Now my method is much simpler.' They demanded a description. I must say they were rapidly converted. The Research Section urged the adoption of the 'statistical method' of wheel setting.

Soon the electrical engineers produced the necessary machines. We called them Heath Robinsons. The engineers were pleased because they were rushing teleprinter tape through the machinery at unprecedented speeds without ever breaking it. Well, hardly ever. Agreements, I was told, were counted photoelectrically. When you see a photograph of a contraption with teleprinter tapes running on pulleys you can be sure that it is comparing $\Delta(C_i + C_j)$ with $\Delta(\chi_i + \chi_j)$ for some i and j.

When the five χ-wheels were all set the χ-key was added to, that is subtracted from, the cipher message to yield the combination $P + \psi$. Now we ran into the problem of 'de-psiing', that is, separating $P + \psi$ into P and ψ. The process was analogous to depth-reading. ψ was not plaintext but it had its own peculiarities. It had a great many repeated letters. Of two consecutive letters it could be said that if they were different they were likely to differ by more than the random expectation. When de-psiing had gone far enough for the ψ-wheels to be set, the process simplified. As a rule there would be only two alternatives for the next ψ-letter. But sometimes confusion would be caused by a repeated letter of ψ that unexpectedly covered a ψ-advance. Most of the de-psiing was done by women of the auxiliary services, who became expert at it. When they were unsuccessful they spoke instead of 'deep-sighing'. When a sufficiently long stretch of ψ was known, the motor-wheels could be set and then further deciphering was routine.

The statistical method worked best on long messages. Fortunately the Germans were sending longer and longer messages at this time. They would put several actual messages into a single transmission. From our point of view that would be a single very, very long message.

Production increased again. But somewhere around this time, the Germans decided to change their wheel patterns every day. Perhaps they were hearkening again to that same inspector. But they could not be relied upon to send a depth every day.

Rectangling

I began to dream of generalising the statistical method. Could it be improved so far as to find unknown wheel patterns instead of merely setting known ones? Even if that could be done in theory, surely it would need a very long message. There on my work table was a cipher message about 15,000 letters long.

First I went along the message, marking off its letters in numbered blocks of, I think, 20. Never must the 15,000 get out of step. Never must I mistake letter number 11,614 for letter number 11,615. I then had to make the familiar statistical assumption that $\Delta(C_1 + C_2)$ agreed, sufficiently often for my purpose, with $\Delta(\chi_1 + \chi_2)$. I had to suppose that effectively $\Delta(C_1 + C_2)$ was a badly damaged version of $\Delta(\chi_1 + \chi_2)$. I hoped that it would still be at least 55 per cent correct. Probably I could use the fact that $\Delta(\chi_1 + \chi_2)$ was the sum of two periodic sequences $\Delta\chi_1$ and $\Delta\chi_2$, of periods 41 and 31 respectively.

The first step seemed clear. I wrote $\Delta(C_1 + C_2)$ diagonally into a rectangle of 41 rows and 31 columns. (Or perhaps it was 31 rows and 41 columns? No matter.) With each successive symbol the sequence would advance one row and one column. The first row was deemed to be the successor of the last, and similarly with the columns. The first symbol of $\Delta(C_1 + C_2)$ went into the first row and first column, and the sequence returned to any given square in just 1271 steps.

At the end of this procedure there were 11 or 12 entries in each little square of the rectangle, less a few corresponding to doubtful letters of the ciphertext. All the entries in a particular little square corresponded to the same settings of the first and second χ-wheels. Each came in the same place of the period of $\Delta\chi_1$, and the same place of the period of $\Delta\chi_2$. Since a symbol of $\Delta(C_1 + C_2)$ was more likely than not to agree with the corresponding symbol of $\Delta(\chi_1 + \chi_2)$, I took a majority verdict in each square. Whichever symbol, dot or cross, occurred most often there, I took to be, most likely, the symbol of $\Delta(\chi_1 + \chi_2)$ for that square. True there were disappointing cases in which the majority was only one. There were even a few in which there were just as many dots as crosses and I could make no decision. But I felt sure that my evaluation of $\Delta(\chi_1 + \chi_2)$

was much more than 55 per cent correct. So I made a new rectangle with my estimates of $\Delta(\chi_1 + \chi_2)$ replacing the original entries.

I now had to decompose the estimated $\Delta(\chi_1 + \chi_2)$ into $\Delta\chi_1$ and $\Delta\chi_2$. To do this I chose a row in which I thought the evidence was unusually strong, and adopted it as a first approximation to $\Delta\chi_1$. Comparing this with each row in turn, I could estimate whether the corresponding symbol of $\Delta\chi_2$ was dot or cross. (Dot for good agreement, cross for marked disagreement.) Thus I got my first approximation of $\Delta\chi_2$. Comparing this with each column in turn, I got a second approximation to $\Delta\chi_1$. Continuing in this way, alternating between rows and columns until the patterns changed no more, I got what I thought were pretty reliable estimates of $\Delta\chi_1$ and $\Delta\chi_2$. True there were one or two entries in these for which the evidence was very weak. Moreover there was the usual ambiguity: did I have the correct patterns or their reverses? For delta-ed sequences this matters.

There were two considerations that allowed me to do some fine tuning. $\Delta\chi_1$ and $\Delta\chi_2$, merely because they were delta-ed periodic sequences, would each have to have an even number of crosses. As you go round a χ-wheel to return to your initial position you must make just as many steps from dot to cross as from cross to dot. That makes an even number of changes, an even number of crosses in the pattern of $\Delta\chi$. Their reverses, those imposters, would each have an odd number. Moreover each χ_i-sequence had to be plausible. So I got estimates of $\Delta\chi_1$ and $\Delta\chi_2$, and thence of χ_1 and χ_2, that I thought reliable. At least I was content to assume their accuracy as a working hypothesis. In the event I did not have to correct them.

I now had to go through the same process again with a different pair of impulses. It was to be feared that the agreement between $\Delta(C_i + C_j)$ and $\Delta(\chi_i + \chi_j)$ would be smaller. On the other hand by making $\Delta\chi_1$ or $\Delta\chi_2$ one member of the pair we could take one of the patterns $\Delta\chi_i$ and $\Delta\chi_j$ as known. In fact I got satisfactory results with my new pairs and soon had the five χ-patterns. Barring any residual errors I now had the χ-key. Accordingly I de-chied the message, getting $P + \psi$. Now for a grand operation of de-psiing!

In my deciphering I was at a disadvantage compared with the wheel setters, since I did not know the patterns of the ψ-wheels. But I made some progress and it soon became clear to me that I had made a lucky choice of message. The text seemed to be in short blocks separated by unnecessarily long sequences of symbols of punctuation. At any rate the sender had been generous in providing blocks of four or more word-spaces. I wish I could remember more about how I separated P from ψ. I know I made an effort to construct the motor-key from the ψ-motion as I went along. At the time of writing (2000) I see clearly that ψ-motion would repeat on the period of the motor key, that is $61 \times 37 = 2257$, and this fact should have been exploitable. If there was here a ψ-letter repeated twice there would likely be the same 2257 places on. If so, one would have 32 possibilities for a triplet of plaintext there, and only one might be plausible. I was equally capable of seeing this when I was working on that message. But whether I used this observation or neglected it in favour of some procedure that I have now forgotten, I cannot say. All I can be sure of now is that I did get enough information about ψ, its stoppages and its starts, to determine the patterns of the ψ-

wheels and the motor-wheels. What was left of the message could then be routinely deciphered.

I remembered taking this message, with its wheel patterns and wheel settings, to the Testery. To emphasise what I considered the importance of the occasion I told Ralph Tester, 'This is the first machine to be broken on a depth of one.'

Statisticians improved upon this 'rectangle method'. Instead of taking the majority verdict for a little square they estimated the probability of $\Delta(\chi_1 + \chi_2)$ being cross, and wrote that number there. In getting the first approximation to $\Delta\chi_2$ they would not make a crude estimate of dot or cross but work out probabilities. And so on for further approximations. (The process became that of finding an eigenvector for a rectangle-matrix.) More wheel patterns were found.

Clearly the refined rectangle method would be too tedious to be done routinely by hand. If it was to be of real use mechanisation would be necessary. However, our Post Office engineers were steadily improving their Fish-breaking apparatus and they went on to design an electrical machine that could find χ-patterns by the rectangle method. That was Colossus II.

The Coming of Colossus

I remember being introduced to Colossus. With other members of the Research Section, I was taken to a large room, where a large box-shaped object, sheathed in sheet metal, stood upon a wet floor. If it was $16 \times 3 \times 5$ in feet, that would not contradict my memory. 'That,' we were told, 'is Colossus.' Gerry Morgan, gazing at the wet floor, remarked that it had not been house-trained yet. We were told that those valves generated heat and the apparatus had to be water-cooled. Alas, there was some leakage. (See page 76—Ed.)

One of my memories of early Colossus-time is still vivid. It is of Max Newman exclaiming with an air of surprise, 'You know, this thing could do logical operations!' (Silent upon a peak in Darien.)

I cannot remember any further work I did with Fish. I knew of various complications the Germans now put into their cipher machines. They took the form of additions to the motor-key. Sometimes a χ- or ψ-impulse from a few letters back would be added to it. Sometimes even a delayed impulse of plaintext would be added. The latter device was called an autoclave. From the German point of view it had the advantage of making depth-reading impossible. On the other hand a single wrong letter could wreck the remainder of the message. It seemed that the autoclave, when used, gave more trouble to the Germans than to the Bletchleyites. These new devices did not prevent the breaking of the χ-wheels, but they made de-psiing and ψ-breaking more difficult. On the whole, however, Bletchley kept on top of Fish until the end of the German war, armed as it was with Colossus. Not all messages were read, but there was a statistical test for deciding early on whether the one under investigation was likely or not to yield. If not, then it was rejected.

Professor Cumlatly

Sometimes in phantasy I envisage a future university department in which, for reasons unfathomable to this century, they are devoted to the study of how Fish was broken and, more importantly, of how it ought to have been broken. There is Professor Cumlatly, lecturing at his Annual Cryptographical Meeting of 2253. I cannot distinguish what he is saying, though a few phrases sound like 'Turing's method', 'rectangle method', and 'HQIBPEXEZMUG-method'. He seems to be pouring scorn on all of them. One sentence comes through quite clearly. 'And yet Sturgeon could have been broken so easily.' There is another brief interval of clarity at question time. Someone asks, 'Johnny, wouldn't it have been quicker and easier to break those keys from the depths and near-depths of 1942 by the rectangle method?' The Professor answers, 'That is a good question. I already have a graduate student working on it.'

In this phantasy I have expressed my fear that cryptographic historians, having mulled over their problems for a few years, will express pained surprise at the cryptanalytic crudities of the 1940s and will marvel at the obtuseness of their practitioners. If so, let them remember that our customers wanted results quickly; the first method that gave any results at all would have to go right away into general use.

I put in a reference to Sturgeon, the teleprinter cipher machine that I have said we did not break. Sturgeon's physical machine, it is now known, had one disastrous weakness. There was a switch that put the wheels back to their original setting. When an operator had sent a message, he was tempted to use that switch and so send the next message on the same key. It saved him the trouble of turning the wheels to a new setting. So depths of four or five became common in the Sturgeon traffic. With depths of that profundity messages could be read, permutation or no permutation, wheel patterns could be deduced, and the working of the machine laid bare. Deep depths were common enough to yield a supply of decodes. So it could be said that Sturgeon was broken. But to workers on Tunny and its analogues, a month would not be considered broken until we had some way of decoding messages that were not in depth, as by dragging, Wyllie's method, the statistical method of wheel setting, or the rectangle method. We never got that far with Sturgeon. Eventually it was decided at a high level that the flow of information from Sturgeon was less satisfactory, in volume and in content, than that from Tunny-type traffic. We were instructed to concentrate on the latter. In spite of its fantastic misuse by its German operators I can think of Sturgeon as 'the one that got away'. In my phantasy I express my misgivings that perhaps, by some method that we missed, Sturgeon could have been made as tame as Tunny.

The question and answer that I put into my phantasy record a question I have often asked myself. But let the answer be Cumlatly's own. Having got a key K, we can write

$$\Delta(K_1 + K_2) = \Delta(\chi_1 + \chi_2) + \Delta(\psi_1 + \psi_2).$$

But $\Delta(\psi_1 + \psi_2)$ is about 70 per cent dot. Hence $\Delta(K_1 + K_2)$ must be in 70 per cent agreement with $\Delta(\chi_1 + \chi_2)$. And the agreement would still be 70 per cent for other pairs of impulses. Surely with 1000 or so letters of key the rectangle method would have resolved $\Delta(K_1 + K_2)$ into $\Delta\chi_1$ and $\Delta\chi_2$? I suppose I could check this if I went to enough trouble. But what would be the point now, so long after the last Fish message was sent? On second thoughts the problem could be reformulated as one in pure mathematics and so made worth solving. It would not be the first of Bletchley's little problems to undergo such a transformation.

If I were asked to state the main weaknesses of the Fish machine I would comment first on the separation of the five impulses, each being effectively controlled by only two wheels. Actually the two motor-wheels made four but our cryptanalytic methods did not have to consider the motor patterns in their early stages. In Sturgeon, because of the permutations, all ten wheels were involved in the production of a single impulse of ciphertext. The second main weakness was that the ψ-wheels moved in step. Had they moved independently, each with its own motor pattern, then Turing's method would not have worked, and the statistical method and the rectangle method would not have applied.

Appendix 5

The Tiltman Break

Friedrich L. Bauer

Tunny Compromised at Birth

In the summer of 1941 the German army tested an experimental Tunny link (see Chapter 3 and Appendix 1). The link used *Hellschreiber*, an early form of fax. Each message was preceded by a 12-letter indicator in clear language, as shown in Figure 1—the indicator MGLOBLCOODKQ is written by hand across the top of the 'Red

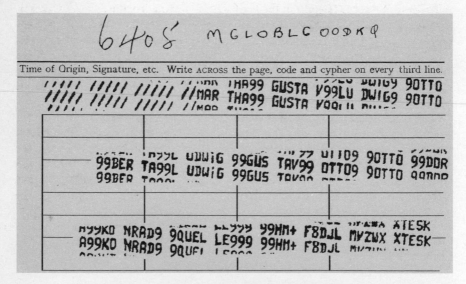

Figure 1. British *Hellschreiber* recording of the start of a Tunny message (8 August 1941). The five-letter groups read: ///// //MAR THA99 GUSTA V99LU DWIG9 9OTTO 99BER TA99L UDWIG 99GUS TA?99 OTTO9 9OTTO 99DOR A99KO NRAD9 9QUEL LE999 99HM+ F8DJL MVZWX XTESK.

Source: Bletchley Park Archives

Form' produced by the intercept station (see Chapter 7). The sloping text, which is pasted to the Red Form, is typical of a *Hellschreiber* record.

When the British studied these enciphered signals, they found hints—in particular when some of the message indicator spellings were corrupted in a message sent out on 22 July 1941 ('h0inrich' for 'heinrich', 'th0o3or' for 'theodor')—that a Vernam-type encryption based on teleprinter machines was involved (see Appendix 12). It was observed that the corrupted name and its correct form had 5-bit teleprinter representations differing only in the first bit. This could be explained by the existence of some fault in the teleprinter machine. The cipher machine was evidently not the Siemens T52—'Sturgeon'—described in a German patent of 1930, since this used ten keying wheels, leading to an indicator consisting of ten letters, not twelve.

Lack of discipline is the enemy of good cryptography and the hope of the unauthorised decryptor. Thoughtlessness and laziness are dangerous. Many test messages were sent on the experimental *Hellschreiber* link—and since these contained no information that should have been kept secret, nobody on the German side was troubled when depths occurred. These depths would compromise the whole Tunny cipher system. On 3 July 1941, a depth of two with the indicator DKTNFQGWAOSH was found by the British and nicknamed WAOSH. It was clear to the British that the two messages must be in depth, since the same indicator was transmitted in clear at the beginning of each. Another depth was found on 21 July; with the indicator KONPAENGFQBZ, this one was nicknamed GFQBZ.

The British recorded depths in the hope that something like the Siemens *Geheimschreiber* with a letter subtractor cipher was used. By July 1941 their assumptions were confirmed. A group 33zzz11 (meaning +++), which had appeared occasionally in clear preambles, was tried as clear at the beginning of one message—and the clear of the other message came out as seven letters of the word *spruchnummer* (message number), usually found at the beginning of a message. This was enough evidence that an additive system was being used on the *Hellschreiber* link.

Notice the typical doubling of the teleprinter control characters 3 and 1 in the group 33zzz11. In this appendix, the symbols '1', '2', and '3' are used for the control characters 'letter shift', 'space', and 'figure shift', respectively. This is in accordance with the International Teletype Alphabet (see Appendix 12). At Bletchley Park, the symbols '8', '9', and '5' were used instead (see Appendix 2). These are merely different linguistic conventions and there is no difference in substance. The reason for doubling was that wireless transmission often led to mutilations. Similarly the German operators were instructed to precede a 2 by a 1, i.e. for word separation the pair 12 was used. (This was a weakness exploited by Beurling in his attack on T52 traffic; see Chapter 26.)

HQIBPEXEZMUG

On 30 August 1941, a German telegraphist made an error and two rather long messages were sent with the same indicator, HQIBPEXEZMUG. Two messages of roughly 4000 characters, in depth and coinciding in the first seven characters, were recorded.

As it turned out, the first message was corrupted by atmospheric noise and had been sent again. It should have been repeated identically, but this is not easy and the operator made minor deviations.

This compromise allowed Colonel (later Brigadier) John Tiltman to deduce the two plaintexts, p' and p'', from the result d of subtracting the two ciphertexts, c' and c''. His deduction was based on the fact that, since the two messages have the same key, $p' - p'' = c' - c''$. Tiltman used a painstaking zigzag method to reveal the plaintexts.

The first 120 characters of the two messages are shown in Figure 2, together with the results of the subtractions that Tiltman performed. (The subtractions can be verified by means of the Table in Appendix 3, remembering that for this cipher system addition and subtraction are the same thing.)

```
        1  2  3  4  5    6  7  8  9 10   11 12 13 14 15   16 17 18 19 20   21 22 23 24 25   26 27 28 29 30
c"    J S H 5 N   Z Y M F S   0 1 1 5 I   V K U 1 Y   U 4 N C E   J E G P B
c'    J S H 5 N   Z Y Z Y 5   G L F R G   X O 5 S Q   5 D A 1 J   J H D 5 O
d     0 0 0 0 0   0 0 f o u   g f l 4 m   a q s g 5   s e k z r   0 y w h e

        31 32 33 34 35   36 37 38 39 40   41 42 43 44 45   46 47 48 49 50   51 52 53 54 55   56 57 58 59 60
c"    M N T Q M   A 0 U 4 Y   L 1 Q I J   L Y V I N   U B 2 3 R   5 W E V G
c'    B K S U C   B T T O 5   E 4 T S L   E 3 F G Z   Y U H V H   3 H E E O
d     s a y t l   g t q t q   w q u a b   w c w m x   l v t s v   b u 0 1 g

        61 62 63 64 65   66 67 68 69 70   71 72 73 74 75   76 77 78 79 80   81 82 83 84 85   86 87 88 89 90
c"    Q I 2 4 5   G R J M L   C Y 5 0 H   K A S 1 I   S 5 X U N   S R Z Z B
c'    T G 2 H H   1 Q J X V   K 1 B J M   K 2 O M Z   Y V I N 3   H M C 3 D
d     u m 0 m p   s x 0 e n   e r 3 j 4   0 u x a q   t m 3 j q   z p 1 r t

        91 92 93 94 95   96 97 98 99 00   01 02 03 04 05   06 07 08 09 10   11 12 13 14 15   16 17 18 19 20
c"    D B B 1 C   L S Q H H   U H 5 X D   0 F N 3 J   3 V O C A   D J C D N
c'    U Q 3 4 Z   R 2 M R M   O H 5 J Q   P W U E Y   C P R G 1   L D A T I
d     c c 5 q 1   o e j v 4   1 0 0 p v   p v j g v   y 4 l h m   3 5 f b r
```

Figure 2. The first 120 characters of the two messages.

The next task is to choose a probable word and test for its occurrence in one of the messages. Perhaps Tiltman would have tried the very frequent word geheim2 (secret). If he did, he would have succeeded twice in finding an intelligible counterpart:

```
        61 62 63 64 65   66 67 68 69 70   71 72 73 74 75   76 77 78 79 80   81 82 83 84 85   86 87 88 89 90   91 92 93 94 95
p"    * * * * g   e h e i m   2 * * * *   * * * * *   * * g e h   e i m 2 *   * * * * *
d     u m 0 m p   s x 0 e n   e r e j 4   0 u x a q   t m 3 j q   z p 1 r t   c c 5 q 1
p'    * * * * n   2 d e u t   s * * * *   * * * * *   * * e r a   t t a c *   * * * * *
```

n2deuts can easily be supplemented to an2deutsch, and erattac leads to 2militaerat-tache2 (military attache). The gap is filled by an2deutschen (German). There results a probable fragment for p' with a length of 29 characters:

```
      61 62 63 64 65  66 67 68 69 70  71 72 73 74 75  76 77 78 79 80  81 82 83 84 85  86 87 88 89 90  91 92 93 94 95
p''   * * * * g e h e i m 2 * * * * * * * * * * * * g e h e i m 2 * * * * * *
d     u m 0 m p  s x 0 e n  e r e j 4  0 u x a q  t m 3 j q  z p 1 r t  c c 5 q 1
p'    * * * a n 2 d e u t  s c h e n 2 m i l i  t a e r a  t t a c h  e 2 * * *
```

The probable fragment of p' produces 29 consecutive characters of p'' as well:

```
      61 62 63 64 65  66 67 68 69 70  71 72 73 74 75  76 77 78 79 80  81 82 83 84 85  86 87 88 89 90  91 92 93 94 95
p''   * * 1 1 g  e h e i m  2 2 k r 2  2 3 3 z z  0 1 g e h  e i m 2 2  k r * * *
d     u m 0 m p  s x 0 e n  e r e j 4  0 u x a q  t m 3 j q  z p 1 r t  c c 5 q 1
p'    * * 1 a n  2 d e u t  s c h e n  2 m i l i  t a e r a  t t a c h  e 2 * * *
```

This illustrates a pet silliness on the German side: *geheim* was doubled. The doubling of the complete group lgeheim22kr2233zz leads to an extension for p', which makes sense apart from two discrepancies, at positions 94 and 98:

```
                 81 82 83 84 85  86 87 88 89 90  91 92 93 94 95  96 97 98 99 00
p''   0 1 g e h  e i m 2 2  k r 2 2 3  3 z z 1 2
d     t m 3 j q  z p 1 r t  c c 5 q 1  o e j v 4
p'    t a e r a  t t a c h  e 2 i (w)2  a t (g)e n
```

The discrepancies are probably the result of sloppiness and can be corrected.

One could continue in this zigzag fashion. However, at this stage, if not earlier, the suspicion arises that the rest of the message p' is simply shifted against p'' by 39 positions, since repeating an2deutschen2militaerattache2 from position 103 of p'' makes sense again, producing in p' lagg11nr33mwoou211g. In readable form, and with a typing error corrected, this fragment is *lage nr. 2997⊔g*, where ⊔ represents a space ('site number 2997').

```
      86 87 88 89 90  91 92 93 94 95  96 97 98 99 00  01 02 03 04 05  06 07 08 09 10  11 12 13 14 15  16 17 18 19 20
p''   e i m 2 2  k r 2 3 3  3 z 1 1 2  * * a n 2  d e u t s  c h e n 2  m i l i t
d     z p 1 r t  c c 5 q 1  o e j v 4  1 0 0 p v  p v j g v  y 4 l h m  3 5 f b r
p'    t t a c h  e 2 i n 2  a t h e n  * l a g g  1 1 n r 3  3 m w o o  u 2 1 1 g
```

The continuation can now be produced mechanically by looking ahead 39 characters, until such time as new deviations occur. It is reported that Tiltman finished the deciphering in ten days. This may have been because further errors caused by noise made the break more difficult than a retrospective analysis shows. Anyhow, a continuous message was constructed. Luck was on Tiltman's side— normally only isolated parts of a message will be found by this 'cross-ruff' technique. That was why his attempts with the earlier depths had failed.

There remain positions 1 to 62. If the probable word nummer2 (number) is tried in p'' there is promise at positions 7 to 13:

```
      1  2  3  4  5   6  7  8  9 10  11 12 13 14 15   16 17 18 19 20  21 22 23 24 25  26 27 28 29 30
p''   *  *  *  *  *   *  n  u  m  m   e  r  2  *  *    *  *  *  *  *   *  *  *  *  *   *  *  *  *  *
d     0  0  0  0  0   0  0  f  o  u   g  f  l  4  m    a  q  s  g  5   s  e  k  z  r   0  y  w  h  e
p'    *  *  *  *  *   *  n  r  2  3   3  u  p  *  *    *  *  *  *  *   *  *  *  *  *   *  *  *  *  *
```

nummer2 can most likely be extended to spruchnummer2 (message number). The change in p' from nummer2 to nr2 suggests that p' continues in the same way as p'' but shifted by 4 positions:

```
      1  2  3  4  5   6  7  8  9 10  11 12 13 14 15   16 17 18 19 20  21 22 23 24 25  26 27 28 29 30
p''   s  p  r  u  c   h  n  u  m  m   e  r  2  3  3    u  p  *  *  *   *  *  *  *  *   *  *  *  *  *
d     0  0  0  0  0   0  0  f  o  u   g  f  l  4  m    a  q  s  g  5   s  e  k  z  r   0  y  w  h  e
p'    s  p  r  u  c   h  n  r  2  3   3  u  p  w  u    2  e  *  *  *   *  *  *  *  *   *  *  *  *  *
```

```
      1  2  3  4  5   6  7  8  9 10  11 12 13 14 15   16 17 18 19 20  21 22 23 24 25  26 27 28 29 30
p''   s  p  r  u  c   h  n  u  m  m   e  r  2  3  3    u  p  w  u  2   e  *  *  *  *   *  *  *  *  *
d     0  0  0  0  0   0  0  f  o  u   g  f  l  4  m    a  q  s  g  5   s  e  k  z  r   0  y  w  h  e
p'    s  p  r  u  c   h  n  r  2  3   3  u  p  w  u    2  e  p  x  i   2  *  *  *  *   *  *  *  *  *
```

And so on.

The plaintext piece nr233upwu2epxi2, in readable form $nr \sqcup 7027 \sqcup 30/8$, seems to contain the date. Given the German predilection for doubling important pieces of text, p' can be tested for further occurrences of upwu2epxi2. There is success at positions 29 to 38, and a repeated fragment upw shows up in p'':

```
      6  7  8  9 10  11 12 13 14 15   16 17 18 19 20  21 22 23 24 25  26 27 28 29 30  31 32 33 34 35  36 37 38 39 40
p''   h  n  u  m  m   e  r  2  3  3    u  p  w  u  2   e  *  *  *  *   *  *  *  w  q   p  2  z  z  2   u  p  w  *  *
d     0  0  f  o  u   g  f  l  4  m    a  q  s  g  5   s  e  k  z  r   0  y  w  h  e   s  a  y  t  l   g  t  q  t  q
p'    h  n  r  2  3   3  u  p  w  u    2  e  p  x  i   2  *  *  *  *   *  *  *  u  p   w  u  2  e  p   x  i  2  *  *
```

Prefixing the second occurrence of upwu2epxi2 in p' by 2 has the consequence in p'' of prefixing wqp2zz2upw by q. This suggests searching for an occurrence of qwqp2 in p'. Success comes at positions 22 to 26, with the counterpart pmim2 in p'':

```
      6  7  8  9 10  11 12 13 14 15   16 17 18 19 20  21 22 23 24 25  26 27 28 29 30  31 32 33 34 35  36 37 38 39 40
p''   h  n  u  m  m   e  r  2  3  3    u  p  w  u  2   e  p  m  i  m   2  *  q  w  q   p  2  z  z  2   u  p  w  u  2
d     0  0  f  o  u   g  f  l  4  m    a  q  s  g  5   s  e  k  z  r   0  y  w  h  e   s  a  y  t  l   g  t  q  t  q
p'    h  n  r  2  3   3  u  p  w  u    2  e  p  x  i   2  q  w  q  p   2  *  2  u  p   w  u  2  e  p   x  i  2  q  w
```

The remaining gap from positions 41 to 62 can be closed similarly:

$$
\begin{array}{llllllllllllllllllll}
& \text{41 42 43 44 45} & \text{46 47} & \text{48 49 50} & \text{51 52 53 54} & \text{55} & \text{56 57 58 59 60} \\
p'' & \text{2 e p m i} & \text{m 2} & \text{q w q} & \text{p 2 z z} & \text{1} & \text{1 3 3 2 *} \\
d & \text{w q u a b} & \text{w c} & \text{w m x} & \text{l v t s v} & & \text{b u 0 1 g} \\
p' & \text{q p z 1 1} & \text{k r} & \text{2 k r} & \text{2 g e h e} & & \text{i m 3 3 *}
\end{array}
$$

Doubling and the occurrence of probable words both contributed to the break. The abundance of teleprinter control characters also helped. Most helpful of all, though, was the fact that large parts of the plain messages were merely shifted:

p'' reads: *spruchnummer$\sqcup$7027$\sqcup$30.8.$\sqcup$*1210$\sqcup$++$\sqcup$7027$\sqcup$30.8.$\sqcup$*1210$\sqcup$++$\sqcup$*** geheim$\sqcup\sqcup$kr$\sqcup\sqcup$++geheim$\sqcup\sqcup$kr$\sqcup\sqcup$+an$\sqcup$deutschen$\sqcup$milit.....*

p' reads: *spruchnr$\sqcup$7027$\sqcup$30/8$\sqcup$*1210$\sqcup$*$\sqcup$7027$\sqcup$30/8$\sqcup$1210+kr$\sqcup$kr$\sqcup$geheim*** an$\sqcup$deutschen$\sqcup$militaerattache$\sqcup$in$\sqcup$athen*lage nr.2997$\sqcup$g.....*

A complication in the deciphering could have been that the date in p', 233upwu2-epmim2 (in readable form $nr\sqcup7027\sqcup30.8.\sqcup$), was written slightly differently in p'', namely 233upwu2epxi2 (in readable form $\sqcup7027\sqcup30/8\sqcup$).

The two messages themselves were most likely of little value. What was important was that a fragment of about 4000 characters of key, generated by the hitherto almost unknown machine, was exposed (since $c' = p' + k$ leads to $k = c' + p'$). The first 120 characters of key are shown in Figure 3 overleaf.

Given the reconstructed key fragment, it was possible to analyse the key generator of the Tunny machine. First the periods of the individual keying wheels had to be found. (The existence of keying wheels could be inferred by analogy with the Siemens machine.) One could hazard a guess from the fact the indicator HQIBPEXEZMUG had 12 letters that there were 12 keying wheels. Since none of the five channels of the key had a period of length less than 100, it could be assumed that each channel was enciphered by a composition of (at least) two keying wheels. Tutte found the periods of the chi-wheels by an examination of periodicity—a standard practice that Friedrich Kasiski had introduced in 1863. Figure 4 on page 377 shows the investigation of the periodicity of the χ_1-wheel. The rest, as they say, is history.

Analysis of the depths WAOSH and GFQBZ (in March 1942) went much faster in the light of the experience that ZMUG (as it was nicknamed) had brought. The codebreakers found that the wheel order in WAOSH was the same as in ZMUG, and that the patterns of the psi-wheels in WAOSH were identical to the psi-wheel patterns of ZMUG, but the patterns of all the other wheels were different.

```
     1  2  3  4  5   6  7  8  9 10  11 12 13 14 15  16 17 18 19 20  21 22 23 24 25  26 27 28 29 30
 k   C  W  V  S  5   S  B  3  Z  B   E  Y  3  B  H   B  B  H  O  Z   I  V  T  4  X   K  *  F  S  C
 1   0  1  0  1  0   1  1  1  1  1   1  1  1  1  0   1  1  0  0  1   0  0  0  0  1   1     1  1  0
 2   1  1  1  0  1   0  0  1  0  0   0  0  1  0  0   0  0  0  0  0   1  1  0  0  0   1     0  0  1
 3   1  0  1  1  0   1  0  0  0  0   0  1  0  0  1   0  0  1  0  0   1  1  0  0  1   1     1  1  1
 4   1  0  1  0  0   0  1  1  0  1   0  0  1  1  0   1  1  0  1  0   0  1  0  1  1   1     1  0  1
 5   0  1  1  0  0   0  1  1  1  1   0  1  1  1  1   1  1  1  1  1   0  1  1  0  1   0     0  0  0
```

```
    31 32 33 34 35  36 37 38 39 40  41 42 43 44 45  46 47 48 49 50  51 52 53 54 55  56 57 58 59 60
 k   R  4  E  I  O   2  P  H  K  Z   P  V  E  G  F   C  Z  D  Y  3   Z  X  Y  R  Y   X  4  G  G  *
 1   0  0  1  0  0   0  0  0  1  1   0  0  1  0  1   0  1  1  1  1   1  1  1  0  1   1  0  0  0
 2   1  0  0  1  0   0  1  0  1  0   1  1  0  1  0   1  0  0  0  1   0  0  0  1  0   0  0  1  1
 3   0  0  0  1  0   1  1  1  1  0   1  1  0  0  1   1  0  0  1  0   0  1  1  0  1   1  0  0  0
 4   1  1  0  0  1   0  0  0  1  0   0  1  0  1  1   1  0  1  0  1   0  1  0  1  0   1  1  1  1
 5   0  0  0  0  1   0  1  1  0  1   1  1  0  1  0   0  1  0  1  1   1  1  1  0  1   1  0  1  1
```

```
    61 62 63 64 65  66 67 68 69 70  71 72 73 74 75  76 77 78 79 80  81 82 83 84 85  86 87 88 89 90
 k   *  *  3  Q  O   3  V  R  G  C   R  Z  F  R  T   J  O  V  C  Q   S  X  U  I  O   2  N  F  Y  X
 1         1  1  0   1  0  0  0  0   0  1  1  0  0   1  0  0  0  1   1  1  1  0  0   0  0  1  1  1
 2         1  1  0   1  1  1  1  1   1  0  0  1  0   1  0  1  1  1   0  0  1  1  0   0  0  0  0  0
 3         0  1  0   0  1  0  0  1   0  0  1  0  0   0  0  1  1  1   1  1  1  1  0   1  1  1  1  1
 4         1  0  0   1  1  1  1  1   1  0  1  1  0   1  1  1  1  0   0  1  0  0  1   0  1  1  0  1
 5         1  1  1   1  1  0  1  0   0  1  0  0  1   0  1  1  0  1   0  1  0  0  1   0  0  0  1  1
```

```
    91 92 93 94 95  96 97 98 99 00  01 02 03 04 05  06 07 08 09 10  11 12 13 14 15  16 17 18 19 20
 k   I  W  X  2  Y   D  H  4  J  T   M  I  E  Z  P   D  N  J  I  C   Y  R  B  5  U   Y  F  M  K  M
 1   0  1  1  0  1   1  0  0  1  0   0  0  1  1  0   1  0  1  1  0   1  0  1  0  1   1  1  0  1  0
 2   1  1  0  0  0   0  0  0  1  0   0  1  0  0  1   0  0  1  1  1   0  1  0  1  1   0  0  0  1  0
 3   1  0  1  1  1   0  1  0  0  0   1  1  0  0  1   0  1  0  0  1   1  0  0  0  1   1  1  1  1  1
 4   0  0  1  0  0   1  0  1  1  0   1  0  0  0  0   1  1  1  1  1   0  1  1  0  0   0  1  1  1  1
 5   0  1  1  0  1   1  1  0  0  1   1  0  0  1  1   0  0  0  0  0   1  0  1  0  0   1  0  1  0  1
```

Figure 3. Key exposed by Tiltman.

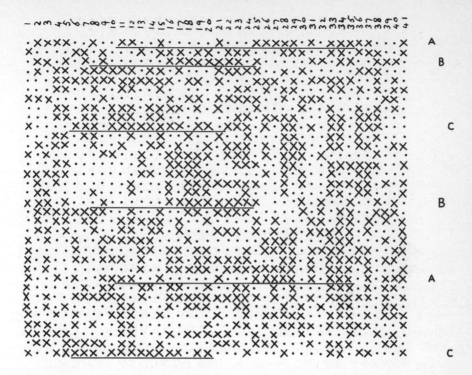

Figure 4. Periodicity examination of the χ_1-wheel, whose length is 41. Kasiski repetitions: A, B, C.

Source: Bletchley Park Archives

Appendix 6

• •

Turingery

Jack Copeland

Turing and Enigma

Turing took up residence at Bletchley Park the day after Chamberlain's announcement of war. He joined Dilly Knox's Research Section, and during the first weeks of the war he designed the machines that would turn Bletchley Park into a codebreaking factory—the Bombes. (See photograph 25.)

The crux of the Bombe design was Turing's ingenious method of dealing with the substitutions created by the Enigma's plugboard (see page 17). Turing described his method in notes known at Bletchley Park simply as 'Prof's Book'. These were declassified in 1996 and the relevant parts were published in 2004 in my book *The Essential Turing*. In its mature form, the Bombe contained 36 replica Enigma machines, with ten miles of wire and a million soldered connections. The prototype, named 'Victory', was installed in March 1940. By November 1941 there were 15 Bombes: at the end of the war there were several hundred. (From August 1940 the Bombes included Gordon Welchman's invention known as the 'diagonal board'. Turing describes the diagonal board in *The Essential Turing*.)

The Bombes attacked Enigma messages by means of cribs. Cribs—words predicted to occur in the message—arose because of the stereotyped nature of the messages. For example, weather stations regularly sent messages beginning WETTER FUER DIE NACHT ('Weather for the night'). Sheer stupidity also played a role in the generation of cribs. One station transmitted the confirmation FEUER BRANNTEN WIE BEFOHLEN each day ('Beacons lit as ordered').

The Victory seems to have been used exclusively by Turing and his assistants in their effort to read Naval Enigma. During 1940 German air force traffic was read in large quantities by Bletchley Park, but naval traffic—including the all-important messages to and from the wolf-packs of U-boats in the North Atlantic—remained cloaked. If this traffic could be broken, the positions of the wolf-packs would be known and the convoys bringing food, raw materials, and other supplies across the Atlantic from North America could be routed around them. From the outbreak of war to December 1940 a devastating total of 585 merchant ships were sunk by U-boats, compared to 202 merchant vessels sunk by aircraft during the same period.

When Turing arrived at Bletchley Park in September 1939 no work was being done on Naval Enigma, which was generally considered unbreakable. As late as the summer of 1940 Denniston, the top man at Bletchley Park, declared to Birch, head of the naval section in Hut 4, 'You know, the Germans don't mean you to read their stuff, and I don't suppose you ever will.' This was certainly not the opinion of Birch and Turing. Alexander noted in his history of the attack on Naval Enigma (written at the end of the war but declassified only recently): 'Birch thought it could be broken because it had to be broken and Turing thought it could be broken because it would be so interesting to break it.' Alexander added, 'Turing first got interested in the problem for the quite typical reason that "no one else was doing anything about it and I could have it to myself" '.

Naval traffic was so difficult to break because the sender enciphered the message setting—the trio of letters denoting the positions of the Enigma machine's three wheels at the start of the message—by two different methods before transmitting it to the sender. The message setting was enciphered once by means of the Enigma machine itself, and once by hand, using a table of letter-pairings issued to the operators. These were called 'bigram tables' at Bletchley Park. By the end of 1939 Turing had deduced how this complicated system worked, a remarkable piece of cryptanalysis. However, his discovery could not be used to read naval traffic until the bigram tables were known. Here the codebreakers depended on the Royal Navy. Thanks to several 'pinches' of material from German vessels during 1940 and 1941 (described in Chapter 2), Turing and the other members of Hut 8—Turing's section dedicated to breaking Naval Enigma—slowly gained control of the code.

Hut 8's ability to break the U-boat messages had an immediate effect. During June 1941, when the traffic was read currently for the first time, re-routings based on Hut 8 decrypts were reportedly so successful that the North Atlantic U-boats did not sight a single convoy for the first 23 days of the month.

Another of Turing's fundamental contributions to the breaking of Naval Enigma was his hand method called *Banburismus*. He invented this on the same productive night in 1939 that he broke the system for enciphering the message setting. The aim of Banburismus was to identify two of the Enigma's three wheels. This meant that fewer wheel combinations had to be tried on the Bombe, so saving huge amounts of Bombe time. Hut 8 was dependent on Banburismus until 1943, when Bombes became more plentiful. (*ismus* is a German suffix equivalent to the English *ism*. The name 'Banburismus' arose because a printing company in the nearby town of Banbury manufactured the special sheets, marked with the alphabet, that were used to apply the method. The sheets themselves were called 'Banburies'.)

Turing left Bletchley Park for the United States in November 1942. There he liaised with the US Navy's codebreakers and Bombe-builders. From that time Turing did no further work in Hut 8 (by then headed by Alexander). When he returned to Bletchley Park in March 1943, he held a wider brief, including scientific policy adviser. Towards the end of 1943 he took on the problem of speech encryption, setting up a laboratory at nearby Hanslope Park, where he worked until the end of the war.

Banburismus and Tunny

Banburismus was the source of a concept used later in the attack on Tunny. This was Turing's measure of probability known simply as the 'ban'. A cryptographic dictionary written at Bletchley Park in 1944 (and declassified in 2000) gives the following definition. 'Ban: Fundamental scoring unit for the odds on, or probability factor of, one of a series of hypotheses which, in order that multiplication may be replaced by addition, are expressed in logarithms. One ban thus represents odds of 10 to 1 in favour, and as this is too large a unit for most practical purposes *decibans* and *centibans* are normally employed instead.'

Michie, echoing Newman, describes this concept as Turing's 'greatest intellectual contribution during the war'. Michie notes that Turing's method anticipated the statistical tool now known as *sequential analysis*—a tool that is usually said, by those with no knowledge of Turing's wartime work, to have originated in a post-war book by Abraham Wald (who coined the name 'sequential analysis').

Although a part of Banburismus, a procedure specific to Enigma, Turing's scoring method was itself completely general. When key members of Hut 8—Good, Hilton, and others—moved across to Tunny, they took Turing's method with them, and it was used extensively in the Newmanry. A Newmanry rule of thumb was that a promising pair of wheel settings became 'certain' if the odds of their being correct reached about 50 to 1. On Turing's logarithmic scale, odds of 50 to 1 in favour are represented by a positive score of 1.7 bans, or 17 decibans (since the logarithm of 50 is 1.7).

Michie reports that Turing's method 'percolated the general practice of Newmanry people, first as a minor mental aid in a variety of jobs and then as a major aid in the chi-wheel pattern breaking which became a central activity of the Newmanry in the era initiated by the installation of Colossus II'. Turing's method, Michie says, 'routinely supported the duty officer's use of Colossus for rectangling, previously do-able only as a very slow wholly manual operation in the Testery'. Rectangling is described in Appendix 9.

Turingery

During 1942 Turing's talent for ground-breaking work was needed once again in the Research Section. It was while on loan from Hut 8 to the Research Section in July 1942 that he invented the method of attack on the Tunny wheels that became known simply as *Turingery*.

While 'Turingery' was the 'official' name for Turing's method, used in *General Report on Tunny*, another name was also employed: *Turingismus*. Michie explains that 'three of us (Peter Ericsson, Peter Hilton, and I) coined and used in playful style various fake-German slang terms for everything under the sun, including occasionally something encountered in the working environment. Turingismus was a case of the latter.' Turingismus and Turingery are one and the same method. Turingery/Turingismus is not to be confused with Banburismus or its sequential-analysis-style derivative just discussed.

The function of Turingery was wheel breaking, starting from a stretch of key obtained from a depth. (Wheel-breaking is the finding of the pattern of the cams, operative or inoperative, around the wheels—see Chapter 3.) Turingery was a hand method, involving paper, pencil, and eraser. It enabled the breaker to prize out from the key the contribution that the χ-wheels had made. The cam-patterns of the individual χ-wheels could be inferred from this. Further deductions led to the cam-patterns of the ψ-and motor-wheels. Once gained via Turingery this information remained current over the course of many messages: at first the Germans changed the cam patterns of the χ-wheels once a month and of the ψ-wheels quarterly, and then from October 1942 the ψ-wheel patterns were also changed monthly. (From August 1944 all wheel patterns were changed daily, but by that time Colossus, not Turingery, was being used for wheel breaking.)

Basic to Turingery—as to Tutte's later method for finding the chi-wheel settings of messages not in depth (Chapter 5)—was the idea of forming the *delta* of a stream of characters. Delta-ing was also called 'differencing'; the concept is explained in Chapter 5. Turing introduced the concept in July 1942, observing that by delta-ing a stretch of key he was able to make deductions which could not be made from the key in its un-delta-ed form. Turingery worked on delta-ed key to produce the delta-ed contribution of the χ-wheels. Tutte discovered, a few months later, that delta-ing was also the way in to wheel setting (see Appendix 4).

Turing's discovery that delta-ing would reveal information otherwise hidden was essential to all that followed in the Newmanry. The algorithms implemented in Heath Robinson and Colossus depended on this simple but brilliant observation. In that sense, the entire machine-based attack on Tunny flowed from this fundamental insight of Turing's.

How did Turingery work? The method exploited the fact that each impulse of the chi-stream (and likewise its delta-ed form) contains a pattern that repeats after a fixed number of steps. Since the number of cams on χ_1 is 41, the pattern in the first impulse of the chi-stream repeats every 41 steps. In the second impulse the pattern repeats every 31 steps (the number of cams on χ_2), and so on for the other three impulses, whose wheels have 29, 26, and 23 cams respectively. Therefore a hypothesis about the identity, dot or cross, of a particular bit in, say, the first impulse of the chi will, if correct, also produce the correct bit 41 steps further on, and another 41 steps beyond that, and so on. Given 500 letters of key, a hypothesis about the identity of a single letter of the chi (or delta-ed chi) will yield approximately 500/41 bits of the first impulse, 500/31 bits of the second impulse, 500/29 bits of the third, and so on—a total of about 85 bits.

Turingery is described in detail in the final section of this appendix, which is an extract (written by Michie) from *General Report on Tunny*. In outline, the method is this. The first step is to make a guess: the breaker guesses a point in the delta-ed key at which the psi-wheels stayed still. Whatever guess is made, it has a 50 per cent chance of being right. Positions where the psis did not move are of great interest to the breaker, because at these positions the delta-ed key and the delta-ed chi are identical. (The reason for this is that the delta-ed contribution of the psis at such positions is /

or •••••, and adding / to a letter does not alter the letter: $\Delta K = \Delta \chi + \Delta \psi'$ (ψ' being the extended psi), so where the letter of $\Delta \psi'$ is /, $\Delta K = \Delta \chi$.)

Since the key is known, the letter of the delta-ed chi at the guessed position is also known—assuming, of course, that the guess about the psis not having moved is correct. Given this single letter of the delta-ed chi, a number of bits can then be filled in throughout the five impulses, by propagating to the left and right at the appropriate periods.

Now that various bits of the delta chi are filled in, guesses can be made as to the identity of others letters. For example, if one letter of the delta chi is •???• and the corresponding letter of the delta key is •×××• (C), the breaker will guess that this is another point at which the psis stood still, and replace •???• in the delta chi by •×××•. This gives three new bits to propagate left and right. And so the process continues, with more and more bits of the delta chi being written in.

Naturally the breaker's guesses are not always correct, and as the process of filling in bits goes on, any incorrect guesses will tend to produce clashes—places where both a cross and a dot are assigned to the same position in the impulse. Guesses that are swamped by clashes have to be revised.

With patience, luck, a lot of rubbing out, and a lot of cycling back and forth between putative fragments of delta χ and delta ψ', a correct and complete stretch of delta χ eventually emerges.

Misconceptions about Turing and Colossus

Earlier accounts pointed to Turing as the key figure in the design of Colossus. In a biographical article on Turing the computer historian J. A. N. Lee said that Turing's 'influence on the development of Colossus is well known', and, in an article on Flowers, Lee referred to Colossus as the 'cryptanalytical machine designed by Alan Turing and others'. Lee asserted: 'Newman fully appreciated the significance of Turing's ideas for the design of high-speed electronic machines for searching for wheel patterns and placings on the highest-grade German enciphering machines, and the result was the invention of the "Colossus".' Even a book on sale at the Bletchley Park Museum states that at Bletchley Park 'Turing worked . . . on what we now know was computer research' which led to 'the world's first electronic, programmable computer, "Colossus" '. *Time* magazine says, 'At Bletchley Park, Alan Turing built a succession of vacuum-tube machines called Colossus that made mincemeat of Hitler's Enigma codes.'

The view that Turing's interest in electronics contributed to the inspiration for Colossus is indeed common. This claim is enshrined in codebreaking exhibits in leading museums; and in the *Annals of the History of Computing* Lee and Holtzman state that Turing 'conceived of the construction and usage of high-speed electronic devices; these ideas were implemented as the "Colossus" machines'.

However, *General Report on Tunny* makes matters perfectly clear: 'Colossus was entirely the idea of Mr Flowers.' By 1943 electronics had been Flowers' driving passion for more than a decade and he needed no help from Turing. Turing was, in any case, away in the United States during the critical period at the beginning of 1943 when Flowers proposed his idea to Newman and worked out the design of Colossus on paper. Flowers emphasised in an interview that Turing 'made no contribution' to the design of Colossus. Flowers said: 'I invented the Colossus. No one else was capable of doing it.'

Some authors confuse Turingery (Turingismus) with Tutte's method for wheel setting. Martin Davis wrote:

Some of the methods to be used were playfully called *turingismus* indicating their source. But turingismus required the processing of lots of data and for the decryption be [sic] of any use, the processing had to be done very quickly. . . . Under the direction of Flowers and Newman, a machine, essentially a physical embodiment of turingismus, was rapidly brought into being. Dubbed the Colossus and an engineering marvel . . .

Turing's method of wheel-breaking from depths and Tutte's method of wheel-setting from non-depths were distant relatives, in that both used delta-ing. But there the similarity ended. Turingery, Tutte said, seemed to him 'more artistic than mathematical'; in applying the method you had to rely on what 'you felt in your bones' (see Appendix 4).

Conflating the two methods, Davis erroneously concludes that Colossus was Turingery in hardware. But Turingery (Turingismus) was a hand method; it was Tutte's method that 'required the processing of lots of data'—so much, indeed, that carrying out the method by hand was completely impractical (see Chapter 5). It was Tutte's method, not Turingery, that was implemented in Colossus and in its precursor, Heath Robinson. 'Turingery was not used in either breaking or setting by any valve machine of any kind,' Michie underlined.

Excerpt from *General Report on Tunny**

Turingery introduced the principle that key differenced at one, now called ΔK, could yield information unobtainable from ordinary key. This Δ principle was to be the fundamental basis of nearly all statistical methods of wheel-breaking and setting. Many improvements and refinements of technique have since been made enabling very much shorter lengths of key to be broken than the 500 [characters] or more required by original Turingery. . . . The original method is described here. The description gives a certain amount of rationalisation of the process which could certainly not have been given at the time since the principles involved had not been studied and understood to the extent that they were later.

The property used throughout is simply

$$p(\Delta\psi'_{ij} = \bullet) = b,$$

or, in different terms,

$$\Delta K_{ij} \xrightarrow{b} \Delta\chi_{ij}.$$

* This material, which is from pages 313–15 of *General Report on Tunny*, is Crown Copyright. Words in square brackets have been added by the editor.

ΔK is written out in ink on squared paper. The 5 rows of squared paper beneath are regarded as corresponding to the 5 TP [teleprint] impulses and each impulse is marked off with an upright ink line according to the chi length of that impulse. All subsequent work is done in pencil. A letter of ΔK is arbitrarily chosen and assumed to have $\Delta\psi' = /$. On the Tunny machine of the time the psis came in at the second letter and moved on automatically from the second to the third place. So the third place of ΔK was the first possible TM dot [total motor—see Appendix 10]. At the assumed $\Delta\psi'$ / position we enter the $\Delta\chi$ letter in impulses (= ΔK since $\Delta\psi' = /$), and the 5 $\Delta\chi$ signs [bits] thus derived are entered on their respective chi-periods throughout the ΔK. These signs are underlined to distinguish them from other $\Delta\chi$ signs deduced from them. Now from every $\Delta\chi$ sign thus entered we can use the property $\Delta K_{ij} \to \Delta\chi_{ij}$ to deduce one $\Delta\chi$ sign on each of the other four impulses. For if the underlined $\Delta\chi$ character is on impulse i and gives $\Delta\chi_i = \Delta K_i$, then in accordance with the above property we deduce $\Delta\chi_j = \Delta K_j$, for j = each of the other 4 impulses, thus obtaining 4 fresh $\Delta\chi$ characters which each have probability b, provided that the position originally selected is in fact a TM dot. Similarly if we find $\Delta\chi_i \neq \Delta K_i$, we assume $\Delta\chi$ on the other four impulses to be the opposite of ΔK. These deduced $\Delta\chi$ signs are written into 5 'cages' of width 41, 31, 29, 26 and 23 respectively. Thus all signs deduced for $\Delta\chi_3$ from underlined $\Delta\chi$ signs on impulses 1, 2, 4 and 5 are written out on a width of 29. An example of a $\Delta\chi_3$ cage is given [in Figure 1].

It will be seen that the underlined $\Delta\chi_3$ sign is also written into the cage each time it occurs as a check against inadvertently sliding the cage to right or left when entering. We now use these 5 cages as a test of the original assumption of a TM dot. For if the original assumption is correct the ratio of agreements to disagreements among the signs in each column of the cage will be $b^2 + \overline{1-b}^2$ to $2b(1-b)$, or $(1+\beta^2)$ to $(1-\beta^2)$. [β is the 'proportional bulge' of $\Delta\psi = \bullet$] We therefore write the number of agreements and the number of disagreements at the bottom of each column (see [Figure 1]) and add up the total excess of agreements over disagreements for all 5 cages. Each excess contributes a factor of $\dfrac{1+\beta^2}{1-\beta^2}$ to the theory that the original position has $\Delta\psi' = /$ (or $\Delta\psi' = 8$ which merely makes all our $\Delta\chi$'s inside out). It the result is poor we scrap the cages, erase the workings and take the next ΔK letter as our $\Delta\psi' = /$ assumption. If it is good we accept the original assumption. In that case the cage entries each have a probability b of being correct and can simply be totted up in columns, and written at the bottom as ringed or unringed numbers according to whether they are scores in favour of the particular $\Delta\chi_i$ character being dot or cross (see [Figure 1]). Accepting scores ≥ 2 we form rudimentary $\Delta\chi$ wheels with which we de-chi the ΔK to give rudimentary $\Delta\psi'$. We examine [this] $\Delta\psi'$ to find a character with 3 or more dots, not counting dots generated by an original underlined $\Delta\chi$ sign. This we assume to be another position where $\Delta\psi' = /$, and re-apply the cage test described above. If the proportion of agreements is poor we try another assumed $\Delta\psi'$ /. If it is good we derive $\Delta\chi$ scores as before by summing the columns and combine these with the previous scores by straight addition, provided that the agreement between scores is

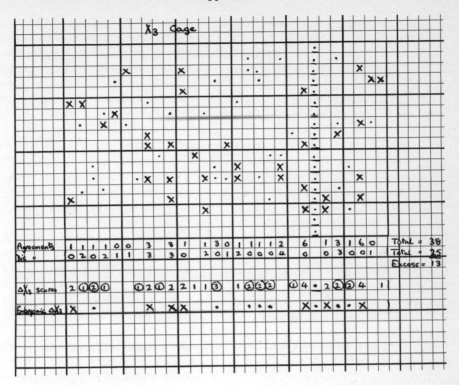

Figure 1. Example of a $\Delta\chi_3$ cage.

reasonably good. Again taking a standard of ≥ 2 we form 5 embryonic $\Delta\chi$'s from the combined scores, with which we de-chi the ΔK to give embryonic $\Delta\psi'$.

We make a 'count' for $\Delta\chi_5$, which is the shortest wheel and therefore will accumulate the most evidence per character. The system of scoring is as follows. For each $L_{m,n}$ in $\Delta\psi'$ (considering only the other 4 impulses) (where $L_{m,n}$ is a letter with m dots and n crosses) we score $m - n$ for the theory that $\Delta\psi'_5 = $ dot, and that therefore $\Delta\chi_5 = \Delta K_5$ at that place. Thus if the $\Delta\psi'$ letter reads ×?•× in the first 4 impulses, and the ΔK letter is Q we score ① for $\Delta\chi_5 = $ dot. We write in all these scores throughout the key on a width of 23, and add up the columns to give an improved $\Delta\chi_5$. With this we de-chi ΔK_5 in place of the earlier $\Delta\chi_5$ used, and count for $\Delta\chi_4$. This process continues, going back to $\Delta\chi_5$ after $\Delta\chi_1$, until all the $\Delta\chi$'s are completed. These $\Delta\chi$'s must obviously integrate into legal undifferenced chis, the even or odd number of crosses in the $\Delta\chi$'s will tell us whether the original assumption was a $\Delta\psi'$ / or 8. With the undifferenced chis obtained, from the $\Delta\chi$'s we de-chi the undifferenced K to give ψ', from which we derive the psi wheels by taking out the extensions.

Appendix 7

$\Delta\chi$-Method

Max Newman

Editor's Introduction

Extraordinarily, two very secret wartime documents in Newman's handwriting were removed from Bletchley Park by unknown means. These documents set out the fundamentals of Tunny breaking. One of them, which Newman entitled '$\Delta\chi$-Method', is reproduced in this appendix.

Jack Good describes the rediscovery of the two documents:

In October 1994 I received a letter from David Whitehead who he said had serviced equipment developed by Flowers and Chandler prior to their work on Colossus. One of his colleagues, Ron Batch, who had worked at BP for a short time, had come across twenty sheets of hand-written notes which Dr Arnold Lynch thought might be of interest to me. (Arnold Lynch was a pre-war friend and one of the designers of the photoelectric reader used in Colossus.) Whitehead sent photocopies of those notes to me. There are two documents, one of twelve pages, and one of eleven. I think Newman must have given the documents to engineers, especially Flowers. Both documents were obviously written after there had been some experience in the use of Heath Robinson. The first document was written by Newman and me. It describes 'Expected values, set totals and necessary lengths'. The second document, written by Newman, is headed '$\Delta\chi$-Method'. I think it fair to say that both documents are based on ideas of Newman, Michie, and me, and also on Newman's and Michie's experience in the Testery. Michie once said to me during the war that when he has a good idea he tries to make Newman think he thought of it himself because that strategy speeds up the effective use of the idea!

I. General Ideas

1. <u>Notations</u>. P = plain language, Z = cipher, '5' is used for 'fig-shift', as [on page 349], '+' for actual addition, i.e. A + P means A added to P, not three letters.

   If M is any message, ΔM is got by adding M to itself displaced one, thus:

This transcription of Newman's handwritten material is published by permission of William Newman. Material in square brackets has been added by the editor. The diagrams have been redrawn.

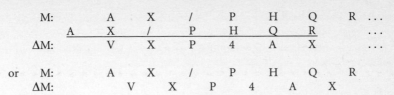

	M:		A	X	/	P	H	Q	R	...
		A	X	/	P	H	Q	R		...
	ΔM:		V	X	P	4	A	X		...

| or | M: | | A | X | / | P | H | Q | R |
| | ΔM: | | | V | X | P | 4 | A | X |

Note that a <u>repeat</u> (the same letter twice in succession) in M corresponds to a <u>blank</u> (/) in ΔM.

2. The machine methods of setting are based on counting letters or signs which are commoner in plain language than in random stuff, and therefore commoner when wheels are added in the right position than in the wrong. For example '9' (space) occurs in random series no more often than any other letter—i.e. about once in 32 times; whereas in most plain texts it occurs about once in 4 or 5. If it were possible to decipher the text with all possible settings of the 12 wheels, one after another, the true settings would stand out by giving one '9' in 4 or 5. But to set all 12 wheels at once would entail examining

$41 \times 31 \times 29 \times 26 \times 23 \times 37 \times 61 \times 43 \times 47 \times 51 \times 53 \times 59$ positions, roughly 10^{19}.

It is therefore necessary to break up the search.

The simplest idea is to look at one impulse at a time. For example, the dot in

impulse 1 of $\dot{\times}$ makes dots more common than crosses in impulse 1. If then Z_1 is

deciphered with all possible positions of χ_1, ψ_1, μ_{37} and μ_{61}, the true settings will be those that give the most dots as against crosses in the resulting P_1. But this would still involve looking at $41 \times 43 \times 37 \times 61 =$ about 4 million settings. Our machine [Robinson—Ed.] will do the count of about 2000 involved in looking at one position in 1 second, and 4 million seconds is about six weeks, too long for setting one message.

The following more complicated scheme, which is the one actually used, enables us to set only <u>two</u> wheels at once and hence look at only about 1000 settings. It makes use of two facts.

(1) <u>Repeats</u> are very common (about 1 in 5) in certain kinds of traffic (but not in all). It arises chiefly because these lines double all their stops, spaces, letter shifts, etc. On RB (Rome Bream) the operator always sends 99, 88, 55 etc.; but at the Berlin end of the same line only single stops, 9, 8, 5 are used, and the property fails.

(2) All the ψ-wheels stop when there is a motor-dot, and move when there is a motor $\times$. This means that $\Delta\psi = /$ for all positions where there is a motor dot, and this is ·3 of all positions. Now

$$\Delta P = \Delta Z + \Delta\chi + \Delta\psi$$

and therefore $\Delta P = \Delta Z + \Delta\chi$ when $\Delta\psi = /$; i.e. if we assume $\Delta P = \Delta Z + \Delta\chi$ we shall be right in about ⅓ of all cases. But there is a chance of 1 in 5 that $\Delta P = /$. The effect of all this is that if $\Delta\chi$ with correct settings is added to ΔZ, there is a stronger chance of its being / than if $\Delta\chi$ with wrong settings is added; and this still remains true if only two impulses are looked at.

The upshot is, then, that if we consider

$$\Delta Z_1 + \Delta Z_2 + \Delta\chi_1 + \Delta\chi_2,$$

with various χ settings, the true settings will give • for the value more often than the wrong settings; i.e. if we count the number of dots, the settings giving the highest total are likely to be correct.

This is what the machine does. It calculates ΔZ_1 by adding the Z_1-impulses in two successive letters, and then adds $\Delta Z_1, \Delta Z_2, \Delta\chi_1, \Delta\chi_2$.

3. When 3 (or 4) χ-positions have been found there is a different method of finding the last two (or one). If the message is de-χ-ed on the known positions (say χ_1, χ_2, χ_4) the other two settings may be looked for as those giving the <u>greatest number of repeats</u> in the clear. That is, we are given the five impulses

$$\Delta Z_1 + \Delta\chi_1 = \Delta P_1$$
$$\Delta Z_2 + \Delta\chi_2 = \Delta P_2$$
$$\Delta Z_3 = \Delta Z_3$$
$$\Delta Z_4 + \Delta\chi_4 = \Delta P_4$$
$$\Delta Z_5 = \Delta Z_5$$

the χ's being correctly set. If $\Delta\chi_3$ and $\Delta\chi_5$ are added to ΔZ_3 and ΔZ_5 in their <u>right</u> positions, the resulting five impulses are those of ΔP, which is / whenever P has a repeat — i.e. about once in 5 or 6 times. Hence the settings of these two wheels are given by taking those that make ΔP, as calculated from them, have the most /'s.

The advantage of this method is that it uses the very strong property of having repeats in all the five impulses separately.

4. <u>Finding the motor-setting</u>. Suppose all the χ-settings known. Let the message be de-χ-ed. For reasons given above, all repeats in P that fall on motor dots appear as repeats in the de-χ-ed message. Hence among the motor dots there is 1 repeat in 5 in the de-χ, whereas among the motor crosses there is only 1 in 32. Thus the motor-position will be found as that in which as many dots as possible are opposite repeats in the de-χ.

e.g.	de-χ:	A	B	P	Q	Q	X	R	R	R	S	H	H	V	V	O	A
	'good' posn. of M:	×	×	×	×	•	×	×	•	•	×	×	×	×	•	×	×
	'bad' posn. of M:	×	×	×	×	×	•	×	×	•	•	×	×	×	×	•	×

Sometimes it can be seen by inspection that certain short stretches of de-χ (say 60 letters) have exceptionally heavy repeats, say 12 in 60. This probably means that a single letter occurs 30 or 40 times in the clear. In this case nearly all these repeats correspond to motor dot, and the setting can be found by hand in a few minutes, simply by sliding a (printed) copy of the motor-key along the stretch of 60 till a good fit is obtained.

5. <u>Finding the ψ-settings</u>. This is done more easily by hand in many cases. It can be tried by the machine as follows when χ- and motor-settings are known.

First <u>contract</u> the de-χ, i.e. cut out those letters that are opposite motor-dots. This cuts out all the extra repeats that come through on motor dots, so that the repeats should be about random once more. If now $\Delta\psi_1$ and $\Delta\psi_2$ are correctly combined with $\Delta Z_1 + \Delta\chi_1$ and $\Delta Z_2 + \Delta\chi_2$ (already known) giving ΔP_1 and ΔP_2, these will both be 'dot' more often than 1 in 4, the random frequency—provided the plain language is favourable.

II. Tape Routines

<u>Long and short runs</u>:

(α) When neither of the settings of the two wheels on a tape is known, a length of message-tape <u>prime</u> to the two wheel-lengths must be used. The simplest way to secure this is to make the message actually prime (but see below).

The length of such a run will be from 15 to 75 minutes. The exact time (in minutes):

$$\frac{\text{wheel tape length} \times \text{message tape length}}{2000 \times 60}$$

E.g. $\chi_1 + \chi_4$ against message 3373 long:

$$\text{time of run} = \frac{1066 \times 3373}{60 \times 2000} = 29 \text{ minutes.}$$

For such <u>long runs</u> the wheel tape is set at $(1,1)$:

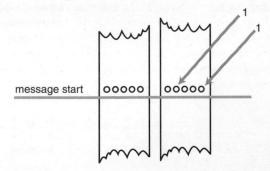

(β) If the (χ_1, χ_4)-tape is run against a message whose length is a multiple of 41 ("41χ-tape") the χ_1-setting will remain fixed. Hence if the χ_1-setting is known (say 27), the χ_4-setting may be found by running the (χ_1, χ_4)-tape against a 41×-message with χ_1 set at the correct position:

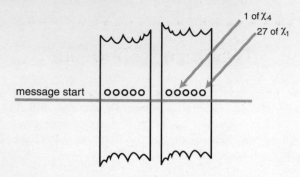

The length of these <u>short runs</u> is only a few minutes. E.g. χ_1 and χ_4 against 3373 is

$$\frac{26 \times 3373}{2000 \times 60} = 3/4 \text{ minute.}$$

Actually two or more complete cycles should be done to check the recurrence every 26 counts.

In favourable cases the χ's can be found, in either of two ways, by two long and one short run.

(a) 1.   Run χ_1, χ_2 against prime length (<u>long run</u>).

(If this is not successful it is better to abandon the message altogether.)

   2.   Run χ_1, χ_4 or χ_2, χ_5 on known χ_1 setting (<u>short run</u>).
   3.   De-χ on three known χ's and set other two χ's by counting repeats (<u>long run</u>).

or

(b) 1.   Run χ_1, χ_2 (long run)
   2.   Run χ_4, χ_5 (long run)
   3.   De-χ on impulses 1, 2, 4, 5 and find χ_5 [*sic*] by counting repeats (short run).

It is advisable to begin a new message $(\chi_1 \chi_2)$ while the de-χing is in progress.

Appendix 8

Newman's Theorem

Friedrich L. Bauer

Counting Coincidences

The idea of the 'index of coincidence' between two texts (often abbreviated IC) goes back to the American cryptologist William Friedman in 1925. The index of coincidence, here called simply *kappa*, is the number of coinciding characters divided by the total number of characters. Kappa for two arbitrary ciphertexts (based on an alphabet of 26 characters) is normally close to $1/26 = 3.8$ per cent. It is usually much higher when two texts are in the same natural language—about 7 per cent for English or German. This is so even if the two texts are encrypted (in phase) by the same key.

Two 5-bit characters a and b coincide if and only if their sum modulo 2 is •••••, i.e. / (see Appendix 2). Counting coincidences between two texts therefore amounts to counting the number of occurrences of / in the sum modulo 2 of the two texts. Figure 1 illustrates this in the special case where the second text is simply the first text shifted by one character. Coincidences are marked by an asterisk. The text is part of a German message dated 13 July 1943, from Generaloberst Keitel to Generalstab des Heeres. Figure 1 shows 440 characters of the message, beginning 'der fuehrer' (the Fuehrer). (In this appendix, the symbols '1', '2', '3', '4', and '5' are used for the teleprinter control characters 'letter shift', 'space', 'figure shift', 'carriage return', and 'line feed', respectively. This is in accordance with the International Teletype Alphabet (see Appendix 12). At Bletchley Park, the symbols '8', '9', '5', '3', '4' were used instead (see Appendix 2).)

The sum modulo 2 shown in Figure 1 is in fact the delta of the German plaintext. Following the procedure set out by Newman in Section 1 of Appendix 7, the delta is formed by shifting the text by one character and adding. Coincidences occur where the delta is /.

There are only 14 letter coincidences, producing a kappa of $14/440 = 3.2$ per cent. This is because the index of coincidence for plaintexts shifted by one place is lower than the usual kappa of 7.6 per cent for plain German. However, if a count is made of all 32 symbols in the delta, the following surprising distribution is obtained:

```
/  a  b c  d e  f g  h  i  j  k  l  m  n  o p  q  r  s  t  u  v  w  x  y  z  2  3  4  5  1
14 10 2 6 11 3 33 15 5 10 30 14 7  0 10 9 13 9 17 9  5 22 14 17 7 21 16 12 61 17 15 6
```

```
d e r 1 2 f u e h r e r 1 2 h a t 1 2 f u e r 1 2 d i e 1 2 w e i t e r e 1 2 k
e r 1 2 f u e h r e r 1 2 h a t 1 2 f u e r 1 2 d i e 1 2 w e i t e r e 1 2 k a
4 j y 3 d r i y v j j y 3 t q w k 3 d r i j y 3 f k u v 3 q l u p z j j v 3 j a

a m p f f u e h r u n g 1 2 a u f 1 2 s i z i l i e n 1 2 f o l g e n d e 1 2 r
m p f f u e h r u n g 1 2 a u f 1 2 s i z i l i e n 1 2 f o l g e n d e 1 2 r i
1 r 3 / r i y v f j p s 3 u 2 r l 3 e a q q h h u f w 3 d y r 4 3 f s 4 v 3 c n

i c h t l i n i e n 2 b e f o h l e n y y 2 3 3 q m l 1 1 2 n a c h 1 2 a u s f
c h t l i n i e n 2 b e f o h l e n y y 2 3 3 q m l 1 1 2 n a c h 1 2 a u s f a
4 g 2 5 h r r u f 4 x o n y n i w f b / z 1 / o 1 c f / 3 4 k f g j 3 u 2 5 4 c

a l l 1 2 d e r 1 2 m a s s e 1 2 d e r 1 2 i t a l i e n i s c h e n 1 2 k r a
l l 1 2 d e r 1 2 m a s s e 1 2 d e r 1 2 i t a l i e n i s c h e n 1 2 k r a e
z / f 3 f 4 j y 3 o 1 i / 2 v 3 f 4 j y 3 5 p w z h u f r a j g y f w 3 j s d 5

e f t e 1 2 i m 1 2 a n g r i f f s r a u m 1 2 r e i c h e n 1 2 d i e 1 2 d e
f t e 1 2 i m 1 2 a n g r i f f s r a u m 1 2 r e i c h e n 1 2 d i e 1 2 d e u
n x z v 3 5 g a 3 u k p t n j / 4 k d 2 3 a 3 c j u 4 g y f w 3 f k u v 3 f 4 i

u t s c h e n 1 2 k r a e f t e 1 2 a l l e i n 1 2 a u c h 1 2 b e i 1 2 g r u
t s c h e n 1 2 k r a e f t e 1 2 a l l e i n 1 2 a u c h 1 2 b e i 1 2 g r u p
q y j g y f w 3 j s d 5 n x z v 3 u z / w u r w 3 u 2 d g j 3 x o u b 3 v t f z

p p e n w e i s e r 1 2 z u s a m m e n f a s s u n g 1 2 n i c h t 1 2 m e h r
p e n w e i s e r 1 2 z u s a m m e n f a s s u n g 1 2 n i c h t 1 2 m e h r 1
/ q f 1 l u a 2 j y 3 y p 5 i 1 / x f e c i / 5 j p s 3 4 r 4 g 2 k 3 o x y v y

1 2 a u s y 1 2 u m 1 2 d e n 1 2 g e l a n d e t e n 1 2 f e i n d 1 2 i m 1 2
2 a u s y 1 2 u m 1 2 d e n 1 2 g e l a n d e t e n 1 2 f e i n d 1 2 i m 1 2 a
3 u 2 5 t r 3 a 3 a 3 f 4 f w 3 v 3 w z k s 4 z z f w 3 d n u r s p 3 5 g a 3 u

a n g r i f f 1 2 i n 1 2 d a s 1 2 m e e r 1 2 z u r u e c k z u w e r f e n x
n g r i f f 1 2 i n 1 2 d a s 1 2 m e e r 1 2 z u r u e c k z u w e r f e n x 1
k p t n j / l 3 5 r w 3 f r i g 3 o x / j y 3 y p f f i k e v p h l j u n f z 5

1 2 m i t 1 2 w e i t e r e n 1 2 f e i n d l a n d u n g e n 1 2 a u c h 1 2 i
2 m i t 1 2 w e i t e r e n 1 2 f e i n d l a n d u n g e n 1 2 a u c h 1 2 i m
3 o g p k 3 q l u p z j j f w 3 d n u r s 3 z k s c j p 3 f w 3 u 2 d g j 3 5 g

m 1 2 w e s t e n 1 2 d e r 1 2 i n s e l 1 2 m u s s 1 2 g e r e c h n e t 1 2
1 2 w e s t e n 1 2 d e r 1 2 i n s e l 1 2 m u s s 1 2 g e r e c h n e t 1 2 w
a 3 q l 2 y z f w 3 f 4 j y 3 5 r d 2 w f 3 o 3 5 / g 3 v 3 j j k g o f z k 3 q
```

Figure 1. Where the two texts coincide a / appears in the sum modulo 2.

f occurs in the delta with kappa of 7.5 per cent, j with 6.8 per cent, and 3 with a thumping 13.9 per cent (the average is 1/32 = 3.125 per cent). In short, the delta shows a much bigger deviation from randomness than the German plaintext itself. This is the starting point of the delta process that Max Newman describes in Appendix 7.

There are also significant deviations from randomness when a count is made for each one of the five impulses (tracks) of the delta, as Table 1 shows.

Table 1. Frequency count of dot and cross in Δp

impulse	1	2	3	4	5
count of × (per cent)	61.6	60.5	43.4	57.3	47.0
count of • (per cent)	38.4	39.5	56.6	42.7	53.0

Notation

Some special notation is used in this appendix. p is the plain letter stream, c is the cipher letter stream, k is the key stream, and d is the de-chi. $\hat{\psi}$ is the extended ψ-stream (written ψ' in Bletchley Park notation—see Appendix 10). The sum modulo 2 of a and b is written $a \oplus b$; + is used for ordinary addition.

Taking our cue from Newman's 'Expected values, set totals and necessary lengths' (see Appendix 7), the notation

$$\text{Prob}[\Delta\hat{\psi}_i = \bullet] = \tfrac{1}{2}$$

is used to abbreviate 'the probability of dot occuring in the ith impulse of $\Delta\hat{\psi}$ is 50 per cent'.

This useful notation can be employed to capture the information in each cell of Table 1. For example, $\text{Prob}[\Delta p_1 = \times] = 0.616$.

German Efforts to Achieve Randomness

The Germans must have realised that since each chi-wheel had a constant period, an opponent could discover the period by means of a small number of tests, say 41 for the wheel χ_1. The Germans hit on the idea, first implemented in March 1942, of selecting the cam patterns of the motor-wheels and the psi-wheels so that $\Delta\hat{\psi}$ was 'close to random'. (This is described as '$ab = \tfrac{1}{2}$' in the timeline in Appendix 1.) 'Close to random' means that for each $\hat{\psi}_1, \hat{\psi}_2, \hat{\psi}_3, \hat{\psi}_4, \hat{\psi}_5$, the probability of $\Delta\hat{\psi}_i = \times$ and of $\Delta\hat{\psi}_i = \bullet$ coincide:

$$\text{Prob}[\Delta\hat{\psi}_i = \times] = \text{Prob}[\Delta\hat{\psi}_i = \bullet] = \tfrac{1}{2}.$$

By 1943 the Germans were implementing this procedure regularly.

Newman's Theorem

Newman's handwritten notes smuggled out of Bletchley Park (see Appendix 7) contain a basic theorem on the probabilities of the occurrence of • and × in the modulo 2 sum of two bit-streams a, b. The theorem is:

$$\text{Prob}[a \oplus b = \bullet] = \tfrac{1}{2} + 2 \times (\text{Prob}[a = \bullet] - \tfrac{1}{2}) \times (\text{Prob}[b = \bullet] - \tfrac{1}{2}),$$
$$\text{Prob}[a \oplus b = \times] = \tfrac{1}{2} - 2 \times (\tfrac{1}{2} - \text{Prob}[a = \times]) \times (\tfrac{1}{2} - \text{Prob}[b = \times]).$$

The proof of the theorem runs as follows:

Since $a \oplus b = \bullet$ when and only when either $(a = \bullet$ and $b = \bullet)$ or $(a = \times$ and $b = \times)$,

$\mathrm{Prob}[a \oplus b = \bullet] = \mathrm{Prob}[a = \bullet] \times \mathrm{Prob}[b = \bullet] + \mathrm{Prob}[a = \times] \times \mathrm{Prob}[b = \times]$

$= \mathrm{Prob}[a = \bullet] \times \mathrm{Prob}[b = \bullet] + (1 - \mathrm{Prob}[a = \bullet]) \times (1 - \mathrm{Prob}[b = \bullet])$

$= 2 \times \mathrm{Prob}[a = \bullet] \times \mathrm{Prob}[b = \bullet] - \mathrm{Prob}[a = \bullet] - \mathrm{Prob}[b = \bullet] + 1$

$= \frac{1}{2} + 2 \times (\mathrm{Prob}[a = \bullet] \times \mathrm{Prob}[b = \bullet] - \frac{1}{2}\mathrm{Prob}[a = \bullet] - \frac{1}{2}\mathrm{Prob}[b = \bullet] + \frac{1}{4})$

$= \frac{1}{2} + 2 \times (\mathrm{Prob}[a = \bullet] - \frac{1}{2}) \times (\mathrm{Prob}[b = \bullet] - \frac{1}{2})$.

Similarly for $\mathrm{Prob}[a \oplus b = \times]$. *End of proof*

Applying the Theorem

According to Newman's Theorem, the probability of the occurrence of $\times$ in a modulo 2 sum of two bit streams is $\frac{1}{2}$ if it is $\frac{1}{2}$ for one of the bit streams. It follows that, for $i = 1, 2, 3, 4, 5$

$$\mathrm{Prob}[\Delta p_i \oplus \Delta \hat{\psi}_i = \times] = \tfrac{1}{2}$$

and thus

$$\mathrm{Prob}[\Delta c_i \oplus \Delta \chi_i = \times] = \mathrm{Prob}[\Delta c_i \oplus \Delta \chi_i = \bullet] = \tfrac{1}{2}.$$

A desire to achieve this balanced situation was presumably a reason for the introduction of the motor wheels. But there was a snag. Tutte revealed the surprising fact that although each bit stream was in itself 'close to random', the two taken together could provide information about the corresponding pair of chi-wheels.

This can be seen mathematically as follows. Since

$$\mathrm{Prob}[\Delta \hat{\psi}_i = \times] = \mathrm{Prob}[\Delta \psi_i = \times] \times m, \text{ where } m = \mathrm{Prob}[\text{motor wheels move}] < 1$$

and

$$\mathrm{Prob}[\Delta \psi_i = \times] \times m = \mathrm{Prob}[\Delta \psi_j = \times] \times m = \tfrac{1}{2},$$

it follows that

$$\mathrm{Prob}[\Delta \psi_i = \times] = \mathrm{Prob}[\Delta \psi_j = \times] = q, \text{ where } q \times m = \tfrac{1}{2}.$$

This means that there is a common value $q > \frac{1}{2}$ for all five streams. To avoid this, the Germans should have used five motor wheels in place of the single second motor wheel (see Appendices 10 and 11). ($q = 0.71$ was indeed observed by BP in March 1942, while in August 1941 $q = \approx \frac{1}{2}$ had been observed.)

Newman's Theorem enables the derivation of an important result concerning Δd, the deltaed de-chi. Since

$$\Delta d = \Delta \hat{\psi} \oplus \Delta p,$$
$$\mathrm{Prob}[\Delta d_i \oplus \Delta d_j = \bullet] = \mathrm{Prob}[(\Delta \hat{\psi}_i \oplus \Delta \hat{\psi}_j) \oplus (\Delta p_i \oplus \Delta p_j) = \bullet].$$

According to Newman's Theorem,

$$\mathrm{Prob}[\Delta \psi_i \oplus \Delta \psi_j = \bullet] = \tfrac{1}{2} + 2 \times (\mathrm{Prob}[\Delta \psi_i = \bullet] - \tfrac{1}{2}) \times (\mathrm{Prob}[\Delta \psi_j = \bullet] - \tfrac{1}{2})$$
$$= \tfrac{1}{2} + 2 \times (q - \tfrac{1}{2})^2.$$

Furthermore, $\Delta\hat{\psi}_i \oplus \Delta\hat{\psi}_j = \bullet$ results if:

either the wheels do not move, probability $(1 - m)$;
or they do move and $\Delta\psi_i \oplus \Delta\psi_j = \bullet$, probability $m \times (\frac{1}{2} + 2 \times (q - \frac{1}{2})^2)$.

Altogether:

$$\text{Prob}[\Delta\hat{\psi}_i \oplus \Delta\hat{\psi}_j = \bullet] = (1 - m) + m \times (\frac{1}{2} + 2 \times (q - \frac{1}{2})^2).$$

But surprisingly, m drops out. Since $q \times m = \frac{1}{2}, \frac{1}{2} = \text{Prob}[\Delta\psi_i = \times] \times m$:

$$(1 - m) + m \times (\frac{1}{2} + 2 \times (q - \frac{1}{2})^2) = 1 + m \times 2 \times q \times (q - 1) = 1 + (q - 1) = q.$$

Therefore

$$\text{Prob}[\Delta\hat{\psi}_i \oplus \Delta\hat{\psi}_j = \bullet] = \text{Prob}[\Delta\psi_i = \times] = q > \tfrac{1}{2}. \tag{A}$$

This shows that $\Delta\hat{\psi}_i \oplus \Delta\hat{\psi}_j$ is not random.

Continuing the derivation, let r be the proportion of repeated letters in the plaintext. $\Delta p_i \oplus \Delta p_j = \bullet$ can come about in the following ways:

(1) $\Delta p_i = \bullet$ and $\Delta p_j = \bullet$ because of a repeat, with probability r.

There remains the case of a non-repeat, with probability $1 - r$. $1 - r$ is divided equally among the four possible values of $(\Delta p_i, \Delta p_j)$, $(\bullet, \bullet)$, $(\bullet, \times)$, $(\times, \bullet)$, $(\times, \times)$. Thus:

(2) $\Delta p_i = \bullet$ and $\Delta p_j = \bullet$, with probability $\frac{1}{4}(1 - r)$;
(3) $\Delta p_i = \times$ and $\Delta p_j = \times$, with probability $\frac{1}{4}(1 - r)$.

Altogether:

$$\text{Prob}[\Delta p_i \oplus \Delta p_j = \bullet] = r + \tfrac{1}{4}(1 - r) + \tfrac{1}{4}(1 - r) = \tfrac{1}{2}(1 + r). \tag{B}$$

Applying Newman's Theorem to (A) and (B):

$$\text{Prob}[\Delta d_i \oplus \Delta d_j = \bullet] = \tfrac{1}{2} + 2 \times (q - \tfrac{1}{2}) \times (\tfrac{1}{2}(1 + r) - \tfrac{1}{2})$$
$$= \tfrac{1}{2} + (q - \tfrac{1}{2}) \times r > \tfrac{1}{2},$$

since $r > 0$ for meaningful plaintext streams Δp_i and Δp_j.

This shows that the sum of two Δd impulse-streams is not random. In short, despite the German attempt to achieve randomness, Tunny was unsafe.

The deviation from $\frac{1}{2}$ (known as the 'bulge' in Bletchley jargon) is proportional to the deviation of $\text{Prob}[\Delta\psi_i = \times]$ from $\frac{1}{2}$ and to the proportion r of repeated characters in the plaintext.

Typically, $q = 0.75$, $r = 0.2$. Thus $\text{Prob}[\Delta d_i \oplus \Delta d_j = \bullet] = 0.55$. It follows that a probably correct wheel setting is obtained, for a text of length n, if the score for $\bullet$ in a stream $\Delta d_i \oplus \Delta d_j$ is about $0.55 \times n$—a figure not so far away from the random case $0.5 \times n$.

Rectangling

Frank Carter

Tutte's Method

The first method for wheel breaking, using only information from a single message, was devised by Tutte, and was a remarkable development of his earlier method for wheel setting (see Appendix 4). The new technique, which became known as 'rectangling', was a lengthy and complicated procedure, and the following account covers only the basic principles. The objective is to find the cam patterns on the χ_1 and χ_2 wheels, and Tutte's approach was to begin by finding the corresponding delta patterns for these wheels. Once the delta patterns of the wheels were found it was a relatively simple task to recover the original cam patterns (this was known as 'integrating' the wheel). Even though rectangling was a hand method, it was carried out in the Newmanry.

Rectangling depended on the remarkable theoretical principle, deduced by Tutte, that if the χ_1 and χ_2 wheels are set to their correct starting positions, the binary elements ($\times$ or $\bullet$) given by the expression $(\Delta Z_1 + \Delta Z_2) + (\Delta \chi_1 + \Delta \chi_2)$ are more likely to be dots than crosses (where Z_1 and Z_2 are the first and second impulses of the cipher character). Since the dots occurred only when $\Delta Z_1 + \Delta Z_2 = \Delta \chi_1 + \Delta \chi_2$, it followed that if a known binary element, derived from a cipher character by means of the expression $\Delta Z_1 + \Delta Z_2$, was used as an estimate for the corresponding (unknown) binary element represented by the expression $\Delta \chi_1 + \Delta \chi_2$, then there was a greater chance of the estimate being correct than of it being wrong!

Constructing a Rectangle

The fact that the binary elements obtained by using the expression $\Delta Z_1 + \Delta Z_2$ could be used as estimates for the corresponding binary elements represented by the expression $\Delta \chi_1 + \Delta \chi_2$ was applied in the following way. Suppose that a cipher message consisted of $41 \times 31 = 1271$ characters (i.e. exactly same as the number of possible combinations of χ_1 and χ_2 wheel positions), and that the sequence of 1271 dots and crosses of $\Delta Z_1 + \Delta Z_2$ had been written out in a continuous line. These dots and crosses were then copied in the same sequence one by one into the cells of a rectangular table drawn on a large sheet of paper, made up of 41 rows of cells and with 31 cells in each row in a way now to be described and explained.

Entering the characters into the cells

The positions of the cells in the rectangle were defined by using their row and column numbers as coordinates, so that the cell in the top left-hand corner was described as cell $(1, 1)$, and the cell in the bottom right-hand corner as cell $(41, 31)$, and each entry was placed into the cell of the rectangle that had coordinates representing the corresponding positions of the χ_1 and χ_2 wheels. The χ_1 wheel completed a revolution after stepping through 41 positions, and the χ_2 wheel completed a revolution after stepping though only 31 positions.

The first entry into the rectangle would be made in cell $(1, 1)$, the second in cell $(2, 2)$, the third in cell $(3, 3)$, and so on diagonally down the rectangle until one had been made in cell $(31, 31)$, and then the next entries were made in the sequence of cells: $(32, 1), (33, 2), (34, 3), \ldots, (41, 10)$. After placing the next entry in cell $(1, 11)$, the following ones would be made in the sequence of cells: $(2, 12), (3, 13) (4, 14), \ldots$ and so on. In this way the entries were made in sequences of cells that formed diagonals down and across the rectangle, the last entry being placed in cell $(41, 31)$. When this stage had been reached, all the 1271 cells in the rectangle would contain a single entry.

The result of this process was a rectangular table of cells in which a cell entry had been made for every possible pair of positions of the two wheels. Each cell contained a single estimate of $\Delta\chi_1 + \Delta\chi_2$ for the elements $\Delta\chi_1$ and $\Delta\chi_2$ of the two wheels, at the positions on the wheels given respectively by the two coordinates of the cell.

Strengthening the evidence

The single estimates obtained in this way were too unreliable to be of any use, because each had only slightly more than an even chance of being correct. However, it was possible to obtain several independent estimates to enter into each cell, so that they could be combined to obtain a more reliable single estimate. This was done by using a much longer cipher message. If, for example, a message contained 12,710 characters, the entire process just described could be repeated ten times, so that ten estimates for each cell would be obtained, and the majority score of dots over crosses could then be determined. Three illustrative examples are shown in Figure 1.

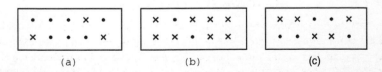

(a) (b) (c)

Figure 1. Typical final entries for three cells: (a) majority = 4, (b) majority = −6, (c) majority = 0.

These majority values were recorded in the corresponding cell in a new 41×31 rectangular grid, as illustrated in Figure 2, with a majority of dots being recorded as a positive score and a majority of crosses as a negative one (a tie was recorded as zero).

At this stage none of the elements of either the $\Delta\chi_1$ or $\Delta\chi_2$ patterns were known, and so these are represented by the '?' symbols shown along the top and left-hand sides of the rectangle. However, in many rectangles the majority scores in a large number of the cells provided accurate estimates ($\times$ or $\cdot$) of the sum of the corresponding pairs of these elements. These majorities were subsequently used as the basis of another procedure, shortly to be described, from which accurate estimates for the *individual* elements of both the $\Delta\chi_1$ and $\Delta\chi_2$ patterns were obtained.

Before giving a description of the process for finding the individual elements of the $\Delta\chi_1$ and $\Delta\chi_2$ patterns, a simple introductory analogy may be helpful. The tabulations in Figure 3 show the results of adding together certain pairs of positive whole

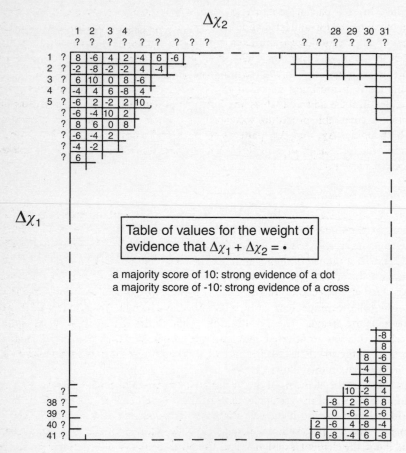

Figure 2. A 41×31 rectangle for the χ_1 and χ_2 wheels.

+	?	?	?	?
?	8	6	9	4
?	7	5	8	3
?	6	4	7	2
?	9	7	10	5

+	5	3↓	6	1
3	8	6	9	4
2	7	5	8	3
1	6	4	7	2
4	9	7	10	5

An addition table for pairs of unknown numbers

If one number is known then all the others can be deduced

Figure 3. A simple analogy of a rectangle.

numbers. In the first table the results of all the additions are given, but the individual numbers in each pair are not. These unknown numbers are represented by the '?' symbols along the top and left-hand side (this table is analogous to the rectangle). The values of all these unknown numbers can be found if any one of them is known, as shown in the second diagram. Here, as an example, the number (indicated by the arrow) is 3. All the other individual numbers can now be deduced, as shown.

This analogy must not be taken too far since, in contrast to the exact values contained in these addition tables, the information contained in a rectangle was less precise. A remarkable procedure was developed which enabled close approximations for both of the $\Delta\chi_1$ and $\Delta\chi_2$ patterns to be found, commencing with a 'starting pattern' which consisted of estimates of a few of the elements in either the $\Delta\chi_1$ pattern or the $\Delta\chi_2$ pattern.

Starting the procedure

It was very important that the estimates in the starting pattern were accurate, and several methods were devised by means of which these elements could be identified as either dots or crosses, with a high probability of correctness. The method described here is the least refined of these, but it has the advantage of being simple.

Suppose the objective is to try to obtain accurate estimates for some of the elements of $\Delta\chi_2$. First an inspection is made of all the rows of the rectangle and, by temporarily discarding all the minus signs, a row is identified in which the sum of the resulting cell numbers is the greatest. Then, continuing to ignore the minus signs, about eight of the cells in this row are selected on the basis of containing larger numbers than any of the others in the row. The cells in this row are then used to derive a fragmentary $\Delta\chi_2$ starting pattern, in the following way.

Assume that the elements of the starting pattern are to be placed below the corresponding columns of the rectangle. Each of the selected cells in the identified row is considered in turn, and if the cell originally had a positive majority score then the element of the $\Delta\chi_2$ pattern immediately below the column containing it is designated •, and if not, the element is designated ×. The other elements of the starting pattern are not designated. The designation just made is arbitrary, and the correct value may be the opposite of the one chosen. That is to say, the final $\Delta\chi_1$ and $\Delta\chi_2$ patterns obtained may have their crosses and dots interchanged. It was easy to discover if this had happened at a later stage of the wheel breaking process, and to make the necessary corrections.

The resulting fragmentary $\Delta\chi_2$ pattern would consist of, say, 23 unknown elements and eight elements to which either × or • had been assigned, each assignment having a high probability of being correct (subject to the caveat just mentioned concerning the possible interchanging of × and •). This fragmentary pattern was used in conjunction with the information contained in the rectangle to find a first approximation to the complete $\Delta\chi_1$ pattern.

Figure 4 shows a small part of the rectangle in which each cell contains the majority score of dots or crosses, together with the most probable cell entry (× or •) based on the score. Five of the elements of an initial fragmentary $\Delta\chi_2$ pattern are shown underneath the rectangle.

By taking an element of the $\Delta\chi_2$ pattern and comparing it with the entry (× or •) in a cell of the rectangle that is located above it, a deduction can be made about the identity of the $\Delta\chi_1$ element in the same horizontal row as that cell. For example, the element of $\Delta\chi_2$ below the fourth column of the rectangle in Figure 4 is ×, and the entry in the cell just above it, at the bottom of the fourth column of the rectangle, is •; so, for this cell, $\Delta\chi_1 + \Delta\chi_2 = •$. Since $\Delta\chi_2 = ×$, it follows that $\Delta\chi_1 = ×$.

The deduction that $\Delta\chi_1 = ×$ has been entered into the corresponding cell in Figure 5, in the bottom row of the fourth column, together with the weight of evidence for the deduction. The weights of evidence are obtained from the majority scores after discarding any negative signs. All the deductions shown in Figure 5 were obtained in the same way.

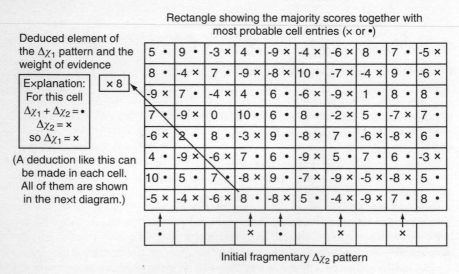

Figure 4. Finding the χ_1 pattern—first stage.

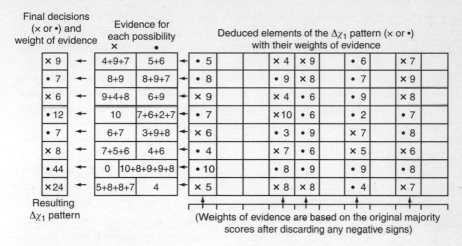

Figure 5. Finding the χ_1 pattern—second stage.

The evidence relating to each element of $\Delta\chi_1$ given in each row can be combined. For example, the combined weight of evidence that the element of $\Delta\chi_1$ in the bottom row is a cross is $5 + 8 + 8 + 7$, while the weight of evidence that it is a dot is 4, giving a total in favour of cross of $28 - 4 = 24$.

Figure 5 shows all the outcomes that can be obtained in this way, together with the corresponding weights of evidence. Only eight rows of the rectangle are shown, but if the complete rectangle is used then this process can be extended to produce a set of estimates for all 41 elements of $\Delta\chi_1$.

An algorithmic approach

This rather complicated procedure can be reduced to the following algorithm:

1. Consider in turn each column of the rectangle for which there is an assigned element of the $\Delta\chi_2$ pattern at its base. If this element is × then change the signs of all the majority scores in that column.
2. Determine all of the row sums from the resulting numbers (i.e. the sums of the numbers in each row taking into account the changes in sign).
3. If a row sum > 0 then the element of $\Delta\chi_1$ to the left of the row is designated •; otherwise this element is designated ×.

Convergence

This algorithm can also be used to obtain an estimate for the $\Delta\chi_2$ pattern given an initial estimate for the $\Delta\chi_1$ pattern. The only modification required is to interchange the references to rows and columns.

After finishing the task of finding estimates for all 41 elements of the $\Delta\chi_1$ pattern, the same process can be carried out again, but now starting with this $\Delta\chi_1$ pattern, and working with the rows of the rectangle instead of the columns. The new set of outcomes will be the estimates for all 31 elements of the $\Delta\chi_2$ pattern. The entire process can now be repeated several times, alternating between the rows and columns to obtain a sequence of successive estimates for the $\Delta\chi_1$ and $\Delta\chi_2$ patterns. The procedure was known as 'taking the wheel through the rectangle'. The successive estimates frequently converged to two estimates, with no further changes occurring when the process was repeated. The two final estimates were often very good approximations to the true patterns, and sometimes were completely accurate.

A simple example

Convergence is illustrated by means of the highly simplified situation shown in Figure 6.

Diagram (a) of Figure 6 shows the accurate addition table for two 'mini' $\Delta\chi_1$ and $\Delta\chi_2$ patterns each consisting of four elements. (b) shows a plausible rectangle for these two patterns. (Note that most of the majority scores are quite large.) (c) illustrates the first step towards convergence by taking an inaccurate version of the $\Delta\chi_2$ pattern through the rectangle, using the algorithm given earlier, to obtain an estimate for the $\Delta\chi_1$ pattern. (d) illustrates the next step, taking the estimate for the $\Delta\chi_1$ pattern back through the rectangle to obtain a new estimate for the $\Delta\chi_2$ pattern.

A comparison of (d) with (a) shows that both of the final estimates are completely accurate. The example demonstrates the recovery of both the true delta patterns from

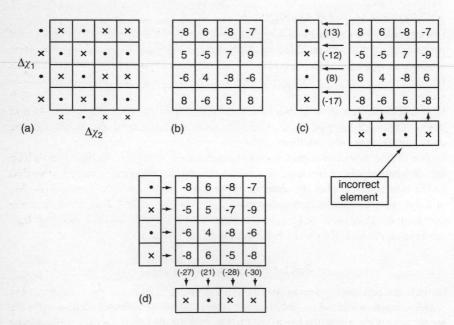

Figure 6. A simple example of convergence.

the rectangle even though the initial version of the $\Delta\chi_2$ pattern used was itself partially incorrect. In practice complete accuracy was not always achieved: a small number of the elements of one or both of the final delta patterns would sometimes be wrong.

If the second estimate found for the $\Delta\chi_2$ pattern is taken back through the rectangle again, the resulting $\Delta\chi_1$ pattern is the same as before—convergence.

The delta patterns for the χ_1 and χ_2 wheels obtained after convergence were then used in other, similar, procedures which yielded estimates for the delta patterns of the other three chi-wheels.

Checking the delta patterns

Some wheel characteristics are constant no matter what the wheel pattern. These could sometimes be useful for checking on the accuracy of the final patterns obtained. The most important of these characteristics was that the true delta pattern for any wheel always contained an even number of crosses.

Level of accuracy achieved by convergence

To achieve a high level of accuracy the starting pattern had to contain very few incorrect elements, and the rectangle had to have large majority scores in a high proportion of the cells. When both these conditions were satisfied, the numerical weight of false evidence arising from any wrong elements in the initial delta pattern or from false information derived from some cells in the rectangle was less than the greater weight of the true evidence.

Statistical evaluation of rectangles

Constructing the rectangles, converging them, and then carrying out the additional procedures used to find reliable estimates for the remaining chi-wheels, was very time consuming. It was therefore important to know at an early stage of the work if a given rectangle was likely to lead to useful outcomes or not. Statistical tests of significance were developed to determine whether a rectangle should be rejected before too much time had been wasted. A considerable amount of research work was undertaken to devise tests for predicting the likely usefulness of rectangles and the accuracy of the delta patterns derived from them.

Two different types of significance tests were developed. One was intended to help decide whether a given rectangle was sufficiently promising to merit further attention before it had been used in the convergence process. Other tests were based on the $\Delta\chi_1$ and $\Delta\chi_2$ patterns obtained from the process of convergence, and so suffered from the disadvantage that they could only be applied after this process had been at least partially completed. They were, however, much more accurate.

Rectangling with Colossus

Initially the process of converging a rectangle was done by hand. Later the majority scores in each cell could be obtained by means of a special run on Colossus. These scores were then transcribed manually to the cells of the rectangle drawn on a large sheet of paper. Colossus II was fitted with a device (the Special Attachment mentioned in previous chapters) which made it possible to produce an automatic printout of the complete rectangle.

In the Newmanry the aim was to produce final versions of the five delta patterns for which the odds of being correct were 1000:1 on. The procedures that were employed to evaluate these odds involved the use of a logarithmic scale whose unit of measurement was called a 'deciban' (see Appendix 6 *Turingery*). On this scale, odds of 1000 : 1 in favour are expressed as +30 decibans (because the logarithm of 1000 is 3, and 3 bans = 30 decibans). This high level of certainty could be achieved provided that a message of about 20,000 characters was available. The task often required the application of more than twenty different algorithms. During this very complex activity, the Wren operators selected the algorithm to use at each stage from an operational sequence prepared in advance by the mathematicians. If there was no successful outcome, the operators consulted a senior cryptologist known as the shift's 'Colossus man', who would attempt to devise an alternative strategy.

Convergence by machine

It was possible to carry out the convergence procedure on Colossus, but it appears that Newmanry Wrens carried out most of this work by hand. '[C]omputer time is often cheaper than Colossus time,' pointed out *General Report on Tunny* (meaning by 'computer' a human working by rote).

How was the convergence procedure carried out on Colossus? Colossus could not store the considerable quantity of information contained in the rectangle, making it impossible to apply the algorithm described above. Instead an equivalent counting procedure was used, in which the characters were read from the cipher tape one by one and processed immediately. This was carried out in such a way that the information derived from one complete run through the cipher tape was equivalent to that contained in one row (or column) of cells in the corresponding rectangle. It was necessary to carry out a number of runs through the tape in order to derive all the required information.

Suppose that a start was made with either a complete or a partial pattern of elements for $\Delta\chi_2$, with the objective of deriving a complete pattern of elements for $\Delta\chi_1$. The first stage of the procedure was to install a 'dummy' pattern for $\Delta\chi_1$ on Colossus's thyratron rings, in which in effect all the elements were set to •. A run was then made using all the characters in the cipher message, making a count of the number of times that the event $(\Delta Z_1 + \Delta\chi_1) + (\Delta Z_2 + \Delta\chi_2) = •$ occurred. This count was called the 'norm'. The first element of the dummy $\Delta\chi_1$ pattern was then changed from • to ×, and a second run made to obtain a new count for the occurrence of the same event. A score consisting of the new count minus the norm was assigned to the first element of $\Delta\chi_1$. If a positive score was obtained, then the first element of the required $\Delta\chi_1$ pattern was taken to be ×, and otherwise to be •.

The first element of the dummy pattern for $\Delta\chi_1$ was then reset to •, the second element was changed from • to ×, and another run was made to give another count, which, after subtraction of the norm, was the score assigned to the second element of

$\Delta\chi_1$. This score was used to determine the second element of $\Delta\chi_1$ in the way previously described.

This process was carried out for all the elements of the dummy pattern. The validity of the results obtained depended upon the fact that the dot counts were expected to be higher when the elements of the $\Delta\chi_1$ pattern were correct, so that if a positive score was obtained when an element in the dummy pattern was changed from • to ×, this implied that × was the best estimate for the corresponding element of the required $\Delta\chi_1$ pattern.

This process is equivalent to the rectangle algorithm described above and gave identical results, providing final estimates of the $\Delta\chi_1$ and $\Delta\chi_2$ patterns that were often very accurate.

Finding the patterns of the other chi-wheels and improving the accuracy of the $\Delta\chi_1$ and $\Delta\chi_2$ patterns

After estimates for the $\Delta\chi_1$ and $\Delta\chi_2$ patterns had been obtained by convergence, a number of similar algorithms were used for the next stage, finding estimates for the $\Delta\chi_3$, $\Delta\chi_4$, and $\Delta\chi_5$ patterns. These algorithms made use of the delta patterns that had already been found. All the algorithms were closely related to those used for wheel setting and the work was carried out on Colossus.

Once estimates for all five delta patterns had been obtained, the final stage of the work involved using some additional algorithms to obtain improved estimates for the five patterns. For example, one algorithm used the estimates of the four patterns $\Delta\chi_2$, $\Delta\chi_3$, $\Delta\chi_4$, $\Delta\chi_5$ previously found to provide a new and improved estimate for $\Delta\chi_1$. Remarkably, by cycling around the delta patterns in this way better estimates could be obtained.

Appendix 10

· ·

The Motor-Wheels and Limitations

Jack Good, Donald Michie, and Geoffrey Timms

Motors

The dots and crosses arranged round the motor-wheels do not mean the same as the symbols usually called dots and crosses.

A dot means STOP

A cross means GO

Mu61 moves on once after each letter is enciphered. When Mu61 has a cross in the active position (before moving) Mu37 moves on once: when it has a dot in the active position (before moving) Mu37 stays still. The character of Mu37 in the earlier active position is the active character of the BASIC MOTOR (BM). In other words, BM = Mu37 'extended by Mu61' = Mu37'.

Example of finding Basic Motor

Mu61: × • × × × • × × • × × × × × × • × ×
Mu37: × • • × • • × × • × • × • • × × •

(a) Number the characters of Mu61 repeating numbers wherever there is a dot:

× • × × × • × × • × × × × × • × ×
1 2 2 3 4 5 5 6 7 7 8 9 10 11 12 12 13

(b) Number the characters of Mu37 (without repeating):

× • • × • • × × • × • × • • × × •
1 2 3 4 5 6 7 8 9 10 11 12 13 14 15 16 17

With the exception of the title 'The Motor-Wheels and Limitations', this appendix is reproduced verbatim from pages 7–8 of *General Report on Tunny* <http://www.AlanTuring.net/tunny_report>.

Material that in the original is underlined has sometimes been replaced by either italics or boldface; and occasionally punctuation marks have been added or removed. Material enclosed in square brackets has been added by the editor.

(c) Replace the sequence of numbers given in (a) by their equivalents given by (b).

```
        1  2  2  3  4  5  5  6  7  7  8  9  10 11 12 12 13
BM:     ×  •  •  •  ×  •  •  •  ×  ×  ×  •  ×  •  ×  ×  •
```

The active character of the Basic Motor—in conjunction with the active character of the LIMITATION—determines the character of the TOTAL MOTOR and this regulates the motion of the psis.

The limitation consists of a sequence of dots and crosses such that when there is a Basic Motor dot *and* a limitation cross in the active position there is a Total Motor dot and the psis do not move. At all other places (e.g. where there is a Basic Motor cross or a Basic Motor dot and a limitation dot) there is a Total Motor cross and every psi moves on once.

Example

```
Basic Motor    ×  •  •  •  ×  •  •  •  ×  ×  ×  •  ×  •  ×  ×  •
Limitation     •  ×  •  ×  ×  •  •  ×  ×  ×  ×  •  •  ×  ×  •  •  ×
Total Motor    ×  •  ×  •  ×  ×  ×  •  ×  ×  ×  ×  ×  •  ×  ×  •
```

Limitations

The sequence of characters defined in [the previous] paragraph as the LIMITATION is a byproduct of the other patterns on the machine or in the P-stream [P = plaintext], and is not generated independently. Four different methods have been used to produce the limitation and the four different types are defined as follows:

(i) $\overline{\chi}_2$ limitation (known for short as χ_2 lim or chi 2 lim).

The active character of the limitation at any position is given by the character of χ_2 which was active in the previous position. This is called chi 2 ONE BACK and written $\overline{\chi}_2$. (NB $\overline{\overline{\chi}}_2$ means χ_2 two back, $\underline{\chi}_2$ means χ_2 one forward etc.)

(ii) $\overline{\chi}_2 + \overline{\psi}'_1$ limitation (known for short as $\overline{\psi}_1$ lim or psi 1 lim).

The active character of the limitation is given by the sum of the characters of χ_2 and ψ'_1 which were active in the previous position. [ψ'_1 is the first impulse of the extended psi; see page 49.]

(iii) $\overline{\chi}_2 + \overline{\overline{P}}_5$ limitation (known for short as P_5 lim).

The active character of the limitation is given by the sum of the character of χ_2 which was active in the previous position and the character of P_5 which was active two positions previously.

(iv) $\overline{\chi}_2 + \overline{\psi}'_1 + \overline{\overline{P}}_5$ limitation (known for short as ψ_1, P_5 lim).

The active character of the limitation is given by the sum of the characters of χ_2 and ψ'_1 which were active in the previous position and the character of P_5 which was active two positions previously.

Limitations involving P_5 constitute an 'autoclave' since the key stream becomes dependent on the Plain Language.

On the earliest model of the Tunny machine there was 'No limitation'. This was equivalent to a limitation stream consisting entirely of crosses, so that Total and Basic motors were the same.

A General Example of Ciphering with $\overline{\chi}_2 + \overline{\psi}'_1$ Limitation

(i)	P: 9 I M 9 K A M P F 9 G E G E N 9	(given)
(ii)	χ: U O 8 X X R J Y W O R / E Q L 3	(given)
(iii)	ψ: N L D E Q / K H B 4	(given)
(iv)	BM: • • × × • • × • × • × × • • • ×	(given)
(v)	χ_2: × • × • • × × • × • × • • × × •	(from ii)
(vi)	$\chi_2 + \psi'_1$: × • • × × × • • × × × • • × × × •	(from v and x)
(vii)	$\overline{\chi}_2 + \overline{\psi}'_1$: • × • × × × • • × × × • • × × ×	(from vi)
(viii)	TM: × <u>•</u> × × × <u>•</u> <u>•</u> × × × <u>•</u> × × × <u>•</u> <u>•</u> ×	(from iv and vii)
(ix)	ψ': N L <u>L</u> D E <u>E</u> <u>E</u> Q / K <u>K</u> H B <u>4</u> <u>4</u> <u>4</u>	(from iii and viii)
(x)	ψ'_1: • • • × × × × × • × × • × • • •	(from ix)
(xi)	K = $\chi + \psi'$: J R F H M J R 4 W Q S H O Y T R	(from ii and ix)
(xii)	Z = P + K: K N Z T W 3 P H V W 8 Y 4 H M C	(from i and xi)

The underlinings in the example show the relation between Total Motor dots and psi extensions.

Note that the ψ' (ix) depends on (vi) which depends on a character in ψ' at a previous place. ψ' therefore depends on its own recent past and can only be constructed letter by letter. Only when the 4th letter of ψ' is known can we tell if there is an extension in the ψ from the 5th letter to the 6th, and so determine the 6th letter for certain. When this is known, and only then, can we start to find out if the ψ is extended from the 7th to the 8th letters, and so on.

Appendix 11

Motorless Tunny

Jack Good and Donald Michie

MICHIE: The motor-wheels were of a different character from the others and exercised a control function. Their task was to govern step by step whether the psi-wheels were to move on *en bloc*, in concert with the chi-wheels, or whether they should stand still for the current step. This elaboration of the Lorenz machine design had the object of further complicating the task of would-be codebreakers. In actuality it had the opposite effect, introducing a subtle element of regularity. If the motor-wheels had been omitted from the German design, it is overwhelmingly probable that Tunny would never have been broken. Pure key could readily have been constructed so as to destroy any practical possibility of reverse-engineering the mechanism that generated it.

Admittedly, with just ten wheels in total (five chis and five psis), the combinatorics get knocked down. The number of possible sets of wheel patterns for the actual Tunny was of the order of 10^{120} and for the motorless version 'only' 10^{95}. The number of possible settings of the twelve wheels of the actual machine was $(41 \times 31 \times 29 \times 26 \times 23) \times (43 \times 47 \times 51 \times 53 \times 59) \times (61 \times 37)$—approximately 10^{20}. In the motorless version this drops to about 10^{16}. But given reasonably prudent restrictions on the properties of the wheel patterns themselves, these reductions still guarantee a sufficient semblance of randomness in the generated chi + psi stream of characters. As it was, the extra and gratuitous touch of having all psi-wheels intermittently stutter in synchrony allowed the entry of a serious and systematic departure from randomness.

GOOD: Michie is right that Tunny without the motor-wheels would be a better machine. I shall discuss this counterfactual matter.

Notice that by making $\mu 37$ all crosses, and having no limitations, the Tunny machine would behave exactly as if it had no motor wheels and ten regularly moving wheels. The German cryptographers might very well have begun by having a ten-wheel machine, with all the wheels moving regularly, and then decided to make it more complicated. I believe that, about sixty years ago, I came across a description of a machine due to the American cryptographer Parker Hitt of just that simpler design, but with a different number of wheels. I have not been able to verify this, but David Kahn informs me that Hitt did patent two cryptographic machines in 1932 and 1936.

If my memory is right, the German cryptographers might have known about Hitt's patents and adopted his idea, just as they had adopted the commercial Enigma and then complicated it.

The ability (just noted) to switch to the demotorised Tunny very easily would enable cipher clerks with a Tunny to communicate with other clerks who had only the motorless form of the machine.

Further evidence that they started with the motorless form is that the ten lengths of the chi- and psi-wheels are mutually prime, even the composite lengths 26 and 51. For the ordinary Tunny I can see little if any advantage in having the psi lengths prime to the chi lengths. (This isn't strong evidence, however: they might have decided it was prudent to have all the lengths mutually prime just in case there was an advantage in doing so.)

Let us consider possible weaknesses of the motorless Tunny. In the first place, depths could be read in precisely the same way as for ordinary Tunny—but would be slightly less likely to occur. That is because the total number of cams would be reduced from 501 to 403, so the cipher clerks would have less of a burden and would be slightly less tempted to use the reset button 'illegally'. The cryptanalysts would read the depths and obtain some pure key.

Perhaps the cryptographers were worried in case there *might* be some way to exploit a long stretch of pure key, without reducing it to the individual wheel patterns. Could the key be combined with the message indicating system to find partial reuse of the key in other messages in the same crypto-period, especially when the crypto-period is a month instead of a day? If this is possible, the technique might branch out to an attack on many messages. Even if such a technique is impracticable, the mere fear that it might be practicable would be a reason to try to improve the motorless Tunny.

Suppose the wheel patterns are approximately 'perfect', containing as large a patch of ••xx••xx as is legal (producing •x•x•x•x•x in the delta). Then, when pure key is available (obtained from a depth), one could try using random patterns in a four-wheel run and perfect patterns for the other six wheels, each tried in only four of its rotations. This could be tried many times with different randomisations and with different selections of the four wheels randomised. (There is an interesting comparison with the 'substantialisation' of sign sequences in X-ray crystallography.)

Whatever the answer to these questions may be, it seems safe to say that the motorless Tunny would have been better than the actual Tunny.

• •

Origins of the Fish Cypher Machines

Friedrich L. Bauer

Baudot and the Teleprinter Alphabet

In the nineteenth century enciphering was done by hand. The first cipher machines appeared around the turn of the century. Since wireless communication using Morse code was the norm, it was sufficient for early cipher machines to allow manual entry of the plaintext via a keyboard, with the enciphered text appearing either at illuminated windows, as in Enigma, or on printed tape, as in the case of the Hagelin machine (designed by the Swede Boris Hagelin and built in large numbers under licence by the US army). The enciphered text was read by eye, and transmitted manually by a wireless operator.

David Hughes invented a 'printing telegraph' in 1855. It was to be a long time before his idea came into practical use. An important step forward was made by the French engineer Jean Baudot. Baudot, one of the great pioneers of modern telegraphy, invented a system where all symbols were encoded by groups of the same length. Thirty-two letters and other symbols were represented by groups of five binary characters, the characters meaning 'current' or 'non-current'. (This kind of encoding can be traced back to Francis Bacon in 1605.) The encoding allowed a simple mechanism for teleprinting, superior to the machine Hughes had invented, with a keyboard on the sending side.

In 1895 August Raps invented a *Schnelltelegraph* (fast telegraph) for the Siemens company. From 1927 a *Springschreiber* (start-stop recorder) invented by Edward Kleinschmidt was built under licence by the Lorenz company in Berlin. Herbert Wüsteney designed equipment for the Siemens company and this came into public use in 1933, through the German *Reichspost* (Post Office). By 1939 the German public telex network had 1500 subscribers.

In 1929 the 'International Teletype Alphabet No. 2' (CCITT 2) was introduced. This originated with Donald Murray in 1900. Figure 1 shows the representations: a dot means 'current', an empty square 'non-current'. The alphabet has 26 letters and 26 other symbols, as well as control symbols for *letter shift* ($\downarrow$), *figure shift* ($\uparrow$), *space* (|||), *carriage return* (<), and *line feed* ($\equiv$). The combination numbered 32, all blanks, was not to be used.

CCITT Nr.	1	2	3	4	5	6	7	8	9	10	11	12	13	14	15	16	17	18	19	20	21	22	23	24	25	26	27	28	29	30	31	32
Letter shift	A	B	C	D	E	F	G	H	I	J	K	L	M	N	O	P	Q	R	S	T	U	V	W	X	Y	Z	<	≡	↓	↑	‖‖	◥◢
Figure shift	–	?	:	✠	3	☐	⊟	⧄	8	⍾	(	)	.	,	9	0	1	4	'	5	7	=	2	/	6	+						
Start bit (A)																																
Data bits 1	●	●		●	●	●				●	●						●		●		●		●	●	●	●			●	●		
2	●		●				●		●	●	●	●				●	●	●			●	●	●					●	●	●		
3			●			●		●	●		●		●	●		●	●		●		●	●		●	●				●		●	
4		●	●	●		●	●			●	●		●	●	●			●				●		●			●		●	●		
5		●					●	●				●	●		●	●	●			●		●	●	●	●	●			●	●		
Stop bit (1½)(Z)	●	●	●	●	●	●	●	●	●	●	●	●	●	●	●	●	●	●	●	●	●	●	●	●	●	●	●	●	●	●	●	●

Figure 1. International Teletype Alphabet No. 2 (CCITT 2).

Teleprinter coding was widely known from the turn of the century. Professional cryptologists were also familiar with it, thanks to the invention by Vernam described below. Thus a precondition for an attack on the Lorenz and Siemens machines—knowledge of the system—was satisfied.

Bitwise Encryption

An encryption by substitution replaces each character by another (or sometimes by the same) character, without altering the position of the character in the text. Usually each such encryption step is uniquely reversible.

In the Baudot system and its successor CCITT 2, there are only two characters. We shall denote them by the bits 0 (standing for an empty square in Figure 1) and 1 (standing for '•'). Figure 2 shows a more systematic reordering of the alphabet, which is useful for decoding. It corresponds to Figure 1 except that the start bit 0 and stop bit 1 are suppressed. In the top row, the control characters are named 0, 1, 2, 3, 4, 5. At Bletchley Park different names were used for the control characters: /, 8 (or –), 9, 5 (or +), 3, 4, respectively. The tiny figures along the bottom row 0 . . . 31 are the base-2 number equivalents of the 5-bit groups.

An encryption by substitution is said to be *monoalphabetic* if there is one and only one replacement to be used, once and for all, and *polyalphabetic* if there is more than one.

0	t	4	o	2	h	n	m	5	l	r	g	i	p	c	v	e	z	d	b	s	y	f	x	a	w	j	3	u	q	k	1	
0	0	0	0	0	0	0	0	0	0	0	0	0	0	0	0	1	1	1	1	1	1	1	1	1	1	1	1	1	1	1	1	1
0	0	0	0	0	0	0	0	1	1	1	1	1	1	1	1	0	0	0	0	0	0	0	0	1	1	1	1	1	1	1	1	2
0	0	0	0	1	1	1	1	0	0	0	0	1	1	1	1	0	0	0	0	1	1	1	1	0	0	0	0	1	1	1	1	3
0	0	1	1	0	0	1	1	0	0	1	1	0	0	1	1	0	0	1	1	0	0	1	1	0	0	1	1	0	0	1	1	4
0	1	0	1	0	1	0	1	0	1	0	1	0	1	0	1	0	1	0	1	0	1	0	1	0	1	0	1	0	1	0	1	5
0	1	2	3	4	5	6	7	8	9	10	11	12	13	14	15	16	17	18	19	20	21	22	23	24	25	26	27	28	29	30	31	

Figure 2. Binary coding of the International Teletype Alphabet No. 2 (CCITT 2). 0: void, 1: letter shift, 2: word space, 3: figure shift, 4: carriage return, 5: line feed.

For bitwise encryption, there are only two possible encryption steps:

the *identity O*: $\begin{smallmatrix} 0 \to 0 \\ 1 \to 1 \end{smallmatrix}$ and the *reflection L*: $\begin{smallmatrix} 0 \to 1 \\ 1 \to 0 \end{smallmatrix}$

Using identity throughout would be futile, and using reflection throughout could easily be deciphered. Thus, there has to be some alternation of the two encryption steps. In other words, nontrivial bitwise encryption is necessarily polyalphabetic. The two 'substitution alphabets' are the two orderings (0, 1) and (1, 0) of the bits.

O and L are used to form a *key letter*. A key letter consists of a group of five Os and Ls. The letter is used to indicate how identity and reflection are to be alternated in a polyalphabetic encryption of a single letter. For example, if

the key letter is $G = OLOLL$
the plain letter c, coded by 01110, is to be encrypted
then the encryption reads 00101, which is the ciphertext letter H.

This is because O in the first and third positions leaves the bits unchanged, while L in the second and fourth positions changes the bit 1 into 0 and in the fifth position changes the bit 0 into 1. (Following traditional cryptological usage, plaintext letters are written in lower case, ciphertext letters in upper case, and key letters in upper case italics.)

Another example:

The sequence of encryption steps	*OLLOL*	*OLOOO*	*LOLLO*
corresponding to the key		*P5F*	
applied to the Baudot sequence	01110	00011	11101
representing the plain message		coq	
yields	00011	01011	01011
which is the cipher text		OGG	

Note that the identity O can be described as 'adding 0' (written $+ 0$) and the reflection L as 'adding 1' (written $+ 1$) according to the 'addition table'

$$0 + 0 = 0 \qquad 0 + 1 = 1$$
$$1 + 0 = 1 \qquad 1 + 1 = 0$$

Mathematicians call this kind of addition *addition modulo 2*. It coincides with the Boolean operation XOR (exclusive or), which is also called *non-carrying* binary addition. It is obtained from normal addition of integers as the remainders after division by 2: even numbers have the remainder 0, odd numbers the remainder 1.

It is natural to use the key letters supplied by Figure 2 for each of the 32 groups of five key elements. The 32 lines of Figure 3 give the different substitution alphabets for the key letters *0 A B C . . . Z 2 3 4 5 1*. Figure 3 displays the resulting encryption table based on the bitwise addition modulo 2 of the 5-bit groups. (Because of its simplicity, the table must be assumed to be known to the enemy codebreakers.)

To give an example of the use of Figure 3: in order to encipher the plaintext letter m using the key *S*, look for the intersection of the line for the key *S* and the column for m. The ciphertext letter B is found.

```
  0 a b c d e f g h i j k l m n o p q r s t u v w x y z 2 3 4 5 1

0  0 A B C D E F G H I J K L M N O P Q R S T U V W X Y Z 2 3 4 5 1
A  A 0 G F R 5 C B Q S 4 N Z 1 K 3 Y H D I W 2 X T V P L U O J E M
B  B G 0 Q T O H A F 1 L P J S Y E K C W M D V U R 2 N 4 X 5 Z 3 I
C  C F Q 0 U K A H G 4 S E M L 5 P O B 2 J V D T X W 3 1 R Y I N Z
D  D R T U 0 4 2 W X K 5 I 3 Y S Z 1 V A N B C Q G H M O F L E J P
E  E 5 O K 4 0 N 3 Y U R C W X F B Q P J 2 Z I 1 L M H T S G D A V
F  F C H A 2 N 0 Q B J I 5 1 Z E Y 3 G U 4 X R W V T O M D P S K L
G  G B A H W 3 Q 0 C M Z Y 4 I P 5 N F T 1 R X 2 D U K J V E L O S
H  H Q F G X Y B C 0 L 1 3 I 4 O N 5 A V Z 2 W R U D E S T K M P J
I  I S 1 4 K U J M L 0 F D H G R V T Z N A P E O Y 3 W Q 5 X C 2 B
J  J 4 L S 5 R I Z 1 F 0 2 B Q U W X M E C 3 N Y O P V G K T A D H
K  K N P E I C 5 Y 3 D 2 0 X W A Q B O S R 1 4 Z M L G V J H U F T
L  L Z J M 3 W 1 4 I H B X 0 C V R 2 S O Q 5 Y N E K U A P D G T F
M  M 1 S L Y X Z I 4 G Q W C 0 T 2 R J P B N 3 5 K E D F O U H V A
N  N K Y 5 S F E P O R U A V T 0 H G 3 I D M J L 1 Z B X 4 Q 2 C W
O  O 3 E P Z B Y 5 N V W Q R 2 H 0 C K L X 4 1 I J S F D M A T G U
P  P Y K 0 1 Q 3 N 5 T X B 2 R G C 0 E M W I Z 4 S J A U L F V H D
Q  Q H C B V P G F A Z M O S J 3 K E 0 X L U T D 2 R 5 I W N 1 Y 4
R  R D W 2 A J U T V N E S O P I L M X 0 K G F H B Q 1 3 C Z 5 4 V
S  S I M J N 2 4 1 Z A C R Q B D X W L K 0 Y 5 3 P O T H E V F U G
T  T W D V B Z X R 2 P 3 1 5 N M 4 I U G Y 0 Q C A F S E H J O L K
U  U 2 V D C I R X W E N 4 Y 3 J 1 Z T F 5 Q 0 B H G L P A M K 5 O
V  V X U T Q I W 2 R O Y Z N 5 L 1 4 D H 3 C B 0 F A J K G S P M E
W  W T R X G L V D U Y O M E K 1 J S 2 B P A H F 0 C I 5 Q 4 3 Z N
X  X V 2 W H M T U D 3 P L K E Z S J R Q O F G A C 0 4 N B I Y 1 5
Y  Y P N 3 M H O K E W V G U D B F A 5 1 T S L J I 4 0 2 Z C X Q R
Z  Z L 4 1 O T M J S Q G V A F X D U I 3 H E P K 5 N 2 0 Y R B W C
2  2 U X R F S D V T 5 K J P O 4 M L W C E H A G Q B Z Y 0 1 N I 3
3  3 0 5 Y L G P E K X T H D U Q A F N Z V J M S 4 I C R 1 0 W B 2
4  4 J Z I E D S L M C A U G H 2 T V 1 5 F O K P 3 Y X B N W 0 R Q
5  5 E 3 N J A K O P 2 D F T V C G H Y 4 U L S M Z 1 Q W I B R 0 X
1  1 M I Z P V L S J B H T F A W U D 4 Y G K O E N 5 R C 3 2 Q X 0
```

Figure 3. Encryption table (Latin square) for the teleprinter characters.

The key letter *0* in the first line of Figure 3 acts as a neutral element, leaving the letters unchanged. The key letter *1* in the last line acts as a reflector, swapping 0 and 1, a and m, b and i, c and z, d and p, e and v, f and l, g and s, h and j, k and t, n and w, o and u, q and 4, r and y, x and 5, 2 and 3. Figure 3 shows that the remaining 30 key letters also have this property. Thus the encryption step and its reciprocal, the corresponding decryption step, coincide. Bitwise encryption is necessarily self-reciprocal. This is a great advantage for practical work.

It can be seen from Figure 3 that the key letter could be reconstructed if a plaintext letter and the corresponding ciphertext letter were given. For example, if the plaintext letter w is encrypted by the ciphertext letter G, the key letter is *D*.

Vernam

Polyalphabetic bitwise encryption as discussed above was proposed in 1919 by the young American engineer Gilbert Vernam. Vernam, an employee of AT&T, had been charged by his boss R. D. Parker to develop a secure method of teleprinter communication.

Since five-channel punched paper tape was frequently employed with teleprinters, Vernam proposed using a tape of key symbols. In effect this meant that the addition table had to be customised for $2^5 = 32$ five-bit combinations. Vernam had no difficulty in designing suitable electromechanical circuitry for performing the bitwise encryption.

As to the key, sender and recipient had to have identical copies, since the encryption was self-reciprocal. The key tape could form a loop, in which case the key would have a periodic repetition. It was clear that for good security the period ought to be quite long. The engineers objected, however, complaining that if the key tapes were long, they would be difficult to cope with.

Parker was in close contact with the US navy. Major Joseph Mauborgne, head of the signal corp's research and engineering division, was informed of developments. A demonstration was arranged and Mauborgne was convinced—except with regard to the key, which he knew should not show repetition, since periodic keys invited a break. A non-periodic infinite sequence would be the ideal, or in practice a finite segment of this, of the same length as the message itself; but this seemed unattainable.

The problem was solved in the following way by an engineer in Vernam's team, Lyman Morehouse. By encrypting twice, using two short loops of tape of 999 and 1000 characters each, Morehouse obtained a key that was 999,000 characters long. Moreover, this key did not show the characteristics present in natural languages—it was senseless.

On 13 September 1918 Vernam applied for a US patent, obtaining one in 1919 (patent number 1 310 719). His idea of bitwise encryption by addition modulo 2 was adopted in diplomatic and military cryptography, for example in a Siemens machine with a double tape reader and 'mixer', and, later, in the US army SIGTOT machine. Commercially, however, the invention was not a success. Code books were more in demand.

The Siemens T52

Around 1928, the Siemens company was contacted regarding the matter of cipher teleprinter machines by Eberhard Hettler, on behalf of the Reichsmarine (German navy). Hettler requested that instead of there being an unwieldy key tape, the key should be generated within the cipher machine by wheels having some form of irregular movement—an idea that had already been used in the commercial Enigma, with which the Reichsmarine was familiar. Periodicity of the key was a likely outcome of this approach, but the German authorities did not have the scruples Mauborgne had had.

The encryption mechanism of the cipher teleprinter machines developed by Siemens (*Geheimschreiber*, British codename 'Sturgeon') worked on the 5-bit code groups of CCITT 2. Apart from 32 different Vernam-type encryption steps operating on the 5-bit code groups, the Siemens machine also created permutations of the 5 bits—transpositions of their order, as described in Chapter 25. This was a remarkable improvement over Vernam, since it led to many more than the 32 substitution alphabets of Figure 3.

The Siemens cipher machine was based on a patent applied for by August Jipp, Ehrhard Rossberg, and Eberhard Hettler on 18 July 1930 (German patent no. 615016); a US patent was granted on 6 June 1933 (no. 1 912 983). The patent openly described the machine. Model T52a (1930) of the Siemens cipher machine was used by the Reichsmarine from 1931. In 1934 the T52a was upgraded to the T52b and this was also used by the Reichsmarine. Model T52c (1938) was first used by the Luftwaffe (air force). It was later replaced by the variant T52ca, which was used generally by the Wehrmacht (and by mid-1943 was again called simply T52c). Models T52d and T52e appeared in 1942–3. It is estimated that about 1000 T52 machines were built between 1930 and 1945.

The T52d and T52e featured an optional *Klartextfunktion* (see Chapter 25). Abbreviated KTF by the British, this was a tricky device where the encryption step was influenced by the 5th bit of the plaintext character two characters back ($\bar{\bar{P}}_5$ in the notation of Appendix 10). This idea originated with the Swedish inventor Arvid Damm in a 1919 patent application. KTF not only caused difficulties for the code-breakers, but on noisy transmission channels also for the authorised recipient. $\bar{\bar{P}}_5$ was introduced experimentally for the Lorenz *Schlüsselzusatz* in March 1943, and broken by the British in April 1943 (see Appendix 1).

One way of attacking a crypto-system had been known since 1883, when the Fleming Auguste Kerckhoffs published his famous article 'La Cryptographie Militaire' (see Chapter 1). Kerckhoffs called his cryptanalytic method *superimposition*, meaning that if a number of messages encrypted polyalphabetically with the same key (depths) were brought 'in phase', they could be compared position for position and reduced to monoalphabetic cases. Kerckhoffs assumed that the substitution alphabets were not known.

In the absence of prior knowledge of the substitution alphabets, about a dozen or so messages are usually required for a reasonable depth. If the substitution alphabets are known, however, even the extreme case (not treated by Kerckhoffs) of a superimposition of only two ciphertexts encrypted with the same key is not hopeless. This was outlined for the first time in 1918 by the great American cryptologist William Friedman. The polyalphabetic encryptions amenable to this form of attack are, mathematically speaking, encryptions having a *key group*. (This means that, for each two key elements, there exists a third key element such that the composition of the first two elements results in the same substitution as the third.) While this feature of a crypto-system may simplify the encryption–decryption process considerably, it also makes cryptanalysis easier. Both Sturgeon and Tunny have a key group; this arises naturally from the particular properties of teleprinter code.

When Jipp, Rossberg, and Hettler applied for the *Geheimschreiber* patent in 1930 there was no indication of this danger in the unclassified literature. But intelligence services studied the description of the machine in the patent, and it can safely be assumed that the British and the Swedes discovered weaknesses of the *Geheimschreiber*.

The Lorenz *Schlüsselzusatz*

The Lorenz SZ40 and its successor the SZ42 were cryptologically simpler than the T52. The Lorenz machine (Tunny) performed only Vernam substitutions—in fact a double Vernam encryption, one substitution being performed by the chi-wheels and one by the psis. Correspondingly, the encryption was self-reciprocal: if repeated a second time, the original message was restored.

In the case of this machine, there are just 32 possible encryption steps, the 32 substitutions of the 5-bit code group (named by the alphabet letters in Figure 3). Moreover, the ith letter of key k_i is now uniquely determined by a pair consisting of plaintext letter p_i and ciphertext letter c_i—it is in fact the bitwise difference $k_i = c_i - p_i$, as indicated by Figure 3. Since subtraction coincides with addition for addition modulo 2, Figure 3 shows a matrix which is symmetric with respect to the diagonal.

The double Vernam encryption of the Lorenz machine could not really match the degree of protection offered by the permutations that the Siemens machine introduced (and the Lorenz's two motor wheels turned out to be no great barrier either). The British were lucky that the Siemens machine was not meant to be used for wireless communications—the messages that they could intercept were for the most part encrypted with the weaker Lorenz machine.

The Olivetti Machine

Much less is known about the practical use of a cipher teleprinter machine built by the Olivetti company (Italian patent 387 482, 30 January 1941). This had five cipher wheels and two motor wheels, producing only a weak irregularity.

The Siemens T43

Towards the end of the war, a cipher teleprinter machine with the denotation SFM T43 was built by Siemens. Only a few copies were made. It used one-time key, and was therefore much closer to Mauborgne's philosophy. The T43 is almost certainly identical to the member of the Fish family that the British codenamed '*Thrasher*'.

Notes and References

NOTES TO INTRODUCTION

PAGE

1 *tight-knit group*: Coombs, Flowers' assistant, describes the group as 'a happy few, a band of brothers'; Coombs, A. W. M. 'The Making of Colossus', *Annals of the History of Computing*, vol. 5 (1983), pp. 253–9 (p. 259).

'eyes dropped out': Flowers in interview with Copeland (July 1998).

2 *British industry suffered as a result of the total secrecy*: see ch. 3 of Copeland, B. J. (ed.) *Alan Turing's Automatic Computing Engine: The Master Codebreaker's Struggle to Build the Modern Computer* (Oxford: Oxford University Press, 2005).

photographs of the Colossi: the photographs were released to the National Archives/Public Record Office (PRO) in Kew, Richmond, Surrey (PRO reference FO 850/234). Several of the photographs are reproduced in Chapter 5.

hardware of the first Colossus: Flowers, T. H. 'The Design of Colossus', *Annals of the History of Computing*, vol. 5 (1983), pp. 239–52.

Flowers was told by the British authorities: personal files of T. H. Flowers (24 May 1976, 3 September 1981).

3 *he was instructed to remove these*: personal files of T. H. Flowers (3 September 1981).

General Report on Tunny: PRO reference HW 25/4 (Vol. 1), HW 25/5 (Vol. 2).

4 *'On thirtieth November by order of the Fuehrer'*: British message reference number CX/MSS/T400/79 (HP 9622); PRO reference DEFE 3/318. (Thanks to William Newman for supplying me with a copy of this document.)

word-for-word translation of an intercepted Tunny message: British message reference number CX/MSS/2499/T14; PRO reference HW1/1648. (Thanks to Ralph Erskine for assistance in locating this document.) Words enclosed in square brackets do not appear in the original.

von Weichs, Commander-in-Chief of German Army Group South: Hinsley, F. H. et al. *British Intelligence in the Second World War*, vol. 2 (London: Her Majesty's Stationery Office, 1981), p. 624.

passed along the 'Squid' radio link: copy of CX/MSS/2499/T14 in HW5/242, p. 4.

British analysts deduced from the decrypt: 'A Postponed German Offensive

(Operations ZITADELLE and EULE)' (anon., GC & CS, 7 June 1943; PRO reference HW13/53), p. 2.

conveyed directly to Churchill: documents from GC & CS to Churchill, 30 April 1943 (PRO reference HW1/1648). (An earlier decrypt concerning *Zitadelle* (13 April 1943), and an accompanying note from 'C' to Churchill, are at HW1/1606.) *On 30 April an intelligence report based on the content*: tape-recorded interview with Harry Hinsley (Sound Archive, Imperial War Museum, London (reference number 13523)).

Cairncross was sending raw Tunny decrypts: Cairncross, J. *The Enigma Spy: The Story of the Man who Changed the Course of World War Two* (London: Century, 1997), p. 98; Hinsley, H. 'The Counterfactual History of No Ultra', *Cryptologia*, vol. 20 (1996), pp. 308–24 (pp. 322–3); interview with Hinsley (see above).

6 *launched operation Zitadelle on 4 July*: Hinsley, *British Intelligence in the Second World War*, vol. 2, p. 626.

practically every panzer division on the Russian front: ibid., p. 625.

On 13 July Hitler called off: ibid., p. 627.

'completely frustrated': ibid., p. 627.

NOTES TO CHAPTER 1

10 *in his famous article 'La Cryptographie Militaire'*: Kerckhoffs, A. 'La Cryptographie Militaire; ou, Des chiffres usités en temps de guerre avec un nouveau procédé de déchiffrement applicable aux systèmes à double clef' (Military Cryptography; or, ciphers used in times of war, with a new procedure of deciphering, usable for systems with double key), *Journal des Sciences Militaire*, vol. 9 (Jan./Feb. 1883), pp. 5–38, 161–91.

11 *Arab philosopher al-Kindi*: see Al-Kadi, I. A. 'Origins of Cryptology: The Arab Contributions', *Cryptologia*, vol. 16 (1992), pp. 97–126.

14 *discovered a flaw*: Franksen, O. I. 'Babbage and Cryptography', *Mathematics and Computers in Simulation*, vol. 35 (1993), pp. 327–67; Kahn, D. *The Codebreakers* (New York: Scribner, 1996).

NOTES TO CHAPTER 2

18 *'the orderly Teutonic mind'*: 'History of Military Intelligence Directorate 1920–21' (National Archives/Public Record Office (PRO), Kew, Richmond, Surrey; document reference WO32/10776). Digital facsimiles of all PRO documents referred to in this chapter are available online in The Turing Archive for the History of Computing <www.AlanTuring.net>.

19 *Zimmermann telegram*: 'Records of W. F. Clarke of Room 40 and Head of Naval Section, Government Code and Cypher School' (PRO document reference HW3/182); Nigel de Grey's account of how he worked on the Zimmermann telegram in Room 40, January 1917 (PRO document reference HW3/177).

'the loss of efficiency to both departments': 'Record of Conference Held at the

Admiralty on 5 August 1919 on amalgamation of MI1b and NID25' (PRO document reference HW3/35); and de Grey, N. 'Notes on Formation of GC & CS', p. 1 (PRO document reference HW3/33).

Two Royal Navy intercept sites: Denniston, A. G. 'The Government Code and Cypher School Between the Wars', *Intelligence and National Security*, vol. 1 (1986), pp. 58–9; Johnson, J. *The Evolution of British Sigint 1653–1939* (Cheltenham: HMSO, 1997), pp. 45, 50.

GC & CS came under the control: Denniston, op. cit.; de Grey, 'Notes on Formation of GC & CS', p. 1.

'a poor relation of SIS': Denniston, op. cit., p. 50.

20 *'Like many other recruits . . .'*: Cooper, J. E. S. 'Personal Notes on GC & CS 1925–39', pp. 1–2 (PRO document reference HW3/83).

delegation used the one-time pad system: Denniston, 'The Government Code and Cypher School Between the Wars', p. 54.

Very little interest was shown in naval or military messages: Johnson, *The Evolution of British Sigint*, pp. 50–3; de Grey, 'Notes on Formation and Evolution of GC & CS', pp. 1–2.

21 *intercepts*: Kenworthy, H. C. 'A Brief History of Events Relating to the Growth of the Wire Service' (PRO document reference HW3/81); Sinclair-Williams, C. L. and Kenworthy, H. C. (unpublished paper kindly provided by Mrs Hazel Sinclair-Williams).

asked Hugh Foss: Foss, H. R. 'Reminiscences on the Enigma', p. 2 (PRO document reference HW25/10).

22 *Foss later recalled*: ibid.; see also Johnson, *The Evolution of British Sigint*, p. 55.

A year after Foss's investigation: de Grey, N. 'Enigma History', p. 2 (PRO document reference HW25/10).

23 *until the French lent a hand*: de Grey, op. cit.; handwritten memo by J. E. S. Cooper on de Grey's 'Enigma History' (PRO document reference HW25/10).

'Scarlet Pimpernels': Cooper, op. cit.; Cooper, 'Personal Notes on GC & CS 1925–1939', pp. 16–17.

24 *'Dilly, who had a taste for inventing . . .'*: Peter Twinn in interview with Michael Smith (April 1998).

'Knox kept muttering to Denniston': Foss, 'Reminiscences on the Enigma', p. 3.

25 *able to solve 75 per cent*: Rejewski, M. 'How the Polish Mathematicians Broke Enigma', Appendix D of Kozaczuk, W. *Enigma: How the German Machine Cipher Was Broken, and How It Was Read by the Allies in World War Two* (London: Arms and Armour Press, 1984, trans. C. Kasparek).

'As the danger of war became tangibly near': Mayer quoted in Stengers, J. 'Enigma, the French, the Poles and the British', in Andrew, C. M., Dilks, D. N. (eds) *The Missing Dimension: Governments and Intelligence Communities in the Twentieth Century* (London: Macmillan, 1984), pp. 130–2.

Knox was furious to discover: Denniston, A. G. 'How News was brought from Warsaw at the end of July 1939' (PRO document reference HW25/12).

Twinn recalled: Twinn in Smith, M. *Station X, The Codebreakers of Bletchley Park* (London: Channel 4 Books, 1998), p. 19; see also Hinsley, F. H., Stripp, A. (eds.), *Codebreakers: The Inside Story of Bletchley Park* (Oxford: Oxford University Press, 1993), p. 127.

26 *described taking the British copy to London*: Bertrand, G. *ENIGMA ou La Plus Grande Enigmé de la Guerre 1939–1945* (Paris: Plon, 1973), p. 60.

Cooper said: Cooper, J. E. S. 'Reminiscences on GC & CS at Bletchley Park', pp. 17–18 (PRO document reference HW3/83).

Soon the various sections: de Grey, 'History of Air Sigint', chapter II, pp. 77, 91 (PRO document reference HW3/95).

27 *Turing managed to break five days*: Turing, A. M. 'Mathematical theory of ENIGMA Machine', p. 136 (PRO document reference HW25/3).

Turing was sent to see them: de Grey, 'History of Air Sigint', chapter II, pp. 77, 91.

suggested that the codebreaking operation needed to be much larger: Welchman, G. 'From Polish Bomba to British Bombe: The Birth of Ultra', *Intelligence and National Security*, vol. 1 (1986), pp. 73–5.

When Cooper suggested: Cooper, 'Reminiscences on GC & CS at Bletchley Park', pp. 27–8.

Welchman was given the go-ahead: Welchman, G. *The Hut Six Story: Breaking the Enigma Codes* (2nd edn., Cleobury Mortimer: M & M Baldwin, 1997), pp. 84–5.

28 *top London banks*: de Grey, 'Notes on Formation of GC & CS', pp. 2–3.

recalled Joan Nicholls: Nicholls in Smith, *Station X*, p. 41.

The main pre-war intercept sites: Kenworthy, 'A Brief History of Events Relating to the Growth of the Wire Service', pp. 7–10.

29 *Banister Lists*: Taunt, D. 'Hut 6 From the Inside', in Erskine, R., Smith, M. (eds.) *Action This Day* (London: Bantam, 2001), p. 82.

said Twinn: Twinn in interview with Smith (April 1998).

'We had these Typex machines': Clarke in Smith, *Station X*, p. 34.

set up in Hut 3: Lucas, F. L. 'History of Hut 3', vol I, pp. 1–74 (PRO document reference HW3/119).

30 *Turing used the correct data*: de Grey, 'History of Air Sigint', chapter II, p. 90.

'On a snowy January morning . . .': Lucas, F. L. 'History of Hut 3', vol II, p. 75 (PRO document reference HW3/120).

prove to be an important break: de Grey, 'History of Air Sigint', chapter II, p. 91.

'Yellow': de Grey, ibid., pp. 102–3.

31 *teleprinters allowing direct contact with MI6*: ibid.

said Ralph Bennett: Bennett in Smith, *Station X*, p. 39.

Hut 3 totally rewrote the messages: Lucas, 'History of Hut 3', Vol I, pp. 26–7; de Grey, 'History of Air Sigint', chapter II, p. 89.

'If the intercept sites could send us . . .': Herivel in Smith, *Station X*, pp. 42–3.

recalled Peter Calvocoressi: Calvocoressi, P. *Top Secret Ultra* (London: Cassell, 1980), p. 70.

settings which spelt out words: Erskine, R. 'Cillies', in Erskine and Smith (eds.), *Action This Day*, pp. 453–7.

32 *The first Bombe*: de Grey, 'History of Air Sigint', chapter II, pp. 88–90.

'*because I could have it to myself*': Alexander, C. H. O'D. 'Cryptographic History of Work on the German Naval Enigma', p. 20 (PRO document reference HW25/1).

33 *Turing struggled*: Erskine, R. 'Breaking German Naval Enigma', in Erskine and Smith (eds), *Action This Day*, p. 177.

Foss managed to break: ibid.

Hut 8 enjoyed sporadic breakthroughs: ibid.

The solution came when Harry Hinsley: Hinsley, F. H. 'Bletchley Park, the Admiralty, and Naval Enigma', in Hinsley and Stripp (eds), *Codebreakers*, p. 79.

on top of Dolphin: Erskine, 'Breaking German Naval Enigma', pp. 179–80; Smith, *Station X*, p. 64.

34 *Hinsley later said*: Hinsley, F. H. 'The Influence of Ultra in the Second World War', in Hinsley and Stripp (eds), *Codebreakers*, p. 6.

'*Shark Blackout*': Smith, *Station X*, pp. 109–14; Hinsley, F. H. et al. *British Intelligence in the Second World War*, vol. II (London: HMSO, 1981), p. 548.

the solution to Shark: Smith, *Station X*, pp. 109–14; Erskine, 'Breaking German Naval Enigma', pp. 182–3.

NOTES TO CHAPTER 3

36 *The Enigma cipher machine*: Copeland, B. J. 'Enigma', in Copeland, B. J. (ed.) *The Essential Turing* (Oxford: Oxford University Press, 2004).

WEWA: Mahon, P. 'The History of Hut Eight', Bletchley Park (June 1945), in Copeland, *The Essential Turing*, p. 303.

BINE: Mahon, 'The History of Hut Eight', p. 299.

38 *Murray modified Baudot's original form of the code*: Murray, D. *Murray Multiplex: Technical Instructions*, Manual no. 1: *General Theory* (Croydon: Creed and Coy, no date), p. 8. (I am grateful to Don Hobbs for drawing my attention to this book.)

during the second half of 1940: Kenworthy, H. C. 'The Interception of German Teleprinter Communications by Foreign Office Station Knockholt' (GC & CS, March 1946), p. 1 (National Archives/Public Record Office (PRO), Kew, Richmond, Surrey; document reference HW3/163).

39 *unbreakable Thrasher*: see section 93 of *General Report on Tunny*. <http://www.AlanTuring.net/tunny_report>

mainly by the German army: there is a discussion of the use of Tunny by the German navy in Erskine, R. 'Tunny Decrypts', *Cryptologia*, vol. 12 (1988), pp. 59–61.

The Tunny machine: the physical machine is described in section 11 of *General Report on Tunny*, and in Davies, D. 'The Lorenz Cipher Machine SZ42', *Cryptologia*, vol. 19 (1995), pp. 517–39. The machine's function and use is described in sections 11 and 94 of *General Report on Tunny*.

numbered the wheels 1 to 12: ibid., p. 10.
40 *numbers of positions*: ibid., p. 6.
The first Tunny radio link: ibid., p. 14. ibid., mentions that the first messages on the experimental link passed between Vienna and Athens (p. 297).
thought that the Germans had abandoned the Tunny machine: ibid., p. 320.
a new link: ibid., pp. 14, 320, 458.
most stable and widespread state: ibid., p. 14.
26 different links: ibid., p. 14.
42 *The two central exchanges*: ibid., p. 395.
such as Paris: ibid., p. 5.
two trucks: ibid., p. 4.
Sometimes a land line was used: ibid., p. 5.
the Tunny network became increasingly disorganised: ibid., p. 15.
transported from Berlin to Salzburg: ibid., p. 15.
last Tunny message: ibid., p. 15.
45 *correlations were different for each individual wheel*: ibid., p. 14.
Each month, a different set of correlations: ibid., p. 14.
new procedure was introduced: ibid., p. 14.
QEP book: ibid., section 94.
typical QEP book looked like this: the example is from a QEP sheet intercepted on the Whiting link on 13 November 1944; ibid., pp. 498–9.
46 *the complete process of transmission*: ibid., p. 13.
48 *Different links used different wheel patterns*: ibid., pp. 12–13.
Prior to the summer of 1944: ibid., p. 14.
monthly from October 1942: ibid., p. 458.
The motor-wheel patterns were changed daily: ibid., p. 14.
After 1 August 1944: ibid., p. 14.
contained each character of the teleprinter alphabet approximately an equal number of times: ibid., p. 6.
49 *In the SZ40, it was solely*: ibid., p. 10.
In the SZ42A and SZ42B: ibid., p. 10.
'autoclave': ibid., p. 8.
50 *recollected one of the Tunny group*: Jerry Roberts, typescript (2001).
51 *on loan to the Research Section from Hut 8*: Tutte on p. 359.
the three strokes of genius that Turing contributed: Copeland, 'Enigma'.
'might have lost it without him': Jack Good in interview with Pamela McCorduck (McCorduck, P. *Machines Who Think* (New York: W. H. Freeman, 1979), p. 53).
The codebreakers were thrown back on depths: General Report on Tunny, p. 28.

NOTES TO CHAPTER 4

53 *Given a desk job to recuperate*: *Dictionary of National Biography*, s.v. 'Tiltman, John Hessell'.

Tiltman years later said: 'Some Reminiscences by Brigadier John H. Tiltman', p. 3 (US National Archives and Records Administration (NARA), College Park, Maryland; document reference NR 4632, Historic Cryptographic Collection, RG 457).
more like a detective than a modern cryptanalyst: ibid.
'I say, old boy': Filby, P. W. 'Bletchley Park and Berkeley Street,' *Intelligence and National Security*, vol. 10 (1983), pp. 408–22.

54 *broke the hand cipher used by the German Police*: 'History of the German Police Section' (National Archives/Public Record Office (PRO), Kew, Richmond, Surrey; document reference HW 3/155).

55 *'the greatest cryptanalytical feat of World War II'*: Ralph Erskine in interview with Budiansky (December 2000).
important reassurance to Allied commanders: Hinsley, F. H. et al. *British Intelligence in the Second World War*, vol. 3, part 2 (London: Her Majesty's Stationery Office, 1988), pp. 53, 799.

57 *'men of the professor type'*: Erskine, R. 'GC and CS Mobilizes "Men of the Professor Type" ', *Cryptologia*, vol. 10 (1986), pp. 50–9.
as Twinn facetiously put it: Andrew, C. *Her Majesty's Secret Service: The Making of the British Intelligence Community* (New York: Penguin, 1987), p. 453.
couldn't even read his own writing: Mahon, P. 'The History of Hut 8' (NARA document reference NR 4685, Historic Cryptographic Collection, RG 457), pp. 23–4. A digital facsimile of the original typescript is available in The Turing Archive for the History of Computing <http://www.AlanTuring.net/mahon_hut_8>.
mathematically adept recruits would be needed: 'Memorandum to Commander Denniston', 18 November 1939 (PRO document reference HW 14/2); Welchman, G. *The Hut Six Story* (rev. edn., Cleobury Mortimer: M & M Baldwin, 1997), p. 84.

58 *virtually every message was read*: *General Report on Tunny* (PRO document reference HW 25/4, HW 25/5), p. 28. <http://www.AlanTuring.net/tunny_report>
Building on an initial insight by Turing: op. cit., pp. 313–15.

60 *In the spring of 1943*: Donald Michie in interview with Budiansky (December 2000).

61 *'was fairly sure it was codebreaking'*: Jack Good in interview with Budiansky (December 2000).
'tea party': *General Report on Tunny*, p. 439.

63 *Flowers pointed out*: Flowers, T. H. 'The Design of Colossus', *Annals of the History of Computing*, vol. 5 (1983), pp. 239–52 (p. 252).

NOTES TO CHAPTER 5

64 *as much as several hundred years*: Newman in interview with Christopher Evans ('The Pioneers of Computing: An Oral History of Computing', London: Science Museum).
designed by C. E. Wynn-Williams: Wynn-Williams, C. E. 'The Use of Thyratrons

for High Speed Automatic Counting of Physical Phenomena', *Proceedings of the Royal Society*, series A, vol. 132 (1931), pp. 295–310; Wynn-Williams, C. E. 'A Thyratron Scale of Two Automatic Counter', *Proceedings of the Royal Society of London*, series A, vol. 136 (1932), pp. 312–24. (See also Hull, A. W. 'Hot-cathode Thyratrons', *General Electric Review*, vol. 32 (1929), pp. 390–9; de Bruyne, N. A., Webster, H. C. 'Note on the Use of a Thyratron with a Geiger Counter', *Proceedings of the Cambridge Philosophical Society*, vol. 27 (1931), pp. 113–15.)

65 *The section was housed*: Thurlow, N. 'The Road to Colossus', in The Turing Archive for the History of Computing <http://www.AlanTuring.net/thurlow>.
Smoke rose: information from Harry Fensom (see Chapter 24).
Dollis Hill made: letter from Harry Fensom to Copeland (4 May 2001).

66 '*knowledge of "Tunny-German"* ': *General Report on Tunny*, p. 22. <http://www.AlanTuring.net/tunny_report>

68 *delta was first introduced by Turing*: *General Report on Tunny*, p. 313.

69 '1 + 2 break in': ibid., p. 20.

71 '*intolerable handicaps*': ibid., p. 328.
taking several hours: Newman in interview with Evans.
prevented Heath Robinson from obtaining results at all: *General Report on Tunny*, p. 328.
joined the Telephone Branch of the Post Office: 'Mr T. H. Flowers, M.B.E., B.Sc., M.I.E.E.' *Post Office Electrical Engineers Journal*, October 1950, p. 156.

72 *During the 1930s Flowers pioneered*: unless indicated otherwise, material in this chapter relating directly to Flowers derives from (1) Flowers in interviews with Copeland, 1996–98 (2) Flowers in interview with Christopher Evans in 1977 ('The Pioneers of Computing: an Oral History of Computing', London: Science Museum).

73 *as he himself remarked*: Flowers in interview with Copeland (July 1996).
would automatically decipher the message: Flowers in interview with Copeland (July 1998).
design of the combining unit: Flowers in interview with Copeland (July 1996); *General Report on Tunny*, p. 33.

74 *in February 1943 he presented Newman*: Flowers in interview with Copeland (July 1996); Flowers, T. H. 'The Design of Colossus', *Annals of the History of Computing*, vol. 5 (1983), pp. 239–52 (p. 244).
entirely his idea: *General Report on Tunny*, p. 35.
received with 'incredulity': Flowers, T. H. 'Colossus – Origin and Principles', typescript, no date, p. 3; Coombs in interview with Christopher Evans in 1976 ('The Pioneers of Computing: An Oral History of Computing', London: Science Museum). 'Incredulity' is Flowers' word.
'*too unreliable to do useful work*': Flowers, 'Colossus – Origin and Principles', p. 3.
'*in the face of scepticism*': Flowers in interview with Copeland (July 1996).
'*without the concurrence of BP*': ibid.
'*BP weren't interested until they saw it working*': ibid.

'the whole resources of the laboratories': Flowers, 'Colossus – Origin and Principles', p. 3.

in lorries and reassembled: Myers, K. 'Dollis Hill and Station X', in The Turing Archive for the History of Computing <http://www.AlanTuring.net/myers>.

Flowers' original plan was to dispense with the message-tape as well: General Report on Tunny, p. 35.

75 *'I don't think they really understood . . .'*: Flowers in interview with Evans.

working at Bletchley Park in the early part of December 1943: Flowers, 'The Design of Colossus', p. 245; Flowers in interview with Evans.

at Bletchley Park on 8 December 1943: Flowers in interview with Copeland (July 1996); Flowers in interview with Darlow Smithson (no date); Flowers in interview with staff of the Imperial War Museum, London (1998).

'Colossus arrives to-day': Newman, M. H. A. 'Report on Progress' (Newmanry, 18 January 1944; in the National Archives/Public Record Office (PRO Kew, Richmond, Surrey; document reference HW14/96), p. 4.

'I seem to recall it was in December': letter from Harry Fensom to Copeland (18 August 2005).

Colossus immediately doubled: General Report on Tunny, p. 35.

76 *only a trickle of messages*: ibid., p. 34.

Newman's machines were essential: ibid., p. 28.

they were demanding twelve: ibid., p. 35.

order for Robinsons was curtailed: ibid., p. 35.

'from the highest level': Flowers, 'The Design of Colossus', p. 246.

caused consternation: ibid., p. 246.

'did nothing but work, eat, and sleep': ibid., p. 245.

about one per month: ibid., p. 246.

'dilly-dallying' . . . 'staggered at the scale of the effort': Flowers in interview with Copeland (July 1996).

top priority for everything: note from Donald Michie to Copeland (27 May 2002), reporting a disclosure by Coombs in the 1960s.

In February 1944 Michie and Good: General Report on Tunny, p. 461.

referred to as the 'Mark 2' Colossi: Flowers' personal diary, 4 May 1944.

on 4 May 1944: ibid.

assemble and test Colossus II at Bletchley Park: Chandler, W. W. 'The Maintenance and Installation of Colossus', *Annals of the History of Computing*, vol. 5 (1983), pp. 260–2 (p. 261).

intermittent and mysterious faults: Flowers, 'The Design of Colossus', p. 246.

dispersed at 1 a.m.: Flowers' personal diary, 31 May 1944.

around 3 a.m. Chandler noticed: letter from Chandler to Brian Randell, 24 January 1976; unpublished manuscript by Gil Hayward (2002).

77 *'Colossus 2 in operation'*: Flowers' personal diary, 1 June 1944.

had to don gumboots: Hayward, op. cit.

wiring in a few extra resistors: Flowers, 'The Design of Colossus', p. 247.

'band of brothers': Coombs, A. W. M. 'The Making of Colossus', *Annals of the History of Computing*, vol. 5 (1983), pp. 253–9 (p. 259).

By mid-July . . . : Hinsley, F. H. et al. *British Intelligence in the Second World War*, vol. 3, part 2 (London: Her Majesty's Stationery Office, 1988), maps 'OVERLORD' (frontispiece) and 'September position 1944' (facing p. 365).

unparalleled window on German preparations: some crucial decrypts are listed in Hinsley, *British Intelligence in the Second World War*, vol. 3, part 2, ch. 44 and appendix 10.

three were dedicated to wheel breaking: *General Report on Tunny*, p. 36.

Flowers was a regular visitor: Flowers' personal diary for 1944.

all 12 wheel settings: *General Report on Tunny*, p. 35.

considered the offer derisory: Peter Hilton in interview with Copeland (May 2001).

NOTE TO CHAPTER 6

82 *a German scientist and engineer came to see me*: Flowers is probably referring to Konrad Zuse (Ed.).

NOTES TO CHAPTER 7

84 *top-secret cryptographic dictionary*: 'A Cryptographic Dictionary' (anon., GC & CS, July 1944; in the US National Archives and Records Administration (NARA), College Park, Maryland; document reference RG 457, Historic Cryptographic Collection, Box 1413, NR 4559), p. 94. A digital facsimile of the Dictionary is available in The Turing Archive for the History of Computing <http://www.AlanTuring.net/crypt_dic_1944>.

Foreign Office signals interception programme and Scotland Yard: Kenworthy, H. C. 'The Interception of German Teleprinter Communications by Foreign Office Station Knockholt' (GC & CS, March 1946; in the National Archives/Public Record Office (PRO), Kew, Richmond, Surrey; document reference HW3/163), p. 4.

develop wireless for police vehicles: 'Wireless Telegraphy – Possible Use by Police' (notes of a conference held at the Home Office, 29 October 1925; PRO document reference MEPO 5/128).

Foreign Office started to finance: Kenworthy, 'The Interception of German Teleprinter Communications', p. 4.

85 *'any curious type of transmission'*: ibid.

first intercepted German non-Morse transmissions in 1932: ibid.

first wartime encounter with non-Morse: ibid, p. 1.

put aside, owing to a shortage of cryptanalysts: ibid.

teleprinter code and Hellschreiber: ibid., p. 2.

Some transmissions were supersonic: ibid.

transmissions were sent via Hellschreiber: *General Report on Tunny*, p. 14. <http://www.AlanTuring.net/tunny_report>

wired to a tone transmitter: *General Report on Tunny*, pp. 14, 457.

Assistance was provided by a small outstation: Kenworthy, 'The Interception of German Teleprinter Communications', pp. 2–3.

in May 1942, a farmhouse: ibid., p. 4.

altitude of about 600 feet: Small, A. 'Report on British Attack on "Fish" ' (US Navy Department, Washington DC, May 1945; NARA document reference RG 457, Historic Cryptographic Collection, Box 579, NR 1407), p. 17.

86 *over 800 people worked there*: Kenworthy, 'The Interception of German Teleprinter Communications', p. 18.

30 receiving sets: *General Report on Tunny*, p. 281.

about a quarter of them women: Small, A. 'Knockholt Intercept Station' (23 December 1944; NARA document reference RG 457, Historic Cryptographic Collection, Box 1424, NR 4682), p. 2.

managed the recording equipment: Small, 'Report on British Attack on "Fish" ', p. 17.

Two receiving sets were needed: ibid.

A dozen or so priority links: ibid.

search the airwaves for Tunny transmissions: *General Report on Tunny*, p. 281.

morning meeting at Bletchley Park: ibid.

priorities set by Bletchley exceeded Knockholt's capacity: ibid.

Knockholt intercepted . . .: *General Report on Tunny*, p. 394.

suspected depths were teleprinted immediately: ibid., p. 281.

'hitherto unknown degree of accuracy': Kenworthy, 'The Interception of German Teleprinter Communications', p. 13.

A single wrong or omitted character: *General Report on Tunny*, p. 281.

87 *25 or so available frequencies*: Gaschk, M. 'Non-Morse Operating Procedure' (16 October 1944; NARA document reference RG 457, Historic Cryptographic Collection, Box 880, NR 2612), p. 11.

teleprinters available at Denmark Hill were too slow: Kenworthy, 'The Interception of German Teleprinter Communications', p. 1.

30 words per minute: 'Non-Morse Activity' (anon., no date (*c.* May 1944); NARA document reference RG 457, Historic Cryptographic Collection, Box 880, NR 2612), p. 1.

speed of Tunny transmissions was 66 words per minute: Gaschk, 'Non-Morse Operating Procedure', p. 10.

88 *German operator would often use plaintext*: Gaschk, ibid. p. 11.

'civilian girls': 'Non-Morse Activity', p. 1.

a contemporary report said: Gaschk, 'Non-Morse Operating Procedure', p. 10.

'Red Form': Small, 'Report on British Attack on "Fish" ', p. 17; *General Report on Tunny*, pp. 269–70.

operator switched off the teleprinter: Gaschk, 'Non-Morse Operating Procedure', p. 4.

200 people at Knockholt whose job was to read: Small, 'Knockholt Intercept Station', p. 2.

Slip Reading Room: Gaschk, 'Non-Morse Operating Procedure', p. 6.

two months' training was necessary: ibid., p. 10.

slip produced by the Set Room was never read: Kenworthy, 'The Interception of German Teleprinter Communications', p. 18.

In the Perforation Room: Gaschk, 'Non-Morse Operating Procedure', p. 8.

transmitted twice to Bletchley Park: ibid.

by motorcycle despatch rider: Hinsley, F. H. et al. *British Intelligence in the Second World War*, vol. 3, part 1 (London: Her Majesty's Stationery Office, 1984), p. 479.

NOTES TO CHAPTER 9

101 *'the first electronic computing machine'*: von Neumann, J. 'The NORC and Problems in High Speed Computing' (1954), in Taub, A. H. (ed.) *Collected Works of John von Neumann*, vol. 5 (Oxford: Pergamon Press, 1963), pp. 238–9.

'the birth of electronic machines with ENIAC': Bell, C. G., Newell, A. *Computer Structures: Readings and Examples* (New York: McGraw-Hill, 1971), p. 42.

102 *'disciplined but unintelligent manner'*: Turing, A. M. *Programmers' Handbook for Manchester Electronic Computer* (Computing Machine Laboratory, University of Manchester, 1950; in the National Archive for the History of Computing, University of Manchester; a digital facsimile is in The Turing Archive for the History of Computing <http://www.AlanTuring.net/programmers_ handbook>), p. 1.

Lovelace envisaged: Lovelace, A. A., Menabrea, L. F. 'Sketch of the Analytical Engine Invented by Charles Babbage, Esq.' (1843), in Bowden, B. V. (ed.) *Faster than Thought* (London: Pitman, 1953).

103 *'Difference Engine'*: Babbage, C. *Passages from the Life of a Philosopher*, Vol. 11 of Campbell-Kelly, M. (ed.) *The Works of Charles Babbage* (London: William Pickering, 1989); Randell, B. (ed.) *The Origins of Digital Computers: Selected Papers*, 3rd edn. (Berlin: Springer-Verlag, 1982), ch. 1.

'Difference Engine No. 2', *designed during 1846–9*: Swade, D. *The Difference Engine: Charles Babbage and the Quest to Build the First Computer* (New York: Viking, 2001), pp. 173–7.

'Analytical Engine': Babbage, *Passages from the Life of a Philosopher*; Lovelace and Menabrea, 'Sketch of the Analytical Engine Invented by Charles Babbage, Esq.'; Randell, *The Origins of Digital Computers*, ch. 2; Bromley, A. 'Charles Babbage's Analytical Engine, 1838', *Annals of the History of Computing*, vol. 4 (1982), pp. 196–217.

Vannevar Bush and Howard Aiken: Bush, V. 'Instrumental Analysis', *Bulletin of the American Mathematical Society*, vol. 42 (1936), pp. 649–69; Aiken, H. 'Proposed Automatic Calculating Machine' (1937), in Randell, *The Origins of Digital Computers*.

mealtime discussion at Bletchley: Flowers in interview with Copeland (July 1996).

104 *ENIAC*: Burks, A. W. 'From ENIAC to the Stored-Program Computer: Two Revolutions in Computers', in Metropolis, N., Howlett, J., Rota, G. C. (eds) *A History of Computing in the Twentieth Century* (New York: Academic Press, 1980); Goldstine, H. H. *The Computer from Pascal to von Neumann* (Princeton: Princeton University Press, 1972); Goldstine, H. H., Goldstine, A. 'The Electronic Numerical Integrator and Computer' (1946), in Randell, *The Origins of Digital Computers.*

up to three weeks to set up and debug: Campbell-Kelly, M. 'The ACE and the Shaping of British Computing', in Copeland, B. J. (ed.) *Alan Turing's Automatic Computing Engine: The Master Codebreaker's Struggle to Build the Modern Computer* (Oxford: Oxford University Press, 2005), p. 151.

given by Newman: Newman in interview with Christopher Evans ('The Pioneers of Computing: An Oral History of Computing', London: Science Museum).

'which could naturally be regarded as computable': Turing, A. M. 'On Computable Numbers, with an Application to the Entscheidungsproblem', *Proceedings of the London Mathematical Society*, series 2, vol. 42 (1936–7), pp. 230–65 (p. 249); reprinted in Copeland, B. J. (ed.) *The Essential Turing* (Oxford: Oxford University Press, 2004).

105 *emphasised that the Analytical Engine was universal*: Turing, A. M. 'Computing Machinery and Intelligence', *Mind*, vol. 59 (1950), pp. 433–60 (p. 450); reprinted in Copeland, *The Essential Turing.*

works on both using exactly the same operations: Gandy, R. 'The Confluence of Ideas in 1936', in Herken, R. (ed.) *The Universal Turing Machine: A Half-Century Survey* (Oxford: Oxford University Press, 1988).

Turing was later to suggest: Turing, A. M. 'Lecture on the Automatic Computing Engine' (1947), in Copeland, *The Essential Turing*, p. 393.

Right from the start: Newman in interview with Evans.

Differential Analyser: Bush, V. 'The Differential Analyser: A New Machine for Solving Differential Equations', *Journal of the Franklin Institute*, vol. 212 (1931), pp. 447–88; Bush, V. 'Instrumental Analysis', *Bulletin of the American Mathematical Society*, vol. 42 (1936), pp. 649–69.

106 *Electromechanical program-controlled digital computers*: Stibitz, G. R. 'Early Computers', in Metropolis, Howlett, Rota, *A History of Computing in the Twentieth Century*; Aiken, H. H., Hopper, G. M. 'The Automatic Sequence Controlled Calculator', parts I–III (1946), in Randell, *The Origins of the Digital Computer*; Zuse, K. 'Some Remarks on the History of Computing in Germany', in Metropolis, Howlett, Rota, *A History of Computing in the Twentieth Century.*

Atanasoff–Berry Computer: Atanasoff, J. V. 'Computing Machine for the Solution of Large Systems of Linear Algebraic Equations' (1940), in Randell, *The Origins of the Digital Computer.*

In 1941 John Mauchly: Burks, A. R. *Who Invented the Computer: The Legal Battle that Changed Computing History* (Amherst: Prometheus, 2003), pp. 52–3.

107 *'much more of a computer than ENIAC'*: Flowers in interview with Copeland (July 1996).

'program store consisted of a bank of binary mechanical switches': Flowers, T. H. 'Colossus – origin and principles', typescript, no date, p. 5.

'didn't really understand much of it': Flowers in interview with Copeland (July 1996).

question of waiting until he 'got out': see next reference.

'in close touch with Turing': letter from Newman to von Neumann (8 February 1946) (in the von Neumann Archive at the Library of Congress, Washington, DC; a digital facsimile is in The Turing Archive for the History of Computing <http://www.AlanTuring.net/newman_vonneumann_8feb46>).

lectures 'on valve theory': Turing, S. *Alan M. Turing* (Cambridge: W. Heffer, 1959), p. 74.

108 *'Proposed Electronic Calculator'*: reprinted in Copeland, *Alan Turing's Automatic Computing Engine*; a digital facsimile of the original typewritten report is in The Turing Archive for the History of Computing <http://www.AlanTuring.net/proposed_electronic_calculator>.

'First Draft of a Report on the EDVAC': reprinted in Stern, N. *From ENIAC to UNIVAC: An Appraisal of the Eckert–Mauchly Computers* (Bedford, Mass.: Digital Press, 1981).

'information in the "First Draft" was of no help': letter from Harry Huskey to Copeland (4 February 2002).

not fully working until 1952: Huskey, H. D. 'The Development of Automatic Computing', in *Proceedings of the First USA–JAPAN Computer Conference*, Tokyo (1972), p. 702.

'I have read Wilkes' proposals . . .': memo from Turing to Womersley, c. December 1946 (in the Woodger Papers, National Museum of Science and Industry, Kensington, London (catalogue reference M15/77); a digital facsimile is in the Turing Archive for the History of Computing <http://www.AlanTuring.net/turing_womersley_cdec46>).

109 *'obsessed with the idea of speed on the machine'*: Wilkinson in interview with Evans (1976) ('The Pioneers of Computing: An Oral History of Computing', London: Science Museum).

much effort had gone into writing programs: Copeland, B. J. 'The Origins and Development of the ACE Project', in Copeland, *Alan Turing's Automatic Computing Engine.*

'greeted with hilarity': Michael Woodger in interview with Copeland (June 1998).

'one machine would suffice to solve all the problems': Darwin, C. 'Automatic Computing Engine (ACE)' (National Physical Laboratory, 17 April 1946; in the National Archives/Public Record Office (PRO), Kew, Richmond, Surrey (document reference DSIR 10/275); a digital facsimile is in The Turing Archive for the History of Computing <http://www.AlanTuring.net/darwin_ace>).

Flowers said that a 'minimal ACE' would be ready: anon. 'Status of the Delay Line Computing Machine at the P.O. Research Station' (National Physical Laboratory, 7 March 1946; in the Woodger Papers (catalogue reference M12/105); a digital facsimile is in The Turing Archive for the History of Computing <http://www.AlanTuring.net/delay_line_status>).

'too busy to do other people's work': Flowers in interview with Copeland (July 1998).

Turing suggested that the NPL: Turing, A. M. 'Report on visit to U.S.A., January 1st – 20th, 1947' (National Physical Laboratory, 3 February 1947; PRO document reference DSIR 10/385; a digital facsimile is in The Turing Archive for the History of Computing <http://www.AlanTuring.net/turing_usa_visit>).

inter-departmental rivalry: Copeland, 'The Origins and Development of the ACE Project', pp. 65–70.

'probably as far advanced 18 months ago': Minutes of the Executive Committee of the National Physical Laboratory for 20 April 1948 (NPL library; a digital facsimile is in The Turing Archive for the History of Computing <http://www.AlanTuring.net/npl_minutes_apr1948>).

pioneering work on Artificial Intelligence: Turing, A. M. 'Intelligent Machinery' (National Physical Laboratory Report, 1948; in the Woodger Papers; reprinted in Copeland, *The Essential Turing*).

'very fed up': Robin Gandy's description of Turing in interview with Copeland (November 1995).

110 *principles of Turing's ACE design were used in the G15*: Harry Huskey in interview with Copeland (February 1998).

G15: Huskey, H. D. 'The ACE Test Assembly, the Pilot ACE, the Big ACE, and the Bendix G15', in Copeland, *Alan Turing's Automatic Computing Engine.*

first G15 ran in 1954: letter from Huskey to Copeland (20 December 2001).

Other derivatives of the ACE: Bell and Newell, *Computer Structures*, pp. 44, 74; Froggatt, R. J. 'Logical Design of a Computer for Business Use', *Journal of the British Institution of Radio Engineers*, vol. 17 (1957), pp. 681–96; Yates, D. M. *Turing's Legacy: A History of Computing at the National Physical Laboratory 1945–1995* (London: Science Museum, 1997).

MOSAIC: digital facsimiles of a series of technical reports concerning the MOSAIC, by Coombs, Chandler, and others, are in The Turing Archive for the History of Computing <http://www.AlanTuring.net/mosaic>; see also Coombs, A. W. M. 'MOSAIC', in *Automatic Digital Computation: Proceedings of a Symposium Held at the National Physical Laboratory* (London: Her Majesty's Stationery Office, 1954).

MOSAIC first ran a program: 'Engineer-in-Chief's Report on the Work of the Engineering Department for the Year 1 April 1952 to 31 March 1953' (Post Office Engineering Department; in the Post Office Archive, London).

'it was just Chandler and I': Coombs in interview with Evans (1976) ('The Pioneers of Computing: An Oral History of Computing', London: Science Museum).

111 *approved in July 1946*: Council Minutes, Royal Society of London, 11 July 1946.

'It was one room in a Victorian building . . .': Williams, F. C. 'Early Computers at

Manchester University', *The Radio and Electronic Engineer*, vol. 45 (1975), pp. 237–331.

designed the input mechanism and programming system: letter from Williams to Randell (1972), in Randell, B. 'On Alan Turing and the Origins of Digital Computers', in Meltzer, B., Michie, D. (eds) *Machine Intelligence 5* (Edinburgh: Edinburgh University Press, 1972), p. 9.

programming manual: Turing, *Programmers' Handbook for Manchester Electronic Computer.*

'*Artificial Life*': Turing, A. M. 'The Chemical Basis of Morphogenesis', *Philosophical Transactions of the Royal Society of London*, Series B, vol. 237 (1952), pp. 37–72; reprinted in Copeland, *The Essential Turing.*

programming digital computers to think: Turing, A. M. 'Computing Machinery and Intelligence', *Mind*, vol. 59 (1950), pp. 433–60; reprinted in Copeland, *The Essential Turing.*

not as 'ideas men': Peter Hilton in interview with Copeland (May 2001).

112 '*Now let's be clear before we go any further . . .*': Williams in interview with Evans (1976) ('The Pioneers of Computing: An Oral History of Computing', London: Science Museum).

'*Tom Kilburn and I knew nothing about computers . . .*': Williams, 'Early Computers at Manchester University', p. 328.

Turing and Wilkinson gave a series of nine lectures: Turing, A. M., Wilkinson, J. H. 'The Turing–Wilkinson Lecture Series', in Copeland, *Alan Turing's Automatic Computing Engine.*

Among the audience was Kilburn: Bowker, G., Giordano, R. 'Interview with Tom Kilburn', *Annals of the History of Computing*, vol. 15 (1993), pp. 17–32 (p. 19).

Kilburn . . . usually said: letter from Brian Napper to Copeland (16 June 2002).

'*Between early 1945 and early 1947*': Bowker and Giordano, 'Interview with Tom Kilburn', pp. 19–20 (I am grateful to Napper for drawing this passage to my attention).

first report on the Manchester computer work: Kilburn, T. 'A Storage System for Use With Binary Digital Computing Machines' (1 December 1947; in the National Archive for the History of Computing, University of Manchester).

'*number of different computing projects is now so great*': Turing, 'Report on visit to U.S.A., January 1st – 20th, 1947'.

contract with the US Army Ordnance Department in June 1943: Goldstine, *The Computer from Pascal to von Neumann*, p. 150.

113 *Goldstine circulated the 'First Draft'*: Stern, N. 'John von Neumann's Influence on Electronic Digital Computing, 1944–1946', *Annals of the History of Computing*, vol. 2 (1980), pp. 349–62 (p. 354).

was working by the summer of 1951: Bigelow, J. 'Computer Development at the Institute for Advanced Study', in Metropolis, Howlett, Rota, *A History of Computing in the Twentieth Century.*

Von Neumann became familiar: Copeland, B. J. 'Computable Numbers: A Guide', in Copeland, *The Essential Turing*, pp. 21–2.

114 *'the great positive contribution of Turing'*: letter from von Neumann to Wiener (29 November 1946) (in the Library of Congress Manuscript Division, Washington, DC).

'I know that in or about 1943 or '44 . . .': letter from Frankel to Randell (11 February 1972). (First published in Randell, 'On Alan Turing and the Origins of Digital Computers', p. 10. I am grateful to Randell for giving me a copy of this letter.)

gave his engineers 'On Computable Numbers': letter from Bigelow to Copeland (12 April 2002).

'The person who really . . .': Bigelow in a tape-recorded interview made in 1971 by the Smithsonian Institution, Washington, DC (released in 2002). (I am grateful to Bigelow for sending me a transcript of excerpts from the interview.)

NOTES TO CHAPTER 10

116 *moved to the MIT campus in 1958*: Levy, S. *Hackers: Heroes of the Computer Revolution* (Garden City NY: Anchor Press/Doubleday, 1984), pp. 14–25.

120 *Colossus printed English plaintext from German ciphertext*: Ifrah, G. *A Universal History of Computing: From the Abacus to the Quantum Computer* (New York: John Wiley, 2001), p. 218.

122 *Colossus had circuits that computed XOR and OR*: figures 4 and 9 in Flowers, T. H. 'The Design of Colossus', *Annals of the History of Computing*, vol. 5 (1983), pp. 239–52 (pp. 243, 247).

'performing the logical functions': Flowers, T. H. 'Colossus – origin and principles', typescript, no date, p. 5. (Thanks to Jack Copeland for supplying me with this quotation.)

Flowers mentioned a one-valve inversion unit: Flowers, 'The Design of Colossus', p. 249.

123 *designated the ALU*: figure 16 in Flowers, ibid., p. 252.

124 *data in semi-permanent memory*: Flowers, ibid., p. 247.

125 *Flowers stated that the output of a thyratron ring*: Flowers, ibid., p. 248.

Flowers and Coombs affirmed increasing flexibility: Flowers, ibid., pp. 251–2; Coombs, A. W. M. 'The Making of Colossus', *Annals of the History of Computing*, vol. 5 (1983), pp. 253–9 (pp. 256–8).

126 *four structures that show some qualifications*: diagrammed in figure 16, Flowers, 'The Design of Colossus', p. 252. (The unnamed box lying to the left of the output counter is the 'combining unit'.)

127 *within heat limits according to Chandler*: Chandler, W. W. 'The Maintenance and Installation of Colossus', *Annals of the History of Computing*, vol. 5 (1983), pp. 260–2 (p. 262).

legend about the speed of Colossus: Fox, B., Webb, J. 'Colossal Adventures', *New Scientist*, vol. 154, no. 2081 (10 May 1997), pp. 38–43 (p. 43).

128 *asynchronous designs*: see e.g. Fant, K., Brandt, S. 'Null Convention Logic, A Complete and Consistent Logic for Asynchronous Digital Circuit Synthesis',

Proceedings of the International Conference on Application Specific Systems, Architectures, and Processors (ASAP '96) (Los Alamitos, California: IEEE Computer Society Press, 1996), pp. 261–73.

129 *reached the set total*: *General Report on Tunny*, p. 337. <http://www.AlanTuring.net/tunny_report>

131 *fantasy improvements*: *General Report on Tunny*, p. 331.

132 *According to Flowers, there was a temporary data store*: figure 16 in Flowers, 'The Design of Colossus', p. 252.

aided electronic circuits transforming the approximately rectangular pulses: Flowers, ibid., p. 243; Coombs, 'The making of Colossus', pp. 254–5.

133 *even visual output*: *General Report on Tunny*, p. 338.

five-row punch: ibid., pp. 326, 351.

135 *configured to facilitate this parallel programming*: Flowers, 'The Design of Colossus', pp. 251–2.

only parallel use described by Flowers: Flowers, ibid., pp. 245–6, 247, 249, 251–2.

136 *'multiple test' feature*: *General Report on Tunny*, pp. 337, 342, 345–50, 421.

two vague references to multiple reading: ibid., p. 337.

The two parallel modes seeem incompatible: ibid., p. 345.

throwing 'the multiple test switch': ibid., p. 345.

Flowers said that the programs tended to become hardwired: Flowers, 'The Design of Colossus', p. 251.

137 *special-purpose 'gadgets'*: *General Report on Tunny*, pp. 330, 349–51.

138 *improved Q panel*: ibid., pp. 333, 342.

Flowers said that the direct, wired coding: Flowers, 'The Design of Colossus', p. 252.

Functionality depended on the location: Copeland, B. J. (ed.) *Alan Turing's Automatic Computing Engine: The Master Codebreaker's Struggle to Build the Modern Computer* (Oxford: Oxford University Press, 2005), pp. 231, 245.

139 *'a degree of general-purpose programmability'*: Andresen, S. L. 'Donald Michie: Secrets of Colossus Revealed', *IEEE Intelligent Systems*, vol. 16, no. 6 (Nov/Dec 2001), pp. 82–3 (p. 83).

'problem domains far beyond the original': ibid.

140 *virtual Colossus and a virtual German Tunny machine*: inspired by Tony Sale's Virtual Colossus and Virtual Tunny available at: <http://www.codesand ciphers.org.uk/anoraks/lorenz/tools/>.

universality of computation on Colossus: Wells, B. 'A Universal Turing Machine Can Run on a Cluster of Colossi', *Abstracts of the American Mathematical Society*, vol. 25 (2004), p. 441.

NOTES TO CHAPTER 11

141 *book on the origins of digital computers*: Randell, B. (ed.) *The Origins of Digital Computers: Selected Papers* (Heidelberg: Springer-Verlag, 1975).

Turing's pre-war work: Turing, A. M. 'On Computable Numbers, with an Application to the Entscheidungsproblem', *Proceedings of the London Mathematical Society*, series 2, vol. 42 (1936–7), pp. 230–65.

an article by Jack Good: Good, I. J. 'Some Future Social Repercussions of Computers', *International Journal of Environmental Studies*, vol. 1 (1970), pp. 67–79.

The result of this investigation: Randell, B. 'On Alan Turing and the Origins of Digital Computers', in Meltzer, B., Michie, D. (eds) *Machine Intelligence 7* (Edinburgh: Edinburgh University Press, 1972).

142 *wartime photographs of Colossus*: National Archives/Public Record Office (PRO), Kew, Richmond, Surrey; reference FO 850/234.

my presentation: Randell, B. 'The Colossus', in Metropolis, N., Howlett, J., Rota, G. C. (eds.), *A History of Computing in the Twentieth Century* (New York: Academic Press, 1980).

143 *The Secret War*: Johnson, B. *The Secret War* (London: British Broadcasting Corporation, 1978).

Flowers was in charge: Flowers in interview with Randell (17 December 1975).

'work was fired at us': ibid.

special-purpose digital calculator: Beevers, C. A. 'A Machine for the Rapid Summation of Fourier Series', *Proceedings of the Physical Society (London)*, vol. 51 (1939), pp. 660–3.

early contact with digital computation: Flowers in interview with Randell (31 October 1975).

On the analogue side: ibid.

device for anti-aircraft ranging: Flowers in interview with Randell (17 December 1975).

144 *to work on a problem for Bletchley Park*: ibid.

first Post Office people to be initiated: letter from Flowers to Randell (21 January 1976).

Flowers' next six months: Flowers in interview with Randell (17 December 1975).

interacted with Turing: ibid.

Turing paid a number of visits: ibid.

brought in to help with this project: Flowers in interview with Randell (31 October 1975).

Broadhurst had . . .: Broadhurst in interview with Randell (11 November 1975); letter from Broadhurst to Randell (20 January 1976).

device that Flowers and Broadhurst built for Turing: Flowers in interview with Randell (17 December 1975).

a lot of the data and logic: Flowers in interview with Randell (31 October 1975).

nothing in the way of arithmetic or programming: Flowers in interview with Randell (17 December 1975).

turned out to have been a mistake: ibid.

wasted his time: ibid.

145 *joined the Research Branch at Dollis Hill in 1936*: Chandler and Coombs in interview with Randell (10 November 1975).

He had begun his career in 1930: Chandler, W. W. 'The Installation and Maintenance of Colossus', *Annals of the History of Computing*, vol. 5 (1983), pp. 260–2 (p. 261).

worked on long-distance signalling and dialling: ibid.

Flowers described Chandler: Flowers in interview with Randell (31 October 1975).

involved in a different project: Flowers in interview with Randell (17 December 1975).

direction from Turing: ibid.

electronic forms of relays: ibid.

spent some time at Letchworth: ibid.

valves instead of relays: ibid.

solution was not adopted: letter from Flowers to Randell (21 January 1976).

leading exponents of electronics at Bletchley: Flowers in interview with Randell (17 December 1975).

at about the time the first Colossus was commissioned: Broadhurst in interview with Randell (11 November 1975).

After leaving Glasgow University: Chandler and Coombs in interview with Randell (10 November 1975).

into the Foreign Office cipher work: ibid.

Wynn-Williams had assembled: letter from Wynn-Williams to Randell (16 March 1976).

Wynn-Williams undertook: Flowers in interview with Randell (17 December 1975).

146 *was thus that Morrell*: letter from Morrell to Randell (3 February 1976).

Post Office's 'Speaking Clock': Lynch, A. C. 'The "Transmitter, Telegraph, Mark I" ' (unpublished memorandum, 1976).

Speight and Lynch had previously designed and produced a teleprinter tape reader: unpublished manuscript by Gil Hayward (2002).

'Transmitter, Telegraph, Mark I': Lynch, 'The "Transmitter, Telegraph, Mark I" '.

2000 characters per second: letter from Flowers to Randell (23 January 1976); letter from Chandler to Randell (24 January 1976).

TRE and Dollis Hill halves: letter from Wynn-Williams to Randell (16 March 1976).

Flowers was confident: Chandler and Coombs in interview with Randell (10 November 1975).

'the basic thing about Flowers': ibid.

147 *mainly by Flowers and Chandler*: Broadhurst in interview with Randell (11 November 1975).

redesigned version of the one used in Heath Robinson: letter from Flowers to Randell (16 February 1976).

developed before the war by W. B. Lewis: Lewis, W. B. 'A "Scale of Two" High-Speed Counter Using Hard Vacuum Triodes', *Proceedings of the Cambridge Philosophical Society*, vol. 33 (1937), pp. 549–58.

book on counting circuits: Lewis, W. B. *Electrical Counting: With Special Reference to Alpha and Beta Particles* (Cambridge: Cambridge University Press, 1942).

When Flowers tried out: Chandler and Coombs in interview with Randell (10 November 1975); Flowers in interview with Randell (17 December 1975).

later patented: Flowers, T. H. 'Pulse Counting Circuits', UK Patent No. 584,704 (17 November 1944).

Tests were made using short loops: letter from Chandler to Randell (30 January 1976).

partially unwired prior to transportation: Chandler and Coombs in interview with Randell (10 November 1975).

team of junior technicians: Flowers in interview with Randell (31 October and 17 December 1975).

happened to take only ten minutes: Flowers in interview with Randell (17 December 1975).

'They just couldn't believe it ': ibid.

Historically significant features: letter from Flowers to Randell (26 May 1976).

148 *An additional counter was provided . . .*: letter from Flowers to Randell (26 May 1976).

design work was divided up: Chandler and Coombs in interview with Randell (10 November 1975); Flowers in interview with Randell (17 December 1975).

half the total workshop: Flowers in interview with Randell (31 October 1975).

would take two or three weeks: Chandler and Coombs in interview with Randell (10 November 1975).

Design work continued: Chandler and Coombs in interview with Randell (10 November 1975); Broadhurst in interview with Randell (11 November 1975).

Coombs was placed in charge: letter from Michie to Randell (18 March 1972).

probably less programmable: letter from Flowers to Randell (16 February 1976).

could not be mechanised: letter from Newman to Randell (20 March 1976).

149 *Flowers designed at least one other machine*: letter from Flowers to Randell (26 May 1976); letter from Michie to Randell (18 March 1972).

solved by Morrell: Flowers in interview with Randell (17 December 1975); letter from Flowers to Randell (21 January 1976).

then electronically synchronised: letter from Flowers to Randell (26 May 1976).

Robinson remained indispensable for 'crib runs': General Report on Tunny, p. 330. <http://www.AlanTuring.net/tunny_report>

Newmanry began to use it in June 1944: General Report on Tunny, p. 36.

A successful crib run usually produced: ibid., p. 331.

four Super Robinsons were ordered: ibid., p. 331.

four bedsteads and a plugboard: ibid., p. 26.

'span' and 'set total': ibid., p. 26.
completed by 8 May 1945: ibid., p. 36.

NOTES TO CHAPTER 12

150 *brief descriptions by Flowers, Coombs, and Chandler*: Flowers, T. H. 'The Design of Colossus', *Annals of the History of Computing*, vol. 5 (1983), pp. 239–52; Coombs, A. W. M. 'The Making of Colossus', *Annals of the History of Computing*, vol. 5 (1983), pp. 253–9; Chandler, W. W. 'The Maintenance and Installation of Colossus', *Annals of the History of Computing*, vol. 5 (1983), pp. 260–2.

152 *rebuild is on public display*: <www.bletchleypark.org.uk>; see also <www.codes andciphers.org.uk>.

NOTES TO CHAPTER 13

157 *immediately set up under Major Ralph Tester*: *General Report on Tunny*, p. 28. <http://www.AlanTuring.net/tunny_report>
read nearly every message from July to October: *General Report on Tunny*, p. 28.
Research Section renewed its efforts against Tunny: ibid., pp. 28, 320–2.
Newman was given the job: ibid., pp. 28, 322–3.

158 *Newmanry would be responsible for breaking and setting the chi-wheels*: ibid., p. 28.
two or three messages were being set each week: ibid., p. 276.
26 cryptographers, 28 engineers, and 273 Wrens: ibid., p. 276.
two Americans joined the cryptographic staff: ibid., p. 277.
'declared that it was impossible to break that code': Coombs in interview with Christopher Evans (1976) ('The Pioneers of Computing: An Oral History of Computing', London: Science Museum).
the Newmanry moved: *General Report on Tunny*, p. 276.
Wheel breaking took place in Block H: ibid., p. 30.
wheel setting was carried out in Block F: ibid., p. 30.
preparing and copying the tapes: ibid., p. 30.
print out the resulting de-chi: ibid., p. 30.
put in a bag: information from Peter Edgerley.
used for motor-setting and psi-setting: *General Report on Tunny*, pp. 29, 462.
responsibilty for psi-setting passed formally from the Testery to the Newmanry: ibid., p. 463.

159 *'It is regretted that it is not possible . . .'*: ibid., p. 327.
from HMS Pembroke V: ibid., p. 278.
'mathematics in School Certificate or "good social recommendations"': ibid, p. 278.
between 17 and 20 years of age: ibid., p. 278.
where they received up to a fortnight's training: ibid., p. 278.
nine per cent of Newmanry Wrens had received a university education: ibid., p. 278.
'cheerful common sense': ibid., p. 278.

'Wrens (unlike men)': ibid., p. 278.

The Report notes approvingly: ibid., p. 278.

167 *'Then there were the engineers'*: Newman in interview with Christopher Evans ('The Pioneers of Computing: An Oral History of Computing', London: Science Museum).

'[W]e used to go out regularly': Coombs in interview with Evans (1976).

168 *maintenance engineers were also supplied by Dollis Hill*: *General Report on Tunny*, p. 278.

recruited from the best available Post Office telephone engineers: ibid., p. 278.

'[W]e went round pinching good people': Coombs in interview with Evans (1976).

recruits worked first: *General Report on Tunny*, p. 278.

aged between 20 and 22: ibid., p. 279.

shifts of 70 hours a week or more: ibid., p. 279.

running stories about a Mrs Miles: Myers, K. 'Dollis Hill and Station X', in The Turing Archive for the History of Computing <http://www.AlanTuring.net/myers>.

170 *a fire on 15 November 1944*: *General Report on Tunny*, p. 462.

173 *British codebreaking headquarters was transferred from Bletchley Park*: Freeman, P. 'How GCHQ Came to Cheltenham' (undated, GCHQ), p. 8.

'Government Code and Cypher School', was formally changed: ibid.

during 1952–4 GCHQ transferred its personnel and equipment: Freeman, ibid., p. 30.

Two Colossi made the move from Bletchley Park: unpublished manuscript by Gil Hayward (2002).

two of the replica Tunny machines: ibid.

'I heard that Churchill . . .': letter from Jack Good to Henry H. Bauer (2 January 2005).

NOTES TO CHAPTER 14

178 *As Andrew Hodges has told*: Hodges, A. *Alan Turing: The Enigma* (London: Burnett, 1983), pp. 90–113.

179 *'Max has no job here . . .'*: letter from Lyn Newman to her parents (9 November 1937) (papers of Max and Lyn Newman, St John's College, Cambridge).

When she realised that Max's proof had failed: personal communication from Barbara Whitehead (2001).

180 *'every able-bodied man ought to be carrying a gun'*: letter from Lyn Newman to Max Newman (24 February 1941) (papers of Max and Lyn Newman).

'The man I mentioned to you . . .': letter from Blackett to John Godfrey (13 May 1942) (ibid.).

'some work going at a government institution': letter from F. E. Adcock to Newman (24 May 1942) (ibid.).

181 *'I rang up a friend in the Ministry of Reconstruction'*: letter from Blackett to Newman (22 June 1942) (ibid.).

Blackett wrote back: letter from Blackett to Newman (26 July 1942) (ibid.).

'*I gather from Blackett . . .*': letter from F. L. Lucas to Newman (27 July 1942) (ibid.).

182 *to lead research on special codebreaking machinery*: 'Most Secret. D.D. (S) Serial Order No. 80' (Bletchley Park, 1 February 1943); National Archives/Public Record Office (PRO), Kew, Richmond, Surrey (document reference HW 14/66).

on first-name terms, despite Max's insistence: personal communications from Donald Michie and Jack Good (16 November 2001).

183 *Flowers' 'more ambitious machine'*: letter from Newman to E. W. Travis (12 March 1943) (PRO document reference HW 14/70).

made visits to Knockholt: letter from Newman to Travis (22 August 1943) (PRO document reference HW 14/86).

184 *Max had had to argue diplomatically*: letter from Newman to Travis (28 November 1943) (PRO document reference HW 14/92).

a detailed argument for more staff: letter from Newman to D.D.I. (12 March 1944) (PRO document reference HW 14/99).

'*genial colleague, but he knew what he wanted*': letter from Ralph Tester to William Newman (10 January 1997).

intolerance for 'horseplay': file of documents on the official inquiry into a disturbance outside Max's office in December 1944 (Bletchley Park Trust).

186 '*I was, in fact, also offered an OBE*': letter from Newman to Norris McWhirter (18 August 1982) (papers of Max and Lyn Newman).

187 *unguarded remarks of Alan's*: *The Times*, 11 June 1949.

describing the more mundane computing work on checking Mersenne prime numbers: *The Times*, 14 June 1949.

188 *working on a paper that was to surprise many*: Newman, M. H. A. 'On the division of Euclidian n-space by topological (n–1)-spheres', *Proceedings of the Royal Society of London*, series A, vol. 257 (1960), pp. 1–12.

'*suspended animation*': Max quoted by Lyn Newman in a letter to Nancy Blackburn (22 March 1961) (papers of Max and Lyn Newman).

NOTES TO CHAPTER 15

189 *letter to Churchill*: 'Letter to Winston Churchill', in Copeland, B. J. (ed.) *The Essential Turing* (Oxford: Oxford University Press, 2004).

192 *Jack Good pointed out*: Good, I. J. *The 1998 'Computer Pioneer Award' of the IEEE Computer Society*, Technical Report 98–11 (IEEE Computer Society, 1998).

I exaggerated Turing's role: Hilton, P. 'Reminiscences of Bletchley Park, 1942–1945', in *A Century of Mathematics in America*, part I (American Mathematical Society, 1988), pp. 291–301.

197 *Max Newman*: further remarks about Max Newman may be found in my obituary of him in *Bulletin of the London Mathematical Society*, vol. 18 (1986), pp. 67–72.

198 *volunteered for the Local Defence Volunteers*: Andrew Hodges asserts on page 231 of his biography of Turing (*Alan Turing: The Enigma*, New York: Simon and Schuster, 1988) that 'The authorities quaintly insisted upon the Bletchley analysts doing soldierly work in their spare time.' I have no recollection of such a fatuous order.

NOTES TO CHAPTER 16

206 *'remarkably effective in an ugly and contorted style'*: Milner-Barry, S. 'C. H. O'D. Alexander—A Personal Memoir', in Golombek, H., Hartson, W. R. *The Best Games of C. H. O'D. Alexander* (Oxford: Oxford University Press, 1976), p. 1.

207 *'Fuzzy Bayes'*: Good, I. J., Lewis, B. C. 'Probability Estimation for 2 by S Contingency Tables and Predictive Criteria', *Proceedings of 43rd Session* (Buenos Aires, 1981), *Bulletin of the International Statistics Institute*, vol. 49 (1983), book 1, pp. 97–113.

   Max Planck's resolution: Van Fleck, J. H. 'Quantum mechanics', *Encyclopaedia Britannica*, vol. 18 (1951), pp. 814–27 (p. 815).

   simplicity in scoring: Alexander, C. H. O'D. 'Cryptographic History of Work on the German Naval Enigma', no date (*c.*1945) (National Archives/Public Record Office (PRO), Kew, Richmond, Surrey; document reference HW 25/1), p. 94; a digital facsimile of Alexander's typescript is available in The Turing Archive for the History of Computing <http://www.AlanTuring.net/alexander_naval_enigma>.

208 *In April 1943*: *General Report on Tunny*, p. 276. <http://www.AlanTuring.net/tunny_report>

210 *Hilton gave too much credit to Turing*: Hilton, P. J. 'Reminiscences of Bletchley Park, 1942–1945', in *A Century of Mathematics in America*, part I (American Mathematical Society, 1988), pp. 291–301; 'Working with Alan Turing', *The Mathematical Intelligencer*, vol. 13 (1991), pp. 23–5.

212 *in the penultimate paragraph of his article of 1981*: Rejewski, M. 'How Polish Mathematicians Broke the Enigma Cipher' (trans. Stepenske, J.), *Annals of the History of Computing*, vol. 3 (1981), pp. 213–29 (with comments by C. Devours (pp. 229–32) and I. J. Good (pp. 232–4)).

   the US navy built 120 electronic Bombes: Lee, J. A. N., Burke, C., Anderson, D. *The American Bombes: NCR, Joseph Desch, and 600 Waves* (typescript, 1 June 1998), p. 11.

215 *with some algebra*: the algebra is set out in sections 21 and 22 of *General Report on Tunny*.

   calculus of finite differences: Jordan, C. *Calculus of Finite Differences* (New York: Chelsea, 1939).

216 *Wheel setting*: see section 23 of *General Report on Tunny* for a much more complete account of wheel setting.

217 *Chandler once said*: Chandler, W. W. 'The Maintenance and Installation of Colossus', *Annals of the History of Computing*, vol. 5 (1983), pp. 260–2 (p. 262).
218 *As Chandler remarked*: Chandler, ibid., p. 261.
   article on infinitely long games of chess: Euwe, M. 'Set Theory, Observations on Chess', *Proceedings of the Academy of Sciences, Amsterdam*, vol. 32 (1929), pp. 632–42.
219 *coalescence*: *General Report on Tunny*, sections 23N, 23X.
   Markov Chain Monte Carlo (MCMC) method: Casella, G., Lavine, M., Robert, C. P. 'Explaining the Perfect Sampler', *The American Statistician*, vol. 55, no. 4 (2001), pp. 299–305.
   'Colossus rectangling has been slightly disappointing': *General Report on Tunny*, p. 330.
220 *When T. H. Huxley first heard of the theory*: Milner, R. *The Encyclopedia of Evolution* (New York: Facts on File, 1990), p. 22.

NOTES TO CHAPTER 17

223 *Codebreaking and Colossus*: this chapter is a modified and updated version of the author's 'Colossus and the Breaking of the Wartime "Fish" Codes', *Cryptologia*, vol. 26 (2001), pp. 17–58.
234 *first mention appeared in the open literature*: Good, I. J. 'Pioneering Work on Computers at Bletchley', in Metropolis, N., Howlett, J., and Rota, G. (eds) *A History of Computing in the Twentieth Century* (New York: Academi Press, 1980).
240 *Newman remembered*: letter from Newman to Brian Randell (26 November 1975).

NOTES TO CHAPTER 22

281 *extended three floors into the ground*: unpublished manuscript by Gil Hayward (2002).
282 *The electronics coped, but the paper tape disintegrated*: Flowers in interview with Christopher Evans in 1977 ('The Pioneers of Computing: an Oral History of Computing', London: Science Museum).
284 *by the British Tabulating Machine Company in Letchworth*: 'Enigma – Position' and 'Naval Enigma Situation', notes dated 1 November 1939 and signed by Knox, Twinn, Welchman, and Turing (National Archives/Public Record Office (PRO), Kew, Richmond, Surrey; document reference HW 14/2).
287 *counter that W. B. Lewis had described*: Lewis, W. B. *Electrical Counting, With Special Reference to Counting Alpha and Beta Particles* (Cambridge: Cambridge University Press, 1942), p. 91.

NOTES TO CHAPTER 25

307 *Siemens T52 existed in four functionally distinct models*: Davies, D. W. 'The Siemens and Halske T52e Cipher Machine', *Cryptologia*, vol. 6 (1982), pp. 289–308; Davies, D. W. 'The Early Models of the Siemens and Halske T52 Cipher Machine', *Cryptologia*, vol. 7 (1983), pp. 235–53; Mache, W. 'The Siemens Cipher Teletype in the History of Telecommunications', *Cryptologia*, vol. 13 (1989), pp. 97–117; Mache, W. 'Der Siemens-Geheimschreiber—ein Beitrag zur Geschichte der Telekommunikation. 1992: 60 Jahre Schlüsselfernschreibmaschine' (The Siemens Secret Writer—A Contribution to the History of Telecommunication. 1992: 60 years of the Cipher Teleprinter Machine), *Archiv für deutsche Postgeschichte*, no. 2 (1992), pp. 85–94; Weierud, F. 'Sturgeon, The FISH BP Never Really Caught', in Joyner, D. (ed.) *Coding Theory and Cryptology: From Enigma and Geheimschreiber to Quantum Theory* (New York: Springer-Verlag, 2000), pp. 18–52.

first revealed that Sweden had broken the T52: Boheman, E. *På Vakt. Kabinettssekreterare under andra världskriget* (On Duty. Under-Secretary of State During the Second World War) (Stockholm: Norstedts och Söners Förlag, 1964); Kahn, D. *The Codebreakers* (New York: Macmillan, 1967), pp. 482–3.

only in 1984 that the British officially acknowledged: Hinsley, F. H. et al. *British Intelligence in the Second World War*, Vol. 3, Part 1 (London: Her Majesty's Stationery Office, 1984), pp. 477–82.

308 *BP decided to concentrate on Tunny*: Hinsley, op. cit., p. 477; Hinsley, F. H. 'Cracking the Ciphers', *Electronics & Power IEE*, vol. 33 (July 1987), pp. 453–5; Hinsley, F. H. 'An Introduction to Fish', in Hinsley, F. H., Stripp, A. (eds) *Codebreakers: The Inside Story of Bletchley Park* (Oxford: Oxford University Press, 1993), pp. 141–8.

309 *Lorenz worked on the development of an improved machine*: European Axis Signal Intelligence in World War II: Vol. 2 – Notes on German High Level Cryptography and Cryptanalysis, Army Security Agency (1 May 1946). (Thanks to David Alvarez for supplying me with a copy of this document.)

'*Sägefisch*': Maas, F. J. 'Der Stand der Funkfernschreibtechnik in Deutschland bis 1944' (The State of Radio Teleprinter Techniques in Germany up to 1944). Unpublished manuscript (15 February 1946). (Thanks to Wolfgang Mache for supplying me with a copy of this manuscript.)

310 *called the 'Sturgeon' link*: 'Sturgeon Type Ciphers', anon., BP Research Section (November 1944), an addendum to Captain Walter J. Fried's Report No. 116 of 17 November 1944 (National Archives and Records Administration (NARA), College Park, Maryland, USA; document reference RG 457, NSA Historical Collection, Box 880, NR 2612).

Crum analysed the depths: Wylie, S. 'Breaking Tunny and the Birth of Colossus', in Erskine, R., Smith M. (eds.) *Action This Day: Bletchley Park from the Breaking of the Enigma Code to the Birth of the Modern Computer* (London: Bantam, 2001), p. 319.

gave many of the more obscure codes new meanings: Fried, W. J. 'Fish Notes (Non Morse Army Q Code)', Report No. 122 (29 November 1944) (NARA document reference RG 457, NSA Historical Collection, Box 880, NR 2612).

314 *impulses always summed to zero*: 'Sturgeon Type Ciphers', anon., BP Research Section (November 1944), addendum to Fried's Report No. 116 of 17 November 1944 (NARA document reference RG 457, NSA Historical Collection, Box 880, NR 2612).

315 *BP was initially confronted with the T52c*: Davies, 'The Early Models of the Siemens and Halske T52 Cipher Machine'; Mache, 'The Siemens Cipher Teletype in the History of Telecommunications'; Mache, 'Der Siemens-Geheimschreiber— ein Beitrag zur Geschichte der Telekommunikation. 1992: 60 Jahre Schlüsselfernschreibmaschine'.

316 *broken from the depth of five*: Fried, W. J. 'FISH Notes (Sturgeon)', Report No. 68 (29 July 1944) (NARA document reference RG 457, NSA Historical Collection, Box 880, NR 2612).

318 *each switch interchanged two wheels*: Davies, 'The Early Models of the Siemens and Halske T52 Cipher Machine'.

319 *Two of the wheels were controlled by a plaintext cross*: 'Sturgeon Type Ciphers', anon., BP Research Section (November 1944), constituting Fried's Report No. 116 of 17 November 1944 (NARA document reference RG 457, NSA Historical Collection, Box 880, NR 2612). (This logic is described in detail in Davies, 'The Siemens and Halske T52e Cipher Machine', and in Davies, D. W. 'New Information on the History of the Siemens and Halske T52 Cipher Machine', *Cryptologia*, vol. 18 (1994), pp. 141–6.)

known from German sources: Mache, 'The Siemens Cipher Teletype in the History of Telecommunications'; *Die Siemens Schlüsselfernschreibmaschine SFM T52d (T typ 52 d)* (The Siemens Cipher Teleprinter Machine SFM T52d), Oberkommando der Kriegsmarine, Berlin (March 1944) (M.Dv. Nr. 35IV, D.(Luft) T.g.Kdos. 9105d).

main instruction book for the use of teleprinter cipher machines: *Schlüsselfernschreibvorschrift* (Cipher Teleprinter Regulations), Deutsche Wehrmacht (1 December 1942) (H.Dv.g 422, L.Dv.g 704/3b, M.Dv. Nr. 924a).

On 17 October 1942 an Enigma message: message on Red (the main German air force) key, 121–2–3, 17/10, 6610.

322 *message from Madrid to Paris*: message on the Abwehr link Madrid–Paris, RSS 6713/2/43.

new set of instructions for using the T52: message on the German army's Bullfinch II (Italy) key, 1735/18/2/43.

On 19 February another message: message on the German army's Merlin (Southern Europe) key, 19/2/43.

on 6 March two messages: messages on Red Nos. 322/4 and 387/7, 6/3/43.

On 14 June 1943 there was a message: German navy message 14/6/43, 77, Mediterranean.

324 *'This officer has been of great service'*: Ulstein, R. *Etterretningstjenesten i Norge*

1940–45 (Intelligence Service in Norway 1940–45), vol. 2 (Oslo: Cappelen, 1990), p. 361 (note 3).

'The Swedish Bureau had had considerable success': 'Memo to the Head of the G.C. & C.S.', anon. (15 November 1941) (National Archives/Public Record Office (PRO), Kew, Richmond, Surrey; document reference HW 14/22). (Thanks to Ralph Erskine for supplying me with a copy of this document.)

325 *Enigma was used by the Security Police*: Haarstad, G. *I Hemmelig Tjeneste* (In Secret Service) (Oslo: Aschehoug, 1988), p. 70.

use of Enigma by the East German State Police: Lewis, A. 'Deciphering on the M8 – Top Secret SUEDE', part of the file 'The Setting Rotor' (NARA document reference RG 457, NSA Historical Collection, Box 950, NR 2805). ('Deciphering on the M8', itself undated, is written on ASA (Army Security Agency) Form 781-C10S with the date 6 July 1951. In the margin there is a handwritten note: 'Used for deciphering E. German Police Enigma on the tape-printing Sigaba. Not applicable to other machines being used as ?. 22-May 1952. MKS'.)

'In accordance with the Minutes . . .': Abrook, R. H. 'Service Trials of the G. Schreiber – Headquarters No. 26 Group, Air Staff Memorandum, Task No. 817, Appendix X' (PRO document reference AIR 25/563).

326 *In 1946 the Norwegian Cipher Office*: Selmer, E. S. 'The Norwegian Modification of the Siemens and Halske T52e Cipher Machines', *Cryptologia*, vol. 18 (1994), pp. 147–9.

would be left with the Norwegians: 'No. 8801 Air Disarmament Wing, Operations Record Book', Royal Air Force (1945) (PRO document reference AIR 26/508).

about 380 T52 machines survived: Mache, 'Der Siemens-Geheimschreiber—ein Beitrag zur Geschichte der Telekommunikation. 1992: 60 Jahre Schlüssel-fernschreibmaschine', p. 92.

they were only dismantled: Mache, 'Der Siemens-Geheimschreiber—ein Beitrag zur Geschichte der Telekommunikation. 1992: 60 Jahre Schlüssel-fernschreib-maschine', p. 92.

Willi Reichert: the firm was Willi Reichert, Elektronik und Electromechanik, Trier, Petrisberg; later it became Willi Reichert, Werkstätten für Radio und Fernmeldetechnik, Trier, Güterstrasse 1.

to the French Foreign Office: Mache, 'Der Siemens-Geheimschreiber—ein Beitrag zur Geschichte der Telekommunikation. 1992: 60 Jahre Schlüsselfernschreib-maschine', p. 92.

327 *a manual cipher called TAPIR*: 'Schlüssel für den Fernschreibverkehr' (Encryption for Teleprinter Traffic), Ministerium für Staatssicherheit (Mf S), Berlin (21 October 1950). (Thanks to Jürg Drobick for supplying me with a copy of this document.)

a United States Intelligence report: Kimbrell, G. T. 'Communications in the Soviet Zone of Germany' (18 July 1951) (indexed as 'Three German Language Radio Communication Reports'; NARA document reference RG 457, NSA Historical Collection, Box 1112, NR 3457).

NOTES TO CHAPTER 26

330 *Stockholm was no exception*: McKay, C. G. *From Information to Intrigue: Studies in Secret Service based on the Swedish Experience 1939–1945* (London: Frank Cass, 1991).

332 *Hinsley has singled out*: Hinsley, F. H. 'An Introduction to Fish', in Hinsley, F. H., Stripp, A. (eds) *Codebreakers: The Inside Story of Bletchley Park* (Oxford: Oxford University Press, 1994).

NOTES TO APPENDIX 1

339 *German precaution*: *General Report on Tunny*, pp. 11–12. <http://www.AlanTuring.net/tunny_report>

341 *first of six Research Logs*: *General Report on Tunny*, p. 1.

342 $\hat{\chi}_2$: ibid., p. 169.

343 *Garbo*: ibid., p. 369.

344 *slide-run*: ibid., p. 435.

      flag: ibid., p. 413.

347 *the 5202*: ibid., pp. 469–80.

NOTE TO APPENDIX 5

372 *deduce the two plaintexts, p′ and p″, from the result d*: Good, I. J. 'Enigma and Fish', in Hinsley, F. H., Stripp A. (eds) *Codebreakers: The Inside Story of Bletchley Park* (Oxford: Oxford University Press, 1993), p. 161.

NOTES TO APPENDIX 6

378 *day after Chamberlain's announcement*: letter from A. G. Denniston to T. J. Wilson of the Foreign Office (Government Code and Cypher School, 7 September 1939; National Archives/Public Record Office (PRO), Kew, Richmond, Surrey, document reference FO 366/1059).

      during the first weeks of the war he designed the machines: Knox, A. D., Twinn, P. F. G., Welchman, W. G., Turing, A. M. 'Enigma – Position' (Government Code and Cypher School, 1 November 1939; PRO document reference HW 14/2).

      'Prof's Book': 'Mathematical theory of ENIGMA machine by A M Turing' (Government Code and Cypher School, no date (*c.* summer 1940); PRO document reference HW 25/3). Chapter 6, 'Bombe and Spider', is in Copeland, B. J. (ed.) *The Essential Turing* (Oxford: Oxford University Press, 2004). A digital facsimile of Turing's typescript is in The Turing Archive for the History of Computing <http://www.AlanTuring.net/profs_book>.

      ten miles of wire and a million soldered connections: Mahon, P. 'The History of Hut Eight', Bletchley Park (June 1945), in Copeland, *The Essential Turning*, p. 291.

installed in March 1940: 'Squadron-Leader Jones' Section', anon. (Government Code and Cypher School, no date (*c.* 1945); PRO document reference HW3/164), p. 1.

15 Bombes: Alexander, H. 'Cryptographic History of Work on the German Naval Enigma' (Government Code and Cypher School, no date (c. 1945); PRO document reference HW 25/1), p. 35. A digital facsimile of Alexander's typescript is in The Turing Archive for the History of Computing <http://www.AlanTuring.net/alexander_naval_enigma>.

From August 1940 the Bombes included: Hinsley, F. H. et al. *British Intelligence in the Second World War*, vol. 3, part 2 (London: Her Majesty's Stationery Office, 1988), p. 955.

WETTER FUER DIE NACHT: Mahon, 'The History of Hut Eight', p. 296.

FEUER BRANNTEN WIE BEFOHLEN: Mahon, ibid., p. 303.

used exclusively by Turing: 'Squadron-Leader Jones' Section', p. 2.

merchant ships were sunk: Roskill, S. W. *The War At Sea 1939–1945* (London: HMSO, 1954), pp. 615–16.

379 *no work was being done on Naval Enigma, which was generally considered unbreakable*: Mahon, 'The History of Hut Eight', p. 279.

'the Germans don't mean you to read their stuff': Morris, C. 'Navy Ultra's Poor Relations', in Hinsley, H., Stripp, A. (eds.) *Codebreakers: The Inside Story of Bletchley Park* (Oxford: Oxford University Press, 1993), p. 237.

'Birch thought it could be broken': Alexander, 'Cryptographic History of Work on the German Naval Enigma', p. 19.

'Turing first got interested': Alexander, ibid. p. 20.

once by means of the Enigma machine itself, and once by hand: Mahon, 'The History of Hut Eight', p. 272.

By the end of 1939 Turing had deduced: Mahon, ibid., p. 285.

'pinches' of material: there is an account of the pinches in Copeland, B. J., 'Enigma', in *The Essential Turing*.

re-routings based on Hut 8 decrypts were reportedly: Hinsley, F. H. et al, *British Intelligence in the Second World War*, Vol. 2 (London: Her Majesty's Stationery Office, 1981), p. 171.

hand method called Banburismus: Mahon, 'The History of Hut Eight', pp. 281–5.

invented this on the same productive night: Mahon, ibid., p. 281.

dependent on Banburismus until 1943: Mahon, ibid., p. 285.

United States in November 1942: Turing, S. *Alan M. Turing* (Cambridge: Heffer, 1959), p. 71.

liased with the US Navy's codebreakers and Bombe-builders: Turing, A. M. 'Visit to National Cash Register Corporation of Dayton, Ohio' (Government Code and Cypher School, no date (*c.* December 1942); US National Archives and Records Administration (NARA), College Park, Maryland; document reference RG 38, CNSG Library, 5750/441). A digital facsimile of the report is in The Turing

Archive for the History of Computing <http://www.AlanTuring.net/turing_ncr>.

did no further work in Hut 8: Alexander, 'Cryptographic History of Work on the German Naval Enigma', p. 42.

returned to Bletchley Park in March 1943: Turing, *Alan M. Turing*, p. 72.

scientific policy adviser: Don Horwood in interview with Copeland (October 2001).

380 *'Fundamental scoring unit'*: 'A Cryptographic Dictionary', anon. (Government Code and Cypher School, 1944; NARA document reference RG 457, Historic Cryptographic Collection, Box 1413, NR 4559), p. 4. A digital facsimile of the original typescript is in The Turing Archive for the History of Computing <http://www.AlanTuring.net/crypt_dic_1944>.

'greatest intellectual contribution during the war': Michie, D. 'Colossus and the Breaking of the Wartime "Fish" Codes', *Cryptologia*, vol. 26 (2001), pp. 17–58 (p. 27).

post-war book by Abraham Wald: Wald, A. *Sequential Analysis* (New York: John Wiley, 1947).

used extensively in the Newmanry: *General Report on Tunny*, index, p. 408. <http://www.AlanTuring.net/tunny_report>

Newmanry rule of thumb: Carter, F. 'The Use of Probability Theory in the Newmanry' (unpublished manuscript).

'percolated the general practice of Newmanry people': letter from Donald Michie to Copeland (28 November 2001).

'routinely supported the duty officer's use of Colossus': ibid.

'three of us (Peter Ericsson, Peter Hilton, and I)': letter from Michie to Copeland (29 July 2001).

381 *the Germans changed the cam patterns*: *General Report on Tunny*, pp. 14, 458.

written by Michie: letter from Michie to Copeland (28 November 2001).

382 *'influence on the development of Colossus is well known'*: Lee, J. A. N. *Computer Pioneers* (Los Alamitos: IEEE Computer Society Press, 1995), p. 671.

'cryptanalytical machine designed by Alan Turing': Lee, ibid., p. 306.

'Turing's ideas for the design of high-speed electronic machines': Lee, ibid., p. 492.

'on what we now know was computer research': Enever, E. *Britain's Best Kept Secret: Ultra's Base at Bletchley Park* (2nd edn., Stroud: Alan Sutton, 1994), pp. 36–7.

'Turing built a succession of vacuum-tube machines called Colossus': Golden, F. 'Who Built the First Computer?', *Time*, March 29, 1999, no. 13, p. 82.

'these ideas were implemented as the "Colossus" machines': Lee, J. A. N., Holtzman, G. '50 Years After Breaking the Codes', *Annals of the History of Computing*, vol. 17 (1999), pp. 32–43 (p. 33).

'Colossus was entirely the idea of Mr Flowers': *General Report on Tunny*, p. 35.

383 *'made no contribution'*: Flowers in interview with Copeland (July 1996).

'I invented the Colossus': ibid. (July 1996).

'Some of the methods to be used were playfully called turingismus . . .': Davis, M.

The Universal Computer: The Road from Leibniz to Turing (New York: Norton, 2000), pp. 174–5.
Michie underlined: letter from Michie to Copeland (28 November 2001).

NOTE TO APPENDIX 8

395 *Prob*$[\Delta d_i \oplus \Delta d_j = \bullet] = 0.55$: *General Report on Tunny*, p. 322. <http://www.AlanTuring.net/tunny_report>

NOTES TO APPENDIX 9

396 *'integrating' the wheel*: Small, A. 'Report on British Attack on "Fish" ', US Navy Department, Washington, DC (May 1945) (US National Archives and Records Administration (NARA), College Park, Maryland; document reference RG 457, Historic Cryptographic Collection, Box 579, NR 1407), p. 74.

404 *odds of being correct were 1000:1 on*: ibid., p. 76.
'computer time is often cheaper than Colossus time': *General Report on Tunny*, p. 122. <http://www.AlanTuring.net/tunny_report>

NOTES TO APPENDIX 11

410 *'perfect'*: *General Report on Tunny*, p. 425. <http://www.AlanTuring.net/tunny_report>
'substantialisation' of sign sequences in X-ray crystallography: Good, I. J. 'On the Substantialisation of Sign Sequences', *Acta Crystallographica*, vol. 7 (1954), p. 603, and 'Randomized and Pseudorandomized Substantialization of Sign Sequences', *Acta Crystallographica*, vol. 12 (1959), pp. 824–5.

NOTES TO APPENDIX 12

415 *Siemens company was contacted*: Mache, W. 'Geheimschreiber', *Cryptologia*, vol. 10 (1986), pp. 230–42 (p. 231).

416 *US patent was granted on 6 June 1933*: Davies, D. W. 'The Siemens and Halske Cipher Machine', *Cryptologia*, vol. 6 (1982), pp. 289–308 (p. 290).
Models T52d and T52e appeared in 1942–3: Mache, 'Geheimschreiber', p. 233; Weierud, F. 'Sturgeon, The Fish BP Never Really Caught' in Joyner, D. (ed.) *Coding Theory and Cryptography* (Berlin: Springer-Verlag, 2000), pp. 20–34.
encryptions having a key group: Bauer, F. L. *Decrypted Secrets: Methods and Maxims of Cryptology* (Berlin: Springer-Verlag, 2002, 3rd edn.), p. 156.

Sources of Photographs

Frontispiece Kenneth Flowers. **1–2** Government Communications Headquarters, Cheltenham. **3** Beryl Turing and King's College Library, Cambridge. **4** William Tutte. **5** Royal Society of London. **6** Catherine Caughey. **7** Dorothy Du Boisson. **8** Jack Good. **9** Eleanor Ireland. **10** Donald Michie. **11** Karin Dawe. **12** Helen Currie. **13** Peter Hilton. **14** Jerry Roberts. **15** Harry Fensom. **16** Gil Hayward. **17** Bletchley Park Trust. **18–20** Science and Society Picture Library, National Museum of Science and Industry, London. **21** Barbara Eachus and Government Communications Headquarters, Cheltenham. **22** Wladyslaw Kozaczuk, *Enigma* (Arms and Armour Press, 1984). **23** Beryl Turing and King's College Library, Cambridge. **24** Picture Library, Imperial War Museum, London. **25** National Archives and Records Administration, College Park, Maryland, USA. **26–29** Picture Library, Imperial War Museum, London. **30–39** National Archives Image Library, Kew (Crown copyright). **40** Government Communications Headquarters, Cheltenham. **41** Jack Copeland. **42** J. Lyons and Co. **43** Science and Society Picture Library, National Museum of Science and Industry, London. **44** School of Computer Science, University of Manchester. **45** National Physical Laboratory, Teddington (Crown copyright). **46** Harry Huskey. **47** Royal Mail Group plc (Crown copyright). **48** School of Computer Science, University of Manchester. **49** Collections of the University of Pennsylvania Archives, USA. **50** Alan Richards/Archives of the Institute for Advanced Study, University of Princeton, USA. **51-52** Frode Weierud.

Photo processing by Dustin Barrett.

Index

Numerals in **bold** indicate Plate numbers.

1+2 break in 51, 58–9, 64, 66, 67–70, 157, 216, 340, 363–5, 383, 386–90
5202 (cryptanalytical machine) 347

'$ab = \frac{1}{2}$' principle 339, 393, 407–8
ACE *see* Automatic Computing Engine
Adcock, F. 180
Aiken, H. 103, 106
Aire, C. 208
Aitken, J. 199
Alexander, C. H. 28, 53, 61, 189, 199, 204, 205–6, 207, 208, 235, 379
al-Kindi, A. 11
Analyser (decoding machine) 73, 78, 144, 284, 285, 302
Analytical Engine 103, 104, 105
Anderson, L. 234
Andrews, J. 221–2
app (apparat) 329, 331
Aquarius (cryptanalytical machine) 131, 301–2; *photograph* **38**
Arnhem 167
Artificial Intelligence 105, 109, 111, 187, 235
Artificial Life 111
Ashcroft, M. 208, 209, 244
Atanasoff, J. 106
Atanasoff–Berry Computer 106
Atkin, O. 209
autoclave 49, 314, 367
Auto-Teller 146, 221, 297
Automatic Computing Engine (ACE) 108–10, 112
    Pilot Model of 109, 138; *photograph* **45**

B-tube 186

Babbage, C. 14, 101, 102–3, 105, 108, 114; *photograph* **43**
Babbage, D. 28
Bacon, F. 411
ban *see* deciban
Banburies 379
Banburismus 33, 206–7, 379–80, 381
Banister list (Blist) 29
Banister, M. 29
Barbarossa 329; *see also* Battle of Kursk, Russian front, *Zitadelle*
Barratt, R. 253, 270
Batch, R. 386
Baudot–Murray code *see* teleprinter code
Baudot, J. 38, 411
Beevers, C. A. 143
Bendix G15 110, 116; *photograph* **46**
Benenson, P. 199, 208, 237, 250, 253
Bennett, R. 31
Berlin, fall of 6, 262
Bertrand, G. 26
Beurling, A. 328–9, 371
Bigelow, J. 114
Birch, F. 18, 379
Blackett, P. 178, 179, 180, 181, 185
Bletchley Park (BP)
    acquired by GC & CS 26
    and Knockholt 86, 88
    Babbage discussed at 103
    changes course of history 81
    life at 160–7, 168–9, 171, 172–3, 181, 196, 197–202, 210, 233, 234, 250, 258–9, 265–7, 292, 352
    Museum 150, 151, 275, 382
    photograph (of Mansion) **17**

Bletchley Park (BP) (*cont.*)
    see also Government Code and Cypher
        School, Station X
Block F 158, 160, 161, 168, 169, 270, 342,
        343
Block H 152, 158, 172, 209, 344
Boheman, E. 307, 332
Bolam, D. 289–90
Bomba 25, 32, 212
Bombe 32, 33, 34, 51, 62, 73, 78, 145, 168,
        189, 206, 212, 284, 285, 292, 325, 378,
        379; *photograph* **25**
Booker, E. *photograph* **33**
Borelius, C.-G. 331
Bradshaw, D. 352
branching 103, 128–30; *see also* Colossus,
        branching in
Brett-Smith, H. 208
British Tabulating Machine Co. 32, 145,
        284
British Tunny machine 66–7, 158, 162, 170,
        173, 250–1, 252, 254, 264, 265–6, 270,
        291–3, 295–6, 329, 341, 343;
        photograph **30**
Broadhurst, S. 142, 144, 147, 148, 286, 291,
        292, 294, 295, 296, 301
Brown, T. 34
Bruce, A. 297
Budapest 4
Bureau Szyfrów 24, 25
Bush, V. 103, 105
Butler, L. 200

'C' (Chief of the Secret Intelligence
        Service) 4
Caesar cipher 9–10, 12, 13
Cairncross, J. 4
Calvocoressi, P. 31
Campaigne, H. 209
Campbell, D. 146
Carlbom, L. 331
Caughey, C. 160, 165–6, 166–7, 171;
        photograph **6**
CCITT 2 411–12, 416
Chamberlain, A. 208, 244
Chamberlain, M. 199
Chamberlain, N. 157, 378
Chandler, W. 76–7, 110–11, 127, 142,
        144–5, 147, 148, 150, 217, 218, 287,
        291, 292, 301, 386
Château de Vignolles 27

chess 61, 198, 199, 204, 205, 218, 235, 254
Christie, J. 250, 253, 270
Church, A. 178
Churchill, W. 2, 4, 76, 171, 172, 173, 189,
        201, 270, 281, 295, 324
Cicero 9
Clarke, D. 29
Clarke, J. 208
Clarke, W. 21
Clifford, A. 208
coalescence 219, 345
Cobra (cryptanalytical machine) 284,
        285
Collins, T. 294
Colossus
    and D-day 77, 80–1
    architecture of 117–39
    as personal computer 116–17, 118, 139,
        218
    branching in 103, 128–30, 220
    broken up 2, 140, 172–3, 295
    building of 1, 74–7, 80, 147–8, 170, 286,
        287, 289–90, 291, 300, 301
    compared with ENIAC 220, 302
    compared with IAS computer 113
    date of first operation 75, 343
    flexibility of 62, 76, 107, 120, 123, 125,
        139, 148, 149, 192, 218, 220, 302
    function of 66–70, 97–8, 123, 124, 158,
        191–2, 219, 257, 364, 386–90
    impact on future of computing 62–3,
        64, 79, 81, 82–3, 106–7, 110, 111, 112,
        114–15, 139, 172, 221, 302
    initial reception of 74–5, 76, 147, 286–7
    interrupts in 128, 130, 221, 244
    Mark 2 74, 76–7, 80, 147–8, 151–2, 169,
        244, 245, 290, 292, 301, 343, 367
    memory of 93–6, 132–3, 345
    number of 2, 62, 77, 81, 119
    operation of 162–5, 168, 169, 170, 218,
        303–4, 404
    parallelism in 74, 100, 133–6, 221, 282
    pleasures of 159
    post-war secrecy of vi, 2–3, 81, 82–3,
        101, 110, 141–3, 150–1, 171, 172–3,
        176–7, 201, 233–4, 246, 259, 268, 285
    post-war use of 2, 173–5, 295
    programming of 62, 76, 104, 107, 123,
        124, 125, 127, 129–30, 132, 136–8, 139,
        148, 218, 220, 221, 243, 244, 302, 303
    rebuild of 140, 150–2

rectangling with 209, 244–5, 343, 367, 344, 346, 380, 381, 403–5
reliability of 146, 169–70, 217, 287
set total facility 98, 129, 149, 303, 304
span counter 99, 123, 149, 220, 343
speed of 100, 126–7, 152, 217, 282, 301
statistical method and 66, 243, 383
structure of 96–7, 121–38
Turing and 192, 210, 218, 381, 382–3
photographs **32, 33, 34, 35, 36, 37**
see also de-chi, Newmanry, rectangling, shift register, statistical method
Colvill, T. 250, 252, 253
Coombs, A. 110–11, 125, 142, 145, 148, 150, 158, 167–8, 222, 288, 289, 290, 291, 292
Cooper, J. 19–20, 21, 23, 26, 27
Cowgill, S. 208
Crawshay-Williams, R. 187
Creasy, C. 179
crib
  definition of 11, 22
  use of against Enigma 22, 378
  use of in Bombe 31–2, 378
  use of in Robinson 149, 344
  use of in Testery 192, 196, 224–5, 229–30, 236–7, 255–6, 257–8, 271–7
Cripps, S. 332
Crofts, F. 295
Crum, M. 209, 310
Cunningham, A. B. 166
Cunningham, A. D. 166
Currie, H. 233; *photograph* **12**

Damm, A. 416
Darwin, C. 109, 110
Davies, M. 253, 270
Davis, M. 383
D-day 34, 55, 77, 80–1, 82, 166, 245, 249, 291, 332, 344
de Grey, N. 18, 180–1
de-chi, definition of 66–7
  example 276
deciban 206, 207, 380, 404
decision problem 104, 178
delta (Δ), definition of 67–8
  examples 226–7
Denmark Hill 21, 28, 85, 86, 87
Denniston, A. 18, 19, 20, 24, 26, 27, 56–7, 379; *photographs* **1, 21**
depth, definition of 50

Desch, J. 212
DEUCE (Digital Electronic Universal Computing Engine) 109
Deuxième Bureau 23
diagonal board (in Bombe) 32, 378
difference *see* delta
Difference Engine 103, 105
Differential Analyser 105
director 300
Dobbins, H. 250, 253, 270
Dollis Hill (DH) *see* Post Office Research Station
Donald Duck (cryptographic machine) 174
Double Playfair 250
double-banking 28
Doust, J. 282, 283
dragging (a crib) 225, 229–31, 236, 273, 275, 294, 360–1, 363, 368
Dragon (cryptanalytical machine) 236, 275, 293–4
Du Boisson, D. 160, 162–3, 167, 172; *photographs* **7, 33**
Duff, P. 352

Eastcote 173, 295
Eccles–Jordan trigger circuit (flip-flop) 95
Eckert, P. 106, 108, 112–13
Eden, A. 166
Edgerley, P. 250, 251, 253
EDSAC (Electronic Delay Storage Automatic Calculator) 108, 221
EDVAC (Electronic Discrete Variable Arithmetic Computer) 108, 113, 115, 301
Eisenhower, D. 80–1, 166
El Alamein, Battle of 310
Elliott, P. 208
EMI Business Machine 110
ENIAC (Electronic Numerical Integrator and Computer) 2, 82, 101, 104, 106, 107, 112–13, 114, 151, 172, 302; *photograph* **49**
Enigma
  Air Force 29, 30, 31, 32, 34–5, 61, 378
  Army 29, 30, 31, 32, 34, 61
  as Vigenère cipher 15–16
  between the Wars 21–5
  Bombe and 31–2, 33, 34, 51, 62, 73, 285, 378–9

Enigma (*cont.*)
　compared with Tunny 1, 36–7, 39, 40,
　　79, 210–12, 213, 332
　decrypts 3–4, 31, 293, 319, 322, 323
　description of machine 15–16, 17, 21–2,
　　23, 36, 40, 314–15
　development of attack at Bletchley Park
　　26–35, 157, 189, 378–9
　diagram of 17
　Naval 27, 32–4, 51, 61, 78, 205, 378–9
　Poles and 23–5, 26, 27, 29
　post-war use of 325
　photographs **18, 19, 20, 24**
　see also Bomba, Bombe, crib, Herivel tip,
　　pinch, Sigaba, Zygalski sheets
Ericsson, P. 208, 234, 237, 250, 251, 253,
　254, 380
Erskine, R. 55
Euwe, M. 218–19
extended psi, definition of 49

Fairweather, A. 143
Fasson, A. 34
female (in Enigma) 25
Fensom, H. 72, 75, 164, 166, 245, 284–7,
　295; *photograph* **15**
Ferranti Ltd 115
Fish, as code-name 39
Florin, B. 331
Flowers, T.
　and ACE 109
　and Enigma 73, 78, 144, 145, 284, 285
　and MOSAIC 110
　and Robinson 73–4, 145, 149, 183, 297
　and Sturgeon 284
　and Turing 73, 78, 109, 144, 145, 302,
　　382–3
　as architect of Colossus 1, 2, 71, 74, 75,
　　76, 77, 122 *passim*, 142 *passim*, 150,
　　151, 174, 183, 192, 221, 289, 290,
　　300–1, 303, 383
　influence on Turing and Newman 62–3,
　　83, 107, 112
　nearly blinded 288
　on ENIAC 107
　post-war life and career 2–3, 73, 77,
　　82–3, 143, 201, 281
　pre-war achievements 71–3, 106, 143,
　　281, 282
　photograph ii
Foss, H. 21, 22, 24, 203

Frankel, S. 114
Freedom of Information Act 151
Friedman, W. 391, 416
Friendly, A. 196

Garbo (cryptanalytical machine) 343
GC & CS *see* Government Code and
　Cypher School
GCHQ *see* Government Communications
　Headquarters
Geheimschreiber 191, 325–6, 328, 331, 371,
　416, 417
General Report on Tunny
　declassification of 3, 151, 245
　writing of 3, 246, 267
Gill, E. 18
Gödel, K. 59, 178, 179
Goldstine, H. 113
Golombek, H. 28, 199
Good, I. J. 3, 51, 61, 62, 63, 76, 141, 158,
　　164, 173, 186, 192, 194, 199, 235,
　　239–40, 242–3, 244, 245, 380, 386;
　　photograph **8**
Government Code and Cypher School
　(GC & CS)
　becomes GCHQ 173, 295
　during first months of war 26–31
　moves to Bletchley Park 26, 57
　prior to Second World War 18–26
　see also Bletchley Park, GCHQ
Government Communications
　Headquarters (GCHQ) 2, 20, 173–5,
　246, 295
GP 28 cipher machine 326
Gray code 219
Grazier, C. 34
Green, M. 187
Green, S. 187, 209
Grigg, J. 223
Guderian, H. 4; *photograph* **24**
Gyldén, Y. 323

Hagelin cipher machine 284, 324–5, 353–5,
　411
Hagelin, B. 411
Hallamaa, R. 324
Hanslope Park 379
Hayward, G. 146, 164, 253, 281, 282–3,
　288, 297; *photograph* **16**
Hawking, S. 102
Heath, E. 141

Heath Robinson
  design and construction of 65, 74,
    145–6, 284, 297–8, 341
  enhancements to 131, 149, 183, 286, 342,
    343, 344
  first proposed 64–5, 146, 157, 182, 238,
    341
  function of 66, 69, 146, 158, 162, 215,
    216–17, 219, 238–9, 240–1, 242, 243,
    298–300, 364, 386–90
  handicaps of 71, 73–4, 79, 125, 149, 162,
    183, 214–15
  later models 74, 76, 131, 149, 168, 169,
    286, 298, 342, 343, 344
  location of 165, 168, 239
  optical tape reader of 65, 134, 146, 147,
    221
  output of 71, 158, 272
  parallelism in 133–4, 146
  rebuild of 153
  reliability of 71, 75, 146, 162, 214–15,
    298, 299
  speed of 65, 146, 298, 300
  statistical method and 66, 364, 383
  structure of 65, 168, 298–9, 301
  use with cribs 149, 344
  photograph (of Old Robinson) **31**
  see also Super Robinson
Hellschreiber 85, 370, 371
Herivel tip 32, 184
Herivel, J. 27, 31, 184, 209
Hettler, E. 415, 416, 417
Highgate Wood telephone exchange 73
Hilton, P. 187, 208, 209, 210, 231–2, 250,
    251, 253, 256, 266, 268, 271, 274, 380;
    photograph **13**
Hinsley, H. 34, 208, 332
Hitler, A. 4, 6, 42, 54, 77, 80, 81, 82, 249,
    274, 300
Hitt, P. 409–10
HMS *Pembroke V* 159, 161, 173;
    see also Woburn Abbey
Hodges, A. 178, 442
holocaust 54
Holtzman, G. 382
Hughes, D. 411
human computer 103, 104, 106, 112, 113,
    344, 404; *photograph* **42**
Huskey, H. 108, 110, 221
Hut 1 32
Hut 3 29, 30, 31, 33, 252, 262, 270

Hut 4 32, 33, 270, 379
Hut 6 27, 28, 29, 30, 31, 32, 34, 270
Hut 8 32, 33, 34, 51, 190, 205, 206, 208, 379,
    380
Hut 11 65, 168, 239, 298, 342
Hut 15 360
Hut 15A 270
Huxley, T. H. 219–20

IAS (Princeton) computer 113, 114, 115;
    photograph **50**
IBM 650 123
IBM 701 115
IBM PC 116ff
impulse, definition of 38
index of coincidence 391–3
indicator (in Tunny) 45, 51, 56, 58, 85, 157,
    192, 355–63, 370–1, 375
Institute for Advanced Study (Princeton)
    113, 179, 180, 328; *see also* IAS
    computer
Ireland, E. 160–2, 163–4, 172;
    photograph **9**
Ismay, H. 189

Jacobs, W. 209
Jefferson, G. 187
Jeffreys, J. 26, 28
Jenkins, R. 208, 224, 250, 253, 270
Jipp, A. 416, 417
Julius Caesar 9

Kahn, D. 409
kappa *see* index of coincidence
Kasiski, F. 14, 375
Kasiski repetition 356–7, 375, 377
Kedleston Hall 271, 345
Keen, H. 32, 145
Keitel, W. 249
Kendrick, F. A. 25
Kenworthy, H. 21, 86, 87
Kerckhoffs, A. 10, 416
Kerckhoffs' principle 10
key (in Tunny), definition of 39
    example 44
key group 416–17
Kilburn, T. 111–12, 172
Kjellberg, B. 331
Kleinschmidt, E. 411
Knockholt 85–8, 162, 165, 171, 183, 271,
    342, 343, 345, 346

Knox, D. 18, 21, 23, 24, 25, 26, 27, 28, 157, 378
Kursk, Battle of 4–6, 332

LeCouteur, K. 209
Lee, J. A. N. 212, 382
Lefschetz, S. 179, 180
Letchworth 32, 145, 284
Levenson, A. 253, 270
Lewis, W. B. 145, 147, 287
limitation (in Tunny) 49, 76, 129, 219, 232, 257, 274–5, 341, 342, 343, 344, 345, 367, 406, 416
Lindstein, V. 329, 331
Ljunggren, T. 331
Lorenz SZ40/42 cipher machine *see* Tunny
Lovelace, A. 102, 114
Lucas, F. 30, 181, 182
Lynch, A. 146, 151, 297, 386

Mache, W. 326
Macintosh, A. 236
Mahon, A. P. 208
Manchester computers 2, 63, 109, 111–12, 114–15, 172, 185–7, 221
  Ferranti Mark I 115; *photograph* **48**
  Manchester Baby 109, 111–12, 186; *photograph* **44**
  Manchester Mark I 111, 115
Manchester University 2, 63, 106, 107, 109, 111–12, 143, 172, 185ff, 197
Manhattan Project 112, 114
Markov Chain Monte Carlo (MCMC) method 219
Masters, V. 250, 251, 253
Mauborgne, J. 415, 417
Mauchly, J. 106, 108, 112–13
Mayer, S. 25
Menzies, S. 26
MI1b 18
MI5 28
MI6 19, 23, 26, 29, 30
Michie, D. 3, 60–1, 62, 65, 76, 139, 141, 158, 164, 194, 208, 209, 210, 215, 218, 219, 251, 253, 267, 380, 383, 386; *photograph* **10**
microprogramming 62, 221
Milner-Barry, S. 28, 61, 189, 204, 206
MIT TX-0 116
Model, W. 249
Molien, T. 209

Molotov–Ribbentrop pact 26
monoalphabetic cipher 14, 412, 416
Montgomery, B. 166
Moore School of Electrical Engineering 112–13, 114
Morehouse, L. 415
Morgan, G. 157, 352, 356, 363, 364, 367
Morgan, J. P. 208
Morgan, S. 352
Morrell, F. 64–5, 72, 73, 146, 149, 282, 284, 297
Morse code 16, 37, 54, 165, 264
MOSAIC (Ministry of Supply Automatic Integrator and Computer) 110, 302; *photograph* **47**
Mrs Miles (cryptanalytical machine) 168, 170, 343; *photograph* **39**
Murray, D. 38, 411
Myers, K. 164, 166, 169, 172

National Physical Laboratory (NPL) 108, 109, 110, 141, 186
National Security Agency (NSA) 151, 173, 246
Netzverfahren (grid system) 25
Newman, L. 178ff
Newman, M.
  and decision problem 104, 178, 185–6
  as computer pioneer 52, 63, 83, 105, 106–7, 109, 111–12, 114, 172, 185, 186, 187, 218, 221
  as manager of Newmanry 61, 158, 160, 162, 165–6, 167–8, 182–3, 184, 196, 197, 205, 215, 218, 232, 242, 243, 245, 386
  declines OBE 77
  joins attack on Tunny 59, 181–2, 208
  pre-war life and career 177–9
  post-war life and career 176–7, 185–8, 197
  proposes and oversees electronic attack on Tunny 59–60, 62, 64–5, 66, 71, 74, 146, 157, 182, 192, 208–9, 238–9, 240, 272, 292, 297, 340, 363, 364, 367, 386, 391–5
  recruited to Bletchley Park 180–1
  photograph **5**
Newmanry
  end of 171–3, 202–3, 222, 262
  engineers in 158, 164, 165, 166, 167–71
  expansion of 158, 342

fire in 170–1, 298, 345
foundation of 65, 157, 158, 209, 239, 341
nature of work undertaken in 66, 149,
  157–8, 191–2, 195, 227–8, 242–3, 245,
  380, 396, 403–5
relation to Testery 66, 194, 195, 208, 209,
  232, 257, 270, 342, 343, 346
use of Banburismus in 380
Wrens in 158, 159–67, 168, 169, 170,
  171, 184, 218, 239, 243, 341, 346, 404
  photographs **30, 31, 33, 34, 35, 36, 37, 38,
  39**
Newman's Theorem 393–5
Nicholls, J. 28
NID25 18
Nightingale (cryptanalytical machine) 284,
  285–6
Noskwith, R. 208
Nygaardsvold, J. 324
Nyman, B. 331

Official Secrets Act vi, 2, 19, 26, 110, 161,
  171, 172, 223, 265, 284, 289
Olivetti cipher machine 417
one-time pad 20, 61, 173–4, 192, 332
Oswald, D. 250, 253

Packard-Bell PB250 110
Packard-Bell personal computer 116
Parker, R. D. 415
parallel processing *see* Colossus, parallelism
  in
Pendered, R. 208
Penny, J. 208
Penrose, L. 178, 180, 188
Penrose, M. 178, 188
Perkins, A. 199
pinch (of Enigma material) 32, 33, 34, 379
Planck, M. 207
Poincaré conjecture 179, 180
polyalphabetic cipher 14, 16, 412, 416
Post Office Research Station at Dollis Hill
  65, 67, 71ff, 78, 79ff, 109, 110, 114, 142,
  143ff, 158, 167ff, 221, 222, 281–90,
  291–4, 297, 299; *photograph* **41**
Preston, G. 209
'Prof's Book' 378
psi, extended *see* extended psi
Pyry 24

Q-code 46, 310–11

QEP number (in Tunny) 45–6, 47, 51, 75,
  157, 192, 310, 311, 340, 345, 362
Quande, E. 324
Quatsch 195–6, 271, 273–4, 339

Radley, W. G. 74, 144, 284, 301
Randell, B. 188
Raps, A. 411
rectangling 76, 77, 152, 158, 244–5, 340,
  341, 343, 344, 345, 347, 365–7, 368,
  369, 380, 396–405
Red Form 88, 265, 370–1
reflection order 218
Rees, D. 186, 194, 209, 244
Rejewski, M. 24–5, 27, 206; *photograph* **22**
Research Logs 55, 61, 182, 210, 341
Research Section 27, 50, 51, 157, 181–2,
  190, 208, 232, 338, 340, 341, 352ff, 378,
  380
RISC 109
Roberts, J. 253; *photograph* **14**
Rollo, C. 253, 270
Rommel, E. 80–1, 232, 249
Room 40 (Admiralty) 18, 20, 56, 254
Roots, 'Tubby' 252, 253, 264
Roscher Lund, R. 323–5, 330
Rossberg, E. 416, 417
routiner 300
Royal Arsenal 71
Royal Radar Establishment 110
Royal Society of London 111, 186
Rowe, A. 145
Różycki, J. 24, 206
Russell, B. 187, 209
Russian front 4–6, 249, 310, 329, 332
Rylands, Sergeant 352, 360

Sägefisch 309, 322, 355
Saunders, M. 30
Scarlet Pimpernels 23
Scherbius, A. 15
Scheutz Difference Engine 105
Schmidt, H.-T. ('Asché') 23, 25
Schnelltelegraph 411
Secret Intelligence Service (SIS) 19
sequential analysis 380, 381
Shark 34
shift register 100, 126, 127, 131, 132, 134–5,
  147, 148, 222, 301
Siemens and Halske T43 cipher machine
  307, 326, 417; *see also* Thrasher

Siemens and Halske T52 cipher machine
    see Sturgeon
Sigaba cipher machine 446
SIGTOT cipher machine 415
Sinclair, H. 19, 21, 26
Sixta 270, 343
slide, definition of 87
Smith, H. 28
Source Boniface 31
Spanish Civil War 23
Speight, E. A. 146, 282, 288, 297
Sprague, R. 352
Springschreiber 411
Stalin, J. 4, 6
Stalingrad, Battle of 4
Stanmore 171, 285
Station X 26, 86, 159, 295; *see also* Bletchley
    Park, Government Code and Cypher
    School
statistical method 66, 67–70, 71,
    240–3, 340, 363–5, 368, 369, 383,
    386–90
Stibitz, G. 106
Stordahl, N. 326
stored program concept 52, 57, 63, 104–5,
    107, 108, 109, 111–14, 117, 125, 138,
    302
Sturgeon 35, 39, 55, 143, 204, 209, 284,
    307–27, 328–33, 341, 368, 371,
    415–17
    post-war use of 325–7
    photographs **51, 52**
substitution cipher 9–12
    frequency analysis and 11
Super Robinson 149, 344, 346, 347
Swade, D. 103

TAPIR 327
tea party (Newmanry) 61, 182, 210
Telecommunications Research
    Establishment (TRE) 64, 65, 74, 111,
    145–6, 172, 286, 297, 299
teleprinter code (Baudot–Murray code) 16,
    37–9, 87, 225, 348–9, 371, 411–12
    encryption of 42–4, 47–9, 327, 350–1,
    412–17
Tester, R.
    as manager of Testery 184, 196, 232–3,
        250, 251–2, 260, 262, 292, 367
    founds Testery 60, 157
    photograph **11**

Testery
    ATS girls in 250–1, 252, 254, 260, 264–7,
        293
    end of 202–3
    formation of 157, 223–4, 250, 339
    management of 250–2
    nature of work undertaken in 67, 148,
        192, 195, 219, 229, 245, 251, 252–4,
        255–8, 270–7, 340, 341, 380
    relation to Newmanry 66, 157–8, 184,
        192, 194, 195, 208, 209, 232, 257, 270,
        342, 343, 346
Testery report 245–6
Thompson, J. 250
Thrasher 39, 307, 346, 417;
    see also Siemens and Halske T43
    cipher machine
Thurlow, N. 168–9, 172–3, 282, 284, 344
Tickle, M. 253, 293
Tiltman, J. 24, 53–4, 55, 57, 59, 60, 181,
    224, 250, 259, 324, 356, 372, 373, 376;
    photograph **21**
Timms, G. 3, 62, 139, 219, 220
Tirpitz 167
Tovey, J. 166
Travis, E. 21, 182, 183, 209; *photograph* **2**
Tunny
    auto mode 37, 39, 46, 241, 271, 272, 273
    Banburismus and 380
    broken by Swedes 331–2
    captured machine shown to Bletchley
        codebreakers 172, 214, 347
    compared with Enigma 1, 36–7, 39, 40,
        77, 210–12, 213, 410
    compared with Sturgeon 35, 39, 143,
        307, 308, 309, 310, 311, 313, 319, 368,
        416, 417
    decrypts 3–6, 275–6, 293
    description of machine 16, 36–7, 39–40,
        42–4, 47–50, 66, 213–14, 292, 296,
        350–1, 355, 357, 363–4, 406–8
    encipherment equations for 363–4, 368,
        387–8
    first break 50, 55–6, 57–8, 85, 157, 338,
        339, 355–8, 363, 370–7
    first intercepts 1, 40, 55–6, 85, 338,
        470–1
    frequency counts 227–8, 239, 240–1,
        242–3, 342
    fundamental weakness in 70–1, 215–16,
        369, 394, 409–10, 417

hand mode 37, 46, 271, 272, 273, 274
interception of 85–8, 309, 310, 311
map of Tunny network 41
network 40–2, 45, 338, 340, 343, 344, 346, 370
operating procedure 36–7, 44–7, 192
post-war secrecy of 3, 82–3, 141–3, 172–3, 174–5, 246
post-war use of 174–5, 262, 325–6
significance of breaking 1, 4–6, 35, 39, 55, 77, 80–1, 249, 308, 332
version SZ42c 309
using cribs to break 192, 196, 224–5, 229–30, 236–7, 255–6, 257–8, 271–7, 343, 344, 360–1, 371–7
using depths to break 50, 51, 56, 58, 75–6, 157, 192–4, 224, 229–30, 238, 241, 255–6, 271–2, 338, 340, 355ff, 371–7
virtual 140
wheel pattern changes in 48, 51, 77, 163, 191, 244, 257, 272, 340, 344, 365, 381
photographs **28, 29**
see also 1 + 2 break in, autoclave, British Tunny machine, depth, extended psi, impulse, indicator, key, limitation, QEP, *Sägefisch*, teleprinter code, Turingery, wheel patterns, wheel settings
Turing, A.
  and atomic bomb 206
  and Automatic Computing Engine 108–10
  and Babbage 105
  and Banburismus 206, 379–80
  and Bombe 32, 33, 51, 62, 73, 284, 378, 379
  and Flowers 73, 78, 109, 144, 145, 382–3
  and Manchester computers 109, 111–12, 114, 186–7
  and speech encryption 379
  and Turingery 51, 380–2, 383
  as computer pioneer 52, 57, 63, 83, 104–5, 106–15, 138, 141, 382
  builds electromechanical multiplier 106
  discovers delta 68, 363, 381, 383
  early work on Enigma 24, 25, 26, 27, 29–30, 32, 57, 62, 157, 378–9
  on fundamental nature of computer 102
  personal characteristics 50, 178, 187, 197–9, 205–6, 208, 235
  pioneers computer programming 109
  plays key role in development of attack on Tunny 381
  pre-war work on computability 62, 104–5, 107, 112, 113–14, 141, 178
  receives OBE 185–6
  stored program concept and 104–5, 106–7, 108, 112, 113–15
  writes 'Proposed Electronic Calculator' 108, 138
  work on Naval Enigma 26, 32–3, 51, 57, 78, 205, 235, 378–9
  work on Tunny 58, 68, 192, 197, 208, 359–60, 380–5
  writes to Churchill 189
  photographs **3, 23, 48**
Turingery 51, 68, 157, 229, 230, 238, 272, 339, 360, 363, 369, 380–5
Turing machine 62
  universal 104–5, 106, 107, 113–14, 140
Turingismus *see* Turingery
Tutte, W. 50, 51, 57–9, 64, 66, 67, 68, 69, 70, 71, 77, 152, 157, 158, 181, 182, 224, 229, 239, 244, 340, 375, 381, 383, 394, 396; *photograph* **4**
Twinn, P. 24, 25, 26, 29, 32, 57
Typex cipher machine 22, 29

U-boat 32, 33, 34, 51, 73, 378–9
  U-33 32
  U-110 33; *photographs* **26, 27**
  U-559 34
undulator tape 87–8
universal computer, definition of 104–5
universal Turing machine *see* Turing machine

Veblen, O. 180
VENONA 61
Vernam, G. 212, 412, 415, 416, 417
Vernam encryption 212, 371
Vigenère, B. de 12
Vigenère cipher 12–16
Vincent, E. *photograph* **21**
von Neumann, J. 101, 107, 108, 112–14, 115, 179, 185, 206, 301, 303; *photograph* **50**
von Runstedt, G. 55, 249
von Weichs, M. 4–6

Wald, A. 380
Walford, J. 252, 253
Welchman, G. 27, 28, 32, 144, 189, 204, 378
Weyl, H. 179, 180
White, F. 178
Whitehead, A. 209
Whitehead, D. 386
Whitehead, J. H. 178, 209, 244
wheel-breaking (in Tunny), definition of 191
wheel patterns (in Tunny), definition of 47–8
wheel-setting (in Tunny), definition of 191
wheel settings (in Tunny), definition of 44
Wiener, N. 114, 187
Wilkes, M. 108, 185, 221
Wilkinson, J. 108, 112, 221
Willi Reichert Elektronik und Electromechanik 326–7, 447
Williams, F. C. 111–12, 172, 186
Williams tube 111, 113, 115, 302; *photograph* **50**

Wittgenstein, L. 184–5, 209
Woburn Abbey 161ff
Womersley, J. 108, 109
Wormwood Scrubbs 282–3
Wüsteney, H. 411
Wylie, J. 232
Wylie, O. 209
Wylie, S. 148, 172, 194, 205, 208, 209, 220, 244
Wyllie, J. 362, 368
Wynn-Williams, C. 64, 65, 69, 72, 145–6, 147, 299

Y Service 19, 21, 27, 28, 84–8; *photograph* (of Flowerdown Y Station) **40**
Yoxall, L. 208

Zimmermann telegram 19, 20, 181
Zitadelle 4–6
Zuse, K. 106, 428
Zygalski, H. 24, 25
Zygalski sheets 26, 27, 29, 31